RED
CHINA
TODAY

*The Other Side
of the River*

BOOKS BY EDGAR SNOW

Far Eastern Front
Living China
Red Star Over China
The Battle for Asia
People on Our Side
The Pattern of Soviet Power
Stalin Must Have Peace
Random Notes on Red China
Journey to the Beginning
Red China Today:
The Other Side of the River

RED
CHINA
TODAY

REVISED AND UPDATED EDITION OF
The Other Side
of the River

EDGAR SNOW

Vintage Books
A Division of Random House
NEW YORK

A strange justice that is bounded by a river! Can anything be more ridiculous than that a man should have the right to kill me because he lives on the other side . . .

— BLAISE PASCAL, *Pensées*

Men will not receive the truth from their enemies and it is very seldom offered to them by their friends; on this very account I have frankly uttered it.

Placed between the conflicting opinions that divide my countrymen, I have endeavored for the time to stifle in my own bosom the sympathy or the aversion that I felt for either . . .

The subject that I wished to cover by my investigations is immense, for it includes most of the feelings and opinions produced by the new condition of the world's affairs. Such a subject certainly exceeds my strength, and in the treatment of it I have not been able to satisfy myself.

— ALEXIS DE TOCQUEVILLE, preface to
Democracy in America, Volume II

To Bennett Cerf, Donald Klopfer, Mao Tse-tung, Chou En-lai, Rewi Alley, and Gardner Cowles, who helped make it possible for me to return to China.

And to countless Chinese, Americans and Europeans who contributed in various ways to this report — for which no one is responsible except the facts and myself.

Contents

Contents

Contents

A Note on Chinese Pronunciation

IT is not necessary to strangle over the pronunciation of Chinese names if one observes a few simple rules in the rather arbitrary but workable Wade-Giles system of transliteration (romanization) of the language into English. Each Chinese character represents only one sound and homonyms are innumerable. Chinese is monosyllabic, but combinations of characters in the spoken language may form a single idea or equivalent of one foreign word and thus in a sense the spoken language is polysyllabic. Chinese surnames come first, given names (usually two words) follow, as in Teng Hsiao-p'ing. Aspirates are represented in this book by apostrophes; they indicate a soft consonantal sound. Examples:

Chi (as in Chi Chao-t'ing) is pronounced 'Gee', but *Ch'i* (as in Liu Shao-ch'i) sounds like 'Chee'. *Ch'in* is exactly our 'chin'.

Chu is roughly like 'Jew', as in *Chu Teh* (Jew Duhr), but *Ch'u* equals 'Chew'.

Tsung is 'dzung'; *ts'ung* with the 'ts' as in 'Patsy'.

Tai is our word sound 'die'; *T'ai* – 'tie'.

Pai is 'buy' and *P'ai* is 'pie'.

Kung is like 'Gung' (-a Din); *K'ung* with the 'k' as in 'kind'.

J is the equivalent of 'r' but roll it, as *rrrun*.

H before an *s*, as in *hsi*, is the equivalent of an aspirate but is often dropped, as in Sian for Hsian.

Single Chinese words are always pronounced as monosyllables. Thus *Chiang* is not 'Chee-yi-ang' but a single sound, 'Geeang'. *Mao* is not 'may-ow' but pronounced like a cat's 'miaow' *without* the 'i'. *Chou En-lai* is 'Joe Un-lie' but the last syllable of his wife's given name, *Ying-ch'ao*, sounds like 'chow'.

Vowels in Chinese are generally short or medium, not long and

flat. Thus *Tang* sounds like 'dong', never like our 'tang'. *T'ang* is
'tong'.

a as in *father*	There is also a 'ü' as in German and an 'ê' as in
e – *run*	French. I have omitted Wade's umlaut and
eh – *hen*	circumflex markings, which are found in Euro-
i – *see*	pean latinizations of Chinese.
ih – *her*	
o – *look*	
ou – *go*	
u – *soon*	

These sounds indicate Chinese as spoken in *kuo-yu*, the northern
(Peking, mandarin) speech, which is now the national language,
taught in all schools. Where journalism has already popularized
misspellings or variants in other dialects, such as Chiang Kai-shek
for Chiang Chieh-shih, etc., I have followed the familiar version.

Chinese words frequently encountered in place names are :

sheng – province; *hsien* – county; *hsiang* – township; *ching* (or
king) – capital; *ch'eng* – city; *ts'un* – village; *chiang* (kiang) – great
river; *ho* – river; *hu* – lake; *k'ou* – mouth; *pei* – north; *nan* – south;
tung – east; *hsi* (or *si*) – west; *chung* – central; *shan* – mountain.

Such words combine in the following examples :

Peking (properly, *Pei-ching*, pronounced 'Bay-ging'), meaning
'northern capital'. Peking was renamed 'Pei-p'ing' (Peiping or,
erroneously, Peping), 'northern peace' (or tranquillity), by the
Kuomintang régime, which made its seat in Nanking (southern
capital), but the historic name remained in general use and was
formally restored in 1949.

Shantung means east of the mountains.

Shansi – west of the mountains.

Hankow – mouth of the Han (river).

Sian – western peace (tranquillity).

Hopei – north of the (Yellow) river.

Hunan – south of the lakes.

Yunnan – south of the clouds.

Kiangsi – west of the river.

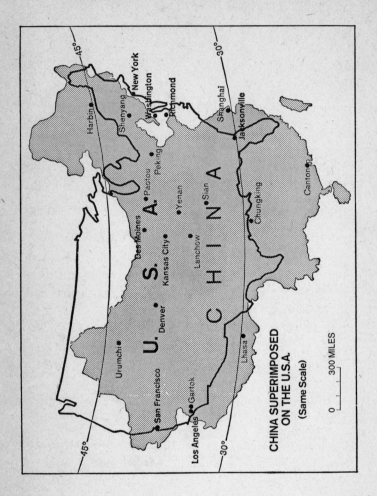

CHINA SUPERIMPOSED
ON THE U.S.A.

(Same Scale)

0   300 MILES

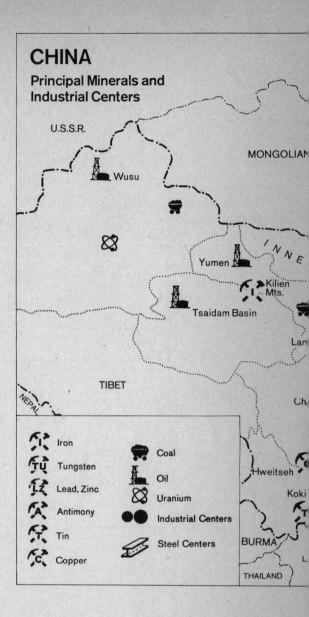

CHINA
Principal Minerals and Industrial Centers

U.S.S.R.

MONGOLIA

Wusu

Yumen

Kilien
Mts.

Tsaidam Basin

Lan

TIBET

NEPAL

Ch

Hweitseh

Koki

BURMA

THAILAND

Iron		Coal	
Tungsten		Oil	
Lead, Zinc		Uranium	
Antimony		Industrial Centers	
Tin		Steel Centers	
Copper			

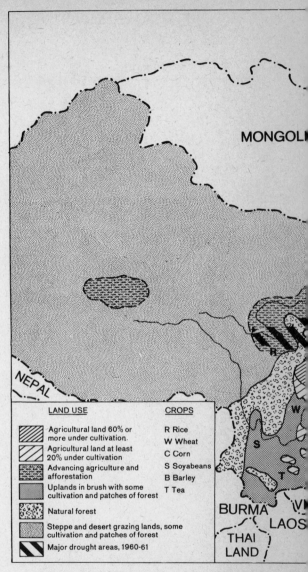

MONGOL[

LAND USE

/// Agricultural land 60% or more under cultivation.

/ Agricultural land at least 20% under cultivation

Advancing agriculture and afforestation

Uplands in brush with some cultivation and patches of forest

Natural forest

Steppe and desert grazing lands, some cultivation and patches of forest

Major drought areas, 1960-61

CROPS

R Rice
W Wheat
C Corn
S Soyabeans
B Barley
T Tea

NEPAL

BURMA

LAOS

THAI LAND

Sources for this map include a land-use map by Alle... Ginsburg, ed. © 1958. Prentice-Hall, Inc., Englewood C...

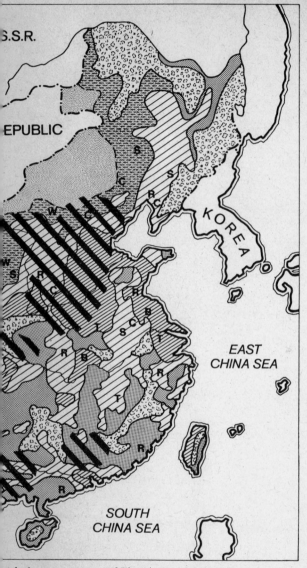

S

C

W C

W
S
R C

R

S C B

R

B

R

T

R

T

R

KOREA

EAST
CHINA SEA

R

SOUTH
CHINA SEA

rick, from pages 174–5 of *The Pattern of Asia*, Norton

National Autonomous Regions

Inner Mongolian Autonomous Region: Mongols

Kwangsi Autonomous Region: Chuang

Ninghsia Autonomous Region: Mohammedans (Hui)

Sinkiang Uighur Autonomous Region: I-li (Kazakh), K'e-tzu-le-su (Khalka), Ch'ang-chi (Hui)

Tibetan Autonomous Region: Tibetans

Larger Provincial Minority Autonomous Districts (Chou)

Hainan
South: Li and Miao

Hunan
West: Tuchia and Miao

Kirin
East: (Yen-Pien border): Korean

Kweichow
South east: Miao, Tung
South: Puyi, Miao

Szechuan
West (Kan-tzu, A-pa areas): Tibetan

South (Liang-shan). Yi

Tsinghai
West (Kuo-lo, Yu-shu): Tibetan
Northwest (Hai-hsi): Mongol, Kazakh, Tibetan
East (Hai-pei, Hai-nan, Huang-nan): Tibetan

Yunnan (Shan)
South: Thai, Chingpo, Hani, Yi
Northwest: Lisu, Tibetan
West: Pai, Thai, Chingpo, Chuang, Miao
Central: Yi

Introduction

JOURNEY TO THE BEGINNING,[1] an autobiographical account of adventures in ignorance (not necessarily all mine), contains enough details of my personal history to satisfy any reasonable reader's curiosity – and considering the subject of this book you have a right to be curious. It tells among other things how I went to China when I was twenty-two and there began my career as a foreign correspondent, with Colonel McCormick's *Chicago Tribune*.

What is relevant here is that I happen to be well known in China because I was the first person to penetrate a civil war blockade and interview and photograph Mao Tse-tung, Chou En-lai and other leaders of the old Chinese Red Army. That was a century ago (1936), a year before the Communists and the Nationalists under Chiang Kai-shek called a truce in their first nine years of mutual extermination, in order to compete in a war of resistance against Japan. I then represented the *London Daily Herald* and the *New York Sun*. My reports on the Chinese Communists also appeared in *Life* and the *Saturday Evening Post*, for which I later became a world correspondent and then was for many years an associate editor.

Mao Tse-tung told me his own story and the history of the Chinese Communist revolution up to that time, which appeared in my book *Red Star Over China*, first published in 1937.[2] A Chinese version of that book came out before the English edition and provided countless Chinese with the first authentic information about Chinese Communists. Among those readers were many youths whom I have met again as second- or third-echelon leaders of Red China.

This background made it possible for me to be given a welcome, despite official hostility between Peking and Washington, when I

returned to China in 1960 for the first time since the end of the
Second World War. Relatively few of the small number of Occi-
dentals who have seen Red China ever lived there before the revolution. I believe I was, among resident American correspondents
who knew China in pre-war days, the first to return.

It might be assumed from the foregoing that it was easy for me
to get a Chinese visa, but several years elapsed before my application was granted – only after reaching the highest level of authority. Some of my reports about Stalin's Russia had caused me to be
barred from that country and I had expressed views on the origins
of the Korean War sharply at variance with the way it looked from
Peking. Other comments on Sino-Soviet relations, on Yugoslavia,
and on communism in general might have made me *persona non
grata* if Peking authorities admitted to China only those who never
questioned their official *People's Daily* version of history. As early
as 1948 (11 December), I had suggested that Tito's heresy marked
the beginning of Communist heterodoxy and foreshadowed today's
Sino-Soviet dispute.

'The Belgrade schism', I wrote in the *Saturday Evening Post* at
that time, when Stalin expelled Tito and his colleagues from the
Cominform,

provides a mirror which clearly reflects the basic aims and limitations
of Russia's policies in Europe [and] likewise gives us a perspective on
events now transpiring in China. There is projected, against the screen
of the remote future, the real possibility* of war between socialist states
even after the 'final' extirpation of capitalism. The possibility first
impressed me a decade ago in China, where the Communist party was
at that time the only one in the world outside Russia which had an
army, territory and real administrative responsibilities of its own. Because of that, it seemed likely that the Chinese would become the first
foreign Communists openly to place their national interests on a level
with those of Russia. But while the Chinese were still deeply involved
in a long and complicated civil war on a continental scale, the Yugoslav
party relatively quickly won absolute internal victory. It thus achieved
all the conditions necessary to enable it seriously to question the paramountcy of Kremlin interests.

* Possibility, not 'inevitability'. In 1957, Mao Tse-tung himself discerned
'contradictions' between socialist national states. See page 377.

As is well known, the Yugoslav Communists were not installed by the Red Army but as a result of a severe internal struggle in which they were armed chiefly by Britain and America. Out of the struggle grew a strong sense of pride and brotherhood bound together in a spirit of self-reliance and self-glorification. Demands imposed in the name of the Kremlin myth [of infallibility] increasingly interfered with the performance of internal tasks which Yugoslav Communists themselves considered necessary to stabilize their power. And it was in bold rejection of the doctrine of Kremlin infallibility that the Yugoslav party reiterated, last July [1948], its conviction that 'the national independence of the people of Yugoslavia is the condition for their road to socialism and their progress in general.'. . .

Insubordination in Marshal Tito and his party could not long be tolerated without encouraging others to place the national interests of their own countries on a level with those of Russia. For there exists, in every Communist party that possesses even a measure of responsible power, a latent but growing will to free itself of the dogma of unconditional obedience. The heresy of Tito marks the end of an era of communism *as an extension of Russian nationalism*. The Kremlin myth has been defied and the infidel has not fallen dead. Tito is the beginning of a true heterodoxy in the Communist 'universal church'. The lesson must have penetrated even the thick walls of the Kremlin, to bring about realization that the satellite countries themselves could not be counted as true assets, rather than liabilities, in the event of an early war. In particular, the potential risks of Poland and Hungary – not to mention Soviet Germany – following Belgrade's example must haunt the Russian high command.

How, then, explain provocative Soviet actions at Berlin and elsewhere? Russian tactics can be viewed primarily as heavy-handed efforts to accelerate a basic settlement recognizing international legality of the new status quo. ... Unless we attempt to drive Russia from Eastern Europe by force there will be no general war between us in the foreseeable future.

That was published on 18 December 1948. Four months later (9 April 1949) I wrote about China in the same precincts :

As a result of the Communists' sovereign victory in China there now exists in East Asia a new set of circumstances with significant implications both inside and beyond the Marxist world. Moscow must deal with a major foreign power run by Communists possessing all the means of maintaining real equality and independence. This becomes important when it is realized that potential sources of friction between Soviet and Chinese nationalisms already exist in Manchuria, Mongolia and Chinese Turkestan, where Russian attrition has been going on for generations. . . .

Far from accepting the role of satellites, either for Manchuria or for China as a whole, the Chinese Communists look upon their country as the potential focus of a new federation of Eastern socialist states, which can exist independently, on a plane of complete equality with the U.S.S.R. While the Kremlin cannot be much happier over such a prospect than it was about Tito's Balkan federation scheme, it would be highly illusory to imagine that the Russians will promptly repeat, in China, the mistakes which lost them effective control in Yugoslavia. They will proceed with extreme caution, hopefully waiting for the Americans to make the blunders on which their own success could be improvised. . . .

If the purpose of American policy is to strengthen China's independence from Russia then it is not likely to be achieved by forcing the Communists to resign themselves to the terms of Russian alliance in self-defense. . . . In any event, in the long run the Chinese Communist Party cannot and will not subordinate the national interests of China to the interests of the Kremlin. *China will become the first Communist-run major power independent of Moscow's dictation. And that in itself would project entirely new perspectives within the socialist camp, as elsewhere* . . . [Italics added.]

Given the opportunity to develop its own resources in arm's length cooperation with other nations such a new Asia might form a bloc of powers important enough to maintain a stable balance between the Russian and American spheres of influence. . . .

Following these remarks I was barred from the U.S.S.R. during Stalin's lifetime, and in one Shanghai journal I was called an agent of American imperialism. Washington likewise rejected the views expressed above; United States policy for a decade was based on quite opposite assumptions that the Peking régime was 'non-Chinese' and a will-less puppet of Moscow, and that the process of Soviet expansion by such means could continue indefinitely. Twelve years later it had become clear to everyone that disputes and rivalries rooted in conflicts of national interest had arisen between Russia and China, and so respected a diplomat-historian as George Kennan was able to draw the following logical inference without fear of contradiction even by his less discerning colleagues in the State Department:

There is no magic by which great nations are brought to obey for any length of time the will of people very far away who understand their problems poorly and with whom they feel no intimacy . . . or understanding. This has to be done by bayonets or it is not done at all. . . . This is the reason why, despite all that is said about Soviet expansion, the power of the Kremlin extends precisely to those areas which it is able to dominate with its own armed forces without involving impossible lines of communication, and no farther. . . . What I am asserting is that universal world dominion is a technical impossibility and that the effectiveness of the power radiated from any one national center decreases in proportion to the distance involved and to the degree of cultural disparity.[3]

Remembering my 'controversial' writings of a decade earlier, the Yugoslavs and other Eastern European Communists in Peking were keenly interested in my admission to China in 1960. They attached significance to it as a straw in the wind of increasingly unfavorable weather in Sino-Soviet relations. In that same year the departure of many thousands of Soviet technical advisers from the People's Republic was to begin to reveal to the outside world the deep tension and open fissures that had grown between the two giants of the Communist bloc over just such rivalries as I have mentioned – disputes formerly held unthinkable by orthodox Marxists who believed as an article of faith that class solidarity was a stronger cement than the atavisms of tribalism which we call nationalism.

Seemingly unaware of such nuances in the Sino-Soviet alliance, the State Department had rebuffed numerous overtures from the People's Republic to reopen communications. My own return was strenuously opposed by the Eisenhower Administration, as had been true of every effort made by Americans on a non-official level who understood something of the historical contradictions, and their portent for the U.S.A., as I have described them. The State Department actually did everything but compel me to go to China illegally, if at all.

Certain State Department press releases had given the impression that the Peking régime alone was responsible for barring Americans from China. The facts were not that simple. Although China now took the position that it was useless to admit correspondents there as long as the United States was unwilling to discuss ending its armed protectorate over Taiwan, it must be noted that formerly the Peking government had offered visas to many Americans, including correspondents and writers. It was Secretary of State John Foster Dulles who then forbade *all* Americans to visit China. By threatening any violators with loss of their passports and possible fines or imprisonment – and by instigating direct Presidential appeal to a few important publishers who were inclined to defy him – the Secretary managed for years to keep America effectively cut off from any direct news of the great story of the Chinese revolution.

In 1957, Mr Dulles finally made up a selected list of 'news media' he considered 'qualified' to send representatives to China – if they could get visas. Peking declined to receive his 'accredited' correspondents unless the United States would accept an equal number of Chinese correspondents. Mr Dulles flatly rejected that proposal, saying that American immigration laws prohibited the issuance of visas to Communists. The evasion was transparent; exceptions had already been made for Soviet and other Communist correspondents. But there the matter rested until after Mr Dulles' death.

Meanwhile the Peking government continued to offer visas to Americans who wished to enter China as ordinary travelers, but the State Department would not permit that, either. During the Eisenhower Administration many distinguished Americans, including Eleanor Roosevelt and Averell Harriman,* were offered visas by China but were prevented from accepting them by State Department warnings that to do so would be violating the law.

By 1958 the Peking government had abandoned what it considered three years of fruitless attempts at conciliation of the United States. Reasons for the change will emerge in these pages. Briefly, as Chou En-lai was later to state to me in most concrete terms, his government had concluded that it was profitless to discuss conces-

---

*Mr Harriman was offered a visitor's visa, but the State Department would not validate his passport. Under pressure he had himself made a State Department-accredited 'correspondent'. The Chinese then declined his application in accordance with the policy noted above.

sions to be made by China unless the United States would agree to mutual rejection of the use of force in the settlement of Sino-American disputes *and* simultaneously recognize, *in principle*, the sovereignty of China over the Taiwan territories.

Part of the new 'firm' policy meant the refusal to receive 'correspondents' of publications and news media 'accredited' to China by the State Department. Peking officially had made it clear that China would now seek no exchange of correspondents unless the United States reconsidered its Taiwan policy. Thus it was already evident, in 1960, that it would be futile for me to apply to enter China as a 'correspondent'. Instead, I asked for admission as a 'writer'. I was so defined on my passport. At the same time I applied to Secretary of State Herter for permission to travel there in the same category, to gather material for a book. China accepted me, but the State Department promptly rejected my request. My problem then was how to confound beadledom without losing my passport or becoming a diplomatic issue which would cause China automatically to withdraw a visa.

At this point my guerrilla publisher, Bennett Cerf, took charge by selling periodical rights to my potential book to *Look* magazine. *Look* then applied to the State Department to 'accredit' me as its 'representative'.

Look magazine was on the Department's 'list', but once *Look* wished to send me to China the publisher was subjected to intense pressure from the Department; certain senators and even the White House were incited to intervene to try to persuade him to withdraw my name. My record was too well known at the State Department for me to be called a Communist. The special reason given for opposing me was that as a correspondent I had known Chinese Communist leaders since my youth, and that I was still acceptable to them; therefore, it was obvious that I could not write a 'satisfactory report'. Anyone else acceptable to Peking might have met the same opposition in Washington.

Of course the Department had no international or domestic legal right to 'accredit' or not 'accredit' *any* news media or correspondents to a government which it did not recognize, and from whom it could make no demands for the normal courtesies granted American citizens abroad. The Department itself in the end tacitly admitted as much in official correspondence with Gardner Cowles, publisher of *Look*, and conceded that it 'had no alternative' but to validate my passport if Mr Cowles insisted. He did. Very grudgingly permission was finally given for me 'legally' to enter China.

After all this difficulty I presented my passport to the Chinese authorities in Europe for a visa. They found it still included a ban against travel in North Korea and North Vietnam, countries friendly to China, which they regarded as unsatisfactory. Ironically, therefore, they gave me a visa on a separate piece of paper, and thereafter ignored my passport.

Officially, China admitted me as a-writer-not-a-correspondent; Washington's view was that I entered as a-correspondent-not-a-writer.

This book of course concerns a land where a dictatorial government quite frankly decides what is good for people to know and what is not, and where reporters shall go or not go. It is a matter of basic principle with Communists in power that they *must* freely utilize all means of communication in the service of a party which claims identity with the interests of 'the whole people' and certainly is identical with the state. Nor is it any news that such control is philosophically justified by a positive faith that communism and public ownership will lead to ultimate human liberation. Just the opposite faith is claimed to be the basis of a democracy, which holds that the truth itself is a greater liberating force than any party and that a free society can exist only if the tools of communication are freely available to all. If by common agreement both the bureaucracy and those individuals who actually own the essential means of communication use them to disseminate only that part of the truth which serves their private interests, however, the cornerstone of what is called 'the democratic process' crumbles, and a basic difference in principle between the two systems we are talking about disappears.

It is true that I might not have been granted a visa by the Chinese People's Republic but for the accident of the special circumstances I have related. Neither would the information in this report have been made available to a wide American public if the State Department's policy had gone unchallenged at *Look* and at Random House, as it did in recreant quarters elsewhere.*

That there existed even one *Look* was enough to prove that state control and self-subjugation of our press were far from complete and far from unified. The area of freedom of inquiry which separates China from the United States is not itself an absolute gulf, however, but a frontier; not something fixed or permanent, not anything ordained by God but a will in men's minds; not a right which may exist forever or has ever existed without constant struggle to maintain it; of wholly negative value if used only to serve narrow interests of private ownership while censoring the general interest of the public enlightenment and welfare; and a freedom which will soon lose all meaning if those who possess it, on the American side of the frontier, do not more energetically use it to reveal the truth about ourselves as well as the black, the white and the gray about people and systems on the other side.

The greater danger which has all along faced America, as Walter Lippmann has eloquently observed, is not communism but whether we can 'to ourselves be true', and whether we can 'find our strength by developing and applying our principles, not in abandoning them'.

It seems to me that any nation which has achieved a democratic system compatible with civil liberties would undergo unmitigated tragedy and evil if it were to lose them. No advantage could possibly accrue from depriving people of existing freedom to change their government by peaceful means. Such a loss, for whatever reasons, could only be regarded as political retrogression, even if

---

*(1969) Under pressure from publishers, scientists, educators and some congressmen, the State Department cautiously increased the number of exceptions made to the administrative ruling which excluded Americans from travel in China. Peking authorities refused to cooperate by granting visas to the State Department's 'exceptional' Americans, however. In 1968 a U.S. Supreme Court decision declared unconstitutional the State Department's practice of denying passports to those who violated its travel bans, but by then the issue had become somewhat irrelevant. China had closed its doors to all but a handful of foreign visitors during the Great Proletarian Cultural Revolution, and Americans were not in that handful. (See Preface, 1970.)

only momentary. That one form of dictatorship or authoritarianism should replace an existing one, however, in a nation which has never known a democratic or free choice between the status quo and a legal opposition, cannot be said to threaten to rob people of any treasure they already possess. It is therefore not a new evil but an old one in a different and lesser or greater degree. China is such a country. Behind its revolutionary choice of today lie reasons of history quite unlike those which made the United States and Western Europe.

We need not believe that Chinese history or its present political products are valid for export in order to give them a fair and realistic examination in their own environment. My purpose is to see why and how this particular government came to be in this particular country, and whether its dictatorial power is being used for any more enlightened aims and results than the dictatorship which it overthrew.

CONCERNING THE REVISED EDITION

Brief passages of new writing have been inserted in the original text, mainly where I have felt it necessary to clarify, or to eliminate anachronisms. Occasional footnotes have been added (1970) for the same reasons. I have made many abridgments and some complete deletions of obsolete material, including several whole chapters and some of the end-of-book documentation, notes, and appendices, all of which may, of course, be consulted in the original edition.

In a new preface, 'China in the 1970s', I have further attempted to bring this edition abreast of the time present. Does the book now serve as a useful record of China of the 1950s and the 1960s, on which tomorrow's China must arise? I should like to think so. But again I am reminded of de Tocqueville's words, that 'the subject certainly exceeds my strength, and in the treatment of it I have been unable to satisfy myself.'

E. S.

Preface: China in the 1970s

BY 1970, three years after the opening propaganda shots of the Great Proletarian Cultural Revolution, Mao Tse-tung had largely dissolved the former Party Central Committee. It was replaced by a new coalition of forces pledged to maintain the absolute authority of the Thought of Mao Tse-tung, prevent the formation of an urban-based class of managerial élite, and return the orientation of the revolution to the peasant and the rural areas, where about eighty percent of the population lived.

The Ninth Party Congress in March 1969 nullified the old Party constitution and adopted one reportedly drafted by Mao himself, wherein Lin Piao, minister of defense and vice-chairman of the Party, was named Mao's official 'successor'. Of the 176 persons named to the presidium of the Congress, only 42 were holdovers from the former Central Committee. Among delegations from provincial and regional revolutionary committees (the 'three-way alliance' of mass organizations, Party 'reliables', and army political work teams which had completed the Party purging) all but two were led to the Congress by men connected with the armed forces. The new Central Committee of 279 members, chosen by the Ninth Congress, included no less than 100 persons of military rank. The long series of antirevisionist struggles had probably displaced from one half to three quarters of the senior cadres who had been in local or central positions of authority before Mao 'bombarded the headquarters' of his former heir apparent, Liu Shao-ch'i, Chairman of the People's National Congress, and constitutional chief of state, now condemned for following 'the capitalist road'.

Thus there was indeed a revolutionary seizure of power. It was to some extent a takeover by a younger generation, albeit led by the Old Man. At every level younger cadres – aggressive, ambitious, more idealistic, certainly less privileged – unseated older cadres held guilty by association with the Liu Shao-ch'i control apparatus. A bureaucratic seniority system, holding majority control in a Central Committee of a Party itself a minority of the populace, was broken up by a revolt in which the Party chieftain called the signals.

Such were the concrete facts. The old system seemed shattered beyond renovation; government by 'revolutionary committees' was 'of' the Party, but not exclusively 'by' it. The new constitution cut many ties with Soviet-patterned parties and its emphasis was on ideological purity. In brief, the Maoist constitution gave maximum authority to the Party leader and a small group at the top to 'produce' whatever administrative and political organs were required to govern. The intention was to maintain a direct 'mass line' of communications with the people throughout the countryside, impeded as little as possible by any legally constituted bureaucratic hierarchical apparatus. One novel feature enabled even the lowest ranking Party member to petition the highest level, including the Chairman, for redress of any grievance or directive he held intolerable. This provision, in contradiction to concepts of Party discipline maintained by other Communist parties, invited comparison with the traditional (though largely specious) right of the people to make direct petition for justice to the emperor.

Among the thousands of China experts and Hongkong-based 'China watchers' not one had predicted the Mao–Liu duel before it became a public spectacle in 1966, and none foresaw the unprecedented Party purge which accompanied it. So much for the unendingly assiduous efforts of Western scholasticism, intelligence and espionage to penetrate the inner realities of political struggle in China. By 1968, however, after about three fourths of Communist China's top bureaucrats had become displaced persons, many foreign Pekingologists were prophesying that Mao would not live to stabilize a new government. Events once again confounded them.

Chinese history teaches us that no régime has collapsed there (in both imperial and republican eras) until: (1) it 'lost the mandate of heaven', or rule by consent of the people; (2) the 'dynastic cycle' ended; it became soft and corrupted beyond hope of redemption or fulfillment of traditional expectations of virtuous rule; and (3) internal contradictions reached a crisis of disunity, faced by armed rebellion or foreign invasion beyond the capability of the régime to resolve. Bizarre though some miraculous results attributed in China to applications of 'Mao Tse-tung Thought' often seemed from afar, however, Mao was personally revered by most of the peasants of China and had gone far toward winning the younger people to his banner; the Cultural Revolution had, in the people's eyes, been necessary to prevent the formation of a corruptible (revisionist) élite; and Mao had behind him the loyalty of the armed forces sufficient to handle internal factors of disunity. Mao still held the 'mandate of heaven'.

It was instructive to note that whereas in Stalin's Russia such a power struggle could have been quickly decided by the physical liquidation of any comrades in opposition, that did not happen in China. Despite three years of a great purge, Liu Shao-ch'i alone was officially named as a renegade and expelled from the Party by Mao's Central Committee in its communiqué of October 1968. For the rest of the top revisionists there presumably remained some hope of rehabilitation. As in past rectifications, efforts at reconciliation followed tension and struggle. The slogan 'Struggle – criticism – transformation' was a feature of the last phase of the Cultural Revolution; with the election of the Ninth Party Congress, 'transformation' was well advanced. The period ahead would seek to restore unity in more orderly implementation of the slogan : 'Grasp revolution and increase production.'

Whatever their genesis, the new organs of Chinese government were bound to uphold the Thought of Mao as a unifying faith. Once the Soviet Party had repudiated Stalinist ikons, the Chinese could no longer invoke the authority of Moscow's infallibility. After 1953 even Liu Shao-ch'i could not but help glorify Mao as the personification of revolutionary creativity, independence, national self-esteem and world prestige. Now, as throughout history, China put a unique Sinitic stamp upon an imported ideology which at first had appeared, to many, as a kind of barbarian conquest. It was not by accident that the patriarchal Mao, depicted as the Red Sun, hailed his people from the Heavenly Peace Gate where the Son of Heaven presided for ages long predating Karl Marx.

Major domestic policies would continue to stress Maoist solutions to the principal contradictions arising from modernization by revolutionary means. The chief domestic contradictions remained: between Party dictatorship and individual responsibility; between urban society and rural society (worker-economy needs v. peasant-economy); between mental workers and physical workers; and between ideological theory and pragmatism in the solution of technico-economic problems of social transformation. The long-range goal remained: to erase the difference between town and countryside, to subordinate selfishness to service, to create a superior and socialist man from poor peasants and the proletariat, to bypass the wastelands of bourgeois society, and to prevent the rise of a new ruling-class élite which could mislead China into those wastelands.

In general economic planning agriculture remained the foundation, with industry as the leading modernizing factor. In industry: State-market rather than consumer priorities; self-reliance, with selective foreign imports; working-class and army leadership, spurred by mixed hortatory (patriotic) and material incentives. In agriculture: poor-peasant commune management balanced between self-help (self-financing) central guidance, increased welfare programs and continuation of some material incentives: a few privately owned pigs and chickens, on small-garden-sized private plots, and privately owned peasant huts. (Ninety to ninety-five percent of the commune economy was collectively owned and operated.) Ideological, cultural, economic and technological factors of modernization in rural China had to be brought much closer to the urban levels in preparation for a true breakthrough to a take-off stage of selfsustaining growth.

Meanwhile, in education: priority for admissions of proletarian students; shortened college and middle-school courses; simplified and Mao-oriented curricula; half-time labor, half-time classroom work; self-support under commune, army, and worker-committee leadership, coordinated with centrally led priority programs for essential technico-scientific specialists. Generally: some physical work for all intellectuals; priority for modernization of the countryside over urban needs; integration of urban youth with rural life, and shifting of advanced elements to backward and frontier areas.

The 'new mandate' placed principal reliance on the army in

implementing all such programs and preventing the formation of bureaucratic élites. In 1949 Mao said: 'The army is a school. Our field of armies of 2,100,000 are equivalent to several thousand universities and secondary schools. We have to rely chiefly on the army to supply our cadres.' Since 1935 Mao had never relinquished his hold over the army – dominated through his Chairmanship of the Party military affairs committee. Once again he used it to reassert his political authority. During the purge Lin Piao retired many veteran senior officers and replaced them, paralleling civilian cadre shifts, with younger officers. With the disintegration of the old cadre-supply system (Liu Shao-ch'i's Party training schools, the Young Communist League, the former labor union educational system) the army emerged as the principal purified prep school for future cadres. Under Lin Piao, 'Mao Tse-tung's best pupil', the People's Liberation Army sought to develop the Yenan style of military and political training: egalitarianism; mastery of techniques and ideals of people's war; versatile service to the people combined with Maoist indoctrination.

Of course the army itself – which Mao saw as the model of true proletarian leadership for the younger generation – could supply only a small percentage of the management personnel needed by the nation. Cadres in or detached from the P.L.A. played a supervisory role. They provided the leaven between recruits newly introduced into leadership groups (through the revolutionary committees) and experienced Party cadres who survived the purge. Army leaders helped distinguish those among the newly educated youths who had completely integrated themselves with the peasants and workers from those still tainted by 'bourgeois intellectualism'.

As for foreign policy? The new Party constitution 'firmly upholds proletarian internationalism'. It committed Party members to 'work for the interests of China and the overwhelming majority of the whole world', and saw no contradiction between the two interests. It provided that China 'unite with all true Marxist-Leninists' and 'oppressed peoples and nations' and at the same time called for 'fighting to overthrow modern revisionism headed by the Soviet renegade clique, and reactionaries in all countries.' Since most Communist Party *majorities* outside the U.S.S.R. itself were either dominated by the Soviet system or tending toward revisionism, the problems of uniting them to achieve the other international objective defined by the constitution – 'overthrow of imperialism headed by the United States' – were formidable.

While the above terms expressed China's long-range strategic aspirations, regional aspirations were nearer realization. 'In the interests of China and the overwhelming majority of the world', Peking wished to halt the advance of the two super-power hegemonies. That is, to win respect for Chinese hegemony in her traditional political-cultural sphere of influence in East Asia : in effect, to revivify some of the old meaning of 'China', which is *chung-kuo* or 'central realm'.

With 'Vietnamization' of the Vietnam conflict reducing the immediate fear of an American attack on China, and with a major domestic campaign safely behind him, Mao was able to focus the nation's attention in the direction of what now seemed the major menace. Intensified fear of a Soviet preventive war, to knock out China's nuclear installations before she might achieve effective deterrent credibility, was by 1970 taken quite seriously in Peking, or at least by China's mass media and those participating in defensive-war preparations. The war talk and the patriotic zeal engendered also served, to be sure, as stimulants to greater efforts in production harnessed to some new Great Leap Forward.

In that perspective, and with Liu Shao-ch'i off the scene, a renewal of Sino-American discourse now seemed plausible. During the 1950s and 1960s the United States followed a policy of armed encirclement or containment of China which aimed to isolate and bring about the collapse of the People's Republic. That policy was founded on the assumption that the Sino-Soviet alliance framed a durable unity, a Eurasian giant bent on armed conquests. During the 1960s, however, that assumption crumbled. China left the Russian orbit and sharply vied with Stalin's successors for ideological world hegemony. The Soviet invasion of Czechoslavakia proved that the Russians would not hesitate to use force in order to secure obedience wherever they held armed dominance. China read the message – and prepared.

In 1969 the frontiers of the U.S.S.R. from Turkestan to the Pacific bristled with arms and Soviet–Chinese skirmishes occurred in several places; in ideological warfare and claims and counter-claims each side sought to isolate the other from credibility in world opinion. New realities, it was argued in Washington, now enabled the United States to modify its own strategy from armed containment and the isolation of China to one of armed containment with limited isolation, tending toward non-isolation and free discourse. Was not the Soviet Union now doing the major share of the work of isolating China? As some saw it, China and Russia were obligingly containing each other, within the ruins of the communist monolith. It was a confrontation which Washington might exploit further by favoring China, the weaker of the two Red nuclear powers, with moves toward a relaxation in tension.

In 1969 the Nixon administration cancelled most of the administrative restrictions against trade with China, as well as against travel, cultural and newspaper contacts. Even before those gestures China had signalled its readiness to revive the suspended ambassadorial talks. Early in 1970, at Warsaw, Chinese and American diplomats resumed discussions concerning terms of peaceful co-existence and the dissolution of the American armed protectorate over Taiwan. The instruments of a potential agreement existed within the two simple principles defined for me by Chou En-lai (see Part One, Chs. 12–14). Sooner or later they would have to be thoroughly and publicly and officially explored. But that time was not yet, as became evident with Nixon's egregious political blunder – which amounted to repeating the tragic Vietnam miscalculation itself – when he plunged into Cambodia in April 1970.

Meanwhile, China had given signs of exercising its long-dormant power of diplomatic maneuver in other directions. After being withdrawn for three years for political re-education in Peking, China's diplomats returned to their posts abroad. Tactical changes in pace and style became apparent in friendlier and more open relationships with officials and the people in Western countries. China wooed Rumania, vilified Russia for invading Czechoslovakia, and wrote an important trade agreement, the first in a decade, with that archetype of revisionism, Yugoslavia. By 1970 Canada and China had come close to an agreement to establish diplomatic recognition.

A most compelling reason why China was likely to be brought

into full international recognition during the 1970s was the necessity to call a halt to the nuclear arms race. Without China's participation in negotiations to limit and control the nuclear Frankenstein, no agreement would be universally enforced. That was further demonstrated when, in 1970, China launched a large space satellite.

The foregoing remarks leave countless questions tabled, but it is hoped that the pages which follow will provide some answers and help to show why and how China's historical problems conditioned the political means available for their solution. Obviously those means would continue to be defined chiefly by what was now officially called 'Mao Tse-tung Thought', a kind of secular religion to which organized opposition was not permissible. The paradox was that Mao Tse-tung's thinking was in spirit deeply populist: his doctrines proclaimed faith in the people, scientific experimentation, and modernization of production, as a trinity of proletarian class values.

The revolutionary purpose was human emancipation, but Mao's way left no room for heterodoxy if the Vision was to be fulfilled: that the poor (and not any Mandarin élite) should inherit the Chinese earth, marching en masse toward an egalitarian and class-free future. Whether Maoism could remain a dominant living force unadulterated by pragmatic and empirical deviations, after Mao's death, was widely doubted. A China without the corporeal Mao was an inescapable fact of the relatively near future, but Maoism was larger than Mao and would survive him. Future revisionists there would doubtless be, but none could altogether erase the impact on history of the life and the legend of Mao Tse-tung.

E. S.

Part One

REDISCOVERING CHINA

AFTER I had been in China four months I spent an evening with a Very High Official. He was an old acquaintance and we spoke off the record. He asked what my impressions were and I mentioned several aspects of China's material and cultural progress.

'But that's only a bird's-eye view of the surface of things,' I said. 'I would have to get a lot closer down to go in deeper than that. What seems obvious is that China is no longer a backward country.'

'You are mistaken,' he said. 'China is *still* a backward country. It is true that China is in better condition than it was under Chiang Kai-shek, but that is not saying much. The old China could hardly have been worse; some improvement was inevitable. The big change is in the people. I believe they have changed fundamentally for the better. But if we speak of economic progress we can only say that China has laid the foundations for fundamental change. We have enormous difficulties to overcome before we can call ourselves a *forward* nation.'

I

Arrival in Peking

EARLY one fair June day I said good-by to Lois and our two children, Sian and Christopher, and left Geneva on a Swiss plane which took me to the sparkling, new, all-window Vienna airport, where I changed to an old Czech copy of a Douglas for Moscow. By the following afternoon at about three I had flown halfway around the world and landed at Peking in a Soviet turbojet manned by a Chinese crew.

At the Moscow terminal my luggage was carried in and I had to go through customs and immigration and be weighed out again. As a through passenger I hadn't expected that, and I protested at the weighing process; like all seasoned travelers I was carrying about twenty-five pounds of overweight on my person and thus far had encountered no discourtesies about it. But here a stiff-necked young official made me divest myself of coat, cameras, films and a small box about the size of a baby grand, and even empty my pockets onto the scale. Ignoring my dimly remembered Russian, he made out a receipt for me and kept repeating '*Pláta, pláta, pozhaluista*' (Payment, payment, please). He demanded, at four times the rate charged Communist-bloc citizens, the equivalent of seventy dollars for my excess.

'Be reasonable, comrade,' I said. 'Every American isn't Rockefeller. I'm paying fourteen hundred dollars to fly to China and back. Is it fair to charge me seventy extra for a bit of fat to bring me even with your Russian passengers?'

He waved me aside, but I saw a sympathetic look in the eyes of his blond assistant and went on to say that the excess was mostly Swiss toys and chocolates for children of people I knew in Peking (perfectly true), which altogether hadn't cost seventy dollars. 'I'd rather leave the gifts here for Russian children,' I said, and I began to unpack. A crowd had gathered nearby to hear a Russian woman peasant demand a free taxi ride for herself, a mountain of baggage, and a child, because the airline bus had left without them. Now the audience deserted her to watch me and among them I saw a number of Chinese dressed as students.

The Sympathetic Blonde engaged her superior in animated debate in which two other women clerks joined on my side. The young stiff-neck dismissed them angrily and told me I could do as I pleased about disposing of my excess but if I carried it I'd have to pay. Then he disappeared behind a door marked *Kontora*.

As soon as he had gone the young woman snorted after him, 'Huh ! The *Chef!*' spoke some fast Russian to the others, and then abruptly turned and packed my things back in the box. 'Simply a blockhead !' I heard her mutter. From snatches of conversation I gathered that 'the Chief' had arrived just the day before.

Without another word she tore up the receipt he had written out, stamped my luggage and ticket and passed me through the barrier. Shortly afterward I saw her order a taxi and send the old peasant on her way.

'*Bon voyage!*' she said as I left, to continue my journey reassured that the sense of humanity is not dead in Russia.

When we took off from Moscow at midnight, one of the Czechs aboard the big Soviet transport spoke to me in broken English. 'So you are an American writer? Going to *China*?' His eyebrows lifted.

As the only 'validated' American at large in the People's Republic during the next five months I was to be greeted by many as a subject of mild wonder and speculation. Why was I there? Was I a secret envoy? Did my presence foretell some change in China's policy? Who knew what explanations of a mysterious mission lay hidden in the leather satchel I kept so carefully locked beside me? (Answer : old clippings, a Marxist handbook, Hamilton's *Mythology*, two Chinese dictionaries, a dozen blank notebooks, my toilet articles, a Hermès, and plenty of aspirin.)

I did less to allay the Czechs' curiosity than they did mine. There were six of them, with stout, bourgeois-looking wives (all wearing Bata shoes), on their way to serve two-year contracts as technical advisers in China – replacements, perhaps, for Mr Khrushchev's Russians who were soon to begin their widely publicized trek homeward. The Czechs settled down to bridge at a few kopeks a point, and for hours I watched the northern lights stretch in a red banner nearly as far as Tomsk. There the true dawn spread over Siberia and its endless dark forests broken by somber black lakes and only occasional signs of human habitation.

We skirted a great new dam and power grid and landed at Irkutsk on a vast field full of the confusion of a half-finished building program. A long wait followed in a barracks-like edifice. Eventually we were fed black bread and a few slices of cold bologna and tea, which reminded me of my wartime days in Russia. Then we slowly passed through customs and immigration. A small host of Chinese youths in dark blue tunics and ballooning trousers joined us and we all entered a Chinese-manned Ilyushin jet, its immaculate interior décor all in familiar Peking style. Chinese stewardesses seated us. They wore dark slacks and high-collared crimson silk Chinese jackets, and their long black braided hair was tied with bright red ribbons. When we were aloft one of them brought me hot coffee and biscuits.

'Ni hao?' she said, in the greeting now universal in China. 'You are well?'

'Wo hao, hsieh-hsieh ni.' My Chinese won a smile. She answered my questions briefly; she was a Peking girl, the daughter of a peasant family, a middle-school graduate, and had been an air hostess for two years. She and her good-looking assistants, who served a savory buffet luncheon, including Chinese wine or beer, made a first impression of courtesy and modern efficiency which I later found to be characteristic of China's main-line air service.

We flew all morning over Siberia and Outer Mongolia but saw only clouds and blue sky until we dropped suddenly over the jade hills of Jehol and crossed the Great Wall. Now the garden-like, well-watered fields of shaded colors and textures and the ancient plaid pattern of rural China unfolded toward the historic capital.

In a few minutes we landed at the new Peking airport, its wide paved runways flanked by a spacious modern terminal building. I knew that no visitor nowadays arrives in China anonymously, and I had supposed that some minor official would meet me. I was touched by an unexpectedly warm reception. Stepping from my plane into the bright dry June day, I saw a small group of people familiar to me from days of auld lang syne. Having been informed of my visit they had troubled to make the long journey out to the airport to welcome me.

I recognized Rewi Alley, a New Zealander who had lived in China for thirty years and had been a Chinese foster father many times over; Dr Chi Ch'ao-ting, a University of Chicago graduate whom I had last seen in Chungking, where he was adviser to Dr H. H. Kung and the U.S. Treasury representative; Huang Hua, whom I knew as a student leader when I taught briefly at the American-supported Yenching University; T'ang Ming-chao, whom I hadn't seen since he was editor of the *Daily News* in New York's China-town; Israel Epstein, a former United Press correspondent in North China, who was now a Chinese citizen and on the staff of *China Reconstructs,* in Peking; Y. Y. Hsu, a old colleague from the Chinese Industrial Cooperative days; and Dr George Hatem, a remarkable American physician whose story I shall be able to tell in these pages for the first time.

We drove back to Peking on a wide macadam parkway, arrow-straight for forty kilometers and bordered by trees and shrubs. Sub-stantial new structures surrounded by thick plantings of willows, acacias, walnut and fruit trees were identified for me : new research institutes, schools, the permanent agricultural exhibition pavilion, new factories, and many community buildings under construction. On the outskirts were long rows of landscaped brick apartments, and soon we passed Wai Chiao Ta Lou, the foreign diplomatic quarter, with its white homes and gardens built in Western style adapted to suit Peking's plans and tastes.

'There are only half a dozen embassies left in the old Legation Quarter,' said Rewi Alley. 'Eventually they'll all be shoved out here. The Quarter is gradually being rebuilt as the space is needed for more and more government office buildings moving that way.' Then he added with a wry smile, 'I'm living in Count Ciano's old quarters – the former Italian Embassy – myself. Quite posh. You'll see it.'

Rewi and George Hatem were the two I knew best in that group. I had first encountered Rewi Alley in 1929. We became friends and later worked together to found Chinese Industrial Cooperatives ('Indusco') during the Second World War, when I wrote a great deal about him.[1] Now he was widely known, especially in the British world, for his work in building early cooperative industry in China; for the unique and self-sufficient Sandan community he organized in the northwest during the war – in some ways a proto-type of the commune ideal; for his knowledge of Chinese character and the books he had written about it; and as the man to whom Joseph Needham, Cambridge's noted sinologue, dedicated the latest volume of his monumental work on China. Alley is, incidentally, one of the few British subjects who has turned down a knighthood. 'Fawncy me wearing a garter, now,' he said when I asked him about it. He had not long since returned from his native home in New Zealand, where he was a guest of the Prime Minister.

Alley was now in his early sixties. His blue eyes had lost none of their sharpness, but his red hair was sparse, his rugged frame sagged somewhat under its heavier weight, and his short sturdy legs were no longer the muscular pistons that had driven him across thou-sands of miles of rural China. Yet just the year before he had made an eight-month trip, he told me, retracing all the footsteps of his youth, to visit every province of the country. I had corresponded with Alley often, and read his books, so that he was no stranger even after twenty years. What had happened to Dr Hatem since Pearl Harbor was much more obscure to me. I turned to him now :

'What about you, Shag? What have you been doing lately?'

'Married a wonderful girl. Two children, nearly grown by now. Bound up the wounds of the revolution.'

'Is that all?'

'I helped wipe out syphilis in China. That's something. You know it's the dream of every doctor to rid a whole country of at least one disease he knows he can beat. We did it! Come over to our institute and I'll show you.'

'Institute?'

'*P'i-fu Hsin-ping Nien-Chih-So.* We translate it, Institute of Venereology and Skin Diseases.'

We had reached my hotel, the new Hsin Ch'iao (Overseas Guest House), a modern six-story edifice built just inside the Tartar Wall near Hatamen Gate, on what used to be Legation Street. Years ago I would ride down this street on my Japanese bicycle, with my beautiful white Kansu greyhound Gobi pulling me at the end of a leash, on daily rounds to press conferences at the foreign embassies. Now it was all-Chinese, like everything else in China.

'Hsiu-hsi!' (Take a rest!) was the welcome advice I was left with at the door. 'You'll need plenty of rest to get ready for all that's ahead of you.' How right that was!

I cannot complain about lack of opportunity to *see* China. I was to travel, if anything, too extensively in the time I had available. In five months I visited scores of factories, hospitals, schools, urban and rural commune enterprises, projects large and small – dams, reservoirs, bridges and power plants under construction, steel mills, coal mines – from huge machine-building plants to porcelain factories. In many thousands of miles of travel I got close to the Siberian border in Heilungkiang, reached the sea at Dairen, retraced old steps in Inner Mongolia and the northwest, traversed the Yellow River country and saw Chungking and West China again, spent some weeks in the Yangtze Valley and got as far south as Yunnan, on the borders of Burma and Vietnam. I saw something of nineteen principal cities in fourteen of China's twenty-two provinces before I left. My interviews with China's leaders, from Mao Tse-tung and Chou En-lai to the youngest cadres, numbered more than seventy. And I talked with soldiers, peasants, workers, intellectuals, students, composers, teachers, doctors, lawyers, scientists, journalists, actors, pediatricians, nurses, gardeners, ex-capitalists, lumbermen, nomads, prisoners, priests, cadres, ex-landlords, research workers, jailers, ballerinas, union leaders, housewives, movie stars, poets, inventors, acupuncturists, engineers, V.D. specialists, state planners, cancer specialists, former acquaintances, harp makers, gentlemen in the park, Mongols, Tibetans, Miaos, Lisus, Mohammedans, assorted foreign diplomats and one ex-emperor.

I talked to many such citizens alone, and often directly in Chinese, but that does not mean that I was given any clairvoyant power to enter into their private thoughts. At formal interviews there was generally an official or an interpreter present, and nobody bares his soul to either one, especially with a foreigner around. Nevertheless, I think I know more about all these people than I could possibly have understood had I never returned to China.

2

The Quiet City

AT the Hsin Ch'iao a small suite consisting of a sitting room, bedroom and bath cost me 24 yuan ($10)* a day, about as much as a highly skilled Chinese worker can earn in a week. A balcony overlooking the Outer City gave a view of the distant triple-tiered, blue-glazed round roofs of the Temple of Heaven, glistening above the carved marble altars where emperors used to offer annual sacrifices and pray for good harvests. I could see it only when the sun was relatively free of the heavy haze from new smokestacks, however, which was not often. The view was not generally worth the price of the suite, so I shifted to a fifth-floor bedroom and bath which, at about half the price, overlooked Legation Street and gave an opportunity to take note of everybody who entered and left the Hsin Ch'iao.

There were now a dozen substantial modern hotels in Peking, besides numerous inexpensive Chinese-style inns, and many new hotels had been built throughout the provinces. In former days Western-style hotel accommodation was scarce in China beyond the seaboard cities, but now it existed in towns I had never visited or scarcely heard of before. All these hotels were now managed by the China Intourist Bureau, and many were built primarily to house the thousands of Soviet advisers who once worked for China. Nearly all offered satisfactory European as well as Chinese cuisine. Food served to foreign hotel residents was not rationed, and I learned that it was often better and priced much lower in the provinces than at the Hsin Ch'iao, where my meals averaged three dollars a day.

For the benefit of tourists planning early trips to Peking, I may

* The official exchange rate, stable for many years, had been 2.44 yuan to U.S. $1.00. For statistical purposes it was generally figured as 1 yuan= U.S. $0.40. See *China's Jenminpi*, Peking, 1969, for a discourse on 'a socialist country without internal or external debt'.

as well add that the Hsin Ch'iao service was fully up to old standards in politeness if not always in quality. The 'foreign-style' cooks and No. 1 boys for which the city used to be famous had scattered to become *maîtres d'hôtel* in the provinces. They were constantly training new staffs. In the Hsin Ch'iao, as in other hotels I visited, kitchens were scrupulously clean and servants were courteous and conscientious. Quick to respond to appreciation, they politely declined all tips.

Menials were not called 'servants', 'waiters' or 'porters' (you could not find a porter at a railway station) but were addressed as *t'ung chih*,' 'comrade', like anyone else.* They were much in earnest. If you wished special attention from a waiter or a room servant it was well to learn his or her name and use it, and to find out what he was studying. Servants didn't spend their idle time playing mah-jongg now but sat by the bell boards studying English or Russian, or other textbooks, getting ready for after-hours classes, or they did *t'ai chi ch'uan* calisthenics. Even old Fatty Wang, the headwaiter at the Hsin Ch'iao (who used to be a 'boy' at the Peking Hotel), could be seen out on the terrace every morning at six-thirty going through the balletlike movements of *t'ai chi ch'uan*.†

'It's good,' he told me enigmatically, puffing in at breakfast one morning, 'for personal contradictions.'

The hotel staff had its party cells, like all state enterprises. On each floor there was a committee in charge of a workers' clubroom decorated with the usual portrait and bust of Mao (rarely of Stalin), posters, photographs, letters of praise (in lieu of gratuities), wall comments and criticisms, a few pieces of furniture, books, a radio and a television set which seemed available for general use when not rented out to some guest. The floor committee held a meeting

---

T'ung chih was now the common form of address to a stranger. Formerly one could address anyone in the countryside as *Lao Hsiang*, 'Old Village(r)', but this had become obsolete, just as *lao pai-hsing*, 'Old Hundred Names', for 'the people', had been replaced by *jen-min*, which carries more connotation of 'the masses'.

† To benefit fully from the seemingly effortless rhythms of *t'ai chi ch'uan* one must understand something of their underlying dialectical principles, which are related to Taoist concepts of unity and harmony as products of tension between opposites. See pages 375–81; see also Sophia Delza's *Body and Mind in Harmony*, N.Y., 1961.

once or twice a week and exchanged criticisms and self-criticisms which I sometimes heard waxing warm when I returned at a late hour. Warm but not boisterous, I thought to myself, when I remembered former Chinese conversations which had often sounded nearest mayhem at their peak of amiability.

Hotel employees also participated in a constant war against flies and mosquitoes, and small boys with butterfly nets competitively chased cicadas in the streets and parks. It was true that these old pests, as well as rats, mice, lice and fleas, were under better control in China than in most countries, and that stray cats and dogs had disappeared. Peking was not only much cleaner, more orderly and more disciplined; it was somehow far quieter. The capital had never rivaled Shanghai or Canton for bedlam, but now that public spitting, yelling, quarreling, gambling, drug dens, brothels, haggling in the market, peddlers' bargaining, and rickshaws had been eliminated, everything was more subdued than I remembered.

After eleven at night theaters closed, the electric buses stopped running, and only an occasional car or bicycle appeared on the brightly lighted broad main streets. Except for a night-long traffic of heavy cargo trucks and endless rubber-tired carts heard on the back roads, it was a silent city until dawn. I missed the old peddlers' chants of daytime, the trained pigeons that used to fly overhead and fill the air with music made by tiny flutes fixed to their tails, and the late-hour noodle vendor with his plangent cry.

Buses were unwontedly chaste and their girl drivers and conductors deferentially polite to the foreigner. Invariably some youth would be stirred to arise and offer me (mistaken for a Russian comrade) a seat which it was not always easy to decline. Buses discreetly sounded horns and pedestrians observed traffic lights and posters instructing them on the right and wrong ways to cross streets. People automatically gave right of way to the two-wheeled miniature buses which carried six or eight kindergarten children tandem behind pedicabs piloted by aging rickshaw men.

Taxis (Soviet, East and West European, and American makes) were available at hotels and the new central railway station. A few two-seater pedicabs also occasionally appeared. Near the Hsin Ch'iao I picked one up, pumped by a neatly dressed gray-haired gentleman who said he had pulled a rickshaw at the old Peking

Hotel in the 'preliberation' days. I managed a bit of local dialect and he responded cheerfully, to ask me how I liked 'new' Peking.

'It's cleaner, more modern, more beautiful,' I said. 'It also seems very quiet.'

'Quiet? Yes, I know what you mean.' He laughed over his shoulder. 'People are quiet – but the radio isn't quiet!'

I asked him how things were with him and he said '*Ma-ma hu-hu*', meaning so-so. Then he added, 'I couldn't afford a wife in the old days. Now I have a wife who makes a few yuan in the commune [*kung-sheh*] factory. Our daughter works in a nursery [*t'ou ehr-so*]. Who ever heard of a nursery in the old days!'

He went on to say that he hadn't been able to work much lately. He was fifty-eight and he had a back ailment for which he regularly took acupuncture (*hsia chen pien*) treatments free of charge; for he belonged to a union now.

'If only we had more to eat; the imperialists –' he muttered. '*Nin shih na-i-kuo jen?*' (What nationality are you?) he suddenly called back.

'I'm an American,' I answered.

He repeated his question and I my answer.

'*Shuo li!*' (Speak reasonably!) He turned, and seeing that I was serious he then pumped on in silence.

At the end of our trip I paid him the small regulation fare, which he accepted politely. 'Truly an American?' I nodded. He smiled, wagged his head and pedaled off.

3

The Big City

AFTER fifteen years of disuse I could still understand simple conversational Chinese but I could not claim fluency. In the written language, all the basic characters which I had once known well enough to translate vernacular literature were now so simplified as to be unrecognizable, and I had no time to learn the new system. Even limited spoken Chinese is useful, however – indispensable as a check on what one is told or not told by interpreters, and to pick up stray bits of conversation here and there.

During my visit no foreigner of any nationality left Peking, or any other city he might be authorized to visit, without a travel permit. Permits were closely restricted in time, space and availability. Every foreigner was regarded as a guest whether he paid his way, as I did, or not. Whether or not travelers spoke any Chinese they were met on arrival anywhere by a Chinese Intourist guide or an official or cadre (state or party functionary) of some kind who escorted them on their scheduled visits. Such attention is not simply surveillance; the average foreign visitor would be completely lost without an interpreter. Where it does amount to interference it is rather pointless; any traveler with good eyesight and some ear for the language learns almost as much that may be unfavorable to the régime as he would learn if he moved everywhere entirely on his own, and sometimes he learns more. One must not forget also that there really are spies in China and elementary precautions are justified. I was spared some of the official overprotection and managed privacy now and then. I also had old friends, Chinese and a few foreign residents, who took time out from busy lives to conduct me on excursions or otherwise serve to alleviate my ignorance. Within municipal limits visitors were generally free to make solo trips, except to a few clearly marked military zones.

The language problem alone is an effective barrier to 'individual' research and most strangers perforce keep on well-worn paths. Heart-to-heart political talks with casual strangers are hardly feasible for anyone as conspicuous in China as a Caucasian, a Negro or any non-Mongolian. Much less can any visiting mogul get to the 'bottom of things' in five days of banqueting and official interviews. Nor could I in five months.

Invited guests of the state did the routine conducted tours; foreign diplomats and correspondents often suffered long delays before even seeing the inside of a factory or school. They complained that for them to get to know any Chinese except embassy clerks on terms of some intimacy was very difficult. They rarely got beyond the capital.

To be 'confined' to Greater Peking, however, was not exactly punishment. Now a small state in itself and administered as such, it was five thousand square miles in area, and ranged from the Grand Canal to the Great Wall. As everyone knows, Peking is one of the world's most beautiful capitals, and physical changes wrought by the new régime had not destroyed the inner harmony and integrity of the older city. The main palace grounds and buildings in the center were intact and well kept. Within them lie the Purple or Forbidden City, and within that the Tartar or Imperial City, which dates back to Kublai Khan's capital, Tatu, and to foundations of more ancient palaces. The central scheme of Peking, a broad south-north road about five miles long, reached from the Temple of Heaven, through a series of gates in the Outer City, to the entrance of the Imperial City at T'ien An Men (Heavenly Peace Gate), which now faced the world's largest paved public square. Here more than a million people could gather or disperse in less than an hour between the imposing new Great Hall of the People, where the National Congress sat, the Museum of History, and the Museum of the Revolution. At T'ien An Men's golden-tiled double roofs the central axis pierces vermilion walls and continues through the Forbidden City, flanked by great palace halls, to a series of artificial lakes and wooded hills surmounted by graceful pavilions and temples now used as public parks and playgrounds. Modern traffic circles had been built around the massive gates, but expansion necessitated eliminating most of the old outer walls, which were being replaced by circuitous new roads. City planning limited building sites and heights and generally sought to preserve the broad and open beauty of the past.

With a population of about seven million, Greater Peking was three times as large as when I called it home for five years in the thirties. As a 'modern' capital it dates largely from the fifteenth century, but it was a political center of North China millennia ago and, if you want to go back to Peking Man, 'people' have been multiplying hereabouts for half a billion years. Bits of *Sinanthropus pekinensis* were housed in a special museum, but the skull and the greater part of the once magnificent collection of fossil bones had disappeared during the Second World War.

Peking had its dozen other notable museums, modern and ancient libraries, its score of lake-dotted parks and pavilions, the temple-strewn Western Hills, numerous new and old theaters, cinemas, restaurants and recreational centers. One new stadium seated eighty thousand people and another, built exclusively for table tennis (now second only to basketball as a Chinese national sport), was completed in time to seat fifteen thousand people for the international ping-pong matches of 1961. Wide streets, lengthened vistas, hundreds of new apartment houses and modern government structures – varying from early Stalin-type revolutionary and pretty bad, to later revolutionary (modified Chinese) architecture and increasingly good – extensive networks of extramural roads and highways running in four directions, and scores of new schools and institutes were transforming all but the old inner walled city.

Peking's famous bazaars and shops were no longer a tourists' paradise. I saw fine rugs, ivories, porcelains and embroideries being made here in state and commune factories, but they were mostly for export. The 'cosmopolitan charm' visitors loved was gone; this was an all-Chinese city now and the old foreign resident would never feel at home – if he could find it. Much of the attraction of Peking for foreigners lay in the old Peking houses, with their walled courtyards and gardens, many of which had been converted into schools, workshops or multiple dwellings, or demolished to widen or erect new edifices that are practical and unesthetic. Like New York.

Perhaps the greatest physical change was that the Outer City and suburbs had become a major industrial and steel metropolis based on nearby iron, coal and copper deposits. Peking now held nearly a million factory workers. Housing had more than doubled in area in ten years but the shortage was still acute. Most families lived cramped in one or two rooms, although newly constructed flats for state-factory workers were larger and better than anything they had known in the past. Fortunately the spacing and landscaping of 'developments' in the suburban city conformed to well-balanced zoning plans.

I shall have more to say about Peking, where I could easily have spent all my time without exhausting its interest; fortunately I was not obliged to do that. At the outset I decided to confine my travel requests to the Foreign Office as much as possible to places I had known under Kuomintang rule. As I had roamed widely and to remote corners of China in the past, that gave me plenty of territory in which to judge changes and whether people were faring better or worse. My program seemed reasonable to Premier Chou En-lai.

Red China is of course merely the current chapter, and an organic part, of a very ancient and rich history wherein one may find pre-Marxist beginnings even of some institutions built by Chinese Communists of today. 'The entire man is to be seen in the cradle of the child,' wrote Alexis de Tocqueville in his classic study of the infant American democracy. 'The growth of nations presents something analogous to this; they bear all the marks of their origin.' In the exciting and radically new society European immigrants were forming in the New World, which shocked and frightened the crumbling aristocracies of the Old World, De Tocqueville discerned 'fundamental causes' in 'the obscurity of the past'. If that was true of a nation so immature and seemingly free to make its own future as the United States was in 1835, how much more mandatory it is to see China today as a point in time and space reached by a great people who have traversed a long, long road from antiquity.

4

Confucius to Mao

To attempt to condense China's long history into a brief chapter may be an affront to scholars but excusable as a service to readers unfamiliar with the rudiments of that history. Confucius thought that if he showed a man one corner of a thing he should be able to discover the other corners for himself.

The stage which has witnessed what is to some 'the world's oldest continuous civilization' and to others 'the world's oldest continuous tragedy' is a multinational country with an area of about 3,705,000 square miles;[1] that is, a country ninety thousand square miles larger than the United States. China reached its present boundaries (including Tibet, Turkestan and Inner Mongolia) many centuries ago; in times past the empire was larger than today. Two thirds of the People's Republic, however, is mountainous, desert, or land otherwise unfit for cultivation. In 1960 slightly less than 12 percent of the total area was utilized as cropland and there were formidable problems to be overcome before substantially more marginal acreage could be brought under cultivation.* By contrast, 17 percent of the area of the United States was cropland (391,000,000 acres, as of 1959[2]) and a large portion of an additional 22 percent (now in grassland pasture) could readily be cultivated. With close to four times as many people as the United States, the Chinese had to feed themselves on 40 percent less cropland. In order to equal American agricultural output, *per person*, China would have to raise her product per acre to almost six times as much – if confined to the present cropland area – as the American output per acre.

If one superimposed a transparent map of China on a map of the United States (see map, page 15), the two countries would corres-

---

* Tibet, Turkestan (Sinkiang) and Inner Mongolia account for a large part of the mountains and desert, of course. Excluding those areas, from 15 to 20 percent of China was under cultivation.

pond fairly closely in latitude and dimensions. Both lie mainly in the temperate zone. In the south, China would extend into northern Mexico and the Caribbean, and in the northeast it would reach far into Canada. China's southernmost point (the island of Hainan) would be at Haiti, and her westernmost area (Sinkiang or Chinese Turkestan) would reach a little beyond San Francisco. Shanghai would lie near Jacksonville, Washington would correspond to Peking, New York to Shenyang in Manchuria, and Los Angeles would be somewhere in western Tibet. The topographies differ greatly. China is landlocked except for her eastern seacoast. The world's highest mountain ranges and plateaus rim her southwest and western borders, and in the north lie the Mongolian desert and a frosty frontier shared with Soviet Siberia.

Until the nineteenth century the Pacific shut China off from, rather than connecting it with, the outside world. China looked inward and was a land power, not a great maritime nation. Mountains and desert both sheltered and isolated her from continental neighbors and Europe. Contacts with the West existed but made little impact on the civilization that grew up along the Yellow River – whose origin, on that superimposed map, would be somewhere around Denver, and its exit near Richmond, Virginia. China developed in almost total isolation from the West. The term Chungkuo, which the Chinese still call their country, means Central Realm. The Ptolemaic conception of the world remains deeply imbedded in Chinese psychology even today.

Legendary Chinese history begins more than five thousand years ago. Dates of the beginning and end of the Shang and Chou dynasties are debatable, but writing on oracle bones and on bamboo offers an increasingly authentic record from the later Shang Dynasty (1523 B.C. onward). The classical period in which the civilization acquired characteristics preserved into our times was the Chou Dynasty (1027–249 B.C.), and K'ung Fu-tze or Confucius (551–479 B.C.) was its outstanding personality. His teachings gradually became state doctrine and after the Later Han Dynasty (A.D. 23–220) Confucianism dominated the social and political thinking and the whole form and style of Chinese civilization for twenty centuries.[3]

Lao-tzu (whose name means 'Old One'), a whimsical mystic said to have been a contemporary of Confucius, preached a rival philosophy of *Tao*, or 'The Way', of harmony with nature, which has little in common with Confucian doctrines. Lao-tzu's teachings embraced a concept of the unity of opposites and dialecticism which had similarities with Platonism and many points in common with Hindu and Buddhistic philosophy. Lao-tzu was not a religious teacher, but his thought was corrupted and combined with traditional geomancy in what became the native religion of China, Taoism. The dialectical nature of the *Tao Teh Ching*, which contains the essence of the 'Old One's' philosophy, suggests analogies with the schematic analytical methods of dialectical Marxism. (The authenticity of writings attributed to both Confucius and Lao-tzu is much disputed by scholars. Lao-tzu is far from established as a historical person.)

Confucius was not a religious teacher either. With some reservations it may be said that China was never essentially a religious country so much as a nation ruled by morals, ethics, conventions and philosophy. 'Respect the spirits,' Confucius is reputed to have said after a dialogue with Lao-tzu, 'but keep them at a distance.' He was China's first great reformer, a humanistic, practical codifier of the inherited wisdom of the ancients. He sought to 'remold' everybody from ruling princes to peasants into 'superior men', although he showed less interest in reforming nobles and aristocrats than in 'undertaking to make men of humble background into "gentlemen" able to hold their own in the halls of state with the most polished courtiers', according to one outstanding Confucian scholar and biographer of the sage, Professor Herrlee Glessner Creel.[4] Confucius himself wished 'to become a man of perfect virtue and to teach others without weariness'.

Confucius lived when the Chou Dynasty was breaking up into the 'Warring States', and Chou sovereignty was only nominal over some five thousand petty principalities somewhat comparable to the contemporary city states of Greece. Chinese scholars revere Confucius for having edited the classics and having written the *Spring and Autumn Annals*, a work of literature as influential as the Bible and equally disputed as absolutely reliable history. A generation or more ahead of Periclean Greece, Confucius concerned himself with the same problems of human intercourse. His social and political teachings were moralistic, benevolent, traditional, realistic and authoritarian in contrast with the dynamism of the ideal republic and other lively abstractions of Socrates, Aristotle and Plato. All were equally concerned with the qualities of virtue in rulers and the attainment of an ideal society, but Confucius found answers very different from those of the Greeks.

He prescribed a code of behavior between all members of the family in which women obeyed and deferred to men, younger brothers to elder brothers, sons to fathers, and patriarchs to men of superior rank. All men rendered homage to the emperor, who was regarded as an embodiment of Confucian virtue and innate wisdom and moral superiority, the Head of the Great Family or Nation. Dynasties rose and fell but the Confucian pattern was changeless. Administration under the emperor lay in the hands of a small Confucian scholar class, access to which was in theory democratic. Anyone who could pass the examinations could qualify, and open opportunity represented the ideal of equality. In practice this meant a monopoly of power held by a gentry-scholar class over peasant masses organized in the family system and kept in order by filial piety, ancestor worship and imperial edicts.

Confucianism provided China with the world's most stable system of bureaucratic power. It was natural for the Chinese to look upon it as the only 'correct' method of regulation of human relations and to regard themselves as superior men. China was never challenged by any advanced civilization until modern times; though sometimes defeated by culturally inferior tribes, she always ended by civilizing and absorbing them. Chinese civilization made original advances in the arts, science, industry and agriculture, and Europe borrowed many of its inventions. Treating their immediate neighbors as vassals, the Chinese conceived of the rest of the world as barbarians, much as Rome looked upon the Huns.

Capsulated Chinese history inevitably leaves the impression that nothing really happened after the Chou and Han dynasties. That would be as erroneous as to assert that in Europe nothing happened after Pericles until Copernicus was born. Immensely important changes, refinements and creative contributions to human culture continued despite long interregnums of regression under barbarian conquerors. As instances become relevant, I shall cite a few as we proceed. For the moment, three examples of Western loss through isolation from the Middle Kingdom: the Chinese were using elaborate water clocks six hundred years before one was independently invented in Europe; water-powered armillaries were turning in China three hundred years before Copernicus; and the Chinese invented printing roughly five centuries before Gutenberg produced movable type. China lost much from isolation also: for instance, Europe invented the mechanical clock in the fourteenth century, but it did not reach China until the seventeenth century; and although China invented gunpowder hundreds of years before the West, she failed to develop the uses of her marvelous firecrackers in time to avoid prolonged humiliation at the hands of the Christians.

For centuries China had some contacts with the West, but nothing her merchants and travelers reported changed her opinion of Europe's inferiority. Occasional envoys were received as representatives of vassal states and a few early Jesuit missionaries at the Manchu court were tolerated more as curiosities than as cultural equals. China's isolation from the West was finally broken in the nineteenth century, when it was invaded from the sea. From the 1840s onward the British and French wars forced China to permit the importation of opium and other trade with the West. Britain took Hong Kong and Kowloon, and extended her control over Burma and Nepal, which had been tributary vassals of Peking. In 1883, France defeated China and ended her suzerainty in Indochina. During the latter half of the century the waning Manchu power was repeatedly humiliated by violence, as China's major ocean and river ports fell under foreign control and she became a semicolony not of one nation but of all the major industrial and naval powers. A series of territorial and political concessions gave the foreigners effective control over China's trade and she seemed destined to be divided among them like India and south-east Asia.

In the middle of the last century there occurred the T'ai-p'ing ('Heavenly Peace') Rebellion, a titanic effort to overthrow the corrupt Manchu Dynasty and establish a revolutionary power. The rebellion, which reached the walls of Peking, was led by an able Chinese Christian convert, Hung Hsiu-ch'uan, who proclaimed himself the younger brother of Jesus Christ. Members of the Peace Corps today might tolerate a revelation of this nature by a promising nationalist in the 'back lands', but it was too much for our rigid nineteenth-century missionaries. They disowned their most promising convert as a sacrilegious impostor. They were even more shocked by some of his Christian reforms. Although there is no evidence that T'ai-p'ing leaders had ever heard of Marx or the *Communist Manifesto*, they had some points of similarity. Reformers in Chinese history from pre-Confucian times had reported (e.g. *Rites of Chou*) early egalitarian societies in which land was held in common and production and distribution were shared by all. T'ai-p'ing leaders made attempts to establish this kind of primitive communism. Land was distributed, with priority given to men between sixteen and fifty. Slavery and the sale of women and children were abolished together with foot-binding, prostitution, arranged marriages and polygamy. The importation of opium was prohibited, and torture and cruel punishments were supposedly forbidden. Armies participated in production and tilled fields in common, much as on the state farms (as distinct from communes) of New China.

After fourteen years of civil war said to have cost forty million lives, the rebellion was finally defeated by the armies of Tseng Kuo-fan, a Chinese scholar-general from Hunan. He was helped by Western mercenaries, first led by an American adventurer, Frederick Townsend Ward, and later by General Charles Gordon and other regular British army and navy officers, supported by the British government. Tseng was helped still more by decay and corruption among T'ai-p'ing leaders, who failed to abide by their own principles. But the suppression of the T'ai-p'ing rebellion was a Chinese victory, and the Manchu Dynasty thereafter was held hostage to the Chinese reactionary landlord-gentry-scholar class, by whom it was assimilated. The victory also increased the subservience of the Manchu Dynasty to Western imperialism, until it finally collapsed from inner rot, more than from outer assault, in 1912.

Japan had meanwhile joined the imperial overlords; in 1895 she defeated China, seized Taiwan, and ended China's suzerainty in Korea. With financial support from the United States, Japan fought Russia over the Chinese territory of Manchuria and defeated her. As prizes she took over the Russian naval base at Port Arthur,

Dairen, and Russian railway rights and concessions in south Manchuria – all of which had also been pried from Peking. Tsarist Russia retained Siberia (annexed the previous century), railway concessions in north Manchuria and a protectorate over Mongolia – where, however, Peking's sovereignty was still nominally recognized.

All through these years the reformist spirit and patriotism of the T'ai-p'ings continued to seed the underground revolutionary movements, as it later also persisted throughout the Nationalist and the Communist periods. In 1900 the secret societies provided the leadership for the fanatical antiforeign Boxer Rebellion. When the Boxers were crushed by an Allied invasion of Peking, the European powers, Japan, and the United States together imposed crushing indemnities on the dynasty which robbed it of all remaining prestige. By the time it faded away not only the major powers but small states such as Belgium, Holland and Portugal had become part of the Western dominance which made China a semicolony. The United States took no territorial concessions but fully shared in the whole system of unequal treaties by securing for its nationals all the privileges of the 'most favored nation' – a euphemism also reflected in John Hay's so-called Open Door doctrine, of equal rights for all, in trade and exploitation. Under the unequal treaties foreign nationals had extraterritorial rights which enabled them to reside and do business in China while remaining accountable only to their own courts.

Following the demise of the Manchu Dynasty, attempts were made to set up a parliamentary republic, for which the nation was wholly unprepared. Western-educated Sun Yat-sen, an exiled hero of the national independence movement, was elected president of the provisional republican government. He lacked armed forces and was obliged to defer to the former chief of the imperial troops, Yuan Shih-k'ai. When Yuan subsequently proclaimed himself emperor he was quickly overthrown by rival militarists. Disunity and chaos reigned as provincial satraps struggled for supremacy and the foreign powers vied with each other to control them. Meanwhile, Sun Yat-sen and the Kuomintang, or Nationalist party, which he had founded, made alliances with various warlords. Repeatedly Sun failed to establish a stable basis for a successor to the weak, corrupt, semipuppet and largely impotent warlord-dominated governments at Peking.

Dr Sun was spurned by all the foreign powers until after the First World War, in which the Peking government had, as a result of great pressure from the United States in particular, joined the Allies. China had expected that the defeat of Germany would result in the rendition to her of Germany's colonial holdings in Shantung; at Versailles the Allied Powers revealed that they had (except for the United States) signed secret treaties awarding the Shantung concessions to Japan. All Chinese patriots were bitterly disillusioned. These included many youths who had volunteered for service in Europe and some who had gone there as leaders of China's labor corps. (Chinese were then considered unfit material for soldiers.) Among the members of this Work-Study movement who became prominent in Red China was Chou En-lai. Mao Tse-tung helped recruit worker-students but at the last moment he chose – a fateful decision – to stay in China.[5]

One result of the resentment aroused by the Versailles Treaty was the May Fourth Movement of 1919, led by Chinese students and intellectuals, in which Mao Tse-tung participated. It had important cultural results – a reform in the written language and rejection of many remaining influences of Confucianism – as well as political consequences. In awakening the patriotism of the nation to resist and finally defeat Japan's effort to reduce China to an outright colony (through the 21 Demands of 1915) students and intellectuals demonstrated an astonishing moral and political power and foreshadowed an end to warlord rule. By exposing the hypocrisy and cynicism of the Versailles powers, the movement opened all China to the inflow of revolutionary ideas stemming from the anti-imperialist Russian revolution. At this time Sun Yat-sen turned to Lenin for help and there at last he received it.

Soon after seizing power the Bolsheviks had made generous overtures toward China. These included voluntary renunciation of the unequal treaties, the return of territorial concessions, and an offer of joint operation of the Chinese Eastern (Manchurian) Railway. Moscow maintained relations with the foreign-dominated Peking régime, but meanwhile Lenin's correspondence with Sun Yat-sen opened another prospect. It led eventually to the Bolshevik implementation of a new strategy to promote world revolution by supporting colonial nationalist leaders.

As late as 1919 the first writings of Lenin appeared in Chinese and it was not until 1920 that the first complete translation of the *Communist Manifesto* was published in China.* Out of the intellectual ferment germinated by changes within China and by the October Revolution, the Kungch'antang or Chinese Communist Party arose in 1921. Following the entente between Dr Sun and the Bolsheviks (represented by Adolf Joffe) in 1923, the Nationalist and Communist parties formed a united front. Its platform was Dr Sun's *San Min Chu I* or 'Three Principles of the People'. These principles were known as 'nationalism, livelihood and democracy'. In brief, somewhat oversimplified terms they meant national liberation and unification; restoration of China's economic independence and the regeneration of rural life; and universal education and enlightenment of the whole nation in preparation for a modern, popular government.

Sun Yat-sen seized a base in Canton and the Russians sent money, arms, military advisers and experts in revolutionary techniques of political organization and propaganda. The Communists were permitted dual membership in their own party and the Kuomintang. In his last days (1925) Dr Sun said of the principle of livelihood, 'It is socialism and it is communism.' Chiang Kai-shek, a Japanese-educated officer and one of Sun Yat-sen's young followers, was sent to Moscow and received special training there. Following Sun's death, Chiang Kai-shek was groomed as his successor by the Russian advisers. In 1927 the Nationalist revolution, under the supreme military leadership of Chiang Kai-shek, was victorious over most of China. In the same year Generalissimo Chiang broke with the Communist party and made membership in it a capital offense.

By 1928 four fifths of the Chinese Communist Party had been exterminated. Forced underground, its urban leaders continued to observe directives from Moscow, while Stalin headed the Comin-

* (1970) Ironically, ten measures proposed by Karl Marx for adoption by the 'most advanced countries' after a world proletarian revolution (in the *Communist Manifesto*) were the first of his writings ever translated into Chinese. They were appended to an article by Chu Chih-hsin in the *Min Pao*, a journal of Chinese revolutionaries in exile in Japan, January 1905. See *Li Ta-chao and the Origins of Chinese Marxism*, Maurice Meisner, Cambridge, Mass., 1967, page 52.

tern, but attempts at proletarian insurrections were disastrous failures. Meanwhile Mao Tse-tung had gone to the deep hinterland, in Hunan, to begin a guerrilla movement with its base in the peasantry. For ten years a civil war as savage as the T'ai-p'ing Revolution – and still claiming direct historical descent from it – raged across South China. The basic 'three principles' remained the common heritage of both the contending parties. The Communists brought to them a Chinese Marxist interpretation of thoroughgoing social revolution while Chiang Kai-shek struggled to retain private ownership as the unalterable fundament of all three principles.

Throughout this whole epoch following the demise of the Manchu Dynasty, China's 'traditional society' underwent a continuous disintegration. What Chiang attempted was to replace it with a capitalist state in China under a military dictatorship. It is a mistake to assume that his struggle with the Communists was over either the restoration of 'traditional society' or its final destruction. 'Traditional society' had already been shattered by the impact of foreign industry, science and capitalism. The struggle between the Reds and Chiang Kai-shek was quite simply over whether China's modernization was to be achieved by private enterprise under the dictatorship of a very weak bourgeoisie, or by a proletarian revolution, led by the Communist party, to establish public ownership over the basic means of production and to mobilize 'the whole people' and their immense labor power.

Chiang Kai-shek and his bureaucracy were not elected but seized power. Before the Japanese occupation, the Kuomintang (membership about two million in 1938) held the cities against the Communists with armed garrisons, police, and some foreign help. As far as the peasant majority was concerned, 'government' simply meant the Kuomintang-appointed county magistrate who ruled as of yore in collusion with the landlord-gentry of the district and their local armed guards – 10 to 20 percent of the population.

In the contest between Chiang and Mao, time was decisive. Modern capitalism had begun more than a century late in China. As the nation reluctantly accepted the superiority of science and mechanized industry, intellectuals despaired of ever catching up by emulating the nineteenth-century West and using its agonizingly slow and painful method of 'capital accumulation' through the private exploitation of labor and national resources. Even so, Chiang might have won against the Communists had they not received 'providential' help from Japanese imperialism.

When Mao said that imperialism had 'prepared the material as well as the moral conditions'[6] for Communist victory in China he spoke literal truth. It was not the Communists but Japanese imperialism whose deep penetration and occupation of urban China (1937-45) crippled the bourgeoisie and destroyed Kuomintang morale. In doing so it opened the countryside to the proselytization and organization of the peasantry by the Communists. Japan's war, originally launched under the slogan 'To eradicate communism in East Asia!' had the double effect of destroying Western colonial dominance in China and making it possible for Mao Tse-tung to arm the massive peasant fist of a renewed T'ai-p'ing Rebellion – this time led by Marxists, not Christians.

As early as 1936 Mao Tse-tung had foreseen these consequences as inevitable, and I myself had summarized his convictions in *Red Star Over China*:

> Thus ... a great [Japanese] imperialist war, which is almost certain to assume the character of a world war, will release the forces that can bring to the Asiatic masses the arms, the training, the political experience, the freedom of organization, and the mortal weakening of the internal police, necessary for a revolutionary ascent to power ...

In this sense Marx's prophecy that 'capitalism digs its own grave' was fulfilled not only in Asia but also in Europe, where two great wars wrecked the old society. As George Kennan observes:

> It was not ... Communist efforts which destroyed the old order in Europe itself in the thirties and forties and eventually delivered the eastern half of the continent into Communist hands; it was Hitler who did this ... And, similarly, in East Asia, it was not Moscow, and least of all Washington, which really delivered China into the hands of the Communists; it was the Japanese ...[7]

Mao Tse-tung did not create or command the forces of Japanese imperialism but his understanding of them enabled him to seize leadership and control over the energies of nationalism and patriotic resistance, to win a sovereign victory for social revolution.

5

Paotou Retrospect

In Peking I was invited to a cocktail party to renew acquaintance with some professors, writers, soldiers and other people who remembered me from former days. My host was Liao Ch'eng-chih, with whom I had worked on Mme Sun Yat-sen's China Defense League in days when China and America were allies. Liao is the son of Liao Chung-k'ai, who was Dr Sun's closest colleague. Liao Ch'eng-chih was now chairman of the Overseas Chinese Commission, a cabinet-level post, and a director of the China Peace Committee, which might be called the Anti-American-Imperialism Committee.

I found myself talking to a thin, hollow-chested guest who gazed out of lashless eyes behind heavy-rimmed glasses. He had a bad haircut and, in blue cotton work clothes, was the most simply attired person there. If he had not been munching hors d'oeuvres from one hand and holding a glass of wine in the other I would have thought he had wandered in by mistake. Yet he looked vaguely familiar; as I knew most of the guests I thought I should remember him.

'What kind of work are you doing now?' I probed.

'I work in the botanical gardens of the Academia Sinica. I specialize in tropical flowers,' he said.

'Oh, you're a horticulturist?'

He spoke some English and must have understood me. Irrelevantly he replied, through an interpreter, in self-accusation: 'My crime helped to cause the deaths of millions of people. I should have died for it. Instead of that I have been given a chance to repent and to work for socialist construction. I am quite happy at my work, very happy for the first time in my life because for the first time I am doing something useful.'

Here was indeed a sinner wearing his remolded thoughts on his sleeve.

'You are,' said the Chinese beside me, having enjoyed my mystification, 'speaking to the former Manchu emperor, Hsuan T'ung.' The boy emperor – P'u Yi. He was now fifty-four. At the age of eight he had been sitting on the Dragon Throne in the Forbidden City when the first revolution forced his abdication. Later he had lived in exile in Tientsin.

In 1935 the Japanese spirited him off to set him up as the puppet emperor K'ang Teh of Manchukuo. Captured by the Russians in 1945, he had been returned to China only a few years ago. I had always assumed that P'u Yi had been kidnaped by the Japanese and I asked now if after all he should really feel guilty.

'Oh, yes,' he told me. 'I worked willingly with them. I felt ashamed to have lost my family's power and I believed the Japanese would help restore it. I cost the lives of millions. Any other country would have killed me. Instead, they have let me work at what was always my hobby – gardening.'*

'And today you support socialism?' I asked.

'Yes, certainly!' he said. 'Socialism is good.' He proposed a toast which was on everybody's lips that day: 'To the friendship of the Chinese and American – people!'

Beginning and end are like a circle, says the *Chuang-tzu*; where there is end there is the beginning. P'u Yi had reached the end.

'Climb in! We're late and trains leave on the dot these days.'

Rewi Alley shifted his big frame to make room for me as I got into the taxi, which took us to the new Peking station. Under a wide translucent dome supported by feathery, powerful lattices of steel, stood China's first escalator and other innovations of the large new terminal: public baths, reading rooms, nurseries and laundry facilities for mothers, various shops, a theater, television, and restaurants with Chinese and European cuisines. The food was expensive for most Chinese (three to six yuan a meal), as was true of all off-ration restaurants, but it was still available to those who could pay. A few months later, with the bad news of massive crop failure, most off-ration restaurants were closed down, although meager meals continued to be available in metropolitan stations to travelers provided with special ration coupons.†

On the walls of an all-sleeper train of pale green cars, trimmed in yellow, were signs in characters as well as romanized Chinese which casually proclaimed: *Peking–Urumchi Express*. In four days

* (1970) P'u Yi died of cancer, in Peking, in 1967. His book, *From Emperor to Citizen*, was published in Peking in 1965 and in New York (under the title *The Last Manchu*) in 1967.

† Ration tickets were required at this time for grain (raw or cooked), oil or fats, sugar, meat, cloth and a few other items. Rationed items were inexpensive and within the means of all. 'Off-ration' restaurants sold food

one could now do a twenty-five-hundred-mile overland journey to Chinese Turkestan. When I lived in Peking, Turkestan was accessible only by camel caravan and months of travel across the Gobi.

Alley and I were not going to Turkestan. We were on a four-hundred-and-fifty-mile trip to Paotou (pronounced Bao Toe), which used to be the frontier end of the line and is now autonomous Inner Mongolia's largest city. I missed by only a year making it the thirtieth anniversary of a summer excursion taken when, still wet behind the ears, I first met Alley during the height of a great famine in the dust bowl of northwest China, between northern Kansu-Shensi and the Mongolian steppe.

From 1938 to 1941 I had spent much of my time and energy helping Rewi Alley and others promote Chinese Industrial Co-operatives. That had meant raising money abroad to keep Alley in the field as chief technical adviser in the organization of those war-time handicraft production units which later helped to maintain and develop successful guerrilla warfare against Japan. Until recently Alley had been director of the Sandan[1] technical training school which he organized in Kansu. It was now headed by one of his adopted children, Alan, a Chinese orphaned by one of the great floods of the thirties. Rewi had many books in print and was constantly writing and translating poetry.

Beyond Peking we passed the growing Shihching Shan (Mountain) iron and steel complex, surrounded by a modern town within sight of the Jade Fountain, the old temples of Patachu, and the imperial hunting parks. All around were green hills now heavily afforested. A new line was being built to encircle and by-pass Peking; this Shihching Shan spur was part of it, on an alternate route to Hualai, on the Inner Mongolian frontier. It was in the process of double-tracking, which involved many tunnels and bridges to get through the Taiheng Mountains. Hundreds of workers were camped in clusters along the blue-green Yungting River, their red flags flying over white tents or marking the day's advance

at prices prohibitive for low-income people except as an occasional luxury or treat.

(1970) By now meat, grain, sugar, oil and most other foods had been in plentiful supply since 1964 but rationing of cloth (still a major export item) and grain continued.

of battalions on the job. In the early evening their campfires flowered along the river bank and some of the men turned to wave to us.

Railway mileage in China had about doubled – to 24,000 miles – in ten years and highways had increased by five times – to 270,000 miles, but both were still far behind the need of so large and energetic a country; reservations on express trains usually had to be made far in advance. (In 1959 the United States had 259,000 miles of railroads and 3,510,000 miles of rural and municipal roads.) China's railways were standard gauge and Chinese factories now made all types of rolling stock. The equivalents of first, second and third classes were soft, medium and hard, the last being simply wooden seats, while medium provided narrow berths ranked in tiers of three. 'Soft' was a compartment with well-upholstered comfort. Fares were about half those in the United States and service considerably better in both quality and spirit. On the other hand, inter-urban bus services were poor and in many areas nonexistent.

We had a compartment finished in blue plush, with a retractable dining table, rose-silk-shaded lamps, and fans. A radio offered Chinese and Western music broadcast on the train, interspersed with pep talks and educational programs; it *could* be disconnected. A hot four-course Chinese dinner (3·50 yuan) was served in the compartment by a waitress, her hair done in pony-tail style, who as usual declined any gratuity. Before you left one of these de luxe trains the headwaiter brought around his guest book, to ask for suggestions and complaints, and beamed with satisfaction at a few words of praise.

'It's better than the old gondola I rode in when I first met you up here, remember that?' asked Rewi. 'Whatever became of that Kuomintang bantam with you that summer – Napoleon Li, or something like that?'

'Wu – C. T. Washington Wu!'[2]

Mr Wu was a technical expert with the Ministry of Railways. I was working for a paper in Shanghai and doing a series of articles on railways then in use, two years after Chiang Kai-shek had established the Nationalist capital in Nanking. The Ministry had lent me Washington Wu's services but he knew very little about railways. He was a Kuomintang 'cadre' of that day, a returned student from America who had been given a sinecure for various family reasons.

What Washington lacked in technical proficiency in one profession he more than made up as a connoisseur in another.

At the end of a hard day of sightseeing he would reach his room in a Chinese hotel and shout for the *lao-kuan-ti*, or 'old-fix-it'. That omnipresent factotum would appear bearing steaming water and hot towels. While Washington was still wiping the dust from his face and hands he would give sharp instructions to the porter, who would *shih-shih* (yes, yes) him and leave. In a few minutes there would be a knock at the door and in would come a young girl or maybe two or three together. Washington would look them over, pinch a behind or two, and make a city man's joke. As a rule he would reject the first offering. 'Old-fix-it' would be rebuked for sending in a flower-face (pockmarked girl), and eventually a rosy-cheeked lass would be found acceptable. He would do her the honor and a few minutes later be ready, the technical expert, for an evening banquet.

'Washington told me that the women of Kalgan were supposed to run horizontally – that old smoking-room joke of the West,' I said. 'I can't remember whether he ever found out.'

In the early 1930s Kalgan had swarmed with prostitutes, and the sale of women was a thriving industry. In the regions of prolonged drought in the northwest millions were completely destitute and boys as well as girls were sold to brokers for indentured labor. Pretty girls found ready buyers as concubines, teahouse waitresses, or common street *piao-tzu*. The most talented and stronger became singing girls and sometimes emerged as prosperous house mothers, but the great multitude had a short life as cheap prostitutes and slaves of their owners and procurers.

All over China the poorer peasants were being steadily driven from the land by confiscatory taxes and excessive rents. Foreigners in Shanghai would say, 'These Chinese are heartless; they think no more of selling a child than a pig.' But in an International Settlement where an official burial detail was continuously on duty and used to bury tens of thousands of corpses annually picked up from the streets and canals – they were mostly victims of infanticide – there were worse fates than being sold into service.

Washington had wanted to end our trip at Kalgan but I insisted that we go on to Paotou; I wanted to see the famine country.

Not far out of Kalgan we came to a small station on a hot dusty plain and drew up beside a gasping locomotive pulling some freight cars packed with wan, half-naked, hungry children and women. No passenger trains were operating. Our caboose had been attached to a west-bound train made up of a few goods wagons and an open gondola or two. Out of a crowd of black-topped Chinese I suddenly saw a carrot-haired foreigner emerge. It was Rewi Alley.

Employed at the time as a factory inspector by the Shanghai International Settlement, he had chosen to spend his annual vacation in the famine region with a handful of foreigners who ran a few soup kitchens and were offering food and shelter to those still capable of working on the Sa Tao Chu irrigation canal near Kueisui. I introduced myself to Alley and after talking to him I asked Washington to let him sleep in one of the unoccupied bunks in our caboose. He refused. He didn't like 'imperialists', especially 'missionaries', and he had an idea Alley was one of them. They were 'always talking about China's backwardness'.

We went on to the end of the line at Paotou and to Wu's disgust I spent several days with Alley riding into the ghost towns and the deserts which had once been fertile plains. There for the first time I saw children dying by the thousands, in a famine which eventually took more than five million lives but was scarcely noticed in the West. Seeing it was an awakening point in my life; it remained the most shocking of all my experiences with war, poverty, violence and revolution until, fifteen years later, I saw the furnaces and gas chambers in which the Nazis, too impatient to wait for mere starvation, exterminated six to seven million people.

Except for the International Famine Relief Commission's canal project, run by O. J. Todd, an American engineer, and Dr Robert Ingram, a medical missionary whose special task was to delouse the labor gangs to keep typhus and plague out of the camps, practically nothing was being done for the hordes of ragged, penniless refugees driven to the dusty mud-walled towns in search of food. Hundreds of last-ditchers sat or lay on the streets or doorsteps dying before my eyes. Relatives were too weak to bury them, but at night they disappeared, consumed by ravenous dogs, rats and – some said – by creatures once men.

Twenty million people were seriously affected in that winter of

1929–30 and in the equally terrible seasons that followed before the drought ended its three-year scourge. Vast acreage passed into the hands of moneylenders and absentee landlords, from the Great Wall southward to the Wei River Valley. During the next dozen years there would scarcely be a time when famine, flood or war did not strike some large area of China. In every case the same confiscatory economics would be at work, the same exploitation of human tragedy going on unchecked, the same degradation of the farmer, the constant growth of a landless peasantry, and the making of recruits for eventual revolution.

The next summer Alley adopted a Chinese orphan he picked up among the human debris of the Yangtze River flood. He called the child Mike and took him to Shanghai to be educated. I remember him as a little fellow with solemn eyes, then as an honor student at St John's University, later as a young engineer working with Rewi when he was building industrial cooperatives to help the guerrillas fight Japan. And now I had just seen Mike in Peking, as friendly as ever, tired from overwork, proud of his talented wife and a promising son and charming daughter. He was in charge of an important project in the Academy of Sciences.

Twilight had fallen while Alley and I reminisced. Here and there the fires of coke ovens or small blast furnaces burned through the night. Before them dark figures moved in silhouette, and on the horizon I could see the giant poles of new high-tension power lines with their multiple arms stretched out like the many manifestations of the Buddha, toward the wide steppe beyond.

At ten o'clock the reading lamps on our train were turned off, as was the custom. Alley was already asleep.

6

Steel in Mongolia

FEW visitors to this land had been even as far west as Paotou during the past decade. As it had now undergone an astounding trans-formation, to become China's main heavy-industry base for the development of the middle northwest, and was also a principal political base in Mongolia, it is worth some detailed notice here.

Kalgan is the gateway to Paotou and to a million square miles of plateau which form historic Mongolia. Ruled as a single nation under China's suzerainty until late in the Manchu Dynasty (1644–1912), Mongolia was divided when the expanding Tsarist Empire set up a semiprotectorate over the northern or 'Outer' half, called Wai Meng Ku. During the revolution the Bolsheviks pursued White Russian leaders into Urga (now Ulan Bator), where they helped create the Mongolian People's Republic after overthrowing the lama priesthood and the princely descendants of Genghis Khan.

Although the Soviet government continued to recognize China's nominal sovereignty over *all* Mongolia, Moscow made an armed alliance with Outer Mongolia and stationed troops there. Mao Tse-tung said in 1936 that when the Chinese revolution was victorious Outer Mongolia would 'automatically become a part' of a socialist federation of China.[1] In 1945, Stalin exacted Chiang Kai-shek's full recognition of Outer Mongolian independence, however, when he signed the Sino-Soviet military alliance against Japan with the Kuomintang government. That alliance died a natural death once Mao Tse-tung achieved victory, but Outer Mongolia retained its independence and status as a military ally of Moscow.

By 1930 the Kuomintang government was actively absorbing southern or 'Inner' Mongolia by incorporating it into Chinese provinces known as Ninghsia, Suiyuan, Jehol and Chahar. The People's Republic formally reversed the Kuomintang's policy of obliterating Mongolia in political geography. Under the Commu-

nists the frontier provinces mentioned above, together with a large
slice of western Manchuria, were 'returned' to the Mongols and
were combined into today's Inner Mongolian Autonomous Region.
In size it is roughly comparable to, and in population (about ten
million) nearly ten times larger than, the Mongolian People's
Republic.

On a map the Inner Mongolian Autonomous Region might thus
impress any Mongols at Urga who still favored unification with
their southern brothers. But the new cities of Inner Mongolia were
largely Chinese, as were most of the advanced agricultural lands,
and in the whole region Chinese now outnumbered Mongols by at
least six to one. The great grasslands and plateau were still pastoral
domains of the Mongol nomads, and where Mongols predominated
they formed a majority in locally elected councils. They were all
subject to directives from the sovereign Communist Party of China,
of course, as was true in all autonomous regions, including Tibet,
but each minority nationality had its own party, also. The term
autonomous was administrative more than political – the minorities
had nothing like independence – but the revolutionary modernization of the Mongols' economy now in process was probably inevitable if they were not to be extinguished as a continuing people.

Possibly more than a third of the population of Inner Mongolia
lived in the area served by the Peking-Paotou section of the railway. Beyond Kalgan the two principal cities were Kueisui, officially
known as Huhehot and now the capital of Inner Mongolia, and
west of it, by about a hundred miles, the sprawling old and new
cities of Paotou. Huhehot and Paotou were now joined (via Tsining)
by a new railway to Outer Mongolia and Siberia. On the map of
China and the United States superimposed (page 15) the location
of Paotou would roughly correspond to that of Des Moines, but its
climate is similar to that of North Dakota and its place in China's
future scheme of economy more like Chicago's or Pittsburgh's.

Passing through this ancient land west of Kalgan I counted fourteen small and medium-sized new iron and steel mills, with power
plants and settlements of workers clustered around them. One of
these, the Shih Hsuan Hua No. 1 Steel Works, was the focus of an
entirely new industrial city built up for about two miles along the
railway. Here and there spur lines came in from the north, bringing

coal and ore from newly developed mines. Near Huhehot the buildings of a large modern rolling mill, under construction, stretched
for nearly half a mile. Around all the metallurgical developments
substantial steel and concrete factories and new brick apartments
were rising. Little building in the old mud-brick style was being
done; brick kilns seemed to be everywhere you looked.

The old Paotou I remembered was a few thousand tumble-down
buildings and a dusty main street. It was now called East Paotou,
and the new or main Paotou railway station lay about five miles
farther west. The area in between was rapidly filling up with factories, residences and streets connected with the new steel town by
a wide macadamized road which would soon be the main thoroughfare of a single city. Scores of tall chimneys on the horizon told the
story of the older town changing at a pace to match the new.

In ten years Paotou had grown from a war-torn and famine-
ravaged frontier town of 90,000 survivors, to a metropolis of
1,320,000 inhabitants.

We put up at the Kun To Lun, a new hotel which covered a city
block. It consisted of one main building of five stories and an annex.
Between them lay a spacious garden complete with fountain and
plaza. The balcony of my room overlooked, on one side, a range
of red-brick apartments; across the road straggled blocks of old
adobe huts with clay chimneys, interspersed with patches of sunflowers (grown everywhere on marginal land for their seeds and
oil) and green vegetables. Two miles beyond, the new road ended
at the huge half-completed Paotou Iron and Steel Works. It was
flanked on both sides by more apartments and by public buildings,
schools, an opera house, a hospital and modern shops fronted with
Mongolia's first plate-glass picture windows. Near a new bridge a
stadium had been completed. Masses of tents clung to the outskirts
and I learned that more than 100,000 people were living in them.
Of these tent-dwellers 17,000 belonged to construction gangs putting up subsidiary buildings for Paokang – the steel mill – and more
housing for its 66,000 workers.

My informant was Li Chih, the mayor. He had invited us to
lunch, together with the deputy manager of Paokang, a Mongol
named Wu Lichi Najen, and some other officials. Mayor Li was a
wiry Hupeh man of forty-five, with a well-shaped shaved pate

burned as brown as his face. He reminded me of Yul Brynner. I knew almost without asking that he was a guerrilla veteran of the old Eighth Route Army, the Paluchun.* There was something different, a quiet self-confidence without arrogance, a genial manner of authority, and usually a sense of humor, which readily distinguished these older combat Communists from the sedentary Party bureaucrats.

'Yes, everybody here was a guerrilla,' Li said, his glance sweeping all the Mongols and Chinese at the table. 'First we fought the Japanese, then we chased out the Kuomintang. When we had won we laid down our rifles and immediately picked up tools.'

Li Chih had been Paotou's mayor since 1951. He said that the Japanese and the Kuomintang had left him with two industries, a power plant of 500-kilowatt capacity and a mill that turned out 200 tons of flour a year. Today there were 273 state and municipal industrial enterprises and more than 1,000 small-scale *kung-shih* production units. Paotou was producing railroad equipment, lathes, heavy machinery, power tools, all kinds of building materials, processed foods (including packed beef and mutton) and textile machinery. Output value in the whole area in 1949 had not exceeded 10,000,000 yuan, according to Mayor Li. The 1960 target was 1,200,000,000 yuan ($500,000,000.) 'And we'll exceed it,' said the same authority.† Quite possibly they did; but the same would not be true in 1961 and 1962, for reasons which develop in further chapters.

Greater Paotou City includes seven *ch'u* (boroughs), and like most of China's new industrial metropolises it embraced suburban agricultural and natural resources around it. The aim was to achieve integrated urban-rural self-sufficiency. Under Paotou's

---

* After the Nationalist-Communist truce of 1937, the Chinese Red Army was reorganized as the Eighth Route Army. With its base in Yenan, in northern Shensi, it carried on guerrilla warfare behind the Japanese lines deep into northern China.

† The figure would mean a per capita output value of about 1,000 yuan yearly, or, at official exchange rates, something like $416 – extraordinarily high for this part of the world, even in an area undergoing rapid industrialization, with emphasis on heavy industry. Here 'output value' would be relatively meaningless unless one had an index of commodity prices related to world market values.

administration was the rich new Mongolian iron-mining center of Pai Yun Shan (White Cloud Mountain), which was directly connected with Paokang by an electric railway eighty miles long. One whole borough was entirely agricultural and pastoral. The regional sugar industry, centered on a large submodern factory far in the suburbs, was also run by the municipality. Mayor Li added that the local beet crop had been largely ruined by drought and a siege of pests new to the area and immune to insecticides in use there. The mill was closed down.

'No, we can't say we have achieved anything like food self-sufficiency here yet – though we have a better meat supply than most areas. Even if we had good weather, farm output wouldn't take care of the tremendous growth. Farms are short-handed; we're behind on the new Paotou-Yellow River canal, which will double local production. We haven't had a real rain all summer – and we get only four months of frost-free weather and one crop a year. It will be a hard winter for us but nobody will starve. Nothing like you saw here in 1929. Paotou is no beggar. We're making things farmers need and we'll trade for food: steel, power equipment, machinery, agricultural tools. We'll soon be making big locomotives, cranes, trucks, tractors, too –'

Staples were already closely rationed in Paotou, as elsewhere, but I saw no beggars, starving people, ragged urchins, or signs of mass famine. Steel workers, miners and other heavy-industry workers stood in top priority on rations all over China, of course.

There was also the problem of housing, and in Paotou's long winters shelter was vital.

'Yes, we're behind in housing,' Mayor Li went on. 'How do you keep ahead of a city that grows fourteen times its size in one decade? The Kuomintang left us nine hundred thousand square yards of mud buildings filled with vermin. Since 1952 we have built five million square yards of clean brick dwellings with lights and running water. We have killed the rats, fleas and lice and wiped out epidemics and venereal disease. But we still have only fifteen square feet of housing space to a person – and we're expecting four hundred thousand more immigrants here within two years! Why? To man new factories we are building, to extend irrigation works, to open up new farms on the steppe. Your government keeps telling you people that China wants war. Oh, I know that, all right, but, Mr Snow, we simply don't have time to fight any wars – except for living space right here at home. Of course we'll give the imperialists more than they're looking for if *they* start any wars against *us* !'

The personable Mongol manager of Paokang took us to see the mill : five square miles of belching smokestacks, acres of pipes, sidings, cranes, and different kinds of steel processing plants. One of 156 major projects undertaken by China with Soviet aid, and built under the supervision of Russian engineers – all of whom had now left – Paokang had begun producing early in 1960. By now it had a turn-out rate of close to a million tons of steel a year and 700,000 tons of iron. With a target of 1,500,000 tons of iron in 1961 and hopes of 2,500,000 tons of steel in 1962, Paokang would rank as one of China's five major metallurgical centers. The largest, at Anshan, Manchuria, had a 1960 output of about 5,000,000 tons of steel – which Paokang planned to reach by 1965; the other main centers were at Wuhan, on the Yangtze, the cluster of small new mills in Anhui, and the large Shanghai mills which in 1960 reportedly produced more than two million tons. Paokang's ambitious targets were destined not to be reached as early as 1962, however.

Slogans on the pipes, walls and buildings exhorted workers to do their utmost, quoting Mao and party texts. Giant white letters on a duct caught Rewi's fancy and he translated them : 'Liberated Thinking Liberates Production.' As we watched steel poured from a great furnace, drums began to beat and gongs were sounded. A detachment of young women and men in white overalls arrived to present a red banner of achievement to a girl I photographed manipulating a mammoth overhead crane. I was told that she had just completed a thousand 'missions' without a mishap.

Somehow none of this meant as much to me as the thousands of shade and fruit trees planted along the highways, around the factories, and running up the low hills. I kept remembering the dying trees, those that were still standing here in 1929, stripped of their leaves and bark for food of sorts, by starving human locusts.

But before I fell asleep that night I thought : It has taken me most of the day to see one steel mill and I know nothing of the communes and the many factories we passed. What one person can learn anywhere in China in one day is sharply limited. I wondered drowsily about how this city of more than a million new inhabitants, dropped suddenly on a relatively backward agricultural base, would be fed. The mayor had said the region could not meet sixty percent of its grain requirements. From how far away would come the needed supply of at least 500 tons a day? What about other mushrooming cities along this same railway stretching westward to Sinkiang and southward to Lanchow – fifteen to twenty million people probably also tight on food? The new single-track railway was hardly adequate even to carry vital industrial materials and products. Imbalances between the demands of a rapid urbanization and industrialization and the supply and transport capabilities of the grain-rich plains and valleys of central China to meet them were certain to develop, it seemed to me.

7

White Cloud

THE mayor assigned Lu Ch'u-tseng to accompany us on a hundred-mile trip into the Mongolian steppe. Lu was a tall, thin Hupeh man who had fought the Japanese around the famous guerrilla base in Wu T'ai Shan, in Shensi, the mountain stronghold of the Eighth Route Army. His dome was shaved smooth as an egg and was shaped like one. He had a friendly grin, large white teeth, and a vast store of energy and local information. Paotou's official chief of protocol, Lu had been chairman of its Support Korea Committee and its Sino-Soviet Friendship Committee. But the Korean War was over and the Soviet advisers had left, and now here he was, a paradox, temporary chairman of the Welcome Old American Friends Committee, membership strictly limited.

We left Paotou in a new green Volga sedan and journeyed northward through dust and construction which reached along twelve miles of paved highway. Then a gravel and dirt road led into a brief stretch of granite hills. A new highway was being built on the flank of a dry river bed, where hundreds of men working on the project were gathering stones by hand. Farther on, turning from an empty country, we came upon a settlement of tents and new brick houses. Everything was covered with red dust, including men and camels hauling loads up a narrow valley stream. On one side engineers were directing work on the scaffolding of a dam and future power plant.

'Iron country,' said Rewi, gazing at the broken ferrous earth. 'These hills are full of it.' Workers stared curiously at our car. Seeing foreign faces grinning back at them, they waved their red arms in greeting. 'This is a spot where bandits used to ambush caravans in the past. Safe as main street now.' In two days of riding across this country we saw no armed guards. I had no personal bodyguards anywhere on my travels, and saw none.

Abruptly we emerged from rocky hills and arroyos into rolling prairie something like our Dakota country. On these irrigated lands, margins of the true steppe, pastures alternated with fields of buckwheat, oats, barley, sorghum, corn and wheat. The air was fresh and cool. We passed one large state farm where tractors and motor-driven pumps were doing most of the work. Throughout North China generally the old water wheels were rapidly disappearing. Here I remember a photograph I missed: a woman dressed in a gay jacket and red trousers, her pigtails flying and her face flushed as she trotted out of green gardens on a black horse, precariously balancing a huge market basket on one knee and a child on the other. Far on the road we passed a Mongol pony pulling a cart heavily laden with produce on the top of which, unexpectedly, were perched two shining new red bicycles; and I missed that picture too. Christmas for somebody, and nomads on bicycles.

Rounded purple mountains gradually lowered into wide grazing lands, the flat-roofed villages thinned out; for a few miles we saw only grazing cattle, sheep and goats and no houses at all. Then in the middle of a vast plain we saw, several hundred yards beyond the gravel road, a village of new brick dwellings erected in a semi-circle around a two-story hall and school building surmounted by a large red star. We stopped and I hauled out my Bolex to take a panorama and a telescopic close-up. From the village a strong young man wearing Mongol boots ambled up the pathway and stood watching me with detached interest. We learned from him that we were at a production brigade headquarters of the Hsing Hsing Hsi Commune made up of Chinese and Mongol farmers and cattlemen. It ran forty miles in one direction and twenty-four in another.

'What do you eat here?' he was asked.

'*Pai mien* [white flour] and greens.'

'What's your ration?'

'Not enough.'

'What's not enough?'

'Fifty-three catties.'

We all smiled and he seemed disconcerted. This was nearly sixty pounds a month, twice the average Peking ration; it seemed nothing to complain about. I did not pursue the matter, but afterward I thought we had not heard his whole story. This was meat-eating country and if he was not getting mutton no amount of flour would substitute.

Mr Lu had urged us on. We were overdue at White Cloud, the iron mine, still some miles beyond. Late in the afternoon there arose a vision of tall chimneys and moving cranes, automatic shovels and bulldozers creeping over iron hills served by an electric railway. It seemed a mirage on this broad prairie sea, but the mine manager who met us was real enough. Wang Yung-shou looked twenty-five but was also an Eighth Route Army veteran and said he was almost forty. He had never seen a mine until he was sent to Pai Yun three years earlier to build this mechanized little city from scratch.

'There wasn't even a yurt * here when we began,' he said.

'How did you learn mine management?'

'Fighting the Japanese – and the Kuomintang.' He grinned. 'We had some Soviet comrades for technical advisers. I learned from them. They've all gone home now.'

A Mongol named Wu Lung was city chairman; he was an ex-guerrilla too, and had been here since the beginning. With pride he took me on a tour. Pai Yun, population twelve thousand, already had a theater, capacity one thousand, a two-story school building and a large workers' club, each building a block long. New dining rooms were displayed; so were the power plant, hospital, new apartment buildings, the small hotel where we spent the night, and the mine itself. Pai Yun's deposits of very rich ore had never been worked before. They were, together with neighboring reserves, said by Director Wang to be adequate to supply Paokang for 'many years'. Output quota for 1960 was 2,400,000 tons, 'which will be overfulfilled'. (I can't recall visiting any mine or factory where 'underfulfillment' was predicted.)

Pai Yun mine was certainly moving at a good rate. The modern plant seemed adequate to goals set for it, and buildings everywhere were already in full use, although paved streets and sewers were just being laid.

Skilled underground miners in China earned as much as many university professors, who were among the highest paid state employees. Work at Pai Yun was mostly above ground and the

* A Mongol tent made of felt and erected over a light wooden lattice, as every crossword puzzler knows.

workers, in two shifts of eight hours each, received a minimum wage of thirty-six yuan a month and a top of 120. Like all state enterprises, Pai Yun offered free medical care and spare-time schooling; unemployment insurance, a pension plan and other welfare benefits were provided by funds to which workers contributed. Rents were minimal and food better than average. Work clothes were furnished gratis. Winter temperatures here reach forty below Centigrade and fur hats, sheepskin coats, padded suits and heavy boots were also supplied free.

Rewi hadn't seen Pai Yun before, but he took its sudden appearance from nowhere much more for granted than I did. 'You'll get used to this; China has built 165 new cities since the revolution,' he said. 'There are also 140 completely rebuilt cities like Paotou. I spent most of last year looking at them in every province but I still missed quite a few.'[1]

I was well satisfied with what I saw of the condition of the Mongols and the respectable role they had in the direction and management of this town and a modern enterprise far beyond their possibilities in the past. At dinner that night I congratulated the young officials, Chinese and Mongol, and Chairman Lu Ch'u-tseng of the Welcome Old American Friends Committee. Warmed by the food and a little wine, my hosts inevitably recited the achievements of socialism, pointed out its obvious peaceful intentions and good will toward the whole world, and then asked me to explain how the American people could tolerate their oppression under an 'imperialist government'. Out of sympathy with the gross and repeated errors of American policy toward China as I was and had been for years, I nevertheless found these moments awkward. Chinese are no different from other people and most of us find it easier to pronounce judgments than to discuss facts.

An old reporter is always uncomfortable when asked whether his neighbor is still beating his wife. The 'American imperialism' question was usually posed in that way. America is a faraway Thingamajig to most Chinese, just as China is to Americans. It is very hard to help anyone understand in a few minutes how a Thingamajig works, if he has never seen one. This is especially true if the person has it firmly fixed in his mind that this particular Thingamajig exists solely for the purpose of launching world wars.

In Pai Yun, I had to solve the problem by bringing up an extraneous matter, the reasons for the problem of overproduction of food in the United States as compared with the current underproduction in China. My hosts were very much interested in what I had to say about the stupidity of the American solution – to subsidize farmers to grow less grain. The reasons why China could not subsidize farmers to grow *more* grain were of course well understood by them – if not yet by me. It was then possible to conclude dinner satisfactorily after I proposed a toast made to me by an old veteran on a collective farm I once visited in Russia.

'To the triumph,' he had said, 'of all that is good in man!'

'*Kan-pei!*' (Bottoms up!) we all said.

8

Mongol Commune

UP at six, we breakfasted on ham, eggs and a local cheese vaguely like Parmesan. By seven we were on our way to Hsinpailike, or New Wealth Springs, a Mongol commune in the Pailingmiao district of Autonomous Inner Mongolia.

For a few miles beyond White Cloud we saw virgin land being cultivated by Chinese farmers to supply the mining town, still largely dependent on imported grain. More than ten million *mou* (1,660,000 acres) of Inner Mongolia were already planted in wheat, I learned from Lu Ch'u-tseng, and output averaged four fifths of a ton per peasant cultivator. Most of this lay far to the east of Paotou. The Mongolian economy was being rapidly agrarianized wherever suitable conditions existed; more and more Mongols were becoming settled farmers and animal husbandmen as cattle breeding and a new dairy industry supplanted the old nomad economy of camels, horses and sheep. Besides exporting beef and mutton, Mongolia now supplied North China with increasing quantities of milk, butter and other dairy products used largely by nurseries, hospitals, sanatoria and hotels.

By far the greater part of the ancient Mongol domain above Paotou remained wide grassland, however, in which we soon found ourselves. For an hour we drove across blue prairie and low hills where herds of horses and flocks of sheep grazed. Here and there were clusters of felt yurts, smoke drifting lazily from their campfires. Then far on the horizon a dagoba spire came into view and soon we arrived at a lama temple called Hsila Tulu. We passed four lamas on horseback and drove beyond some cattle barns to draw up before a whitewashed mud wall. Commune headquarters.

Inside the gate we were met by the young chairman, Jenkejin Noru, small, wiry and rugged. He wore a green cotton gown over black boots, and a gray cap with a bellows top and a long bill pulled low upon his smiling eyes. Committeemen around us were clad in short gowns pulled in at the waist by bright sashes, worn over soft trousers tucked into black leather riding boots. A middle-aged Mongol woman, also in boots, was introduced as a vice-chairman. Her wind-burned face was as dark and seasoned as saddle leather and wreathed by thick hair tightly plaited. On one side of the compound a trio of yurt-shaped whitewashed buildings stood linked together in a row, a doorway opening into the center one. Waiting beside it was a smiling, booted Mongol girl in a long gown of bright green silk, girdled with a sash of pale pink. Her stiff bobbed hair was adorned with another pink ribbon, which matched a silk scarf tied around her buttoned-up collar. She welcomed us at the threshold.

'Our secretary,' said Jenkejin Noru.

Inside the yurt we sat on cushions laid on low benches around a hearth in the middle of one chamber. The floor was covered with clean felt and before each of us was a small red-lacquered table piled with Mongol delicacies, 'all products of the commune'. There were small, rock-like pieces of cheese, fried wheat fritters, brown sugar and a kind of sorghum. All these ingredients, together with some nameless condiments, were mixed in a cup of buttered tea over which the girl secretary, Precious Spring, wielding a giant brass kettle equipped with a foot-long spout, poured a warm, sweet, milky liquid. This was assiduously renewed as fast as any portion of it was consumed. The honorable name for this hors d'oeuvre I cannot now recall, nor do I soon (begging the pardon of my hosts) care to renew an acquaintance. Mongol taste for the ultrasaccharine and for clashing color in costume – like the warmth and earnestness of Mongol hospitality – reminded me of bedouins I had encountered in Arabia.

Trilingual transmission gradually revealed that New Wealth Springs was a cattle commune regionally administered under the Tao Mao Integrated Banner at Pailingmiao, fifty miles east of us. In 1958 five 'advanced cattle cooperatives' here had amalgamated to form the present commune, consisting of four production brigades made up of twelve teams of herdsmen and a few farmers. Population, surprisingly small: 2,200 adults. Animals: 90,000 sheep and goats, 12,000 horses and mules, 7,000 cows, and 2,000 camels.

Grazing lands covered roughly 400 square miles and the commune also cultivated 3,200 acres of grain, mostly for consumption by local livestock.

Flocks and herds and yurts here had been restocked and built up with state loans. Ownership of the cattle and livestock was held by the teams but the commune as a whole owned and operated veterinary, artificial insemination and breeding stations, a meteorological post, a hospital and some health stations, one theater, a telephone line, and a small tractor station. A dairy industry produced dried milk and cheese and there was a small garment factory, a brick kiln, a leather tannery and a blacksmith shop.

Here, as elsewhere in Inner Mongolia, it was claimed that about ninety percent of Mongol children under ten years of age were in primary schools. New Wealth had sent 230 graduates to Huhehot and Paotou to learn more about animal husbandry and combustion engines. In the past, literacy among Mongols was confined almost exclusively to the lamas and nobility, less than ten percent of the population. According to one writer, Inner Mongolia now had twenty 'institutions of higher learning' – including medical, veterinary, engineering and normal colleges; of some 10,000 registered students, more than 1,400 were of Mongol or of other nomadic origin.[1] A substantial number of Mongols, both men and women, had already been trained as technicians. I was told at Paokang that more than 1,500 were learning metallurgy there.

'Last year we had 252 live births in our commune,' said Jenkejin as he showed me around the village. 'In one year before the revolution only one child born in this whole banner lived till the next year. In former times we used to say that we had more women than men, more lamas than children, more old people than young, and always more deaths than births. The animals survived better than people, but anthrax frequently wiped out whole herds. Now things are different. We have modern medicine and hospitalization, our children are healthy, anthrax is under control, plague and syphilis have been wiped out.'

Jenkejin was a Party member, of course. So was his Chinese deputy chairman, who did most of the interpreting from Mongol, as Jenkejin knew little Chinese. This was his story, as I wrote it down :

'Our banner was led by Prince Chimiteh Jenching Kaoerlo, and my parents were poor nomads under him. Princes were all-powerful then; we were Chimiteh's subjects. He was one of the anti-Japanese princes. When he refused to collaborate the Japanese captured him and carried him off to Pailingmiao. There he was tortured and killed. Chimiteh became a Mongol hero and our people still speak respectfully of him. We have no more nobility now, of course, but Chimiteh's children live here and work like other citizens and are much respected.

'After Prince Chimiteh was killed our people hated the Japanese, and many more of us were robbed, tortured and strangled to death by them. The year before the end of the war, when I was eleven years old, my grandfather was arrested and accused of connections with the Paluchun. He had sheltered a few Red soldiers but that was all. The Japanese tortured him but he could not tell them any-thing. They let him out, a wreck, and soon afterwards he died of heart failure. I was beside him and I wept. The Japanese were slaughtering and eating all our animals and we were starving and had no money. My father died next, then my older brother, then my mother. Finally there was only my sister, my grandmother and myself.

'Then I joined the revolution – that is, the Paluchun. I attached myself to a company of Mongolian Red cavalry led by Paluchun men trained at Yenan. At that time I was so small I could not get on a horse when I was carrying a rifle and comrades had to help me. Soon afterward the Japanese surrendered and Kuomintang troops came to replace them. There was no difference except that the Kuomintang was worse. Anybody who had anything left was called a collaborationist or a Red and was robbed and beaten or killed. We had more than a hundred Kuomintang troops feeding on us here at that time. I went back to guerrilla life with the Paluchun and fought until we finally drove the Kuomintang out of here in 1947.'

Back in the commune headquarters we found that a feast had been prepared and set up under the supervision of the versatile secretary, Precious Spring. A baby lamb roasted whole, in Mongol fashion, sat royally mounted on a saddle of white rice. I blanched when I saw it surrounded by more 'products of the commune' such as had already somewhat jaundiced my appetite. But this visit provided for my hosts the excuse of a rare feast, I knew, and I dared not slight it; besides, the lamb was irresistible. With it were served bottles of colored liquor which matched Precious Spring's green and pink color scheme. I think it must have been straight vodka dyed and heavily sweetened. Jenkejin tackled it with the audacity of a guerrilla and there was nothing perfunctory about the sincerity of repeated toasts to his guests – including the first American he had ever seen. As Alley would sip nothing but soda water, I had no choice but to respond to Jenkejin's obvious desire to communicate his good will by this most ancient and honorable language of the cup which binds men in true brotherhood.

'To the friendship of the Mongol and American people,' said he quite without reservation. '*Kan-pei!*'

'To the Mongol,' I returned, 'in all of us.'

The effects were warm and exhilarating and the aftereffects not as disastrous as I had feared. We were still able to spend the afternoon inspecting some of the nearby herds of young horses and watching exhibitions of riding, led by Jenkejin himself, and demonstrations of the Mongol method of lassoing – by a noose fixed to the end of a long pole.

A man about ten years older than Jenkejin rode up and was introduced as a production brigade leader. He wore a mustache and the general air of bravado about him was enhanced by a fur-trimmed silk hat, topped by a large coral button, which crowned his head at a sporty angle. The button, I was told, was formerly reserved for nobles but now was the mark of brigade leadership.

As we inspected some of the commune buildings I heard reports of rapid growth: cattle and livestock increased five times in ten years, commune income up forty-five percent just since 1958, all due to state loans and credits for the purchase of new stock and equipment. 'A hospital, schools, a theater, veterinary specialists, telephones!' said the leathery lady vice-chairman. 'Whoever heard of that around here in the old days?'

These were new things and good things for Mongolia, there was no doubt. There was also no doubt that the general growth was partly explained by Chinese immigration. The Mongol banner families numbered 1,320 adults, an increase of 130 percent since

1949, but of the total of 2,200 inhabitants 880 were Chinese. They were farmers and construction workers, I was told – all enjoying full residential rights. The construction workers, Jenkejin explained, were temporary, but I had a feeling that more Chinese farmers were on the way.

Late in the afternoon we drove down to visit the lama temple I had asked about. Half a dozen lamas still lived in quarters nearby but the temple was closed. While we waited for a lama I was informed that there were five temples in the commune. When I asked whether any of the small party with me believed in religion or attended services I was answered with smiles and negative headshakes.

'That's for the old people,' they said.

'That's for *some* old people,' corrected Madame the vice-chairman.

A monk with a heavy fuzz of beard and wearing rumpled yellow robes appeared and opened the temple, smiling obsequiously at us. Everything was intact, including walls filled ceiling-high with dusty sutras, and a roomful of prayer wheels, gongs, gilded gods and candelabra flanked by vases of paper flowers. At my request the monk picked up one of the brass trumpets, carried it out to the terrace with the help of Jenkejin, and blew a deep blast. It caused a horse to shy. The trumpeter was still a young man. I wondered how he could be a lama.

'Why not?' the chairman answered. 'He has known nothing else since he was a child.'

'But is that still possible today?'

'Certainly not. No children nowadays believe in gods invented by priests. They are taught the truth and know that priests can't help solve man's problems.'

'This is a museum, then, not a living church?'

He shrugged his shoulders. 'You can see, we don't interfere with anyone who still believes.'

As we left they all mounted their ponies and raced beside our car for a few hundred feet, and then suddenly halted, took off their caps, and waved good-by. Behind them the monk quietly closed the doors of the temple.

'Rewi,' I said, 'do you think they really have as many as 12,000 horses and 90,000 sheep in this commune?'

'More or less.'

'But we didn't see that many.'

'Do you want to count all the bloody livestock in the commune?'

No. If some refugee in Hongkong wrote a story saying there were no horses or sheep in Mongolia I could tell you that he is mistaken. But suppose he said that there were half as many as last year or that there were a million people in concentration camps here? I could not disprove that. This does not necessarily show that you can learn more in Hongkong than you can in China and Mongolia, but it indicates the limits of education by travel.

Our visit had been so swift I had not really learned anything about how a commune worked or didn't work. I had permitted my attention to be diverted by Mongol gastronomics. I determined to reform.

9

Why China Went Red

'THE unfortunate but inescapable fact is that the ominous result of the civil war in China was beyond the control of the government of the United States. Nothing that this country did or could have done within the reasonable limits of its capabilities could have changed that result; nothing that was left undone by this country has contributed to it. It was the product of internal Chinese forces, forces which this country tried to influence but could not.' *Secretary of State Dean Acheson, 30 July 1949.*

Vast libraries exist to 'explain' China, and probably the most enlightening words in answer to the question Why Did China Go Red? are those of the man who led the nation to where it is today, Mao Tse-tung. Why Mao himself and other Chinese intellectuals were logically pushed toward Marxism rather than nationalism-capitalism is abundantly clarified in Mao's life story as he related it to me, and in the testimonials of many other Red leaders which I later gathered.[1] A careful study of such information as early as 1938 could hardly have failed to suggest that the whole national experience of China made a Communist victory inevitable unless the Kuomintang underwent a miraculous transformation. Deep and revolutionary changes were needed, beginning with a redistribution of the land during the patriotic war against Japan.

The plain fact was that in China (as in Vietnam, Korea and other semicolonial and colonial countries) the *Communist Manifesto* had a literal authority which in Europe and America had been lost to Fabian gradualism, evolutionary socialist movements, and Keynesian economic practive. When Marx's stirring call to arms first began to be read by young people in China after the First World War, they did not see in it an analysis of conditions in Europe of February 1848, but a true description of their own immediate environment.

'The modern laborer, instead of rising with the progress of industry, sinks deeper and deeper below the existence of his own class,' said Marx. Even in America, relatively civilized labor legislation is scarcely a generation old. In China, with its child and female slave labor, its twelve- to fourteen-hour day, its starvation wages and the absence of any protection against sickness, injury, unemployment and old age, and no serious possibility of collective bargaining, why should people have questioned Marx's prophecies right down to 1947?

The old security under the clan-family and the guild systems had collapsed and now the have-not was literally worth no more than his price tag in the market, 'purely as a means of production'. Back of the defenseless position of labor lay of course the breakup of the old agrarian economy under the impact of Western imperialism and the bankruptcy of handicraft production brought on by machine products. Capital levies in the form of ever rising taxes (sometimes collected sixty years in advance) and usurious interest rates, and the consistent plunder of public revenues by thieving bureaucrats and militarists, had by the twenties and thirties reduced the solvent landowning tillers to a minority. Aided by famine and war, this ruined economy threw millions of 'surplus' sons and daughters of degraded peasant families onto the swollen labor market of unemployed. This process was prophetically analyzed years ago by R. H. Tawney in his *Land and Labor in China*. The reminder here serves to emphasize that the biography of almost every Red soldier I met revealed him to be a direct product of this mass rural bankruptcy.

It required no sharp intuition to comprehend why, in a country where child workers of ten or twelve were often locked up at night, to sleep in rags beneath the machines they operated by day, the *Communist Manifesto* was read as gospel. (I saw this even in Chinese-operated shops in foreign-run Shanghai.) Nor need one ponder why Chinese who met Western democracy only in its role of foreign policeman, defending 'rights and interests' seized by violence in China, could readily accept at full face value Marx's scornful denunciations of its hypocrisy.

China was never a complete colony; rivalries among the European powers and Japan prevented any one power from becoming dominant. But China was treated as the inferior of all and was the responsibility of none. Any foreigner in the 'treaty ports' – even a drunken bum – was legally privileged over the most virtuous Chinese; to be treated as inferiors in their own country rankled for many years.

Thus nationalism, the passion to reassert China's ancient role as a great power, initially played a greater part in attracting literate Chinese to Marxism than it did in Russia. In the West the Communist party had no comparable appeal. The Communist subservient to Stalin's infallibility had to learn to despise 'national patriotism', substituting for it a religious 'belief in a savior abroad'. He had to be essentially a mythomaniac – and often remained so even after he became an ex-Communist.

The program which the Chinese Communist Party adopted soon after its founding called for a two-stage revolution, in accordance with Lenin's classical theses for colonial and semicolonial countries. The first stage would complete the 'bourgeois-democratic' revolution, in a united front of the progressive bourgeoisie, the working class and the peasantry led by the Communist party. It would end foreign imperialist oppression and win complete independence. In rural China it would abolish rule by the landlord-gentry and equalize land ownership. In urban China it would nationalize the property of native reactionary capitalists held to be collaborators of foreign imperialism. Only when these two aims were accomplished would the revolutionary power move on to lay the foundations for the second stage: building socialism.

Programmatic aims of the 'bourgeois-democratic' revolution, as thus defined, made a strong appeal to Chinese nationalists. Within it, sentiments of patriotism, class war and international communism under Russian leadership were readily reconcilable. It must be remembered that at the outset the party founders' acceptance of Marxism coincided with direct Russian help to Dr Sun Yat-sen in his struggle against foreign imperialism. The slogans of anticapitalist class war were also rendered more palatable because of antiforeign and nationalist sentiments. The small native bourgeoisie, including the great landlords linked with it, was in truth largely a collaborator class dependent on the imperialist powers, as events were to show. And it was simpler for the Chinese to believe in Moscow, because Russia's foremost antagonists were just those Western colonial powers who were likewise the immediate enemies of independence movements all through Asia and Africa.

China's outstanding Communists were internationalists' in ideology but no less national patriots than the Kuomintang 'nationalists'. They were not proletarians but for the most part came from the less than five percent of China's millions who possessed some secondary or higher education. The biographies I collected showed that among the fifty 'top' brains of the Communist party and the Red Army only two or three were of true proletarian (as distinct from peasant or intellectual) origin (although by 1945 the proletariat was somewhat better represented). During the united-front period of the Nationalist government at Canton (1924–7) today's Communists were already men of marked ability. If, by some curious digression of history, they had remained in the Kuomintang camp, they might have ultimately provided its top leadership.

Young patriots of that time broke with Chiang Kai-shek not because they fundamentally differed over national independence aims, but because they became convinced that China could never realize those aims without deep internal revolutionary changes which Chiang Kai-shek and the Kuomintang conservatives were determined to prevent. To Chinese intellectuals Marxist revolutionary dogma as applied to the modern world seemed, like the theory of dialectics itself, more new wine in Chinese bottles.[2]

These men were also in a hurry. Their own experiences, combined with their study of European and American history, made them painfully aware of China's weakness, backwardness and imminent peril of total disintegration. In their search for a means of coping with complex problems of individual and national regeneration, young Chinese men and women of initiative and intelligence gravitated toward an authoritarian *and* revolutionary doctrine because other means had been tried and had failed, because they believed time ruled out gradualism, and because Chinese history had repeatedly sanctioned revolution as a means of salvation.

Contrary to opinion held in America, the Kuomintang never posed a clear moral alternative to the Communists but competed with them purely on a basis of efficient use of force. For educated youths joining the Communists it was simply a matter of practical judgment whether their method was the only one which would provide a personal solution as well as quickly close the appalling industrial and scientific gaps between China and the advanced nations of the world. Those who became convinced of this in the early days made a discovery which confounded all previous Marxist theory. They discovered that they could bring the 'proletarian revolution' to power without urban or proletarian insurrections.

Mao's faith in the peasant as the main engine of social revolution developed from objective experience and was not shared by the Russians. Orthodox Marxists elsewhere also continued to believe that a Communist movement could not succeed without an organized industrial proletariat as its main insurrectionary force. In the beginning the Chinese agreed. After their initial disasters (1927–30) in urban insurrections, when the party was all but destroyed, they had no choice but to fall back on the rural areas, where Mao Tse-tung and Chu Teh set up the first peasant sanctuaries. Real events thenceforth made the peasants virtually their sole material and mass support. Out of them came the strength which finally carried the Communists to national power, with minimum help from the heavily policed urban working class.

'Whoever wins the peasants will win China,' Mao Tse-tung told me in Pao An. 'Whoever solves the land question will win the peasants.'

The Reds were never 'agrarian reformers' who believed in land redistribution as an end in itself.[3] They simply saw that only by preliminary 'land reform' could they get the peasants to join in a fighting alliance and later win their support for the main program. Remaining the party of the proletariat in theory and doctrine, the Communist intellectuals became in practice the party of the poorer two thirds of the peasantry whom the Kuomintang, wedded to its landlord supporters, could not claim to represent.

The Communists became in effect a mobile, armed, ubiquitous propaganda crusade spreading their message across hundreds of thousands of square miles of Asia. To millions of peasants they brought the first contacts with the modern world. To youths and women – for the Reds courted them first and last – they opened up unheard-of vistas of new personal freedom and importance. To the poor farmers they promised land and relief from ruinous taxes, usury, starvation, and family disruption. To all they promised equality of opportunity in a new state free of corruption, devoted to the welfare of the common people, and founded on a share-the-wealth and share-the-labor philosophy. *Kung-ch'an-tang,* Chinese for Communist Party, literally translated is 'Share-Property-Party'.

The reasons why the fire at first burned slowly in China were the very reasons why it could not be stamped out. Poor communications – lack of roads, railways and bridges – made it possible to create enclaves of armed struggle in the great spaces between the modern industrial centers dominated first by the Western powers, then by the Kuomintang, and lastly by the Japanese. In the hinterland the Reds could offer leadership and objectives to almost universal rural discontent, agitate and awaken new ambitions, and build an army to fight for their goals. When they actually carried out land reforms, eliminated some of the worst inequalities, turned the old gentry-ruled village hierarchy upside down, and took no personal profit for themselves, the have-not two thirds of the peasants began to accept them and finally merged with them.

'The people are the water and the ruler is the boat,' said the revered philosopher Hsun Tzu twenty-two hundred years ago. 'The water can support the boat but it can also sink it.'

'We are the fish,' said the modern Communist sons of Hsun Tzu, 'and the people are the water of life to us. We do not ride over the people but swim with them.' And of this they made slogans the peasants understood.

IO

Aboard the Premier's Special Train

THE Chinese seem to like springing an important appointment as a surprise. Late one evening my phone in the Hsin Ch'iao gave a long, urgent ring. I was asked to be ready to leave early the next morning for a day's trip north of the capital.

At the appointed hour I was met on platform No. 1 by Dr Chi Ch'ao-ting, my old acquaintance of prewar and wartime days. He was now director of foreign trade promotion, but this was no occasion arranged to discuss commerce. He led me into a special train waiting for a very special passenger. Premier Chou En-lai had ordered it for the day. He had invited me to accompany him to the recently completed Miyun Dam, North China's largest reservoir, power-grid and flood-control project, which nestles under the Great Wall near historic Kupei Pass.

An autumn sun flashed on the amber-colored tile cornices of Peking's marble-walled new East Station as the Premier and his wife drove through a side gate directly to the train. Beneath the quais of the new terminal lay the site of my old home on Kuei Chia Ch'ang, beside the Tartar Wall. Originally that house had been the residence of Dr J. Leighton Stuart, who was America's last ambassador to prerevolutionary China. And to Kuei Chia Ch'ang, when I lived there in July 1937, had come a brave woman, Teng Ying-ch'ao, seeking help. Now she was my hostess for this day's trip. Her married name was Mme Chou En-lai.

It was a three- or four-car train and Premier Chou and his wife disappeared in one direction while I was shown to an observation car and an air-conditioned stateroom of 'my own'. It amounted to an exhibit of New China; this was an all-native train. Peking carpeting covered the floor, a large teak desk and easy chair stood under a lace-curtained window, and a full-size bed filled one side of the room.

'A good place to write a book,' said one of my hosts, smiling.

Adjoining the stateroom was a bathroom with green tile tub, matching lavatories, and a glass-walled shower.

We went on to the observation section and more heavy carpets, silk curtains, and handsomely paneled walls. There was a buffet and a bar, and the chairs and sofa were luxuriously upholstered.

As the train left noiselessly I searched for the haunted Fox Tower near our old house, but that also had vanished in the maw of progress. I recognized few landmarks in this corner of the old capital so familiar to me for five years; even the moat where farmers used to bring their ducks for a morning swim was gone. I wondered what had happened to Lao Chin, our last cook, and to Lao Han, our dignified Manchu *kuan shih-ti* (major-domo), who had somewhat doubtfully shown into our house, that long-ago July day, a Chinese woman wearing dark glasses and long-bobbed hair. She was Teng Ying-ch'ao.

That was the July of the 1937 'incident' at Marco Polo Bridge, of which the Japanese made a pretext to attack and occupy Peking, an action which began the seven-year war. Teng Ying-ch'ao had been living secretly in a temple in the Western Hills outside Peking, convalescing from lung trouble acquired during the Long March, of which she was one of only thirty-five women survivors. Taken by surprise when the Japanese surrounded the Western Hills, Mme Chou had fled, in straw sandals and disguised as a peasant woman, to reach the city just before the gates were closed.

I had met Teng Ying-ch'ao in 1936, during my first trip to the Red districts, and had learned to appreciate her as a highly cultivated and gifted woman – much wanted by the Nationalist police, as well as the Japanese. And there she was, a year later, led to my house by Chiang Hsiao-mei, the vivacious little wife of a friend of mine named Hsu Pin, a professor in Peking. It was Hsu who had given me a letter of introduction to Mao Tse-tung which I carried into Red territory. Years ago I described the circumstances of Mme Chou's escape from Peking at a time when hundreds of Reds and alleged Reds were being arrested.[1] She would have been a rich prize. As a foreigner with extraterritorial privileges I was able to conduct her and Chiang Hsiao-mei, represented as our family *amahs*, through the Japanese blockade by a 'last train' to Tientsin, and thence to safety on a British boat bound for what was then called Free China.

Now, another summer twenty-three years later, we were on a very different train. We went unannounced and no crowds met us anywhere. During the entire excursion, including two hours of boating on the newly created Miyun Lake, I didn't see any armed guards. Once I commented on this to Chou as we climbed a wide flight of stone steps after we had visited Huaijou Dam, en route to Miyun. Our train stood high above us on a trestle spanning a deep ravine; it looked isolated and vulnerable to sabotage.

'All this used to be bandit country when I lived in Peking,' I said. 'Officials who came here in those days would have been loaded with arms and troops.'

'We have plenty of guards, you just don't see them.' Chou's left arm took in some masons working on a wall not far off and some peasants cultivating a hillside. 'Every able-bodied person in China is a militiaman now. We don't need professional bodyguards.' That was but a slight exaggeration.

Our entourage was a modest one. Beside Dr Chi and his wife there was Yung Lung-kuei, who had been a depot manager of Chinese Industrial Cooperatives[2] and who was now secretary of the State Planning Commission's Research Bureau; Hsu Pin and his wife, Chiang Hsiao-mei, who was now chairman of the Peking Women's Federation; Mme Ch'en Yi, the attractive and well-groomed wife of China's Foreign Minister; Mme Kung P'eng, a student leader at Yenching University when I briefly taught there, later Chou En-lai's 'first secretary', and now director of information at the Foreign Office; and a few other old acquaintances of Peking and Yenan days.

Chou En-lai came into the salon car soon after we left Peking. Tanned and healthy-looking, he had only a tinge of gray in his hair and looked ten years younger than his sixty-one. He wore sandals, slacks and a white sports shirt. Remembering our first meeting, I thought how had the lowly risen and how had the mighty fallen.

Chou had been the first important Communist leader I encountered when I crossed the Red lines in 1936. He was in command of an East Front Red Army in a tiny cave village north of Yenan. I had just entered camp when a slender figure in an old cotton uniform came out to greet me, brought his cloth-soled shoes together, and touched his faded red-starred cap in a smart salute. He examined me intently with large dark eyes under heavy brows. His face, covered with a beard of abundant growth for a Chinese, parted in a smile which exposed even white teeth. That was Chou En-lai, the Red bandit for whose head Chiang Kai-shek was then offering eighty thousand dollars.

I had spent two days in long interviews with Chou in that outpost called Pai Chia P'ing, before a day's journey farther on to meet Mao Tse-tung in Pao An. Chou had told me that the Reds wanted to end the civil war and unite with the Nationalists to resist Japan. That would not mean abandoning the revolution, he said, but advancing it. 'The first day of the anti-Japanese war,' he prophesied, 'will mean the beginning of the end for Chiang Kai-shek.'

A year later, when the civil war ended (temporarily) following the Sian Incident, Chou played a key role in negotiations. After he left the Communist areas to become chief of the Eighth Route Army delegation in Nanking, then Hankow, and finally in Chungking, I saw him many times. Few Chinese made a more favorable impression on American officials during the war than Chou En-lai did in Chungking. The grandson of a distinguished mandarin of the Manchu Dynasty, and a former honors student at Nankai University in Tientsin – where he met Teng Ying-ch'ao – he had also studied in Europe and knew some French and English. Chou was thirty-eight when I first met him, boyish despite the beard, a person of charm and urbanity in control of a tough, supple and highly disciplined brain.

Chou explained why the admission of American correspondents to China had now become a question integrally related to negotiations over the major problem created by an American policy which had established a protectorate over Taiwan, an island which 'belongs to China as clearly as Hawaii belongs to the United States'. Until Washington was ready to recognize that fact, Chou declared, American correspondents could not be welcomed by China.

'We don't look upon you as a reporter but a writer,' Chou went on, 'that's why we make an exception. We consider you a writer and a historian, not a correspondent.'

'What's the difference? Every good historian has to be a good reporter, whether you begin with Thucydides or Ssu Ma-ch'ien.'

'All the same, your visit cannot set any precedent for American correspondents in general. We recognize you as a writer and a historian, not a correspondent.'

Historian, writer, correspondent, who cared? The story was the thing.

Having satisfied protocol, if that is the word, Chou picked up the questions I had submitted to him and began our marathon interview. I soon understood that he had been quite serious about treating me as a historian. Three hours later we had not got much beyond history when our talk was interrupted. We had reached Miyun.

'Don't forget your camera,' I was told as I left the train. I could take all the pictures I wanted – but not as a correspondent.

II

New Shores on Ancient Mountains

AT Miyun's exhibition hall we stood before a large wall map which illuminated Miyun's future as a resort and vineyard country, to add to China's growing wine output. Rest houses and retirement homes dotted the lake; interspersed were beaches and swimming pools, pleasure boats, botanical gardens, parks and camping grounds. It looked much like a week-end scene at the lake of Yi Ho Yuan, Peking's Summer Palace – but Miyun is a hundred times larger. It was all still on paper, except that far up the slopes, above the island-studded inland sea, extensive walnut groves were already planted.

'They tell me I'll live to eat walnuts here in ten years, but I don't think so.' Chou shrugged. 'It will take thirty years or at least twenty to see all this dream fulfilled. I won't see it, but' – he pointed to comely Mme Ch'en Yi – 'she may. Certainly her son will.'

Chou remarked that he could be wrong again; they had astonished him with the big dam itself. Originally scheduled for 1965, it had been pushed ahead by five years. Unexpectedly rapid industrial growth in Peking and its tributary farming country had created new demands for both increased water and power. Initiative had also come from nearby communes, which stood most to benefit. Called into emergency council, he said, commune committeemen promised to furnish them enough workers, together with tools, food and wages, to build the entire project. Its importance, he said, had been self-evident to everybody; 200,000 workers had 'volunteered' from twenty-one counties in the area – far more than needed.

We drove up to the main dam and a magnificent view of the broad blue lake enclosed by dramatic, sharp-prowed mountains. The reservoir is seventy-two square miles in area. High above it on the west stood the long serpentine of the Great Wall, studded by five watchtowers. Beneath them twenty-two centuries of history had ebbed and flowed since the first emperor of the Ch'in Dynasty,

Shih Huang Ti, mobilized China's man power to complete the world's mightiest piece of masonry, more than two thousand miles long. As a defense against the barbarian hordes it was a success, but the Ch'in empire (259–206 B.C.) collapsed soon after the great builder's death.

'The stones that went into the Great Wall would have made hundreds of Miyun dams,' I remarked to an engineer with our party.

'Maybe they will yet,' he replied. 'Farther west, dozens of smaller dams are being built with these stones where the Wall is disintegrating.'

Droughts, alternating with abrupt torrents which rose in the rainy season, had always been the scourge of Miyun and its vicinity, as in much of northern China. In flood years the Pai and Chao rivers, whose confluence is the site of the Miyun reservoir, used to inundate more than a million acres of farmland. In years of drought the same land was stricken and starvation followed. The eleven new dams of the reservoir now contained 4,100,000,000 cubic meters of water, which provided a regulated supply for that same million acres, much of which had been converted into rice land.

Like many new reservoirs in China, Miyun was also contributing to a new longitudinal canal system which would eventually join Peking, by way of the central provinces, to Canton, thirteen hundred miles farther south. It would parallel the old Grand Canal system which runs through the eastern or seaboard provinces. In 1961 the Miyun-Peking Canal joined the Peking-Tientsin Canal, to provide a waterway deep enough to carry boats of five hundred tons from the Wall to the China Sea. Primarily a water conservation and irrigation scheme, Miyun also produced 90,000 kilowatts of power to speed up electrification and industrialization. Miyun had already prevented a serious flood, in 1959; in 1960 it minimized regional effects of the severe drought that struck all of northern China.

With its immense basin and eleven dams, the large reservoir was completed in two years, during the first fifteen months of which mainly hand labor was used. Heavy earth-moving machinery arrived in March of 1959, some 8,000 peasants were taught to use it, and a division of troops participated in the final months of work.

An example of China's policy of education combined with practical labor, the whole Miyun project, with its miles of walls and spill-ways, its facilities, locks and canals, was designed by graduate students and professors of the Water Conservation Department of Peking's Tsing Hua University. Student theses provided the thou-sands of working blueprints actually used in the construction.

Miyun was impressive, but it was a modest project compared to the great dam being erected at San Men Hsia on the Yellow River, which I was to see later, and the projected Yangtze River power complex, said to be the world's largest.

Chou turned to speak to the waterworks engineer and then raised his heavy eyebrows.

'I'm out of date again,' he said. 'The engineer tells me there are four other small reservoirs under construction hereabouts. This county has just sent 12,000 volunteers over to help the next county build its reservoir in exchange for help Huaijou got from them last year.'

In random conversation I asked Chou how much land was now under cultivation in China and he gave me the figure 110,000,000 hectares, about 275,000,000 acres.

'How much has it increased since 1955?'

'Not at all. There was a decrease of about 2,000,000 hectares.'

Answering my puzzled look Chou explained :

'The reason is what you've been seeing : new highways, dams, reservoirs, canals; very large urban and rural housing and industrial developments; new streets, schools, hospitals, laboratories; new railways and new double-tracking; large new airports, and so on.'

The area of cultivable land in China has been widely disputed by agricultural experts abroad and the question is worth brief com-ment. Chou's figure would amount to about twelve percent of China's land area, including the mountains and deserts of Tibet, Sinkiang and Mongolia. It seemed fairly probable that the actual cropland in use was even less in 1960; the press several times re-ferred to 107,000,000 hectares (267,000,000 acres) *under cultiva-tion*. Dr Wu Chen, secretary general of the Ministry of Agricul-ture, also gave me the figure of 1,600,000,000 *mou*, or about 267,000,000 acres.

The recent decrease by about 5,000,000 acres which Chou mentioned also traced to other factors. In the euphoria of 1958, official policy encouraged communes to seek increased yields by deep plowing, close planting, more irrigation, more fertilizer, etc., and more double cropping on good land, at the neglect of poorer land. While the government's 'eight-point charter for agriculture', which included such advice, might be sound enough if applied by experienced farmers, bureaucratic and indiscriminate enforcement was probably costly. Second, some commune administrations in 1958 abruptly curtailed or even ended the cultivation of small plots privately owned by the peasants, and these fell fallow. Third, commune diversions of farm labor to nonagricultural projects often caused neglect of available land. Finally, many communes had simply expropriated good land of prosperous peasants for public works without compensation. With the erasure of the last vestiges of private ownership, inducements were lacking to encourage enterprising peasants to combine to exploit new fields.

Thirty years ago, O. E. Baker put the 'ultimate area suitable for cultivation on the basis of climate, land forms, and soils at 700 million acres', but George Babcock Cressey, whose studies were more thorough, concluded that Baker had 'greatly exaggerated the agricultural potentialities of China'.[1] At that time China was thought to have 207,000,000 acres under cultivation, or about 0.4 acre per person. Within recent years the cultivated area had been expanded by about thirty percent, but acreage *per person* remained approximately the same. Dr Wu Chen told me that China could double her croplands within ten to twenty years, and that an additional two hundred million acres of marginal land might be reclaimed with much greater difficulty. Exactly how much new acreage could profitably be opened by *present* available means – before industrialization had reached an advanced stage – was quite another question, however. More than half of the arable land was multiple-cropped, so that the *sown* area was more than 500,000,000 acres annually.[2] As long as it required the labor of twenty to thirty Chinese to produce as much as one American on a modern farm, they might well be more rationally employed on existing croplands rather than on breaking in new low-yield land over really extensive areas.

Nevertheless, very great efforts were renewed in 1961–2 to

develop hillside, plateau and desert land now rendered more cultivable by afforestation and new water conservancy works in the far hinterland, as well as along the southern coast, where rainfall is generally adequate. Swamps were being drained and difficult mountain land terraced in Chekiang, Fukien, and northern Kwantung, where the appearance of regular army labor battalions on a large scale in 1962 aroused fears in Taiwan of an imminent invasion. It takes several years for such land to begin to yield pay-off results, however, and meanwhile the diversion of labor and materials involved often intensified local food demands.

Chou En-lai continued his remarks to me : 'We are not now trying to get a rapid increase in cultivated acreage, although it is going on all the time. You can see' – he pointed to Miyun reservoir – 'that we want first to establish effective control over and efficient use of what land is already under the plow – more scientific agriculture in every respect.'

That meant, first, about twenty times more chemical fertilizer than China produced in 1960 – a figure already about fifteen times the 1952 output. It also meant about twenty times more mechanization than the present level. Scientific agriculture in every respect meant water and soil conservation projects on an immense scale, better seeds, and improved planting and plowing methods. It meant general conversion of small-plot farms into large-scale farm-factory enterprises. But of all this, and of communes and their attempts to improvise speedier answers, more later.

Now, in late August, Chou already predicted a tough year ahead. Nearly forty percent of China's farmland was reported afflicted by prolonged drought, unprecedented floods in the northeast, hailstorms in the south, and other natural calamities. The early crop was far below expectations. In days I could remember this would have meant that famine and death for millions would soon overtake the nation. But China's food resources and supply system were now well organized, Chou asserted; even if the autumn crops also suffered a heavy shortfall, there would be no famine. Further on we shall see how the catastrophe, when it came, was met.

'For us,' he mused as he gazed across the lake, 'the darkest time in history was during our Long March, twenty-four years ago – especially when we crossed the great grasslands near Tibet. Our condition was desperate. We not only had nothing to eat, we had nothing to drink. Yet we survived and won victory.'

When one thought back to the Long March, things had been getting relatively better for Chou, not worse, it seemed to me. 'You must look upon your remaining national problems as by comparison easy to solve,' I said.

'Easy! Nothing about them is easy!' Chou responded curtly. 'Don't ever quote me as saying anything is easy here. Ten years ago, all China began a second Long March. We have taken the first step, that's all – the first step.'

Our barge, pulled along by a motor launch, leisurely crossed the big lake. The steep hills turned deep purple as the sun dropped lower. Presently a squall blew up and a light rain fell. It did not last long.

'These sudden rains are common here,' Chou said. 'Once I was walking around this lake when I got caught in a storm. I took refuge in a nearby house. The housewife invited me to eat some stewed apricots – very delicious. It was a new house, clean and comfortable, and I learned she belonged to one of the families displaced by the dam. Her family had lived there for generations. She said many of the peasants had opposed being moved at first but now everybody was delighted with the change. No more fear of flood or drought, new and better land, electricity – and lake fish to eat! That was an interesting experience.'

That had made him think that the Long Marches, the first one and the one ahead, were worth the struggle, he seemed to say. As he sat relaxed on the deck beside his wife, a stiff breeze blew from the young walnut groves. Tall waves lapped the sides of ancient mountains which had seen many flood waters but had never before had their middle flanks converted into beaches. When we touched shore again at a village called Shadow of Nine Pines on a Hill, I could think of nothing better to write in the guest book than 'Today I saw new shores on ancient mountains.'

12

Chou En-lai and America

ONE might assume that contempt for American imperialism would by now have produced Chinese equivalents of insulting American epithets such as slopeys, slant-eyes and chinks, but such is not the case – not in print, at least. 'American imperialism' is translated by paradoxical characters which literally mean, 'Beautiful-Country imperialist doctrine' – or sometimes by 'Flowery-flag imperialism' – while Britain has its 'Brave-Country imperialists', France its 'Legal-Country imperialists', Germany its 'Virtuous-Country' ditto, etc. This seems oddly consistent with the Communists' oft-asserted principle which distinguishes hatred of a foreign government policy from friendly feelings toward a people and a country.

Similarly, the possibility of educating and redeeming imperialist leaders may be suggested by the Chinese rendering of Eisenhower as 'Forest Hero'. Somehow the picture of 'Forest Hero', chieftain of the 'Flowery-flag imperialists', riding a 'Beautiful-Country paper tiger', does not quite fit into standard Marxist idiom. Both Mr Truman and the late John Foster Dulles bore the same surname, *Tu*, as the illustrious poet, Tu Fu. Truman's given name, *Lu-men*, means Gate to Lu (Shantung) – Confucius' birthplace and China's 'sacred province' – and is highly complimentary.

I had seen Chou En-lai on one occasion before our trip to Miyun and at his request had submitted some questions for an interview. They numbered more than forty. Chou answered most of them while we were on the train and during a later interview I had with him just before I left China. Altogether our conversations covered about twelve hours, not counting 'table talk'. In our formal interviews interpreters were used, so that only about six hours of straight colloquy was accomplished, during which I wrote down some eleven thousand words.* All Chou's comment was offered *ad lib* except for

* (1970) These interviews took place on 30 August and 18 October 1960. For the full text see the unabridged edition of this book – text and appendix – and *Look* magazine, 31 January 1961.

an occasional reference to notes. I submitted my own version of the interviews and at Chou's request corrected it to conform to the official transcript. The latter followed the language of Chou's interpreter, Chen Hui, a Swarthmore graduate who nevertheless insisted upon correcting my 'Taiwan Strait' to the English usage 'Taiwan Straits'. The discrepancies between our two texts were otherwise negligible.

Chou gave me the most comprehensive exposition of Sino-American problems and statement of China's policy yet offered in a public interview. We also discussed Tibet and China's relations with India – difficulties which Chou connected with American influence on New Delhi. Chou gave me the only interview in which any official, Chinese or Russian, had publicly discussed the nature of the 'Sino-Soviet dispute'. I made an undertaking to publish his remarks 'in full or not at all', and they appeared, *in toto*, in *Look* magazine. At that time *Look* was criticized on the ground that the Chinese press would never publish an interview with a high American official. Peking later reciprocated by publication, in the *People's Daily*, of the full text of President Kennedy's interview with Premier Khrushchev's son-in-law.

It will be noticed that nearly all Chou's arguments depend on the logic of nationalism, quite apart from communism. There is no such thing as a 'pro-foreign' Chinese, and even if there were, one would still have to expect a continuing ideological antagonism against the United States among Communists for many years to come. What is probably not comprehensible from abroad is the extent to which even anti-Communist Chinese support Peking on any *nationalistic* issue. The fact that the United States had for a decade followed a policy of armed intervention in China's affairs, that this policy had served to discredit influential Chinese on the mainland once friendly to America and had added great force to Peking's ideological attacks on imperialism – which might otherwise seem as obsolete to Chinese intellectuals as they did to Mr Nehru – had been little understood by those Americans most anxious to bring about the downfall of the Communists.

I shall later have something of my own to say about the contribution which China's policies had made to the embitterment of Sino-American relations. Here I merely act as a reporter, whose job it is accurately to record answers, not to lead a debating team.

Premier Chou considered that my first seven questions were all related and said that he would answer them in a general discussion of the background of Sino-American problems involved, and then in terms of solutions. The seven questions, in slightly condensed form:

1. Would China take the initiative in summoning a conference to discuss Chou En-lai's proposal for a nonaggression pact to create a nuclear-free zone in the Pacific? (This proposal was first publicized by Nikita Khrushchev in 1958 and in March of that year supported by Chinese Foreign Minister Ch'en Yi.)

2. What could be the main points covered by such a pact?

3. If the President were to invite Chou to the United States to discuss such a pact, would he accept?

4. Would China welcome any envoy the President might designate to visit Peking for the same purpose?

5. Would it be possible for China to sign such a pact as long as the United States pact with the Taiwan régime existed?

6. If China was resolutely opposed to the extension of nuclear arming of the world, why was she striving to make nuclear weapons?

7. It was said that China considered that successful negotiation with the United States would be possible only when China possessed the means of manufacturing nuclear weapons. Please comment.

'As one who follows political developments in this country,' said the Premier, 'you must have noted that China signed treaties of peace and friendship with ... the Union of Burma in January, and with the Kingdom of Nepal during my visit to that country in April. In August, when Vice-Premier and Foreign Minister Ch'en Yi visited Afghanistan, a treaty of friendship and mutual non-aggression was concluded with the Kingdom of Afghanistan ... [Earlier there was] the treaty of friendship with the Mutawakelite Kingdom of the Yemen and the joint statements on peaceful co-existence with India, Indonesia, Cambodia and Ceylon.

'The main content of the three treaties this year is based on the

Five Principles of peaceful coexistence, which China has all along advocated. You know these principles: (1) Mutual respect for sovereignty and territorial integrity; (2) mutual nonaggression; (3) noninterference in each other's internal affairs; (4) equality and mutual benefit and (5) peaceful coexistence.

'A peace pact of mutual nonaggression among the countries of Asia and those bordering on the Pacific involves the questions of Sino-U.S. relations and of relations between the four countries of China, the U.S.S.R., Japan and the U.S.A.

'*It is inconceivable that a peace pact can be concluded without diplomatic relations between China and the United States.*

'*It is also inconceivable that there can be diplomatic relations between China and the United States without a settlement of the dispute between the two countries in the Taiwan region.**

'These are two important facts. That is why I said that prolonged efforts were necessary to realize this proposal. Since prolonged efforts are required, why have we repeatedly made this proposal? It demonstrates that the Chinese people and the Chinese Government desire to settle disputes between China and the United States through peaceful negotiations, and are opposed to the U.S. policy of aggression against China. But I would like first to cite one proof of this. After the liberation of China the U.S. Government declared that it would not interfere in the internal affairs of China, and that Taiwan was China's internal affair. [Dean] Acheson said so in the White Paper[1] and it was also admitted by Truman later. As a matter of fact, Taiwan was restored to the then government of China in 1945, after the Japanese surrender. It was taken over and administered by the then Governor of Taiwan, General Chen I, who was later killed by Chiang Kai-shek.

'After war broke out in Korea in June 1950, Truman changed the policy and adopted a policy of aggression toward China. While sending troops to Korea the United States at the same time dispatched the Seventh Fleet to the Taiwan Straits and exercised military control over Taiwan. *Beginning from that time the United States started new aggression against China.* The Chinese Government sternly condemned United States aggression in Taiwan and

* The italics here and subsequently are added to express Premier Chou's original emphasis. Ellipses indicate omissions.

the Taiwan Straits. Shortly afterwards United States troops in Korea showed the intention of crossing the Thirty-eighth Parallel and pressing on toward the Yalu River [China's frontier], and, because of this, the Chinese Government could not but warn the United States Government that we would not stand idly by if United States troops crossed the Thirty-eighth Parallel and pressed on toward the Yalu River. This warning was conveyed to the United States through the Indian Ambassador. The United States Government disregarded this warning and United States troops did indeed cross the Thirty-eighth Parallel and press on toward the Yalu River.

'The Chinese people could only take the action of volunteering support to Korea in its war of resistance against the United States. But this action *was not taken until four months after the United States stationed its forces in the Taiwan Straits and exercised military control over Taiwan*, and not until United States troops had crossed the Thirty-eighth Parallel and approached the Yalu River.[2] ...

'After two years of negotiations an armistice was at last reached in Korea. *By 1958 Chinese troops had withdrawn completely from Korea.* But up to now United States troops are still hanging on in South Korea and will not withdraw. Moreover, the United States is still controlling Taiwan with its land, sea and air forces, and the United States navy and air forces are still active in the Taiwan Straits. ...

'Though the United States committed these acts of aggression against China, *would we use force to settle disputes with the United States? No!* I declared already during the Bandung Conference in 1955 that the Chinese people were friendly to the American *people* and the Chinese Government was willing to sit down and enter into negotiations with the United States Government to discuss existing disputes between the two countries, though the two countries had not recognized each other and had no diplomatic relations. This proposal of ours resulted, through the good offices of Britain, in ambassadorial talks between China and the United States which started 1 August 1955, in Geneva. ...

'Five years have elapsed since the start of the Chinese–United States talks in August 1955. At the very outset, we proposed that disputes between China and the United States, including the dispute between the two countries in the Taiwan region, should be settled through peaceful negotiations, without resorting to the use or threat of force. The United States blocked all news of this proposal, but China later published it. Why did [John Foster] Dulles reject it? Because Dulles realized that reaching such an agreement implied that the next step would be discussions on how and when United States armed forces were to withdraw from Taiwan and the Taiwan Straits.

'We hold that the dispute between China and the United States in the Taiwan region is an international question; whereas military action between the Central Government of New China and the Chiang Kai-shek clique in Taiwan is an internal question. The United States has maintained that the two questions are inseparable. We hold that they can and must be separated. Since it has been possible for China and the United States to hold ambassadorial talks in Geneva and Warsaw, talks can also be held at the same time between the Central Government of China and the Chiang Kai-shek clique. The former is an international question while the latter is an internal question. Parallel talks can be conducted and solutions reached separately.

'In the talks between China and the United States, agreement on principle must after all be reached first before concrete issues can be settled. The two points of principle on which agreement should be reached are :

'(1) *All disputes between China and the United States, including the disputes between the two countries in the Taiwan region, should be settled through peaceful negotiations, without resorting to the use or threat of force; and*

'(2) *The United States must agree to withdraw its armed forces from Taiwan and the Taiwan Straits. As to the specific steps on when and how to withdraw, they are matters for subsequent discussion. If the United States Government ceases to pursue the policy of aggression against China and of resorting to threats of force, this is the only logical conclusion which can be drawn.*

'This is the crux of the dispute between China and the United States. The activities and direction of United States policy toward China have been aimed at manufacturing "two Chinas". In this respect, both the Republican and the Democratic parties aim at the same thing. ... This scheme would probably be opposed not only by mainland China, but also by the Kuomintang in Taiwan and the Chinese in Taiwan. Therefore such an approach would lead nowhere, but in the solution of Sino-U.S. relations it would tie things up in knots.

'We believe that a solution to Sino-U.S. relations will ultimately be found; it is only a question of time. But there is one point: if the United States does not give up its policy of aggression and the threat of war against China, no solution is possible. We do not believe that the people of the United States will allow their government indefinitely to pursue such a policy. *There is no conflict of basic interest between the peoples of China and the United States, and friendship will eventually prevail.*'

Question: 'Does the second principle include as well the question of the time and manner of the withdrawal from Taiwan?'

Answer: 'The United States Government must first agree on the principle before concrete matters can be taken up.'

Q: 'The United States Government has insisted that no agreement is possible without a declaration from the Chinese Government to refrain from the use of force in the Taiwan area, has it not?'

A: 'The United States Government has insisted that the United States and Chiang Kai-shek have "the inherent right of individual and collective self-defense" in the Taiwan region. In other words, it would also legalize United States aggression in Taiwan and the Taiwan Straits, and create the objective reality of "two Chinas". This is opposed by the entire Chinese nation. Suppose someone occupied the Hawaiian Islands and dispatched a fleet to the waters between the mainland of the United States and the Hawaiian Islands, or supposing someone occupied Long Island and sent a fleet to the straits north of Long Island, how would the people of the United States feel in such a situation? You can thus imagine how the Chinese feel. Did not the people of the United States rise up against the Japanese after Pearl Harbor was attacked? ...'

For some minutes a white-jacketed waiter had been hovering discreetly at the door of the salon. When he had finished speaking, Chou looked around and saw him.

'Hungry?' he asked me.

Here was at least one concrete matter we were able to settle at once. I followed him into the dining car, where a table was set for about twenty guests – and one historian.

13

Table Talk

AT the luncheon table I asked the Premier whether he would informally or formally discuss a solution along these lines: neutralization of Taiwan in so far as military bases were concerned, with a commitment by China not to send arms or armed forces to Taiwan for a stipulated time following a United States withdrawal. During such a period, I elaborated, China, the United States, Japan and the U.S.S.R. would seek to enter into a Pacific nonaggression pact – all this to be premised upon simultaneous arrangements to dissolve military alliances (in effect a disengagement operation) in both parts of Korea and Vietnam, and for China's admission to the U.N. and U.S.-China mutual recognition.

Chou answered that such questions would belong in the realm of diplomacy, once principles were agreed upon.

'You,' said he, 'are not the United States Secretary of State. I am not China's Foreign Minister.'

'That I am not the Secretary of State no one will dispute,' I replied. 'As for the truth of the second half of your statement I am far from convinced.' He laughed.

'Who knows, you may be Secretary of State yet.'

'Not,' I said, 'in my time.'

'You are a pessimist.'

'No, sir, an optimist.'

Our conversation turned to random topics. We spoke about swimming. Chou hadn't been able to catch up with Mao; he had broken his right arm many years ago and it had never been reset properly. We talked of his wife's growing interest in photography, at which she had become quite proficient; she had kept a picture I had taken of them in Hankow in 1938, in 'their first home since their marriage'. Then Chou told me something about the language reform.

Han-yu p'in-yin – use of the Latin alphabet for phonetic writing of Chinese – was limited to attempts to break mass illiteracy and to help children get a quick start in characters, he explained. Once they knew the characters they dropped the *han-yu p'in-yin*. There was no literature in the new phonetics and there was no demand for one. The Latin alphabet was used, however, in new written languages created for some of China's minority peoples.

Simplification of character writing was quite another thing. People had been writing abbreviated characters for a long time but it had never before been systematized. Now there was a standard set of abbreviations for a thousand basic Chinese characters. Some old scholars had strenuously objected; they thought the art of calligraphy would be ruined by the simplifications. Chou maintained that even the adumbrated hieroglyphics could be written in beauty. I couldn't agree; I was a reactionary.

I spoke appreciatively of China's widespread interest in Western symphonic and operatic music, unknown in the past. Chou demonstrated some intimate knowledge of the careers and idiosyncracies of John Foster Dulles, of Mr Nixon, of Mr Kennedy, and of sundry others, including Chester Bowles, whom he credited with more influence than I did. I expressed doubt that Mr Bowles's proposal for an independent Taiwan was anything more than a personal view. Chou corrected me by pointing out that Mr Bowles was chairman of the Democratic party foreign policy committee. That had escaped my notice but the fact did not alter my judgment.

As for Mr Dulles, he said they had regretted his passing because he had been such a 'downright reactionary'. He ran so completely true to form that it had never presented any difficulties to anticipate all his 'reactions'. Nevertheless Mr Dulles had, Chou admitted, surprised him once. During the Geneva conference in 1954 Chou had entered the lounge of the conference room ahead of time. No one was there except Mr Dulles, who was 'only an observer' at the conference. In a natural gesture under the circumstances Chou extended his hand. Mr Dulles folded his hands behind his back, shook his head, and left the room. Chou winced as he remembered it. 'That was really carrying even reaction to extremes,' he said.

The legacy of Dulles' policy, Chou thought, had left the U.S.A. in a precarious position. With more than two hundred bomber bases around the world, 'the U.S.A. is now a man balancing an armful of eggs. He can't move or he will lose them *all*.'* The United States was overextended and had lost the mobility to achieve effective concentration on attainable goals.

'You can't catch fleas with your fingers,' Chou said, using a Chinese epigram. He spread his fingers wide apart on the table. 'You can't lift a finger, don't you see, or a flea will get away. Such a man is fundamentally defenseless against all the untrapped fleas, who can choose where and when to mobilize and dine at leisure.' Chou clapped his hands together sharply. 'That,' he said, 'is the way to catch fleas.'

That was the strategy Mao used with success against Chiang Kai-shek's attempt to catch fleas with his fingers. 'Despise the enemy strategically,' said Mao, 'but pay attention to him tactically.' In this connection he had uttered his famous dictum that 'all reactionaries are paper tigers'. Chiang Kai-shek was his first example. Later he applied it to 'American imperialism'. This was oversimplified in the West to suggest that Mao was ignorant of the destructive capabilities of hydrogen bombs. He used the expression figuratively in the way Lenin described old-style imperialism as a 'colossus with feet of clay'.

What Mao actually said was: 'Imperialism and all reactionaries, looked at in essence from a *long-term* point of view, must be seen for what they are – paper tigers. On this we should build our strategic thinking. [That is, the ultimate victory of socialism is inevitable.] On the other hand, there are also living tigers, iron tigers, real tigers which can eat people. On this we should build our tactical thinking.'[1]

The limit to Chou's allegory of the fleas was also plain. In America's case the hands happened to hold down not just fleas but untold megatons of deadly nuclear power. While it is extremely difficult to exterminate a whole species, the lifting of one nuclear finger might release such violence as to destroy not only a flea-harassed U.S.A. but all the precious fleas, both the trapped and the untrapped as well. How far could the man with his fingers down – if his fingers *were* down – be safely provoked?

*The United States later announced the liquidation of a number of the smaller bases.

Was that the essence of the reported disputes between the U.S.S.R. and China over theoretical possibilities of coexistence versus the 'inevitability of war'? Would Premier Chou frankly discuss a subject then filling the Western press with speculations? Reaching for the improbable, I decided to jump across some of my remaining questions when our interview was resumed.

14

Sino-Russian 'Differences' *

At meals we had spoken in mixed Chinese and English; Chou's understanding of English is better than his speaking ability. After luncheon Chou, his wife, and everyone else retired for a brief nap, as is now customary in China, not only among officials but among all the people. Then, back in the salon, we returned to formal colloquy through his interpreters, only occasionally interrupting to question the translation of a phrase of two.

The Premier's remarks on Sino-Soviet relations were made well in advance of the stormy conference of eighty-one Communist parties held in Moscow in November 1960.

I indicated three questions on my list that were related to disputes or disagreements between China and the Soviet Union. These concerned reported differences in the Soviet and Chinese interpretation of the Leninist theory of the inevitability of imperialist war, whether peaceful coexistence between countries of different social systems was the permanent foreign policy of the Communist countries and not merely tactics, and whether peaceful coexistence was unavoidable in a world threatened by nuclear war in which no nation or class could be victorious. And I asked specifically about the 'mass exodus' of Soviet advisers from China.

Premier Chou said: 'I would like to begin by stating that the Communist Parties and Governments of China and the Soviet Union, as well as those of other socialist countries, all believe in Marxism-Leninism and formulate their policy by integrating the principles of Marxism-Leninism with the specific conditions of their

---

* (1970) Chou's statements were the first official admission that Chinese press attacks on anonymous and/or Yugoslav 'revisionists' were in fact directed at Moscow. Chou's mild comments were far exceeded, after 1962, in a long series of diatribes exchanged with Moscow – the Chinese side being personally directed by Mao Tse-tung.

respective countries. Having the same belief and the same system, they share the same overall principles and go along the same general direction.

'But this is not equivalent to saying that the two parties have no differences in the way they look at certain questions, nor does it mean that there is no difference in emphasis in the policies of the two countries. To have no difference whatsoever is impossible in the realm of thinking. Even in the thinking of a single person, one sometimes looks at a question in one way and at another time in another way. In a specified period of time, it is a natural thing that there are some differences between two parties on theoretical questions and on ways of looking at things. To be exactly identical would indeed be something strange and incomprehensible.

'For example, though there are some differences in the Chinese and Soviet press on how to evaluate the situation with regard to war, opposition to imperialism launching a war is our common point. Take the case of the policies of the two countries. The Soviet Union is in the United Nations while China is not. *Proceeding from this point, the actions of the two governments cannot be the same in many respects.* Both China and the Soviet Union are opposed to "two Chinas"; both maintain that the Chiang Kai-shek clique does not represent China, and that only New China can represent the 650,000,000* Chinese people. This stand of the Soviet Union has not yet won majority support although it is backed by all socialist countries and by a number of Asian, African and European countries. So the representatives of the Chiang Kai-

---

*Official census figures for the year 1957 showed a total of 656,630,000, of whom 340,140,000 were male and 316,490,000 female – not including 'Chinese living in Hongkong, Macao and abroad', but including Taiwan (T.G.Y., p. 8). At an increase rate of two percent the mainland population alone should have exceeded 700,000,000 by 1963 – with another 25,000,000 in Taiwan and overseas. See also Chapter 50, 'Of Blue Ants and White'; and, for a more comprehensive evaluation, Leo A. Orleans, *Professional Manpower and Education in Communist China*, Washington, 1961.

(1969) In an interview with the author in January 1965, Mao Tse-tung indicated that China's 1964 sampling census suggested a population of between 680,000,000 and 690,000,000; but Mao considered the figures exaggerated. In 1967 the official press adopted the figure '700,000,000 people'. In 1964 Chou En-lai told the writer that 'the average' population growth rate was 'around two percent'.

shek clique have remained seated in the United Nations. The representatives of the Soviet Union take part in meetings along with them in the General Assembly, the Security Council and subsidiary organs. China, however, in addition to disagreeing that the Chiang Kai-shek clique represents China, will not participate in any meeting or organization in which the Chiang Kai-shek clique is included. If China also took part, it would result in a situation of "two Chinas", which we firmly oppose.

'Here is a case of a difference owing to the different situations of the two countries. ...

'Many such examples can be cited.

'All the socialist countries, including China and the Soviet Union, practice internationalism, supporting and helping each other and holding unity as their common goal. In view of these principles, should the imperialists try to seek any loopholes for driving a wedge and sowing discord among the socialist countries, they would do so in vain and are doomed to failure. *An imperialist attack against any socialist country would be deemed by China as an attack on China and on the entire socialist camp, and in that event China would never sit idly by.*

'This is the general aspect of the situation. Under this principle, it is permissible to have some differences between the two parties on ways of looking at things and in the emphasis of their policies. There is nothing strange about this. ...

'The return of some Soviet experts is a natural thing. Having come to China, they are bound to return some day; surely they can't stay here all their lives. They work in China for definite periods of time and have rendered good service. Perhaps it was because many returned this year that it drew the attention of the Western countries. ...'

Question: 'Have you read any of the recent articles which appeared in the Soviet press written by prominent Communists, in which opponents of the Soviet stand on coexistence and against the "inevitability of war" doctrine were denounced as "left-wing infantilists", "dogmatists", "revisionists", etc.? Though no specific names were mentioned, it was assumed that they must have been directed against some phenomena within the socialist camp, or else they would have been meaningless. Or were they perhaps directed against some strong left-wing forces within the Communist Party of the Soviet Union? How do you explain this rash of articles?'

A: 'In the first place, I have not read many such articles. Secondly, China's explanation differs from that given by you just now. We are not left-wing opportunists as interpreted by the Western press. We consider that the Western press has so speculated because they want to lead on to sowing discord between China and the Soviet Union. We are against attempts to sow discord in Sino-Soviet relations. The Chinese Government and the Chinese Communist Party are against the launching of a war by the imperialists and have advocated peaceful coexistence among countries of different social systems. This has been our stand from way back, and this stand has never changed.'

Q: 'If the comments in the Soviet press are not to be applied to China, what is your interpretation of China's difference in viewpoint from Russia's concerning the Leninist theory of the inevitability of imperialist war?'

A: 'On the question of imperialism instigating wars, we hold that the 1957 Moscow Declaration of the fraternal parties of the twelve countries is correct. The Bucharest (1960) communiqué also supports the theses of the Moscow Declaration. We support the Moscow Declaration and stand firmly by it. There should be no differences in standing firmly by the Moscow Declaration. *The Moscow Declaration states that so long as imperialism exists, there will always be soil for aggressive wars.* Imperialism invariably aims at realizing its domination of the world by instigating wars. But the Moscow Declaration also points out that owing to the mighty strength of the socialist camp, owing to the growth of the anti-imperialist and national independence movements of the Asian, African and Latin American peoples, owing to the growth of the people's struggle in the capitalistic countries for democracy and freedom and owing to the development of the movement to defend peace by the peoples throughout the world, *it is now possible to delay and prevent imperialism from launching war. While preventing imperialism from launching war is one possibility, vigilance must be heightened on the other hand to guard against it.*

'Such a thesis is entirely correct. As China sees it, through the people's struggles we strive on the one hand for a lasting world peace, while on the other hand we remain vigilant and on guard against the danger of war. The mightier the forces of the people, the greater the possibility to defend peace, and the greater the strength to avert war. These are the two aspects of the matter. It is also [a matter of] "walking on two legs".'*

Our train had been sitting on the platform of the Peking station for an hour and it was now nine at night. The Premier excused himself but left with a promise to complete our interview as soon as he could arrange to see me again.

Back in the Hsin Ch'iao that night I reviewed my notes and realized that Premier Chou had given me a historic interview. No previous official acknowledgments of any differences or dissimilarities between the two major Communist leaderships had been made by Peking. Chou's statements remained the only ones of their kind on record during a long period of Sino-Russian fencing by means of Aesopian language.

What the years had revealed was that *nationalism inside the Communist system of states* was a more powerful factor than the bonds of class solidarity which socialist power would theoretically make unbreakable.[1] Premier Chou's statements require further comment – after we have seen more of the conditions inside China which underlie differences between East and West, and both within and beyond the Marxist sphere.†

> *See Chapter 27, 'Two Legs Are Better Than One'.
> † See Chapter 77, 'China and Russia: Point, Counterpoint'.

Part Two

WHERE THE WAVES BEAT

MAO TSE-TUNG on Leadership:

Of all things in the world people are the most important. We believe that revolution can change everything and that before long there will arise a new China with a big population and a great wealth of products, where life will be abundant and culture will flourish.

It is necessary to consult the lower levels first. We should 'not feel ashamed to ask and learn from people below' [Confucian *Analects*]. Be a pupil before you become a teacher. Listen also to the mistaken views from below; it is wrong not to listen to them.

Learn to 'play the piano'. In playing the piano all ten fingers are in motion; it won't do to move some fingers only and no others. But if all ten fingers press down all at once, there is no melody.

'Grasp firmly.' One cannot get a grip on something with an open hand. When the hand is clenched as if grasping something but it is not clenched tightly, there is still no grip.

Don't call a meeting if the preparations are not completed. Be concise and to the point. Meetings also should not go on too long.

Pay attention to uniting and working with comrades who differ with you ... [including] people outside the Party. There are some among us who have made very serious mistakes; we should not be prejudiced against them but should be ready to work with them.

Guard against arrogance. For anyone in a leading position this is a matter of principle and an important condition for maintaining unity.

If [a person's] achievements amount to seventy percent of the whole and his shortcomings to only thirty percent then his work should in the main be approved.

The ancients said, 'The principle of Kings Wen and Wu was to alternate tension with relaxation' [Confucius, *Book of Rites*]. If a bow-string is too taut it will snap.

We must firmly uphold the truth and truth requires a clear-cut stand. A blunt knife draws no blood.

Selected Works of Mao Tse-tung, Volume IV

15

The Big Change

TWENTY-FOUR years ago I first met Mao Tse-tung in a cave dug into the clay hills of the province of Shensi, within the great bend of the Yellow River, where the long story of the Chinese people began. Mao's headquarters were in a ruined town called Pao An, not far below the Great Wall. He was then the leader of a band of fewer than forty thousand 'remnant Red bandits' whom Chiang Kai-shek had already chased thousands of miles across China.

When I stood with other guests on the terrace of the T'ien An Men during the celebration which marked the eleventh anniversary of the triumph of revolution I re-encountered Mao for the first time since 1939. We watched half a million people parade past in a pageant of which Chairman Mao was Hero No. 1. All over China there were two days of festivities and thanksgiving.

'I haven't seen you for a long time,' said Mao, when he shook hands with me. 'How long *has* it been?'

'Twenty-one years,' said I, looking around the spacious old palace room and remembering former circumstances. 'Your cave has slightly expanded in size since then!'

He smiled. 'Things have improved a little.' He invited me to come to see him and in subsequent visits we spent about nine hours speaking of things that had happened in intervening years – and a few things that hadn't happened yet.

When I last saw Mao, his country had been described as a 'mere geographical expression'. Manchuria, economically the most advanced part of China, was a Japanese colony. Below the Great Wall, Japan also held the most important cities and seaboard provinces; the rest of China was weak, disunited and bankrupt. Since then China's Silurian age had ended. 'China has stood up,' as Mao proclaimed on the birthday of the People's Republic, in 1949. The People's Republic had eliminated foreign economic and political control, and was united under a single government for the first time since the collapse of the empire.

To understand where the Chinese had been, what they were doing now, and where they were going, it is necessary to know something about the commanding place Mao Tse-tung held in their daily lives. He was the central personality in all internal struggles as well as in Red China's disputes with the U.S.S.R. and its attitudes toward the U.S.A. and the West. He was also the least known and least accessible of all contemporary world leaders.

Since the death of Stalin, Peking had recognized no mentor but Mao as a Marxist theoretician and ideologist. Unlike Khrushchev, he had been for twenty-six years the continuous and practically undisputed chieftain of a revolution. Like Tito, he won sovereign victory without Russian armed intervention and like Tito he contrived to retain his independence from Stalin's dictation. Unlike Tito, he was never called a traitor or a revisionist by Stalin. Under Mao the Chinese party evolved its own interpretations of Marxist theory, its own strategy and tactics, and its own idiom and 'line' to fit Chinese conditions. Before 1960 Mao's voluminous writings were acknowledged even by Nikita Khrushchev to contain 'new contributions' to Marxist thought.

The nature of Peking's claims to ideological leadership over the 'correct strategy' on the international front was explicitly set forth in 1951 by Lu Ting-yi, propaganda chief and Politburo member. He declared :

Mao Tse-tung's theory of the Chinese revolution is a new development of Marxism-Leninism in the revolutions of the colonial and semi-colonial countries ... Mao Tse-tung's theory of the Chinese revolution has significance not only for China and Asia – it is of universal significance for the world Communist movement. It is indeed a new contribution to the treasury of Marxism-Leninism ... *The classic type of revolution in the imperialist countries is the October Revolution [of Russia]. The classic type of revolution in colonial and semicolonial countries is the Chinese revolution* ... Study of [Mao's theory] will help ... achieve the liberation of all mankind.[1]*

Mao held no official post in the government. He had long made

*Italics added by the author are indicated in the Notes at the back of this book.

his chairmanship of the Communist Party Central Committee the most important job in China. Until 1959 he was also Chairman of the People's Republic; officially, he retired in order to devote more time to 'questions of the direction, policy and line of the party and the state'. There were, it will be suggested later, other internal reasons.

16

Impersonality of Power

FEW Westerners conversed with Mao Tse-tung these days; for him to spare me as much time as he did was very rare. Mao freely answered a wide range of questions but for the most part it was off the record – unfortunately for historians. I remarked that what he said was bound to influence me when I came to write what I think *he* thinks, and he conceded that that was probably unavoidable.

Even if I were licensed to record everything I heard from Mao it would not 'explain China', however. Did Mao himself believe that he was indispensable? As long as he lived, yes. But Mao did not believe in gods or immortality. 'The people and the people alone,' he said, 'are the creative force of world history.'

Anyone who has seen a little history made knows how impossible it is for one man to turn the wheel all by himself. Nor does one leader's death basically change all the infinitely complex forces which gave him power. The individual personality adds something to the mixture, but it takes a whole nation to produce a Stalin, a Hitler, a Gandhi, a Kennedy or a Mao Tse-tung. Each man is the logical outcome of a long history which involves the whole world.

Of course the study of an outstanding person can tell us very much about a whole nation if we study the *people* all the way through, and not just seek to deify a saint or burn a devil. The many days and nights I spent years ago questioning the unknown Mao Tse-tung about his youth and the experiences that made him a Communist were far more important than an interview with him to-day.* In Mao's case the early personal history happened to coincide with the feelings of personal frustration, injured national pride and patriotic dedication of a whole generation of revolutionary youths

*(1970) For a full text of Mao's life story as told to me in 1936, and a biographical sketch up to 1969, see *Red Star Over China* (revised edition).

determined to remake China. And if Mao had been killed, as many
of his comrades were, someone else would now be Mao, doing and
saying many of the same things.

There is an impersonality of power which exists side by side with
man's need to worship an image of himself perfected. If there were
no God, said Voltaire, it would be necessary to invent Him. In
politics, when there literally *is* no god it is necessary to invent the
Power Personality.

That such a person acts within necessities imposed by a historic
impersonality of power and its objectives may easily be illustrated
in China by hypothesizing a situation in which Chiang Kai-shek
had remained godhead. Chiang was born a decade earlier than Mao;
his parents were landlords and Mao's were rich farmers; Mao was
a peasant intellectual, Chiang a warlord and neo-Confucianist; and
Mao became a Communist Marxist while Chiang was converted to
Methodism and capitalism. But there was little fundamental difference between the *national* (as apart from social) aims each man
had to pursue, the aims which most vitally affect China's neighbors.

In his book *China's Destiny*, written in 1943, the Generalissimo
left no doubt that he not only intended to recover all China's lost
territories, including Taiwan, but also to reconquer Tibet. The
1960 China Year Book published in Taipeh showed a border even
farther south in India than Peking claims. Chiang also expected to
Sinicize Inner Mongolia, to 'recover' Outer Mongolia (whose independence he refused to re-recognize in the U.N. in 1961), and to reassert China's ancient close ties with Burma, Vietnam and Korea. If
he held power today history would oblige Chiang to support or seek
to establish satellite or friendly régimes in all those bordering states.
He would doubtless be criticized for murdering Communist intellectuals, conscripting labor, and quarreling with India over the Tibetan
border states or territories. The impersonality of power might find
him demanding unlimited aid from the U.S.A. to feed his anti-
Soviet armies and to police starving peasants and Red bandits. And
if aid were not sufficiently generous he might be blackmailing
Washington with threats to join Russia's camp.

The cult built around Mao was no entirely new phenomenon.
Chiang made a fair start toward self-deification; before him there
was the Sun Yat-sen cult, and before Sun there were the emperors

and emperor worship. Nations which for centuries have been ruled by authoritarianism may cast aside one skin and pick up another but they do not change chromosomes, genes and bodies in a generation or two.

To call Mao either the saint or the devil of China is relevant only to those who see history as a branch of ponerology. It was more certain that Mao had far greater power to do evil than he used, however, than it was certain that he had greater power to do good than he used. The President of the United States seemed to have the power to return Taiwan to China; because he did not do so he was evil in the eyes of mainland Chinese. Mao seemed to have the power to call off the anti-imperialist campaign; because he did not do so he was considered evil by some in the West. But neither man really had the power to do either of those things *alone*, any more than he had the power to launch a war *alone*. This may not be accepted by those who seek a single madman or megalomaniac to explain events of which they violently disapprove, but in truth each man behaves within the pattern set for him by history.

Mao Tse-tung remains the giant of his nation and whatever happens to him henceforth, China will never be the same again. But it was not Mao who made China. Marx observed that man makes his own history but he makes it in accordance with conditions of his environment. Before further considering the changes Mao has made in history it is useful to see something more of the impact of past environment on Mao himself.

17

Flashback to Pao An

IN June 1936, after walking two days across the broken hills of northern Shensi, not far south of the Great Wall, I entered the straggling village of Pao An. There a large part of what remained of the Chinese Red Army, as it was then called, had ended a journey across China known as the Long March. The second column of the Red forces was still fighting its way up from the Tibetan grasslands.

A curious crowd lined both sides of the street before a few dozen ramshackle huts and shops. Red flags bore the hammer and sickle and the marginal inscription of a recently acquired title: 'Chinese People's *Anti-Japanese* Red Army'. Banners in English and Chinese were held aloft proclaiming: 'Welcome the American journalist to investigate Soviet China !', 'Down with Japanese imperialism !' and 'Long live the Chinese Revolution !' At the end of the street waited a group who included most of the Politburo members then in Pao An. Here also I first met Lin Piao, Lu Ting-yi, and Teng Ying-ch'ao (Mme Chou En-lai).

Mao joined us that day at supper. He was then a gaunt, pale figure. Taller than most Chinese, he had large, searching eyes, wide, thick lips, a high-bridged brow and a strong chin with a prominent mole. His black hair was thick and long, on a head for which the Generalissimo was offering 250,000 silver dollars.

I was quartered in a newly built mud-brick house and Mao lived in a hillside cave not far down the road. It had a single window and a door that opened on a lane guarded by a lone sentry. There I soon found myself ending every day, or beginning it. Mao invited me down regularly to have hot-pepper bread – or compote made by Mrs Mao from local sour plums. Afterward we talked for hours, sometimes till nearly dawn.

There was a brief lull in war and politics at that moment and Mao had some leisure. My intense and youthful interest may have won a response in him. I was also a medium through whom he had his first chance, after years of blockade, to speak to the cities of China from which the Reds had long been isolated. He especially wished to proclaim widely the party's new and moderate policy, seeking a restoration of the united front with the Nationalists – a choice which the Japanese invasion itself made unavoidable for Chiang Kai-shek in the following year.

It was only after he had answered scores of questions about many other matters that I finally extracted from him an account of the first forty-three years of his life.

Mao was born in 1893 in the village of Shao Shan, in Hsiang T'an county, Hunan province, south of Hankow on the Yangtze River. His father, Mao Jen-sheng, was an ex-soldier who inherited a small farm but had fallen into debt and lost it. By thrift and hard work he managed to buy back his land and added to it, until he owned 3·7 acres, which gave him the status of a rich peasant. Tiny though his acreage was, labor productivity was so low that he needed a regular hired hand; in busy seasons he took on another. He also used the part-time labor of his wife and three sons, of whom Mao Tse-tung was eldest. The father sold about half his rice for cash and kept his dependents on frugal but adequate rations. Once a month he gave the hired labourers eggs with their rice, 'but never meat', said Mao. 'To me he gave neither eggs nor meat.'

The old man regularly beat his children to secure unquestioning compliance. He was himself barely literate enough to keep books. He sent his sons to school, hoping to see them become good business-men and help him 'amass a fortune' by memorizing the *Four Classics* and the Confucian *Analects*. Their teacher belonged to the 'stern-treatment school' and beat his students. Mao's first remembered act of rebellion was in protest against such treatment when he was ten years old. He ran away from school but was afraid to return home for fear of another beating. He wandered 'in the general direction of the city' until he was found.

'After my return to the family,' said Mao, 'to my surprise conditions somewhat improved. My father was slightly more considerate and the teacher was more inclined toward moderation.'

Mao's mother was wholly illiterate and a devout Buddhist who gave young Mao religious instruction – heavily diluted by his father's skepticism. 'She was a kind woman, generous and sympathetic,' said Mao. 'She pitied the poor and often gave them rice when they came to ask for it during famines. But she could not do so when my father was present. He disapproved of charity. We had many quarrels in my home over this question.' Mao and his mother 'made many efforts to convert him, without success'.

Mao now used political and dialectical terms humorously to depict the 'growing struggle' between himself and Paternal Tyranny.

'There were two "parties" in the family. One was my father, the Ruling Power. The Opposition was made up of myself, my mother, my brother and even the laborer. In the United Front of the Opposition, however, there was a difference of opinion. My mother advocated a policy of indirect attack. She criticized any overt display of emotion and attempts at open rebellion against the Ruling Power. She said it was not the Chinese way.

'When I was thirteen I discovered a powerful argument of my own for debating with my father on his own ground, by quoting the classics. My father's favorite accusations against me were unfilial conduct and laziness. I quoted, in exchange, passages from the classics saying that the elder must be kind and affectionate. Against his charge that I was lazy I used the rebuttal that older people should do more work than younger, that he was over three times as old as myself, and therefore should do more work.'

His father devoted more and more time to buying and selling grain and speculating. Eventually he gathered 'what was considered a great fortune in that little village'. He did not buy more land but he bought many mortgages. His capital grew to two or three thousand dollars.

When Mao was about thirteen his father invited many guests to their home. A dispute arose between them and the old man denounced Mao before everybody, calling him 'lazy and useless'. Infuriated, Mao cursed him and left the house, threatening to commit suicide. His mother ran after him and begged Mao to return, but he continued to the edge of a pond and stood ready to jump in.

'My father also pursued me, cursing me at the same time he

commanded me to come back. Demands and counterdemands were presented for cessation of the civil war. My father insisted that I *k'ou-t'ou* [knock head to earth] as a sign of submission. I agreed to give a one-knee *k'ou-t'ou* if he would promise not to beat me. Thus the war ended and from it I learned that when I defended my rights [dignity] by open rebellion my father relented but when I remained meek and submissive he only cursed and beat me the more. Reflecting on this, I think that in the end the strictness of my father defeated him. I learned to hate him and we created a real United Front against him.' Yet at this distance Mao was able to speak of his father with some objective appreciation. He added that the discipline 'probably benefited me. It made me most diligent in my work; it made me keep my books carefully, so that he should have no basis for criticizing me.'

The same pattern of father rejection runs through the lives of many revolutionists. Mao simply seemed better able to analyze it, and franker about it, than most Chinese. The dichotomy between his father's harsh conservativism and his mother's kindness and compassion, the sympathy established with hired peasants who supported him against his father, his resentment against male domination of his mother, and her submissiveness to fate, all reflected a generation in rebellion against blind filial piety and Confucian traditions no longer suitable for the nation's needs. An end to the feudal and patriarchal clan-family system, opportunity for the poor peasants, equal rights for women, brotherhood in a new freedom that had to be won by hard struggle for one's rights, by defending the interests of the lowly against the mighty: these were ideas which Mao's early life taught him to share with many awakening youths.

Mao had long since outgrown personal hostility toward his father, whom he now saw as a product of a tough world of cannibalism. It was to the perhaps impossible task of changing that world that he had since dedicated himself. Yet he certainly had not forgotten the Old Man when, ten years before I met him, Mao wrote *An Analysis of Classes in Chinese Society*. In it he defined the poor peasantry as a *semiproletariat* indispensable to the success of the revolution. He sharply distinguished it from prosperous owner-peasants whom he thus characterized:

People who, by their manual or mental labor, have an annual surplus over and above what they need for their own support ... are very eager about getting rich and worship Marshal Chao [God of wealth in Chinese folklore] most devotedly ... At the sight of small capitalists who command people's respect their mouths water copiously. They are timid, afraid of government officials, and also a bit afraid of the revolution. This group is a minority among the petty bourgeoisie and constitutes its *right wing*.[1]

From such people, who Mao believed had twisted their lives to adapt themselves to a crumbling society, he had learned that he could expect no help in building a new one. Poor farmers, oppressed women like his mother, allies like his younger brothers and fellow students who thought as they did, 'the great majority', as Mao saw it, these were his friends – and friends of revolution.

An acknowledged beneficiary, in spite of himself, of the petty, shrewd, Marshal Chao-worshiping peasants whom he despised, Mao had educational opportunities then shared by very few of his countrymen. Intermittently his father quarreled with him and opposed his method and subjects of study. Once Mao left farm work and for six months studied at the home of an unemployed law student. After he returned 'things again improved' for a while, but when he wished to enter higher primary school in a neighboring town his father made him put up the money to hire an extra hand on the farm for a whole year. Mao borrowed the money – twelve dollars – from a cousin. Always among the most impoverished students, he nevertheless managed to scrimp through five years in the Hunan Normal School, from which he graduated in 1918. In the interim, and while still in primary and middle schools, he had witnessed famines, revolts, banditry and executions.

From boyhood on he had memorized episodes from romanticized accounts of the 'Warring States' and other turbulent periods, books like the *San Kuo* (*Three Kingdoms*) and *Shui Hu Chuan* (*All Men Are Brothers*). Discussing these legends with old peasants, who also delighted in them, Mao heard them reminisce about heroes of the T'ai-p'ing Rebellion, with whom they had sympathized. Like most of his schoolmates Mao could read such forbidden and subversive works only covertly – hiding them under texts of the classics when the teacher walked past. It was these epics, rich in details of strategy and tactics, and the military experience summarized in *Sun Tzu*, the work of Sun Wu, greatest of the ancient military experts (fifth century B.C.), which were to provide for Mao, in later life, basic understanding of the arts of defense and offense in the prosecution of revolutionary war.

Fired by reading the works of the reformist scholars K'ang Yu-wei and Liang Ch'i-ch'ao, and by Sun Yat-sen's *sub rosa* writings in *The People's Strength*, smuggled into the classrooms, Mao had by 1910 become an antimonarchist in mind and heart. In Changsha he had seen the heads of rebels mounted on poles to strike terror into the people. It was not the first time Mao had witnessed such sanguinary reprisals. As a child he had watched poor peasants, driven by starvation during famine, sack the granaries of the gentry. When leaders of the bandits were captured their heads had also been spiked and displayed as a public warning. By now he fully understood the price of both social and national revolt. But his own principal soon defiantly invited revolutionaries to speak before the students, awaken sorrow and arouse patriotism to 'save China from dismemberment'. As a gesture of dedication to the cause Mao cut off his own queue (a symbol of submission to the Manchu emperor) and helped sever the pigtails of some students less ardent than himself. In 1911 he enlisted in the republican forces after he had witnessed the seizure of Changsha. Six months later he 'resigned'; the emperor had abdicated and a republic was proclaimed. 'Thinking the revolution was over,' he explained, 'I decided to return to my books.' After many vacillations Mao determined to become a teacher.

It quickly became apparent that a mere change from dynastic rule to military dictatorship would not end China's decline. Mao began to spend most of his limited cash on newspapers, in order to follow local and national politics. The famous *New Youth* magazine, edited by Ch'en Tu-hsiu, a returned student from France, made a deep impression on Mao and other students of the time. Echoing Ch'en's revolutionary ideas in Hunan, Mao Tse-tung gathered together some friends to form a 'discussion group', very serious in intent. In some ways, it was the prototype of the *hsueh hsi*, or study groups, which were to become a standard feature of 'thought-remolding' disciplines applied over all China a generation later.

In his college discussion group Mao Tse-tung built up a follow-ing among students and asserted his political leadership for the first time. Everything they did and said 'must have a purpose', he told me. They wasted no words on 'love or romance and considered the times too critical and the need for knowledge too urgent to discuss women or personal matters. I was not interested in women. My parents had married me when I was fourteen to a girl of twenty but I had never lived with her — and never did. I did not consider her my wife and at this time gave little thought to her.

'Quite aside from discussions of feminine charm, which usually play an important role in the lives of young men of our age, my companions even rejected talk of ordinary matters of daily life. I remember once being in the house of a youth who began to talk to me about buying some meat, and in my presence called in his ser-vant and discussed the matter with him. I was annoyed and did not see this fellow again. My friends and I preferred to talk of large matters – the nature of men, of human society, of China, the world, and the universe !'

More unusual for Chinese students of that time, Mao and his friends became ardent physical culturists. They sought to toughen and steel themselves by taking long excursions, living in the moun-tains on a minimum of food, sleeping in the open, bathing in cold streams in November, going shirtless and shoeless, 'seeing the country', 'living as the poor people lived', testing themselves, 'body-building'. One summer Mao and another student walked across five counties of his native province, 'without using a single copper. The peasants fed us and gave us a place to sleep; wherever we went we were kindly treated.' It was always the poor peasants, Mao noticed, who were generous in sharing what little they had. Dis-cussing their lives and problems, Mao learned of hardships and in-justice beyond anything he had suffered.

In these same counties, and to the homes of many of the same peasants who had sheltered him, Mao would ten years later return to launch the peasant movement which provided the first recruits for the Red Army.

Mao first went to Peking in 1918, as a delegate from the New People's Study Society. There, at the age of twenty-five, he tenta-tively stepped upon the national political stage. Provincial educa-

tion in China was sketchy and confused in this time of transition
from Confucian teachings to the first gleanings from the Western
world, but Mao had already made wide-ranging contacts and done
omnivorous reading in the Changsha library. In his self-study he
was guided by his favorite professor, Yang Chen-ch'i, British-
educated, 'an idealist and a man of high moral character'. He taught
Mao the first (among the few) English words he ever learned. Now
Mao found Yang again, as a professor at Peking National University. Through his help Mao secured a job under the university
librarian, Li Ta-chao, who later became a principal founder of the
Communist Party. Here he also fell in love with Yang Chen-ch'i's
daughter, K'ai-hui; they were married in 1920.

Both Li Ta-chao and Mao's youthful and beautiful bride were
executed a few years later, after membership in the Communist
party was made a capital offense.

As an assistant librarian Mao's job was 'so low that people
avoided me'. On his arrival in Peking Mao shared a k'ang with
Professor Yang's gateman. Later he lived 'in a little room which
held seven other people. When we were all packed fast on the k'ang
there was scarcely room to breathe. I had to warn people on each
side when I wanted to turn over.' They could not afford wood for a
fire but shared each other's bodily warmth. Among them they had
one winter coat, and they wore it in turn when they wished to go
out at night.

But 'the beauty of the old capital was a vivid and living compensation,' Mao remembered. 'In the parks and the old palace grounds
I saw the early northern spring; I saw the white plum blossoms
flower while the ice still held solid over the North Sea. I saw the
willows over Pei Hai with the ice crystals hanging from them and
remembered the description of the scene by the T'ang poet Chen
Chang, who wrote about Pei Hai's winter-jeweled trees looking
"like ten thousand peach trees blossoming".'

In spite of his poverty and humble occupation Mao managed to
meet important leaders of the cultural renaissance, including Hu
Shih and Ch'en Tu-hsiu. As an editor and political mentor Ch'en
influenced Mao 'more than anyone else'. Under his spell and that
of Li Ta-chao and other senior intellectuals of that time, the impact
of the Russian Revolution turned Mao from belief in parliamen-

tarism, bourgeois democracy, gradualism and ethical idealism, toward Marxism and a commitment to socialist revolution. In 1918 he had joined a study group organized by Li Ta-chao and there first read some Marxist classics.

'Three books especially carved my mind,' he answered a question for me, 'and built up in me a faith in Marxism from which, once I had accepted it as the correct interpretation of history, I did not afterward waver. These were the *Communist Manifesto*, *Class Struggle*, by Kautsky, and *History of Socialism*, by Kirkup.' By the summer of 1920 Mao considered himself a Marxist, and in the following year he joined Li Ta-chao and ten others to found the Chinese Communist Party.

The ensuing years of Mao's life are largely the history of that party. His leadership was not to assume great national significance until after 1926, but in retrospect it is clear that his experience in organizing the peasant unions of his native province came to dominate his own thinking and, ultimately, the course of the revolution.

From its formation throughout the subsequent years of the first United Front with the Kuomintang and down to the break, in 1927, the line and policies of the Chinese party were largely determined by representatives of the Comintern (Communist International), master-minded from Moscow. During the most fateful period of the Nationalist Revolution, 1926-7, Josef Stalin (under constant attack from Trotsky) headed the Comintern and its agents in China took directives from him. From afar, Stalin perhaps saw the revolution primarily as a useful weapon with which to strike at Moscow's archenemies, the great capitalist powers, which were considering large-scale armed intervention in China. Until China achieved national unification and independence the revolution should remain under the leadership of Kuomintang progressive Chinese bourgeoisie, Stalin believed.

Restraints placed upon the Communists were insufficient, however, to lull the fears of the warlord-landlord-banking interests behind Chiang's controlling right wing of the Kuomintang. The Nationalist forces had reached the Yangtze River by 1926. It was not until after Generalissimo Chiang Kai-shek took Nanking that he turned to the destruction of all Communist-influenced troops. Labor-union organizers had seized the Chinese city of Shanghai (not the foreign settlements) in March 1927. They were attacked and disarmed in a counter coup led by Shanghai gangsters, supported by the arrival of Chiang's main forces early in April. Thereafter Chiang Kai-shek made war on the labor unions and thoroughly smashed their urban mass organizations. In the countryside, and particularly in the province of Hunan, the extirpation of the peasant associations turned out to be far more difficult than anticipated. Here Mao Tse-tung entered the dispute on high strategy with his first open defiance of a Comintern line which he believed had led the party to disaster.

Of all Mao's writings, probably none is more important for a student of history than his *Report on an Investigation into the Peasant Movement in Hunan*,[2] written in February 1927, and urged upon the Politburo, together with proposals to change party policy, in the last days, which unnecessarily frightened the bourgeoisie. But these associations then embraced about half the population of Hunan. Were they all riffraff? Mao listed 'Fourteen Great Deeds' they had already accomplished. *These items clearly reveal what Mao considered 'good' and 'bad' for China and the general aims of the agrarian side of the revolution with which he thereafter identified himself.* One of the most remarkable things about Mao's report was that it scarcely mentioned Western imperialism, the major preoccupation of Comintern strategy of the time; almost its entire emphasis was on the necessity to overthrow landlord-gentry oppression in order to liberate the peasantry from 'feudalism' and inequality.

Greatest of the 'deeds' was that the poor peasants had at last actually organized – a miracle in itself – against 'the local bullies', the 'bad gentry', and 'the corrupt officials'. Among other good deeds they were smashing the political prestige of the landlords; compelling them to 'audit accounts'; forcing them to make contributions to the starving; parading the 'most brutal' oppressors through the streets wearing 'tall paper hats'; prohibiting usury, grain hoarding, speculation, excessive rents; taking over the offices of police chiefs and electing magistrates; taking command of the landlords' militia and its arms; eliminating banditry (by bringing bandits into the peasant associations!); overthrowing feudal clan tyranny of rich over poor; fining oppressive landlords and helping themselves to their provisions; ridiculing superstitious practices; ending male tyranny over women; spreading knowledge of the 'Three Principles'; prohibiting gambling, opium-smoking, sumptuous feasts, expensive weddings and elaborate funerals; sponsoring mass education for illiterates; organizing marketing and credit cooperatives; and building roads and irrigation ditches financed by 'contributions' from the landlords.

'No ancestral temple dare any longer, as it used to, inflict cruel and corporal and capital punishments like "beating", "drowning", and "burying alive",' Mao reported. In instances the peasants had found that 'the only effective way of suppressing the reactionaries is to execute, in every county, at least some of those whose crimes and wrongdoings are most serious' – of whom Mao mentioned, in his own Hsiang T'an, two men he accused of having 'murdered' 'more than fifty' poor men 'euphemistically described as bandits'.[3]

Such was Mao's vision of good and evil in the countryside. Such became the program of history's first Communist-led revolution based on the poor peasantry as its 'vanguard'.

After the Hankow debacle Moscow blamed the hapless Ch'en Tu-hsiu for misinterpreting Stalin's contradictory directives, but the party line continued to rely on the proletariat and insurrections in the cities. Attempts at armed uprisings in Canton and Nanchang were bloodily suppressed. Moscow-trained Communists regrouped the shattered party underground and led it in more putsches of the United Front. Mao had attacked Ch'en Tu-hsiu, the party secretary, for his vacillating and negative directives concerning the peasant associations, the arming of the peasants, and redistribution of land. Ch'en was not opposed to arming the peasants so much as he was concerned with trying to reconcile two contradictory directives from the Comintern, which in essence were: (1) maintain the united front with the Kuomintang by all means; (2) meet the demands of the peasants, especially for land confiscation. The 'united front' with the Kuomintang rested upon the support of militarists who were themselves big landlords. To threaten their land would (and did) end cooperation. In a decisive May meeting Ch'en tabled Mao's report and four months later had him read out of the Politburo. Thus the teacher disowned his disciple; but behind Ch'en loomed Stalin.

The counterrevolution drove Soviet advisers from the country and descended upon mass organizations with a violence particularly savage in Hunan, where numerous peasant leaders and intellectuals were executed. Mao himself escaped, probably only because Ch'en had ordered him not to return to Hunan. Chiang Kai-shek emerged supreme, and the Communist party was driven underground.

Mao's 1927 report had been the result of thirty-two days of travel in five counties of Hunan, starting in his native Hsiang T'an, where he had gathered information to try to convince Ch'en that all the peasants of China were about to 'rise like a tornado' of such force that 'no power, however great, will be able to suppress it'. He announced that the poor peasants of China were 'the vanguard of the revolution' – almost a heresy in the eyes of orthodox Marxists; only an industrial proletariat could be the vanguard of a social revolution. Mao reported that 'the poor peasants comprise seventy percent of the rural population; the middle peasants, twenty percent; the rich peasants and landlords, ten percent.' What was more: the 'enormous mass of the *poor peasants* are the backbone of the peasant associations'. Also, 'being the most revolutionary, the poor peasants have won the leadership. ... This leadership of the poor peasants is absolutely necessary. Without the poor peasant there can be no revolution. Their general direction of the revolution has never been wrong.'

Mao now and henceforth saw himself as their champion.

Party critics (those who bothered to read him) had called his associations a 'movement of the riffraff' and of 'lazy good-for-nothings' (aided by the Comintern), which proved disastrous. By 1932 Chiang Kai-shek and the foreign-policed concessions had made the cities untenable for even a skeletal party apparatus. The bulk of the Central Committee then fled to rural sanctuaries meanwhile built up by Mao Tse-tung and others who believed in the 'poor peasantry as vanguard'.

After the unseating of Ch'en Tu-hsiu, in August 1927, Mao had returned to Hunan, where, still lacking party approval, he evolved a policy based on his own neglected report on the peasant movement. Gathering together the pieces of the peasant associations – their local leadership having been decapitated by the Kuomintang –

he launched the first armed rural insurrection, called the Autumn Crop Uprising. By September it had developed what was called the First Division of the First Peasants and Workers Army. Besides recruits from the shattered peasant unions Mao brought in some miners from Hanyang unions and some Kuomintang forces which revolted against the Wuhan (Hankow) government.

Inexperienced and poorly armed, the little band was quickly surrounded and forced into disorderly retreat. Mao himself was captured by Kuomintang forces but escaped. Fleeing southward at night he was helped by old friends among the poor peasants to re-establish contact with his remnant forces. Rallying about a thousand men, he retreated to a mountain stronghold called Chingkangshan, and there established the first base of the new revolution. In May 1928 he was finally reinforced by the arrival of troops from Nanchang, where Chu Teh (a Kuomintang police commander) had led the ill-fated Nanchang Uprising. From this time on Mao had a trained and able military commander beside him, and he and Chu Teh became inseparable. Mao told me:

'Because the program of the Autumn Uprising had not been sanctioned by the Central Committee, because also the First Army had suffered some severe losses, and from the angle of the cities the movement appeared doomed to failure, the Central Committee now definitely repudiated me. [Behind it, still, were the Comintern experts.] I was dismissed from the Politburo and also from the Party Front Committee. The Hunan provincial committee also attacked us, calling us a "rifle movement". We nevertheless held our army together at Chingkangshan, feeling certain that we were following the correct line, and subsequent events were to vindicate us fully. New recruits were added and the division filled out again. I became its commander . . .'

In the winter of 1928–9, Mao's action during and after the Autumn Uprising finally won approval of the Comintern, still bossed by Stalin. It would be wrong to assume, however, that Mao's general line based on the Hunan report was fully accepted. Mao was reinstated in the Central Committee and the Politburo, but his leadership was not to be conceded till 1935. Meanwhile, Mao himself never openly defied Stalin or challenged orthodox Marxist doctrine, which continued to hold that 'seizure of power' could be attained by the party only through the urban working class. Mao's problem in semantics was one of loyally upholding Moscow's infallibility, and maintaining an orthodox posture, while the party in practice became almost solely dependent on the peasantry. This he managed to do by means of postulating the existence of a 'rural proletariat' and a worker-peasant army under the leadership of the Communist Party itself acting as the vanguard of the true (urban) proletariat. That Mao was able to become an innovator, in Stalin's own time, without again being expelled as a heretic, required great skill in dialectical polemics combined with the ancient Chinese art of 'appearing to move in a straight line while actually taking a curve'. Whether Mao made 'original contributions to Marxist theory' is consequently now a subject which engages many Western scholars and historians in debates as hotly fought as were past ecclesiastical arguments over the question, 'How many angels can dance on the head of a needle?'[4]

The Long March

FROM 1928 onward the peasant war spread rapidly. North of the Yangtze River other guerrilla bases were set up which developed on much the same pattern as those in Kiangsi, and also achieved limited successes. Foremost among the northern partisan leaders was Chang Kuo-t'ao, an old friend of Mao since student days in Peking, and a cofounder with him of the party, at Shanghai.

Mao's own story of the growth of the Red Army, made up entirely of volunteers and based on intensive political indoctrination, with egalitarian brotherhood between officers and men – new ideas in China – has been fully related in *Red Star Over China*. By 1934 six separate soviets, south and north of the river, embraced a population of 9,000,000 people. In the largest area, in Kiangsi, a central government was formed at Juichin. Mao Tse-tung was elected chairman – but he was not then chairman of the party.

The 'mass base' of the soviet movement was built upon the organization of workers' and peasants' unions, with the principal role in the hands of the 'poor peasantry, the vast majority' led by the Communist party, claiming hegemony over the revolution and its ultimate 'proletarian dictatorship'. Its radical policy included outright confiscation of landlords' estates and their distribution among have-not peasants, and the establishment of socialist ownership over means of industrial production. 'Reforms' included correction of most of the evils of corruption and inequality listed in Mao's earlier report on Hunan. Effective leadership required very strict discipline and moral codes and a readiness to share all the hardships of peasant life.

'Gradually the Red Army's work with the masses improved,' Mao told me. 'Discipline strengthened, and a new technique of organization developed.' As early as the Chingkangshan period the army had 'imposed three simple rules: prompt obedience to orders;

no confiscations whatever from the poor peasantry; prompt delivery to the government, for disposal, of all goods confiscated from the landlords.' Eight other rules were adopted and put to music, to be sung and remembered by all troops :

1. Replace doors when you leave a house.*
2. Return and roll up the straw matting.†
3. Be courteous and polite to the people and help them.
4. Return all borrowed articles.
5. Replace all damaged articles.
6. Be honest in all transactions with the peasants.
7. Pay for all articles purchased.
8. Be sanitary : establish latrines at a safe distance from people's houses.

'Three other duties were taught to the Red Army as its primary purpose : first, to struggle to the death against the enemy; second, to arm the masses; third, to raise money to support the struggle ... Red tactics, apart from the political basis of the movement, explained much of the successful military development.' All the elementary rules of consideration were innovations for Chinese soldiers – traditionally contemptuous of the people and regarded by them as a kind of unavoidable scourge and punishment. (Good iron doesn't become a nail, said an ancient Chinese proverb, nor does a good man become a soldier.)

Four simple tactical slogans were early adopted :

When the enemy advances, we retreat.
When the enemy halts and encamps, we trouble him.
When the enemy seeks to avoid battle, we attack.
When the enemy retreats, we pursue.

Whenever the Red Army departed from them, in general, it did not succeed.

'Our forces were small,' Mao explained, 'exceeded from ten to twenty times by the enemy; our resources and fighting materials were limited, and only by skillfully combining the tactics of

---

*Wooden doors of Chinese peasant houses are hung on pegs and easily detachable; placed on wooden stools they serve as improvised beds.
† Used for sleeping.

maneuvering and guerrilla warfare could we hope to succeed' – in capturing arms and ammunition from the Kuomintang forces, the Reds' 'only supply base'. 'The most important single tactic of the Red Army was its ability to concentrate its main forces in the attack, and swiftly divide and separate them. This implies that positional warfare was to be avoided and every effort made to meet the forces of the enemy while in movement, and destroy them.' On the basis of these tactics the Red Army perfected the mobility and power of its 'short attack' – rapid engagement utilizing massive superiority in brief decisive battles of limited scope.

Beginning in 1930 Chiang Kai-shek had launched four major 'extermination campaigns' against Red strongholds. The net results had been only further arming of his adversaries. Late in 1933 he mobilized 900,000 men and deployed about 300,000 well-armed troops in his most systematic effort to encircle and annihilate the Red forces. This time he was successful – almost. Until the 'fifth campaign', which lasted a whole year, the Chu-Mao offensive-defensive had been based on well-developed strategy and tactics of guerrilla-partisan warfare. Now the Generalissimo met them with new methods; he followed the plans of his Prussian advisers, headed by the Nazi general von Seeckt. Instead of rushing into the well-laid traps prepared for him, Chiang slowly built up a series of stone fortresses, extended highways, transported the 'infected' population, built more forts, and gradually closed a vise upon his enemies.

To Chiang's new tactics the Reds also responded differently, and also under the advice of a German general, Otto Braun – in Chinese known as Li Teh – who had been smuggled into Kiangsi by the Comintern. Against the judgment and will of Chu Teh, Mao Tse-tung and most of the experienced native army staff (I was told), Li Teh and the Moscow-oriented Chinese Politburo leaders committed the Red Army (about 180,000 men) to several great battles in positional warfare. They attached excessive importance to holding towns and cities. They 'lost the initiative' and were very heavily defeated.

As the steel encirclement narrowed and tightened, and enemy depopulation tactics shrank the 'human base' itself, the Red leaders made an agonizing decision. After seven years of fighting they abandoned their hard-won soviet republic. They withdrew their main surviving forces (about 90,000 men), leaving only a few thousand Red 'regulars' and partisans to fight rear-guard actions. On 16 October 1934, with what equipment and supplies they could carry on the backs of animals and 5,000 porters, the Red Army began a great strategic retreat by means of which – historic paradox – they eventually 'recovered the initiative'.

It was only now that Mao Tse-tung at last stood forth as the strongest personality of the party. It is one thing to command men in hope of early victory. It is quite another to lead them into such cheerless prospects as faced the defeated Red Army. Completely cut off from all further contact with Moscow, moving into country where the populace had been indoctrinated to fear and hate them, yet dependent on the people for survival, constantly pursued, obliged to give battle nearly every day, to improvise, to maneuver, to double and redouble their tracks to avoid ensnarement, never sure when they would eat again or where lie down exhausted, these were warriors whose lives hung upon morale alone – and faith in their leadership. Many thousands were to desert or fall by the wayside.

The weakest link in the encirclement lay on the west, where the provincial warlords in Kweichow were unable to prevent a major Red breakthrough.

Moving into that opium-soaked province, the Reds captured the governor's headquarters and seized his residence at Tsun-yi. There a historic enlarged Politburo conference in January 1935 unequivocally recognized Mao's leadership. As chairman of the Politburo, he assumed supreme responsibility for strategy. Moscow-trained Po Ku (Ch'in Pang-hsien)* and his supporters stepped down and acknowledged their errors. High among them had been turning over strategic military command to Li Teh during the fifth campaign. Now Mao's strategy (in general, one of capturing the countryside to encircle the cities) was held to have been correct. His summary of the lessons of the period, *Strategic Problems in China's Revolutionary War*, was to become a party classic. Together with two other documents,[1] it forms the bulk of Maoist thought and doctrine of 'the science of combining political struggle with arming the people in colonial and semicolonial countries'.

*Killed in an airplane accident in 1945.

Political differences behind them (for the moment), the Reds now advanced upon the great adventure which was to unite them more firmly than any political élite in our times. Ahead lay unknown dangers, exploration, discovery, trials of human courage, ecstasy and agony, triumph and reverses – and through it all an amazing ardor and optimism, as thousands of youths, most of them still in their late teens or early twenties, marched into the western horizon on an odyssey unsurpassed in military annals.

Mao Tse-tung first spoke to me of the ordeal, now behind him, as the *Liang Wan Wu-Ch'ien-Li Ch'ang Ch'eng* – the Long March of 25,000 *li*. With all its twists and turns, advances and retreats, from the farthest starting point in Fukien to rugged eastern Tibet, and then to the end of the road near the Gobi Desert, some men probably did that distance. An accurate stage-by-stage itinerary prepared for me by the First Army Corps showed a main trek of some 6,000 miles – about twice the width of the United States. This journey on foot led across some of the world's most arduous trails, its highest mountains, and its greatest rivers.

The first critical test was the crossing of the upper Yangtze, the 'Gold Sand' River. As the Reds pulled out of Kweichow they entered the wild mountainous country of western Yunnan, where the river flows treacherous and swift, through gorges thousands of feet deep. The few bridge crossings had all been occupied by government troops, and all ferryboats had been drawn to the north bank. Chiang Kai-shek was well pleased. Advancing in an enveloping movement, he sought to finish off the Red Army forever in these defiles. Far into Yunnan, the Reds started to build a bamboo bridge. Then a commando force countermarched at night through the mountains, covered eighty-five miles on foot in twenty-four hours, and stealthily seized a small Kuomintang garrison at a ferry crossing. Dressed in captured uniforms, they persuaded troops on the opposite bank to send over ferryboats. Under cover of darkness they then crossed the river, seized the fort, and secured a vital route on which the whole army soon escaped westward.

Another strategic river had to be crossed: the Tatu, in western Szechuan. Here the heroes of the *Three Kingdoms* had met defeat, and here the troops of Prince Shih Ta-k'ai, last of the T'ai-p'ing rebels, had been surrounded and completely destroyed with their leader. Mao and Chu Teh had studied both those campaigns; they knew that the main cause of their heroes' defeat had been costly delay. To beat Chiang Kai-shek to the river, they entered the never conquered and forbidding forest domains of aborigines known as the Lolos. All Lolos traditionally hated Chinese, as their oppressors, but there were White Lolos and Black Lolos. To the Black Lolos the Reds declared that their enemies were the White Chinese; they were Red Chinese and the Lolos' friends, fighting for their freedom. Why not unite against their common enemies, the White Chinese? In skillful bargaining led by one commander who knew the native language, the Reds negotiated a treaty and safely passed their whole army through territory the Generalissimo thought impossible for them.

The strategy and tactics by which the dare-to-die band of heroes then seized and captured the last bridge on the Tatu is an exciting chapter in itself. Had they failed, the Red Army would have been forced into high Tibet and there likely have perished in the eternal snows. At the sacrifice of some lives they succeeded. Ahead lay a 16,000-foot pass over the Great Snowy Mountains of western Szechuan, and range after range beyond that. They climbed on. 'On Pao-tung Kang peak alone,' Mao Tse-tung said, 'one army lost two-thirds of its transport animals. Hundreds fell down and never got up again.' So did hundreds of the men and women who braved the trek.

In July the survivors finally emerged in the rich Moukung area and debouched into the Sungpan region of eastern Tibet. Here they met the Fourth Front Red Army which Chang Kuo-t'ao had led up from the abandoned Red districts north of the river in the central Yangtze Valley. They had had an easier retreat and had even managed to augment their forces – estimated at 100,000. And now, in Chang Kuo-t'ao, Chairman Mao met the last rival to his leadership. A clash of wills which almost destroyed the party, it was described to me by both Mao Tse-tung and Chou En-lai as the most critical moment in its whole history.

The crisis was broken by two factors. First, the rapid advance of new forces mobilized by Chiang Kai-shek in Szechuan, moving in from north to south, threatened to drive a wedge between the two Red columns. Second, a sudden rise in the headwaters of one of

Szechuan's rapid rivers, which then physically divided the two forces, completely cut them off from each other. Chang's forces were left on the southern banks.

Obliged to leave Chu Teh a virtual prisoner of Chang Kuo-t'ao, the main Kiangsi column now continued its northward advance under Mao Tse-tung, accompanied by Chou En-Lai, P'eng Teh-huai and Lin Piao. They resumed their march with only 30,000 men.

Into wild lands inhabited by warring tribesmen who opposed them at every step, in and out of thick, gloomy forests and miasmatic jungles, across more headwater marshlands where comrades sank and disappeared, into deep, narrow passes where hostile natives often ambushed them – uninfluenced by the 'Communist policy of equality for national minorities' – they struggled on. For weeks, said Mao, 'to get one sheep cost the life of one comrade.'

By September they were deep in the Great Grasslands, where they saw no human habitation for ten days. Almost perpetual rain falls over these high swamplands, passable by a maze of narrow footholds known only to native highlanders, whom the Reds had to capture to guide them. More animals were lost, and more men. Many foundered in a weird sea of wet grass and disappeared, beyond reach, into the depth of swamps. There was no dry firewood. There was nothing to eat but wild vegetables and herbs. There were no trees for shelter : at night they huddled under bushes tied together. Worst of all, they could get no potable water. 'On occasions men were reduced to drinking their own urine.'

When at last they came down onto the Kansu plain their numbers had been cut to 7,000. Still more critical battles lay ahead before they entered the fertile Yellow River basin. After a brief rest, they broke through weak cordons of Moslem cavalry and replenished themselves. They finally united with local Red forces* in north Shensi, on 25 October 1935, and wearily assessed their achievement.

Out of a total journey of 368 days they had spent 235 in marches by day and eighteen in marches at night. Official army records show that they fought an average of almost a skirmish a day, somewhere along the line, while fifteen days were devoted to major pitched battles. Aside from the long stay in the Sungpan (fifty-six

* See pages 451–2.

days) they had taken only forty-four days of rest, over a distance of about 6,000 miles – one halt for every 114 miles of marching. The mean daily stage was about 24 miles.

Altogether they crossed eighteen mountain ranges, five of them perennially snow-capped, and they crossed twenty-four rivers. They passed through twelve provinces, each larger than most European countries; they broke through enveloping armies of ten different provincial warlords; they eluded, outmaneuvered or defeated Kuomintang troops numbering more than 300,000. They entered and crossed six different aboriginal districts and penetrated areas through which no Chinese army had gone for many years.

One may reject or despise Communist ideology as a universal religion or political faith, but it is impossible not to recognize the Long March as one of the great triumphs of men against odds and man against nature. While the Red Army was unquestionably in forced retreat, its toughened veterans reached their planned objective with moral and political will as strong as – probably much stronger than – ever. They declared and believed they were advancing to lead a sacred national salvation war against the invading Japanese – a psychological factor of great importance to the rank and file. The conviction helped turn what might have been a demoralized rout into an arrival in triumph. History has subsequently shown that Mao was undoubtedly right in taking the Red forces to the strategic northwest, a region which he correctly foresaw was to play a determining role in the immediate destinies of China, Japan and Soviet Russia.

In Yenan, while Mao Tse-tung finished his own eyewitness account to me, the flesh still lean on his bones from the ordeal, far to the west General Chu Teh and Chang Kuo-t'ao (now chastened from the hard winter on the edge of Tibet) were themselves emerging with their own decimated troops from the Great Grasslands and soon to unite once more with the 'vanguard of the poor peasants' who had proved it could be done. Thinking of this happy event, Mao wrote a poem for me which I translated with the help of his English-speaking secretary, Wu Liang-p'ing:

The Red Army, never fearing the challenging Long March,
Looked lightly on the many peaks and rivers,

Wu Meng's range rose, lowered, rippled,
And green-tiered were the rounded steps of Wu Meng.
Warm-beating the Gold Sand River's waves against the rocks,
And cold the iron chain spans of Tatu bridge.
A thousand joyous *li* of freshening snow on Min Shan,
And then, the last pass vanquished, the Armies smiled.[2]

In Peking today I found a whole floor in the newly opened Revolutionary Museum devoted to these exploits, now a part of the David and Goliath legends of the East. Every fifteen minutes, a huge map lights up which traces each stage of the heroic route. A pony-tailed girl guide stands before it and retells the story before yet another audience of youths and wide-eyed tourists.

19

Power Personality

MAO'S childhood resentments seem to have been well-founded protests against tyranny and ignorance, but we have only his side of the story. On his later years there is much more information. It is difficult to separate Mao's adult behavior or writing from the whole Chinese revolution. Should that be considered one vast delusion of persecution? Is everyone who disdains to compromise with the intolerable a paranoid? That would put Patrick Henry in the vanguard. If, after a nation has been exploited, robbed, opium-soaked, plundered, occupied and partitioned by foreign invaders for a century, the people turns upon its persecutors and drives them from the house, along with the society whose weakness permitted the abuses, is it suffering from paranoia? Or would it be schizoid if it did otherwise? Some grave miscalculations in Mao's later years suggest delusions of grandeur. Could they not readily be matched by blunders of bigoted 'normal' statesmen elsewhere which are rationalized as bad judgment? Erik Erikson has described Martin Luther as a great man whose personality found maximum stability only when he discovered his *adult* 'identity' in reasonable heresy; in his rebellion against Rome he found truth in a fully justified good cause. Similarly, Mao had little difficulty in uniting his personality as leader of a 'just war' of liberation.

A man who made a career of nonconformism, Mao was demanding from the nation a degree of conformism unsurpassed anywhere. He was as aggressive as any civilized leader alive, and, like the rest of them, not above wanting a bomb of his own. He would never slap his soft-soled shoe on the table to demand attention, as Khrushchev had done with his Russian boot at the United Nations, but he was not entirely free of the exhibitionism that affects other power personalities. The father of any nation must reflect at least some of the paradoxes of its children as well as those of the outside world.

It was Mao's ability to analyze the experience common to his generation – rather than the uniqueness of his own experience – plus his messianic belief in the correctness of his own generalizations of that experience, which distinguished him from compatriots who became his followers.

There was nothing neutral or passive about Mao, but neither was there any record that he had ever advocated a war of foreign conquest. His concept was that revolutionary war was essentially an offensive-defensive action. When people are held in subjection by armed oppressors they repel them by force. Having 'liberated' China by means of 'struggle', Mao viewed the world as divided between two camps in which justice and right would finally prevail after more struggle. Class war everywhere continued in the capitalist countries; they threatened humanity with imperialist war which could be prevented or defeated only by struggle, as Mao saw it. Because he was the product of a land repeatedly hit by foreign invasion and civil war, and himself a near-victim of counter-revolutionary violence, life taught him to rationalize all revolutionary action as 'blows for peace'.

'War,' he wrote at the time of the Japanese invasion, 'this monster of mutual slaughter among mankind, will be finally eliminated through the progress of human society, and in no distant future, too. But there is only one way of eliminating it, namely, to oppose war by means of war, to oppose counterrevolutionary war by means of revolutionary war, and to oppose counterrevolutionary class war by means of revolutionary class war. All counterrevolutionary wars are unjust, all revolutionary wars are just. Our study of the laws of revolutionary war starts from our will to eliminate all wars – this is the dividing line between Communists and all exploiting classes.'[1]

Generations of Western dominance in Asia had brought not peace but a sword, and Mao summarized the lesson for many of his countrymen when he said, 'All political power grows out of the barrel of a gun.' Not until China learned to use modern guns effectively did the West begin to respect and fear her. It was therefore not likely, alas, that China would be first to lay down her arms.

To Mao Tse-tung Western observers who expected China to
commit suicide by launching aggressive wars of conquest were
hypocrites or fools. 'Sooner or later,' he said, 'these gentlemen will
take a look at a map. Then they will notice that it is not China that
is occupying Western territory, not China that has ringed Western
countries with military bases, but the other way round.'

To a man sincerely convinced that revolutions are 'blows for
peace' – and who had actually seen revolution bring internal
peace to China – the question of war and the nature of its causes
was bound to look very different from the way it looked to those
who believed that counterrevolutions were 'blows for peace'.
Whatever objective results Mao's policies may have in an infinitely
complex world, there was in my own mind little doubt that he
wished to avoid war but greatly feared it might not be possible.
Still less did he believe that a general holocaust could hasten the
construction of socialism – and certainly not in time for him to
receive congratulations. Mao was not mad. Anyone who talked
to him for a few hours saw in Mao an aging warrior deeply conscious of his mortality and aware that he must soon step aside,
leaving behind him the still unfinished edifice of which he had
merely laid the foundations. He knew that it would be long in the
creation but he believed that it would create everlastingly. Even
without the cataclysm of nuclear war the task would take many
years. Fifty? A hundred? What is that, he asked, in the life of
nations – and especially in the life of China?

There was evidence that Mao understood his own country better
than any national leader in modern times, yet his grasp of the
Western world was a schematic one based on methods of Marxist
analysis of classes as they existed in backward economies like the
one he grew up in. He lacked sufficient understanding of the subtle
changes brought about in those classes in advanced 'welfare states'
by two hundred years of the kind of transformation China was
only now entering; just as many well-fed American congressmen
consistently failed to understand that starving have-not majorities
of poor nations would not wait for two hundred years to see their
children fed and educated.

Was Mao a blind and rigid dogmatist? 'Dogma is more useless
than cow dung,' he said. He stressed the importance of concrete

analysis derived from specific and concrete conditions. Did he hold that *only* material conditions determine social behavior and that there is no such force as the spiritual, which preoccupies the idealistic philosophers? No; what Mao said in *On Contradictions* was '. . . while we recognize that in the development of history as a whole it is material things that determine spiritual things, and social existence that determines social consciousness, at the same time we also recognize and must recognize the reaction of spiritual things and social consciousness on social existence, and the reaction of the superstructure on the economic foundation.' Between them contradictions were bound to exist.

Chinese Communists appeared to the Western critic to hold extremely dogmatic positions from which no logic could budge them. That was because, once a party line was formulated, all members parroted it with the same uniformity and seeming lack of individual thought or will. But the line was constantly subjected to re-examination in terms of old and new data. There were repeated examples of changes and reversals of tactical or even strategical approaches to many questions – often accompanied by 'rectification' movements and downgrading of 'antiparty' elements too slow to move with the times. Maoist Marxists, in kinship with all Marxists, did not believe in change but regarded nothing as immune to change. Although they were often slower to modify their analysis to accommodate minor changes than were politicians who lack a basic doctrine – and hence depend more upon improvisation and pragmatism – they could make very sudden and dramatic policy shifts. They might leave an obsolete line hanging on a cliff, to the embarrassment of nonparty sympathizers who supported it for reasons of personal interest or ideals without understanding its transitory character. Acceptance of the new line – which might directly contradict the old – presented no problems to the experienced party member, however, whose disciplined faith enabled him to proclaim the reconstructed 'only truth' on any question with the same zeal and uniformity as he did the old.

In the past few years Communists had been going through an 'agonizing reappraisal' of the 'inevitable imperialist war' thesis – one of the very fundamental formulations of Lenin – based on changed world conditions. Mao had been denounced as a backward dogmatist in this dispute. We shall see, further on, that experiences of China to date give more logical support to his views than many persons living in another milieu can readily comprehend.

Inside China, Mao's record as a prophet is very good but not without blemish. As a recent example of an amazing lapse : his promise made in June 1958, when he set goals 'attainable within one or two years', namely, 'that there should be available each year for each person 1,650 pounds of food grains' and '110 pounds of pork'. In 1960 he told Marshal Montgomery that such Western standards of diet would not be realized for 'fifty years'. How to reconcile the two remarks? Neither Mao nor China yields to any simple analysis, be it by Freud or by Marx.

Serious miscalculations in planning have been attributed to Mao, and he undoubtedly ignored some good advice. Yet he was not too conceited to adopt the ideas of a trenchant critic* by incorporating them into the national 'eight-point charter for agriculture'. In their original aims the people's communes were the most radical attempt to uproot man and remake his environment since the Paris Commune. Observers afar tended to blame the entire food shortage of 1960–62 on the communes and to hold Mao responsible. The communes were not Mao's idea alone, as we shall presently see, yet he could not avoid responsibility for the costly haste of their beginnings.

Foreign critics accused Mao of indifference to the possible loss of millions of lives in nuclear war. It was said that Mao regarded his own 'blue ants'† – a fashionable substitute nowadays for the 'yellow peril', which conjures up the same ancient racist fears and hates – as expendable. Yet under Mao's régime very great and systematic efforts were being made to preserve and prolong human life and to educate people for constructive effort.

Mao had been called stubborn, quick-tempered, egotistical and

* The economist Ma Yin-ch'u.

† The term 'blue ants' seems to have been invented by certain French journalists to describe Chinese Communist society. Visiting photographers and writers were reminded of ant colonies when they observed masses of blue-clad Chinese building great public works. Blue is said to have been widely popularized mainly because of the universal availability of a cheap, fast native vegetable indigo dye favored by makers of homespun textiles. It has been in use for centuries. Modern Chinese wear garments of many

ruthless. Yet some Chinese intellectuals who had used these terms were still walking around free men.* It had been said abroad that Mao's vanity surpassed Stalin's. But in a period when Khrushchev was still dancing jigs to amuse Stalin (according to his own report to his Twentieth Party Congress) and doubtless looking for new rivers to name for the boss, Mao Tse-tung had initiated a Central Committee decision to forbid the naming of provinces, cities or towns for himself or other living leaders, and banned birthday celebrations in his honor.[2]

In order to hold power Stalin had to kill or remove nearly all the Old Bolsheviks left behind by Lenin. Khrushchev removed every member of the 1953 Politburo except Anastas Mikoyan. Mao had worked with much the same Central Committee for nearly twenty years. Except for Kao Kang and Jao Shu-shih, who were accused in the mid-fifties of attempting to set up an independent state in Manchuria (possibly backed by Stalin), there had been no split in the top leadership since 1937. The Politburo was composed exclusively of close comrades of a lifetime, but Mao had at times been bitterly opposed and occasionally defeated. He had not shot his opposition. Following his own advice to others, to 'use means of persuasion', he had either accepted his defeat or recovered by winning a majority in the Central Committee.†

'No man can rule guiltlessly,' said Saint-Simon, and least of all can men in a hurry. If the successes of China's revolution may be personified by one man so must its crimes and its failures. Mao had not held power by devouring his closest comrades, as Stalin did, but he was not without blood on his hands. The amount of killing during a revolutionary change of power varies with the intensity

---

colors and patterns but work clothes are blue – whether worn by peasants, students, intellectuals or officials, male or female. The blue work clothes of French peasants apparently do not make them blue ants.

*See Chapter 49, 'Counterattack and Paradox'.

† (1970) This comment records opinion held among Chinese Communists themselves as well as by outsiders, prior to 1966. The Great Proletarian Cultural Revolution of course shattered all precedents when Mao called for nation-wide 'revolt of the masses' against party leaders and organs which did in fact control a majority of the Central Committee. The G.P.C.R. clearly transgressed the C.C.P. constitution and many rules of inner-party struggle formerly held inviolate. (See Preface.)

of the counterrevolution, and in China that was of long duration. Throughout his twenty-two years of power Chiang Kai-shek was held responsible for the execution of countless rebels and sympathizers, as well as four fifths of the Communist party membership during his 1927 *coup d'état*. In the same sense Mao was responsible for sanguinary excesses no less severe. During the revolution Mao sanctioned 'necessary' executions of 'archcriminals'. His repeated admonitions against killing without 'fair trials' and emphasis on 'the less killing the better' were not indicative, however, of a sadist or a man with a personal blood lust.[3]

'Revolution is not the same thing as inviting people to dinner or writing an essay or painting a picture or doing fancy needlework,' Mao discovered years ago on his first encounter with rebel peasants in action. 'It cannot be anything so refined, so calm and gentle, or so mild, kind, courteous, restrained and magnanimous.'[4]

The image of Mao among the masses was hardly that of an executioner. What made him formidable was that he was not just a party boss but by many millions of Chinese was quite genuinely regarded as a teacher, statesman, strategist, philosopher, poet laureate, national hero, head of the family, and greatest liberator in history. He was to them Confucius plus Lao-tzu plus Rousseau plus Marx plus Buddha. The 'Hundred Flowers' period revealed that he had enemies as well, yet Mao was the only Communist party boss who ever dared open the press and forum to give voice to that popular resentment.*

Some of the hero worship of Mao may have expressed much the same kind of national self-esteem as British idolatry of Queen Victoria in days when the Empire was shouldering the white man's burden. Victoria did no more to discourage that, it may be recalled, than the press did to demolish the Kennedy 'image' in the United States. In so far as the Mao 'cult' was reminiscent of the synthetic beatification of Stalin when he was alive, it was to any Westerner nauseating in the same degree. No public building, no commune, no factory or girls' dormitory was complete without its solemn statue or plaster bust of the man with the mole on his chin. They were as much a part of the furniture in any reception room as the inevitable green tablecloth and bowls of boiling tea. In Szechuan I

*See Chapters 46–9.

even saw a towering simulated bronze statue of Mao made of lacquer so light that a schoolgirl could easily shift it from pedestal to pedestal as occasion demanded.

The truth seems obvious that most nation-families of today still require a national parental image as well as some kind of patriarchal image of God (or History). Sigmund Freud has analyzed religion as a product of the adult need to find a substitute for the child's conceptions of his parents – loving, omnipotent and incomprehensible – which he transfers to the awesome father image of God, with his faith matching the intensity of his yearning for protection. Similarly, the greater a nation's aspiration toward security and recognition, and the more difficult its way there, the more its children may need the reassurance of a national father figure as a projection of their individual and collective self-esteem.

The value of a state father image in the 'democratic dictatorship' had been clearly recognized by the Chinese party. With the break-up of large families as a result of industrialization of both town and country, as well as the replacement of family paternalism by party paternalism, the mantle of national patriarch would inevitably have descended on the shoulders of any leader in a country not far removed from ancestor worship and emperor worship. Mao had become an Institution of such prestige and authority that no one in the party could raze it without sacrificing a collective vested interest of first importance. Probably no one knew that better than Mao himself.

He was also his own best propagandist by practicing the rule of 'physician, heal thyself'. Consider this significant passage :

If you want the masses to understand you and want to become one with them, you must be determined to undergo a long and even painful process of remolding. I began as a student and acquired at school the habits of a student; in the presence of a crowd of students who could neither fetch nor carry for themselves I used to feel it undignified to do any manual labor such as shouldering my own luggage. At that time it seemed to me that the intellectuals were the only clean persons in the world and peasants seemed rather dirty beside them.

Having become a revolutionary I found myself in the same ranks as the workers, peasants and soldiers of the revolutionary army, and gradually I became familiar with them and they with me, too. It was then and only then that a fundamental change occurred in the bourgeois and petty-bourgeois feelings implanted in me by bourgeois schools. I came to feel that it was those unremodelled intellectuals who were unclean while the workers and peasants are after all the cleanest persons even though their hands are soiled and their feet smeared with cow dung. This is what is meant by having one's feelings transformed, changed from those of one class to those of another.[5]

Early in life Mao understood the obvious but neglected facts which brought him to power: 1) that the vast majority of the Chinese people were poor and illiterate; 2) that China's greatest reservoir of creative energy lay in this majority; 3) that the man who succeeded in winning its confidence and effectively organized it could gain political ascendancy; 4) that in this massive labor power lay all the 'capital' necessary to industrialize China and make of it a wealthy and mighty nation.

Unlike many Chinese intellectuals, who looked upon the huge, illiterate, spawning population as their country's greatest liability, Mao saw their 'economically poor' and 'culturally blank' condition as China's greatest assets. Because they were so very poor, he said, things could hardly be worse; any party which brought even a modest improvement would win their support and hold their loyalty. Because they were so 'culturally blank' they were like a clean new sheet of paper. Whoever made the effort to remold their lives for the better would leave sharp, clean and lasting impressions.

'Ninety percent of the people,' Mao often said, 'are without culture and education.' What distinguished him from all previous Chinese leaders, with the exception of Sun Yat-sen, was that he did not mean merely to utilize the peasants in order to attain power, and then drop them back into the mud. The ex-teacher proposed to end the misery and stupidity of illiterate and invertebrate peasant life itself by lifting the peasants onto high levels of education and providing access to tools of a new environment.

To convince the peasants that by determined struggle they could own the land they tilled, and then to convert that sense of ownership into energetic participation in the mastery of their fate through the 'construction of socialism' – these were the not inconsiderable tasks which Mao and his followers assumed, and the results of which are here being examined.

20

Mao at Home

EVERY schoolboy in China was familiar with the major events in Mao's own history, yet the average youth of today knew less about his private life either past or present than the older generation did. Mao had never written any autobiography except as he told me his life story, and many details revealed in my own book were no longer available in Chinese.[1] Few of his countrymen knew his general whereabouts most of the time. For long periods his activities were not mentioned in the press. They often became a subject of speculation by foreign diplomats, who sometimes started rumors of 'serious illness' to smoke him out. A man who walked twenty thousand miles across China, he still liked to keep on the move.

On the day I first visited Mao in the Imperial City I saw only two sentries at the New Gate by which we entered. Just west of it stood the great T'ien An Men, on the wide and busy main thoroughfare called Ch'ang An Chieh (Long Peace Way). Across from it was the marble-columned Great Hall of the People. Mao frequently walked from his home to the Great Hall followed by a few plain-clothes men. Within the compound no guards were visible along a willow-fringed drive that skirted the palace lakes, past beds of gladioli and chrysanthemums, to the graceful old one-story yellow-roofed residence. It was one of a group of palace buildings formerly occupied by court mandarins and later by Kuomintang officials. Most members of the Politburo were similarly quartered, close to each other. The great chambers and audience halls of the main palaces were now museums or playgrounds and in one corner of Pei Hai stood a model nursery.

Mao's family consisted of his wife, Chiang Ch'ing, and their two daughters; and one son, Mao An-ying, by an earlier marriage, to Yang K'ai-hui. (Mao's parents had arranged a marriage for him when he was a child, but he never lived with that bride. His first chosen wife, Yang K'ai-hui, was executed in 1930, as a Communist. He was divorced from his second wife, Ho Tzu-ch'en, in 1937. In 1939 he married, in Yenan, a former cinema actress who took the party name Chiang Ch'ing.) Mao had another son, An-ch'ing (by Yang K'ai-hui), who was killed in the Korean War. The surviving son, An-ying, lived obscurely in China and was said to be an engineer. Mme Mao herself was reported in poor health and was seldom seen or mentioned in the press.*

The large, comfortable living room of Mao's home was tastefully furnished in Chinese style; directly adjoining it were a small dining room and his study and living quarters. The meals he ate and served his guests were a few home-style dishes of Hunanese cooking. He drank with me a bit of *mao-t'ai*, the fiery liquor of Hunan, in raising toasts for the occasion. He also served the Chinese red table wine which was for sale (unrationed) in the liquor stores of North China at one yuan a bottle.

Mao was much heavier than he used to be; he ate moderately and smoked fewer cigarettes. For a man close to seventy, oftentimes reported dead, he was 'holding the status quo', as he put it, and had had no serious illness for many years. He wore a plain dark gray woolen jacket buttoned at the neck, with trousers to match; this had been a kind of official uniform ever since Sun Yat-sen introduced it. Mao had on brown leather shoes in need of a polish, and cotton socks hung loosely at his ankles.

I should not say that Mao's home and the homes of other high officials justified the term 'lavish' used by Taiwan critics to describe their way of life. His 'comforts' were the rough equivalent of those enjoyed in a good ranch bungalow by a successful Long Island insurance salesman. Mao had a staff of secretaries but that was true when he lived in a cave in Yenan. Across the park were imperial Manchu buildings in which he could have outshone the White House, but these were kept for 'people's palaces'. Politburo mem-

---

* (1970) That impression of Chiang Ch'ing had to be drastically revised after 1966, when she emerged as 'first deputy leader of the Cultural Group within the [C.C.P.] Central Committee', in charge of directing and organizing the masses during the Great Proletarian Cultural Revolution. A biographical sketch of Chiang Ch'ing appears in *Red Star Over China* (revised edition).

bers were not interested in personal acquisitions. They did have cars and planes at their disposal, and they could entertain state guests in the Great Hall of the People, which seats five thousand at dinner, and where honored workers and peasants were often invited to superlative food.

These Politburo members had lived communally and eaten in canteens for twenty years or more; they had done their apprenticeship. But they still spent a great deal of time together, still worked twelve to fifteen hours a day, and lived relatively simply. Their wives dressed inexpensively, and did not own sideline banks and businesses such as had engrossed the former ruling families of China. Their worst enemies did not accuse these men of accepting bribes or having bank accounts abroad. They did not indulge in private exchange speculations with public funds or operate on the black market. If there was any taint of personal scandal in their lives it was kept well hidden. But they all had power, and loved it – led by Mao.

Mao could not ride a horse any more or go on long walking expeditions. He exercised by swimming. This may partly explain why Nan Hai and the other imperial lakes were now fed by clean running water and the Summer Palace lake in the Western Hills had become a popular swimming resort. It may also account for a new nation-wide interest in swimming and the many good pools built by cities, schools and communes. In 1957 Mao had horrified the Politburo by announcing his intention to swim the Yangtze near Hankow. The State Council even got the Premier to try to dissuade him; there were treacherous undercurrents; it had never been done before.

One of Mao's slogans that dot the landscape is 'Dare to think and dare to do'. A youthful champion volunteered and succeeded; then a girl did it. Mao followed them and made it easily 'by guerrilla means'; he floated with the current, zigzagging over and back again. Pretty soon the river was full of swimmers. So many were observed near Shanghai that a rumor arose from abroad that China was preparing for an invasion of Taiwan. Mao assured one guest that the report was exaggerated; China would not use a swimming force to take Taiwan.

I should guess that one of the great prices Mao paid for power was lack of personal freedom to see the world. He had often said that he would like to tour America. In Pao An he told me he wished to see the Grand Canyon and Yellowstone Park; his interest in them may have helped inspire recent developments of great national forests in China. When I saw him this time, he said that he wanted to swim the Mississippi and the Potomac before he was too old. He thought that Washington wouldn't consent to the Potomac idea but probably would be glad to let him swim the Mississippi. 'At the mouth,' he added, where it is fifty miles wide.

Chiang Kai-shek was always an extremely tense, tight little man. Mao was still relaxed, deliberate in his movements, quick to perceive any nuance in a remark, and a man with not exactly a twinkle but a quizzical beam in his eye. He had an infectious laugh and thoroughly enjoyed a witty remark. He also had an incandescent temper.

To be a leader dedicated not just to the explanation of history but to the task of changing it – with the lives of a quarter of the human race at stake – is not easy. Jawaharlal Nehru once told me that the only moment he felt 'really free' was 'on top of a mountain'. After Mao's first swim across the Yangtze, at the age of sixty-four, he wrote a poem which at a glance might suggest the same escapist longing for peace :

> I care not that the wind blows and the waves beat;
> It is better than idly strolling in a courtyard;
> Today I am free !
> It was on a river that the Master said :
> 'Thus is the whole of nature flowing !'[2]

'The Master' is Confucius, who wrote in the *Analects,* after reflecting on the bank of a river : 'Thus is the whole of Nature flowing *ceaselessly, day and night.*' It becomes evident on closer reading that here, as in all Mao's poems, there is a political meaning, and that it is far from idealizing withdrawal. As the wind blows and the waves beat Mao finds himself in a scene of elemental change; because he is in the midst of this struggle he feels wholly alive and free.

Mao had always liked to be his own reporter. Now he averaged only four months a year in Peking and was free to travel in China if not America. He visited the big cities regularly and kept in close touch with provincial party leaders and also with the lower ranks. He dropped in on new projects, communes, factories, nurseries and kindergartens, and said that he inspected reform-through-labor farms. He frequently made an unscheduled appearance at a local farm or workshop, where he had long talks with the peasants and tried their food. My talk with him revealed that he knew close to the calorie what the average child and adult were eating; in a time of successive natural catastrophes, he knew how far it was from adequate.

Many of Mao's disappearances from public view were long periods of solitary study. He might spend as much as a whole week reading, a habit acquired in his youth. He once left a middle school he was attending because 'its regulations were objectionable', and spent half a year 'reading every day in the Hunan Provincial Library'.

He told me: 'I went to the library in the morning when it opened. At noon I paused only long enough to buy and consume two rice cakes . . . There for the first time I saw and studied with great interest a map of the world. I read Adam Smith's *The Wealth of Nations*, and Darwin's *Origin of Species* and a book on ethics by John Stuart Mill. I read the works of Rousseau, Spencer's *Logic*, and a book on law written by Montesquieu. I mixed poetry and romances and tales of ancient Greece with serious study of history and geography of Russia, America, England, France and other countries.' Much earlier he had been 'fascinated by accounts of the rulers of ancient China: Yao, Shun, Ch'in Shih Huang Ti, and Han Wu-ti.'

Mao probably had a better knowledge of Western classics, read in translation, than any Western ruler had of Chinese literature. Nor had he confined his reading to political tracts. Recently he surprised a French visitor with an apt allusion to the character of Marguerite Gauthier, La Dame aux Camélias.

Mao was never out of China until he visited Russia and Eastern Europe in late 1949 and early 1950. He had never seen any non-Communist foreign land, not even India or Japan, nor did he speak any foreign language. Up to 1962, only two persons in the Politburo, Lo Fu and Teng Pi-wu, had seen the New World. It was doubt-

ful if anyone on a level lower than the Politburo could make himself heard with theories contradictory to Mao's own concepts of
'American imperialism', which were more rigid and oversimplified
than on most subjects.

According to Lenin's theses 'imperialism' is capitalism in its
'highest stage' of development, or 'monopoly capitalism', of which
the great American banks and corporate empires are held to be
classic examples. In this 'final' stage capitalism seeks world domination by various means of which the traditional colonial system is
but one. 'Oppression', 'exploitation', 'enslavement' and the collection of tribute in the form of super-profits at home and abroad, say
Leninists, can be more effectively imposed by the manipulation of
money power in private hands which direct the capitalist government, than by direct military or colonial power in the same hands.

Both Mao Tse-tung and Khrushchev regarded the United States
as the last and dying champions of world capitalism. They differed
in their concepts of how the sick man was to be eased out of his
misery and who was to administer euthanasia to him to make way
for socialist liberation. They believed that American 'monopoly
capitalists' saw, in the break-up of the older colonial empires, great
opportunities for the extension of American power – a view still not
altogether discounted in Europe.

To Mao, the American position in Taiwan itself fitted definitions
of both old-fashioned colonialism and neoimperialist domination.

That may come as a surprise to many readers of these pages,
who may also need to be reminded that Mao Tse-tung and other
Chinese leaders had known the United States in one direct and
negative way, through their experiences with the American army in
China during the Second World War. The United States used its
influence to prevent Chiang Kai-shek from renewing open civil war
with the Chinese Communists during the Japanese occupation of
China, but throughout that period, when the Communists led the
fight behind Japanese lines, not a rifle or cartridge or even a ban-
dage of U.S. government aid ever reached their forces; all American
equipment was given exclusively to Chiang, who used much of it
to blockade and harass the rear bases held by the Communists.
America's generous support for Chiang in the civil war, her subsequent alliance with Chiang Kai-shek on Taiwan, the economic

embargo which has imposed serious handicaps on China's internal development, American-led exclusion of China from the U.N., and the maintenance of American bases in eastern Asia, all helped enlist mass patriotic sentiment behind the Communists' ideological distrust and hostility.

The 'thought of Mao Tse-tung' as presented to the masses was both complex and simple. It was complex because the politically literate Chinese was supposed to learn to think in 'dialectics' in order to follow 'the Chairman's' complete meaning. It was simple because Mao's writing makes its points by use of colorful paradox, earthy epigrams and epithets, folklore allusions, imperialist paper tigers, and commonplace examples obvious to all. And all must learn the essence of the teaching. 'Not to have a correct political point of view,' said Mao, 'is like having no soul.'

For the man in the street in China acceptance of Maoist doctrine meant identifying himself with the forces of light and progress led by the party, and living by a high moral code devoted solely to advancing the interests of socialism and the revolutionary classes. Toward the enemy, the forces of darkness, entirely different methods had to be used. As Mao explained it:

The [Chinese] people's democratic dictatorship uses two methods. In regard to the enemy, it uses the method of dictatorship, that is: it forbids them to take part in political activities for as long a period of time as is necessary; it compels them to obey the laws of the People's Government, compels them to work and to transform themselves into new people through work. In regard to the people, on the contrary, it does not use compulsion, it uses democratic methods, that is: it must allow the people to take part in political activities, and, far from compelling them to do this or that, use the democratic methods of education and persuasion. This education is self-education among the people, and criticism and self-criticism is the fundamental method of self-education.

That was written in 1952 and quoted by Mao himself in an important policy statement five years later.[3] 'Democracy' and 'self-education among the people' were still going on and so was the 'method of dictatorship'. This paradox will receive further treatment, as will my impressions of Mao's views of the world outside what was 'home' to him.

Part Three

SOCIALIST CONSTRUCTION

... In fact, those two revolutions, the agricultural and the industrial-scientific, are the only qualitative changes in social living that men have ever known. . . . Industrialization is the only hope of the poor. I use the word 'hope' in a crude and prosaic sense. . . . It is all very well for one, as a personal choice, to reject industrialization – do a modern Walden, if you like, and if you go without much food, see most of your children die in infancy, despise the comforts of literacy, accept twenty years off your own life, then I respect you for the strength of your aesthetic revulsion. . . . But I don't respect you in the slightest if, even passively, you try to impose the same choice on others who are not free to choose. In fact, we know what their choice would be. For, with singular unanimity, in any country where they have had the chance, the poor have walked off the land into the factories as fast as the factories could take them. . . .

For the task of totally industrializing a major country, as in China today, it only takes will to train enough scientists and engineers and technicians. Will, and quite a small number of years. There is no evidence that any country or race is better than any other in scientific teachability : there is a good deal of evidence that all are much alike. . . .

Since the gap between the rich countries and the poor can be removed, it will be. If we are short-sighted, inept, incapable either of good-will or enlightened self-interest, then it may be removed to the accompaniment of war and starvation : but removed it will be. . . .

C. P. SNOW, *The Two Cultures and the Scientific Revolution*, Cambridge University Press, N.Y., 1959

21

Steel Decade

COLLECTIVE life in new China was above all change and move-ment.

Elements carried over from the past were engaged in dynamic combination and recombination with new elements of the time-present which was itself always becoming a future something-else. Last year's slum could next year be a new school or a garden sur-rounded by the brick flats of an apartment development. Weather had not been tamed (as some Chinese boasted in 1958), and flood, drought or storms could in one season turn a prosperous commune into at least a temporary failure. A production brigade without modern machines when you first saw it could five months later have electric power and tractors. Food, housing and working condi-tions varied considerably. 'Good' or 'bad' generalizations based on several instances in one part of the country might not necessarily apply everywhere.

Speed-up campaigns slowed down for 'consolidation', then picked up again. Yesterday's mistakes were corrected, to reveal new and unsolved problems of tomorrow. 'Rectification', self-criticism, re-training and restudy among party and nonparty cadres were fol-lowed by shake-ups which affected millions. Everything was subject to revision except Marxism, the changeless 'law of history'. But Chinese Marxism, like all dynamic doctrine, was making laws to fit its own history.

China was not simply a different country; its obsessive haste to catch up with history and to become the world's greatest nation (in more than numbers) was positively awesome to those who could remember a passive China in which time meant nothing. The Com-munists changed China's *ming* or fate when they fought ceaselessly during twenty years of hardship before winning power. For them the condition of combat and struggle became the normal way of life. Because they achieved everything against great odds, it seemed natural to the Communist veterans that a whole nation should follow in the same paths with discipline and faith matched by high fortitude, and distant glory as the ultimate reward. It had not always seemed so 'natural' to the populace. But these were steel decades led by steel men, an era of 'continuation of war by other means' against every obstacle standing in the way of building a modern, mighty, socialist state. Because they arose from the peasants, and were convinced that all they did was solely for the benefit of the common people, these leaders could make far tougher demands on their energies than men from the old ruling class.

Probably Russia, Japan and Germany suffered as much damage as China did during the Second World War, but while those countries (much more advanced technologically) were recovering, China went through three years of heavy civil war before rehabilitation could begin in 1949. India's national debt to Britain was actually erased during the Second World War, and the nation sustained no damage. Germany and Japan received billions in postwar subsidies from the United States, and Russia was at least able to collect reparations in Germany, Eastern Europe and Manchuria. The People's Republic had to start off with a bankrupt nation and a currency in total collapse following Chiang Kai-shek's flight with China's meager remaining gold reserves.

China had only 12,000 miles of railways and 48,000 miles of usable roads, all in chaotic condition and in need of major reconstruction. Livestock and draft animals had been greatly reduced and canals and irrigation works had broken down. Industrial production had declined by fifty-six percent and agricultural output by twenty-five to thirty percent as compared to the hypothetical peak year of 1936.[1] Population had meanwhile increased by tens of millions, to a total of about 550,000,000. Even that 'ideal' 1936 peak production would, if it had been available in 1949, and figured in terms of 1949 population, have worked out at an annual output per person of only 3.3 pounds of steel (compared to 1,130 pounds per head in the U.S.A., 111 pounds in Japan and eleven pounds in India), 6.6 pounds of iron, one-tenth of a ton of coal, ten kilowatt hours of electric power and eight feet of cotton cloth. Output of chemical fertilizer per person would have been at the rate of less than one pound per year, and output of sugar at less than a pound and a half.

The fundamental problem of livelihood in China was (and remains) the imbalance between people and food supply. Despite intensive hand cultivation by intelligent farmers, China formerly never produced better than an average of 3.5 quintals of wheat to an acre, according to a study made by J. Lossing Buck,[2] compared to 8.5 an acre in Britain and 13.2 in Denmark. It cost thirty-four cents a day to feed a draft animal in China but a man's labor was for hire at twenty-four cents a day. Since the nineteenth century China's harvest had rarely been sufficient to feed her whole population even if output had been equally distributed. For fifty years China had been a net importer of grain, famine had been endemic, and millions had died of malnutrition or starvation.

Before the revolution China had only about 230,000 acres under cultivation; in more densely crowded sections the inhabitants per square mile averaged more than 1,300. Much less than one acre of cultivated land was available for each member of the farm population.[3] In 1955, Mao Tse-tung put the average at 0.5 acre per person.[4] Cropland actually harvested in the United States in 1960 was 311,000,000 acres, or sixty-two times more per farm cultivator than in China in 1960, when the total was still only about 270,000,000 acres. In the United States 4,600,000 farm families and about 5,000,000 actual farm workers were sufficient, in that year, to produce abundantly more food than the whole population consumed, while leaving fallow more than as much again farmland as was actually used.[5]

Before 1949 the primitive Chinese rural economy was without state management or support and offered no prospect that parcelized farming could succeed in modernizing the available resources. Redistribution of the land was a means of mobilizing peasant struggle for the revolution; a mere division of that land into strips of fractions of acres owned by bankrupt peasants plainly could do no more than consolidate the political stability necessary to create and utilize altogether new means to solve the food shortage. What was required were combinations of land parcels into large-scale, modern factory-farms, and radically more efficient means and methods of the kind already cited: heavy increases in fertilizer, more widespread irrigation, river control and power facilities, new roads and transport to open up more land and rationalize distribution, better seeds and tools for deep plowing and cultivation, and (eventually) mechanized equipment. China was very poor; she could not hope to import such means on a vast scale; somehow she had to make them for herself. But irrigation, power plants, railways, bridges, trucks, tractors, combines, chemical fertilizer plants, all spelled machines and machines to make machines. Above all they meant steel and iron. With an output of 158,000 tons of steel in 1949,* China stood at twenty-sixth place in the world.

China *had* to build basic industry, and quickly : steel and iron mills, machinery-making plants, power equipment of all kinds, coal and electric capacities, oil, chemical, communications and transport industries. At the same time the people whose labor was to create these genies had to be fed, clothed, housed, educated, cajoled and convinced that the effort was worthwhile and indeed unavoidable if China and they themselves and their children were to survive, not to mention win the enticing rewards of modern life.

China's revolutionary orientation cut her off from American capital and other foreign investment or aid. In 1950 Russia could still offer but modest economic help. What was new about the Communists compared to past leadership was their emphasis on self-reliance. They saw, in what Western observers believed to be the deepest source of China's poverty – too many mouths to feed – their very greatest source of new wealth : a billion hands to labor. Their task was to put all those hands to work, to turn labor into capital, and to exploit the virtually untouched and as yet hardly explored natural resources of the nation.

That the natural resources required for heavy industrialization existed in China on an adequate scale was for long disputed by foreign economists, particularly Americans. By 1960, however, the U.S. Geological Survey acknowledged that 'extensive prospecting' by a 'few well-trained geologists, including some Russians ... *has shown China to be one of the world's chief reservoirs of raw material,*' with 'vast reserves of coal ... a great reserve of seven billion tons of iron ore in the Shansi area of Central China' and three

---

*The Japanese-built mill at Anshan, Manchuria, was then out of production.

billion tons of 'fifty percent iron oxide ore' in Honan. Very rich deposits of molybdenum had been reported, 'making China's reserves the largest in the world'.[6]

Another report, by the Bureau of Mines of the U.S. Department of Interior, entitled *Rich Mineral Resources Spur Communist China's Bid for Industrial Power*, asserted : 'The extent of [China's] resources was largely unknown until extensive geological work, coupled with vast new knowledge gained through active mineral exploitation in recent years, demonstrated that the country has a sufficiently diversified mineral base to become a first-rank industrial power.' The report continues :

'Communist China appears to be more than self-sufficient in most minerals both for the present and for the future. The coal and iron base is very strong; iron ore has proved to be much more extensive than formerly thought ... [At present] petroleum is inadequate but extensive exploration in recent years shows that the country will be prominent in this field five to ten years from now.' Besides finding China in a 'world position of first rank' in coal, coking coal and iron ore, molybdenum, tin, bismuth, mercury, fluorite, graphite, magnesite and minor metals, and possessing 'significant' reserves of copper, aluminum, lead, zinc, gold and silver, chemical and fertilizer materials, this Bureau of Mines survey states that China has 'the world's largest deposits' of tungsten and antimony. 'Under the Communist régime remarkable industrial progress has been achieved. Within a decade the country has been transformed from an economy primarily agricultural to one bristling with industrial possibilities.'[7]

It was not China's 'resource base' but her capital base which was inadequate. In addition to man power plus resources China had one other asset without which the régime would have been enormously handicapped. Russia's contribution in capital aid was negligible but initially (until 1960) China was able to make maximum use of the rich experience of the senior socialist power of the world in the techniques of building a planned industrialization and managing a planned economy. China had to pay in exports of equal value for all the machines and technical help received, but free access to Soviet scientific and industrial knowledge, patents, blueprints and patterns saved her years of trial and error and in-

calculable amounts of time and money. Farther on I shall have more
to say about the meaning to China, in a year of catastrophic food
problems and imbalances between industrial demands and agricultural output, of the withdrawal of Soviet technical assistance and
the denial of emergency aid, which put to the severest tests the
Chinese party's faith in the creative energies of its own 'greatest
asset' – meaning, of course, the Chinese people, the true hero of
China's first steel decade.

22

Reeling, Writing and Arithmetic

BETWEEN 1959 and 1962 the government of the People's Republic lost ground on two vital fronts: internationally, in ideological disputes with its only important ally; and domestically, in its struggles against the calamities of nature and against the nature of its most important internal allies – the peasants.

In 1958 Peking had startled the world with claims of heavenly harvests as a result of the Great Leap Forward and the people's communes. By 1962 the régime's enemies were exulting in the belief that both efforts were grandiose net failures, and that China was caught in a great famine and facing general collapse. If the harvest claims were exaggerated, so were reports of a breakdown in 1961–2.

By 1962 natural catastrophes and disastrous mistakes in take-off phases of the communes had cruelly combined to expose fantastic overclaims for agricultural output in 1958. Repeated poor harvests since then had slowed down the whole rate of economic growth and in certain sectors put it into reverse. Even with favorable weather, several years would now be required to overcome the food shortage. Until then no major new industrial offensives could be expected.

Even before 1958 an extensive literature of controversy existed abroad over the meaning of Chinese statistics. A dusty answer indeed awaited the soul hot for certainty in that world. Keeping up with the controversy could absorb one's full attention without leading to anything more conclusive than the studies among the lobsters in Lewis Carroll's submarine school of 'reeling, writing and arithmetic' – with special attention to attrition, distraction, uglification and derision.

Beneath all the sound and fury there were, however, some solid facts of astounding growth, and those who had actually traveled in China were more prepared to accept Chinese statistics for the *main trends* of industrial progress, on the basis of many kinds of evidence, than those who had not had that advantage. I cannot deny being influenced by what I personally saw of new industry, science, housing, water control, agricultural means, and communications; of improvements in the people's health, dress, education, child care; and other evidence of progress greater than most of my countrymen or even most Overseas Chinese could have believed without seeing for themselves, and much greater than I had expected to find.

The 'mystery' of the gross overestimates of 1958 involved many political as well as psychological, economic and technical factors which will be briefly discussed when we come to the story of the communes. Meanwhile, it should be noted that the highest leaders of the country themselves were apparently deceived.

There was reason for optimism : 1958 was bound to be a bonanza year in industry because many of the 156 major industrial projects built with Soviet material and technical help, particularly in metallurgy, were coming into production for the first time. Years of basic work in subsidiary industries and in irrigation and improved agronomy were ready, in coordination with the 'blowing in' of prime heavy industry, for a maximum effort. Above all, for once the weather all over China was nearly perfect. In the same year came the big psychological push of the Great Leap Forward slogans and the launching of rural communes. The whole party apparatus, and much of the population, was brought to a frenzy of mass enthusiasm and belief in the impossible. The party was deceived by its own.

For the government the consequences were far worse than mere loss of face. Many communes that had made overclaims of output found themselves obliged to dig deeply into money reserves and grain set aside for consumption in order to meet taxes and fill percentage quotas promised the state by terms of obligatory sales agreements. Later they had to admit their exaggerations and call on the state to return grain in the form of food relief. Accounts became chaotic, the government itself did not know the true situation within a wide margin, and the whole economy was thrown off balance and off schedule.

By late 1960 the planning machinery had to be brought to a virtual halt in order to retabulate and restore a realistic relationship between inadequate agricultural output and heavily increased demands of industry, trade, commerce and human consumption. 'Agriculture is the foundation of the economy' became the national slogan as millions of urban workers turned to reinforce rural labor.

For a decade China had been training statistical and accounting personnel with Soviet assistance and a planned economy made some standards of accuracy indispensable. The Central Bureau of Statistics was a large nation-wide organization closely integrated with the State Planning Commission (they shared the same offices), and both carried enormous responsibilities for the functioning of a vast, uneven, groping, complicated and 'leaping' economy. Staffs of these organizations included some highly trained experts working with very modern tools. But good machines and knowledge of sound technique at the top could not guarantee the accuracy of data gathered under the political pressures of 1958 – under the slogan 'politics in command' – as the government itself belatedly realized.

In 1959 the Statistical Bureau was liberated from the rural cadres, but it would take years for confidence to be restored in its reports. Few figures of any kind were published after 1960, and responsible officials showed a healthy respect for understatement. By 1962 it was clear enough that agricultural failures had applied a brake on the entire economy, and that output in industry had also been sharply curtailed and in some items had probably even declined.

The Leap Forward in industry in 1958 and 1959 was nevertheless real enough and would have been remarkable even if the advances claimed were only half true. The 1958 agricultural yield was also an abundant one, although much of the harvest was lost, partly because of the confusion created by the hasty imposition of communes – as we shall see. To understand the lopsided nature of China's economic successes and current critical problems, however, it was necessary to glance back over the road she had traveled since 1949.

23

Of Leaps Forward

WITH a per person income which in 1949 was probably one thirtieth that of the United States, China could never hope to modernize by slowly repeating the two centuries of history whereby private ownership in the West accumulated the capital basis of modern civilization. In 1946 the Kuomintang had planned to develop China by state capitalism; the state then owned many public utilities and communications. Nor could gifts of 'free aid' from abroad or even outright colonialism ever have sufficed to provide the capital investment required by China, which by 1960 already reached the order of $10,000,000,000 to $14,000,000,000 annually, and was still insufficient to maintain balanced growth.

The Chinese Communist Party had long planned to follow the pattern of socialized industrialization established by the Soviet Union. Its leaders were convinced that in no other way could the rate of production be increased faster than the rate of population growth, to lift the people rapidly from backwardness and poverty to prosperity and economic independence and power. When the party took over in 1949 it immediately sought Soviet advice to help realize such a program.

Party leaders anticipated that it would take about three five-year plans, beginning in 1952, to complete 'the marshalling of all efforts and all resources for the development of heavy industry so as to lay down a foundation for an industrialization and a modernized national defence'.[1]

By 1967 the country was to be capable of making everything necessary for indefinite future development. Such an objective inevitably meant concentrating on basic means of production, the machines that make all other machines and tools of agriculture, science and modern living. To achieve such a crash program of industrialization the whole nation would have to dedicate itself for nearly *two decades* to an austere existence. It would take about fifteen years – or eighteen years after the revolution – for the people to begin to enjoy the fruits of this titanic effort.

Economic development thus far divides into these periods: 1949–52, 'recovery and rehabilitation'; 1952–7, the First Five-Year Plan; and 1957–62, the Second Five-Year Plan, accelerated by the Great Leap Forward, 1958–9. During the first period war damages were repaired, state bankruptcy and inflation were overcome, land reform was completed to create a new popular base in agriculture, former state-owned enterprises were brought into production, and control was established over private banking and business. China also fought the Korean War, a process which hastened nationalization of the economy and brought some special military aid from Russia. Beginning with 1953 the government adopted a fully planned economy. It was still very much played by ear, but by 1957 it was claimed that basic goals had been achieved. Agriculture had been largely collectivized and remaining business and commerce nationalized. In the third phase, or the Second Plan, 1957–62, Great Leap Forward drives quite possibly had achieved the main *industrial* production targets *by 1960* – or two years ahead of time – but results could not yet be fully assessed.

The ambitious nature of the whole program may be measured by the amount of state investment in capital construction. State investment represents profits or savings – capital accumulated by the management by withholding 'surplus labor value' payments, in the form of wages or purchasing power and their equivalent in consumer goods, from farm and industrial workers. Between 1953 and 1957 China invested about $19,000,000,000 in new construction. This amounted to $23 out of every $100 of national income. By 1958 it reached as high as $30 out of every $100. If the U.S.A. invested that percentage of income in new construction it would come to nearly $150,000,000,000 a year. It was Peking's hope to average an investment of between twenty and twenty-five percent of ever-mounting income annually for ten years.

That was not to be. China's investment dropped precipitately in 1961 owing to farm failures. Before that it had been growing far

faster than that of capitalist countries during their early industrialization. Only the Soviet Union, in its Second Five-Year Plan,
ever reached as high a rate of investment.

The value of China's entire industrial and agricultural output in
1949 was only about $19,000,000,000. Her first five-year *invest-
ment* plan just equaled that amount. Out of the $19,000,000,000
about fifty-six cents of every dollar invested went into industry and
about fifty cents of every dollar went into *heavy* industry. Agriculture got only 8·2 percent. As a result the production of steel and
metal-cutting machines mounted phenomenally, while light industry and agriculture increased just about enough to keep up with
the growth in population.

Professor W. W. Hollister of M.I.T. estimated China's domestic
investments in new capital construction at 14·9 percent of her
gross national product in 1952, at 17·6 percent in 1954, and at
twenty percent in 1957.[2] On 20 July 1960, I was officially told in
Peking by Yung Lung-kuei, secretary of the Economic Research
Department of the State Planning Commission, that 'capital accumulation' in the Chinese economy had 'averaged twenty-three percent during the First Five-Year Plan' and had 'appreciably risen
since then'. Western economists deplore this as 'forced savings'
under tyranny. Yet during their own periods of greatest expansion
capitalist economies grew at rates of investment which entailed
comparable sacrifices and withholding of values from the effort of
the working population.

The difficulty of stating China's gross national product and its
rate of increase compared to those of Western economies becomes
obvious when one examines the conclusions Professor Hollister
advanced: 'Valuation [of the gross national product] in dollars
overstates China's output relative to that of the United States while
the valuation in yuan understates China's relative output, but it
is not possible to measure the degree of this theoretical overstate-
ment or understatement.' He found that in 1952 China's 'consumption expenditures' valued in U.S. prices indicated 'an aggregate
value of $54 billion and per capita expenditures of $94 (1 yuan
equaling $0·37).'[3] On that basis the American per person expendi-
ture was fifteen times that of China. But if an American resident in
1952 had paid Chinese prices in China for all goods commonly part

of American consumption – such as gasoline, automobiles, freezers and other hard goods – he would have required 4,830 yuan to duplicate average expenditures in the U.S.A. – or fifty-five times the average Chinese expenditure! Reversing the situation, and putting the Chinese in America (without changing the items or the nature of his consumption account), might require him to spend three to four times as much as at home for the same values. Direct comparison by conversions either in dollars or in yuan inevitably 'gives a somewhat distorted impression of the relative productive power of the two countries.'[4]

I shall presently cite examples which show that Chinese-produced trucks, tractors and automobiles seemed to cost about twice as much as American products. But electric cranes cost less, building and construction of most types cost less, food and housing – far less adequate in China than America – both cost much less, and education and basic defense items cost very much less. How do you compare output values between a China where the average person spent twenty-five cents a day for all his meals, where a college education cost the state less than $100 a year, and where a skilled electrician's labor, product value added, was a dollar a day, and a United States where steak cost a dollar a pound, a college education cost parents $2,000 a year per child, and an electrician got eight dollars an hour? All these 'costs' are themselves relative to many variables. The United States 'wastes' infinitely more materials than China but China 'saves' by means which often would seem 'uneconomical' in America.

Mr Hollister computed China's gross national product in 1950 at 55,020,000,000 yuan. By 1952 it was 67,860,000,000 yuan, and he places it at 102,420,000,000 yuan for 1957. Using 1950 as a base of 100, he indicates that China's G.N.P. had increased by eighty-six percent in 1957.[5] China's social accounting supplied no statistics for 'gross national product', however, but only for combined output volume and values which omit important items used by Western economists and which might very considerably increase the Chinese total. In Chinese terms 1959 total output value was reported at 241,000,000,000 yuan or about $153 per person in nominal dollar values. We may compare this with American G.N.P., then approaching $550,000,000,000 or more than $3,000 per head – but that comparison again combines understatement and overstatement.

The truth seems to be that economies changing at different levels and different speeds can be compared only very approximately in terms of gross national product. Economists themselves disagree on interpretations of information about China, and it is 'not possible', in this volume, to reconcile the figures I have used from various Western sources, much less to relate them to all Chinese government figures.

For the years 1952–7, China claimed a total increase in 'combined output' of 76·7 percent,[6] using 1952 as a base. Various Western economists who rather arbitrarily used 1953 as a base cut the rate of increase to between six and ten percent annually. Professor Liu Ta-chung of Cornell reached a rate of 6·8 percent for 1953–7 while Professor Hollister estimated the annual growth rate at 8·6 percent.[7] Let us merely say that six, nine, ten and eleven percent are all exceptionally high rates for undeveloped countries. They are nothing to dwell upon, however, compared to China's final claims for 1958 and 1959.

In an official report in April 1960, the chairman of the State Planning Commission, Li Fu-chun, maintained that China had already fulfilled, in 1958 and 1959, targets set for industry for the whole Second Five-Year Plan, 1957–62. The state was then working on revised figures for *agriculture* which were still much inflated. Official claims for *combined* industrial-agricultural growth for the Great Leap were thus highly suspect. Statistics on *industrial* growth were a different matter. Even in 1961, Soviet economists – who had worked closely with Chinese industry – apparently accepted Peking's official output figures released for selected major items.[8] These continued to show exceptional advances.

Steel was China's first objective in heavy or capital-goods industry. 'China proper', as the provinces south of the Great Wall used to be called, did not smelt enough steel in 1949 to make a skillet per person. Peak production had been 923,000 tons, but more than 800,000 tons of that was made in the Japanese mills at Anshan, Manchuria, which were dismantled by the Russians during their occupation in 1945. In 1949 the all-China output of 158,000 tons was about one tenth of India's production. By 1951, Anshan had been restored (appropriately with Soviet help) and new mills were under construction elsewhere, but China still made less than a million tons of steel.

From 1951 to 1957 China's production increased by six times. With Soviet aid, major mills in Anhui and at Shanghai and Wuhan got under way and smaller modern Chinese furnaces blew in the following year. By 1960 China claimed that several large new furnaces – including the modern Paotou plant – together with seventy-three small and medium plants turned out 18,500,000 tons of steel, and the British Iron and Steel Institute conceded her at least 17,000,000 tons.[9] Both figures excluded steel made by 'indigenous methods' – that is, back-yard furnaces.

The achievement takes on more significance when one remembers that Japan's annual steel product at the time of Pearl Harbor was less than 10,000,000 tons.

China may have already passed Britain in coal production by 1959.[10] In 1960, with a claimed output of 425,000,000 tons (almost nine times that of India), she ranked close to the U.S.A. and Russia. Western observers said that much of it was unwashed coal of poor quality. That was true. China was now building complete sets of mechanized mining equipment, however, and I saw large new open and closed mines using it.

By 1958 China was able to make more than 50,000 metal-cutting machine tools. In 1959 she claimed 70,000 machine tools and in 1960 reported an output of 90,000, thus apparently doubling her entire machine-making plant in two years. China was making her own trucks, cars, tractors and jet planes *in small numbers*, but also substantial quantities of heavy electrical goods and rolling stock – indeed, eighty percent of the equipment needed to manufacture hard and consumer goods of all kinds.

China's textile industry (formerly largely Japanese-owned) increased output from a prerevolutionary peak of 2,790,000,000 meters of cotton cloth to 7,500,000,000 meters in 1959 – about three fourths that of the U.S.A. China's erstwhile peak of electric power was 5,900,000,000 kilowatt hours. By 1953 its output was 9,200,000,000 and in 1959, 41,500,000,000. In 1960 China produced more than 55,000,000,000 kilowatt hours, or slightly more than three times as much as India, and not very much less than France.

It was certainly prudent to make large discounts for substandard and defective products in so young a national industry, and for losses due to carelessness or inexperience in handling and maintenance. I myself saw new motors and parts piled up unprotected in the weather and damaged or ruined because of transport tie-ups or lack of storage facilities. Allowing for inefficiencies as well as for probable overclaims, a few Western analysts cut industrial output values by one fifth to as much as one third. For various technical reasons it would have been impossible to disguise exaggerations of industrial output as high as the 'overestimate' of the harvest in 1958. My own belief, on the basis of what I observed, even a year after the 'anti-buoyant exaggeration' reforms were imposed on cadres, was that the industrial product for the early 'leap' would be more realistically stated at discounts of twenty to thirty percent.

All the items I have mentioned are primary sinews of a modern industrial civilization, the development of which enables a nation to 'solo' as a major industrial power. Until 1961, growth rate and quantitative output figures suggested that by 1967 China might pass Japan and England in steel production and, possibly early in the next decade, become second only to the United States and Russia as a great industrial power. Disastrous reverses soon punctured that illusion as an early possibility. However great the slowdown, it did not change the fact that – starting at a stage of industrialization far behind that of Russia – China had by 1960 apparently possessed herself of more advanced basic industrial means, with exceptions noted, than those with which the U.S.S.R. met Hitler in 1941. But Russia, of course, had done it alone. China had had a great helping hand in Soviet aid, and Soviet protection – an observation which Mr Khrushchev doubtless made to Mao Tse-tung.

24

And Leaps Backward

'THE Chinese people,' said Liu Shao-ch'i during the Tenth Anniversary celebrations, 'raised the proportion of modern industry from 26·7 percent in 1952 to forty percent in 1957.' By the end of 1959, Liu went on, the proportion was about sixty-seven percent industrial output value to about thirty-three percent agricultural value.*

The 1960 state budget provided for an investment in industry seven times greater than that in agriculture, forestry and water conservation. But local investment in the latter areas, made possible by savings imposed on the peasantry, brought the percentage to about one third the sum spent on industry. One result was that China's irrigated lands more than doubled between 1949 and 1960, to cover about three fifths of her total acreage. This of course meant a great increase in *sown* acreage by means of multiple cropping.

Afforestation work was conspicuous to any traveler and amazingly widespread. By 1960 new railways connected all regional capitals except Lhasa and Kunming (of Yunnan), but China's rail transportation system remained far behind her needs. The doubling of mileage impressed Westerners less than Overseas Chinese elders who could remember a hinterland accessible only by donkey or boat. China still had less than 25,000 miles of railways, however, and transport remained her greatest weakness. Telephone networks now served all 24,000 rural communes, navigable inland waterways had been doubled, and public works had seen comparable expansion; but these were amenities long taken for granted in Europe.

None of this could have been achieved on such a rapid scale without Soviet aid. Yet the total value of Soviet loans and aid projects in

*(1970) That rate of industrial growth, if true, was almost certainly attained, however, at the expense of neglect of agriculture and overemphasis on heavy industry – an error which Chinese later were to blame on Soviet advice. From 1961 onward the imbalance was corrected, when agriculture was acknowledged as the 'foundation' of the economy, with industry as the 'leading factor'.

China up to 1958 averaged less than fifty American cents a head annually, compared to the $30 per head which A. Doak Barnett estimated America had invested in nonmilitary aid to Taiwan and its population under Chiang Kai-shek up to 1958.[1] China received no *free* economic aid from Russia; Soviet loans (as apart from trade agreements) amounted to only $430,000,000 (1,720,000,000 rubles), and all were repayable. United States economic aid to Yugoslavia during the same period amounted to more than that, and American loans to India were more than four times as much. Soviet loans and/or 'free aid' for military equipment made during and after the Korean War had been variously estimated in the neighborhood of $2,000,000,000. As Chou En-lai told me that China had received no 'free aid' from Russia (apart from blueprints, patents, etc.), it seemed evident that Soviet military assistance compensated (at least in part) for China's war effort in Korea.

All Soviet loans 'were only enough to pay for thirty-one percent of the necessary equipment and supplies for the original 156 industrial and other projects which the Soviet Union agreed to help China construct', according to one respected economist in America.[2] It was around these 156 very large key industrial plants that China planned her whole development. But Soviet loans covered only 'eleven percent of China's total imports for the eight years from 1950 to 1957. During the First Five-Year Plan the amount of Soviet *credit* available for new investment (1,570,000,000 yuan) constituted merely three percent of the total state investment (49,300,000,000 yuan). By the end of 1957, all outstanding Soviet credit was exhausted, and since then no new loan has been announced ... *ninety-seven percent of the investment for basic development came from the Chinese people themselves.*'[3]

The significance of these figures may be fully appreciated when it is emphasized that, reckoning China's whole investment in heavy and light industries (including about 700 major projects), as well as in plant constructed to accommodate it, the Chinese in ten years themselves produced or reproduced the equivalent of Soviet machinery imports at a rate of between twenty and thirty to one.

In cash income the worker's share of the profits in China remained minimal. Combined output value during the first revolutionary decade increased about four times, while workers' wages rose only about fifty-two percent up to 1959. It was claimed that farmers' income, counted in grain and cash, increased by a little less. That is probably no harsher a rate of exploitation than in the earlier days of capital accumulation in the Western countries, but in China it was imposed on a far lower standard of living. It was somewhat ameliorated by two factors. Workers and peasants had welfare benefits (education, medical care, old-age assistance and guaranteed employment) which came only much later in countries of private capitalism. Second, the worker and peasant, who understood very well how, and to some extent why, they were being relieved of the profits of their toil, had some satisfaction in knowing that no individual or owning class was getting rich on their efforts and that capital was being collected and invested for the benefit of society as a whole and especially for their children.

China's rate of annual accumulation, or forced savings, grew to such proportions that the 1960 plan called for a state investment in capital construction of 38,500,000,000 yuan – about $15,000,000,000 – including 6,000,000,000 allocated to municipalities and rural communes. That sum represented an increase by 21·7 percent over the amount actually invested in 1959. It was eight times as much as China had been able to invest in 1952. More than five times the total of open loans and trade credits made to China by the U.S.S.R. up to 1959, it was also nearly four fifths as large as the entire state investment program projected over the period 1961–6 of India's Third Five-Year Plan.

China's budgeted investment assumed state revenues which included 65,000,000,000 yuan from state-owned enterprises and 4,000,000,000 from the rural communes. Indirect capital accumulated from peasant labor was far greater than those figures suggest, however, due to the government's complete control of prices, credit and commerce. The budget was further premised upon growth proportions officially defined as a 'continued leap forward' which would 'lay the foundations for continued leaps throughout the whole decade of the sixties'.[4]

Obviously those expectations were not fulfilled. The year 1960 was not a great leap in the economy as a whole but a mere hop, made largely on one leg, industry, with the lame leg of agriculture dragged behind it.

The agricultural reverses of 1960–62 compelled China to expend nearly all her foreign exchange to buy food imports instead of machines. The crisis in agricultural output seriously crippled her export program in textiles and cotton – her most important trade item with Russia – as well as in other processed agricultural goods. China was obliged to default on payments due Russia in 1960 in accordance with Sino-Soviet trade agreements and seek a five-year moratorium on amortizations. Although Moscow granted an extension of time, which the Chinese acknowledged with humble thanks, Mr Khrushchev confined his contributions to alleviate China's food shortage to a bit of sugar for Mao's tea (500,000 tons), following the ideological conflicts discussed elsewhere.

So great was the 1960 decline in agriculture that in all probability China's *combined* output value for that year was less – and possibly considerably less – than in 1957.*

For China's capital-starved economy that meant an agonizing setback and a minimal investment available for 1961 and 1962. In January 1961 the Central Committee foresaw '*two or three years*' of '*consolidation*' – years of concentration on 'strengthening the agricultural front' in a policy of 'taking *agriculture as the foundation* of the national economy'.[5] By late 1960 the party had thus clearly reversed itself on the 'continuous leap forward' policy in favor of an 'undulatory development' of the economy. The new directive meant that until 1963 or 1964 no major new offensives on the industrial front were to be undertaken, and then only if the *agricultural foundations* were secure against future catastrophes.

Farther on we shall see something more of the combined effects of the withdrawal of Soviet aid, of natural calamities, and of human resistance to overregimentation, which thus halted the Chinese Communists in mid-passage to the Utopian Communist goal, 'From each according to his ability, to each according to his needs.'

* See pages 588–9.

Yao Wei and Private Enterprise

To accompany me on a three-week trip to Manchuria I was assigned a China Intourist interpreter named Yao Wei, a young Shantung stalwart who had assisted me in several of the interviews I have already recorded.

Yao Wei was a six-footer who could well have served me as body-guard, and once or twice I suspected that he considered that a part of his role, too. If his omnipresence sometimes made me feel over-protected and tended to limit my practice of spoken Chinese, I had to concede that his physique might come in handy in an emergency. In his small valise he carried a two-handled steel-spring exercise device with which he flexed his muscles every morning to keep them in condition. He wore his hair Yale crew-cut style and had a Yale man's walk, too, and though he granted that all provinces produced good men he was glad to be from Shantung. Come to think of it, a Shantung man and a Yale man have a lot in common.

If Yao Wei and his friends had any criticisms to make of the régime, I heard nothing about them. He was as reserved on such matters as an advertising account executive for a tobacco company being interviewed on the subject of lung cancer. By the end of my trip we had become good friends, even though I learned little from him by way of inside information. Perhaps he had none. He was not a party man but he aspired to be – despite obstacles.

What I did learn from Yao Wei was something about what had happened to China's 'national bourgeoisie'. His father, trained as a doctor of traditional Chinese medicine, had a sister who, in the days of the Shantung warlords, had won approval of a rich official named Kao. After she became Kao's No. 2 wife, Kao had made Yao Wei's father chief of the Shanghai bureau of communications under the Kuomintang. Shantung men are enterprising. The doctor quickly amassed a fortune. By 1930, the year Yao Wei was born, his father was able to retire, and the family moved to Peking.

Soon after the Japanese seized Peking, in 1937, they began to take control of the schools. To avoid enemy indoctrination Yao Wei's father put him in the American School at Peking, where he learned English at an early age. He made many American friends, including children of embassy officials, but after Pearl Harbor the school was closed. His family sent him to Tientsin to attend the St Louis Academy operated by the Marist Brothers mission. There he studied Chinese, English and Catholicism until 1947, when civil war reached Tientsin and he went back to Shanghai.

He was seventeen and wanted to do something. A friend whose father was Minister of Finance got him a job as a signal operator at the airport, and subsequently he was shifted to Nanking. During the civil war he found himself in the radio tower giving landing and take-off signals to B-17 and B-24 bombers attacking the Communist armies north of the river, and helping General Claire Chennault's China Air Transport Command ferry men and supplies to Kuomintang troops beleaguered by the advancing armies of Generals Ch'en Yi and Lo P'ing-hui, which encircled and defeated Chiang Kai-shek's forces in the final, decisive battles of the civil war.

Yao Wei hadn't intended to get involved, he said. He was disgusted with the Nationalists and thought of sabotaging some of the bombing missions and joining the Reds, but he didn't know any of them. When Nanking surrendered he faded into the population and eventually made his way back to Peking. There he looked for a job and was assigned to work with a group of normal-school teachers. All of them were required to write a personal history and make a clean breast of things. Yao Wei played it safe by stating that he had been a student at St John's University in Shanghai during the civil war. Unfortunately some of the group had actually studied there, so his stratagem was quickly exposed.

'What happened?' I asked him.

'Nothing much. I confessed. Some of the others had done the same kind of thing. When I told my whole story everybody just laughed. I had been a child during the war, and it also helped that I had voluntarily returned.'

After a period of *hsueh-hsi* or 'thought remolding' Yao was assigned to teach English in a middle school. Meanwhile he had married a former schoolmate who was studying to become a Russian interpreter. He showed me their wedding picture, in which he appeared fashionably dressed in a frock coat and wing collar, she in a bridal veil – a pretty girl.

'What about your father, Yao Wei?'

'Oh, he's still a capitalist and doing very well. He's an old man now, retired, lives in one of his houses here in Peking, and has more money than he knows what to do with.'

He said his father had been fully resigned to losing everything and becoming a pauper. Instead, he had found himself classified by the Communists as a member of the 'national bourgeoisie' and a 'progressive capitalist'. He could now live comfortably on 'dividends' paid to him by the government on his former investments in real estate and industry. He was thus able to patronize the few expensive restaurants still open, take his friends to the theater, and, according to Yao Wei, to 'enjoy life'.

Families still receiving rentals or dividends from the state were chiefly confined to a few big cities. Among the *rentiers* was Han Suyin, the talented author of the lyrical romance, A *Many-Splendoured Thing*, and (somewhat more torrid) *The Mountain Is Young*. She brightened life in Peking for me during the few days our paths crossed at the Hsin Ch'iao.

'I've tried to give my houses to the government,' she said, 'but they won't have them.' One reason for this benevolence may have been that her father was a 'labor hero' and was buried in the Revolutionary Martyrs Park. This is one of the many 'contradictions in class lines' common in China, which in Han Suyin's case help to make her the most interesting labor hero's daughter around – and the most intelligent interpreter of her homeland at large in the world.[1]

Owing to differences in conditions and to fundamental differences in the history of the Communist rise to power in China, the treatment of capitalists and the managerial class generally did not follow the pattern of wasteful, wholesale class liquidation of the Soviet Russian Revolution. Great and partly successful efforts were made by Communists to win the support of the 'progressive bourgeoisie'. Their policy traced back to the 'united front' led by the Communists against Japan, when Mao Tse-tung promised to protect 'honestly acquired private property' and 'patriotic' capitalism during a 'transitional period'. That promise was reaffirmed in the Common Program adopted to guide construction during the early days of the People's Republic, which was itself founded by a coalition of the Communists and allied 'bourgeois-democratic' parties.

Just as the rural population was arbitrarily divided by the party into great, middle and small landlords, and rich, middle and poor or landless peasants, so urbanites were classified as 'bureaucratic' and 'national' bourgeoisie, petty bourgeoisie, and working class, or proletariat. In 1949, Mao Tse-tung still held that the national bourgeoisie – 'progressive' and 'patriotic' – could play a useful role during a transition from a mixed economy to a socialist economy.

'Bureaucratic' capitalists were another matter. They were mainly typified by the very rich 'big four' Kuomintang families (the Soongs, Kungs, Chiangs and Chens) and their close associates in banking, business and politics, who formed an interlocking directorate of government and business. The holdings of such families, together with those of compradores or agents of major foreign firms, Japanese collaborators, usurers, and 'counterrevolutionaries' who fled to Taiwan, Hongkong and elsewhere abroad, were expropriated outright and sans compensation.

The remaining Chinese private capitalists and businessmen (numerically the great majority; as many as 26,000 private firms were engaged in 'industry' in Shanghai alone, according to one source, while another mentions '165,000 business units'[2]) were encouraged to continue production with state protection. Except for Japanese property, most foreign investment was not seized outright but was retroactively taxed, systematically milched of profits and capital, and denied access to raw materials and markets, by policies which amounted to confiscatory discrimination. The Communists' moral defense of such measures was that 'foreign imperialism' had long since recovered its original capital and investment many times over by the exploitation of Chinese labor and resources, without paying taxes to China. They thus took over more than a billion dollars' worth of foreign property.

Beginning in 1951 all Chinese private enterprise, employer-employee relations, and distribution of earnings were brought under state control, as those who bothered to read Mao Tse-tung all the way through had foreseen. Late in 1951 the government launched a national campaign (the 'Five Anti's' – against bribery, corruption, tax evasion, fraud, and theft of state property and 'economic secrets') which indicated that the 'transition' was to be much briefer than the more optimistic capitalists had supposed.

There were many prosecutions. Heavy fines were levied. As the campaign coincided with the Korean War, it was helpful in raising needed funds. To pay the fines and back taxes some 'guilty' owners of large plants had no alternative but to sell, and the state was the only buyer. Others were obliged to seek state aid and leadership, and as a result of coercion of various kinds, state-private partnerships increased. At this time the Western press reported that suicides among ruined businessmen were as common as during the Wall Street crash of 1929.

After some months the campaign subsided. Businessmen's trading and managerial talents were still needed; the government continued to 'remold' them ideologically while supplying them with credits, raw materials and markets. In October of 1953, Peking summoned a congress of representatives of industry and commerce and flatly announced their fate : the private sector of the economy was to be completely absorbed, by stages but not without compensation.

From 1949 on private owners had been subject to controls exercised by workers' committees organized by the government to 'do everything possible to reduce costs, increase output and stimulate sales', while 'giving consideration to both public and private interests'.[3] By 1955 private industrial production was already reduced to sixteen percent of the nation's total (down from thirty-nine percent in 1952), and more than eighty percent of this output had become dependent on state markets.[4] By September of 1956 Chou En-lai was able to assert that ninety-nine percent of formerly privately owned enterprise had entered partnerships with the state.

Control of division of profits had already been in force some years when, in June 1956, the People's Congress approved a policy of payment of 'interest' at five percent on extant capital assets of private enterprise, without regard to profits or losses. Six months later it was announced that these payments would continue for seven years, or until after 1962, the end of the Second Five-Year Plan.* Former owners of stores and plants who continued to function as joint managers or technical directors drew salaries as well as their five percent interest. As the state took direct control, however, all real business decisions and generally the active management were assumed by state employees and administrators. In many cases the original enterprise was broken up or completely absorbed into larger state factories or stores. 'Capitalist' had by now become a swear word and it was fashionable to be a *kung-jen*, or of worker ancestry. Many ex-owners began to wish to shorten the time period of their own change of identity. It is believable that some may have 'voluntarily' requested, as reported by the press, that their remaining interests be transferred to the state without further compensation. In Peking and Tientsin thousands of shops, production units and houses were turned over to the government in less than a week.

By the time of my visit, private ownership of industry and commerce had for all practical purposes entirely ceased to exist. However, Yao I-lin, now Minister of Commerce, told me in Peking that there were still 'about one million people' engaged in petty private enterprise.† They accounted for only a fraction of one percent of output value, were very small 'businessmen' indeed, really self-employed persons : carters, carriers, peddlers, and a few artisans, in widely scattered areas. Even these were being gradually absorbed by commune factories or the handicraft and merchants' co-operatives organized in 1957, a process partly reversed when the surplus-workers-back-to-farms drive, to alleviate the food shortage, began in 1961.

According to Yao I-lin, 'about 300,000' merchants were still collecting their five percent interest from trading organizations operated under the Ministry of Commerce. They constituted 'about thirty percent' of the overall total of capitalists, including indus-

---

* (1970) In practice, at least some 'national capitalists' have continued to receive state support.

† 28 August 1960.

trialists, who received such payments from joint state-private enterprises.

'Excluding self-employed people, then,' I said to Mr Yao, 'China's ex-capitalists number about one million?'

'Not "ex-capitalists" but real capitalists.'

Such they would nominally remain – providing some sort of economic basis for the formal superstructure of a government which continued to give nominal recognition to eight impotent 'bourgeois-democratic' parties in affairs of state.*

From a humanitarian standpoint this was a harsh fate for some honest and industrious men who must have felt that their efforts were building up the country, much as Mr Paul Getty, the Rockefellers, and most large and small capitalists believe. The elimination of capitalists as 'an unnecessary exploiting class' was, however, the logical expectation following the victory of a revolution committed to wholly socialist ownership – unless the leadership was to betray the ideology which brought it to power. The gradual liquidation of Chinese capitalism (as distinct from rural landlordism) largely by political pressure rather than violence, left open a way of reconciliation which preserved many skills needed by the country. In some instances it may even have won genuinely enthusiastic acceptance by 'reformed' capitalists able to sublimate personal interests to the Communist conception of the good of the society as a whole.

* See pages 220–23.

Manchuria: Industrial Heartland

YAO WEI and I spent twenty-three days in China's three 'northeastern provinces', known in the West as Manchuria. Here Japan had set up the puppet empire Manchukuo which dated from her conquest in 1931–2. One reason why the psychology of *Tungpei* (northeastern) people differs somewhat from that of southerners is that they were under Japanese occupation for fourteen years.

After 1949 part of Heilungkiang province was amputated and added to Autonomous Inner Mongolia, but Manchuria remained nearly as large as Western Europe without Spain. This was the homeland of the once nomadic Manchu people, who conquered China in 1644. They forbade Chinese settlement there until shortly before their overthrow. By 1961 Manchuria's population was estimated at 60,000,000, which is relatively sparse for China. Such growth, largely since 1912, gives one an idea of the speed of Chinese settlement of open territory. One is also impressed, however, by the many centuries that elapsed before the Chinese expanded into that neighboring empty, highly promising land – compared, for example, with American settlement west of the Mississippi.

The industrialization of Manchuria was spurred largely by imperial Russian and Japanese railway development when the region was a chessboard of colonial rivalry between them. By terms of the Soviet alliance with the People's Republic in 1950, Stalin renounced Russia's historic interests in joint railway and industrial enterprises – which had been recognized by the 1945 Soviet treaty of alliance with Chiang Kai-shek. In exchange Peking reaffirmed the independence of Outer Mongolia, also first recognized by the Generalissimo's régime in 1945. Soviet control over the naval base at Port Arthur and the city of Dairen was likewise to be relinquished, but the Korean War caused postponement. By terms of a new Sino-Soviet treaty in October 1954, however, Russia surrendered all her positions in Manchuria as well as her shares in Sino-Soviet joint stock companies in Sinkiang (Turkestan).

'The territorial integrity of China is now an ironic phrase,' said Dean Rusk in 1951. (He was then Assistant Secretary of State.) He added: 'China is losing its great northern areas [Manchuria, Inner Mongolia and Turkestan] to the European empire which has stretched out its greedy hands for them for at least a century.'[1] He thought that the Peking régime did not 'pass the first test' of a government of China; it was simply 'not Chinese'. This misconception was shared by the late Secretary Dulles, who continued to base his policy for years on the conviction that the People's Republic was 'a passing phase'. Yet in 1960, for the first time in a century, China's northern frontier areas had been wholly freed of foreign, including Russian, control. It was almost three hundred years since a strong government had arisen in China capable of turning back the Russian *Drang nach Osten*.

In the middle of the seventeenth century the Ming Dynasty broke up from internal decay and corruption and China was conquered by Manchu princes from north of the Great Wall, helped by Ming traitors. They established the Ta Ch'ing (Great Purity) Dynasty. During the interregnum of chaos the Russians had rapidly pushed eastward from Lake Baikal. In 1682, the year Peter the Great was proclaimed emperor, they reached the Amur Valley and built a powerful fort called Albazin in eastern Siberia. In 1683, after the Emperor K'ang Hsi had driven the last Ming general and his Dutch allies from Taiwan, he turned his attention northward to stop the Russians.

Meanwhile, at the Manchu court in Peking, a Belgian Jesuit, Ferdinand Verbiest, had won some tolerance for Catholicism by teaching Chinese scholars Western mathematics and astronomy, but especially advanced European gunnery. By 1685 Father Verbiest had done his work so well that a Chinese-Manchu force of 15,000 men, armed with 150 pieces of field artillery and fifty siege guns made according to the Jesuit's specifications, attacked and destroyed Albazin. The Russians fled west of the Aigun River into the Nerchinsk Mountains. The Tsar subsequently opened negotiations at Nerchinsk, where K'ang Hsi assigned an important role to

François Gerbillon, a Jesuit successor to Father Verbiest. By terms of a treaty (written in Chinese, Manchu, Russian and Latin) signed in 1689, the Russian frontier was fixed at Nerchinsk. Manchuria and eastern Siberia remained under the Chinese Empire.[2]

More than a century elapsed before the tsars effectively resumed their march toward the Pacific. It was not until 1858 that the Russians (taking advantage of China's humiliating defeats by armed forces defending the British opium merchants) obliged Peking to cede them vast territory beyond the Aigun and to the left bank of the Amur, down to its mouth. Two years later Peking conceded Russia the Ussuri region, where she boldly christened a new Pacific port 'Conquest of the East' – Vladivostok.

I retraced many old paths in Manchuria, from near the Siberian frontier to the sea at Dairen. I saw seven large cities and six urban and rural communes.* I sampled heavy industry (steel, ball-bearings, electrical machines, lathes, cables, cranes, locomotives), shipbuilding at Dairen, trains and automobiles and trucks made in Changchun, and a watch factory in Shenyang. I explored open-pit and underground mines and above-ground film studios, made a refreshing trip to the Amur River, where I spent days in the Tailing Forestry-Timber Station and a new mining-petroleum center on the edge of Mongolia. I put in twelve to fifteen hours a day; I was a

---

*(1970) By 1963 'urban communes' had quietly vanished from press mention and, presumably, existence, without any published explanations. In 1965 economists in China privately told me that labor productivity in 'many' urban communes had been so low that output value was less than the cost of feeding the workers, and in those years there was no food surplus to maintain them during a prolonged training period. In Peking, in 1960, Deputy Mayor Wu Han had said, as reported on page 593, that women doing heavy work in urban communes required an average increased food intake of 900 calories, or about sixty per cent more than when they were mere housewives. I did not evaluate his comment as possible indirect criticism of the urban commune until the Great Proletarian Cultural Revolution and purge of 1966, of which Wu Han became an early prime target. He was denounced for his authorship of the play *Hai Jui Dismissed from Office*, held to be an allegorical attack on Mao Tse-tung, but he was also identified as part of an alleged conspiracy which included economists and party officials, headed by Liu Shao-ch'i, excoriated for criticizing the communes and the Great Leap Forward as failures or part failures.

slave laborer. My notes on people and places in Manchuria alone would fill a book; no one but a slave reader would read it and I shall never write it. Yet I saw only a small fraction of that vast collection of mechanized aviaries, where human effort never stops. Manchuria has a greater potential than the Ruhr; it is, on a less developed level, China's New York-New Jersey-Pennsylvania-Ohio combined.

The most fun I had was a day of boating on the Sungari River along Harbin's elaborate waterfront park. I also spent a cheering afternoon with the child crews and administrators of the 'Peking-Moscow' miniature railway in Harbin. The most depressing sight: half a million refugees marooned by floods in Shenyang and its outskirts. Also: a holiday crowd of workers at a formerly fashionable Dairen beach club. They were all dining on nothing but large man-t'ou (steamed rolls) and 'white tea'. It wouldn't have been poignant if they had not been sitting under gaily colored striped beach umbrellas.

My notes show that apprentices' wages started at twenty-five to thirty yuan per month, and experienced processing workers averaged fifty to seventy yuan. Pay scales were based on eight to twelve grades of work; there were several subgrades in each category, depending on the kind of work performed. Medical care for state factory workers was free; it was half rate for their dependents. Welfare benefits for union members included accident insurance and retirement on half pay, at sixty for men, fifty-five for women. Rents and utilities averaged three to six yuan a room and food costs were a bit less than in the south, or eight to twelve yuan per adult.

All the factories I saw operated nurseries, clinics, hospitals, rest homes and part-time schools; all had clubs, theaters, drama teams and bands. Housing varied from miles of newly built cheap brick apartments with modern plumbing (some with shower baths and private toilets) to ramshackle tenement structures. 'Clubs' and theaters might be in buildings specially constructed for the purpose or in old converted houses or shops. Where the service was not covered by the welfare fund (as in state factories) the cost of nursery care (including noon meal) varied from six to ten yuan a month. Nurseries and kindergartens were sometimes well housed in former homes of the rich; others were in mud-brick huts.

In large factories I saw what might be called 'milking stations', to which working mothers came at regular intervals to breast-feed their babies – whom they carried home at the end of the day. A nurse or two or baby-sitters cared for the infants while the mothers, nearby, operated machines. Mothers received fifty-six days of maternity leave and got extra food allowances; those I saw looked healthy. Some factories had their own dairies and supplied milk rations; most of them operated vegetable farms and piggeries and poultry pens.

The workers were paid a 'norm-wage' in accordance with their 'grade' and also received variable bonuses for over-norm piecework production. There was an eight-hour day and a six-day week in most state factories I saw. Plants worked two or three shifts. Housewives working in municipally owned shops as a rule spent only four to six hours on bench work and two to three hours in spare-time schools learning characters and Marxism.

All state and municipal plants had branch party committees whose cadres were responsible for overall management. Administrators were graduates of courses in factory management. Most large plants I saw were jointly run by engineers and party administrators; technical operations were controlled by the former and management-personnel problems were in party hands. More often than not the party man did all the talking in an interview. Where the relationship between political leadership and technical management was a close one the engineer spoke quite freely, and it was usually these plants that were running well.

'Union committees' of workers existed, and plant managers and party leaders were required to consult them in periodic meetings. Production quotas, accounting and all major executive decisions were finally decided by the party committees, however. Both technicians and administrators were required to do shop work one or two months a year, depending on circumstances; in practice that meant four or five days out of a month. In large plants 'administrators' were merely chairmen of administrative committees; deputies took over during their back-to-the-bench days.

Manchuria still held only about one in ten of China's population but its importance in industrialization was about as one is to three. Before the end of the century this region might contain as many people as Western Europe did now. Its ultimate imprint on the formation of modern Chinese character conceivably might be no less important than the influence of the western frontier on American history, as depicted by Frederick Jackson Turner and his eloquent present-day disciple, Walter Prescott Webb. Yet I devote less space to this region than such a role may seem to justify.

In my view the industrialization of Manchuria is, despite its youth as a frontier of mass Chinese immigration, the continuation of a known story. The transformation of some older regions south of the Great Wall to which I direct more attention is much newer and more significant. In truth the industrialization of Manchuria owed much to legacies of tsarist and Japanese imperialism. When as a youth I first saw cities like Dairen, Shenyang, Changchun and Harbin, as far back as 1929, they were already far more advanced than most places of comparable size south of the Wall. They trained many Chinese technicians. Now everything in the northeast was on a much grander scale but it was still more of the same, to have been expected whatever régime had recovered the territory for China. It was less dramatic to find Anshan now turning out five or six times as much steel as it did under Japanese operation than to see Chinese peasant girls assembling tractors in a backwater town like Loyang. The Russian-built Changchun automobile plant was new to Manchuria but I was more impressed by jeeps and buses and generators I saw made in Chinese-built plants in Kunming, far in the mountains of Yunnan, where no motor of any kind was produced before the war. Electric lights in the caves of Yenan, and a print of Botticelli's 'Birth of Venus' in a worker's room in Chungking, meant more to me than a 150-ton multipurpose crane I saw made in Dairen. Similarly, the forest belts I saw in northern Shensi, and the spectacular water conservation works in the Yellow River Valley, represented wholly new victories won in China's three hundred centuries of struggle against nature.

27

Two Legs Are Better Than One

MAKING use of the armed forces in construction is one means of exploiting China's rich resources of man power and native in-genuity. 'Walking on two legs' covers another big chapter in China's transition.

That may sound naïve in Madison Avenue English, but China still has partly bound feet. The bound feet must help the free feet move faster. During guerrilla days the Communists learned to use both feet. I remember when women in Shensi were classified as 'free feet' and 'bound feet', with appropriate work assigned to each. 'Bound feet' spent most of their time sewing or in the fields collecting fertilizer.

'Walking on two legs' in 1958 meant starting tens of thousands of small brick blast furnaces or 'back-yard' hearths. Millions learned the importance of smelting ore. The Western press made sport of the effort, which produced low-grade and often useless pig iron. It caused serious dislocations in the normal routine and interfered with agriculture. Most of the furnaces were abandoned the next season but quite a few, with improved methods, continued to pro-duce iron for locally forged agricultural tools. A more practical result was that many workers trained at these primitive furnaces combined forces and started small modern mills on a wide scale. Two years later these were making fair quantities of pig iron.

Another interesting consequence was the growth of a school of metallurgists who were fostering a whole network of new small and medium-sized blast or electric furnaces. In 1960 China had seventy-three small modern plants using converters with capacities as low as one ton and with annual outputs ranging from 25,000 to 200,000 tons.

On the outskirts of Chengchow I visited a plant built to produce 100,000 tons of iron and steel annually. The manager took me to watch from a distance as iron was poured from one of three open-hearth furnaces which together had a daily capacity of 120 tons. He would not explain the process to me – 'a technical secret'. This was Chengchow's first iron-and-steel works. In 1958 the plant site was a vegetable field. Peasants in the commune villages built 223 native furnaces during the big leap, and in the process hundreds learned something about the technique. Their cooperatives chose 500 people to send to study steel-making in Anhui. One graduate of the Peking Iron and Steel Institute was then assigned by the state to help construct a township plant.

This small-plant trend may be significant for capital-poor under-developed countries with limited transport facilities bent on speedy acquisition of a heavy industry. Small plants can be built in a quarter of the time required for a big one and bring immediate return. The giant furnace requires a big capital outlay, although its advantage, of course, is much greater ultimate output as well as economy of production.

The new technique seemed smart for any country with so backward a hinterland as China's. It made possible a geographically balanced development of heavy and light industry even before adequate transportation developed. Now every province and autonomous region of China had its own sources of steel. Military advantages of this decentralization are obvious.

'Walking on two legs' campaigns recruited many peasant prospectors who were able to furnish useful leads to resources long known to them but hidden out of superstition or fear of losing their land. Geological surveys had scarcely touched China's surface. By 1960 China's 'geological prospecting personnel' numbered 420,000, compared to about 8,000 in Kuomintang times.

A by-product of 'walking on two legs' was the output of cultural treasures. Earth removals for construction of 180,000 miles of new roads, 12,000 miles of new railways, foundations for countless new buildings, reservoirs and thousands of local dams, canals and irrigation works, did incidental spade work for archeologists, anthropologists, and general sinologists which would have required vast outlays and might not have been undertaken for years. In 1959 the published figures for earthwork and masonry completed on water conservation projects since 1952 were equivalent to the building of

960 Suez canals, or 400 Panama canals. Allowing for some exaggeration, that would still amount to digging more than 1,000 elevator shafts from Shanghai through the center of the earth to New York.

Everywhere I saw modern industry working across the street from makeshifts of all kinds. Large modern plants in Changchun and Peking were making trucks and cars on an assembly-line basis; in the machine shop operated by Tsing Hua University, midget cars were being made by the students, and I saw others made in Kunming and Shanghai. In 1960 China produced her first jet planes; she also turned out 10,000,000 rubber-tired handcarts. China had two legs, with one foot still bound, the other wearing winged sandals. Item: In Harbin I saw an ultramodern railway-carriage factory where beautifully finished fittings were being delivered at one end of a working assembly line – by donkeys!

In Manchuria and elsewhere I saw in production generators up to 75,000 kilowatts in capacity; high-precision meters and fine X-ray machines; ball bearings from microscopic to giant sizes; 2,500-ton hydraulic forging presses and television sets; 150-ton cranes; all-automatic cotton-spinning machines; vertical lathes you could drive a fire engine through; complete sets of mechanized coal-mining equipment; and 8,000- to 10-000-ton motor ships built in Dairen.

Yet ninety-four percent of China's land was still cultivated without mechanized equipment, and man power still does most of the hauling. The story is told in those 10,000,000 carts mentioned above. Note that they were rubber-tired. China had become a quieter country – after street radio exhortations were turned off at night. Rubber tires also made an easier life for the cartman, who today might be anyone from a former rickshaw coolie to a professor or a commune chairman doing his stint of manual labor.

Workers and peasants contributed many practical ideas to an economy halfway between manual labor and mechanization. Of numerous rice-planting machines invented by peasants the most popular was operated by two people and was said to transplant more rice seedlings per hour than ten men working by hand methods alone. (China presented all rights to manufacture this machine to Cambodia, Burma and other countries in southeast

Asia.) Greater availability of power and motors encouraged practical innovations. Primitive time-saving conveyor systems were used in many kinds of earth-moving work.

In a crowded rope-making shop run by a neighborhood factory in Loyang I saw motor-driven machines made entirely of wooden parts. Elsewhere I saw insecticide sprayers, threshing machines, seed drills and fertilizer-spreading machines made entirely of wood. Peasants had rigged up small diesel engines on flat cars to pull miniature trains along wooden rails. Near Yenan I saw one that had already shifted to hard rails and durable rolling stock which brought commune produce into the town.

On a large poultry farm a worker invented a stuffing machine which lines up ducks on a treadmill, thrusts a wad of food down their gullets, and rolls them on, dazed but happy, in a process repeated until they are fat enough to be consumed in the dish that made Peking famous. A cook in Shanghai became a national labor hero by inventing a noodle-making machine, and a woman bank clerk drew a large bonus and the same honor by her invention of a bill-counting machine.

Labor productivity in many of these small industries was very low. In a competitive economy many could not survive. China had no capital to spare for imports that could be made at home by idle labor using scrap materials. However high the cost of production, they were less than costs of human maintenance without any production. As capital accumulated, better machines would be purchased and labor productivity would improve. It was low-level growth but better than stagnation and immobility.

But there are practical limits to the application of the best of ideas. When cadres carried the urban commune workshops to extremes – as happens with most directives – too many skilled handicraft workers were drawn into them from rural areas. Thousands had to be resiphoned into the agricultural economy again in 1961 and 1962.*

*See Chapter 71, 'Szechuan, "The Heavenly Land" '.

28

High Society

BACK in Peking, when it became known that I had spent a few hours with Mao Tse-tung and Chou En-lai, the diplomatic circle, which carried on an old tradition of hospitality under austere circumstances, became mildly interested in me. The diplomatic circle was a square. In one corner were the few representatives of NATO powers, in another were neutrals, east and west; the third corner was held down by the Russians and the European satellite powers; and in the fourth corner was a door, often closed, to China.

In the last days of the Victorian hangover of prewar foreign society in old Peking, the foreign dowagers – wives of diplomats or ex-diplomats or wealthy (relatively) heads or former heads of foreign business firms – used to consider that a great honor was bestowed when they invited carefully selected Chinese ladies and gentlemen to their parties, and likewise if they themselves accepted a Chinese invitation. Now that had all changed. Western diplomats were never invited to Chinese homes, while their own invitations even to third- or fourth-ranking officials were usually declined and often unanswered.

It is true that Western diplomats were invited, with bland irony, to attend banquets in the Great Hall of the People held to acclaim visiting anti-imperialists such as Sekou Touré of Guinea and Ferhat Abbas of Algeria. About the only other social life they had with Chinese of ministerial rank, or any rank at all, was on the occasion of an embassy's party or reception to celebrate its own national holiday. Whether the Premier or some other member of the Politburo attended in person or sent a minor deputy seemed regarded as a barometer of Peking's degree of satisfaction with a particular ambassador and his mission.

Representing 'the West' there were the British, the Swedes, the Finns, the Dutch, the Swiss and the Danes. Australia, New Zealand and Canada did not recognize the People's Republic but their nationals visited China as tourists and businessmen; members of the Commonwealth, they shared (as did Malaya) in the benefits of British recognition. In 1961–2 China became the greatest market for Canadian and Australian grain exports. Trade union groups and intellectuals from all Commonwealth countries visited China. Trade with Western Europe had gradually increased, West Germany vying with Great Britain as a leading trade partner. All the nations of eastern Asia except Japan, the Philippines, Thailand, and the southern portions of Vietnam and Korea, now had diplomatic representatives in Peking. So did the countries of the Middle East, except Jordan, Saudi Arabia and Lebanon – which had trade agreements with China – and Iran, which had no contacts at all.

Peking was first to recognize the provisional government of Algeria, and also exchanged diplomats with Morocco, Guinea, Tunisia, the Sudan and Somaliland. Plans for recognition of the Congo were interrupted by the assassination of Lumumba. After China established close relations with Cuba, Peking's activity throughout South America intensified and Latin-American visitors and residents in Peking increased.

All Western observers were regarded as legal spies by the Chinese (perhaps not without reason) and they had few Chinese contacts beyond the printed word. From the Chinese, Western diplomats heard nothing at all about any problems of coexistence with the Russians. But they observed; they exchanged gossip with non-Chinese Communist diplomats; they composed their dispatches; they talked of almost nothing else. Much outside speculation about the Sino-Soviet 'cold war' could be traced to Peking's diplomatic circle, where contributions were made by both East and West. Some Eastern Europeans seemed even more alert to adverse reports than Westerners.

One evening at a cocktail party the atom bomb entered the conversation. I repeated a chilling comment made to me by a Chinese 'high official' after I had mentioned a responsible Western physicist's estimate that the world then possessed a nuclear weapons stockpile roughly the equivalent of forty tons of T.N.T. for each person alive. Wasn't that enough? I had asked. How much longer could nations behave as if anyone could be a victor in atomic war?

'No,' I quoted my 'high official' as having answered, 'I'm afraid it is not enough. It may go on another ten years – until there are four hundred tons of T.N.T. per head.'

The diplomat to whom I was talking at once left me to confer with one of his staff; then they drew in diplomats of two other countries. A few nights later at another reception the bomb came up again and I asked an Asian diplomat his guess as to when China would make it.

'They're very near it,' he answered. 'A high Chinese official just told a friend of mine that China won't join any nuclear weapons ban for ten years. She wants to wait until she has four hundred tons of nuclear T.N.T. for every living person before she even talks about a ban. That means China believes war is inevitable.'

It was the underdeveloped, anti-imperialist Africans, Asians, and Latin Americans, not the overdeveloped imperialist Western diplomats, who got time and attention from the Chinese, including mass audiences with the highest chieftains. At the Hsin Ch'iao hotel there was a continuous pageant of short-time visitors representing labor, writers, peace committees, lawyers, scientists, teachers, students, merchants, and rebel leaders from Iraq, Jordan, Afghanistan, India, Mali, Libya, Kenya, Egypt, Uganda, Tanganyika, the Congo, Bechuanaland, Nyasaland, Nigeria, Niger, Guinea, the Gold Coast, Algeria, Morocco, Japan, Burma, Indonesia, Cuba, Argentina, Mexico, Brazil, and Africa and Latin America generally. European clothes were often conspicuous exceptions in dining rooms gay with every color and costume and coiffure, and skins from jet black to gold to vanilla. There were parties of tourists from Russia, Mongolia and the Eastern countries, and robust teams of ping-pong, basketball, and track athletes – Slavs, Germans, Poles, Koreans. Sekou Touré got the biggest hand of anyone that year, with a million flag-waving people lined up from the airport to the T'ien An Men. Premier U Nu and his party of bewitching Burmese dancing girls came next. Among Latin Americans the Cubans were foremost; there were Mexicans, led by a general; there were Canadians; and there were also a few Britons, Frenchmen, Italians and Swedes. There was a little of practically everything from everywhere – except from the United States, the Philippines and Puerto Rico.

Even East Europeans complained that they found it difficult to meet and know any Chinese; few of them spoke the language, and there were no more pillow dictionaries in China. At the universities, marriages between foreign Communist students and Chinese were rare. And would this change? Yes, it would change – but not very soon.

Among the Hsin Ch'iao's guests I learned something from a Swedish engineer and from a Swiss watch salesman. The young Swede had supervised the erection of a large modern fiberboard plant at Ichun, in northern Manchuria. It made a special type of hard board which had required imported Swedish machinery at a cost of eight million dollars.

'My company has already set up twenty-two such plants in Russia since the war,' he said. 'So you might say Soviet production of this item is at least twenty-two times greater than China's. On the other hand, from what I've seen of industry in Manchuria, I'd say China is now able to copy, from our installations, practically all the plywood-making machines Soviet industry is producing. China won't have to import such machines from Russia.'

The Swiss watch salesman reported that he was doing a brisk business with regional purchasing agencies, but confined mainly to one item: cheap and serviceable but expensive-looking watches. He could no longer sell any good clocks, nor could he sell the cheapest watches; the Chinese were making these for themselves, and were beginning to export them.

'How long will you have any market left here at all?'

'Five years – but it's good while it lasts. After that they'll probably compete with us in every line. And why not?'

29

Science and Education*

CHINA'S advances in the education of specialists in applied technology had been extraordinary. Between 1949 and 1960 she had graduated 230,000 engineers. Progress in advanced science was far less spectacular. Before 1950 fewer than 3,000 Chinese had doctoral degrees in any branch of science and no more than half of them were in China. Only 862 were listed on the roster as natural scientists when the new government was established.

In 1955 the Peking government first seriously confronted the problem of rapidly training advanced research scientists when it drew up a Twelve-Year Science Plan with the help of a large panel of Soviet experts. This called for 10,500 graduate (doctoral level) students in the sciences and two million graduate engineers by the end of 1967. Up to May 1957 Red China had 7,705 students doing graduate study in fourteen countries; the great majority were in the U.S.S.R. The goal of the Twelve-Year Plan was to catch up with the world 'in those branches of

*(1970) This chapter and subsequent comments on science, schools and cultural activity seemed close to the trend of educational content and method until mid-1966, when the Great Proletarian Cultural Revolution put a temporary end to organized education. All universities and secondary schools were closed, to release on the countryside millions of teenagers (initially under the leadership of newly created Red Guards) and other rebels against 'those within the Party who are in authority and taking the capitalist road'. A major propaganda theme of the G.P.C.R. was educational reform. 'Old things, old thoughts, old culture, old ideas', and all vestigial bourgeois influences were to be replaced by teaching of pure proletarian content, methods and ideals. That meant reorganizing the primary and secondary schools in ways which placed teaching and administrative responsibility directly in the hands of committees of soldiers, peasants and workers. Schooling was divided between practical shop and/or farm work and classroom work. Political reliability received priority recognition above demonstrated scholastic ability, in selecting worker-peasant students to receive higher education. In 1970 this new Maoist educational pattern was still in an experimental stage – with the professional teachers working under 'revolutionary committee' directives.

science and technology which are essential to our national economy'. Research in scientific theory or 'pure science' was of low priority. The allocation of some 500 top scientists and 800 engineers estimated to be required for China's priority atomic energy projects[1] made it likely that she would lag behind in new theoretical contributions for some years.

China had modern research equipment, imported from Russia, and was able to make delicate and complex instruments, including those needed in nuclear research. Scientific libraries had been acquired from other countries. The major emphasis continued to be on research institutes connected with industry and communications. In 1958 these were reported as 415 in number, with 14,700 research and technical personnel. In 1959 the Chinese Academy of Sciences had 105 research institutes to Russia's eighty-seven, but only 7,000 members on its research staff, compared to Russia's 14,000.[2]

China's severe shortage of senior scientists would probably persist for a long time, particularly in view of atomic energy construction requirements. The government had been heavily dependent on Soviet aid in the field of science. If existing Sino-Soviet cooperative projects were scrapped China would be gravely handicapped; she had had no important working contacts with non-bloc countries. Even now 150 of her 180 top scientist academicians who sat on high departmental committees were men educated abroad, among whom eighty studied in the United States.

Popular or 'mass line' science was represented by the China Federation of Scientific Societies, which included forty groups ranging from senior scientists to an Agricultural Machinery Society that had recently admitted thirty-six 'peasant inventors'. On a still broader scope, the China Association for the Dissemination of Scientific and Technical Knowledge had a membership of 300,000 professors, engineers, researchers and technicians. It published several mass-circulation popular science magazines. An example of its work: 160 lectures on space satellites were presented by its members to the public in one year in Shanghai alone.[3]

Before the revolution no systematic census was ever taken in China and no exact data on illiteracy was available. Official estimates varied from eighty-five to ninety-five percent, but probably well over ninety percent of the rural population was illiterate, while in a few cities the figure was possibly seventy percent. Kuomintang statistics offered shortly before the Japanese invasion showed 13,000,000 students in primary schools, or thirteen to fifteen percent of children of school age.[4] Even this low level dropped precipitately during the war. In 1949 it seemed probable that not one in ten adults could read and write.

The growth of educational institutions and literacy in China was bound to impress any visitor. My conclusion after visiting many higher, middle and primary schools was that China had made greater progress in liberating masses of people from illiteracy and bringing millions some knowledge of scientific and industrial technique than any nation had ever done in so short a time. The emphasis had been quantitative rather than qualitative, but standards comparable to those in Russia and the West were now imposed in all fields of advanced study.

One of my most profitable days in Peking was spent interviewing Tsui Chung-yuan, Vice-Minister of Education.[5] Mr Tsui, a graduate of Peking Normal College, was in his early fifties, spoke a bit of English, and suffered from eyestrain. He told me he had been working twelve to fourteen hours a day. At the time I first went to the northwest he had been a young teacher in Sian. After the Sian Incident he joined the guerrilla forces and for many years thereafter did educational work among the peasants.

As in the U.S.S.R., the State Budget of China lumped expenditures on 'social services, culture, education and science' as one item, and in 1960 that amounted to 8,620,000,000 yuan, or twelve percent of all expenditures. In 1953 the state budget for education and science amounted to 1,864,000,000 yuan. By 1960, according to Mr Tsui, 6,400,000,000 yuan (about $2,600,000,000) was devoted to education and science, or fifty percent more than the direct budgetary military expenditure. Factories, communes and other enterprises spent about an equal percentage of their local budgets on education (assertedly), so that the total invested might well have amounted to fifteen to twenty percent of the national income.

In 1960 United States expenditure on education at all levels was less than four percent of the national income, or slightly less than the $18,000,000,000 Americans spent for alcoholic beverages and tobacco. The significance of this comparison is somewhat modified by the fact that in China the state budget lumped together both the cost of educational operations and investment in capital construction for educational institutions. Thus in 1960 there was a 47·1 percent increase in expenditures for 'social services, culture, education and science' as compared to 1959; 'of this sum the investment in capital construction increased by 65·7 percent', according to the report of the finance minister, Li Hsien-nien. It is likewise important to remember, as pointed out in an excellent study by Leo A. Orleans, of the Library of Congress, that while 'the Communist Chinese have in fact made great progress in expanding the educational system of the country', in their concept education 'is not distinguishable from 'indoctrination, propaganda and agitation'.[6]

In a general survey Minister Tsui divided educational developments during the past decade into three periods:

First Stage, 1949–52: 'It took us three years to rebuild the economic basis of education. Everything from transport to schools was broken down. The nation was bankrupt. Money was useless; we were reduced to a barter system. All schools were closed. Our task was to put teachers back to work, in both public and private – mostly missionary – schools.'

Second Stage, 1952–7: 'This period coincided with the First Five-Year Plan. We now began to unify and systematize in preparation for socialist construction. There were twenty-one missionary colleges and higher institutions, more than 500 private middle schools, and 1,200 primary schools. Many were using French, English and Japanese texts with little relevance to China. It was necessary to nationalize them and bring them into the broad curricular needs of the nation's public schools. In this period we set up a number of specialized schools of higher learning, giving first priority to science and engineering.

'Our second aim was to decentralize and universalize our higher-education system. Formerly about seventy percent of our college students were concentrated along the coastal regions of East China. Now we have institutes and colleges everywhere; in 1957 some forty-five percent of our students were already studying in the interior.

'The third thing we accomplished in this period was to train both teachers and students in socialist philosophy and morality. This was a big task in itself – not yet completed, but well along.'

Third Stage, 1957 to date: 'At the beginning of the Second Five-Year Plan, the year of the Great Leap Forward, we adopted the motto: "Educate students for overall development – with equal emphasis on mental, moral and physical training." We sought to make every student a worker, and to make students from workers. We stressed theory combined with practice.

'In the past only eighteen percent of our students studied technology and engineering as against thirty-six percent studying art, law, history and social sciences. That was wrong. Today more than a third of students specialize in the physical sciences and engineering. Together with normal-school students they make up sixty percent of the student body. We have introduced many new branches of engineering – fifteen altogether. There are eight branches of geology and survey, instead of one. We have students in schools and institutes specializing in four- or five-year courses never offered before: in mining dynamics, metallurgy, tool building, electronics, power apparatus, heavy engineering, light industry and synthetic fabrics, geodetics, transportation, communications, aircraft, atomics, computer techniques and advanced mathematical engineering. No one can be good in all these. This is an age when we must specialize.'

In twenty years of Kuomintang rule China graduated a total of 185,000 college students, as compared to 431,000 graduated during the first ten years after 'liberation'.

In the organization of her new graduate educational system China made use of 694 Soviet Russian lecturers and specialists, seventeen Germans, ten Czechs, and five Indians. In 1960 there were fewer than 100 foreign teachers – mostly in engineering and higher physics courses – left in all China. Foreign language study was compulsory from senior middle school onward but it was rudimentary until college. In the higher institutes Russian and English predominated and in English literature nineteenth-century classics were used as texts alongside translations of Mao and other masters of Marxism. Science students studied technical texts in foreign languages, of course, and specialists attended institutes of foreign languages.

Full-term middle school students in 1960 numbered 12,900,000. Primary school students in 1959 formed a vast children's army of 'nearly 91,000,000' enrolled in 737,000 schools, with 2,500,000 'teachers and staff'.* Mr Tsui said that primary education was now compulsory in all except the more remote and backward regions, notably certain minority nationality areas. In 1953 China's census showed a total of 89,500,000 children up to four years of age. Anticipated 1960–61 *new* enrollment in primary schools was 21,000,000.

In 1957 Premier Chou En-lai had estimated illiteracy over the whole country at seventy percent. Mr Tsui said that by 1960 the percentage had been reduced, through all efforts (including adult education courses), to about sixty-six percent for the rural areas and twenty-four percent in the cities. If the current rate of advance in mass education was maintained, illiteracy would be rare among persons under the age of forty by 1967.

As a group, university professors were among the most highly paid employees. In 1960 they were divided into twelve grades, with salaries ranging from a top of 345 yuan down to sixty-two for student instructors. A teacher's grade was determined by technical ability, years in service, and general standing, including political factors. Some professors were able to keep private cars at their own expense and many augmented their incomes by writing articles and lecturing for good fees, and with royalties earned from books. Middle school and primary teachers were divided into ten grades, with a salary range of 26.50 yuan, for beginning kindergarten assistants, to 149 yuan for senior teachers.

There had been considerable confusion abroad about the work-and-study system in China. Mr Tsui explained: 'There are three different schedules in use, depending on the type of study. Obviously a student agronomist will spend more time working on a farm than a physics or chemistry research student. The first schedule calls for a one-month holiday, four months of field work, seven months of classroom study. The second schedule provides for a one-month holiday, three months field work and eight months of classroom work. The third calls for a two-month holiday, one month of field work and nine months of classroom study work. We call the first schedule "1-4-7", the second "1-3-8" and the third "2-1-9".

* Figures for primary schools may have included some adult students.

'Field labor actually means field practice. Engineering students work in the construction of dams, bridges, power plants; geology students do prospecting or field analytical work; pre-med students work in clinics and hospitals; chemistry students may help build a chemical factory; and so on. Some colleges operate their own farms, vineyards and dairies. Some have steel plants.

'In middle schools, students do eight to ten hours of labor weekly, wherever they are needed. We start early. Primary school students get in four to six hours a week at school shops or chores assigned by their teachers.'

'Political study goes on all the time, I suppose – field or classroom?'

'More or less. In classrooms about one hour in ten is devoted to socialist education, both in basic Marxist texts and in lectures.'*

'In general, what percentage of a student's university time is devoted to classroom study, apart from labor and politics?'

'About sixty percent to seventy percent – not less than sixty percent.'[7]

Tuition was free in all schools, including higher schools, and there was no room rent. The majority of university students drew a state stipend which paid for their meager basic food and gave them a small pocket allowance.

Very few students from peasant or working-class families ever reached college in former times; as late as 1960 only twenty percent of party members had been to high school or college. The situation had been drastically altered: in 1959 'slightly more than fifty percent' of all college students came from families of peasant and working-class origin – as distinct from 'brain workers' and bourgeoisie. If true, this was a revolutionary change the consequences of which might not be fully understood in the West for another ten years. Adult peasants were encouraged to aspire to high school education through state aid. If they reached college level all expenses were borne by the state, which in addition granted a stipend of forty yuan a month, enough to provide for family care during their period of study.

'What causes your worst headaches, Mr Tsui – aside from eye-

* This was probably an understatement. It had certainly been much higher in the past.

strain? I mean, what are the ministry's hardest problems of the moment?'

'Probably the biggest problem of all is synchronizing educational output with the needs of science, industry and agriculture. We can't keep up with the changes in demand. A few years ago we faced a trying shortage of engineers. That's why we needed so many foreign advisers. We're beginning to catch up with those needs but we're far behind in pedagogues and specialists in natural sciences.

'What will our needs be in 1965 and 1966 for the students we enroll in college next year? We get close guidance from the State Planning Commission at all times, but no plan is good nowadays for more than a year. All kinds of unexpected shortages develop. We have be able to shift students from one line to another in a year or two to fill new gaps that may appear quite suddenly. To do that without upsetting and confusing the whole curricular system is a delicate task.'

'College applicants don't get to make their own choice of a career or specialization, then?'

'Not always. Category quotas are set in high school, of course, and students begin fairly early to aim at one thing or another. They all get to express preferences, but the decision is made by the authorities, on the basis of the national need.'

In ten years the primary school annual enrollment increased by almost four times, the number in middle schools by ten times, and the number in higher institutions by about seven times. A primary school student now had one chance in seven of entering high school and a high school student about one chance in sixteen of reaching college. This was truly a great improvement in opportunity. But the literate base of the education pyramid had so vastly expanded that competition for available places in secondary and higher schools was extremely severe. Scholastic qualification alone was not enough to guarantee success. Between two students of equal scholastic competence, it is obvious from the following official criteria, the preference would go to the one most 'politically advanced':

In order to guarantee quality of new students, authorities and institutions of higher education in various localities should, in accordance with the unified regulations, strictly examine the political background, academic standing, and state of health of new students, and give priority to their admission on this basis. After new students have been admitted the institutes of higher learning should also conduct a re-check of their *political and health standards.* If they prove unable to meet requirements in these *two respects* they shall be disqualified from continuing study.[8]

In 1958–9 more than thirty-five percent of all university students were in teacher training courses. Engineering came next, with thirty-one percent; agriculture and forestry were third, with 6·9 percent; and medicine and other branches of science came fourth. (By 1961 medical students were more than ten percent.) Fine arts was last, with less than half of one percent of all students. Total new enrollment of students in higher educational institutions rose from 65,900 in 1952 to 280,000 in 1960.[9] Although students were required to enter the schools designated for them, they might, as Mr Tsui stated, express preferences – three in fields of study, and five in institutions – which were taken into consideration.

'What would you consider the greatest mistake made in this decade of new education?' I asked Minister Tsui.

'We made one big mistake and are correcting it. We tried to build up a huge mass educational system without sufficiently integrating it into the needs of production. Today we have 91,000,000 children in primary school, next year it will be more. Logically, we should expect that within ten years 50,000,000 or more will be in high schools. But obviously our economy could not tolerate the withdrawal of so many people from the labor force.

'*From now on secondary and higher education has to be combined with rational solutions of man power distribution problems in our basic socialist construction. In the future there will be more labor-and-study combinations, not less. Experience has taught us that is the only way. It is the fundamental concept of our educational system today.*' (Italics added.)

Fifty million high school students! United States enrollment in high schools in 1960 about equaled that in secondary schools in China. If China's rate of increase in the fifties continued, however, she would by 1970 have five or six times as many high school students *and* college students as the United States. Who would feed them? It was now fully realized that the rate of growth of the economy could not support any such massive sacrifice of labor power to a wholly food-dependent educational system.

The enforcement of universal compulsory primary education within only ten years brought about serious contradictions between the demand for higher education and the state's continuing need for farm labor and increased need for skilled industrial labor. In old China even primary education was so rare that any graduate was considered an 'intellectual'. Now many new graduates were discovering that they must go back to the farms and shops.

Probably nothing had been more misunderstood or distorted abroad than the attempt in China to combine practical work with education and to fit education to the realistic needs of a country engaged in a transition from semifeudal society. Blunders and stupidities occurred in implementing the slogan, 'Intellectuals become manual workers; manual workers become intellectuals.' It may be doubted, for instance, that any good was accomplished by sending a microbiologist I know to dig latrines in the countryside. But the law of gravity itself would prove an erroneous directive in the hands of some Chinese bureaucrats I have seen. The principle of respect for toil and of combining book knowledge with related practical work was sound and necessary in China. If it did nothing but prevent the return of a small élite literati with notions that manual labor is beneath it, the effort would be worthwhile. This disdain for labor and the peasantry was the curse of the rulers of Kuomintang China almost as much as among the Confucian mandarinate (and the Brahmans of India), and it explains much about the near-downfall of the nation.

The aim was not to reduce intellectuals to the level of laborers, but to teach them the meaning of labor. The 'workers become intellectuals' slogan meant to lift the working class to a level where comprehension of the work of intellectuals and its practical applications was possible for all. For this purpose there existed in China a parallel system of schools – highly improvisatory as yet – called Spare-Time Education, of which little was known abroad.

30

'Ministry' of Spare-Time Education

'TRADE union bosses in America would tell you that our unions are run by Communists, that they are tools of the Communist Party. Is that true? Yes, it is absolutely correct. We are tools of the Communist Party. In America I doubt if any union leader would say that about his union?'

Vice-Chairman Li Chi-po, of the All-China Trade Union Federation,* grinned at his little joke. It was eight o'clock in the evening in the big trade union headquarters building on Peking's Fifth Avenue, Long Peace Street. Li was in his late forties, a ruggedly built man in a dark woolen tunic, matching trousers and black leather shoes. A young woman sat taking notes and doing side errands until we finished talking at midnight. He had already had supper in his plainly furnished office. He noticed me looking at a cot in an adjoining room.

'I'm going to sleep there tonight,' he said, motioning toward it. 'I often work sixteen hours a day – my regular office duties, and then all the meetings. I have been talking all afternoon to some provincial union leaders and we finally agreed at supper and now they've gone home.' I learned that Li was a veteran of Yenan Academy who had specialized in labor affairs for twenty years as a protégé of Liu Shao-ch'i.

He went on : 'The reason our unions are under Communist Party leadership is that it is the workers' party. If union leaders in

*(1970) The system of centrally directed spare-time education described here was abolished in 1966 when the All-China Trade Union Federation itself was dissolved as part of the Cultural Revolution's struggle to break up the Party administrative bureaucracy headed by Liu Shao-ch'i. The Ministry of Education itself underwent a revolution in personnel and system. For an indication of these changes consult the Preface and see footnote, p. 226. The chapter is retained here for its comparative historical interest.

America told the truth they would say that they are under capitalist leadership; they are tools of capitalism. Under capitalism, even honest craft unions can do no more than carry on struggles for small temporary gains which cost the capitalists nothing; they merely pass on increased wages by raising prices at the expense of society as a whole. Under socialism, manager, workers and government all belong to the working class; they cooperate for the benefit of society as a whole.'

'I understand the theory,' I said, 'but what happens if, say, a union of shoemakers wants to strike for higher wages to make shoes for the army?'

'You understand the theory but you don't understand that under socialism the unions' main task is educational. Let me explain it. We operate almost as many schools as the Ministry of Education. In fact, you might call the Trade Union Federation a ministry of part-time education. Our schools have two main purposes. The first is to provide political education, which means education in socialist history and principles, in Marxism-Leninism, in the theory and practice of Mao Tse-tung, and in state policies and contemporary affairs. The second purpose is to provide technical and cultural education. The end objective is to prepare men and women who are politically, technically and culturally fitted to manage the national economy.

'We have two auxiliary tasks: to organize the workers in support of production movements in every way, to maintain morale and enthusiasm. Our four guiding principles in this work are: compare yourself with others; study constantly, never stand still; emulate those who are more advanced than you are; help those who lag behind you. This is the philosophy of our educational effort and what we seek in daily life.'

Good Boy Scout principles, too, I thought. Incongruous as it may strike many, a lot of China was like that.

'Our other task is to raise the living conditions of the working class both materially and culturally. We propose wage adjustments and work out wage systems with the government. Because of our work wages have doubled in ten years.'

Li asserted that campaigns in the federation's *Workers Daily* had exposed some sweatshop working conditions in both state and private industries which had led to important reform, including the eight-hour day. (With periodic overtime labor and spare-time study many workers were still committed, however, for ten to fourteen hours a day.) In 1955, for example, the *Workers Daily* revealed that alleged gains made in 'speed-up' drives by shocking overuse of labor were more than offset by heavily increased losses in manpower output due to sickness, accidents and absenteeism.

'Are managers actually members of trade unions?' I asked Li.

'It depends on the trade. In some cases everybody in the government ministry is a member: for example, the Minister of Railways and all his staff are union members.'

We did not get back to the shoemakers' strike for a couple of hours, until after Vice-Chairman Li – obviously an executive of great energy and detailed grasp of his work – had further explained his main preoccupation with *yueh-yi*, or 'spare-time study'.

Prewar unions were nearly all under Kuomintang control, as they were now under Communist control. Their 1947 membership was about 5,000,000. In 1960 there were 'about 40,000,000 members' of trade unions. That included 4,000,000 urban handicraft workers and 17,000,000 members in heavy or state industry – as apart from office workers and employees in 'local' enterprises. About 25,000,000, or sixty percent, were receiving education of some kind in trade union schools which reduced illiteracy among organized urban workers from eighty-five percent in 1949 to fifteen percent by 1961, according to this Walter Reuther of China.

At the lowest level were literacy classes in which workers learned the 1,500 basic characters required to read a newspaper. Not all workers could pass the course, said Li. Many had to repeat and people above fifty often found it impossible. Those who succeeded went on to:

(1) Elementary primary schools where 13,000,000 literates were taking streamlined courses in literature, mathematics, natural science, geography, history and politics (Marxism). 'No time for singing, dancing, music or sports,' said Li gravely. Fast learners finished in two years, some took four. State regulations required that workers and peasants in such schools be guaranteed at least 240 hours a year for study.

(2) Elementary middle schools and technical middle schools. Four

million workers were being taught essential mathematics, science and shop engineering combined with politics. The courses lasted eighteen to twenty-four months and graduates continued to:

(3) High schools, for another eighteen to twenty-four months. Courses offered: mathematics, science, engineering, accounting, shop management, plus lectures in history and Marxism. Here 1,500,000 workers were enrolled in preparation for:

(4) Spare-time colleges, with a current attendance of 400,000 and five to six years of advanced study for those capable of covering full college-level curricula. From these would come technicians, engineers, scientists, factory managers, mathematicians, planning experts and full-fledged Communists.

The spare-time educational program began as early as 1951, but the present system, which covered peasants as well as workers, traced to 1955. A joint conference called in that year by the Ministry of Higher Education, the Ministry of Education, and the Trade Union Federation adopted plans aimed at eradicating illiteracy in a decade. In January 1960 the State Council set up a spare-time education committee (representing the Ministries of Education, Culture, Science, Economics, Defense; trade unions; and party and other organizations) to unify all such activities throughout the nation. Six months before I interviewed Mr Li it was reported that 130,000,000 peasants were enrolled in literacy and primary spare-time schools, made possible largely by newly opened commune mass-education facilities.[1]

'Do you think you can turn out really competent scientists and engineers from a spare-time education system of this kind?' I asked Li.

'We have made studies of the class background of fifty great scientists and inventors,' he replied. 'Forty of them – including your Edison and Ford – came from the working class and were largely self-taught or spare-time students.'

Extension study is nothing new in the modern world, of course, but there may not be anything elsewhere quite as intensive as this on a mass scale. Students spent two to four hours a day in classroom work and study. Added to the shop day that meant ten to twelve hours of work six days a week – which burns up a lot of calories. Teachers also put in at least that many hours and possibly more.

The whole program had a full-time faculty of only 30,000. All China was teacher-short and the union schools borrowed, from the Ministry of Education, 70,000 professionals for part-time work (at extra pay). I saw many spare-time schools. As a rule they used clubs or factory dining or recreation rooms, but often the workshops themselves became classrooms. I saw workers holding meetings in corners of machine shops, apprentices being lectured by veterans around the lathes they were learning to operate, groups of workers conferring over blueprints on the grassy lawns of new factories, and party leaders delivering Marxist courses under the scaffoldings of new bridges and dams. Every worker carried a notebook and pencil and often you saw a textbook protruding from his back pocket.

For those who did not qualify for higher education, there was a gap between the elementary graduation age of thirteen, and the lower middle school graduation age of sixteen, and the legal minimum full-time working age of eighteen. Half-time work-and-study schools continued the education of adolescents, who spent half-days in shop or farm work. These students might also alternate work and study for full days, or spend three days at the bench or plow and three days in school.

Two other types of experimental schools were run under federation auspices, both for sixteen- to eighteen-year-olds: 'school-factories', of four hours shop work and six hours study, and 'factory-schools', which combined six hours of shop work with four hours of study. In the factories with a six-hour work day, there was no lunch period and workers got a full day's pay. 'Production,' said Li, 'is not less than in eight-hour factories, efficiency is at a higher level, and enthusiasm is maximum. So far the experiment has involved only 100,000 workers in industries of a high technical level.'

Included among the federation's activities was the operation of 32,000 workers' 'palaces' or clubs. Some of them were no more than barns but all new satellite towns had clubs of a sort. In Port Arthur I visited a maritime workers' social center with a 2,000-seat theater, a large library, a cafeteria and a big hall for weekly dances. On the Sungari River at Harbin I saw a tile-roofed structure really elaborate enough to be called a palace; it combined boating, swimming, ping-pong, dancing and other recreational facilities with various 'cultural' attractions. Unions had organized 39,000 amateur drama and opera groups; the accent was quantitative, to involve as many people as possible. There were 200,000 athletic associations with 3,000,000 participants and about 30,000 union libraries with 84,000,000 books. Unions also operated 210 rest homes and sanatoria. I saw a rest home for miners on the Dairen waterfront comfortably installed in a former brothel for Japanese officers. Another home had once been a club for tired Japanese businessmen.

Important benefits of union membership were free medical care, spare-time education, accident insurance and old-age and sickness insurance. The unions were financed by a small percentage of profits remitted to enterprises by the state at the rate of ·015 to ·03 of the total wage bill. Members paid a registration fee of twenty-five fen* to one yuan, depending on their wages. Dues were one percent of a member's wages. All union activities were closely coordinated with the Communist party and with Young Communist propaganda campaigns to arouse and maintain enthusiasm for the fulfillment of production quotas and organizational directives. Every union and branch union had its committees to prepare banners, placards, wall newspapers, drawings and cartoons which echoed the party line on everything from 'factory front support agricultural front' to the current phase of the struggle against imperialist aggression and the battered American paper tiger in Taiwan. They formed teams to strike gongs and drums to applaud and congratulate labor heroes during shop hours. They kept account of each person's rate of progress right down to the latest item of piecework and posted notices and awards of honors won by fast quota-makers. They filled the factory with music and slogans and they were tireless organizers and joiners.

Unions were formed in accordance with the Trade Union Law of the People's Republic. Elections followed the same pattern as the state elections. Any place with ten or more workers or employees could set up a union and elect a chairman and subcommittees. Union sub-branches elected delegates to local labor federations or congresses who in turn elected regional and municipal congresses, and so on to the top. The National Labor Congress elected an executive committee which ran the All-China Federation and had

*One yuan equalled 100 fen.

broad supervisory powers to dissolve or reorganize any union. At every step workers were led by cadres and altogether they formed an administration which corresponded to labor bureaucracies in other countries.* Federation leaders and the Ministry of Labor were also practically indivisible.

What about that shoemakers' strike? The answers I got may be condensed as follows:

The right to strike was guaranteed by law and there had been occasional strikes on a local scale. Labor disputes in China were 'contradictions among the people', however, not class struggles. When an unsettled grievance led to a strike or slowdown it was due to faulty leadership on the basic level and differences were settled at the next level. A national strike was inconceivable. 'Strikes for higher wages cannot occur if workers have been properly educated to understand that wages are based on fair standards of values of production set by the state, which makes no profit for itself but merely acts for "the whole people" to reinvest national savings for the future enrichment of all.' But if shoemakers still wanted higher wages? Their views would be considered when general wage adjustments were made. Meanwhile, the shoemakers might need more political education. They could also work harder for bonuses or attend spare-time schools and learn higher techniques and perhaps qualify for better-paying jobs.

'Labor unions cannot fight for the narrow interests of any particular craft union at the expense of the whole people.' The unions were tools of the Communist party, as Mr Li said, and the party represented 'the whole people'. That was the theory, anyway, and I gathered that if I didn't understand it I might need more education.

But education of the workers was not a one-way street, as Mao Tse-tung had often stressed; the educators themselves must be educated by the workers:

In 1956, small numbers of workers and students in certain places went on strike. The immediate cause of these disturbances was the

---

*Trade-union leadership virtually dissolved during the Great Proletarian Cultural Revolution, in many cases being superseded, at first, by the Red Guards. Trade-union law, like the constitution of the C.C.P. itself, was to be heavily revised after the Ninth Congress of the Party, held in April 1969.

failure to satisfy certain of their demands for material benefits, of which some should and could be met ... But a more important cause was bureaucracy on the part of those in positions of leadership. In some cases, responsibility for such bureaucratic mistakes should be placed *on the higher authorities*, and those at the lower levels should not be made to bear all the blame ... In the same year, members of a small number of agricultural cooperatives also created disturbances, and the main causes were also bureaucracy on the part of the leadership and lack of educational work among the masses ...

The guiding spirits in disturbances [including strikes] should not be removed from their jobs or expelled without good reason, except for those who have committed criminal offences or active counterrevolutionaries who should be dealt with according to law. In a big country like ours it is nothing to get alarmed about if small numbers of people should create disturbances; rather, we should turn such things to advantage to help us get rid of bureaucracy.[2]

31

Steel, Sex and Politics

EVERY province had its own higher educational system, but Peking was still regarded as the Athens of China and attracted more than 100,000 college students, or about fifteen percent of the current national enrollment.* They still tended to think of themselves as China's intellectual *crème de la crème*. Old Peking had eleven colleges and about 10,000 students, and foremost of the colleges was the Pei-ta, Peking National University, which produced the foremost founders of the Communist party. Pei-ta was still the goal of ambitious arts and sciences students and graduate research workers. Enrollment was now about 11,000. Outside the city, near the Summer Palace, was the 'rich man's university' of Yenching, founded by missionaries; nearby was Tsing Hua, which also had a foreign background. Yenching, now absorbed by Pei-ta, was a greatly enlarged university with an enrollment exceeding 7,000. I revisited both of them, and went on to the new institutes north of the city walls.

The focus of this recently developed university city was the Chinese Academy of Sciences, which embraced institutes of meteorology, economics, geophysics and physics, linguistics, philology and others. Around it were the spacious new campuses of universities, institutes and colleges specializing in medicine, normal training, petroleum technology, aeronautics, agriculture, mining and metallurgy, music and art. As an illustration of their impact, the new geological institute now had more students than the total number of graduate geologists produced in all the years before 1949.

*(1970) The whole university educational machine was halted abruptly in 1966, when the Cultural Revolution challenged most of its premises and practices. It is not inconceivable that much of what has replaced it (see Preface, and footnote page 226) may itself in time be modified by still another cultural revolution. For the record, then, this chapter is retained as a valid description of university life in the sixties.

At the Iron and Steel Institute, Hu Ying was both chief administrator and party leader, a combination I had learned to welcome. One could accomplish one's business much more smoothly and rapidly wherever a party man was in titular as well as factual control rather than operating under some euphemism such as secretary. The party man might or might not answer all one's questions, but he was in a better position to make the decisions. Hu Ying proved so cooperative that I returned to the school a second time to get a picture story of student daily life.

Director Hu was a Manchurian born in Fushun, the coal town, and educated at Shenyang Normal College. As a young teacher during the war he had joined the anti-Japanese underground, at first simply as a national patriot, so he said. Later he escaped to the hills and the partisans and there became a Communist and fought with the guerrillas until victory. Assigned to help establish the Iron and Steel Institute in 1953, he had been there ever since. The chancellor and vice-chancellors were professional engineers, but Hu Ying was boss. Wearing blue slacks and a blue cotton shirt, Hu received me in a spacious reception room furnished with semi-modern Chinese furniture, the walls decorated with Sung and Ming paintings, the windows draped in silk with golden bees embroidered on it. He offered me innumerable cups of scalding tea served by a student assistant.

The institute's well-landscaped campus covered thirty acres and its plant included forty-one completed buildings, with eleven more under construction. It had 6,000 students, of whom 916 were women. The largest institute of its kind in the country, it had a staff of 700 professors, assistants and instructors. It operated fifty-seven laboratories, more than ten experimental factories, and a small modern steel plant with an electric blast furnace where men and women students were trained. The plant had a 1962 target of 100,000 tons. In the middle of the campus were adequate athletic fields and a large swimming pool built by spare-time student labor – as was common now at many universities.

'Our curriculum includes twenty-three subjects,' said Hu, 'and all varieties of steel processing. We train research specialists and teachers. The full course is five years and we offer one and two years of post-graduate work. There are more than thirty different student activity organizations such as photography, radio, dancing, opera, dramatics, orchestra, chorus, Chinese and Western music appreciation –'

'How about cooking – or is it going to become a lost art in an age of communal eating?'

'There is a cooking club; also a sewing club.'

Hu went on to say that tuition and rent were paid by the state, and that eighty percent of the students drew a stipend which covered the cost of food – twelve and a half yuan a month – and provided pocket money of three yuan for undergraduates and five yuan for graduate students. The other twenty percent of the students, who came from families with an income of more than sixty yuan per month (that excluded most peasants), were obliged to pay for their food in whole or in part, 'depending on circumstances'. Institute students included forty-three Mongols and 'about fifty' assorted Moslems, Uighurs from Turkestan, Chuangs from Kwangsi, and Thais from Yunnan.

'There must be stiff competition to get into a school like this. How are students selected?'

'That's right. The demand is greater than the supply. High schools annually yield from two to three hundred thousand graduates who are qualified to apply, but our own institute can't admit more than about fifteen hundred a year. Applicants are judged by scholarship, character and health status.'

'Children from ex-landlord families, too?'

'Yes, we have some. But most of our students come from peasant and working-class families. We also admit a limited number of students who are substandard in scholarship – most of the minority nationalities students, for example. They get special tutoring or spend an extra year or two with us. An especially promising peasant from a revolutionary family, or the son of a veteran, naturally has a good chance to be recommended.'

'By the party?'

'By the party – and the school authorities, too.'

'Your teachers must average out pretty young?'

'Most of them are under forty. Quite a few were educated in Russia. We have about sixty "old boys" – over forty – trained before the war.'

'Would you say your teaching methods follow Soviet lines or develop independently?'

'In some basic respects they are the same; we use a lot of translated Russian texts. But the teaching revolution going on here now is our own development. We call it a three-in-one technique. It combines, in all grades, teaching, practical research work, and actual production. All students spend some time in our factories where we make some of the materials used in the buildings you see being constructed here. We designed and helped build our steel plant. You'll see it, if you wish. We are working on more than a hundred research projects – real, exciting, practical problems passed on to us by various industries. We also send students to outside factories to study and work. In 1958 we sent two thousand students to build small blast furnaces during the first Great Leap Forward drive.'

'Do you count that a waste of time, materials and money? Critics said the people fell behind in their regular work, the backyard furnace product was useless, the whole thing had to be abandoned. What about that?'

'You have to remember two things. First, our steel output in 1957 was less than a fourth of this year's target. The movement was launched in a countryside where the level of understanding of industry was very low. Many peasants looked upon steel-making as a mystery; they were afraid of it. When the campaign ended, millions of people had learned the principles. Do you know how to smelt iron or steel, Mr Snow?'

'Never touch the stuff.'

'Well, lots of our peasants are ahead of you. You may not need to know, that's true, but in a socialist country just beginning to industrialize, it's important for the people to know what's going on, and what they're working for.'

'But your government admitted that 3,000,000 tons of the pig iron smelted was unfit for industrial purposes.'

'Yes, there was waste, but not all waste. Don't forget, China can always use scrap iron. We have a big shortage. The educational result of the campaign was not the only thing. Our two thousand students helped build 25,000 furnaces –'

'Out of 600,000 all told, as I remember the claim?'

'Most of those were tiny brick hearths intended only for demonstration purposes. With the furnaces our students built we trained 67,000 skilled workers. The best furnaces were then combined and modernized. Last year China's small blast furnaces made 5,000,000 tons of usable iron and steel. That's more than our whole national production a few years ago.'

Hu took me through some classrooms and labs. They were less impressive within than outside; interiors were cheaply finished and furnished and classroom equipment seemed mediocre, if adequate. The labs had good instruments; China now made most of her scientific equipment, including microscopes and some fine lenses. The library held 300,000 books, with journals in foreign languages.

Men's dormitories were two-story brick buildings where students lived in cramped quarters: four to six in a room, with double tiers of bunks, and not much working space. (Not much more, in fact, than I later saw in the Peking jail.) The showers and washrooms, dining rooms and kitchens were clean, Spartan and as dreary as army barracks.

This was the school routine: 5.30 a.m., ablutions, dress; 6.00-7.00, physical exercise, en masse; 7.30-8.00, breakfast; 8.00-11.30, classrooms, lab, or workshops; 11.30-13.30, lunch, rest and study hours; 13.30-16.30, classroom study or workshop; 16.30-17.30, play or study; 17.30-18.00, supper; 18.30-22.30, study, club meetings, political lectures; 22.30, curfew. Saturdays and Sundays were free days used for study, club activities, sports, theater or special group projects. There was a college dance every Saturday.

'Would you like to see the girls' dormitories?' asked Mr Hu as I was about to leave.

I hadn't talked to a girl engineer since I left Russia. I had never talked to a Chinese girl engineer. I said, 'Of course.' That's how I happened to meet Small Lightning and her roommates.

The next day Hu Ying led me down a willow-lined path to a girls' dormitory, a long brick building with a simulated tile roof and numerous casement windows. Two girls in maroon slacks and white cotton pullovers, their hair braided, were hanging laundered underwear on the unpainted wooden stairway banisters. They

looked up and laughed confusedly. The student house chairman
appeared and led us to the second floor, where some girls skipped
past, their long hair damp from a shower.

'Is it all right to just walk in like this –?'

'They're expecting us,' said Mr Hu. The house chairman cried
out our arrival and mobilized girls in half a dozen rooms that were
in order; she invited me to inspect any of them. I looked into two or
three, and their occupants bowed invitingly. Then a girl with an
engaging smile above two pigtails called out, 'Wo-men ch'ing nin
tao li-pien lai', welcoming me to visit them, and three roommates
behind her nodded affirmation.

Inside were two sets of double-tiered bunks in a room ten feet by
twelve. Under the French windows and between the bunks was
a work table covered with a white cloth and on it stood a small
lamp and the usual teapot and statuette of Mao Tse-tung. Under
the bunks was just enough space to store the regulation small
canvas or wooden traveling boxes which contained the girls'
personal belongings. There were two cheap chairs and another
small table. From the white walls in rough plaster hung a few
dresses, slacks and coats. Overhead there was one unshaded light
bulb.

The girl who had beckoned to me was slightly pockmarked and
not very pretty, but she radiated personality. She had bright,
merry, bold eyes – not so much bold as direct. Women of her province, Honan, are not shy or cringing but are noted for their independence. Most Honanese women are also large and deliberate in
their movements, but this girl was diminutive and quick; she was
Chiang Chu-hsing.

I asked the same questions of six girls who crowded into the
room and here quote their answers from my notes.

First (Chiang): Born near Chengchow (northern Honan, central
China). Age twenty-two. Daughter of poor tenant peasants. Neither
could read or write; mother now just able to read Small Lightning's
letters. Two brothers, one sister. During childhood Chiang Chu-
hsing worked as a scullery maid in local landlord's house. One
year's schooling before 'liberation' (1949), when she was eleven.
'Liberation' obviously had literal meaning for her. She had worn
only rags till then. She remembered a famine year of a diet of tree

bark. Never owned a dress. (Now owns three.) Her parents got some land and security; she was sent to school; life completely changed, 'like crossing a bridge to heaven'. Worked hard, with party support. Now a sophomore, three years older than average in her class. Will graduate at twenty-six. She belongs to the Communist Youth League.

Second (Ho): Born Hopei province (where Peking is situated). Age nineteen. Parents small landlords; left home and went to Tangshan, mining town on the Hopei coast, during war. Land confiscated; they stayed in Tangshan. Now both parents work in factory there. 'They like it.'

Third (Lin): Born Hunan (South China). Age nineteen. Pretty girl. Daughter of small landlords. Land redistributed – taken by village cooperative. Parents went through six months of 're-education' and then rejoined community. No discrimination against her? (She would have been a small child at the time.) Not at all, she says. Went through regular schools, won place at institute on high scholarship after close examination. Now in her third year.

Fourth (Sung): Born Kiangsu (where Shanghai is located). Age twenty. Father an 'intellectual'. Meaning, middle school teacher. Nonparty but helped revolution. He now teaches in Yangchow. Three younger brothers. She is sophomore – and a Young Communist.

Fifth (Wang): Born Shantung (east coast). Age twenty. Third year. Father a railway worker. Two brothers, also railway workers, both party men.

Sixth (Hsu): Hopei girl, age eighteen. Father was scavenger – peddler of coal balls (made of coal scrap) in Tientsin. After liberation he became skilled worker. Mother and father both work in factories, have good three-room apartment, new building, living 'better than ever dreamed'.

'Why did you choose to become engineers?' Some answers:

'We want to build socialism.' 'Heavy industry is the foundation of socialism.' 'We want to build China into a strong modern nation and help the world get rid of imperialist oppression.' 'Engineers are the spine of a modern nation.'

'Those answers are out of a book,' I said. 'Before you ever heard

of heavy industry, socialism or imperialism, you must have formed
an ambition. I met a nurse at a hospital recently who told me she
had begun to long to be a nurse from the moment when, as a small
child, she first saw a woman wearing a cool, crisp, clean white uniform, "looking like one of the immortals". Don't any of you remember wanting to be an engineer before you knew the country
needed them?'

Small Lightning spoke up, the most articulate of the group.

'When I was a very small girl I saw a truck for the first time in
my life. I said, "I'd like to drive that truck." My older brothers
laughed at me. For a long time I was determined to be a truck
driver. After liberation, going to and from school, I saw many
trucks, tractors and bulldozers working on a dam but I saw that it
was the engineers who told them what to do, and where to put
their loads. I knew that I couldn't compete with those strong men
driving bulldozers, but by using my brains I could become an
engineer.'

Freudians may recognize some familiar patterns in that frank
statement.

'Many men would say that women shouldn't be engineers,' I said
provocatively, 'especially iron and steel specialists. The work is too
tough. Research, draftsmanship, building design, maybe, but can
women really do the heavy jobs?'

They all heatedly asserted that they did everything men students
did. There was a tendency to give them light work but they all did
their time at the furnaces, the same carrying work, the same risks;
they wanted complete equality in working assignments. Did I know
who was the first volunteer to carry a cable across the Yellow River
rapids at San Men Hsia at the start of the big dam there? A woman
engineer!

They were beginning to boil when I apologized by saying that I
had already heard from factory chiefs and engineers that women
make better operators of heavy-duty cranes than men and are more
reliable at tasks where a precise sense of timing may mean the
difference between life and death. I quickly put myself on record
as being in favor of women engineers.

'I hope you will admit,' I said, shifting to safer ground, 'that two
sexes are better than one. Better a two-sex institute than a one-sex

institute, for example? There must be advantages in being a girl student in an institute with nine males for every female?'

Nobody denied that coeducation was a good thing. 'Much better than an all-girls' school.' 'Very nice!' 'Sex doesn't come into our work here. We are all engineers!' 'There is no sex discrimination here.'

'Do many girls get married while they are students?'

'Very few. Usually we get married right after graduation.' The others laughed at the pretty Hunanese girl, Miss Lin, who said that. 'You mean *you're* going to get married,' they said. Student marriages were distinctly discouraged now. Although the legal age for marriage was twenty for men and eighteen for women,* these young ladies considered the 'correct' age to be at least twenty-two or twenty-three for a man and twenty-one for a woman.

They said they usually dated for Saturday night dances, for Sunday walks, for games or sports like swimming. They often paired up on 'teams' for field-work assignments. 'We have most of our fun in collective living rather than dating.'

Mr Hu had gone off somewhere, so I asked my interpreter's advice about whether anyone would be offended if I asked their views on birth control. He thought I might try.

'Do any of you object to family planning?'

'Certainly not,' said Miss Chiang. The rest looked blank.

'Let me put it this way. How many children do you intend to have when you get married?'

'That won't be my decision alone but my husband's – and the needs of socialism,' said the Shantung girl. 'Personally, I think two are enough.'

'Two!' 'Three!' 'Two!' The small family was definitely preferred.

*In practice this usually meant what the Chinese consider twenty-one and nineteen, since Chinese traditionally count a child one year old at birth, reckoning age from the time of conception.

(1970) During the 'hardship years' (1961–3) state and party urged young men not to marry before age twenty-seven and young women not before twenty-five. Birth control propaganda accompanied the advice. Admonitions have continued against early marriage and numerous offspring, the 'ideal' number now popularized being two children per couple.

'What if you have two or three and they're all daughters? Won't you need at least one boy?'

'That's feudal thinking! We don't make such distinctions any more,' said the little Honanese spokesman. They all joined in pouncing on the old attitude that males have superior value.

A few more questions elicited the information that birth control techniques were understood by all, from group discussions on social hygiene. It was also pointed out that the 'facts of life' were discussed on daily radio programs which explained contraceptive methods, for listeners of any age, in most precise detail. I was tempted to solicit their views on premarital relations, but this was not a clinic. I had already learned that such questions were often regarded as too prying and rather shocking, even to some fully matured adults. I deferred them for another occasion.

'This is too one-sided,' I said. 'You're doing all the answering. Would you like to ask me any questions for a change?'

They shouted in a chorus and held up their hands.

'You said you lived in Peking before, and taught at Yenching University. How do things in New China impress you?'

'Infinitely more opportunity for the poor, that's obvious. Certainly a poor peasant woman in college was almost unheard of. College was mainly for the upper class.'

'How is it in America? Can women study engineering in your schools?'

'They can, and do, but I'd say the cards are stacked – I mean there's a lot of prejudice against that.'*

They all smiled. It was what they had expected to hear.

I asked, 'Do you think you are happier than American students?'

Howls of derision greeted this, laughter and exclamations of surprise. 'What an odd question!' 'How could American students possibly be happy – slaves of American capitalism!' Just like that. Right out of the book. 'Besides, in your country only daughters of the rich get to college. Would any peasant have a chance?'

---

*In the U.S.A. in 1965–6, 13,602 master's degrees in engineering were granted, seventy-six to women; 146 women and 35,669 men received bachelor's degrees as engineering majors. One woman and 713 men received doctor's degrees in engineering. (U.S. Office of Education, World Almanac, 1969.)

This was going to be a hard one. How explain that the average American farmer never thought of himself as a peasant? That it takes only about 5,000,000 farmers to produce more than enough to feed America? That on the same percentage basis only 20,000,000 farm workers should be needed to feed China instead of the 200,000,000 to 250,000,000 now required? Well . . .

'Yes, farmers go to college – yes, they do.'

'Poor peasants can go to college?'

'Not so many poor peasants – I mean poor *farmers*. Of course it takes money to go to college –'

'That's the difference. Here education is free, it's for the working class. In America colleges are run for the rich – and to make money.'

'No, it's more accurate to say they are run to teach *students* how to make money. But let's not forget that America had a free educational system long before any other country. We have free primary and high school education – compulsory, in most places. But at good colleges and universities students have to pay for their tuition, room, board, everything. That's where discrimination in favor of the rich comes in.'

'Naturally,' said Small Lightning. 'Marx said that bourgeois education means bourgeois class domination. That's the kind of system we used to have in China.'

'A high percentage of Americans from working-class families get through college with the help of scholarships and part-time jobs. It's quite possible. You believe in struggle, don't you?'

'Struggle is important but it has meaning only if it's conscious class struggle. Individualistic struggle in bourgeois society only means that the one who succeeds joins the exploiters.'

The normal suppertime had come and gone and I had been pressed to eat with them. Each time I was invited I had declined, because I had a late dinner engagement, but whenever I rose to leave they insisted that I stay. They were genuinely curious, perhaps even more curious about me than I was about them; three of them had never seen an American. I could not leave without finding out a little more about how well they had learned their Mao Tse-tung.

'It may surprise you,' I said, 'to hear that few American youths believe they live under a system of imperialism. The average American believes imperialism means owning colonies, and Americans think they own no colonies. Students of history might ask you why, if America is an aggressive imperialist country, it supported Russia during the war against Hitler. After victory America had half the wealth of the world, fresh armies of fifteen million men, the best navy, the strongest air force, and men in occupation of a dozen countries and colonies. Why didn't America hold them and build a colonial empire?'

'The imperialists were afraid of Russia.'

'Russia was bleeding then, and truly very weak. And she had no defense against the atom bomb.'

They were silent for a moment. Then one of the younger girls, who had said little, remarked thoughtfully, 'The American people would not have supported such a thing.'

Small Lightning would not leave it at that. 'Of course imperialism is not just owning colonies in the old way,' she said. 'It means monopoly capital ownership of the means of production in countries economically colonial to it. It means keeping economic control and enslavement of peoples in order to make great profits. The people's revolutions were becoming powerful in some countries and American imperialism's role was to prevent revolution and to support counterrevolution, in that way maintaining its control.

'America did not really leave any of those countries. She tried to defeat revolution in China and she failed – except in Taiwan, for the moment. She tried to defeat it in Korea and failed. She is trying the same kind of aggression in Vietnam and Laos and she will fail there, too. There are American advisers and bosses in Pakistan and others in India, giving Nehru money to fight socialism. America has two hundred military bases, all the way from Germany to Japan, combining its forces with the native reactionaries to protect U.S. investments and profits and to hold down the people. What we don't understand is why American students tolerate all that – and the great risk of war that goes with it.'

'Why? Some of them would agree with some of what you say, but most would say that these bases are necessary defenses against the danger of Communist aggression –'

'Communist aggression ! Is China's fleet occupying Hawaii, or is

China flying planes over America? Are Chinese troops in Canada or Mexico? No! We haven't a soldier on foreign territory. Are Americans in Taiwan, Japan, Laos, Vietnam? Yes!'

What about Korea? Yes, what about it? That could have meant another six hours and it was really late. I had heard enough to know that these young people, the generation being prepared for leadership, were well indoctrinated in the politics of the land.

I promised to continue the discussion when I returned on Saturday, but that day was full of activity. Small Lightning was the star in a picture story I did of a day in the life of a student. She was a good actress: getting up, eating breakfast, working in the lab, walking in the park with a boy friend. She wore a light summer frock and black pumps and had her hair put up. In the afternoon we went to the steel mill, where she donned white overalls, helmet and glasses and pulled out half a dozen testings of flaming metal before it was poured. I went with her to the swimming pool, which was crowded with students. Finally she took me for some shots of her, with another partner – she was not sticking to one – dancing decorous fox trots and waltzes.

All this, I had persuaded her and the college authorities, would greatly interest youth in America, and help to correct some distorted impressions there about the slave lives of Chinese students. The pictures were not bad, but American magazine editors did not consider them worth using. Like the Chinese students, they already had the right answers – though not the same ones.

32

Swan Lake *in Peking*[*]

PERFORMING artists in China were enjoying high social prestige. Many younger artists had reason to be grateful to the new state, which had welcomed talent and opened wide opportunities for it to develop. More than 80,000 professional artists and musicians were guaranteed full-time employment, above average wages, special privileges and continuous higher studies.

In China, of course, all forms of artistic expression have an ancient history, to which the Communists had been adding new content and reviving some old. Foreign visitors might disagree about other things there but few would have disputed that theater, dancing and music were reaching the masses of the people as never before.

Every state factory of any size had an amateur dramatic club and so did colleges and middle schools. There was an average of seven amateur performing groups in each of the 24,000 communes. Hundreds of new theaters had been built in China. Peking had half a dozen opera houses and many first-class companies performed there and on the road. Nearly every province maintained at least one company to carry on its own opera in the several regional styles, dialects and traditions; these also toured as far as Yunnan and Manchuria. The spoken drama was flourishing; considering its infancy in China, technique and acting ability were promising. Propaganda was much more overt and blatant in drama than in the

---

* (1970) After 1966 foreign ballets were seen no more in China; traditional Chinese opera was also overhauled to make it conform to Yenan principles. Mao Tse-tung's dicta, *Talks at the Yenan Forum on Art and Literature*, became the guidelines for stage and screen performances. In brief: 'art to serve the masses'; art presenting proletarian heroes engaged in overcoming evil personified by their reactionary and counterrevolutionary class enemies. (Stanislavsky, go back to Russia !)

older opera, with which the audience was too familiar to tolerate much tampering or extraneous moralizing.

But I began this chapter to say something about Chinese ballet.

I apologized to Miss Chen Chiang-ching, vice-director of the Peking School of Dance. 'I appreciate your letting me come here on such short notice.'

'It's true that ordinarily you might have had a long wait,' she replied, not smiling. 'We have had so many visitors we must ration ourselves to only a few now.'

She was of medium height, about forty, slender, bobbed haired, rather severe in manner, olive skin drawn tightly over high cheek-bones. Probably once pretty, now Authority. She had been a specialist in folk dancing but here she was the responsible party administrator.

'Until now, you never had any ballet in China, did you?'

'No Western ballet. Of course every province has its dance groups but ours is the first school to specialize in ballet. We teach other kinds of dancing, too. Dancing is an art; art is to serve the people. We train teachers as well as artists to meet the demands of the masses.'

'Does that include ballroom dancing?'

'Yes, our people like mixed dancing. There are other instructors to teach that.'

I remembered then that in the Hsin Ch'iao hotel as well as in hotels in the provinces I had several times watched dances in ballrooms reserved for the evening by clubs of office and factory workers. Taxi dancers and night clubs had disappeared, but social dancing was more widespread. China now made all Western band instruments, and each of these parties had its own offerings of Chinese versions of swing, fox trot and even calypso. Square as could be, that's true. No twists and no cheek-to-cheek business, but some attractive young people in their party best. In Changchun I had tried to crash such a dance but was politely told it was a private affair, Sino-American peoples' friendship notwithstanding.*

---

*(1969) Social dancing of the Western type, by couples, disappeared in China soon after the break with Russia, and by 1962 was considered decadent and bourgeois. What might be called proletarian folk dancing became 'the thing' during the G.P.C.R.

Miss Chen had been with the Peking School of Dance since its inception in 1950; straight from Yenan, she had helped recruit teachers from all over the country. They had begun ballet in 1954. The ballet master was a Moscow student and some other teachers also studied there. A few Russian instructors who came to Peking had since left. Now the school had 340 students. For the 1959–60 term, about one hundred new students were accepted, sixty of them to specialize in ballet, forty in folk and social dancing. The school admitted children of the primary school ages, eleven to thirteen. They spent six to eight years as boarding students, in arts and sciences courses and dancing and theater techniques. A tough regimen kept them busy ten to twelve hours daily.

Something about their performance of *Swan Lake* had puzzled me. It was in one of the new Peking theaters – seats hard, furnishings simple but adequate, orchestra fair, lighting and staging excellent, costumes brilliant. The dancing was technically perfect, the leaps and pirouettes as lively as any I had seen. Yet compared to a Bolshoi or a City Center performance it was strangely lacking in force, oddly innocent and unevocative. Probably virginal is the word for it. I now learned that all the dancers were still at school and their average age was seventeen. The oldest, Miss Pai Ssu-hsiang (the celebrated prima ballerina of China), was twenty.

Miss Chen permitted herself a brief smile at my comment. 'They aren't fully mature, of course. Our dancers have been doing ballet six years – the Bolshoi a hundred. When ours are better we may do a world tour. By then we hope to have perfected some all-Chinese ballets we're now rehearsing. Some things closer to our own people and the revolution.'

As happens everywhere else, hundreds aspire to the stage in China for one who qualifies for a scholarship. Here, too, fond mothers pressed the case for their offspring, of real or imagined talent. Many runaways turned up at Miss Chen's school, begging admission.

'Usually we send them back after a scolding but there are exceptions.' Good! I thought. 'The teacher you saw leading the second dancing class is one. She ran away from her home in Szechuan when she was fifteen, to come here. She was good and we couldn't refuse her.'

In general, students were recruited through recommendations made by athletic directors, in all parts of the country, who looked out for comely children with long straight legs, supple waists and good shoulders. Indeed, the increased stature of Chinese youths was striking to returning visitors who expected to see runts produced by years of starvation diet. Several times I found myself traveling on trains with girl basketball teams beside whom I felt a dwarf; they averaged around six feet.

Miss Chen wanted one thing understood. The aim was not simply the attainment of perfection by a few professional performers. It was to train great numbers of instructors who could bring to the multitudes of China's youth – from childhood up – the bodily graces and disciplines that come from actual participation in some form of dancing.

'What is good dancing,' asked the mistress, 'except skill and discipline contributing to a collective artistic achievement? Dancing is good socialist training.'

Schools for artists and teachers of opera, drama and music in Peking and in some provincial cities, echoed the same philosophy. 'Art is to serve the people.' And socialism.

33

Doctor Horse

I SPENT several days with Ma Hai-teh, a quiet, gentle American physician with whom I had shared a great adventure.

Dr Ma – who was born George Hatem, in Buffalo, New York, in 1910 – knows more about Red China and its leaders than any foreigner alive.

Ma means 'horse' and is a family name especially common among Chinese Moslems, but Ma Hai-teh is an American of Syrian descent. *Hai* means 'sea' and *teh* means 'virtue'. The term could mean 'great virtue' but in this case the combination was probably intended to imply 'virtue from overseas'. These two words are also a phonetic rendering of the surname Hatem. Why Dr Hatem was y-clept Horse in Shanghai I do not know, but his nickname was Shag, and something about his thick black hair, a beard which the closest shave could not altogether efface, and his large, dark, warm eyes, did remind one of a Mongol pony.

In the hot June of 1936, when I met George Hatem in Sian, the capital of Shensi province, he began a journey which entirely altered his life. Had he not undertaken it he would never have met Chou Ssu-fei, one of the most beautiful and charming women in China, nor would they today have a daughter called Liang-p'i, or 'Second Horse', and a son, Yu-ma, which means 'Little Pony'.

Elsewhere I have told how I made contact with the Red underground in Peking in that same year,[1] and was given a letter to Mao Tse-tung, written in invisible ink. Armed with that, I went to Sian and put up at the Guest House, where I was told to expect a call from a certain 'Pastor Wang'. He would arrange to have me smuggled through the Nationalist lines into the Red districts, a hundred miles to the north. Soon after my arrival George Hatem introduced himself and told me that he was aware of my mission; he was also waiting for a call from Pastor Wang.

Shag had been in Shanghai a couple of years but had seen nothing else of China before this trip. I liked him. He hoped that we were 'going in' together and so did I, but we didn't know. For two impatient weeks we spent most of our time playing rummy and talking. Few foreigners except missionaries then visited Sian, and to satisfy the hotel manager's curiosity we told him we were going on a scientific expedition into Chinghai as soon as the rest of our party arrived. I was after a story. Dr Hatem was a missionary in search of a mission.

A healthy, uncomplicated bachelor of twenty-six, Shag possessed a shrewd intelligence that had already penetrated the glossy surfaces of society to its ugliest sores. Beneath a superficial cynicism he was serious about one thing. He wanted to find some purpose to his work as a doctor. Hitler had also sent him up to Sian – as, in a way, he had sent me. The world was no longer a pretty place for young people who understood where Hitlerism was leading it, and in the East the Japanese, going in the same direction, threatened to take Chiang Kai-shek (who at that time had German and Italian fascist advisers) with them. At that time communism seemed about the only force interested in fighting fascism. Since Hitler and Japan hated communism so much, Shag thought there must be some good in it. He had also developed a strong distaste for existing society in Shanghai.

'My father didn't starve himself to educate me for what I've been doing,' he told me.

'Meaning?'

'Fighting V.D. with a pea shooter. Now, venereal disease is one thing that can easily be prevented and can be cured. Shanghai exists to breed and spread it. It's a big business there run by organized gangs with the full protection of the police in both the foreign settlement and the Kuomintang-run Chinese city. There's a lot of money in the doctor's end of that business, too. I could make a fortune there treating nothing but chancres and blueballs for the rest of my life. In fact I've been doing very well. But I didn't spend my old man's money learning to become a V.D. quack for a gangster society. Maybe these people up north are interested in putting an end to the whole business. I want to see what they're like.'

It was not Marx but life experience that had made an emotional radical out of Dr Hatem before he reached China.

At the turn of the century a labor contractor paid a small sum of money to an impoverished illiterate family in Lebanon. In exchange, George Hatem's father, then a boy of fourteen, also illiterate, was shipped to Massachusetts to work in a textile mill in Lawrence. After paying off his parents' debt Hatem became a wage-earning apprentice and then a skilled worker. In a few years he saved enough to return to Beirut to find a bride. He took her back to settle in Buffalo, went to work in another mill, and started an American family.

'Life was a succession of good times when we had enough to eat, and bad times when there were layoffs. My sister became a permanent invalid because of lack of nourishment and medical attention we couldn't afford. Probably that's why the old man wanted me to become a doctor. My sister and I were very close. In a period of prosperity in the early twenties my father saved enough to start me in medical school. I finished my pre-med work in three years and won a scholarship to the American University in Beirut, where I studied until I won another scholarship to the University of Geneva. I didn't have money for railway fare but I had a bicycle and I rode it all the way to Switzerland.'

Besides learning medicine – in Latin, Greek, French and German – Shag managed to have a lot of fun. During summer vacations he waited on tables in tourist hotels and then cycled through Europe with schoolmates. In 1933 he and two other young American doctors in Geneva decided to set up practice in China. Why China? From Oriental students at the University of Geneva, Shag had heard a lot about China, which had come to fascinate him. He wanted to get to some place where basic medicine was needed. One of his classmates had wealthy parents. He put up the money to finance the trip to Shanghai, and to open a joint office.

'We discovered that V.D. specialization was the quickest way for young doctors to get started in Shanghai. Our practice flourished, but first one of my partners went home because of family troubles and then the other followed, to marry a rich girl and become a society doctor. I stayed on, and took a job as staff doctor for the Shanghai International Settlement police force. Examining girls from the brothels and cleaning them up till the next dose. A lot of the cops were in the same clinic. They wanted *their* whores clean.'

Shag helped write a pamphlet on health conditions in Shanghai and through that he met Agnes Smedley,[2] then correspondent for the *Frankfurter Zeitung*. Miss Smedley had gradually established contacts with the Chinese Red underground, through whom she got more information about the civil war than anyone else. One day she introduced Shag to a young Red engineer named Liu Ting, who 'awakened' him with accounts of egalitarian life in the forbidden Communist areas. Doctors, he learned, were desperately needed in there. He was about to go home, but after long discussion and thought he determined to go to the northwest to see whether people there really were trying to do something as worthwhile as the engineer had made it sound.

As we waited, a strange city smoldered around us. Sian was then headquarters of the 'bandit extermination' (anti-Red) forces of the northwest, under 'Young Marshal' Chang Hsueh-liang, who was the Kuomintang's deputy commander-in-chief for all China. Shag and I soon learned that highly important Reds were secretly living in Sian under the personal protection of Chang Hsueh-liang. By the time we left Sian for the North, a budding conspiracy was obvious to us. Within six months it was to erupt in the 'Sian Incident', when Marshal Chang led a mutiny, seized the Generalissimo and his staff during an inspection tour, and held them captive for two weeks.* They changed the fate of China. As a consequence of the 'Incident', Chiang Kai-shek had to postpone his 'final extermination campaign' against the Reds and in another year Japan launched her major invasion. The Nationalists perforce once more became temporary allies of the Reds.

Shag and I carried these secrets, unknown to the outside world, with us when we entered Red China. I also agreed to keep Shag's own whereabouts completely confidential, even from his family. Nor could I, for a long time, reveal the manner in which we were smuggled northward in a Nationalist army truck and dumped at the edge of no man's land, which we crossed on foot.

*Marshal Chang personally flew the Generalissimo back to freedom in Nanking; he was arrested and remained Chiang's personal prisoner. A contemporary account of the Sian Incident appears in *Red Star Over China*.

Now, in Peking, in the small living room of an old house of two courtyards standing on Hou Lake, north of the Winter Palace, I sat sipping Chinese brandy with Dr Horse one afternoon in what he liked to call his stable. We spent hours talking about our experiences together and bringing his story up to date since that high summer when I had left him, a mere quarter of a century ago. Mrs Ma sat beside him.

'I don't think I ever shook inside more than I did in that first Chinese village when we crossed to the Red side,' he said. 'No one knew who we were or what we were doing there. Huddled up on that k'ang in a cave, surrounded by a bunch of strange peasants. They kept looking at your cameras and our watches. I told you they looked like bandits to me.'

'They were bandits,' I said.

'That's right, Red bandits. Red Spears, they called themselves. But there were White bandits around too. That was why we had missed the escort Chou En-lai sent out to meet us,' he explained to Ssu-fei. 'They ran into some White bandits on the way and had to chase them. We heard that later.'

'What bothered me was that these peasants kept saying "*Hai-p'a*", and *hai-p'a* to me meant "I'm afraid". It upset me like hell. Why should *they* be afraid?'

'You told me that, all right,' Shag said. 'Then we went on with one muleteer who left us in a temple in the woods and disappeared for the night. At dawn he came to wake us up and tell us we'd better get a move on. I was really low then. I realized for the first time we'd put our lives in the hands of people we knew nothing about. Maybe we would end up in a couple of cannibal pies. A few hours later we met our first Red soldier on the road and from then on everything was okay.'

'I finally learned that *hai-p'a* in north Shensi dialect means "don't understand".'

Ssu-fei laughed. She said she had been fooled the same way when she first arrived in Yenan.

'I still meet people in the villages,' said Shag, 'who take one look at me, assume I don't speak Chinese, and from then on don't hear a word I say. Sometimes I have to repeat, "I'm talking *Han-hua! Chung-kuo hua!*" several times before they begin to listen.'

Shag and I had traveled together for two months and he had sat in on many of my interviews. We were each given a horse, an automatic, and a cotton uniform.

'You were the only person around who managed to put a hat on Mao Tse-tung,' Shag remembered. 'His hair was very long then and he wouldn't wear a hat.'

'I forgot about that.'

'Yes, you were taking photographs and insisted that he put on a hat. He didn't have one and you put yours on him because it was the only one that looked at all like an army hat. That was the best picture ever taken of Mao. It's been in books and papers for years, and now it's in the Revolutionary Museum.'

We had ridden over northern Shensi, Kansu and Ninghsia together, with P'eng Teh-huai's army. Then Shag went on farther west to meet the Fourth Front Army, breaking through from Szechuan at the end of the Long March, and I went back to Pao An. On the road Shag taught me how to use a hypodermic needle. I practiced by jabbing him with plague and typhoid germs we had brought along as vaccines.

'I still feel that first needle you gave me. Wham! You left a bump the size of a duck egg,' he said now.

At the start Shag couldn't ask for a bowl of water without my help, but in an amazingly short time he began speaking some Chinese. He had a gift for languages, a good ear for them. Almost at once he felt completely at home. He became popular with the 'little Red devils' of that youthful army – the orderlies and mess boys, who used to hang around us and listen and laugh and try to pick up a few words of our ridiculous language.

'I wonder what happened to Shang Chi-pang, that little Beau Brummel orderly of Li K'o-nung's. Remember him?'

'Sure! They used to kid him by pronouncing his name in the wrong tone, so it meant "penis".'

'He asked me to be sure to spell his name correctly when I wrote about him – just as if he were a general.'

'No idea where he is, but I can tell you where Tai Ch'un-ch'i is. Remember him? A bright kid, medical orderly in P'eng Teh-huai's camp in Ninghsia? He looked like a baby but he must have been fourteen or fifteen by then. You took some pictures of him.'

I did vaguely recall Tai. 'What about him?'

'He's a doctor now, working right here in the Skin Diseases Hospital with me. Deputy director, no less, and a crackerjack skin-cancer specialist. You'll meet him.'

Before I left Shag that summer he had made up his mind that that was the life he wanted. His arrival doubled the Western-trained medical force. The only qualified doctor in the whole army then was Fu Jen-chang, a product of a Methodist missionary hospital in Kiangsi. Shag was a much overworked man until the outbreak of the Japanese war, when the Yenan Hospital was set up with the help of funds raised abroad by Mme Sun Yat-sen. Some Western-trained Chinese and a few foreign doctors went in to augment the force. A remarkably ingenious Canadian heart specialist, Dr Norman Bethune,[3] organized front-line guerrilla medical services for the Eighth Route Army. He did the work of twenty men until he died of septicemia for lack of penicillin. There were years when amputations and other operations on wounded men were performed without anesthesia, as in American Civil War days. Many a battle, Shag told me, was fought to capture Japanese penicillin and other medicines.

Shag also did his muleback medical assignments at the front, but his main work was in the organization of the army's base hospital and medical training system. It was in Yenan that he met his wife, when she came up as a volunteer. In prewar Shanghai she had been a movie star.

He said, 'The minute I saw Ssu-fei I dropped whatever I was doing, yelled "There goes my wife", and got on my horse to follow her. She was training theatrical troupes and hardly noticed me. I kept after her for weeks and made no headway. Every bachelor in Yenan had the same idea and I was an ugly American. I was getting desperate, when her best friend went to the hospital to have a baby. It was a difficult birth and I was called in. Ssu-fei watched me deliver the baby and it made a big change in her. She must have decided I was useful for something.'

'I didn't think any foreigner could be that gentle,' said Ssu-fei, laughing and blushing.

'It was the most rewarding delivery I ever made. Ssu-fei couldn't understand half my Chinese then, but we were married a few days later. She's been teaching me ever since – says my tones are still lousy.'

'What do you call him?' I asked her. 'Hai-teh?'

'No, just Ma.'

'Just – Ma?'

'No,' she corrected me, pronouncing it in the third tone, '*Ma!*'

After Japan's surrender there was a period of nearly two years when Communists and Nationalists coexisted and attempts were made to form a coalition government. UNRRA brought in relief supplies and medicines which were supposed to be divided impartially, but they were distributed by the Kuomintang-controlled CNRRA. Dr Ma became Dr Hatem again briefly when he represented Paluchun's relief organization for the guerrilla districts.

'We had no luck with UNRRA,' Shag went on. 'Some of the Americans wanted to help us but the Kuomintang controlled everything and either kept it or sold it on the black market. After a year in Peking all I got was four hundred tons of supplies which turned out to be two-thirds toilet paper. Toilet paper! We still had people dying for lack of penicillin. Six hundred UNRRA workers protested against the scandalous corruption and sale of their supplies on the black market. It all came out in Mayor La Guardia's report when he resigned as head of UNRRA – and it had no effect in China. After the truce broke down I went back to Yenan. Civil war began again.

'That was in 1947. By March, Yenan was surrounded and we had to evacuate and start donkey-back medicine again. Mao Tse-tung gave us a picture of Chiang Kai-shek's strategy, and his own. We had already lost Kalgan and were evacuating most of the cities and railways we held. The Nationalists were bombing hell out of us in their American planes. Naturally I was worried about Ssu-fei and the children. After Mao finished listing all the places we were giving up, things looked pretty grim to me.

'"We're winning!" Mao said. "If Chiang goes on making mistakes like this he will be finished in three to five years."

'Sure enough, by the winter of 1948 I was sitting in the Summer Palace, outside Peking, waiting for Fu Tso-yi to surrender peacefully. We occupied the capital without a battle. So – here we are.'

Shag had never been back to America and he was full of questions. He had some recent books but nothing that explained it all to him. How could people still tolerate racism? What about Mc-Carthyism? Neglecting schools and public health while the state paid billions to farmers not to grow food? What was wrong with youth? Juvenile delinquency? Beatniks? No motivation for life? How could labor tolerate American policy toward China?

I noticed a copy of C. Wright Mills's *The Power Élite* in his small library and I asked Shag if he had read it. He said he had.

'That answers your questions better than I can. Anyway, you've been detached from the American scene for a long time, Shag. Your interest must be mainly academic by now. I suppose you're a Chinese citizen, aren't you?'

'Certainly not.' He went to his desk and came back with a fresh green American passport. 'I got it just before I left Peking for Yenan, in 1947,' he said. 'At General Marshall's headquarters. Fellow named Walter Robertson* gave it to me.'

I looked inside the cover and saw that it was *not* stamped *verboten* for travel in China, since it had been issued before Mr Dulles' ukase on the subject. I smiled. 'Nobody can say you are not a legal resident here.'

'I'm here legally and still an American – unless it's treason to wipe out syphilis.'

Dr Hatem had even more than that to answer for.

---

*Walter S. Robertson later became Assistant Secretary of State under John Foster Dulles. Presumably Mr Robertson procured Dr Hatem's passport for him from the U.S. Consulate General in Peking.

34

Subversive Medicine

THE next day I went over to visit Shag at the Institute of Venereology and Skin Diseases. Laboratories and hospital employed a personnel of about six hundred and Dr Hatem had been the institute's chief of staff during a successful national war against syphilis and gonorrhea. He was now a deputy director and engaged in campaigns against skin diseases and malaria.

At the door I was introduced to a tall, thick-haired, good-looking Chinese wearing a white uniform. He stared at me intently and shook his head.

'No, I wouldn't have recognized you,' he said. 'You had a beard when I met you in Ninghsia with Dr Ma.'

'I have no advantage over you, Dr Tai. You came only to my shoulder then. Your uniform was two sizes too large and you wore a cap that hung down over your ears.'

Dr Tai Ch'un-ch'i, now also a deputy director of the institute, was the grown-up 'little devil' whom Shag had mentioned to me. After Director Fu Ching-kuei and other members of the staff had taken me through the institute I heard some of Dr Tai's story.

He was a native of Fukien, on the South China coast, one of four children born in a family of poor tenant peasants. The Tais were ragged and hungry when Red partisans briefly occupied their village in 1933. The landlords fled and the Reds gave land and food to the peasants. Everything 'turned upside down' and life suddenly became 'lively and hopeful'. When the Reds were driven out again, Tai and some other children ran off with them.

'In a better time my parents had managed to send me to school for two years, so I knew characters. That's why I was put in the Juichin base medical school and given a few months of training as an orderly. I was thirteen then. After a year of changing bandages and giving injections I returned to Juichin and spent six months studying elementary anatomy, biology and pathology. Then we were surrounded and began the Long March. At the end of it, when I met you, I was fifteen. I was a full medical assistant under Dr Fu Jen-chang. You remember him, the ex-Methodist? He's Vice-Minister of Public Health now.'

Tai went on to say that from 1936 until 1949 he had had no more classroom training. He read a few books but otherwise learned everything in the field, where he had to treat all kinds of cases and do minor surgery, as well as fight. He acquired the title 'acting doctor' and went all through the anti-Japanese and revolutionary wars without a scratch. 'I was lucky. Most of the orderlies you met in the northwest are dead.' In 1949 he was finally sent to a medical school in Shenyang, Manchuria, where a few other surviving 'little devils' got their first real medical education.

'Of course I had a big handicap, studying with young people who had had full pre-medical educations. For two years I don't think I slept more than three hours a night. I had so much to learn: biology, medicine, math and physics. But I did have two assets.' He smiled. 'I didn't have to spend much time in political training classes. And after the first two years, when we got into clinical practice, I was far ahead of the others. Even the teachers often had to ask me for practical advice.'

While he was at medical school Tai found a wife. 'Ten years behind Dr Ma,' he said. 'But on children I'm already one ahead of him.' Dr Ma and Dr Tai had been with the institute since its inception in 1953, and from then on their story was a joint one. Several years earlier, however, Shag had helped to begin the war against V.D.

'Our first goal was to eliminate the chief carriers, the prostitutes,' said Shag. 'We started off in the Peking-Tientsin area, with a team of about a hundred doctors and assistants. Women party workers first went into the brothels and explained the program. It wasn't hard to win support; most of the girls were slaves who had been sold into the houses. In some instances women party cadres went in and lived with them to gain their confidence. The seriously ill were sent to hospitals immediately but the rest were allowed to receive guests for a while, until the younger women were organized and ready to burn their contracts. They told their stories and what they would like to do. No guilt was attached to anyone and no punishment involved.

'When everything was prepared we closed down every brothel in Peking in one night. The women were taken to hostels specially set up for them, where they were thoroughly examined and treated. Most of the brothel owners and pimps had fled; a lot of them went on to Shanghai and later to Hongkong. Those who remained were rounded up and treated. About eighty percent of the 70,000 whores in the Peking-Tientsin area were infected with V.D. My own team treated and cured as many as 1,200 cases every two weeks. That's about all it takes with penicillin : ten to fifteen million units does the job. The follow-up work took a lot longer, of course, but that wasn't our responsibility.'

'What did happen to all these Suzie Wongs?'

'Some went back to their villages, some to work in factories, quite a few were young enough to be sent to primary school. We made medical helpers out of the more intelligent. We produced several very able laboratory and research workers from among them. Nobody refers to their past and there's no stigma attached. Many of them have married.'

The campaign was soon duplicated in Shanghai, Hankow, Canton and other cities. In the process medical assistants were trained in the techniques of diagnosing and treating syphilis and gonorrhea, and the anti-V.D. forces quickly expanded. Within two years most of urban China was cleansed of the chief carriers. Work was extended to the rural towns and then to the whole country.

'I read a story about a reformed sing-song girl,' I said, 'who has just been made a hero of labor in Shanghai. She's in charge of a sanitation squad. Sounds kind of dull after the bright lights.'

'That's naïve, my friend. I'll bet that girl had V.D. – that's why she's in a clean-up squad. Most of them were owned body and soul by the brothel keeper. A few high-class singing girls, a few women kept by rich merchants, that was different. Those went off to Hongkong with the brothel keepers and opened business there.'

'Where do the unmarried men go now for what Dr Kinsey called "outlets"? Unmarried women are certainly not getting any more promiscuous and permissive!'

'Promiscuity? Very rare. So is premarital intercourse. Social discipline is all against it. What's different now is that everybody gets married – so-called coolies, too. You know coolies and poor peasants couldn't afford a wife in the past. They used to save coppers for weeks to get ten minutes with a two-bit lay. Now you will find very few men or women still unmarried at twenty-five. Before that, they do without – they're kept busy, no time to fool around, minds and bodies occupied.'

I learned later, in the Peking prison, that the horizontal type of livelihood had not absolutely disappeared, but it would take an extremely clever woman to succeed at it in present conditions.

'While we were getting rid of V.D.,' Shag went on, 'the Ministry of Health organized mass campaigns for personal hygiene, and against pests and epidemics. With the backing of the whole government we have now got control over flies, mosquitoes, bedbugs, rats, mice and lice. Mass vaccination was carried out against smallpox, plague, cholera and typhus. We haven't had a case of plague for years – 1951 was the last I remember – and smallpox, cholera and typhus are extremely rare. Malaria is greatly reduced.

'Parasitic and skin diseases are still a major problem – and that's where the institute comes in.'

We examined the institute's large basic medical library, which included many Western scientific journals, and then we made an aromatic visit to the department of research in Chinese medicine. Thousands of catalogued boxed specimens stood row upon row: countless varieties of tree ears, fungi, wild spices and herbs, dehydrated seeds and leaves – and doubtless bats' ears, wasps' stings, linnet hearts, tiger bones, dragon dung and other choice items (by hearsay) in the Chinese pharmacopoeia. Among them Western doctors had discovered the rare chaulmoogra nut, the oil from which supplies what was for long the only known cure for leprosy (a speciality of the house, in this case), and ephedrine, a plant extract.

When we sat down again Shag went on with the story.

'In 1949,' he said, 'China had fewer than 40,000 trained doctors. That included army doctors such as Dr Tai and wartime trainees who had had only three or four years in medical school. If we confine it to doctors who'd had six years or more in college, we started with fewer than 10,000. Four years later we still had only about 50,000 doctors but we had 70,000 "middle-doctors" or assistants with two or three years of training each, and about 60,000 nurses. In that year all the villages of Ningtu were organized as advanced agricultural cooperatives, and each of them had some kind of medical team – say, one or two doctors, or just doctors' assistants, for every 5,000 people.

'Our institute team of specialists set up a mobile demonstration center where we gathered the Ningtu local medical teams to instruct them. We used lectures, slides and moving pictures to show symptoms of the disease and how it develops, and then demonstrated treatments. We combined training and retraining courses with practice. We got each village medical team to bring in a dozen to fifteen men and women – both medical and nonmedical personnel – and ran over the routine with them.

'We got the technique down to where we could teach the average fifteen-hundred-character person the whole thing in three days. That included learning how to take blood tests and urine tests, and how to diagnose V.D. We had the full cooperation of local peasant leaders, leaders of the women's organizations, and branch party secretaries, of course. Women and men were divided into separate groups; women wouldn't discuss symptoms before men, naturally. Resistance to examination was overcome until no one felt any disgrace involved. Well, as I said, we covered the whole two million population that way in forty days.'

'I think you'll find a lot of skepticism in the West about such claims, Shag. Even with a disease as relatively easy to diagnose as V.D., the margin of error among amateurs must be pretty high.'

'We thought so too. So we spent another forty days spot-checking all over the county. We tested the "trainees" and then the results. We did find that our method wasn't perfect. The percentage of misses was about 15 in 100. But nearly eighty percent of the cases overlooked were latent. That average would not be high anywhere – except for venereology specialists. On the basis of our findings we ran the whole process once more. After that, I'd say Ningtu was about Ivory-Soap pure. There were probably only a few very latent cases left.'

The institute team quickly repeated the experiment in widely scattered areas, while other medical groups sent observers with them. Branches of the institute were established in every province, under the provincial health ministries. These branches now trained medical cadres to teach more village health teams, until the practice became universal. They made full use of about 300,000 Chinese-style doctors.

'By 1957 our national and provincial teams had covered the whole country except for Tibet. The Dalai Lama opposed examination and treatment there on religious grounds; he claimed there wasn't any V.D. in Tibet. Last year for the first time our people started working there. They've found syphilis widespread.'

Director Fu Ching-kuei had come in on his American colleague's story. 'Yes, there is practically no venereal problem left,' he said. 'Dr Ma has done such a good job, professors in medical schools are mad at us. They say that since 1957 they can't find any more active venereal cases even for classroom observation work. We've had to import some from Tibet!' He added soberly, 'We've got plenty of diseases to conquer yet. Some of them are going to take many years. Get Ma *Tai-fu* to tell you ...' His voice trailed off as he left us.

My friend from Buffalo continued: 'In 1957 we took a large institute team back to Ningtu county, to try to develop a method of mass treatment of the six common skin diseases. These are kala azar, schistosomiasis, filariasis, hookworm, ringworm and leprosy. Using the technique we had developed for venereal disease we worked out basic means for easy identification of these parasitic diseases. We used the stages of approach as before. This time people were organized into small teams of a dozen families, each under a discussion leader, to carry out the diagnoses. In this way a competitive spirit was aroused between the small teams to see which would be the first to be declared cured and competently healthy. They made a game out of it.

'I don't know whether it would work anywhere else, but it worked here. In one month we were able to diagnose and begin treatment of 300,000 cases.'

'How many could you cure?'

'We cleared up nearly everything but schistosomiasis and leprosy. The number of lepers was very small. Our surveys show leprosy is less prevalent than was thought in the past. There are probably not more than 350,000 cases in all China and they're practically all known now and already under treatment. We have stopped the spread of the disease. The same goes for schistosomiasis – and kala azar. But to stamp them out altogether – as we did V.D. – will take more time.

'Our problem was how to cut down on time of diagnosis, how to run more and faster tests, and how to get these diseases under control more effectively and more quickly. That's when we developed what the ministry calls the "mass line in medicine". We worked out a very much simplified system of elementary diagnosis for parasitic diseases. We boiled it down to a set of only *one dozen questions*. With this questionnaire as the basis, our institute became the training and testing center for a great new experiment.

'What the mass line in medicine means is that millions of people are getting an elementary understanding of what public health work is all about and the important part every one of them plays in it. With full understanding of the peasants we get cooperation never possible in the past. The villages are now able to make serious attacks on the breeding grounds of snails and sandflies, worms and malarial mosquitoes. Snail-infected canals and ponds and swamps are being drained and filled in and latrines properly sanitized. New cases are diagnosed quickly and isolation and quarantine are enforced because everybody is taking part.

'This is even true of lepers, who used to hide and were shielded by others. Now they know they are not going to be punished or made into pariahs. Our system of handling lepers is to keep them integrated in useful social life. We help them build clean new villages right in the midst of production brigades. They run their own communities and take part in farming and other work while they are being treated.'

That about completes the subversive-medicine story of Shag Hatem from Buffalo. At a minimum, the counts of indictment against him would have to include participation in the service of China against the following foreign powers: syphilis, gonorrhea, malaria, kala azar, ringworm, hookworm, schistosomiasis, filariasis and leprosy. Not to mention his voluntary contribution of two sturdy young *ma* to the Chinese cavalry.

Talking to George Hatem was more illuminating than I am able to convey here : he helped me understand the logic of some things that had puzzled me in China. He knew the faults and failures of the régime but he also knew the misery of Old China and the enormity of the problems it presented. Because he was the one American who had for twenty-five years intimately shared the ordeals of the men and women who fought for the responsibility to bring China to her feet, his continuing faith in what they were doing merits attention.

'China simply could never have stood up in any other way,' he said. 'Nearly everything done has been necessary and nearly everything necessary has been done. And all in all it's a success.'

Full stop and question mark. From afar, China's failure seemed more evident than its success. It was seen abroad as a land of starvation, overwork, commune blunders, cultism, belief in 'inevitable war', shrill propaganda reflecting the fears and tensions of a harassed leadership, forced labor, brain washing and persecution of individualism. American cold-war propaganda has overstated these charges but perhaps no more than Communist propaganda distorts its picture of the American scene by overemphasis of news on crime, racketeering, government corruption, racial oppression, narcotics addiction, juvenile delinquency and commercialized pornography.

But in the quiet of Dr Hatem's tiny garden beside the still lake I was reminded of something overlooked by those who mistook China's current food crisis as the sum total of the revolution. That was the simple fact that behind all the propaganda stood millions of unknown and unsung men and women who had successfully and devotedly carried out the real work of releasing half a billion people from a heritage of dense ignorance and superstition, widespread disease, illiteracy and universal poverty. The task was far from accomplished, but the *foundations* of a modern civilization had been laid, with little outside help, and against handicaps to which Americans had made heavy contributions. These foundations would last regardless of what government ruled in the future – unless, of course, it was destroyed by war and all people perished with it. China is bigger than any government. Because this government had been doing things for China it had been able to command support even from many who were opposed to communism.

35

I See the Army

OUTSIDE Chungking I visited the Szechuan Art Institute, where large white letters on a huge red pylon proclaimed: 'Art to serve the masses, art to serve socialism!' That eliminated quite a few questions about art to serve art.

The school was divided into two departments, 'creative' and 'applied' art. On a large campus thickly planted in vegetables, eight main buildings housed four hundred high school art students and two hundred advanced students enrolled for four-year terms. Graduates become teachers (starting at fifty to sixty yuan) in schools or state institutions, including factories, where workers attend spare-time art courses. Peking had always had good art schools but now every province had one or more and the Chungking institute ranked high among them.

Courses in traditional art included Chinese painting; oil painting; carving in wood, stone, linoleum and metal; and sculpture. Applied arts were: design in all materials; lacquer work; porcelain and pottery; decorative and folk art; and furniture-making. China now baked porcelain as fine as any in her history. Old masters of color and composition were honored and had spread their knowledge widely. I saw superb porcelain exhibited in Peking, Shanghai and Hankow. Most of it was exported or went into state buildings. High quality was also being attained in lacquer, ivory and other applied arts – as demonstrated in the magnificent interior decoration of Peking's Great Hall of the People.

'Paint' was a different story. No masterpieces had yet appeared among works of 'new ideological content'. No one can surpass Chinese painters in technique, however; tractors and power plants may be dull subjects but the execution of them was often very good. Stylistic imitators of Ch'i Pai-shih's enchanting flower and insect paintings were legion, as were those of Hsu Pei-hung's thrilling horses. Both Ch'i and Hsu were best-sellers in China as well as abroad. At one lithograph shop I visited in Liu Li Ch'ang, Peking's street of art, I learned that Hsu's most famous horse had been master-blocked there for print reproductions no less than eight hundred times in ten years.

'Art to serve the masses', inevitably becomes highly pictorial, and poster art in China today showed greater vigor, imagination and talent than more ambitious efforts. Traditional Chinese symbolism and impressionism require a high degree of intellectual participation for full enjoyment. Here was a nation not yet literate, but now becoming literate in Marxist language which had little to do with the mysticism and philosophical concepts underlying much of China's classical art. Was it surprising that literal coinage, à la Norman Rockwell, really did serve mass taste better than abstract concepts?

While the Marxist vision of the perfect society is probably the ultimate abstraction, few men engaged in building the stairway to it appreciate abstract art. Stair building is an intensely concrete task. 'What does it mean?' Chou En-lai asked me about abstract art. 'If it has no meaning, what value has it for the people?'

'What contemporary European painters do you study?' I asked an instructor in oil whose students were painting an old peasant model.

'Very few,' he said. 'We have a long history of art experience and we are trying to develop our own schools and techniques in oil, too. But we do admire Picasso.'

'In what period?'

'We like his Peace Dove,' he said.

My request to interview and photograph the army was ignored in Peking until one evening I met a high official and said: 'I spent four months with the old Red Army in days when you had only one rifle for two or three men and were all in straw sandals. I don't think it did you any harm. How is it that you won't let me see your army now when you've got much more to show?'

He thought it over and smiled and said: 'Yes, you are right. Why not? Ordinarily we don't permit foreigners on army reservations for reasons of security, but there are exceptions.' I was then told to get ready to spend two days with the army. I expressed interest in seeing a mechanized force and/or an ordinary infantry training school. One late October morning at seven the Hsin Ch'iao room boys were greatly impressed when four officers called for me, led by Colonel Li Hsin-kung, army liaison officer of the Foreign Ministry, and Captain Kuo Kung, an English-speaking graduate of the Foreign Languages College.

Once the decision was made, the army received me courteously and even warmly. I was the first Westerner permitted to take still and moving pictures inside Chinese military establishments in many a year. Except for those who were Korean veterans most of the officers had never seen an American, and for the veterans I was the first specimen of Americana they had encountered outside a hostile field.

On every occasion when I could talk long enough to get past formalities I found much greater curiosity in them, from generals down, about how America really 'worked' than I usually encountered among civilians. Coupled with this was an eager determination to have it understood that the army was *not* anti-*American* and did *not* seek a war with the United States. Naturally, that in no way affected their solid support of China's stand against 'American aggression'. They (as distinct from the government) seemed convinced that if the American people could just be made to understand the necessity for the United States to pull its armed forces out of Taiwan, Japan, Korea and South Asia generally, world peace could be assured. Of the absolute reasonableness of these demands they had, of course, no doubts.

The army I saw – if we omit nuclear weapons for the moment – represented what many considered the third greatest military land power in the world.

This remarkable transformation had happened even within my own memories of China. In the thirties Evans Carlson and Joseph Stilwell were the only U.S. Army observers who believed that the Chinese fighting man 'could become the equal of any in the world', and both said so for the record. Chiang Kai-shek had made the first attempt to prove this, with Soviet Russian aid (1924–7), before he broke his alliance with the Communists. From then on he still tried to unify China largely by military means. Throughout his struggles with provincial warlordism, 'communist-bandits', and finally with the Japanese, Chiang remained essentially an old-fashioned militarist. He was never able to subordinate the Bonaparte in himself either to the political discipline of a Napoleon or to the needs of mass support. With all the money and arms given to him by Americans he failed to reconcile the existence of a personal army with the requirements of a modern revolutionary state.

This was always Chiang's chief handicap in coping with the old

Red Army and later with the People's Liberation Army. From the
guerrilla beginning of the Communist forces on Chingkangshan in
1927 the military head was subordinated to the political brain. The
relationship was very close between Chu Teh, the army commander, and Mao Tse-tung, the party leader. They jointly signed
all orders and for years the press referred to 'Chu Mao' as the 'commander leader' of the still little known 'communist-bandits'; many
people believed they were one. Throughout Communist history a
party political commander has stood beside every operational commander, and the 'Chu-Mao' twinship symbolized the ideal.

Now, in this pattern the military arm was regarded as only one
of several means; it could be effective only when coordinated with
economic, political and social factors synthesized by broad strategic
planning under party leadership. All military operational concepts
and principles and general battle orders derived their authority
from the party leader – although they were actually the product of
joint thinking of army and political specialists. Of further significance: Mao Tse-tung, as *de facto* commander-in-chief, had never
taken a military title.

In this fundamental relationship the People's Liberation Army of
1960 was not different from the Red Army of the thirties; it was
still the right army of the party brain. That coordination was by
no means perfect or without its own inner 'contradictions',
however.

My first day with the People's Liberation Army was spent at a
tank school near the Marco Polo Bridge, where the Sino-Japanese
War began. Part of the barracks here traced to Japanese days. The
establishment had been greatly enlarged to include tank practice
and gunnery fields and a farm which supplied part of the school's
food. A military expert would have learned much more; I myself
could bring only a correspondent's amateur view with a general
sense of military efficiency picked up from observation of many
armies in many countries.

I was probably not shown latest weapons. Those I did see were
Chinese variants of standard training equipment in use by Soviet
or American forces up to the missile age. Tanks, now made in
China, were copies of the Soviet T-34, with long low bodies, wide
double-mesh tracks, and a 45-degree climb capability. I was told a

later model (T-54?) was in production. Tanks in maneuvers looked effective.

Before the Korean War, China had no tank command school. The Marco Polo school was founded under Russian advisers in 1950. China's modern tank artillery and jet aircraft industries were begun in 1954 with equipment and advisers also furnished by the Russians. At both the tank school and an infantry regiment I later visited there were no more Soviet advisers.

The 1,200 students here were junior officers of platoon and company grade and three cadet groups in the training department. Two other departments were command and political; they offered twelve courses including tactics, gunnery, signal, mechanical, and ordnance. There were also 'cultural' courses. All students had had battle experience but their 'knowledge of mechanization and their cultural level' was low, I was told. Classrooms I saw in cheap brick buildings were spick-and-span, battlefield models for tactical study were well mounted and electrically animated, and weapons and ammunition models in cross-section detail were also well arranged for dismounting and assembly practice.

The commandant here was Chao Chi, from the old Fourth Front Red Army; his vice-commandant was Ho Feng, also a Long March veteran. Both had had special training under the Russians. As in other army camps, students spent two to three months of the year on 'socialist construction' jobs and working on the school farm. Officers were supposed to participate in rank and file projects of this kind but I had no way of knowing how much was token work and how much realistic practice.

My stay at the tank school was cut short by a phone message which called me back to Peking for another interview with Chou En-lai.* The day after the interview I went with Colonel Li Hsin-kung and Captain Kuo Kung to visit an infantry regiment stationed about ninety miles east of Peking. We drove on a narrow macadam road that skirted the Peking-Gulf canal and in about three hours reached the suburbs of Tientsin. En route, I briefed myself with information available on the People's Liberation Army.

Until 1950 the P.L.A. remained essentially an army of irregulars, chiefly dependent on captured American and Japanese equipment.

*See note, page 113.

In its ranks were many ex-Nationalist troops, still poorly indoc-trinated and assimilated. The Korean War was a baptismal en-counter with a first-class Western army equipped with the latest weapons, which taught China many lessons. Obsolete equipment and ex-Nationalist troops were expended. Material losses were made up by Russia while the P.L.A.'s most reliable cadres were trained in modern technique and re-equipped with up-to-date weapons. Manchurian war industry and transport were also restored by Russian wartime aid, the exact amount of which remained un-known. East European estimates given to me placed it as high as two billion dollars.

By 1960 China's armed forces had their own high-priority mili-tary industries which maintained the supply and modernization of basic weapons of conventional warfare. The pre-Korean army de-pended largely on volunteers. Conscription began during the crisis and was regularized in 1954. Officially, today's regular army totaled about 2,500,000; foreign military observers believed it did not much exceed that. The air force was estimated at a quarter of a million and naval personnel at about the same. All citizens between eighteen and forty were now subject to conscription, and in addi-tion a reserve of many millions of 'citizen militiamen' was being built up. Army service was for three years, air force four years, and navy five.

Conscripts for the regular armed forces did not, I was told by Chinese officers at Fangshun, exceed one in twelve of the eighteen to twenty-five group. Between five and six million young men reached eighteen each year; the army chose its conscripts from the pick of the physically fit, literate, and otherwise mentally qualified. There were many advantages of military service in China for both the soldier and his family. The 'selected' were genuinely envied and congratulated by their native villages and service was regarded as an honor, not a sacrifice. The army was popular and officers were held in a kind of awe which in the U.S.A. is reserved only for head-waiters, church trustees, Elizabeth Taylor and the *Wall Street Journal*.

Just outside the headquarters of the 196th Division at Fangshun we passed a long caravan of rubber-tired, wheat-laden army wagons pulled by horses boosted by many windmills – the only time I saw use of the old land sails in China; evidently motorization of supply was still far from complete. Then we were surrounded by broad fields ribbed by settlements of the new motel-like barracks, and cottages where officers lived with their families. In a moment we entered the outer gates of the reservation and were met by the division commandant, and by Colonel Li Yung-kuei, commander of the 587th Infantry Regiment. Colonel Li took over my tour and acted as host.

The 196th Division consisted of 'not over 12,000 men' organized as follows: regiments: 3 infantry, 1 artillery, 1 tank; battalions: 1 anti-tank, 1 medical, 1 engineers, 1 signal: special companies: 1 reconnaissance, 1 anti-gas, 1 chemical warfare, 1 vehicle training, 1 artillery command; 1 training group.

This is a regular division. China had experimented with separate tank and artillery commands but returned to divisional integration. The navy and air force were also under unified top army command, which was directly responsible for weapons concentration on the corps level.

Item 1. By a rotational system the division was cultivating about 1,700 acres of land and had built a reservoir stocked with ten million fish. Everybody in the division was 'normally' required to work one month a year in the fields, and one month in army shops or on state construction projects. All the vegetables and meat and 'part of the grain' consumed by the division was produced by its own labor, with the help of a few thousand full-time resident peasant families.

Item 2. The guaranteed daily food allowance was 3,200 to 3,400 calories per man, or about one third more than the basic food ration over the country as a whole. This included 1·6 pounds of grain products and 1·6 pounds of vegetables per day but only half a pound of meat and six grams of oil per month. The average recruit weighed 120 pounds on admission and had gained ten to twenty pounds on his separation. Soldiers averaged 5 ft 7 in. in height (well above the Chinese mean), six-footers were common, and general physical condition seemed equal to Western standards. If their food consumption was typical, my calculation shows that between four and five hundred thousand acres were required to produce food adequate to supply the armed forces.

Item 3. Marshals and generals were the highest paid of government employees.* The monthly pay scale given to me may be converted into U.S. dollars as follows: privates started at $2·50; corporals got $4; platoon leaders, $5; second lieutenants, $20; first lieutenants, $24; captains, $29–$33; majors, $39–$44; lieutenant colonels, $51–$60; colonels, $62–$64; senior colonels, $62–$84; lieutenant generals, $144–$160; full generals, $192–$236; marshals of the army, $360–$400. All food, uniforms, quarters and transportation expenses were, of course, provided gratis, and general officers had the use of a car. This was no longer the egalitarian army of guerrilla days, and yet the tradition was kept alive when officers did their annual month in the rank and file.

Item 4. There wasn't a fall-out shelter in all of Fangshun – nor in all China as far as I could learn. The People's Republic was as backward as Europe in this respect.

For two hours I questioned four husky soldiers (eighteen to twenty), and a sergeant of twenty-five. I asked each about his background and education and then asked collectively about army training and their ambitions. They were all from poor peasant families, parents illiterate; they themselves had all been to primary schools. They were 'happy' to be chosen for the army; 'satisfied' that their families were being well cared for in the communes; 'grateful' to be getting 'better' education (political, technical and cultural) than they would have got at home; and enjoyed sports and were certain that 'socialism is good'. All had memories of hunger and poverty in their childhood. I asked one how he explained his fine white teeth if he had been undernourished. (They all had good teeth.) What had he eaten as a child? 'Kaoliang'; that was all he remembered. Sons of ex-landlords were not accepted by the army, I learned, but there was no bar against sons of ex-capitalists. Women were not recruited for combat training except

---

*(1970) All officer titles, from marshal down, were abolished in 1962, epaulets and other marks of distinction were removed, and unit leaders became known merely as 'commanders', as in the preliberation Red Army. Differentiations in pay and privileges were greatly reduced in Defense Minister Lin Piao's army reforms. The army became a 'great school for the teaching of Mao Tse-tung thought', in preparation for its leading role in completing the Great Proletarian Cultural Revolution, 1966–9. See Preface.

as parachutists (why, I don't know) but a few were used in auxiliary tasks, like W.A.C.s.

'Do any of you gamble?'

They did not understand the term. The interpreter gave an elaborate explanation. Yes, they played cards, but they had never heard of playing for money.

'I know you may not believe that,' said Colonel Li Hsin-kung, the Foreign Office liaison, who was more sophisticated than anyone there. He smiled. 'I saw American soldiers gambling when I was at the Panmunjon truce talks. Your officers' drivers spent their waiting time throwing dice and gambling for money. When one of them lost he would swear and get angry and red in the face. Our drivers watched them and couldn't understand but thought it very funny. I explained that it was different in the American army from our army. The American soldier is worried about his future security so he tries to get together a lot of money, hoping to buy a small business when he gets home. In our army every man is guaranteed good employment when he leaves.'

I could not help laughing at the picture he drew but I said that American soldiers I knew would probably say they'd prefer to take their chances with the dice. 'Isn't a little sideline gambling to be expected inside the bigger gamble of the combat zone itself?' I ventured. A good commander never gambles with the lives of his men, I was reminded in fine copy-book phraseology. Communist leaders are not gamblers or adventurers, like monopoly capitalists.

'What about the woman problem?' I asked. It existed in all armies I had seen, including the Russian. Here also the soldiers mingled with the people – in the fields and at entertainments. (Chinese didn't use the old word *ping*, or 'soldier', any more; the P.L.A. had only *chan-shih*, or 'fighters'.) What happened if a soldier got a local girl 'in trouble'?

My question elicited stunned silence. The green youths looked genuinely puzzled. The officers exchanged glances as if something indecent had happened.

It was Colonel Li, smiling but serious, who again had the answer:

'You may find this hard to believe, too, but that is no problem with us. A man is free to marry at twenty.* Before that he is kept

*See note, page 252.

too busy to think about it. General opinion is very strongly against anyone playing with women. In our army men are taught a stern moral code; we still follow the "Eight Rules of Good Behavior Among the People" which you knew in the old Red Army.* A man wants to marry a pure woman, he doesn't want to have someone else spoil his wife. An army with socialist ideals won't dirty its own nest. I won't say it never has happened but it really is very rare.' He turned to the regimental commander, who added stiffly : 'We have simply never had a case of the kind in the five years I've been here.'

A situation which I was more convinced the young soldiers had never heard of was 'conscientious objection'. An officer took a long time to explain 'C.O.' to them. I heard him saying that this was something that used to happen in the old Kuomintang armies as well as in the United States. The men exchanged glances, in some awe, as if to ask each other whether the American army could really be as bad as that.

I asked whether they had ever heard the expression, 'My country, may it always be right, but right or wrong – my country.' This took plenty of explanation, too. Then I said : 'Could you imagine your country being wrong? Would you still fight for it?'

Here was something that obviously had never arisen in political discussions or 'self-criticism' meetings between men and officers. They were all struck absolutely dumb. How could Mao Tse-tung, the party and the army leadership ever be wrong in any war? China would never start a war but China would always destroy any invader. To try to explain that a C.O. would not fight for his country even if he believed it to be 'right' –? It was inconceivable.

*The Eight Rules (revised since Kiangsi days) were now : speak politely; pay fairly for what you buy; return everything you borrow; pay for anything you damage; don't strike or swear at people; don't damage crops; don't take liberties with women; don't ill-treat captives. They were still a popular army song.

The Family: Fact and Fancy

ON the long midnight drive back to Peking I rode in a new Simca sedan with Colonel Li Hsin-kung. We had dined well and had drunk a number of cups of *mao-t'ai* in apolitical toasts to peace, to the brotherhood of man, to the friendship of the Chinese and American peoples, and to the 'restoration of normal relations between countries'. *Mao-t'ai* is a rice brandy with a strong sting, and the best quality comes from Kweichow; sealed in attractive earthen jugs, it was in growing demand abroad. Mellowed as we were by the wine or by the bright moonlit autumn night, our conversation took a personal turn.

'How many children do you have?'

'Five – four girls and a son.'

'The son was No. 5, I suppose?'

Li nodded and grinned with some embarrassment at this revelation of ancestral atavisms. 'How many children have you?'

'A boy and a girl.'

'That's just ideal!' he exclaimed, holding up his right thumb. 'You're very lucky. I'd have stopped right there if the boy had come earlier.'

'Are you having any more?'

'No more! We have adopted absolutely foolproof precautions,' he said. 'Double insurance.'

Not unimpressive in his well-tailored uniform, with braided epaulets, Li looked his role of diplomatic military attaché. He was proud of his guerrilla past. Born into a rich peasant family of Shansi, he had enlisted in the Eighth Route Army in 1937, when he was seventeen. From 1938 to 1940 he studied at the 'Anti-Japanese College' in Yenan; afterward he joined the staff of General Nieh Jung-chen.

'My family married me when I was sixteen, to a woman fourteen years older than I. It was a kind of swindle. The woman was my cousin by marriage and her mother, my aunt, had land and money. This aunt wanted her daughter married off to someone she could control; she was afraid of fortune hunters. She thought her daughter would be safe with me and my mother thought it would be a good thing for our family, financially. I refused to live with this wife. The marriage was one of the reasons I left school and joined the guerrillas. After the war I married a woman of my own choice, a teacher at Tsing Hua University. It has been very successful.'

'Suppose it were not a success, would you get a divorce?'

'How could it fail? We knew each other, we chose each other of our free will, we were not oppressed. Of course it had to be a success.' It was difficult to get a well-trained Chinese Communist to answer a question which hypothesized a situation he knew to be the incorrect outcome of reform.

'Arranged marriages existed in the past because of social and economic oppression,' he explained. 'Parents betrothed daughters at the earliest opportunity rather than risk seeing them end up as spinsters. Now girls legally marry only at eighteen and do not rush into marriage until they know their own minds. Poor peasants formerly sold their daughters to pay off debts to landlords or to raise cash. It happened many times in my own town. If parents waited too long to betroth their daughters then the landlords sometimes claimed first rights. After that, who would marry them? Yet to sell them as concubines might be better than having them go into prostitution. Marriages to strike a good bargain, to acquire land, to pay off debts, to gain family position, to buy sons out of the army, without consulting the feelings of the betrothed, with great differences in ages and temperaments – this is what caused misery in the family. Now we don't have any of that.'

'Yet a man might still fall in love with another woman. Could he divorce his wife?'

Li was silent for a moment before he answered quite seriously: 'Legally it is possible to dissolve any marriage by mutual request. If there are children and there is no mutual consent it is another matter. The kind of divorce you mention would be capricious and not liked. I know it sometimes happens but it is very rare. It is like adultery and premarital sex. You asked about that earlier. These things do happen but I have not experienced a case among comrades personally known to me.'

'I remember hearing Westerners in China in the past say that early betrothals and early marriages prevented homosexual and other sex deviations and were intended to do so. What about that?'

'There are fewer unmarried men and women now than before. Since women are not treated as property or commodities, since everyone can afford a wife, everyone can get married. For a man not to be married is looked upon as abnormal. People feel sorry for him and try to help him find a wife. This is a new society with a new moral code. We are all influenced by socialist ideals. We are against bourgeois decadence of all kinds.'

'To have no posterity was the greatest of all filial sins, according to Mencius,' I reminded Li. 'Everyone used to approve if a man with a barren wife took a concubine or a second wife, and often his first wife would be the one to suggest it. Is that a justification for divorce?'

Li squirmed uneasily. 'We Communists look upon children from a Marxist point of view – not as a man's personal property but as wards of society as a whole. To love children one need not bear them; we love others' children as we love our own. Discarding a wife because she does not bear offspring is not a good reason for divorce.' I knew childless party people whose marriages had lasted for years – among them, Chou En-lai and Teng Ying-ch'ao. Yet Li was aware of the contradictions in his own practice; had not that personal son been a matter of necessity for him? The instinct to maintain the patrilineal descent was still strong among both party and nonparty people.

Since the introduction of the reformed marriage law in 1952 much had been said abroad about the Chinese Communists 'breaking up families' and 'destroying the fine old family system'. In a very real sense the whole Chinese revolution, beginning in the nineteenth century, had been a revolt of sons against fathers – against various evils traced to patriarchal tyranny and attributed to 'Confucian ancestral worship'. (There is little evidence that Confucius himself was interested in the so-called joint family.) Chinese Communists, like Marxists everywhere, accepted Engels' classical analysis of the origins of the family, seen as a basic production unit, with both matriarchal and patriarchal power historically founded on ownership and control of the means of production. To say that the Communist aim was to destroy the stem family or the conjugal family or to 'separate husbands and wives' was, however, akin to folklore about 'common wives' in Russia. Communists did teach that the individual owes his first loyalty to society as a whole (to the state and the party), as Colonel Li said. They were by no means the first to reject ancient codes of filial rites and a joint family system which disintegrated long before 1949.

In *My Country and My People*, Dr Lin Yutang criticized family cultists for the absence of Chinese civic pride, indifference to the sufferings of others, bribery and nepotism. 'Seen in modern eyes,' he wrote, 'Confucianism omitted from the social relationships man's social obligations toward the stranger, and great and catastrophic was the omission. ... In the end, as it worked out, the family became a walled castle outside of which everything was legitimate loot.' The American-educated sociologist H. D. Fong concluded that the 'walled castle' was 'one of the most serious obstacles to industrialization'.[1]

Anyone who wishes to understand the 'fine old family system' as it actually appeared to Chinese even half a century ago should read Pa Chin's shattering descriptions of its tyrannies and stupidities in his novel, *The Family*.[2] Even the medieval classical family novel, *Dream of the Red Chamber*, depicts heroines who so abhorred the conventional marriage relationship that they preferred to be nuns, while in the nineteenth century a 'girls' revolt' against family-arranged matches became so widespread that the government was obliged to set up separate homes for virgins who refused such contracts.[3]

Historically, China had three basic types of families: the conjugal or nuclear family of husband, wife and children, if any; the stem family, which consisted of parents, their own unmarried children, and no more than one married son and his wife and children; and the joint family, of parents, their unmarried children, several married sons and their wives and children. In a few enlarged joint families a fourth or even a fifth generation, and sometimes one other fraternal stem family's descendants, might live under a single patriarchal rule or that of an eldest surviving son.

The enlarged joint family practically disappeared in China two thousand years ago, at the time generally reckoned as the end of the true feudal period, when the Ch'in state abolished the nobility, broke up the great estates, and divided the land among the tillers. Thereafter, although wealthy landed families arose again and tended to be larger than poor ones, 'the family for the overwhelming majority was relatively small', usually five or six persons and seldom more than eight living in a household corresponding to the conjugal or stem family.[4]

The conjugal family was now the commonest form in China, as in most countries; there were also very many stem families. Close extrafamilial ties existed between kinfolk in villages, of course. Formerly a loose clan organization was maintained by the gentry, who exploited their control of ancestral temples (now disappearing) as a means of autocratic authority. Even now, in thousands of Chinese villages named after a distant common progenitor (among the some 470 'old families'), a majority of the citizens might have the same surname although they had long since lost track of their direct blood ties. No doubt these ancestral clan traditions were often effective in preserving cultural cohesion and continuity in times of catastrophe and foreign conquest, but their parochial virtues weakened and dissolved under the impact of capitalism and machine invasion and had to be superseded by broader concepts of solidarity.

The entire revolutionary process since 1911 had vastly raised the horizon of political consciousness for the half-billion people now dwelling in the rural areas. Remembering the reforms of the T'ai-p'ing Rebellion we know that efforts to end parental despotism, to liberate women, and to replace Confucian concepts with higher-than-family loyalties had been embattled slogans a century before the Communists appeared on the scene. The first modern civil code to embody such aims was promulgated by the Kuomintang régime, in 1931, when the whole legal structure of the family was nominally altered. Ancestral worship was abolished, along with male authority and male worship; equality in property rights, inheritance and divorce were promised to women. As with many Kuomintang decrees, however, 'The new legislation ... had little actual effect on the traditional family system because the laws remained largely on paper', according to reflections which appear in *China*, a symposium by Chinese and American scholars.[5]

The basic family law (called the marriage law) of the People's Republic had gone much further and had been energetically, if not completely, enforced. It did not at all abolish the family but rather explicitly defined its basis in a marriage contract freely made between individuals whose equality of rights as citizens was guaranteed. The law banned arranged marriages and matchmakers, concubinage, bigamy, child betrothal, and sale of daughters and wives. Spouses shared ownership and management of family property, and responsibility for the care and support of their children as well as aging parents. This law thus sanctioned both the conjugal and the stem family household.

The right to divorce was guaranteed both parties; vigorous campaigns to encourage its use by discontented women resulted in a total of 409,000 divorces in 1951 – a rate almost one third as high as that in the United States. Violent reactions among some rejected spouses were strongly suggested in a government report, in 1952, that between seventy and eighty thousand people were killed or committed suicide in a single year in China over marriage difficulties.[6] The party propaganda campaign to encourage divorce abruptly ended. In recent years the rate had greatly declined and – as Li's comments indicate – divorce was now distinctly unfashionable among the party élite.

More important than any mere law in changing the marriage relationship was the distribution of land equally among men and women. Following that, collectivization deprived the male of opportunities to use ownership as a means of oppression or exploitation. Women's equality in the right to education and equal pay for equal work further established their 'independence'. Among young people the evidence of a new mutual respect was everywhere apparent.

A new usage which indicated change in status and feeling between men and women was the word *ai-jen*. It had replaced the exalted *fu-jen*, *t'ai-t'ai*, etc., formerly correct when a member of the gentry referred to another person's wife, as well as such terms as *lao-p'o*, meaning 'old stick', when a person hypocritically disclaimed any distinction in his own wife. *Ai-jen* means 'beloved'. It was now nearly universal among young people when either spouse spoke of the other. Old Communists introduced it, as it had long been common usage among the leaders. 'Where is your beloved, Comrade Mao?' was perfectly acceptable – though a bit shocking to the 'old sticks'.

Few who saw China today doubted that the régime's success in deeply involving women in all the nation's work and social life had enormously enriched it culturally as well as economically. All these factors, combined with the general economic and social integration of rural and urban life after industrialization by socialist means, had virtually ended any surviving idealization of 'the family system'. In politics the evils attributed to that system – nepotism, bribery and embezzlement – had not entirely disappeared, as constant rectifications had shown. But current vigilance was unprecedented and deviations among senior officials were virtually unheard of, whereas they formerly provided the worst examples. Chicanery is practically impossible in a state where money cannot buy lawyers, and so is the sale of office. It seemed a real handicap rather than an advantage to be the sibling of a high official, and none achieved prominence because of family connections. Even Chou En-lai refused to interfere to save his obscure older brother's father-in-law from village prosecution and punishment as an alleged oppressive landlord.

Winding up our conversation, on the way back to Peking, the young army officer remarked: 'For China, government by the family system ended with Chiang Kai-shek. Chiang and all his in-laws and sworn blood brothers – the Kungs, the Soongs, the Chens – ruled by the feudal codes of family first. They became millionaires by robbing poor families also named Kung, Soong and Chen. China is through with family-system government.'

Back in the Hsin Ch'ao hotel I met some Canadian visitors, among whom was the distinguished child psychiatrist, Dr Denis Lazure, of the University of Montreal. During his numerous visits to Chinese schools, nurseries, crèches, hospitals, public parks, private homes and communes, Dr Lazure was making a special study of changes in child attitudes toward the family and state as a result of twelve years of revolutionary orientation. He was able to conduct thematic apperception tests (T.A.T.) on a number of children aged ten to sixteen. He questioned them individually about their values, actions, dreams, memories, choices, anxieties, passions, sentiments and wishes. I need not here intrude a layman's interpretation of his arresting discoveries, which are now medical literature.[7] A mere sampling of his observations may at least help fill in the pattern of youthful thinking in China which replaced overdependence on the family.

On the basis of 'most frequent answers' to his questions, Dr Lazure found that 'adolescents seem to place particular value on patriotism, diligence in their studies and in their work in general, altruism, and accepting constructive criticism.' Among 'best acts' they could perform, typical were to 'help an old person carry his packages', 'to return a lost article to police' and 'to contribute to the success of the agricultural plan by growing a garden'. As for sins, 'It is impossible for a Pioneer or a good student to commit a bad act', the psychiatrist was repeatedly told, until he conceded a widespread 'unconscious denial of all unacceptable behavior' which 'astonishes most Western visitors to China'.

Among fifteen subjects he questioned individually only two admitted having any 'feelings of sadness'. One, a girl, said, 'I feel sad when one of the leaders of our country or another socialist country dies.' A boy of sixteen reported a dream in which he was playing 'but the next morning I was too tired and got up too late for school. I was very sad.' Worries? 'All subjects replied that they had none.' Typical was the answer of a girl of thirteen, who said: 'I have no fear or worry. I know that Chairman Mao and the Party are concerned with my welfare and can protect me against any danger.' Hostility normally directed against parents or the environment seemed to Dr Lazure to have been successfully transferred and projected against capitalism and American imperialism, as 'symbols of aggression and cruelty'. There also 'seems to be a remarkable capacity in these subjects to sublimate their aggressive impulses in hard work and for personal improvement and for advancement of the country'. Parental figures 'are constantly perceived as affectionate and supportive, in marked contrast to the T.A.T.'s of North American adolescents'.

What Dr Lazure described as his 'most significant conclusion' about Chinese youth was that 'their leaders have very effectively accomplished the revolution of transferring the emotional investment formerly reserved for the family to society as a whole and to the role which the individual will play in building his society. ... The family as an institution has certainly lost importance in all socialist countries based on the Russian model but this is even more true in China. ...' On the other hand Dr Lazure dismissed the belief that 'the mass exodus of women to the factories and fields' was a 'principal factor in weakening family ties'. He observed that the mother was now 'able to devote her time entirely to her children when she arrives home from work. ...

'The child and the teenager appear to be more concerned with socio-political themes than with conflicts which would exist in their relationship with their parents.' There seemed 'little variation in the theme frequency of psychotic conditions' as compared to the West, but there was, paradoxically, 'probably a marked decrease in psycho-neuroses, character disorders, and anti-social behavior'.

A note of warning. No one should take adolescents' claims that they have 'no problems and no worries' at face value nor imagine that China 'has achieved a utopia' for them. 'It is more realistic,' Dr Lazure emphasized, 'to presume that the State has been highly successful in creating an image of happy youth and that the young people, in their desire to conform, have accepted that illusion.'* Their goals and ambitions showed a 'remarkable diversity of choices' of future careers but it should not be supposed that they were any less outer-directed than the status-seeking sons of Madison Avenue. Dr Lazure observed that it was precisely 'in these countries, China and the United States, that the adolescent of today experiences the strongest pressures toward conformity. For the American teenager the norms of the peer-groups are all-compelling, while the young Chinese wants at any price to be identified with the norms of the Five Year Plan and the Party slogans.'

* (1970) A renewal of Dr Lazure's inquiry would be of interest following the Great Proletarian Cultural Revolution, when youth was taught that 'to rebel [against revisionist authority] is justified'. As the instruction came down from Mao, the unrivaled father image of the land, joining the rebellious Red Guards may not, in fact, have fundamentally shaken the 'desire to conform'.

Medical History, Personal
and Otherwise

I HAD four occasions to make some use of Chinese medical facilities. On my arrival at the Peking airport I discovered that my immunization card was missing; apparently it had not been returned with my passport in Moscow. I signed an affidavit declaring that I had received all necessary inoculations; they were repeated at the airport by a Chinese doctor, and in twenty minutes I had a new certificate. Charge, one yuan, or forty cents.

In Changchun, Manchuria, I consulted a hotel physician about an eye infection which looked like possible trachoma. He diagnosed it as conjunctivitis but as he was only a 'middle doctor' he called in a neighborhood specialist. She quickly and efficiently confirmed his diagnosis, dressed the eye, provided me with a bathing solution, and left within ten minutes. Charge, twenty cents. She had no time to stay for a cup of tea because she was due at a clinic where 'fifty people' awaited her. My eye was well in two days.

In Peking I had a recurrence of a latent infection, the history of which traced to that same city far back in 1936. I had had a small kidney stone removed cystoscopically at the Peking Union Medical College. The operation was a success but postoperative treatment was inadequate and it took months to cure an infection. Ever since then there had been recurrences under conditions of extreme fatigue. On my return from Manchuria the bug made a particularly painful reappearance. I went back to the old P U M C, now part of the Peking Medical Institute. When I entered the office of the chief urologist he had before him a file of my complete medical history to 1937, the year I had left Peking. He reminded me of a lot of complaints that I had forgotten and of some false alarms, including suspected T.B. on my first consultation there, in 1929! He then gave me a thorough examination, complete X-rays on the latest Chinese machines, found nothing serious, prescribed some antibiotics, and I was well again in a few days. Fees, $2·00, standard rates for the noninsured.

While visiting Peking's Chest Surgery Hospital, a new and ultra-modern institution, which trains two hundred internes a year and has American-educated surgeons among its directors, I discovered a small dental clinic in one of its ten wards. The equipment was up-to-date ('jet-powered' drills), all made in China. I sat down in a chair and asked a doctor to take a location-shot picture of me. A young dentist not only posed with me but took advantage of the time to look over my mouth; to his satisfaction he found trouble between two back teeth. He X-rayed me and made an appointment. I returned and he did a difficult excavation of a tiny needle-like cavity that ran to the very edge of the root canal. When I had to ask for novocaine he was astonished. I heard him say to the nurse : 'These foreigners can't stand the slightest pain. No Chinese would feel that !' He completed the work expertly and I have had no trouble since. Charge, $1·00, at standard rates.

The reader now has my medical history up to my departure from China and, I am happy to add, up to this writing. As a nonpatient I visited a dozen other large modern hospitals in or near Changchun, Shanghai, Paotou, Wuhan, Kunming and Chungking, as well as rural health stations and clinics beyond recall. I had an unusual experience at the new and large (900 beds; 3,800 students) T'ung Chi Medical College and Hospital in Hankow. There I watched, through glass theater ceilings, five operations going on simultaneously, three of them for cancer of the esophagus. One was conducted by a woman surgeon with four women assistants.

The rate of death in childbirth had been reduced to about thirty-two per thousand in urban China, according to the head of the pediatrics department at T'ung Chi, where the rate was 'under twenty'. (It is much higher over the nation as a whole.) Obstetrics facilities and maternity care there appeared to be almost as good as at Doctors Hospital in New York, where my own children were born. Control of preventable and communicable diseases combined with state protection and care of mothers had sharply reduced the adult death rate while increasing live births. Critics who yesterday condemned backward China as shamefully indifferent to excessive mortality now expressed concern that too many Chinese go on living.

Nine British doctors who toured China in 1957 largely confirmed basic Chinese claims in public health. Dr T. T. Fox, distinguished editor of *Lancet*, considered the Chinese even then ahead of British public health work in certain aspects of 'mass line' effort. In one area, for example, infant mortality had been reduced to twenty-two per thousand births, as contrasted with about twenty-five in London.[1] Detailed evidence was also reported by American doctors at an American Association for the Advancement of Science symposium. Using both his personal knowledge of China and an examination of data from foreign doctors recently there, as well as research in specialized medical journals of China (twenty-five of 'major importance'), a senior surgeon of the U.S. Public Health Service, Dr William Y. Chen, summarized for the symposium the staggering dimensions of the historical problems faced by the Communists as well as some results of their efforts.

'Before the Communist régime took control ... in 1949,' writes this authority, 'medical and public health organizations were still in their infancy and far below modern standards. Poverty and disease were the rule.'[2] Four million people a year died from 'infectious and parasitic diseases' and sixty million people required 'facilities for daily treatment'. The scope of the problem was indicated by Dr Chen's estimate of China's needs at what he considered 'a minimum standard' of one doctor for 1,500 people and five hospital beds for 1,000 persons. *That would mean 466,000 doctors and 3,500,000 beds for China's population.*

'The total number of scientifically trained doctors [in 1949] was estimated to be only 12,000; for about 500 hospitals, the country was only capable of producing 500 medical graduates per year ...' and it had a total of 71,000 hospital beds.

'Because eighty-four percent of the total population in the rural area was incapable of paying for private medical care, the only early solution of such a tragedy was believed to be a system of state (or socialized) medicine.' That opinion was held by leading Chinese doctors as early as 1937,[3] and 'the idea of the county health centre system was planned, shaped and conducted mostly by American-trained doctors; many of them are now still living in China and, in fact, form the backbone of China's medical and health structure.'

Dr Chen does not understate the case when he says that 'the Communists were desperately in need of medical man power'. He goes on to report their use of the '370,000' (today 500,000) traditional (herbalist) Chinese doctors, as Dr Hatem has already explained. At the same time they emphasized 'quantity rather than quality' in the medical colleges. Dr Chen reports 43,000 graduates from higher medical colleges in the first ten years and 153,000 'graduates from secondary medical schools and secondary public health schools, which provided only two to three years of medical training'. (Ministry of Health records for 1959 showed 48,474 medical college graduates and 263,000 'middle doctors' with 'four years' of medical training. By 1960 there were 1,200 hospitals with 467,000 beds, as distinct from about 200,000 clinics and health stations in the rural communes.[4]) Dr Chen described in detail rural health facilities which now fulfilled the county health center system about as originally planned by the American-trained doctors.

Hospital beds and doctors qualified in Western terms thus increased four to five times in ten years. This is far below Dr Chen's 'minimum standard', but he reports 'greater strides in the improvement of sanitation, health education, and prevention [work] ...

The mortality rate of tuberculosis has also dropped rapidly. For example, T.B. declined from 230 per 100,000 in 1949 to forty-six per 100,000 in 1958 in Peking. Syphilis and gonorrhea are no longer menaces to health due to the proper practice of personal hygiene and effective treatment. ... Extensive medical and industrial health work has been done to check the widely prevalent silicosis, and much progress in its diagnosis and treatment has been related. ...

Having been successful in combating infectious and parasitic diseases the Communists have also realized the importance of preventing and controlling chronic diseases. ... Mass detection of cancer, especially of the uterus and cervix, oesophagus and nasopharangeal cavity, was started in 1958 ...

British medical reports are informative on results of 'the successful control of flies, the litterless streets and fanatical household cleanliness'. Professor Brian Maegraith, dean of the Liverpool School of Tropical Medicine, found that they were 'having a profound effect on the spread of gastro-intestinal infections'. He described the mass work of village health committees and street sanitation and hygiene enforcement much along lines already mentioned by Dr Hatem. A single paragraph may be particularly arresting to anyone who knew the squalor of rural China of the past. Dr Maegraith says:

One further method of control [of schistosome snails], which goes on all the time, illustrates the degree of general cooperation obtained [from the people]. Until artificial fertilizers can be developed on a big enough scale, human excreta remains the cheapest and most valuable manure. Fortunately the dangerous schistosome eggs do not live long if left in faeces without contact with water. Storage thus renders the material non-infective. Thanks to skillful propaganda, this essential conservation of night soil is becoming an economic and social fact. Each family now has its own privy, a portable gaily-colored pot. Every morning the contents are poured into large communal earthenware containers, which are sealed when full and left for the appropriate time necessary for the ammonia generated to kill the eggs, after which the faeces are safe for use in the fields. The collection of family night soil is assured by paying the family for it pro-rata, so many cents a day per person, according to age. This scheme is also being used for the control of water pollution by fishermen, for each boat now has its own collecting pot, which is regarded as a source of income.[5]

38

From John D. to Acupuncture

A GENERATION ago the Rockefeller Foundation established the Peking Union Medical College and brought over a small staff of American doctors and teachers to work in its new Chinese-roofed buildings off Morrison Street. John D. Rockefeller had various reasons for setting up his foundation, but he might have said the heck with it and just let the Treasury Department collect inheritance taxes on his estate if he had known that Chinese Communists, acupuncture and moxibustion were to end up as his beneficiaries. Traditional Chinese medicine was looked upon by the founders of the PUMC in much the same way missionaries regarded Confucian rites as paganism.

I learned something about the renaissance in the Chinese empirical sciences when I returned to the PUMC for a long inspection tour and discussion with its vice-director, Dr Hsu Hung-t'u, and his staff. Dr Hsu was a small, dynamic, cheerful man, who continually rubbed his head and grinned, exposing some missing teeth, whenever he was perplexed. He had graduated from the old Medical College of Peking National University and was now in his fifties; his professional qualifications were probably inferior to those of many of the younger doctors on his staff. He indicated quite frankly that his duties as staff administrator were more political than professional.

The PUMC was still an important hospital. It was now a branch of the large China Medical College, one of ten divisions of the Academy of Medical Sciences. All the institutes had provincial branches. Like the other hospitals and medical colleges in China, they were under the general administration of the Academy of Medical Sciences, which was itself part of the national Academy of Sciences or Academia Sinica.

Since 1958 most medical colleges had offered six- and eight-year courses, but the majority of students were still graduated as 'secondary doctors' after four years. This would continue as long as the emergency demand existed in public health and hygiene work. Secondary doctors took spare-time courses and might later return for advanced academic work. The China Medical College (about 3,600 students) and some provincial affiliates now offered eight-year courses only : three years in basic sciences; two years in basic medicine; two years in clinical medicine, including Chinese medicine; and one year in field work. Russian and English were required subjects for all medical students. As in other professions, medical and pre-medical students had to do their 'down on the farm' period. Each year they spent two months in the villages assisting rural medical workers; they ate and lived as peasants did.*

The former PUMC, now Peking Hospital, was not a college any more but a large polyclinic combined with an institute of gynecology and pediatrics. New buildings had doubled the number of beds (560) but there was little more room for expansion. Newer hospitals and institutes were centered in the suburbs and around the headquarters of the Academy of Sciences. About one third of the doctors of Peking Hospital had been educated under the American PUMC administration. The whole staff consisted of about 250 doctors, nearly half of whom were women.

At its peak the PUMC used to handle 100,000 patients a year, according to Dr Hsu. It was then the only first-class hospital in all North China. Now this hospital was 'processing' 500,000 people annually. That was nearly one in fourteen of the Peking population, I pointed out. Dr Hsu explained that it was 100 percent of Tung Hua, the only district for which the hospital was now responsible. Doctors here worked in close collaboration with neigh-

*(1970) During the Great Proletarian Cultural Revolution (1966–9) Mao Tse-tung insisted on extending medical services to the remote hinterland. He said that urban areas were getting 85 percent of the benefit of modern medical facilities. A system of 'peasant doctors' was set up. Hygienists were trained for short periods in district or county hospitals to serve as simple therapists; to diagnose and care for common diseases, burns, accidents, etc. They were then returned to the commune farms from which they were recruited. Integrated with the professional medical staffs and hospitals, they performed essential liaison and first-aid functions which helped compensate for an absence of skilled personnel.

borhood street committee health and sanitation teams, and 'processing' did not necessarily mean treatment.

Each block of residents elected persons to organize and carry out the daily removal of garbage and refuse, to keep sidewalks and pavements swept, and to supervise sanitation and hygiene routine in dining rooms, nurseries, schools, and so on. Under the supervision of the municipal health authorities these teams also co-operated in immunization work of all kinds, and periodic pest-clearance drives. Each family was required to report all illnesses to these street teams, which diagnosed where possible, and arranged for clinical examination or hospitalization. Public health was supervised in this way by hospitals in different districts of the city. The same system had been built up around county hospitals and beneath them were the rural district centers, and commune, pro-duction-brigade and village health teams.

'How much has this cut down on hospital efficiency?'

'If we look at it only from a technological standpoint,' answered Dr Hsu, 'the level is lower. That is, the few specialists might be better equipped than our present average. If we consider the total number of patients handled and the average level of community health or the recovery rate, it is much better. In the past the re-covery rate of hospitalized patients was less than thirty percent. Now it is above eighty-two percent. Of course we are taking in many more patients than formerly and many patients who would never have been admitted.'

Hospitalization and medical care were free for those with full union sickness insurance. Emergency patients were admitted at once. Other cases were registered through street committees or the patient's employing organizations. For private patients ward beds cost a yuan a day – and wards I saw were extremely crowded. Dr Hsu said, for example, that an appendicitis operation and hospital-ization averaged twenty to thirty yuan. A childbirth averaged five yuan; if difficult enough to require a week's hospitalization it would be fifteen yuan. These fees were higher than prevailing rural rates. Medicines here as everywhere were sold at cost or below cost: penicillin and antibiotic preparations, for instance, at ten to twenty cents a prescription. But doctors' salaries were also low. The assis-tant chief of surgery, Fei Li-min, an American-trained P U M C doctor, got 150 yuan (U.S. $65) a month; his wife, also a doctor, got the same.

The hospital thus offered one doctor for every 2,000 persons in the Tung Hua district, and fewer than two hospital beds per thousand. The rate was higher for Peking as a whole because of numerous smaller clinics and specialized hospitals in addition to general hospitals. Of the latter the best was probably the large (600-bed) Friendship Hospital built and staffed by the Russians for their advisory community; it had been turned over to all-Chinese personnel.

'Another reason we are able to take care of more patients,' went on Dr Hsu, 'is because we combine traditional Chinese medicine with Western practice, and because our doctors are trained in dialectical materialism.'

'How's that again?'

'Chinese medicine and a knowledge of dialectical materialism help a great deal in diagnosis and therapy.'

I learned that since 1958 all Western-trained doctors had been required to devote at least six months to the study of Chinese medicine. During my visit two department heads at the Peking Hospital had been detached from duty to attend courses in the Traditional Chinese Medical Institute.

For three hours I questioned Dr Hsu on theories of Chinese herbal medicine, acupuncture and moxibustion.* During my former residence in China I had never made a serious attempt to understand any of this; I considered it quackery, as did most foreigners. Dr Hsu reminded me that it has a written history of 2,200 years and includes thousands of volumes of medical writings, prescriptions and empirical treatments. For comment on traditional Chinese medicine we may refer again to the U.S. Public Health authority, Dr Chen. His report states:

Traditional Chinese medicine is an empirical healing art based on 4,000 years of practical experience. Its simple concept of health and

---

*'Moxibustion' is derived from a corruption of the Cantonese word *mongsa*, for Chinese wormwood (*Artemesia moxa*). The leaves of moxa are prepared in a soft woolly mass and used as a cautery for burning on the skin, as part of an ancient empirical science similar to the cauterization healing said to be still practiced in parts of Europe.

disease is the functional bodily harmony or disharmony between two forces, Yin (the negative) and Yang (the positive). Anatomically and physiologically traditional Chinese medicine has practically nothing to offer; yet the vast volumes on herbs and drugs and medical treatises recording observations of diseases are precious. The results of the use of these drugs and healing arts of acupuncture, moxibustion, massage and breathing therapy certainly have their empirical value. . . .

Acupuncture . . . consists of the introduction of hot and cold needles into the body at specific points. The needles may be either fine or coarse, short or long (from 3 cm. to 24 cm.). . . . When the needles puncture and stimulate different tissues or organs at various depths, they cause physiological reactions and thus produce healing results.[1]

Acupuncturists were now required to learn aseptic techniques and basic anatomy and science in courses comparable to those given 'secondary doctors'. They practiced only in hospitals, nearly all of which now had acupuncture specialists. Many of them used low-voltage electrically charged needles. Treatment was sometimes combined with radiotherapy. Dr Chen goes on :

The hypothesis is that stimulation from punctures is conducted from the peripheral nerves to the brain cortex and suppresses pathological irritation in the brain. Such an explanation seems to be in harmony with the Pavlovian theory of conditioned reflex.

Acupuncture has been widely used in practically all kinds of diseases ranging from surgical conditions such as appendicitis to chronic conditions such as diabetes. It is believed that it produces best results in illness of the nervous system or those of neurological origin. Good results have been reported in the treatment of facial paralysis, arthritis and eczema. One Russian physician reported that his long history of miserable arthritis was much improved by acupuncture. A doctor from India who went to China and studied acupuncture in 1958 entertained certain doubts as to its value at first. However, he believed afterwards that the integration of traditional medicine and western medicine had already accomplished remarkable success. He was also treated successfully by acupuncture for his acute sinusitis.[2]

I myself met patients in hospitals in Peking, Hankow and Dairen being treated by traditional means for appendicitis, eczema, rheumatism, sinusitis, tuberculosis, migraine headaches, bronchitis and various kinds of neurasthenia. All expressed preference for the

Chinese-style treatment and several were in satisfied convalescent stages. In Hankow I met a patient who had arrived at the hospital unconscious with what Western-trained surgeons had diagnosed as acute appendicitis. Treated by empirical medicine and acupuncture, he was being dismissed as cured – or so I was told.

Coexistence of the supposedly black art and scientific medicine side by side in modern hospitals strikes the foreigner as bizarre. At the Chest Surgery Hospital I saw a patient receiving acupuncture treatments for bronchitis. In the same hospital two heart surgeons showed me a convalescent child who had had an unusual and successful heart operation to relieve a 'tetralogy of Fallot', or blue-baby condition, involving a 'right ventricular hypertrophy, pulmonary stenosis, interventricular septal defect and overriding aorta'. The operation had required prolonged use of both an artificial heart and lung. The child told me, incidentally, that his father was a maritime worker in Dairen and that he had been sent all the way from their home at union expense. (The operation mortality rate at this new hospital was given as 4·1 percent for 1959.)

Chinese herbal medicine and acupuncture work together and herbalists were often needle men as well. Semantics renders it impossible quickly to explain Chinese medical theory, but the *yin-yang* concept of 'contradictions' is basic. The body is organic unity; illness is caused by imbalances between different organs or their extensions, and cure consists in restoring balance and harmony. This is done by relaxing 'antagonisms' among eight principal lines of tension which are: *yin-yang* (negative-positive), *piao-li* (outer-inner), *leng-je* (hot-cold) and *hsu-shih* (empty-solid).

Without getting in any deeper it may be said that the body is charted in terms of those principles and of 'life forces' of balance between them. Normally 'contradictions' of a nonantagonistic nature exist in an equilibrium. When 'disunity' (disease) occurs, one organ or set of functions has been overworked, overstimulated, injured or otherwise disturbed. The doctor's task is to restore the balance by removing the cause of the antagonism or congestion.

'Diseases have inner and outer causes,' said Dr Hsu Hung-t'u, who had got himself into a great sweat to explain this much to me. 'The higher nervous system of the brain affects the general physiology, of course. What we call *ni-ch'u chung-kuan* [anger-in-a-state-of-fury-burns] * may cause organic pains and injuries else-where. A patient may arrive complaining of pains which a Western diagnosis may show to be heart hypertension but a Chinese doctor may treat by a combination of medicine and acupuncture.

'A Western-style doctor often only asks the medical symptoms and medical history. A Chinese doctor looks upon the person as a unity subject to both outside and inside tensions. He wants to know about the person's family, his relations with his parents, whether he likes his wife, how his work goes, what his personal resentments are, where disharmony exists in his life, whether he is a native of the city or is a southerner or a northerner. All these go into diagnosis.'

'South or north? That makes a difference?'

'Yes, certain medicines "hot" for a northerner give the south-erner a "cold" reaction.'

'Such an inquiry would also have to touch upon the patient's political thought, I presume?'

'Of course – conflicts of all kinds are discussed.'

From this and subsequent conversations it became clear to me that the Chinese pathologist was something of an analyst and psychiatrist as well and that acupuncture was often used as shock therapy. Whether illnesses caused by unresolved stress or anxiety were greater in China than in the frenetic competitive system of America I do not know. Dr Chen reported that the incidence of heart hypertension – for whatever this proves – was about the same in both countries.[3] I had no statistics on neurasthenic diseases in China but the number of cases I encountered in hospitals and sanatoria seemed very high. The inner tensions caused by social pressures of the kind of system Communists were trying to create were obviously severe, outlets were few, and it is not surprising that the demand for consultations with Chinese therapists was great.

'Whether the Communists will succeed in their ambitious en-deavor to produce a new Chinese medical science by incorporating traditional medicine with modern scientific medicine only time can tell,' concluded Dr Chen. 'Whatever the outcome, its development is worthy of our constant attention.'

*The general idea, not an exact translation!

Aldous Huxley reported that 'International Congresses of Acupuncture are now convened', and that several hundred European doctors were trying to 'combine the science and art of Western medicine with the ancient science and art of Chinese acupuncture.' He wrote that among the pathological symptoms 'on which the old Chinese methods work very well' were 'various kinds of undesirable mental states – certain kinds of depression and anxiety, for example – which, being presumably related to organic derangements, disappear as soon as the normal circulation of energy is restored. Results which several years on the analyst's couch have failed to produce may be obtained, in some cases, by two or three pricks with a silver needle.'[4]

Enthusiasm for the therapeutic benefits of both acupuncture and herbalism may be kept within bounds when it is remembered that strictly Chinese medical literature offered scarcely any knowledge of such basic sciences as bacteriology, microbiology, parasitology, epidemiology, endocrinology, venereology, etc., and only primitive concepts of asepsis. Chinese medical doctrine was virtually useless in the prevention of smallpox, typhus, tuberculosis, plague, dysentery, cholera, tetanus, kala azar, malaria, filariasis, syphilis and some other diseases. It was too early to say whether those in China who opposed the policy of integration of native and Western therapies might not be proved justified in their prejudices. It seemed to me that some I encountered in hospitals were embarrassed by the prestige being given to traditional methods. All must have resented the *compulsion* to study them. (Something like requiring all American doctors to learn osteopathy?)

Dr Fei Li-min, the assistant chief of surgery at Peking Hospital, obviously was no enthusiastic supporter of the policy. (Admittedly, surgeons are least likely to sympathize with any un-anatomists.) He was a Shanghai man – gaunt, solemn, in his thirties, and to me he looked very tired. There were thirty surgeons and they needed sixty he said, and twice as many beds. He had graduated from the PUMC when it was located in Chungking during the war, and later had come to Peking when the hospital was used as truce-team headquarters by Generals Marshall and Wedemeyer in 1946–7. He had also briefly studied Chinese medicine. How had he found the time?

'Do you function more efficiently than you did before?' I asked him. He understood English but he answered – or evaded – my question through an interpreter.

'Our technical equipment and operations are all about the same as before,' he said. 'What has changed is our relationship with the patient. Formerly the doctor decided what to do and that was that. Now if a patient doesn't like it he tells us so and we try to find some other way. Take colostomy. People don't like it. In the past if they wouldn't accept it we would send them home. Now we have to explain, persuade – or find other means.'

'Like acupuncture?'

'Yes, sometimes.'

'Do you ever recommend it?'

'They use it for appendicitis and hemorrhoids. It's good for relief of pains in the gastrointestinal tract. It helps overcome post-operative spastic condition in the ureter.' (That I was told every-where.)

'But do you personally function more efficiently than before?'

There was a long pause. I repeated the question and the inter-preter repeated the question.

Finally Dr Fei said, 'The relationship has changed between the doctor and the patient. If the patient cooperates we can do a good job. If he wants to argue there is much wasted time.'

Dr Hsu was still smiling but his face was flushed.

'Would you say it is less efficient?' Translation again. Pause. Repeat the question.

'In past years the head surgeon had time to talk to his staff,' said Dr Fei. 'Now everyone in the hospital has a voice in meetings, even the lowest member of the staff. We accomplish less.'

Speaking of mortality rates in operations Dr Fei said they were five to seven percent in the past and about the same now. 'We can't compare it with the past. We used to limit admissions to those with a chance to recover. Now we admit people in the last stages of lung cancer.'

'But the rate of recovery in cirrhosis of the liver is much higher than before!' Dr Hsu broke in, still smiling but still red. 'Even with cases we wouldn't have admitted before.'

Cirrhosis of the liver can be treated by acupuncture. Obviously some patients would express a preference for it, even if Dr Fei were of another opinion. Who would decide the issue? I had penetrated, if only slightly, into unresolved contradictions between partisans of *Han-yao* and *yang-yao*, Chinese and foreign medicine.

My question had beaten a sparrow out of a tree but decent consideration of my hosts required that I let it go. I changed the subject, to the evident relief of both doctors.

Part Four

THE DEMOCRATIC DICTATORSHIP

THE Kuomintang was the precursor of the Chinese Communist Party in seeking to train a new type of scholar-bureaucrat in a new ideology, so as to revive the functions once performed by the Confucian literati and the classics. ... Mao in his turn unified the country as a hero risen from the people, like the founders of the Han and Ming [dynasties]. ... His ideology claimed the Mandate of History if not of Heaven.

The reader can continue for himself to recognize echoes of the past in China today. C. P. Fitzgerald, for example, has summarized the traditional social concepts as embracing 1) a single authority conterminous with civilization, 2) a balanced economy basically managed by the state, 3) an orthodox doctrine which harmonizes and guides all forms of human activity, including the selection of intellectuals for state service ... As of 1952, he suggests that these concepts, destroyed during modern times in their traditional form of expression, have found expression again under Communism. ...

[But it would be] simple-minded to conclude that it is merely another in a long succession of dynasties ... Ancient evils of bureaucratism lie in wait for Peking's mammoth administration at any time its morale declines ... Secondly, Communist China's methods for ensuring universal conformity ... are far more intensive than anything old China ever devised ... [but] a third and conclusive consideration, which seems to lock the Chinese people irrevocably into their struggle to increase production through their conformity and at the expense of personal freedom, is the rate of population increase. Every year, famine waits around the corner ... Like it or not, there is no alternative [to some kind of centralized and dictatorial planning and controls] by which to feed them, employ the youth, and satisfy the national pride.

John K. Fairbank, *The United States and China*, Harvard *University Press*, Cambridge, 1948, 1958

39

State and Superstructure

SOME differences in the theory and structure of the People's Republic of China and the U.S.S.R. traced in part to the prolonged 'united front' policy pursued by the Chinese Communist Party during the war against Japan (1937–45). In modified form the policy was continued during the subsequent struggle for power against Chiang Kai-shek.

The New Democracy,[1] which Mao Tse-tung wrote in 1940, sought to win the support of all 'progressive elements' in a Communist-led war, first to defeat the foreign aggressor and then to eliminate 'feudal forces' inside China. In 1945, Mao's *On Coalition Government*[2] foresaw a long period during which the Communist party and the 'bourgeois-democratic' parties would work together in a reformed presocialist society. After the revolution both theory and practical experience taught the necessity for a policy of limited class collaboration until the peasantry could be won over to collectivization and a new generation of workers indoctrinated to build toward communism.

In 1949 the Communists summoned a meeting in Peking of the Chinese People's Political Consultative Conference – which had first been organized with Kuomintang permission, but with tireless promotion by Chou En-lai and other Communists. Attended by 662 delegates nominally representing all the anti-Chiang Kai-shek forces, classes, professions and nationality groups in China, and excluding only landlords and 'bureaucratic capitalists' (those directly linked with the Kuomintang hierarchy), that conference adopted an Organic Law for its own existence, a preliminary Organic Law of the People's Republic, and a 'Common Program'. These three documents were the fruit of many earlier discussions between the Communists and their non-Communist supporters. They embodied Mao's concepts of a future constitution to provide for the state superstructure of a 'democratic dictatorship'. The term 'The People's Republic of China' had been used in Mao's address to the preparatory committee of the 'New People's Political Consultative Conference' in June 1949.

Thus the new Peking government was provisionally set up on the basis of organic laws adopted by the P.P.C.C. During the next four years the government tried out and gradually stabilized an administrative apparatus adequate to carry out the tasks of the 'Common Program'. Meanwhile the people were organized at the village level to elect congresses which could choose delegates to district, regional and provincial congresses and, finally, delegates to a national assembly. The Communists were the first to create an electoral machinery as an organic part of the state. The party was at all times in control of that machinery, but it worked with considerable success to enlist nonparty people to help operate it.

By 1953 the government was ready to draw up a formal charter of state. Under the existing organic laws it formed a constitutional drafting committee with Mao Tse-tung as chairman. The committee had thirty-two members, of whom nineteen were leading Communists and thirteen were non-Communists chosen mostly from members of the P.P.C.C. and of eight 'bourgeois-democratic' parties. In the spring of 1954 the committee adopted a constitution and announced that elections would be held in September to choose a National People's Congress. Registered voters numbered 323,000,000 (excluding nearly 10,000,000 still unrehabilitated 'class enemies'[3] and it was claimed that eighty-five percent cast ballots. On 20 September 1954, the First National People's Congress adopted the constitution for the People's Republic of China.

Of the 1,220 deputies elected to the first congress, 680 represented villages and rural towns as against 300 delegates from urban areas and 150 from the minority nationalities; armed forces were represented by sixty and Overseas Chinese by thirty.

The Chinese constitution was closely patterned after but not identical to the constitution of the U.S.S.R. A preamble defined the Chinese People's Republic as 'a people's democratic dictatorship'. In the text of the constitution it was 'a people's democracy ... based on the alliance of workers and peasants'. The U.S.S.R. is a 'socialist state of the workers and peasants' founded on 'the con-

quest of dictatorship of the proletariat', but the Chinese Constitution maintained that *'all power belongs to the people'*. The bicameral Supreme Soviet provided for a separate house to represent the constituent republics and nationalities in a 'unified multinational state'.

Here it is worth noting that use of the word 'unified' in the foregoing phrase carried with it a distinction of high significance to Chinese Communists. Their theory was that China had not been an 'imperialist state' since it was unified by the Han Dynasty more than two thousand years ago. Until the revolution all China was a semicolonial, oppressed nation. Now all its minorities were of dual nationality; they had a local or subnationality – *Li, Lisu, Miao,* etc. – while only *Han* were Chinese. But all were also *Chung-kuo jen* – or 'men of China', and all were Chinese nationals. Chinese Communists asserted that Russia was an example of proletarian revolution in a modern 'imperialist nation' which oppressed colonial peoples, and that China was an example of revolution in a semicolonial country oppressed *by* imperialism. Relations between the Russians and ex-colonial peoples were thus different from those between the Han majority and the China minorities. Hence there were no national autonomous *republics* in China; there was only one 'unified' republic in which all were equal.* This distinction also explained why the Chinese officially used the term *'national* minorities' instead of 'minority nationalities'. As far as is known, this theory was unique to China among world Marxists and accepted only by Chinese.

From the National People's Congress all authority – legislative, judicial and executive – was to be constitutionally derived. Also, the Chinese constitution recognized three kinds of ownership: state (ownership by the whole people); cooperative or collective (ownership by 'the working masses' at basic levels of production); and capitalist (private ownership by individuals). Nevertheless, this constitution clearly provided for a managed transformation 'by law' of the entire economy, 'gradually replacing capitalist ownership with ownership by the whole people'.

*Interpretation based on an interview with Professor Lin Yao-hua, director of the History Department of the Institute of National Minorities, 9 July 1960. See Chapter 73, 'National Minorities'.

The People's Republic was organized politically and administratively at four basic levels: (1) villages, under district or commune (township) governments; (2) counties, municipalities, provinces and autonomous regions and (3) large municipalities and autonomous areas directly under the (4) central authority. There was direct election of government at the lowest level, where congresses (commune councils) were chosen every two years.* Every four years these congresses elected delegates to a new county congress; county congresses elected provincial congresses; and so on. Representation was thus escalated right up to the National Congress. Official administrative bodies were formed when congresses at different levels elected executive councils. These councils in turn chose chairmen from village heads to mayors and governors. This system was hierarchical or 'democratic centralism' (in which the central government council (behind it, the Party) retained broad supervisory and veto powers amounting to appointive powers. Each executive council had similar power over councils on the next level below it.

The National People's Congress elected its own chairman, who became head of an elected Standing Committee which served as a supreme executive council. In practice the Standing Committee had little real power, although it acted for the Congress as a whole when it was recessed – which it generally was except for a week or two once a year.† Both the National Congress and its Standing Committee were dominated by a Communist majority which served as a transmission belt of directives handed down from the Party. The nominal authority of the National Congress and its Standing Committee was transformed into realities of power only in the person of the Chairman of the Republic.

Russia had no exact equivalent of the Chairman of the Chinese

---

*The special municipalities and areas directly under the central government also held elections biennially.

†(1970) No National Congress was convened from 1964 to date. One reason was that its chairman, Liu Shao-ch'i, had been denounced as a 'renegade' and 'scab' and expelled from the C.C.P. and his former position as No. 2 there. See Preface and see footnote, page 333 et seq. A full explanation of the extraordinary complex Great Proletarian Cultural Revolution cannot, of course, be attempted in the limited space available in margins of this volume.

People's Republic. He was elected once every four years by the National Congress. Once elected, he alone could form a government. Neither the Congress nor its Standing Committee had any power to nominate a premier. It could only approve (theoretically it could also disapprove) a premier nominated by the Chairman of the Republic. The Premier (perennially Chou En-lai) then nominated his ministers to form the State Council, and the Congress or Standing Committee approved them.

The State Council, which was the cabinet, included a minister of defense. But the Chairman of the Republic was the commander in chief of the armed forces and head of the powerful National Defense Council. Only he could summon a Supreme State Conference, enlarging the Congress membership at his discretion. He could remove the Premier. He could also remove the Defense Minister or any minister. He had broad 'democratic centralist' powers of supervision over the entire government.

On paper the Chairman of the Republic looked like the final boss. But in practice nearly all important legislative, budgetary and planning decisions, as well as judicial and all other important appointments, originated in the Politburo. Mao Tse-tung was the first man to serve (1954–9) as Chairman of the Republic under the constitution. The office seemed designed for him especially – to combine first responsibility for the state superstructure with top leadership of the ruling party. When he declined to serve a second term but retained his chairmanship of the party, however, it became obvious to anyone who doubted it that party leadership remained paramount over any administrative office.

Yet neither the Chinese nor the Soviet constitution gave any specific authority to the Communist party. The Communist party held its authority by claiming for itself, in theory and practice, the sole right to represent the 'workers and peasants' – the immense majority. By a combination of persuasian and coercion it monopolized political leadership – but not necessarily political or managerial office – at every point.

Marxists refer to the government administrative apparatus as a 'superstructure'. Mao Tse-tung defined it as including 'our state institutions of people's democratic dictatorship and its laws and socialist ideology under the guidance of Marxism-Leninism'. Its sole purpose was to play a 'positive role in facilitating the victory of socialist transformation and establishment of a socialist organization of labor ... suited to the socialist economic base'.[4] There was no room at all here for parliamentary opposition nor was such intended. In the Marxist-Leninist theory of the state no government can 'stand above classes' but is bound to be an instrument of class rule – either the dictatorship (open or masked) of the bourgeoisie, under capitalism, or that of the proletariat, in preparation for universal socialist democracy. Only when classes are 'abolished' by communism can the superstructure be eliminated – a millennium described as 'the withering away of the State'.

China was in theory still a 'unified front' government, but in practice the state apparatus and the party administrative apparatus were, as in Russia, practically identical. There were, however, a number of nonparty persons in high office, and persons who were party members of low rank. When a responsible official was not also an important party person he followed directives issued by a party deputy at his side, his alter ego. In practice the party was both the basic structure and the superstructure, with the government its instrument, and the substructure was the production system or mass society itself.

The extent to which the party permeated and directly controlled offices of the highest rank was indicated by the official positions occupied by the nineteen members and six alternate members of the Politburo. Mao Tse-tung himself was the only one who did not hold either a ministerial or cabinet post or the rank of marshal of the army. (Seven Politburo members were marshals.*) China had *sixteen* vice-premiers, almost one to every province or nearly one to every two ministries. Of these, eight were Politburo members while the other eight were, with one exception, party veterans directly in lines to fill Politburo vacancies when they occurred. Of the thirty-four ministries and four commissions of cabinet level, fewer than ten were run by non-Communists or Communists below Central Committee rank.

The question arose then : were not all the popular elections simply irrelevant façade? The answer must be, not entirely so. The

---

*(1970) Until the rank of marshal was abolished after Lin Piao replaced P'eng Teh-huai (1959) as defense minister.

picture I have shown much resembles, it is true, the superstructure of Chiang Kai-shek's government as set up by his own Kuomintang party political committee; Chiang also borrowed techniques from the Russians. But a significant difference lay in the manner in which vast numbers of nonparty people at the mass level were brought to participate in the Communist administration. The Communist dictatorship organized its bases among the have-not peasants and working people and deeply *involved* them in the revolutionary economic, social, political and administrative tasks of building a socialist society. The peasant might have nothing to say about the choice of the Chairman of the Republic,* but he participated in the choice of local administrations; by that action he committed himself to the whole process of power delegated by proxies to the higher administration.

The Chinese constitution was designed to involve not only all the have-nots; originally it also sought to reconcile and positively involve the 'reformed elements' of the former owning classes – capitalists, intellectuals and other middle-class people 'tainted' by bourgeois mentality.

The eight small 'bourgeois-democratic' parties which still existed in China supposedly spoke for such minorities – but they did so under the guidance of the united-front department of the Communist party! In civil war days these parties sided with Mao Tse-tung against Chiang Kai-shek and later helped form the first 'coalition' government. Now the party could easily have snuffed them out but saw a real necessity for their preservation as long as 'remnants' of bourgeois thinking survived. The most important of them were the Revolutionary Kuomintang Committee, which included many former Nationalist generals and officials, and the Democratic League.

The continued existence of the Revolutionary Kuomintang Committee and participation by its leaders in the National Congress and the government provided a device that would be useful if there should ever be a pro-Peking *coup d'état* on Taiwan. The Generalissimo himself had been offered a post as a vice-chairman of the

*(1970) That is, he could not, in 1966–9, be held directly responsible for the choice of Liu Shao-ch'i ('China's Khrushchev') as chairman of the Congress, in 1957. See note, page 330.

Peking government or a governorship, I was told by General Ts'ai T'ing-k'ai, vice-chairman of the Revolutionary Kuomintang Committee.

Nominally, the splinter parties also represented the non-Communists among the intellectuals carried over from the previous régime. 'Intellectual' is loosely used in China to describe practically anyone who earns a living by brain work rather than manual labor. Mao Tse-tung in 1957 stated that 'several million intellectuals who worked for the old society' had come over to socialism. Actually the highly qualified older intellectuals and scientists who studied abroad or in state or missionary-sponsored Chinese colleges numbered scarcely 100,000. Out of disgust with the Kuomintang, or sympathy with the Communists, or for patriotic or other reasons, about ninety percent[5] of those intellectuals stayed on after the revolution. While building up a new generation of university-trained cadres the Chinese Communists wooed these precious brain workers and made heavy use of their scientific or administrative skills and talents.

No one knew how far the thinking of any of the 'bourgeois-tainted elements' had been changed by years of ideological remolding efforts. Party control of communications provided little if any possibility for voices of dissent to be heard openly. Two years after the adoption of the constitution (1954) its guarantees of work, sex equality, educational and welfare benefits and electoral machinery had been at least partly fulfilled, but a certain Article 87 bore no semblance of life whatsoever. Article 87 unequivocally guaranteed all 'citizens' rights of 'freedom of speech, press, assembly, association, procession and demonstration'. Any Western-educated person had to regard this article as at worst a cynical fraud or at best a mere expression of distant aspiration.

Then, early in 1956, Communist leaders suddenly began to urge intellectuals and prominent nonparty Chinese to exercise these freedoms. Mao Tse-tung himself appeared before a Supreme State Conference of party and nonparty leaders and invited critics openly to express themselves in a campaign designed to rectify party mistakes. It was a bold experiment, without precedent in the history of any Communist country, and one that revealed, among other things, the extraordinary degree to which traditional and national concepts of correct relations between the rulers and the people had survived the invasion of Marxist thought and given to Chinese Communist ideology certain national characteristics found in no other Communist party.

40

The 800

MAO and other top leaders had often said that 'nine tenths of the people are with us, only ten percent are opposed to us'. During the 'Hundred Flowers' period, a brief open season for critics, far less than ten percent raised their voices in public protest. It was a minority more significant than its numbers but it did not necessarily prove or disprove whether the rest were for or against. What the experiment undoubtedly did prove was that no dictatorship, however 'democratic' (or republican, for that matter), can safely permit even a minority to carry on prolonged debate about the basic contradiction of its physiology: the necessity to monopolize power and at the same time demand free and spontaneous unity.

If no more than ten percent of the population of China were opposed to the 'democratic dictatorship' that would be astonishing. By the Communists' own reckoning twenty to thirty percent belonged to the 'exploiting classes' and suffered material losses (or worse) in the upheaval. Ten percent or even thirty percent is a negligible opposition in most nations, but ten percent of China exceeded the populations of Great Britain and Canada combined. Ten percent of China's *adult* population (eighteen and over) was a formidable figure – say 40,000,000.

How large a percentage of the people actually made up the ruling leadership and its dedicated followers? A man very high in the party remarked to me in a moment of reminiscence: 'There were 50,000 of us at the start of Chiang Kai-shek's counterrevolution in 1927. After the killings there were only 10,000 left. Today there are about 800 of us – survivors of all the years between. By and large the country is being run and for some years will be run by those 800.'

That was as candid a definition as one could have got of the meaning of 'democratic centralism' and of the enormously important role played by the top hierarchy of the party in relation to its rank and file and the country at large. Decisions that matter were finally made by 'those 800': near the summit, 193 members of the Central Committee (ninety-seven full members and ninety-six alternate members, elected at the Eighth Party Congress, in 1956); directly beneath them, the reserves of veterans ready to succeed them in the years ahead. At the very peak stood the chief Democratic Centralizer; forming the summit around him were the nineteen other members and six alternate members of the Politburo.

The Standing Committee of the Politburo consisted of Mao Tsetung, Liu Shao-ch'i, Chou En-lai, Chu Teh, Ch'en Yun and Marshal Lin Piao. Teng Hsiao-p'ing was also a member as General Secretary of the Politburo. This Standing Committee controlled the fate of more millions than any similar governing body in the world. With Chairman Liu Shao-ch'i clearly designated* as Mao's 'logical successor', Chou En-lai was obviously No. 3, although in public he deferred to Marshal Chu Teh. The usual seating arrangement and order of photographs put Marshal Lin Piao in fifth place but sometimes it was Ch'en Yun or Teng Hsiao-p'ing. They were all of about equal rank below the top level – except that Lin Piao was there as the top leadership's current choice as the army's spokesman. ('The gun will never be allowed to command the Party,' said Mao.)

'Consult others first', 'don't gossip behind comrades' backs', 'exchange information', and 'don't call a meeting until preparations are completed', are among Mao's precepts of leadership. Years ago I was practically Mao's next-door neighbor for some weeks in Pao An. Preceding any important Politburo meeting I used to see members visit Mao's cave, one by one at first, then two or three together, for discussions which lasted several hours. When Mao called a meeting he knew how to present a synthesis to include different points of view. The full meeting usually took less time than meetings between individuals.

Yet the Politburo had frequently been bitterly divided over

---

*(1970) The arrangement of photographs reflected the number of votes received by the C.C.P. Central Committee in the choice of the Politburo. But by 1966 it became clear that Mao by no means did or ever had viewed Liu Shao-ch'i as his logical successor'.

domestic and foreign policy matters; deadlocks had been carried to the Central Committee to bridge differences. This was not a faceless rubber-stamp committee packed with yes-men, but was made up of strong personalities many of whom had commanded troops in battle and had at times held discretionary power over forces that could have destroyed or overthrown Mao. It was clear from party records that Mao had sometimes been defeated and had had to accept compromises. By keeping opposition inside the highest party organs rather than forcing it outside or underground Mao had been able to bridge most differences and maintain an outer front of unity.

At its highest level of leadership the party thus had an impressive record of unity. There had been no open split for twenty-five years, although there were severe splinterings. No member of the Politburo had a party history of less than thirty years, and this applied to most members of the Central Committee as well. The spectrum covered by their common experience was narrow. Nearly all the higher echelon were men educated empirically by revolution and a closed system of thinking. Yet in a postrevolutionary crash construction period, united and positive action in support of a clear-cut program had a better chance of success, even if some of its assumptions were wrong or oversimplified, than the vacillation, delay and disunity which had failed in China again and again.

Disagreements on tactics and personality rivalries obviously existed. The 'severe splintering' in 1954 involved a dozen men in very high positions. Kao Kang, a Politburo member and former chief of the regional government of Manchuria, was chairman of the State Planning Commission. His vice-chairman, Jao Shu-shih, former head of the East China regional government, was also head of the powerful party Organization Bureau. These two were the only members of the Central Committee expelled (Kao Kang committed suicide), but five governors and several former regional chiefs were also dropped from the party.

Kao was formally charged with warlord ambitions in Manchuria and foreign reports suggested that he had Stalin's backing in an attempt to displace Mao. No doubt Soviet relations were involved but the intraparty struggle went much deeper than that. It seems unlikely that Kao or Jao – whose following among lower cadres extended all over North China – had any ambitions to overthrow

Mao. Competition with Liu Shao-ch'i for control of the younger party cadres could well have existed without implying disloyalty to Mao, and a certain balance of power among the three men might not have been entirely undesirable for him. In any case it was Liu who benefited. He clearly emerged as No. 2 in the Politburo and in effective supervisory control of party organization.*

Did Mao initiate all major policy decisions and domestic programs and decide the manner in which they were carried out by the cadres? These were questions not so easily answered. Although the 'Mao cult' had grown enormously since 1949 there were earlier indications that he had not held, and may not even have wanted, the role of absolute power often attributed to him.

During the war Mao was supreme commander in chief and sometimes made critical decisions alone. In September 1948 (eight years before Mr Khrushchev's 'collective leadership' speech), when it became apparent that national power was within grasp, the Central Committee passed a resolution, *under Mao's chairmanship*, which declared:

The Party-committee system is an important Party institution for ensuring *collective leadership and preventing exclusive control by any individual*. It has recently been found that the practice of exclusive control ... by individuals prevails in some leading bodies. ... This state of affairs must be changed. Hereafter ... all important matters must be submitted to the committee and fully discussed by the members present.[1]

Six months later another Central Committee meeting, 'at the suggestion of Comrade Mao Tse-tung', made the decision prohibiting birthday celebrations for party leaders and the use of party leaders' names to designate places, streets and enterprises. Speaking in 1956, Teng Hsiao-p'ing recalled that this decision had 'a wholesome effect in checking the glorification and exaltation of individuals'.

It had 'become a long-established tradition in our Party to make decisions on important questions by a collective body of the Party and not by any individual.' Violations had been 'frequent' but

---

* (1970) This still seems a logical assessment, but it does not fully concur with charges made against Liu in 1969 when he was expelled from the Party following three years of Great Proletarian Cultural Revolution.

'when discovered' had been 'criticized and rectified'. History is 'made by the people', not by individuals, but Teng went on to say, in the only official explanation ever offered for the glorification of Mao:

Marxism never denies the role that individuals play in history; Marxism only points out that the individual role is, in the final analysis, dependent on given social conditions. ... Undoubtedly their authority, their influence and their experience are *valuable assets to the Party*, the class and the people. ... Such leaders emerge naturally ... and cannot be self-appointed. ... Precisely because of this they must set an example in maintaining close contact with the masses, in obeying Party organizations and observing Party discipline. Love for the leader is essentially an expression of love *for the interests of the Party*, the class, and the people, and not the deification of an individual. ... Of course the cult of the individual is a social phenomenon with a long history, and it cannot but find certain reflections in our Party and public life. It is our task to continue to observe faithfully the Central Committee's principle of opposition to the elevation and glorification of the individual ...[2]

If the contradictions in that speech clearly showed that the tendency of one-man rule was ever present and had more than once been curbed by Mao's colleagues, it also revealed not only that Mao himself recognized the danger[*] and had concurred in its 'rectification' but that the party had a vested interest in Mao as an

---

[*](1970) In 1965 I was able to ask Chairman Mao whether a cult of personality existed in China. Mao replied that there might be something like that. Stalin was said to have had a cult, while Khrushchev had had none. Perhaps, Mao added, Khrushchev had fallen from power because of that. ... Teng Hsiao-p'ing's opposition to 'glorification of the individual' obviously was irreconcilable with deification of Mao demanded by the Great Proletarian Cultural Revolution from 1966 onward. Teng became, after Liu Shao-ch'i, the second most important leader deposed during the G.P.C.R. He was not, however, specifically vilified and expelled from the party. That disgrace was reserved for Liu Shao-ch'i, at the twelfth plenary session of the Eighth Central Committee meeting, in October 1968. Red Guard and other information published during the G.P.C.R. indicated that Mao had not agreed with certain changes in the party constitution adopted in 1956. Party resolutions a decade later (August, 1966) which launched the G.P.C.R., however, demanded recognition of the 'absolute authority' of the Thought of Mao Tse-tung. The new constitution produced by the Ninth Party Congress (April, 1969) established the 'study and application' of Mao's Thought as first of the 'main tasks' of the C.P.

Institution. Promotion of the cult of leadership was by inference acknowledged to be inherent in the system of 'democratic centralism' itself. Since then the cult had grown rather than diminished. With intensification of the double crisis of China's relations with Russia and internal economic problems, Mao's infallibility was invoked as never before.

I can affirm that Mao Tse-tung was asked, in a direct question, what lessons he personally drew from Khrushchev's speech denouncing the cult of Stalinism. Mao's reply was that two articles in the *People's Daily* exactly expressed his impressions. The articles were entitled 'The Historical Experience of the Proletariat', 'based on' discussions at enlarged meetings of the Politburo held in April and December, 1956.[3] Since Mao often wrote for the official party paper, it could reasonably be surmised that he himself wrote the articles mentioned. Following are some significant excerpts from his own thoughts on the problem of the cult of personality :

Marxist-Leninists hold that leaders play a big role in history. . . . But when any leader of the Party or the state places himself over and above the Party and the masses instead of in their midst . . . he ceases to have an all-round, penetrating insight into the affairs of the state. . . . Leaders of Communist Parties and socialist states are duty-bound . . . to be most prudent and modest, to keep close to the masses, consult them on all matters . . . and constantly engage in criticism and self-criticism. . . . It was precisely because of his failure to do this that Stalin made certain serious mistakes . . . became conceited and imprudent . . . made erroneous decisions on certain important questions . . . exaggerated his own role and counterposed his individual authority to the collective leadership . . . accepted and fostered the cult of the individual and indulged in arbitrary actions . . . took more and more pleasure in this cult of the individual, and violated the Party's system of democratic centralism . . . failed to pay proper attention to the further development of agriculture and the material welfare of the peasantry . . . made a wrong decision on the question of Yugoslavia . . . showed a tendency toward 'great nation chauvinism' . . . even intervened mistakenly, with many grave consequences, in the internal affairs of certain brother countries and parties . . .

In all this criticism there was implicit and explicit recognition of the same dangers arising in China. 'The cult of personality is a foul carry-over from the long history of mankind [and] . . . even after a socialist society has been founded, certain rotten, poisonous ideological survivals may still remain in people's minds for a very long time. ... We must therefore give unremitting attention to opposing elevation of oneself, individual heroism, and the cult of the individual.' How was this to be done? By firmly adhering to the 'mass line' on the question of leadership, as defined in a Central Committee resolution recalled from 1943 :

... Correct leadership can only be developed on the principle, 'from the masses to the masses'. This means summing up (coordinating and systematizing after careful study), then taking the resulting ideas back to the masses, explaining and popularizing them until the masses embrace them as their own, stand up for them and translate them into action by way of testing their correctness. Then it is necessary once more to sum up the views of the masses ... and so on over and over again.

Despite these grave criticisms the articles assessed Stalin's career as 'nevertheless the life of a great Marxist-Leninist revolutionary'. If a person's 'achievements amount to seventy percent of the whole', according to Mao, 'and his shortcomings to only thirty percent, then his work should be in the main approved'. Was that the margin by which Mao wished to be judged? Probably. 'There has never been a man in the world completely free from mistakes.' Stalin's crimes were not viewed as inherent in any contradictions of 'democratic centralism' itself, but as the failure of the party properly to apply the 'mass line'.

Meanwhile it should be emphasized that no intelligent person in China imagined that Mao Tse-tung had not used the cult of his own personality to impose his will inside the party. That would require a non-ego or a Taoist recluse seeking oblivion; even Mahatma Gandhi repeatedly used his own mass cult to overrule his colleagues. That there was a governor at work inside Mao, however, which had thus far saved him from megalomania and enabled him to maintain an equilibrium between personal dictatorship and group leadership was also evident. The clearest expression of Mao's awareness of his own vulnerability and replaceability seemed to be the party's choice of a successor during Mao's lifetime.

Until Liu Shao-ch'i was nominated Chairman of the Republic in

1959 many foreign observers believed Chou En-lai was the heir apparent. Following the important Lu Shan meeting of the Central Committee in 1959 it became evident that Liu Shao-ch'i was firmly installed on the second rung of the ladder.*

Liu was the only leader besides Mao who had in effect already managed a Politburo – actually, a 'branch Politburo'. In the last war with Chiang Kai-shek, Liu was chairman of a group of Politburo members, including Chu Teh, who were sent from Yenan to take charge of party affairs in the Central Plains and Manchuria. He built up the machine in a vast territory stretching from the Yangtze Valley to Manchuria and from the China Sea to the Yellow River while party membership increased from 40,000 in 1937 to 5,800,000 by 1950. Very many of those 'new' members – today already veterans – were trained and won promotion under Liu Shao-ch'i's chieftainship of the northern and central China bureaus.

Five years younger than Mao and a year older than Chou En-lai, Liu was a thin, wiry, gray-haired man with a rather sharp face, and slightly shorter than Mao. He was born only a short distance from Mao's home, in 1898, in Ninghsiang county, Hunan. His father was a primary school teacher, an educated man, unlike Mao's father. Liu attended Hunan First Normal School (where he enrolled after Mao had left) and joined the New People's Study Society founded by Mao. Like Mao, Liu was a rebel against parental control; he was first married by a family arrangement which he refused to recognize. His second wife was executed during the civil war, in 1933. After the Communist victory he married Wang Kuang-mei, a physics teacher in Peking.

Lin was too young to participate in the 1911 revolution. By 1914 he was a radical student; in 1920 he helped form the Socialist Youth League, precursor of the Communist party. After entering the

---

*(1970) Mao was not, according to remarks attributed to him during conferences of G.P.C.R. leaders which appeared in Red Guard publications (1966–69), originally opposed to the line of succession established at the Eighth Party Congress (1956). Mao's reasons for finally breaking with Liu (1966) summed up as his conviction that Liu had misused the power and trust given to him; he had led the party toward revisionism and capitalism. The above text is now highly anachronistic and is preserved here as a matter of historical interest.

party, the next year he was assigned to the secretariat of the China Labor Federation and began his career as a labor specialist.[4] Comintern representatives in Shanghai sent Liu to Moscow, where he studied for more than two years. In Canton and Shanghai he worked closely with Chou En-lai during the organization of the revolutionary trade unions, until their suppression in 1927, then led the underground labor movement until, in 1932, he entered Soviet Kiangsi with Chou En-lai, Po Ku, Lo Fu, and other members of the Politburo, to which Liu Shao-ch'i was elected for the first time. In Kiangsi he became head of the trade union federation (consisting mostly of rural workers, the 'semi-proletariat').

Liu began the Long March and got as far as Tsunyi, where he backed Mao's election as chairman of the party. Then he was sent to contact guerrilla forces north of the Yangtze River and to head the party underground in North China. He was partly responsible for preparing the way for Mao's arrival in Shensi. In 1937 he again joined Mao, in Yenan, and sided with him in the expulsion of Chang Kuo-t'ao from the Politburo in 1937. From this time on Liu's position as urban spokesman and chief of the North China organization in the 'white' areas steadily improved. After the Japanese invasion he took charge of party affairs in enemy-occupied areas. In 1943 he was elevated to the seven-man secretariat, or inner Politburo, where he replaced Wang Ming. Throughout the war with Japan and the subsequent civil war, he was the Politburo chief (or first commissar) among all the Communist forces in eastern and northeastern China.* Relatively little known to the Chinese public until he was chosen vice-chairman of the provisional government in 1949, Liu became a figure of international importance in communism when he was elected chairman of the Reds' world trade union federation. From 1958 on a planned effort was apparent to prepare people for eventual acceptance of Liu as a party chieftain. It seemed that such a transition might not greatly affect the administrative apparatus,

---

*(1970) Formation of a 'branch Politburo' headed by Liu Shao-ch'i during World War II had the effect of dividing the Red political command into first and second fronts, said Mao in 1966. Party unity thereafter was never fully restored, according to Mao. Eventually it caused the total breakdown in communications between 'two fronts' which had to be resolved by elimination of Liu's 'front' and restoration of Mao's 'absolute authority'.

since many governors, important mayors, ministers, and probably a majority of the Central Committee could be termed 'Liu's men' – although their primary loyalty seemingly remained to Mao Tse-tung.

Liu was the only man besides Mao whose doctrinal works, such as *On Inner Party Struggle* and *How to Be a Good Communist*,[5] were used as basic catechismic texts. Less frequently quoted was Liu's *Internationalism and Nationalism*,[6] written in 1948, which was then an orthodox Marxist statement of the distinction between bourgeois nationalism and international proletarianism. Speaking before a conference of Australasian trade unions called in Peking, in 1949, Liu Shao-ch'i had provided a kind of 'export formula' that embodied what the Chinese saw as the lessons of their own revolution most applicable to colonial and ex-colonial countries. Its four points can be summarized as follows:

1. The working class must join all other classes in a nation-wide 'united front against imperialism and its lackeys'.

2. The united front must be organized by the working class under its own party, the Communist party, and not by wavering nationalistic elements in the bourgeoisie.

3. Long struggles are necessary to build up and educate a Communist party capable of correct leadership for such a revolution. For this purpose

4. It is necessary to set up a Communist-led army. Mass struggles may be conducted by other means but 'armed struggle is the main form of struggle for national liberation in many colonies and semi-colonies. ... This is the basic way of Mao Tse-tung which may also be the basic way ... where similar conditions prevail.'[7]

All Chinese foreign policy, however it veered or tacked, was aimed at facilitating use of this strategy in the underdeveloped countries, which Mao Tse-tung had long seen as decisive in changing the world balance of power. It was one nexus of Mao's quarrel with Khrushchev that in these areas Mr K. followed policies which *divided* the united front against imperialism.

If Mao won his position largely as a peasant leader, Liu Shao-ch'i's support derived more particularly from his knowledge and control of workers' organizations and urban China. If China was moving rapidly from a predominantly peasant economy to an industrial economy it seemed logical that Liu should be Mao's successor.

Foreign diplomats who had spoken with Liu Shao-ch'i considered him a first-rate politician – shrewd, practical, clear-thinking, un-emotional and exceptionally able in the quick analysis of compli-cated problems in simple language clear to all. For example, the Indian Ambassador, Shri G. Parthasarathy, told me: 'Liu Shao-ch'i at first gives a superficial impression of mediocrity. Five minutes of conversation reveals a man with an extremely logical mind cap-able of quickly penetrating to the heart of a question and organizing his answers simply yet with great force and thoroughness.'

China's leaders were accused of ignorance of the outside world, and yet eleven Politburo members had traveled or studied abroad before the revolution. Although none of the 'top seven' had ever seen America except in movies, Premier Chou En-lai knew English and Foreign Minister Ch'en Yi had studied in France. 'The 800' leading old Bolsheviks were men (and a few women) now in their late fifties or past sixty. Second and third waves of party leadership consisted of the younger survivors of the Long March (not over 10,000) and veterans of both the war against Japan and the 'libera-tion war' – about one million. It was these men, now in their forties, who held jobs of top responsibility everywhere in the state and production. They relied for immediate assistance on the young-est generation of 'combat Communists' – veterans only of the last civil war and the Korean War, mostly now in their late twenties or early thirties.

Anyone who has outgrown childhood myths knows that in final analysis nearly every land is ruled by a very few. In China 'the 800' had greater power over management and profits than the combined interlocking directorates of all American corporations. Yet there also stability ultimately rested on organized mass support. Of what did it consist?

41

The Party and the People*

'OUR party,' said Chairman Liu Shao-ch'i on 30 June 1961, 'now has more than 17,000,000 members. Eighty percent of them have joined the Party since the founding of the People's Republic of China and seventy percent have joined since 1953. They are the Party's newest blood but lack experience and many of them have not yet had a systematic Marxist-Leninist education.'[1] This high percentage of youthful members also underlines the necessity for 'democratic centralism' in maintaining senior leadership.

If Chairman Liu's figure did not include party 'alternates' the total party members and candidates might have exceeded 20,000,000. But in October 1960, Premier Chou En-lai had furnished me some data on current membership which included a figure markedly below 17,000,000.† An extremely intensive membership drive must have been quietly going on during subsequent months. I was at that time also informed that there were 'more than

---

*(1970) Ravages made upon the party structure by the G.P.C.R. from 1966 onward rendered much of this chapter obsolete, but it is retained here for what is deemed its useful historical and reference value in assessing new claims for a rebuilt party. Although Mao declared that he believed 95 percent of the party cadres could be redeemed for continued work it was noteworthy that the entire Young Communist membership in 1966 was by-passed when Mao summoned nonparty Red Guards to effect changes in leadership which he was unable to bring about through existing party forces. By 1970 party unity was again the theme, as older and experienced cadres were urged by the new leadership to return to the fold.

† These data were supplied to me at the Premier's request by Mme Kung P'eng, chief of the government information department, who put the October 1960 party membership at 'not over 13,000,000'. Her figure would indicate a drop of one million since 1959, when party membership was reported at 13,960,000 (*People's Daily*, 28 September 1959). Asked for an explanation when she was attending the conference on Laos in Geneva, one year later, Mme Kung P'eng replied that the figure given to me in

25,000,000 Young Communists' (aged fourteen to twenty-five) and 'more than 50,000,000 Red Pioneers' (nine to fourteen). According to the same source, Communists of 'intellectual' background (defined as 'teachers, students, engineers, technicians and professional people') had increased from about five percent since 1956 to about fifteen percent in 1960. Working-class membership was also fifteen percent and 'minority nationalities' accounted for four percent. Peasant membership still heavily predominated but had dropped from nearly seventy percent to sixty-six percent. All peasant members were listed as 'educated' but 'very few in a formal way'. In all, less than twenty percent of party members had attended high school or college. With an inrush of younger members that percentage doubtless rose soon afterward.

Party membership was not forced on anybody in China but was a highly selective process. Nevertheless, recent pressure on intellectuals, particularly among students in state institutions of higher learning, probably accounted for the sharp rise (to an indicated 2,550,000) in their membership. The increase was also notable in view of the party's continuing campaign against 'rightism'; among intellectuals, nonmembers were obviously being increasingly isolated. If it was also true (as I was told on what ought to be good authority) that as many as a million party members had been dropped or put on probation during the 1957-8 rectification campaign, subsequent increased membership combined with a higher educational level might be reflected in a gradual growth of maturity and sophistication in the party personality as a whole.

If the 'Establishment's' support were limited to party members these figures would not be numerically impressive, but the extent of its organic control went much beyond that. Accepting 700,000,000 as a guess about China's total population (concerning

---

Peking was up-to-date but had not included 'candidate' or 'alternate' members, 'many of whom were admitted to full party membership during the past year'. Possibly the 1959 figure had included both members and alternates. If Liu Shao-ch'i's '17,000,000' included only full party members then it might be surmised that an additional three to four million 'alternates' had since been recruited. It is just as possible that Liu's figure included both alternates and full members.

which foreign demographical experts were in 1961 as far apart as 50,000,000[2]), it could be crudely estimated that about four in 100 Chinese adults over the age of eighteen were now party members. But about seven in 100 between eighteen and forty were party members, and about fourteen in 100 in the fourteen-to-forty age group were either party members or Young Communists. If combined Communist, Young Communist and Red Pioneer membership now amounted to 90,000,000 to 100,000,000, that was probably more than twenty in 100 of the ten-to-forty age group.*

Any estimate of para-Communist strength also had to consider 21,000,000 members of the industrial trade unions,† 3,000,000 to 4,000,000 in the armed forces and public security units, and in excess of 25,000,000 in the armed militia and reserves. Allowing as much as twenty percent for overlapping membership, those organizations might augment the ranks of the 'dependables' by about 40,000,000. One also had to include another 19,000,000 persons in the nonindustrial trade unions and remember the support of activists among the scores of millions of members of the All-China Federation of Democratic Women, and of secondary party aspirants, or dependents of party members. Those under direct *organic* response to the Communist hierarchy in all ways probably amounted to more than half the 'effective' population of the country. Beyond that it would be sheer guesswork to estimate how many people who had no particular emotional commitment to 'build socialism', and might strongly resent hardships imposed on them, still preferred the Communists to the old régime.

China used to be a country ruled by venerable gentry; now it was a land where youths in their twenties had greater authority and responsibility than anywhere in the world. Many Chinese youths of twenty were now better trained than their fathers and could produce and earn more. The condition of 'youth in command' was as universal as 'politics in command'. Average life expectancy in

* These very rough estimates of my own are based on China's 1956 census data. There was a great deal of overlapping membership between the party and the two Communist youth organizations, with perhaps ten percent of Red Pioneers concurrently in the Young Communists, and ten percent of the latter in the party.

† According to figures given to me by the vice-chairman of the All-China Trade Union Federation, in an interview on 26 October 1960.

China was believed to be still under forty,* and population distribution was heavily weighted on the side of youth; forty-one
percent of all Chinese were under the age of seventeen. *In this
group, memory of a pre-Communist period was already dim or
nonexistent.*

Men who at forty-five were still outside the party and had no
technical qualifications obviously did not have much influence. No
longer a landowner and nowadays often having little more earning
power than his wife, the older male had a much narrowed economic
base for his senior authority. In spite of the great efforts being made
to reduce the intellectual gap between educated youths and older
workers by the vast expansion in part-time educational facilities,
this general perspective suggested that discontent among people
over forty or forty-five was much higher than among younger
people. Ex-landlords and former 'rich' or 'middle' peasants had lost
the patriarchal satisfactions of ancestor worship, without being
able to look forward to living to see the fruitions of socialism. This
would apply less to the many millions of formerly completely
impoverished peasants. Retirement pensions or lighter work
for the aged, medical care, recreation and entertainment facilities,
rest homes and the 'iron rice bowl' – filled at least to subsistence
level – had done much to make growing old less frightening for
the poor.

'Youth in command' in industry and science was probably inevitable in a country which had to start almost from scratch, but in
agriculture there is often no substitute for experience. Learning
Mao Tse-tung by rote could not provide talent where it was lacking, or the imagination to 'fit directives to local conditions' and
'combine flexibility with firmness', as was constantly demanded of
cadres. One of the party's problems in personnel management was
the millions of primary and middle school graduates who could not
qualify for higher education and had to be reintegrated with the
working class and the peasantry at the 'basic level of production' –
that is, hard labor. Even though entering the party did not relieve
them of work at the bench or in the field, many of them sought to
become cadres for prestige and an ultimate future as office

*But the 1956 census showed 1,850,000 persons more than eighty years
old, and 3,384 over a hundred. One was registered as born in 1798!

bureaucrats – a tendency which Teng Hsiao-p'ing had deplored
several years earlier.[3]

If twenty percent of the members had attended high school that
was well above the national average, but it meant that eighty percent had gone no further than primary school, although younger
members would average higher, and nearly all party members were
required to 'raise their cultural level' by attending spare-time 'Red
and Expert' schools. General directives issued in Peking were broken
down into simpler language for peasant cadres. Yet consider what
a party secretary of provincial level had to bear in mind and *reconcile* in practice:

In 1960 we should further affirm agriculture as the foundation and
industry as the leading force in the national economy, combine the
priority development of heavy industry with the *rapid* development of
agriculture and correctly handle the relations between agriculture, light
industry and heavy industry; we should mobilize *without exception*
the forces of the industrial, communications, commercial, cultural and
educational departments, to give vigorous support to *agricultural* production; we should go all out for mechanization and semi-mechanization
and automation of all trades and strive for higher labor productivity;
we should carry through policies of *simultaneous* employment of modern
and indigenous methods and *simultaneous* development of big, medium-
sized and small enterprises; we should further consolidate and develop
the rural people's communes, take active steps to set up people's communes in the cities, organize in a comprehensive way the production
and people's livelihood in both urban and rural commune areas and
consolidate and develop community dining-rooms; we should make
vigorous efforts to *increase production* and *practice economy*, mobilize
the broad masses against *corruption, waste,* and *bureaucracy,* conscien-
tiously *rectify the style of work of the cadres* and raise the level of their
political understanding and the ideological consciousness of the masses.[4]

At the same time, however, 'all our economic work is subordinate to politics' read another directive. One must 'dare to think and
dare to act'. 'With regard to the system of distributing goods for
individual consumption, the Party and the Government carry out
the principle "to each according to his work" while at the same time
teaching the masses of the people to struggle for great future
objectives *without being particular about personal remuneration.*'

Criticism and self-criticism through large-scale airing of views and opinions, big debates and putting up *dazibao* [posters in large characters] are carried out in government and people's organizations, in schools, enterprises and undertakings, as well as in the people's communes for the self-education of the masses. This guarantees that every man can constantly keep up plenty of enthusiasm and drive, stoutly surmounting all difficulties, and be boldly creative.[5]

It would take either a highly talented magician or a doggedly devoted and sincere cadre to combine those two sets of directives into the kind of local leadership to inspire 'boldly creative' enthusiasm for the masses. Beneath the superficial sameness great differences of appearance and personality existed in China: the hot-tempered and the cool, the warm-hearted and the cold-hearted, the passive and the passionate, the taller, slower, more Mongoloid northerner and the smaller, enterprising, aboriginal-mixed southerner, the opportunist and the devoted, the weak and the strong, the mediocre and the gifted. All were represented in a party in which struggles of personality continued, as mutual criticism meetings constantly testified.

The leadership was constantly in danger of falling victim to cadres' misleading reports of success. Ninety-five percent of the party cadres worked at the county level* or below, and at every stage there had been peasant cadres holding back or sabotaging on the right, as well as 'overfulfilling' enthusiasts bearing too hard on the left. After land distribution many cadres were found to have become rich peasants, exploited hired labor 'under the pretext of mutual aid', refused to join mutual aid or cooperative groups themselves, worked solely for personal gain, used their position to seize control of cooperatives and make money, and even engaged in usury. On the left, *kanpu* ignored the principle of voluntary participation and mutual consent, forced peasants into cooperatives instead of 'educating and persuading', and collectivized by 'commandism' far beyond the party's intention.[6] The ability to steer a middle course, to hold the sympathy of one's fellow workers yet meet party quotas and demands, to balance persuasion with coercion and retain majority support, to be a good politician without ever being corrupt,

*The 'living allowance' of a party secretary at this level was 140 yuan monthly, or the equivalent of a doctor's wage.

to be thoughtful without ever being in opposition to the leadership or finding its directives unworkable – all this was not the kind of ability found every day or universally, especially among twelve million peasant-born cadres!

The party control committee spent much of its time in rectification work: evaluating and criticizing the performance of members, retraining some, and weeding out others. Yet there were always more waiting in line to join.

42

Security*

THE 26,000 communes, although now largely relieved of many of their former controls over production, were still the basic administrative units (townships) of rural China. Scarcely a person was not answerable to or dependent upon some subcommune authority in the countryside or its equivalent in the urban areas. China was now a living colossus none of whose organs, including the whole vast external surface or skin, could be touched without sending a message through the nervous system of the giant.

Under the Ministry of Public Security there were police officers at every administrative level down to the village, but security did not depend solely or even primarily on professionals. Parallel to the police were 'people's security committees' led by cadres in every factory, production brigade, commune and government office. In the cities their function was performed by street committees and subcommittees. They maintained order, mediated disputes, and might even undertake local thought remolding of individuals. They helped gather the census and kept a record of each family. Their offices were not secret but elective. They did humble chores such as checking on sanitation and street cleaning, family health, school attendance and equable rationing; they helped straighten out domestic quarrels and distributed special rations or fuel to needy people. Like the police, they provided social services combined with social supervision. 'Basic level' public security personnel were required periodically to call mass meetings in order to hear complaints

*(1970) In 1966 Lo Jui-ch'ing, chief of the security forces, was denounced by Mao as a renegade and fired from all authority. Meanwhile Mao declared, 'It is right to rebel' (against revisionists) and the police became powerless to control the Red Guards. Curiously there was, however, little increase in crimes against persons and property. The vast majority (mostly in the countryside) continued to live their normal self-policed lives (out of habit, perhaps) until the security system was restored in 1968.

as to whether they were violating any of the 'eight rules and ten points' of good police behavior.

China had known close security systems in the past. During his visit to Cathay in the thirteenth century Marco Polo noted that every household had to display on its portals the tablets of identification of everyone resting there for the night. But probably no security organization in China's history had equaled the present one in omnipresence and efficiency.

It was extremely difficult for anyone to get lost in this country. Everybody and everything were accounted for. Why steal a car? It was impossible to drive it without papers and gas coupons. A stolen fur coat or a bicycle would at once be noted. How did the owner get it? A hoard of food, a sudden splurge of spending, or a non-routine absence from work or home, were soon known 'on the street'. People could travel freely from city to city but they couldn't stay long anywhere without a valid reason. The inn or hotel wanted papers and explanations. A private guest was soon known to neighbors. A person looking for work must register with the labor pool. Where would a murderer hide? What would a bandit do with his loot? How would an embezzler invest or waste his money? How could an illicit affair long transpire in a communal flat without being observed? The party, its satellites, and the security committees permeated all society.

Thieves and pickpockets were formerly as common in Chinese cities as in America today. Now, when I left money and valuable articles in various rooms I occupied, I never locked a door. My luggage may have been searched but I never missed anything. I discarded a fountain pen in a hotel room in Shanghai; it was handed to me a few days later in Hankow. Two or three times I forgot or misplaced pieces of equipment; invariably they were found and returned.

Nowhere today were people more regimented, more disciplined, and more quickly brought to order by other citizens in instances of public misbehavior. There was very little overt sign of armed force. I never saw armed truckloads of gendarmes or riot squads rushing through the streets. One did see small squads of citizen militia drilling but not making armed demonstrations of terror. Security troops were strategically garrisoned of course, but seldom in evidence. During parades crowds were held back by civilian monitors or Red Pioneers. Most of the uniformed police were traffic cops and the majority seemed to be young girls in long braids. This was a well-patrolled society – from within. No policeman ever interfered with my taking pictures but twice I was firmly ordered to desist by housewives acting as voluntary street officers. This happened to me in Dairen, where I was told by the mayor that the regular police force numbered 'no more than 600'. (The population of the greater municipality was given as 3,600,000.) He quickly added : 'It is the duty of every Communist, Young Communist and Red Pioneer – indeed, of every good citizen – to maintain order and respect for the law.'

The People's Republic published no comprehensive crime statistics. I asked Judge Wu Teh-fang, chairman of the association of politics and law, why it wasn't done. His reply was, 'The figures are so low that they would not be believed abroad.' There was Chou En-lai's statement several years before that 830,000 'enemies of the people' had been 'destroyed' during the war over land confiscation, mass trials of landlords, and the subsequent roundup of counterrevolutionaries which ended, as a 'campaign', in 1954.* (Incidentally, the term *hsiao-mieh*, usually translated as 'destroyed', literally means 'reduced', 'dispersed' or 'obliterated', but not necessarily physically liquidated.) This figure, according to the Chinese, was merely used as a basis for 'fantastic distortions and exaggeration by our enemies'.

Eight hundred thirty thousand is far from a bagatelle in human life, but the figure, *if true*, is not large in proportion to the population – about 1,400 per million† – compared to the costs of other

*In reply to an inquiry I made concerning the total casualties on *both* sides during the two civil wars in China, Rewi Alley, who was in China throughout the whole conflict, wrote to me from Peking on 19 May 1956 : 'I have myself estimated that the deaths through political executions, Kuomintange "cleaning up" in Kiangsi, Fukien, etc. [1930–34, during five anti-Communist expeditions], in man-made famines [blockades] in Hunan, Honan, etc., in "incidents" [armed clashes or "border warfare" before the outbreak of renewed major civil war in 1947] and following the K.M.T.-C.P. breaking of armistice negotiations, then in the general [civil war] struggle subsequently, all add up to something like fifty million from the break [counterrevolution] in 1927 up until 1949.'

† On a population base of 600,000,000.

catastrophes, such as the American Civil War, the French Revolution, and the Russian Revolution, not to mention Hitler's Germany. Counterrevolutionaries were still being arrested. I was told by Judge Wu that they were executed only if their action had caused the death of a citizen. Notices of executions appeared in the provincial newspapers – apparently *pour encourager les autres* – and Western correspondents kept a tally on them. In 1960 these notices of executions varied from eight to twelve a month, mostly cases of allegedly well-paid assassins and saboteurs caught in Fukien or Kwangtung, across the strait from Taiwan.

There were two other types of capital crime: (1) murder or assault with intent to kill motivated by class hatred, or violence of an especially cruel nature; and (2) rape, of a victim under the age of fourteen. In such cases the death penalty was now said to be suspended for two years, during which the prisoner could repent and reform. At the end of that period his case was reviewed and he might receive a reduced sentence.

Certainly no one outside the Ministry of Public Security could effectively confirm or dispute the assertion made by Judge Wu that the total prison population of China was 'well below a million'. Without attempting to assess his figure I should say from what I was able to see or learn in conversation with other foreigners that statements made abroad of 'twenty-five million' or 'fifteen million' executed in China could only be guesswork of the highest subjectivity.[1]

Despite all I have said of the tightness of organized security, despite Wu Teh-fang's claims of a greatly reduced crime rate, and despite every appearance of a matchless tranquillity of public behavior which very few visitors ever saw disturbed, it was obvious that repressive measures were still carried out on a national scale. The law provided for 'reform through labor' institutions and they existed in every province and near every large city. These were both urban and rural and industrial and agricultural prisons. All inmates, both ordinary and political, were required by law to work. To say that it all added up to 'one vast slave labor camp' is another matter. There were many contradictory aspects of the term 'forced labor' in China, as I shall suggest in the next chapter.

Wu Teh-fang, a delegate to the National Congress and also to the People's Political Consultative Conference, had been mayor of Hankow until 1954 and was now on the Wuhan University faculty. He told me that there were three thousand Chinese lawyers, all of whom had teaching jobs and spent only a few days a year in court. Three thousand lawyers for 700,000,000 people? Some explanation lay in the Chinese court system. At its apex stood the Supreme Court, made up of a president and associate justices all elected by the National Congress and its Standing Committee. Under it were local, special, appeals and provincial courts, with their presidents and associate judges elected by local congresses and councils. Any literate citizen could be elected. On the same levels there were the Supreme People's Procurator and local and regional procurators and their associates, chosen by similar means. The chief procurator was roughly the equivalent of an attorney general and local procurators acted as district attorneys.

Chinese law followed the French code in that once a person is arrested he is presumed guilty until proved innocent. If the police found a case against a citizen, the procurator drew an indictment and held an examination. The great majority of minor cases were decided at this level. If the crime was serious or the prisoner maintained innocence there was a court trial. The accused could select his own lawyer or ask the court to appoint one or call upon the services of a friend to defend him and summon witnesses. He paid his lawyer five yuan to draw up his brief and five yuan a day expenses. If the defendant couldn't pay, the court bore the costs.

There was the right of one appeal – to the court of the next highest level. According to Mr Wu, only about five percent of the verdicts were appealed and 'not over twenty percent' were reversed. That is, once on trial the defendant's chance of acquittal was one in a hundred. Whenever a case was ready for trial it was heard at once and few trials lasted longer than a day or two. There was no backlog of cases and courts were recessed for days at a time because of no business. I was told this in every city I visited. Shanghai was the first place I managed to find a court in session and was able to hear a trial.

Three kinds of detention were provided for : imprisonment in a municipal jail; work on a state reform farm; and restricted freedom or work under surveillance. Prisoners up for less than three years or more than ten were put in standard jails; those serving between three and ten years were assigned to state reform farms or mobile labor teams based on them; those sentenced for less than a year usually got 'work under surveillance'. This third category was for first offenders and minor crimes. The transgressor returned to his usual abode and work, but he was accountable for his daily behavior and movements to his street security committee or a group of ten fellow workers.

Well over ninety percent of all Western courts spend their time hearing litigation over property ownership and types of cases which no longer appeared in Chinese courts. Chinese individuals could not sue the government against any kind of socialization of ownership authorized by law. Property disputes now usually involved petty theft. Theft of state property was more serious than theft of private property, and theft for resale was a graver offense than theft for personal use. Many types of crime simply no longer occurred, according to Mr Wu, because of the elimination of private estate ownership.

Whether a society could long exist without the motivation of material aggrandizement (under control) remained an unknown of the Communist future, but the effective denial to the would-be criminal of any market for his plunder (or at least any market commensurate with the risks involved) was one reason why gangsters and racketeers had virtually disappeared in China. Even more important as a deterrent was the knowledge that no amount of wealth or expensive legal talent could influence the courts. Yet it was obvious that the judiciary in China was subject to the same 'democratic centralist' principle of party magistry as the legislative and executive authorities. Mme Shih Liang, the Minister of Justice, said that 'as the People's Tribunals are one of the weapons of the democratic dictatorship of the people, we could not take up and use, unaltered, the reactionary institutions of the old-time courts, but were obliged to destroy them completely.' Party members were no exception to the law, however; if arrested they were suspended and if convicted they were expelled.

For all criminals incarceration was the beginning of a long period of 'education or re-education in the morals and purposes of socialist society'. But the concept of law as an instrument of reform, education and ethical indoctrination was not wholly alien to traditional patterns of Chinese thought. Confucians generally believed that those who understood the difference between good and evil had the duty to teach others by positive example, as well as the duty to manage society, especially during periods of crisis. Mao's sense of ethical values had churned the content of old teachings, but he also had held that man can be perfected by education. In this he was closer to Mencius, who believed that most men are inherently good, than to Han Fei-tzu, who believed that nine out of ten are bad, but even Han Fei-tzu agreed that man can be taught to be good – which is the underlying principle of thought reform.

In a casual conversation during my visit Mao remarked (but without any reference to Confucian concepts), 'Most men are good; only the minority is bad. Even bad men are not bad all the time and can be made better, just as good men can be made bad by negative example. The difficult thing is to discover what is good and how to teach it to others.'

The Chinese Communist attitude toward the processes of justice as sanctions against enemies of socialism could also readily be compared with supralegal or extralegal sanctions imposed in Confucianist society. In old China there were no guarantees of civil liberties, of trial by jury, or of certain tenets of Western law descended from Roman times. Litigants carried their disputes before formal courts of the official magistrates only as a last resort. Mediation, arbitration and penalties in the great majority of cases were handled unofficially by the gentry (scholars, landlords and merchants) in the interests of hierarchical and class stability. Except for a brief period when 'Legalist' philosophers dominated, centuries ago, justice was theoretically based on the Confucian classics and commentaries which expounded *li*, *yi*, *lien* and *ch'ih* – the four principles of right relationships between men, and between man and the sovereign power. Decisions of the local gentry were socially binding on the majority of poor illiterates, who could not quote the Books; usually, only the rich and powerful dared to use the more formal courts.

On paper, the Kuomintang promulgated a Western-style legal code, but most litigants still followed the old practice, especially in rural China. There was thus a distinct connection between the traditional system of discipline imposed extralegally by the gentry, and the discipline now imposed by the group under party leadership. Marxist-Maoist doctrines of 'right relationships' and the party had replaced Confucian doctrine and the gentry. Both reflected the past – but as two planets reflect the sun.

43

'Slave Labor'

I SAW thousands of men and women engaged in major construction jobs on roads, railways, dams and other projects. If they were prisoners there were no armed guards around them. Who could speak to them all personally? Twice during about 11,000 miles of travel inside China I saw groups of a dozen or so men being marched along guarded by a soldier or two. I was told that they were regular prisoners from state reform farms assigned to field work. I did not see anything that looked like the barbed-wire-enclosed concentration camps I frequently saw in Stalin's Russia, guarded by high towers with machine guns.

The round number of 'twenty-five million' slave-laborers in China was offered as a Kuomintang guesstimate submitted by the Taiwan government to a world study of that subject made by the International Labor Organization and published by the United Nations in 1957. The I.L.O. report itself assumed no responsibility for the Taiwan document, and noted that no nonpartisan source and no government having diplomatic relations with the People's Republic transmitted corroborating information. The figure 'twenty-five million' was nevertheless widely quoted in the press as supposedly authenticated by the U.N. On the basis of information other than the Taiwan document, however, the I.L.O. did conclude that the People's Republic had 'set up a highly organized system of forced labor in prisons and labor camps, for the purpose of political coercion and education', and was using the system 'on a vast scale for carrying out State programs of economic development'.[1]

How 'vast'? Also, just what is 'forced labor'? Does it include everybody obliged to do work he does not wish to do, or only those formally sentenced to 'corrective camps' without pay? Even the Kuomintang's own 'twenty-five million' guess included three million homeless refugees from flood areas and eight million 'civilians used as corvée labor'.

Nearly everybody in China *was* obliged to do some kind of manual labor, from the professor to the coolie. Whether it was voluntary or involuntary depended somewhat on the person's state of mind. But this part-time communal labor was obviously not the Western conception of slave labor. On the other hand there was an unknown number of 'irregular' persons, who, although they might never have been convicted of a political offense or a criminal felony, were doing full-time compulsory 'education through labor'. This was acknowledged by a State Council decision enacted as law by the National Congress of 1957.[2]

According to this law, 'to transform idlers into new men' and 'to promote order and favor socialist construction' persons could be 'taken in hand and subjected to education through labor' without incurring criminal liability if they were found to engage in

vagrancy ... violate the rules of public order and do not mend their ways despite repeated efforts to educate them; (b) having been expelled from [their] organization, group, enterprise, school or other body to which they are responsible, have no means of existence; (c) refuse over a long period to work although they are fit to do so, or who violate discipline and, having been expelled, have no means of existence; (d) do not conform to the provisions concerning work and assignment to other work, or who refuse to be directed in production work, who interfere with public tasks ... and who do not mend their ways despite repeated efforts to educate them. ...
Education through labor is a way of achieving compulsory educational reform; it is also a way that makes it possible to provide offenders with an occupation.

Such persons received 'a salary in accordance with their work'. They had to provide for their families or save in order 'to found a family'. They were educated in 'socialism', in 'patriotism, and glory of work', to become skilled in 'techniques of production ... and self-supporting'.

This may explain what happened to some professional beggars, malingerers, truants, recalcitrant landlords, 'troublemakers', and those who formerly 'lived by their wits'. It was clearly also a powerful deterrent against people who wouldn't work where and when they were told to work and against habitual nonconformist 'non-cooperators' or 'violators of discipline' in general. Not only the Ministry of Public Security, but any head of family, street committee, organization, school, or group to which the offending person belonged, could place him in this category of reform-through-labor service, subject only to the approval of local governing bodies and without going to court.

Such persons might either be assigned under surveillance to special work in organizations from which they had been expelled or be used in labor construction teams. According to Judge Wu the maximum period of labor surveillance was one year. If the person deserted his tasks he was tried by the courts and sentenced to a regular prison term.

It is hardly necessary to point out that the law to 'transform idlers' could also be applied to expelled party members. It was equally obvious that it was wholly irreconcilable with the existence of civil liberties or guarantees against search or seizure without a warrant – despite the constitution.

According to the 'State Regulations on Reform Through Labor'[3] adopted in 1954, prisoners could be used in any kind of work for 'nine to ten hours a day'. By a supplementary law[4] such prisoners 'could be kept on by the Labor Reform Group and re-employed' even after they were released and their rights restored. This might be at the prisoner's request or if 'the prisoner's sentence has expired in a vast, sparsely inhabited region, where settlers are needed to work and found families'. Since a party member must go anywhere he is sent, said the party, why not an ex-prisoner – or anyone else? Reform through labor was justified as more humane than enforced idleness. In a report which accompanied the Regulations, the Minister of Public Security, Lo Jui-ch'ing, declared:

There have also been established a good number of labor corps which undertake hydraulic works, build railways, fell trees and build houses for the nation. All the production work is not only directly profitable to the development of the various construction undertakings of the nation but also saves the nation great expense and is a real source of wealth.

The use of prisoners for labor of all kinds was thus beyond dispute; the only questions were how many and under what conditions. From an ethical standpoint such information may seem no more relevant than in many other countries where the same practice is followed but in China it was politically significant.

As I have said, no outsider could *know* the answers to those questions. After Khrushchev confirmed the worst reports about Stalinist concentration camps in Russia and Eastern Europe (and from what was known of camps in South Vietnam under Ngo Dinh Diem) no one was entitled to assume that 'reform through labor' in China was administered by humanitarians. A self-constituted 'International Commission' in Europe published a *White Book*[5] about persons who had been released by or escaped from Chinese mainland prisons up to 1953. Of the 'hundreds' of alleged former prisoners whom investigators claimed to have interviewed, they apparently found only eighteen 'case histories' suitable for presentation in the *White Book*. Obsolete and inconclusive for a nation of 700,000,000, this report is nevertheless valuable for its compilation of legal and historical documents and official statements. These leave no doubt about the thorough integration of the prison system with both production needs and the ceaseless campaign to bend men's minds and wills to serve the ends of the régime.

Yet a visitor to China finds paradoxes even in the jails. The *White Book* compilation includes a map which lists 292 'concentration camps' alleged to have existed in China. Locations of most of them suggest that they may have been temporary construction camps; others are in the neighborhood of state farms. One is shown at Sanmoshu, a suburb of Harbin. It so happened that I visited a large state experimental farm near there. It was a hurried trip and I had seen so many farms and farmers that I neglected looking into the workers' living quarters but spent my time inspecting the poultry breeding and automatic pig-feeding 'innovations'. As I left I noticed two armed sentries at the lower gate. It occurred to me only later that mixed prison and free labor might have been employed there. The law quoted above gave reason to suppose that mixed labor was at least sometimes used on state farms – a fact which was officially confirmed for me.

One thing could be reported with reasonable certainty: there were no more child slaves in China. Before the war legions of children were sold to owners of mines or shops or into household drudgery or prostitution. This practice was also general in French Indochina, and still continued in South Vietnam. All the miners in Yunnan's tin mines were formerly boy slaves.[6] In her absorbing prewar Mather Foundation (Yale University) study, *Chinese Family and Society*, Olga Lang reported that: '... child labor represented seven percent of the total employed in Shanghai textile factories but many small workshops ... employ children almost exclusively.' In Peking, she found that 'only a few apprentices receive as much as fifty cents or a dollar [yuan] a month. ... Beriberi, scurvy, and other diseases caused by malnutrition are common', and little workers 'sleep on wooden planks ... or under the tables which other shifts continue to use for their work; others sleep on the streets.' In the mines near Peking, Miss Lang saw (as I had) children who 'emerged from the dark shafts almost completely naked, their thin bodies showing through their skin ... carrying on an average thirty-five-pound loads. The boys looked not older than nine or ten although there were some fourteen- and fifteen-year-olds among them.'[7] Such was life in the thirties, when Miss Lang also reported widespread sale of widows and poor men's wives as well as girl children to become household slaves, prostitutes and concubines.

Under the Kuomintang millions of peasants were forced into labor service; in the countryside I often saw (as did many other foreigners) men yoked together like cattle, with ropes tied around their necks, being dragged along by military police. No foreigner I met in present-day China had seen anything like that. We also forget that the Kuomintang introduced 'thought correction' camps as early as the mass depopulation of Kiangsi Soviet and Hupeh, in the thirties. Official correspondence released by Washington in 1962 revealed that in 1943 the State Department was aware that '"thought correction" camps exist in at least nine provinces in Kuomintang China'. They were not used for labor reform but solely for detention; 'torture is practiced' and it was reported that those fortunate enough to be released were 'usually broken in mind and body'.[8]

44

Hsueh-Hsi *and* Reform-Through-Labor

I WAS told, and resident foreign diplomats believed, that the entire Peking area had only one prison. There was also a mobile labor brigade of 'a few hundred' and there was the state reform farm; both were also under the Peking security bureau. Wu Teh-fang told me the farm had about 2,000 prisoners. That was the same estimate made for me by a resident diplomat. A number of foreigners had seen it; apparently it was not very different from any other state farm. Besides the main prison there was also a 'detention house' in the Peking inner city, near the National Library, in Ts'ao Lan Tze Hu-t'ung, the Lane of the Grass Green Mist. Here some two to four hundred political prisoners were held for interrogation and thought reform prior to a formal trial and verdict.

I could have found the Peking jail without a guide if anyone had told me that it was the old 'model prison' I had last visited in 1935, when some students I knew were incarcerated there. It was built sixty years ago, a great improvement over the filthy windowless dungeons then in general use; that particular prison reform did not spread very far. The prison stands beyond the eastern suburbs and from a distance seemed unchanged : the same gray brick walls. But the outer gate was now open and I saw no sentries until we reached the inner wall, where one soldier stood in a pillbox. An unarmed guard opened the iron gate and Yao Wei and I passed through a flower garden into a reception room which fronted on part of the inner prison walls. The deputy warden, Mr Wang, was a serious-minded party man in his mid-thirties who had had 'special training' for his job. He offered me the usual tea and preliminary briefing.

There were 'about 1,800 prisoners' of whom about forty percent were 'counterrevolutionaries' (aged mostly between thirty-five and forty-five); more than a hundred prisoners were women. Sixty of the inmates were under suspended sentences of death. The prison operated three factories: a hosiery mill, a mill for plastics articles, and a machine and electrical shop. I was told that the prison routine was eight hours of shop work, two to three hours of study and lectures, eight hours of sleep, four or five hours for dining, physical exercise, reading, recreation and 'discussion' (thought remolding). Prisoners got one holiday every two weeks, when they could receive visitors or do as they wished. They had their own band, an opera troupe, an outdoor theater, and movies once a week. Men and women ate in the same dining rooms and could attend plays and sports contests held inside the prison compound.

With that said we toured the prison cells and then the shops. The buildings were one-storied and made of brick, with two rows of cells on either side of a central aisle. I noticed that all bars had been removed from the windows and that every cell door was open. The rooms, with two to four long k'angs in each, were white and clean, and all had neat piles of bedding. One man, off on a free day, was lying in bed reading; his door was also open. He was in for two years for embezzlement of state funds.

In the shops machinery was antique but better than in most urban commune shops I had seen. Women handled the knitting machines and a few worked in the plastics rooms with the men. They wore blue or black cotton clothes issued by the prison, with no special markings to differentiate them from other working people. They paid strict attention to their machines and did not look at us except when I paused here and there to ask a question; then they replied politely and not sullenly. Some of the young women were rather pretty. I asked one of them why she was there. 'Fraud,' was the answer I got. I was puzzled, but the deputy warden later enlightened me.

Shops were run by prisoner foremen supervised by prison staff members; I saw no armed guards among them. Prisoners also managed their own barber shop, mess rooms, a canteen, shower baths and a library. In various courtyards and grounds I saw half a dozen soldiers, but none was posted in guard towers or on the walls which enclosed gardens where prisoners cultivated vegetables. Perhaps the other guards were removed for my benefit? Perhaps. But Sing Sing would consider that rather risky as a public relations stunt.

'It looks easy enough to get out of here,' I said to Wang. 'Do many try it?'

'We've had several runaways in the past year. Usually they are brought back by their families.'

Beside a round-roofed pergola in one corner of a compound near the clinic, half a dozen women were eating rice with their chopsticks, laughing and chattering. They didn't seem to belong.

'They are ex-prisoners,' Wang explained. 'Two of them work in the clinic, another is in charge of the laundry, one works in the office.'

I stopped to take some pictures, to which they made no objection; one or two gave embarrassed smiles. They confirmed that they had stayed on voluntarily after their sentences expired and were working for wages. They felt 'at home' here. One was a married woman who lived nearby; her husband worked in a neighborhood factory. I had no time to pursue what might have been a fascinating study of the psychology behind their choice of a place to work – if it *was* their choice.

Around the basketball court and a stage which prisoners had built were bulletin boards posted with *ta tzu-pao* such as you see before any Chinese factory: essays, rhymes, praise and mutual criticism, lists of model workers and their awards. Prisoners got no wages but received an allowance of three yuan a month pocket money, which they could double by outstanding work. The money bought a few cigarettes or other items in the canteen. The kitchen was preparing a noon meal of soup, spinach and steamed bread which looked like a Salvation Army handout.

Back in the reception room to ask more questions, I learned that the political prisoners were generally serving long sentences up to 'suspended death' – alleged Kuomintang agents, spies, saboteurs or 'despotic landlords' sentenced by 'people's courts' in their villages. Many had been here since the revolution, while others had 'awakened', completed reduced sentences, and been released.

Among civil felonies the commonest was theft of state property for resale or personal use; next came embezzlement, chicanery, forgery and the usual crimes of violence: assault, rape and robbery. There were 'very few' new cases of murder. More than half the women prisoners were in for *p'ien-lai lao-ti*, which means to 'obtain something by fraud'. What was it they had obtained? I asked Mr Wang. Money, clothing, provisions, gifts of all kinds. And by what means?

'An adventurous woman pretends to be in love,' he said, 'with several different men at the same time. She does it solely to get money. She goes from one man to another, deceiving him, but she won't marry any of them.'

'That sounds like a very ancient profession. Isn't prostitution the word?'

'No, no, it isn't prostitution,' he insisted stiffly. 'It is just fraud. There is not necessarily any sex involved. There are many different kinds. These women are very clever at it. They are put in prison only after repeated offenses.'

I should have liked to pursue the matter in a personal interview with one of the defrauders. Mr Wang said that the women would be embarrassed and besides it was their noon rest period (quite true), so I can offer no further particulars, except that they get light sentences, one to three years. When asked whether I would like to question any other prisoner I chose a political offender under suspended death sentence.

He was a Shantung man, rugged in build, heavy-featured, middle-aged and solemn. I asked him what he had done. He answered that as a Kuomintang policeman in Tsinan he had led an anti-Red squad and arrested many suspects. Urged by Wang to elaborate, he added, face downcast, that he had personally killed four revolutionaries, one of whom was a pregnant woman. His crime was graver because he had not come forward after the revolution when everyone was given an opportunity to confess, repent, and ask for punishment. Instead, he had gone north, taken a job in a Peking textile mill and pretended to be an ordinary worker. One day in 1958 he was recognized by another Shantung man who denounced him and had him arrested. Did he feel he had been fairly treated?

'I ought to be dead,' he said.* 'I deserved death but instead I have been given back life. I am being educated and I can now handle machines and do useful work. I am doing my best to remold myself to show my gratitude.' He seemed thoroughly humbled and re-morseful, and deep tension was written on his face. One needed little imagination to share some of the awareness that must have filled his days that one bad mistake might be his last. To know with reasonable certainty that salvation depended entirely on his own repentance and reform must in some ways have placed far heavier burdens on him than would be on a condemned man in an Ameri-can prison. Realizing that nothing he can do by way of inner awakening can alter matters, the latter need not undergo the agony of attempted self-reform but can hold society or his lawyers at least partly responsible for his fate.

When the prisoner and his unarmed escort left, Wang said that he was a good worker. He had been in jail for two years; his sen-tence would probably be altered to life imprisonment.

The theory held, and the law supported it, that the starting point for all prisoners was sincere repentance, recognition of the crime, and welcome of the sentence as 'good'. Until this happened they were kept under stricter confinement. The next step was the 'genuine desire' to reform. Many prisoners were 'really ignorant and understood nothing about the revolution or what the govern-ment was trying to do for the people.' Tours were organized to take them to visit communes, factories and schools, to show the good things being done and to awaken 'a sense of shame'. Illiterates were taught to read and write and all attended political lectures. Much of the education and indoctrination was done by 'advanced' prisoners put into cells with new arrivals and backward ones. Truly 'reformed' prisoners received special privileges; the more successful their political work the better their chances of release. By means of cadres organized within the prison blocks, order and disciplined study were maintained. Political prisoners did the same shop work

---

* (1970) The same thing that the ex-emperor, P'u Yi, said when I met him in Peking shortly after he was released from prison. He had been detained ten years as a 'war criminal' – serving the Japanese as puppet monarch of Manchukuo. See pages 70–71.

as others but were subject to much more intensified thought remolding in cells led by reformed 'politicos'.

In only a few instances did prisoners refuse to 'recognize the roots of their errors'; if these silent resisters worked well and were not political prisoners they would also be released when their sentences expired, although there was no chance for a shortened term. Punishment consisted of overtime work or loss of holidays, but Wang maintained that violence was never used and that solitary confinement 'in no case exceeded a week'. Obviously his statement is no proof that Chinese jailers are any exception to the general rule in prisons everywhere: 'no force, absolutely, when anyone is looking'. The Peking prison looked like a tolerable fate but who can know from the outside looking in? I am much aware of the testimony of Chinese who have been through the wringer of thought remolding, and I have talked to several Americans who were also subjected to it.

An American psychiatrist, R. J. Lifton, has made a study of brain washing which attempts a Western scientific explanation of its pathological and psychological effectiveness.[1] It is worth noting in passing that in the twenty-five cases Dr Lifton examined he found that curiously even among those who remained most hostile to the Communists nearly all said that they had in some ways personally benefited from the experience. Dr Lifton was unable to trace any pattern of influence by Freud, Adler or Pavlov in Chinese thought-remolding techniques, which seem to depend primarily on guilt associations with traditional ethical concepts and fears rooted in Chinese psychology.

Probably no American is better qualified to testify concerning thought remolding than Harriet Mills, who went through four years of the process. She was born in China, in a family of Presbyterian missionaries, and spent twenty-five years of her life there. A graduate of Wellesley College, she was back in China as a Fulbright scholar when arrested and charged with espionage, in 1951. When I spoke to her in 1962 in New York she was teaching Chinese at Cornell University.

In 'Red China', a special issue of the *Atlantic*, Miss Mills described the remolding process with great authority: 'The Communists know that only if people are truly persuaded of the justice of [their] position will they release their spontaneous and creative energy and cooperate not from necessity but from conviction.'[2] Physical violence cannot achieve genuine moral reform and sincere changes in *thinking,* which are basic objectives. 'In serious cases where criminality is involved thought-reform and punishment are combined but the essential aim remains *redemption through criticism.* ... [Original emphasis.]

'They are determined to negate a fundamental tenet of Chinese thinking formulated by Confucius 2,500 years ago : "Who works with his mind rules; who works with his hands is ruled." Reform by labor goes hand in hand with reform through study in rehabilitation of prisoners [and] the right to labor comes only after a certain level of reform through study has been achieved.'

In her article Miss Mills traced 'two main lines of experience' in the techniques of group study. The first derived from the Communists' twenty years as guerrilla fighters when recruits had to be taught to 'use weapons, obey commands, live together, and protect the country people', making sure that 'each man understood not only how but why'. Small groups (of six to ten) went over all questions until everyone understood. By similar means the program of land and social reform and future benefits was patiently explained to the peasants. 'Thus, they persuaded the peasants to cooperate in resisting Japan or the Kuomintang,' and the result was 'high morale'.

The second method, the organization of party cells for group study of Marxist ideology, is standard among Communists everywhere. From 'the fusion of these two traditions – Chinese persuasion and Communist dogma' – evolved the 'ubiquitous working mechanism of thought reform in China'.

All study groups reported to the party and *no* citizen was exempt from participation. There was no freedom of silence. Parroting answers was not enough; one must apply the new theory and self-knowledge as a continuous life process. Criticism was the main weapon. Those who resisted or lacked sincerity might face *toucheng* (struggle) with the rest of the group – 'a humiliating combination of loud criticism, interlarded with sarcasm, epithet and – very rarely – with minor violence'. Ostracism from the group was the worst punishment.

Self-criticism was even more important than criticism of others. And self-criticism in public, a form of confession of all one's doubts, wavering, weaknesses, bad habits and antisocial tendencies, was the most effective form of self-criticism.

'Group study can even be exhilarating ... a sort of catharsis.' The most difficult to redeem had been the higher intellectuals. Communist policy toward this strategic group 'has consistently aimed at securing effective utilization of their knowledge. Zigzagging steadily toward this goal, the Communists have now attacked, now united, now criticized' – while training their own 'new group both Red and expert'.

'Most important of all' was the appeal to

a sense of nationalism, a patriotic pride in China's new posture of confidence and achievement. That China, which in 1948 was economically prostrate under runaway inflation, maladministered by a weak and corrupt government totally dependent on American aid, incapable of producing motorcycles, much less automobiles, can ... fight the United Nations to a draw in Korea, maintain the world's fourth largest air force, produce trucks, jet planes, even establish a nuclear reactor, is an intoxicating spectacle to the Chinese. This pride, in turn, has generated a remarkably effective and spontaneous code of public honesty, courtesy, and civic sense unknown in old China.

To be asked whether an incorrect idea is really worthy of the new China can make one feel guilty. Thousands have asked themselves, 'What right have I to disagree with those who can achieve so much?' As a professor of English, remembering China's internal disintegration and international humiliation, explained to me in the spring of 1951, 'Now we can again be proud to be Chinese!'

Miss Mills wrote primarily of *hsueh-hsi*, or the technique of thought reform – not of reform under coercion. *Hsueh-hsi* in principle was the same wherever practiced, but in prison there was the omnipresent *threat* of force and humiliation, combined with the demand for self-regeneration. In conversation with me, Miss Mills further emphasized the distinction between prison reform – 'corrective imprisonment' – and the ideological remolding undertaken by social organizations in a kind of group therapy. 'Corrective imprisonment' is no exercise in nonviolence. Armed guards, handcuffs, 'solitary', and standing motionless for long periods might all be used 'on occasion', but the assault on the human sense of social guilt was the basic means. According to Miss Mills, food was never withheld or used as a weapon and physical punishment was not practiced as an end in itself. But the knowledge of it held in reserve certainly sharpened the prisoner's response to accusations of his selfish behavior, and the combination left him aware that his only hope of redemption lay in a genuine soul-searching and exposure of past errors. Most people have some sense of guilt if they really face the truth about themselves. The paradox Miss Mills discovered was that 'even strong-willed persons who might never bend before force, alone, did undergo slow, stage by stage, and finally dramatic and wholly convincing transformations'.

That men and women interned under such grave conditions might yet manage literally to 'rethink their way out' and eventually be assigned to reform through labor was gradually seen by most of them to be a 'marvelous thing'. They then tended to become strongly competitive in their desire to be recognized by the interrogator-confessor as 'more progressive' than their cellmates. They became genuinely proud of their own 'creative efforts' in the process of re-examining their past to qualify themselves for a return to society. Finally to be given the right to work, unguarded, on a dam or a bridge or something else 'useful to the people' whom they had 'wronged', could (in the objective opinion of Miss Mills) then indeed mean a kind of 'freedom' in which they might rejoice as a reward, not a punishment.*

---

*(1970) P'u Yi's book, *From Emperor to Citizen*, has become available since the above was written (published under the title *The Last Manchu*, New York, 1967). It provides corroborative evidence of the process of 'transformation' under *hsueh-hsi*, of especial interest in its revelations of competition in self-denunciation.

45

Pre-Teen Delinquents

I SPENT an afternoon in the 'Children's Study-Work School' where 185 children between ten and fifteen were being reformed by gentler methods of thought remolding. Peking had one other reform school, with about 100 juvenile delinquents aged fifteen to eighteen, which I did not see. The Children's Study-Work School had some notable features worth reporting. Its roomy compound was in a good residential neighborhood not far from the Winter Palace. There were no guards except one elderly gateman and no special precautions to prevent escapes. 'Usually they come back voluntarily,' I was told by Mme Wang Ssu-yen, the principal. She was a diminutive woman dressed in a white blouse and dark skirt, her black hair bobbed and caught in curls behind her ears. Her energy and enthusiasm for her job, in contrast with her stature, reminded me of my own spirited grade school principal.

'The methods we follow here,' said Mme Wang, 'are in accordance with the principles laid down by Mao Tse-tung for all primary school teachers. We must love our students like parents, combine affection with strict justice, respect them as much as adults, understand each one as a distinct individual, and inculcate in them socialist ideals of service and unselfishness. The cause of delinquency in children nearly always lies with their parents. All our teachers here realize that the most important thing is to set an example. We participate down to sharing the dirtiest chores such as cleaning floors and toilets. All the work in the school is done by the children and teachers.'

Mme Wang considered that her charges were all reflections of the failure of the 'old society' and 'hangovers of capitalism', but 'class background' figures she gave me did not seem conclusive evidence. According to her, forty percent of the little delinquents came from working-class families; twenty percent were orphans or from broken homes or had lived with old people too disabled to work or look after them; twenty-five percent were the children of *kanpu* (party workers, cadres); and fifteen percent were from homes of 'former capitalists or policemen'. I expressed interest in the quarter from families of cadres. Forty-six in a city of more than seven million was not many, but the relative percentage was high. Weren't cadres themselves supposed to be models of deportment?

'They may work for socialism but still be bad parents,' she said. 'Remember that they also come from the old society and may backslide in their domestic life. When parents are too busy to look after their children, when they neglect to give them love, the result is always the same; the children become wilful, spoiled, aggressive, and do things to win attention. They begin to lie and steal and get into trouble.'

The delinquents here had been habitual thieves or had committed acts of vandalism, cheated or caused disturbances in schools, refused to study or work, or had violently quarreled with their grandparents, who, in some cases, had asked that they be put into the school. (Mao Tse-tung was a rebellious child. What would have happened if he had been sent to such a school? The party's answer would be that Mao lived in a feudal society against which it was morally correct to rebel.)

'The majority of our children are unusually bright, not stupid.' Mme Wang spoke of their 'unusual pride' and 'vanity' and how readily they responded when given recognition and responsibility. One 'bad' boy had refused to study or work for two months. 'I can stand sitting through just one class,' he said. 'Then I have to hit someone.' One day he contrived to tie his teacher's feet to his desk so that when he tried to stand up he was thrown to the floor. The boy expected to be beaten but the teacher dismissed class to talk to him. The teacher thought that he was a clever boy to be able to do that trick without being detected. He thought he had ability and would like to help him. The boy had been abused by his father and hated him, but gradually the teacher won his confidence. A year later the same boy found a gold watch on the street (children are allowed to return, unescorted, to 'home' or the equivalent for two days once a month). He was much tempted to sell it or to take it apart. He was a very curious boy. Instead, he brought the watch to his teacher. When the owner recovered the watch he came to congratulate the youth and they became good friends. By the time he graduated after three years he was chairman of his class.

Mme Wang told several more stories of this kind to support her account of their successes, which seemed to owe much to two basic control devices. There was a pupils' association with many management tasks. Among these was responsibility for helping the 'new ones' learn correct behavior. The 'new ones' were put on two months' probation by the 'old ones'. If they were then voted into the organization they received emblems of membership. If their performance was unsatisfactory they were put on probation for another two months. To be accepted as a 'full pupil' was a 'glorious moment', said Mme Wang. The élite of the students belonged to the Young Pioneers – thirty-two out of a total of 150 boys and thirty-five girls. Membership was extended to students who received 'Five S's' or superior marks in study, athletics, workshop, recreation and hygiene-sanitation, and socialist study and consciousness. These Young Pioneers seemed to play a role similar to that of cadres in adult life.

Shop work was required for two hours in the afternoon: carpentry for boys, sewing and embroidery for girls. The rest of the day was devoted to the usual primary school subjects: classroom from 7:30 to 12:00 in the morning, athletics and recreation for two hours in the afternoon. I visited the shop, where boxes of various sizes were being made to fill commercial orders; the boys worked under the supervision of a male teacher. Half the money earned for their products was kept in a welfare and recreation fund, the other half distributed as wages and bonuses. From the welfare fund they had bought instruments for the school band, which did a march and savaged some military airs for me.

Here, also, tours of factories, farms and museums were arranged and movies and speakers were brought in. The children preferred to listen to military heroes, said Mme Wang. They were very patriotic and most of the boys were especially interested in aviation. They got more than an ordinary dosage of political indoctrination in the spirit of socialism, of course. Gangsterism? Yes, there was always that tendency among new arrivals. The staff depended upon the monthly meetings of the pupils' association and on Young

Pioneer leadership to break it up. Once troublemakers were criticized and called upon by the group to explain themselves they began to see the advantages of 'membership' and compliance with the rules. Much depended on the way teachers helped to support adolescent leadership at such meetings; it was important for the pupils themselves to be in charge.

After graduation from higher primary grades here, students were eligible either for middle school or for half-work, half-study jobs in factories. Would they be admitted to regular schools without discrimination? Mme Wang smiled confidently. 'Our students are especially welcomed – those who have the necessary qualifications. Among Peking schools with Five-S students ours ranks among the top ten. It is well known that during the steel-making campaign in 1958 we built four furnaces in three days and two nights and smelted 2,962 catties [one and a half tons] – the record amount produced by any primary school.' Drawing herself up to her full five feet, she glowed with pride as she concluded : 'On top of that, the Children's Study-Work School is famous for having won, two years in a row, the West Peking Red Banner for primary schools in sanitation work !'

It was not easy for a stranger to question these children about their past errors – for which they were far from fully responsible – without embarrassing them, and I soon desisted. They seemed to work well together and were cheerful and looked healthy. 'Disturbed children' and 'incorrigibles'? No, said Mme Wang, they had no special methods for handling them, except plenty of *ai-hsin* (love) and 'to follow a cool line' with them. They responded to the reward system as the others did. Teachers (three male and four female) were all qualified normal school graduates who had been given special training in a party school before coming here, but they were not using any foreign or Russian system of child psychology. The worst form of disapproval was the threat of expulsion from the pupils' association – loss of 'membership', ostracism and disgrace. Mme Wang said that in three years she had never had to expel a child from the school itself. That was fortunate, she added; she would have to turn him back to the courts and she was not clear herself what would then happen.

On further reflection the principal said that yes, there was one particularly difficult case of a 'disturbed' girl. She was seventeen now and the oldest child there; she had failed in her studies and had had to repeat. She was not really stupid but incredibly shy and reticent; her real reason for failing seemed to be fear of returning to 'the outside'. She had had a completely loveless childhood, full of beatings and abuse, had been raped when a small girl, had never known a home before she came here, and now dared not face the world. She was pointed out to me at one of the sewing tables. She held her head down and I watched her embroider for a moment; her work was exquisite, far more skillful than the others'.

'What will you do with her?' I asked when we moved on.

'I don't know yet. We are trying to decide.' Mme Wang obviously took a more than casual interest in this young woman. I wondered what kind of childhood she herself had had but I never found out. 'If Lin-ling were a little brighter,' she went on, 'we might find some kind of assistant's job for her here, but maybe that would be begging the question. However, we'll find a solution.'

Thought remolding had its limitations no less than 'the couch'.

Prelude to the Hundred Flowers

BY 1960 a small mountain of foreign commentary[1] had grown from the unique 'Hundred Flowers' period in China, when the Communist party urged 'the people' to express themselves freely and made available 'the necessary facilities'. Because the hiatus had occurred there was less mystery in China today than in most Communist countries about what both people and 'unpeople' found unbearable. One could not count the opposition but there was plenty of evidence of its character. Whether these estimates are correct may continue to be debated. It remains mandatory for anyone who wishes to understand something about the why and the how of Red China and the theory, technique, psychology and philosophy of its leadership to know at least the main facts, motivations and objectives behind this daring solicitation of mass criticism.

How daring was it? True, nothing like it had been seen before or since under any dictatorship; but it would also have been highly unusual in any land where the 'necessary facilities' for the expression of public opinion are owned not by the state but by private capitalists. Something like the equivalent of China's 1957 'rectification' method would occur if the owners of America's largest, nation-wide means of communication turned them over entirely to the views and demands of nonowners: working men, peacemongers, socialists, students, scholars, intellectuals, professional people, farm laborers, Negroes and other minorities – advice and dissent from 'the whole people' including John Birchites and 'comsimps', but drawing the line at outright Communists. Wholesale withdrawal of advertising subsidy and financial ruin would doubtless follow and the political repercussions would be very interesting.

The Chinese Communist press had never been completely devoid of self-criticism. Policy mistakes, blunders, incompetence, dishonesty and cases of bullying of the people by cadres were frequently exposed, and the open publication of such material formed the basis of many of the foreign attacks on the régime. Party 'rectification' campaigns, launched periodically ever since 1942, had often revealed much inner strain and dissension. At such times there seemed no attempt to conceal the worst facts against some party members, and they were often more damaging than any isolated refugee tales. During the 1953 rectification campaign, for example, cases of village cadres who had beaten up and robbed peasants, raped their daughters, and driven others to suicide were widely publicized in the open government press. But never had the leadership invited such wholesale public denunciation as it did in 1957. Why?

For Communists the world over, 1956 and 1957 were years of confusion and intense crisis. Khrushchev made his Twentieth Congress speech denouncing Stalin as a murderer and overthrew 'the cult of leadership' with devastating effects on the monolithic structure of Stalinist communism. While Khrushchev consolidated his own power in Moscow the controls loosened over satellite Eastern Europe, where Stalinist bosses fell before the assaults of 'revisionist' opponents seeking 'different roads to socialism'. The Soviet party itself was unprepared for de-Stalinization, and Peking was still less so. The complete text of Khrushchev's speech (February 1956) was not published in China (nor was it openly published in Russia). The first news reached the Chinese public when *Pravda*'s article denouncing 'the cult of personality' was reprinted in the official press in March. By then the Chinese Politburo had adjusted itself. Subsequent articles 'reaffirmed' the collective leadership principle in the Chinese party. That in no way negated Mao Tse-tung's 'great role', however – as the leader of the collective.

In 1956 the Chinese party had anticipated Khrushchev by absorbing some lessons of the post-Stalinist period. Witnessing Mr K.'s murderous fight within the Soviet Politburo following the despot's death, might not Mao logically have begun to think of avoiding a repetition of it by dividing his own power and naming a successor in his lifetime? Mao had already, in January 1956, declared it his party's intention to invite criticism and debate in an attempt to resolve 'contradictions among the people' – a promise made at a Supreme State Conference of 1,800 members of the

National Congress and party and nonparty representatives. After congratulating the nation on its unity and rapid advance toward socialism, he enigmatically discussed a policy of 'letting a hundred flowers bloom and a hundred schools of thought contend'. This was a month before Khrushchev's denunciation of Stalin.

Mao's speech of January 1956 was not published but Lu Ting-yi, the party propaganda chief, assumed the task of explaining. He declared that Mao had meant: 'To artists and writers we say, "Let a hundred flowers bloom". To scientists we say "Let a hundred schools of thought contend." '[2] He defined this as 'freedom among the people', and predicted that 'as the people's political power becomes progressively consolidated such freedom should be given even fuller scope.' Remember that this was before Mr K.'s anti-Stalinist speech.

Mutual criticism conferences between party and nonparty people were called. A drive against excessive bureaucracy had also begun early in 1956. It now branched out slightly to include criticisms of modern China's excessive conformism.[3] Satire was again raising its head. Official reporters ventured to quote a comment made at a meeting of the Chinese Writers Union. 'The themes of literary works should be unlimited,' said the speaker. '*One may either praise the new society or criticize the old.*'[4] In these words all China recognized a parody of Lu Hsun* in his best 'wild grass' period of anti-Kuomintang irony. In an official paper, also, a writer complained that 'if everybody is made to conform to the same pattern it will not only violate the laws of objective beings but also be detrimental to the cause of communism.'[5]

Still, Lu Ting-yi's 'interpretation of Mao' was not taken seriously. He had both raised and dashed hopes of a 'new freedom'. His speech was too ambiguous to smoke out twice-bitten intellectuals harboring grievances. Whether the 'Hundred Flowers' would have gone beyond party self-criticism had it not been for the Hungarian uprising is debatable.

Peking had welcomed Khrushchev's early attempts at reform. At the same time the party pressed for greater recognition of its own position as a political co-equal and sought to fill the vacuum of

---

*Lu Hsun, often called 'China's Gorky', was the most influential literary figure of the revolution until his death in 1937. He remained a national hero.

theoretical leadership left by the collapse of Stalinist absolutism. Khrushchev had yet to make a significant statement as a Marxist theoretician. It was not until the Hungarian events that China's importance to Khrushchev's fight for supremacy became apparent.

Peking's reaction to the first phase of Hungary, in October 1956, was one of sympathy for those who overthrew the Stalinist leadership there. That the East European parties were satellites in a colonial relationship toward Russia was of course well known in Peking, but Chinese theorists could not reconcile it with Marxist theory. Khrushchev's decision to pull out Soviet troops resolved the contradiction for them. In welcoming the restoration of sovereignty in Hungary, Mao's press went so far as to describe the former Soviet position as one of 'great power chauvinism' that was fairly close to imperialism itself. China for once echoed criticisms from Belgrade.

But Mao Tse-tung and his Politburo could not really be expected to understand a Hungarian party which had had no experience at all in leadership but only in obedience. They could not foresee that when Khrushchev momentarily left the helm the junior party would be lost. Having won power by their own independent struggle the Chinese found it difficult to follow the dilemmas of Hungarians obliged to administer a revolution without the prestige of having won a revolution. Once the Budapest Communists lost control and were forced to form a coalition which transferred elements of real power to petty bourgeois, anti-Communist and pro-Western groups, Peking abruptly changed tune. The Hungarian nationalist revolution threatened the dissolution of the whole Communist world bloc. Continued unity and the economic support of the bloc seemed indispensable for the stability of China's own leadership.

Chou En-lai was called back from a trip to Indonesia and India to rush to Budapest. Chou then also threw his weight against anti-Soviet party forces in Warsaw. The Premier's arrival on the Danube marked the first 'intervention' of an East Asian power in Europe itself since the days of Genghis Khan.

Unity—Criticism—Unity

THE downfall of Stalinism, Khrushchev's on-again, off-again flirtation with heretic Tito, the uprising and spreading disaffection in wavering Poland, with echoes in East Germany, and the naked exposure of the Hungarian régime's dependence on Soviet arms alone: all these occurrences could in no realistic sense be reconciled with orthodox Communist dogmas of the past. Circumstances had compelled Khrushchev to relax tensions within the satellite empire; yet as soon as he had done so events had proved how much mightier were the forces for national freedom within the captive states than any proletarian loyalty to the Soviet ideological pattern. Fighting for his life in the Kremlin, Mr K. was unable to offer any adequate theoretical formulation of his difficulties.

Now an answer was advanced in China when, on 29 December 1956, the second and much longer part of the official treatise, *The Historical Experience of the Dictatorship of the Proletariat*, appeared in the *People's Daily*. By this means Mao presented an international doctrine essentially evolved from his 1937 lecture *On Contradiction*, which he had delivered at Yenan, to analyze the class forces then at war with each other in China. 'Contradictions', said the 1956 thesis, exist not only inside bourgeois society and between socialist forces and capitalist forces, but contradictions also exist between government bureaucracies and the people inside socialist societies, and exist even between fraternal parties and socialist states at different levels in their growth toward communism. When such contradictions are allowed to reach the point of 'antagonism' or violence even a socialist state could be overthrown by its own people — misled and confused by foreign imperialists, of course.

Following Khrushchev's revelations of the Soviet party's isolation from the people under Stalin, Mao Tse-tung had ordered a widespread check on his own cadres and their 'style of work' with the masses. Under circumstances similar to those in Budapest could counterrevolution possibly occur in China, too? How dependable were the people, the intellectuals, the students – some of the responsible leaders themselves? How could anyone know unless dissenters were induced to speak truthfully under guaranteed immunity?

Tensions of this nature under Stalinism had always been resolved by secret arrests, mass purges, deportations and executions. Mao Tse-tung took a new and subtler approach when he elaborated, at the Eleventh Supreme State Conference of party and nonparty representatives on 27 February 1957, on his speech of a year before. As later published (June 1957) it bore the title *On the Correct Handling of Contradictions Among the People*, and it is a document of first importance in the literature of contemporary Marxism.

Two points might be stressed before considering Mao's speech. First, it was the opening shot of an official 'rectification' or *cheng-tung tso-feng* movement (usually shortened to read *cheng-feng*). The exact meaning is 'evaluate-rectify work-style'. The word evaluate is often overlooked but the purposes of these movements have been threefold: to assess results, to recognize merit, and to expose and correct mistakes. They aimed primarily at *party* purification.

The rectification campaign conducted in 1942 (which became a model for cyclical repetitions) is described by a party historian as follows:

Under the Leadership of the Central Committee all Party members, by practising criticism and self-criticism, made a thorough analysis of their own thinking and work, and examined the Party leadership, special emphasis being laid on opposing tendencies to subjectivism, sectarianism, and [meaningless] Party jargon. Mao Tse-tung's lectures entitled *Reform Our Study*, *Rectify the Party's Style in Work*, *Oppose the Party 'Eight-Legged Essay'* and *Talks at the Yenan Forum on Art and Literature*, and Liu Shao-ch'i's speeches, *How to Be a Good Communist* and *On Inner Party Struggle* – all played an important role in guiding the campaign.[1]

The second point is that Mao made the first (and thus far the only) attempt by any major Communist leader to draw a lesson from and provide a theoretical explanation for the Hungarian events. In doing so he evolved a kind of coping mechanism to enable his party to maintain national unity while avoiding the gross errors which he believed had led to the Hungarian uprising or, as Communists see it, 'counterrevolution'.

Mao reasserted that 'contradictions' or conflicts of interest exist not only between the socialist state and its class enemies at home and abroad, but also 'among the people'. In Mao's words:

> Contradictions do exist between the government and the masses. These include contradictions between the interests of the state, collective interests and individual interests; between democracy and centralism; between those in positions of leadership and the led, and contradictions arising from the bureaucratic practice of certain state functionaries in their relations with the masses.[2]

These truths were later rejected by Khrushchev, who in effect held them to be local problems of the Chinese Communists only, not applicable to Russia and its subordinate states.

If such terms are not to remain mere mumbo-jumbo to the non-believer it may be useful to recall again, briefly, how Marxist dialectics find tangents in traditional Chinese thought. Greek dialectical method, which Marx borrowed via German Hegelianism, had its counterpart in Chinese philosophy before and during the time of the ancient 'Warring States' (403–221 B.C.). Thoughts attributed to Heraclitus of Ephesus (examples: 'Everything is on the move'; 'God is day-night, winter-summer, war-peace, satiety-famine'; 'Tension or strife of Opposites ... out of this, harmony is created'; and 'Beginning and end are general in a circle') are remarkably comparable to those of the Chinese Taoist sages.[3] The phrase 'Let a hundred flowers bloom, let a hundred schools of thought contend' is a quotation from one of the thinkers of the lively 'Warring States' period. It does not mean literally 'a hundred' of anything but 'free struggle' of ideas in general.

The idea of 'unity of opposites' is especially manifest in the concept of Tao as depicted in the *I-Ching* (*Book of Changes*), the *Chuang-tzu* and other classics, and in symbols such as the *pa-kua*, or eight trigrams, and the more familiar *yin-yang*.

Tao is the Absolute that contains the total life force, or *T'ai Chi*. The halved circle, one side light, the other dark, indicates all the opposing stresses constantly being transformed and harmonized or synthesized in the Oneness of Nature : light (*yang*) and darkness (*yin*), male and female, dynamism and passivism, growth and decay – unity in division and a perfect dialectical symbol. Taoist symbolism permeates Chinese art, literature and science. Mao Tse-tung has frequently drawn attention to dialectical images in China's folklore in helping to popularize Marxism. Thus :

> All contradictory things are interconnected and they not only coexist in an entity under certain conditions but also transform themselves into each other under certain conditions; this is the whole meaning of the identity of contradictions ... The innumerable transformations in mythology, for instance, Kua-fu's racing with the sun in the *Book of the Mountains and Seas*, Yi's shooting down of the nine suns in *Huai Nan Tse*, the Monkey King's seventy-two metamorphoses in *Pilgrimage to the West* ... [are] transformations of opposites into each other as told in legends.[4]

Dialectical materialism used in analyzing any given historical situation – posing a thesis locked in a struggle of contradictions with an antithesis from which emerges a synthesis or continuity – was thus readily acceptable to Chinese minds conditioned by philosophical rather than theistic concepts. To Chinese Marxists, as to Marxists anywhere, the present stage of history (one of basic class antagonisms between the bourgeoisie owners and the working class nonowners) can end in unity only when the contradictions are resolved in a universal Communist society. Inside this mystique, history is not an aimless cycle of rises and falls, as in the Toynbeean mystique of chance 'challenge and response', but a set of phenomena which behave in accordance with organic laws ascertainable through Marxism.

In 1957, Mao concluded that the contradictions between the state and ex-capitalists and intellectuals and groups influenced by bourgeois thought were mainly 'nonantagonistic' or 'within the people'. There was, nevertheless, a hangover of 'antagonistic' (irreconcilable) conflict also. But in China those 'antagonistic' groups had on the whole been benign patriotic citizens who now supported socialism. That is, their nationalist sentiments which coincided with Communist aims overbalanced their anti-Communist sentiments. It was dangerous to leave any contradictions unresolved, however. If they were not met and overcome in debate they might become predominantly 'antagonistic' and result in tragedies such as Hungary.

'Marxists should not be afraid of criticism.... Quite the contrary, they need ... the storm and stress of struggle,' said Mao. 'Carrying out the policy of letting a hundred flowers bloom and a hundred schools of thought contend will ... strengthen the leading position of Marxism. ... We should not use methods of suppression ... but should argue with [critics] and direct well-considered criticism at them. ... Contradictory forces among the people are the very forces which move society forward.'

But:

'The essential thing [for critics] is to start with a desire for unity. ... In 1942 [5] we worked out the formula "unity-criticism-unity" to describe this democratic method of resolving contradictions ... inside the Communist Party.' Now it was time to extend it to the whole people. 'What is correct always develops in the course of struggle with what is wrong.' However, one must begin debate 'only to achieve a new unity on a new basis'. 'Without this subjective desire for unity, once the struggle starts it is likely to lead to ... murderous blows.'

Thus it was obvious enough that Mao did not intend to license 'antagonists' or 'evil-doers' to seek to oppose or dissent from the basic system of 'democratic dictatorship' to achieve socialism. But how can a dictatorship be run democratically? Mao's explanation: democracy means 'freedom for the people', *and* it means 'dictatorship for the enemy of the people'. Said Mao:

'*Within the ranks of the people democracy* [*stands relative*] *to centralism, and freedom* [*stands relative*] *to discipline. ... Our democratic centralism means the unity of democracy and centralism and the unity of freedom and discipline.*'[6]

It is easy to dismiss these paradoxes as sheer demagoguery. It is not so easy to recognize the underlying pretensions here to an ethical system of 'distinguishing between right and wrong' which identified party leadership with the traditional Chinese expectations of perfect righteousness in its authoritarian rulers, representing the synthesis or Unity of Opposites.

We should remind ourselves again that China did not have even the weak but important liberal tradition of nineteenth-century

Russia, which somewhat affected Lenin but never Stalin. No government in China had ever been 'liberal' enough to legalize an opposition. (Tsarist Russia belatedly attempted it.) China felt little impact from the two centuries of liberating ferment which stirred Europe from Descartes through Mill, Hume, Rousseau, Proudhon, Comte and others. But China had its own humanist tradition which idealized harmony with nature, including the nature of power. Marxism made its strongest appeals to the Chinese desire for both individual and national equality (anti-imperialism); egalitarian social unity imposed at the expense of individual liberty or license was in the logic of Chinese philosophical tradition.

According to the *Gorgias*, when Socrates prevailed in debate with the three wisest men in Greece his concluding moral was that oratory and all activity 'must be employed in the service of the right'. Moreover, said Socrates, 'if a man goes wrong in any way he must be punished and the next best thing to being good is to become good by submitting to punishment'. Mao and Socrates might never have agreed on what *is* right, but for Mao also the 'knowledge of right' carries with it the duty to 'correct' what is wrong within oneself and others and to deprive evil of its freedoms.

Mao's concepts are meant to apply to *both* party and nonparty people. In the published version of his speech he laid down six explicit 'criteria' by which critics' 'words and actions' could be 'judged correct'. All of them left no doubt that to be accepted as 'nonantagonistic', criticism must not 'undermine' but must 'help to consolidate all aspects of democratic centralism' and 'the socialist path and the leadership of the Party'.

Mao admitted that 'some mistakes' had been made by the party. During the 'suppression of counterrevolutionaries' there had been 'excesses'. He called for a comprehensive review of sentences and disfranchisements and asked that 'wrongs be righted'. He acknowledged that planning errors had resulted in 'imbalances' between supply and demand and guaranteed a stabilization of the state grain tax at the existing level. He warned party members against 'doctrinarism' and arrogance toward the people. He took note of recent 'disturbances' (strikes and conflicts between farmers and cadres) and said that 'the root cause of all disturbances was bureaucracy'. What was 'very bad' was the appearance among 'many of our personnel' of 'an unwillingness to share the joys and hardships of the masses, a concern for personal position and gain'. Mao warned such cadres that 'a considerable number of them will return to productive work' – out of the offices and into the farms and ditches.[7]

Mao's speech certainly invited the public to enter complaints against officials and party members guilty of 'bureaucratic practices, dogmatism and sectarianism'. For two months *after* he spoke that was the theme of countless meetings to discuss his meaning. The *People's Daily* and other papers summarized the 'contradictions' theory and party functionaries everywhere made known its contents to a delighted but still skeptical public. 'Bourgeois-democratic' parties summoned conferences and began to voice their criticisms.

On 30 April 1957 the Central Committee had issued a directive officially authorizing the beginning of an 'evaluation-rectification' campaign to correct the party's 'style of work'. Now the whole country broke out in a rash of forums called by newspapers, magazines, schools, factories, unions, all kinds of organizations, where party leaders listened and lesser party people and nonparty people spoke. The 'three evils' – bureaucracy, dogmatism and sectarianism – were freely denounced by those who had become convinced that they could do so not only with impunity but *with approval*. In an access of euphoria some critics forgot that neither Mao nor the party had authorized 'counterrevolutionary' demands for an end of 'democratic centralism' itself. They put forward ideas for a 'multiple party' system which exposed them as unreformed 'bourgeois democrats'.

At any rate Mao was not long in learning that not all his contradictors were 'nonantagonistic' – not by a long shot.

48

Wild Flowers

In Peking and elsewhere I spent many hours reading criticisms[1] published during the thaw and I talked to Chinese who had participated in the group 'discontent' meetings. The great bulk of protests was hurled against the Communist party cadres, the functionaries, the bureaucrats – against their arrogance, sectarianism, dogmatism, doctrinarism and abuses of power as an entrenched élite. They ranged from 'constructive' comment to outcries of bruised egos and from citations of grave injustices and inefficiencies to outright counterrevolutionary exhortations.

'Bourgeois-democratic' party leaders asked for the right to recruit students, peasants, workers and groups from other than the dying capitalist class to which they were obliged to confine themselves. A few proposed a two-chamber parliament and an end to 'democratic centralism'. Dr Lo Lung-chi, vice-chairman of the China Democratic League and then minister of the timber industry, summed up the case of the displaced intellectuals:

> There are students of philosophy who work on the compilation of catalogs in libraries, students of law who take up bookkeeping work in offices, students of dye chemistry who teach languages in middle schools, students of mechanical engineering who teach history. Among the higher intellectuals there are also returned students from Britain who earn their living as cart-pullers and returned students from the United States who run cigarette stalls.[2]

Not very many of the older and senior intellectuals made outspoken criticisms of the government or party, perhaps because of distrust of the promised immunity. But many thousands of younger 'brain workers' vociferously voiced complaints. Scientists and teachers protested against nominal responsibility in positions where real authority lay in the hands of party incompetents. Editors and journalists protested against denials of access to officials and freedom to report facts. They cited the sterile press filled with official propaganda instead of news. Housewives complained that army officers' wives wore leather shoes and 'put on airs'. Artists protested against being obliged to turn out stereotyped works of 'socialist realism'.

Teachers hated the long hours required at Marxist study meetings. Students denounced arrogant party cadres who took charge of all activities and suppressed all opinions contrary to their own. Businessmen exposed disastrous orders from party administrators in charge of their plants or shops where they had to retain nominal responsibility. Religious leaders asked for freedom to propagate the faith without having their children excluded from Red Pioneer activities in the schools. Scientists, teachers, civil servants and all groups complained of unqualified people advanced to high positions solely because of party connections while competent nonparty men suffered in the inferior ranks. Instances were cited of heavy overwork and of women deprived of adequate rest before childbirth. Some small businessmen bitterly complained that allowances to them were not adequate to support their families.

All these attacks were published in government newspapers and periodicals or broadcast over the radio. For *six weeks* no attempt was made to answer or suppress them. The party's earnestness in seeking to know exactly what the 'ten percent' thought of it is hardly to be doubted. Even demands for rights for 'counterrevolutionaries' and threats of violent overthrow of the government appeared in the official *People's Daily*. Consider this sample – by a young lecturer at the China People's University – printed on 31 May:

China belongs to the 600,000,000 people *including the counterrevolutionaries*. [Italics added.] It does not belong to the Communist Party alone. ... If you carry on satisfactorily, well and good. If not, the masses may knock you down, kill the Communists, overthrow you.

Most protests did not sound like people seeking 'unity' but people fed up with unity too long imposed by censorship. Some resembled standard out-of-office grumbling but with one very important difference. In China out-of-office meant out-of-influence in practically every field of social endeavor where the individual can command prestige. There were many expressions of agonized frustration by men who aspired to rank and role from which they were barred by the monopoly of power held by the party élite, access to which was denied them except at a low level.

A basic resentment among older Western-educated people who had assumed that they had learned something was the discovery that in Communist eyes they were ignorant. Many knew nothing of Marxism and some were simply not interested in politics but only in their specialized tasks. Now they often had to play student to party dogmatists whom they considered their intellectual inferiors – and who often were their inferiors.

Second, nearly all the alien flowers that bloomed were variations of a single species: lack of freedom – to speak, to move, to publish, to disagree. Among students the demand for civil liberties was uppermost. In the universities of Peking thousands of *ta tzu-pao* – wall papers – appeared. Many youths stopped attending classes to hear antiparty speeches and a few professors were attacked. Some students demanded the right to choose their own teachers and curricula; they wanted free food for all, and no more work in the countryside.

Children of landlord and capitalist families were later blamed for student agitation. Perhaps a few did take part but most of them were only too aware of thin ice beneath them. Many peasants are distantly related to former 'great families', however; scratch a peasant and you find a landlord's cousin. It would therefore be easy to establish 'bad class background' in almost any case.

On 25 May Mao Tse-tung reminded a meeting of the Communist Youth League that '*All words and actions that deviate from socialism are completely mistaken*'. Clearly, anyone opposed to the existing system would be following a dangerous line. Many seemed not to have heard or read what Mao said. But still the party did not counterattack. Letters and articles flooded into the press.

Some party youth leaders also joined the chorus of critics. A few protested against Soviet intervention in Hungary. The chief of the Communist Youth League propaganda department at Shenyang Normal College was reported in the Shenyang *Daily* on 11 June as having uttered these profoundly antiparty sentiments at a forum:

> The suppression of counter-revolutionaries was necessary and timely but too many persons were put to death ... Many were formerly military and political personnel of the so-called Manchukuo and Kuomintang and landlords but they were not guilty of heinous crimes ...

> The cause behind the mistakes of the campaign for rounding up counter-revolutionaries will be traced to the Party centre. ... All kinds of important questions are decided upon by six persons [the Standing Committee of the Politburo]. ... The destiny of 600 millions is directed by the pen of these six persons. And how can they know the actual situation? At best they can make an inspection tour of the Yellow River and swim the Yangtze. Even if they talked to the peasants the peasants would not tell the truth and could only say: 'Chairman Mao is great.' ... The party has never criticized itself publicly since the founding of the Republic. ... The National People's Congress must be made an organ for exercising genuine power ...

Although many critics thus took a 'line' that actually *was* 'rightist', or counterrevolutionary, in Mao's context, few objected to the socialist aims of the state. Relatively few complained of personal hardships, food shortages, or long hours of work. Many demanded trials of party men held responsible for wrongful punishment of alleged counterrevolutionaries. (Mao himself had called for a 're-examination'.) Charges of general police brutality, corruption, bribery and immorality were rare. Some labor union members accused the party of 'commandism' (coercion without discussion and persuasion) and cited demands for overtime work without pay. The 'Hundred Flowers' was mainly a blooming among both party and nonparty intellectuals. It unfortunately evoked little direct testimony from the less articulate peasants, still the vast majority of the people – as well as the party! But 'rightist peasants' were later to come in for a different kind of thought remolding which began with the communes.

There were many thousands of *ta tzu-pao* tacked on bulletin boards before schools, farms and factories of which only a few could see print. Many nonparty editors given freedom to publish what they liked must have retained themselves within self-imposed bounds of discretion. Despite these limitations the party had by early June accumulated enough data to keep it occupied in rectifications both inside and outside the organization for many months to come. On 8 June the *People's Daily* launched a counterattack. 'Correct criticisms' were still invited but the publication of Mao's speech on 17 June, with addenda including the 'six criteria' of loyalty, left no doubt that many had already violated those sanctions.

The party turned the tide. Meetings continued to be held but their purpose now was to denounce 'rightists' and to praise the party in 'evaluations' with which 'critical critics' had forgotten to sweeten their 'evaluation-rectification' of 'work-style'.

49

Counterattack and Paradox

ONE curious thing about the Hundred Flowers period was the intensity of the party campaign to evoke criticism of itself. It almost seemed that quotas had been handed out to selected groups of intellectuals, with bonuses for overfulfillment promised to the energetic.

Another puzzling aspect was that even after new criticisms were cut off in mid-June the government press and radio continued to broadcast attacks against itself. For months the 'rightist' speeches or essays were published while their authors were being haled into forums. The difference now was that they were met with counterattacks from party supporters. Here is one excerpt from a 10,000-word open letter to Mao Tse-tung written by Yang Shih-chan, an obscure teacher of accounting in Hankow:

> During the campaign for the suppression of counterrevolutionaries in 1955 an untold number of citizens throughout the country were detained by the units where they were working (this did not happen to myself). A great many of them died because they could not endure the struggle [thought remolding].... This is tyranny! This is malevolence! ... articles on human rights have become a kind of window-dressing to deceive people ... I admit that in seven years ... achievements are predominant. However, on the particular question of our policy toward intellectuals I should say our policy has been a failure. In the last seven years ... the intellectuals who chose to die by jumping from tall buildings, drowning in rivers, swallowing poison, cutting their throats, or by other methods, were innumerable ...[1]

If that letter had been published before the restoration of official censorship it would be an understandable part of the editor's discretionary responsibility. But it was not easy to see what function it served *for the government* in the post-blooming period. I asked an official about it. His reply was, 'If we did not publish the lies of the rightists how could the masses be aroused to the danger and take action?' How could he be so sure that the 'masses' would recognize them as 'lies'? His answer did not satisfy me but I should have to stay longer in China than I did to find an adequate explanation.

That the party's legions had been kept silent for so long a period doubtless intensified the severity of the response when it came. Prime targets were Lo Lung-chi and Chang Po-chun, the two most outspoken ideological critics and leaders of the Democratic League. There was no legal indictment. Instead, they were subjected to merciless attacks in meetings of their own peers which were fully reported in the press. Hundreds of students and intellectuals whose views were linked with those of Lo and Chang – who were accused of striving to restore bourgeois democracy and capitalism – were disgraced and called to account in public meetings.

Both Chang and Lo were obliged to make humiliating confessions of having held 'incorrect views'. An excerpt from Lo Lung-chi's *mea culpa* delivered before his peers in the National People's Congress must suffice to illustrate the nature of 'rightism'. He said:

I am a guilty creature of the Chinese People's Republic. I have spoken and acted *against the Communist Party and socialism*. ... I am to be held culpable for egging on and adding fuel to the subversive acts of rightists and even reactionary and counter-revolutionary elements. ... I did not ask the *original Party organs* to reverse the wrongs done [against counterrevolutionaries] but worked for the establishment of a *new organ* to do it. Here I attempted to *negate the leadership* of the basic level of the party. ... I had attempted to ... expand the organization and *raise the position* of the China Democratic League, thereby acquiring a relatively big voice in national affairs. ... This was where my dream stopped. I do not have and have never had any scheme for the overthrow of the Party and socialism or for the reinstitution of capitalism ...[2]

Thus it became clear that, in Mao's view, any critic who did not seek to help the party leadership, but opposed or competed with it, was committing a crime. It is odd, of course, that anyone as sophisticated as Dr Lo could have concluded otherwise from Mao's speech. But here is an anomaly. Neither Lo nor Chang ever admitted the charges of a 'conspiracy against the state', which were eventually dropped. Indeed, Dr Lo was permitted to go to Ceylon even after the antirightist campaign began; he would scarcely have returned if he had feared entrapment in a conspiracy. Both Lo and Chang lost their ministerial portfolios but both were restored to their positions in the Political Consultative Conference and took part in the discussion of a successor to Mao Tse-tung held in April 1959.

Thousands of people who had gone beyond 'seeking unity' were denounced as rightists in counterattack meetings led by party wheelhorses. Many who had allegedly 'struggled against' the party's leadership were removed from positions of responsibility by 'the masses' in the form of votes of no-confidence at meetings of their organizations led by Communists. Very often they were suspended from their posts or had to take inferior jobs while attending weekly study groups and expiating their guilt. Passage of the Law of 17 August 1957 also made it possible for those expelled by their organizations to be subject to 'corrective labor'. The timing of the legislation suggests that it may have applied to many 'rightists' undergoing thought remolding. No complete statistics were published on the number of 'rightists'. In October 1959 the government announced that the label had been lifted from 26,000 – which I was told unofficially was 'the great majority'.

Among 'rightists' shifted by 'their own organizations' to work in the communes was Hsiao Ch'ien, a British-educated novelist and editor who was an old friend of mine from Yenching University days. He had had the misfortune to be editor of the *Wen Yi Pao*, a literary paper which published some slashing attacks on party cultural leaders and their policies. I inquired about Hsiao Ch'ien when I met Lau Shaw (Hsu Shih-yu), whose *Rickshaw Boy* was a wartime Book of the Month in America. He had so far overcome that handicap that he was now vice-chairman of the Writers Union. He told me that Hsiao Ch'ien was 'happily working in a commune' and 'no longer much interested in writing', a change of character which I could not at all imagine. He insisted that only a 'small minority' of members of the Writers Union had been sent to do farm labor.*

By contrast, I dined in town with a group of students and professors I had known years ago; they were all in their forties or

*(1970) Lau Shaw himself committed suicide in 1966 when he was attacked by Red Guards as a 'revisionist' and 'capitalist roader'.

fifties now. I ran over a list of names of party and nonparty people. One was now a deputy mayor; one was a vice-minister; one was an ambassador; one was a publisher, another an editor; there was an engineer here, a doctor there, a few teaching, others retired, some killed in the war or dead from natural causes, four or five in Hong-kong, and quite a number in the National Congress.

A Very High Official told me quite flatly that only persons engaged in counterrevolutionary 'acts of violence' were arrested and that no mere dissenter, individualist or critic of party mistakes was punished. (That may depend on whether one considers public denunciation punishment.) According to him the promise of immunity was fully observed. In *The Hundred Flowers* Roderick MacFarquhar offered no evidence of any executions during the period beyond those of three student leaders of a 'revolt' near Wuhan. Accused of leading physical attacks on officials and police and attempts at organizing 'armed rebellion' in the countryside, these students were executed before 10,000 people. MacFarquhar thought that they were singled out because the government was more concerned about disaffection among students – traditionally the leaders of popular discontent in China – than among any other group.[3]

There is nothing conclusive about all this, but from what I could learn in China I could say that it was not fear of physical liquidation or even of concentration camps which tormented those intellectuals still unable freely to adhere to the party, but the far subtler and socially more complicated means of securing conformance. Thought remolding, or 'brain washing' as it is called abroad, conducted not in concentration camps but by one's peers; a choice for stubborn 'reactionaries' between social ostracism and the anguish of public recantation; a spell of down-on-the-farm at the recommendation of one's own organization; and various other measures which in the past would have been called public 'loss of face': these were the main instruments of pressure.

'You can have no idea how agonizing these self-criticism and group meetings can be,' I was told by one American-educated intellectual who returned to China a decade ago and joined the party. 'Everybody in my bureau from the office boy or scrubwoman up can tell me how bourgeois I am, criticize my personal habits, my family life, my intellectual arrogance, the way I spend my leisure, even my silences. I have to sit and take it.' He paused to grimace. 'Some people prefer suicide rather than submit to it. It took me years to get used to it but now I believe it has been good for me. I needed it – how I needed it! I am seldom a target any more. I am a lot humbler than I was. I value people more. I am better able to help others.' And he, I repeat, was a party member in good standing.

A notable thing about the public denunciations of intellectuals during the 'anti-rightist' campaign was that they were aimed at very few, if any, senior scientists or academicians and practically no graduate scientists or engineers of any kind. That the party was especially scornful of Lo Lung-chi and other nonscientists – men with degrees in law, social studies and the arts – was doubtless partly because such men also represented the only political leadership-potential capable of offering an alternative to the régime.

Conversely, it is certain that the 'blooming' was genuinely intended by the leadership to induce 'useful' intellectuals to express their grievances in the hope of reconciling them and drawing more such men into the party.

Another paradox. From the volume of denunciation poured forth against a mere handful of nonparty critics and 'bourgeois democrats' it was evident that such people as Lo Lung-chi and Chang Po-chun furnished convenient pretexts for a major overhaul of membership in the party itself. *The rectification affected immeasurably more Communists than non-Communists* and reached as high as provincial governors and committeemen, many of whom were dismissed from their posts. Thousands of party members were denounced for the 'three evils', as well as for 'rightism'. As many as one million cadres may have been put on probation. In one province the governor, judges of the supreme court, an army general and even the first secretary of the party were removed. Statements published against them *by the open press* included a report that the first secretary had made publicly such utterances as 'famine occurred continuously', 'we are sitting on top of a volcano', 'the problem of food production will not be solved in ten years', 'the peasants are beasts of burden, human beings harnessed in the fields' and 'girls and women pull harrows with their wombs hanging out.'[4]

Final paradox. To this same province, a few months later, came Mao Tse-tung on a personal fact-finding tour, part of the time in Liu Shao-ch'i's company. Of all the consequences of bloom-and-contend and 'search for unity' none was more momentous than this. Here in a province of party dissension there now began an experiment – the people's rural communes – which would in less than a year shake Chinese society more fundamentally than anything that had happened since the revolution.

Part Five

NORTHWEST: OLD CRADLE
OF NEW CHINA

THE party secretary in Honan province wrote an article in which he said that the attainment of communism for the 'whole people' would some day be marked by the commune's ability to satisfy each person's ten basic needs: free supply arrangements covering all accommodations for marriage, birth, food, clothing, shelter, education, health, theater (entertainment), burial services – and 'haircut', meaning cosmetics and adornment. Leo Tolstoy wrote a story called, 'How Much Land Does a Man Need?' His penniless hero wandered to a tribe which possessed limitless grassland, and there the good-natured chieftain promised the visitor all the land he could walk around between sunrise and sunset. The poor man's greed far exceeded his strength; by sundown he had run so hard to complete his boundaries that upon his return he fell dead at the feet of the chief. He was buried in a six-foot plot of land, which was all he then needed.

In prophesying a time of 'each according to his need' which would correspond to a 'withering away of the state', Marx could not avoid, despite his hard-headed realism, the temptation to hold forth the image of man finally perfected, as have all great religious teachers. All the experience of modern civilization to date, whether under socialism or communism, tells us that the greater become the means of the attainment of equality among men, the greater becomes the necessity to curb and reform mankind's incessant greed and selfishness.

Yet one can of course envisage a distant Utopia where the 'whole people' have become one with and consumed the entire state apparatus and its rulers into their selfless selves. That time would seem to await the day when men and women of great nations like China, Russia and the United States could amicably agree on the meaning of 'how much' is 'in accordance with need' – in simple matters like food, for example, or a haircut. The most encouraging fact in the list of the ten necessities was the omission of any kind of weapon.

Of Blue Ants and White

BEFORE investigating the people's communes one needs to see something of the hard logic of large-scale collectivization in China in relation to her fearfully difficult demographic problems. Over-population was not something invented by the Communists but was inherited. By greatly increasing mass employment and intro-ducing the first effective rationing system ever known in China, the Communists had so far prevented the traditional annual har-vest of deaths by mass starvation. The paradox was that imbalances between population and food supply seemed to be intensifying everywhere in the world, almost in proportion to the success of measures to prevent disease, increase longevity, and improve con-ditions for legalized sexual activity. The dilemma at times made one wonder, with Graham Greene, if God was entirely serious when he gave man the sexual instinct. (Mr Greene reminds us that it was St Thomas Aquinas who said that He made the world in play.) Whether we were to regard the situation as tragic or merely amus-ing might depend upon whether the condition was permanent or temporary. Chinese Communists – perhaps fortunately for the rest of the world – believed that it could, in China at least, be remedied.

Overpopulation is a relative term. If China were as densely popu-lated as England, Belgium, the Netherlands or Japan, there would be between three and four billion Chinese, or more than the present world population. *Studies on the Population of China, 1368–1953*, a remarkable book by Ho Ping-ti,[1] vividly suggests that this might well have happened if the Chinese had colonized the New World or otherwise escaped natural and man-made catastrophes. In his classic *Histoire de la Chine*, René Grousset gave census figures gathered in the Ming and Ch'ing dynasties as follows: 104,700,000 in 1661; 182,076,000 in 1766; 329,000,000 in 1872.[2]

'Are the Chinese,' many worried Malthusians asked me on my return to America, 'doing anything at all about birth control?' Not enough, no doubt. But the Chinese government was doing a lot more about it than the government of the United States.

China is slightly larger in area than the United States. In 1870 the American population was 38,000,000. By 1960 it had increased by about five times while China's population merely doubled. Europe and China are almost equal in area. China had about 200,000,000 blue ants at the time the white ants of Europe (with a population of less than 50,000,000) began migrating on a mass scale. Since then Europeans have filled three 'new' continents (and parts of a fourth) with an aggregate population of 420,000,000. If we combine that with the 1960 population of Europe (including Russia) we get more than a billion people and see that the imperiled West has been doing its share of propagating.

In this perspective there was some irony in European fears of a yellow peril from a people that had taken five thousand years to fill out China's present frontiers on one continent while Europeans were seizing and populating most of the world. In the 1960s the Chinese increase was at about the same rate as that of the United States. But China's base was so large that *les fourmis bleues* might number a billion by 1980. By then the white ants would be two and a half billion, however, if fruitful pullulation continued at current tempos.

Thomas Malthus maintained that human ants of all kinds inevitably 'multiply faster than the means of subsistence'. If he was right, crowded stay-at-home peoples – the Indians, Japanese and Chinese – are doomed to famine or wars of expansion. Such catastrophes are not likely to be confined to the East. Before the revolution modern contraceptives were known and used by only an infinitesimal fraction of the Chinese population but 'native methods' were practiced. Abortion was illegal but frequent; infanticide was the 'guaranteed method' widely in use by the poor. In China, impoverished families had fewer children than 'well-to-do', the reverse of the usual situation in the West.[3] More than a century ago Marx ridiculed Malthus, and Russian Communists have done likewise. Before taking power the Chinese party rejected birth control on

Marxist grounds that man could produce his means of subsistence faster than he reproduced himself. After six years of effort to double the rate of food output compared to population growth, with erratic success, the Communists adopted a more realistic policy. In 1956, Peking recognized the practical necessity to limit births 'in order to lighten consumption by nonproducers during the present period of socialist construction', as one advocate put it. A nation-wide campaign spread knowledge of modern 'family planning' methods to every village and town. Graphic posters, picture books, movies and demonstration lectures carried the methods right into the peasant's home. After a trial period these efforts waned at a time which coincided with the development of commune plans.

From conversations with Women's Federation leaders I concluded that the campaign encountered mass resistance due to the following reasons: The peasants and some peasant-minded workers 'weren't ready for it yet'; they still associated offspring with old-age security. (By law children were still obliged to help support their parents.) Sex and childbirth are matters of private management which people are reluctant to turn over to the state. Competent instructors were not yet available on a mass scale. Despite greatly lowered infant mortality rates, peasants still wanted extra children as insurance against high infant-mortality rates as remembered from the past. Peasants asked how it benefited them to live in a welfare state if they didn't use their right to reproduce. Latent sentiments of filial piety and centuries of male-ancestor worship could not in one decade be submerged by the Marx-Engels concept of the family.

As with nearly everything else, party cadres overfulfilled their quotas on mass birth-control propaganda. Too much and too soon, it ran into the same kind of opposition met by earlier campaigns to enforce the new marriage law which legalized 'on-demand' divorce. In the past divorce for women was practically unknown in China. Sudden party insistence on women's use of their new rights went to such extremes as developing 'fronts' among husband and wives, and calling 'frank confession' meetings in public. After dissatisfied concubines had shed their aging husbands and numerous men and women had dissolved misalliances arranged by their parents, divorce ceased to be popular. The campaign boomeranged until the marriage law became known as the 'divorce law'.

Contraceptives were on sale for both men and women. At various hospitals and clinics I found that standard devices were available at the equivalents of twenty to thirty American cents. I was told that they were supplied gratis when necessary. In remote Szechuan at a rather primitive clinic I was shown charts, demonstration equipment and plentiful supplies but was also told that the demand for instruction was 'light'. A pessary there cost thirty cents. Existing supplies would doubtless prove inadequate if the population applied en masse, but for those presently 'planning' there seemed to be no shortage.

Both abortion and sterilization were as easily available in China in 1956 during the 'family planning campaign' as advice on contraception. In 1960, while the advice was still disseminated through radio talks and literature, sterilization was obtainable only through a doctor's recommendation and abortion was discouraged although still performed on the same condition.* The extent to which people may submit to sterilization was indicated by experience in India, where significant cash inducements were offered together with free surgery. By 1960 only 22,000 cases were reported, or about one in 20,000.

A British-educated Indian demographer, S. Chandrasekhar, of the Institute of Population Studies of Madras, visited China in 1959. Like most travelers, he was 'continually impressed by how clean and neat everything was', but he drew attention to the consequences for China's food economy. In the *Atlantic Monthly* of December 1961, Mr Chandrasekhar wrote that in 1959 the birth rate had attained forty per thousand while the death rate had been reduced to 'twelve per thousand, an incredibly low figure for an Asian country. The infant mortality rate, a sensitive index to a community's level of public health, environmental hygiene, and total cultural milieu, was around fifty per thousand births every year.' Mr Chandrasekhar elsewhere said in effect that this repre-

---

*(1970) In 1964 the author learned while in China that abortion had become available on demand of the expectant mother alone. A machine now widely in use enabled the performance of abortion by vacuum removal, a supposedly speedy, safe and relatively painless method.

sented a reduction of about seventy-five percent as compared to prerevolution estimates.

Mr Chandrasekhar's figures did not apply to the country as a whole; as stated above, China's annual increase was about two percent, if the 1953 census was correct.[4] This figure was also given to me as 'average' by Chou En-lai in 1960.[5] Even if China's increase dropped to as low as the Japanese rate (1.01 percent;[6] the United States rate was forty percent higher than Japan's) the result would be six to seven million more Chinese annually.

Literature and radio broadcasts continued to publicize techniques of birth control and periodicals urged young people to use contraceptives for family planning. Many workers and peasants I questioned, as well as the college girls I have mentioned, said that they were 'planning' for no more than two or three children. Party members told me that within the party 'undisciplined' procreation was frowned upon. Most high-ranking party members had small families, although I knew at least one who (somewhat embarrassedly) as late as 1960 celebrated the birth of his seventh child in quest of a son! The two-child family was regarded as ideal and party functionaries received no extra allowances* for more children.

A means of 'planning' which might not work in another society but had produced a noticeable effect in China was the officially sponsored social approval for late marriages. For an ambitious student, early marriage could be a handicap, as in the West, and now everybody was supposed to be an ambitious student. The prestige of the party and the press behind marriage for men at twenty-five to twenty-seven and for women at twenty-one to twenty-three as 'ideal' had made it stylish among the closely party-led youths. Their example might eventually impress the 'outer-directed' peasant masses, who also did not like to be found behind the times or 'old-fashioned'. The party did not 'select brides and grooms', as reported abroad, but young people often consulted group leaders as well as parents before they married.

---

* Party and nonparty cadres or state employees were divided into eight 'grades' which corresponded to workers' levels in salaries and rations, but they got extra allowances, usually small, in accordance with the different demands of their tasks.

There was thus no 'reversal' of policy, nor could anything like an increase-the-race campaign now be seen.* What had happened was that the Chinese realized that far more immediate solutions to problems of underemployment, underproduction, and maldistribution of man power were needed than family planning could provide. China's already existing millions were a fact of *Realpolitik* which could not be changed by a command from Mao Tse-tung. Nor was it good politics, in China any more than elsewhere, to tell one's constituents that they should never have been born. That Mao and other leaders had repeatedly declared China's numbers to be her 'greatest asset' also presented a contradiction to overdependence on birth control and spurred them on to seek other solutions.

No long-range adjustment could change the facts that more than sixty percent of China's vast territory stood above 6,600 feet and another fifteen percent might prove nonarable because of climate and topography. Until advanced industrialization made more extensive and intensive farming possible, the immediate problem would remain the overpopulation of China's available cropland. On the North China plain the average density was more than 1,000 per square mile. In parts of Szechuan and the Yangtze delta it reached 3,000 per square mile. The national average was now not more than 0.39 of an acre of farmland per inhabitant (assuming a 1962 population of 700,000,000).

Yet China's agronomists by no means saw the outlook as hopeless. Japan stood as proof to the contrary. With only about 8,000,000 acres of grain croplands (or scarcely more than half an acre per cultivator) Japan now turned out annually about 20,000,000 tons of basic cereal food, most of it rice.[7] If China could equal Japan's performance, her annual harvests (considering her higher percentage of multiple cropping) would indeed quadruple. If, furthermore, China's cultivable farmland could eventually be doubled – as her leaders now asserted – she could not only satisfy her own needs but become a major grain exporting country for the first time in history.

---

*(1970) By this date birth-control clinics and propaganda centers had reached into virtually every urban street organization and rural commune, and Premier Chou En-lai had declared China's aim to be reduction of the rate of population growth to about one percent per year.

Britain and West Germany had only half as much cropland per inhabitant as China; Denmark, the Netherlands, Japan and Belgium all had even less than that. Yet the per person income of China was from one tenth or less to one third or a fourth as high as in those countries. The difference was of course explained by the degree of industrialization, modernization of agriculture, and trade development. The farmers of China were not less capable, and the I.Q. of its people was no lower than that of any other people; historically its society had demonstrated an efficiency higher than that of most nations. China's natural resources were now known to be not inferior to those of the countries cited above; they were markedly richer than those of Japan, where the effective organization of human labor had been the foundation of present wealth.

Japan had achieved her gratifying grain output by the most intensive kind of scientific cultivation, including the use of ten or more times as much chemical fertilizer per acre as China, and by extensive application of power, mechanization, crop protection and government grain controls. (As in China, farmers in Japan were required to make fixed grain deliveries to the state.) By 1958 China's industry was not yet producing modern means of agriculture on anything like the scale required. In that year the Great Leap Forward and the organization of the people's communes were launched for a variety of reasons. Among them lay the hope that communes would reward the party's search with at least interim answers to the problem which plagued many countries besides China: too many people living on land producing too little to feed them.

Co-ops to Communes

ON 29 August 1958 the Party Central Committee published its earthshaking directive which called for the establishment of People's Communes: 'It seems that the attainment of communism in China is no longer a remote event. We should actively use the form of the people's communes to explore the practical road of transition to communism.'

Up to this date China had not yet completed even the first stage of what Mao Tse-tung had called *semisocialist* rural cooperatives. Suddenly:

agricultural cooperatives with scores of families or even several hundred families can no longer meet the needs of the changing situation ... the establishment of people's communes with all-round management of agriculture, forestry, animal husbandry, sideline occupations and fishery, where industry, agriculture, exchange, culture and education, and military affairs merge into one, is the fundamental policy to guide the peasants to accelerate socialist construction, complete the building of socialism ahead of time, and carry out the gradual transition to communism.[1]

The directive demanded prompt merger of all producers' cooperatives into large units embracing whole townships (*hsiang*) each 'comprising about 2,000 peasant households'. Township governments and township party committees were to become commune governments and take control of former cooperatives.

Share funds were to be pooled and assets and debts consolidated. While some cooperatives were richer than others, the 'cadres and masses' should 'be educated in the spirit of communism' and 'not resort to minute squaring of accounts, insisting on equal shares and bothering with trifles.'

The transition from collective ownership to ownership *by the people as a whole* may take less time – *three or four years* – in some places, and longer – five or six years or even longer – elsewhere ... differences between workers and peasants, town and country and mental and manual labor ... will gradually vanish. After a number of years ... Chinese society *will enter into the era of communism* where the principle from each according to his ability and to each according to his needs will be practiced.[2]

Community dining rooms, kindergartens, nurseries, sewing groups, barber shops, public baths, 'happy homes for the aged' and agricultural middle schools were to be organized. 'Large-scale agricultural capital construction and more advanced agricultural technique and rural mechanization and electrification', and cooperation 'which cuts across the boundaries between cooperatives, townships and counties', should be realized by the new commune governments with pooled labor, tools and resources.

In the whole history of the People's Republic there had never been such an abrupt and sweeping change ordered by so loosely worded a directive. Editorials and articles in the press offered much more radical and explicit authorization for the communization of remaining private property. In particular, the 'Regulations' followed by the first people's commune to be publicized – called Weihsing (Sputnik) in Honan province – provided an exact prototype. In September the Honan party secretary wrote :

Amid the high tide of water conservancy [building of dams, reservoirs, irrigation canals, by mass labor during the Great Leap Forward] and increased production, people in the whole province broke down the boundaries between counties, townships and cooperatives; extensive socialist cooperation involving millions of individuals was organized in the cities and countryside, and mountain areas and plains, brushing aside personal considerations ... and remnants of private ownership.[3]

The Honan 'Regulations' required each village co-op to 'turn over all its collectively owned property'. That included co-op shares – which would 'bear no interest' – and 'privately owned plots of farmland, house sites and other means of production such as livestock, tree holdings, etc.', to be surrendered 'on the basis that common ownership of the means of production is in the main in effect'. Co-op members could 'keep a small number of domestic animals and fowls as private property' but no more.

Communes must build more irrigation works, apply more manure, provide better seeds, breed animals, fight pests, 'develop industry as rapidly as possible', open up mines, iron, steel, farm tool and fertilizer plants, build electric power stations and roads, establish telephone and radio networks, take over education and the militia, organize supply and marketing departments, deliver grain quotas to the state at fixed prices, and control all trade for the whole system of cooperatives. Everyone would be provided for 'in accordance with his work'.

'The commune shall institute a system of centralized leadership, with management organs at various levels, in order to operate a responsible system of production.' Village co-ops were to be grouped as production brigades under multiple-village 'production contingents'. The production brigade was to become 'a basic unit for organizing labor' under commune direction.

The commune administration was to improve medical establishments and build 'housing estates' that would gradually replace individual homes from which 'bricks, tiles and timber' would be used by the commune 'as needed'. Owners were not to be compensated for the old houses or house sites or for their land used for public works. From the yearly income, welfare funds 'not exceeding five percent of the total income' were to support cultural, health and public services, and grain stocks 'sufficient for one to two years' were to be accumulated. All food would be supplied by the commune, with wages paid to 'ensure high speed of expanded production'. When members reached an average 'living standard equivalent to that of well-to-do middle peasants the rate of increase in wages should be reduced to ensure the rapid growth of industry, the mechanization of farming and electrification of the rural areas in the shortest possible time.'

Fantastic? No. Within the context of China's demographic and land problems, it was in theory highly logical. Even today it seemed possible that the rural commune more or less as originally envisaged might eventually provide a rational solution for China. What went wrong?

What threw the communes for a great initial loss was the incredible haste with which they were established; the lack of adequate experimentation and preparation; the suddenness of the mass leveling imposed on prosperous villages and prosperous individual farmers when they were equalized with poorer ones; the lack of incentives to replace the drastic withdrawal of autonomous village control; the threat to home life before a broader community life had been fully established to replace it; the enormous technical responsibility and initiative demanded from inexperienced and poorly trained cadres; and the ruthless disregard of 'the principle of voluntariness' by a vast army of township bureaucrats who mushroomed overnight and began to take charge of every hour of the people's lives. When unbelievably bad weather added its powerfully negative vote, the communes were rapidly driven back into a preparatory stage which the party had tried to jump over in 1958 – at great cost to production.

Who was responsible for the hasty and euphoric directive of 29 August? At first glance it looked like Mao Tse-tung. Yet with special reference to the organization of co-ops Mao himself in 1955 had repeated an old wartime slogan: 'Fight no battle that is not well prepared, no battle whose outcome is uncertain.' He said that 'a great deal of spade work' was necessary before even producers' cooperatives could be accepted over all China.[4] As late as June 1957 Mao still thought a period of *five years or a bit longer* would be required merely to 'consolidate the cooperatives and end these arguments about their not having any superior qualities'. He added, 'It is estimated that it will take roughly *four or five* five-year plans [i.e., till 1972–5] ... to accomplish, in the main, the technical transformation of agriculture on a national scale'.[5]

Yet only a year later the party was leading the universal establishment of the ultraleftist communes (promising 'ownership by the whole people' in three or four years), and Mao's name was being invoked to sponsor them! This was one of many threads of mystery yet to be untangled. Before touching a few more of them a review of the main stages of agricultural transformation may help establish some perspective on the communes.

Remember, first, that 0.39 of an acre of farmland was available per rural inhabitant! For the Communists the equalization of private land ownership was merely a first step to an end, and so their party program openly declared. To win 'majority' support they had, for purposes of 'agrarian reform', divided the rural population into great, middle and small landowning families, about ten percent of the population; rich and middle peasants, twenty percent; and poor peasants, tenants and farm laborers, seventy percent of the population – the 'have-nots'.

By 1952 the landlords had lost most of their land, the owner-tillers had retained most of theirs, and 300,000,000 peasants (sixty percent to seventy percent) had received 118,000,000 acres* or forty-five percent of the cultivated land. Parcels handed out varied from only .15 to .45 acres per person.[6] The Communists thus sought to make allies of roughly 300,000,000 peasants, and to neutralize about 100,000,000 more. 'In the land reform we can and must unite about ninety-two percent of the households or about ninety percent of the population in the villages,' Mao lectured the party cadres in 1948. 'In other words, unite all the rural working people to establish a united front against the feudal system.'[7] On the support of these millions of 'rural working people' – and especially on the support of women and youths who shared in the distribution – the Communists heavily depended in every subsequent phase of the transition toward large-scale farming.

The new owners lacked good seeds, animals, livestock, fertilizer, tools, scientific methods – and capital. Individual earnings from fragmentary subsistence plots could never secure these necessities. Even before the land distribution was completed an all-China campaign began for mutual-aid cooperatives such as had been long established in the old Red bases in the northwest.[8] Coercion was used by extending or withholding state loans and by state control of the market. Poor peasants who pooled labor, animals and implements in group cultivation and harvesting, and in general tasks of community interest, got maximum state assistance. Advantages were obvious and probably most peasants readily joined cooperatives in self-interest – as they did also in the next stage, conventional farm cooperatives.

From 1952 to 1956 rural cadres, using a combination of persuasion and such coercive means as described, led the peasants from agrarian reform to mutual-aid teams to elementary cooperatives and finally to the stage of 'advanced' producers' cooperatives. Under the elementary co-ops the villagers pooled their land, animals and

* 700,000,000 *mou.*

other resources in exchange for shares which represented the value of their individual investments. Their income was based on share value plus their labor contribution. The 'advanced' co-op was a whole village – sometimes several villages – of 100 to 200 families who elected a local council ('congress') which chose its own managers. The peasants turned in their deeds and resources, income was collectively owned and invested for the whole village, and wages were paid in accordance with work performed.

The advanced co-op had many advantages, particularly when several villages formed a big one. Council management could join small plots into large ones, decide what land was best suited for orchards, pasture, and irrigation, how much was needed for cash crops like cotton, how much for consumption, and how much to invest in new equipment and construction. All this had to be co-ordinated with plans at the township and county levels but the village retained much power of decision. Farmers still lived on land to which, although it was now held in common, they felt individual or ancestral attachments of ownership. No one could know from afar, however, with how much heartache and trepidation the individual peasant gave up the security of the land deed, in exchange for purely hypothetical advantages to come from the collective. Retention of minuscule private garden plots helped somewhat – but only somewhat – to compensate for loss of that sense of personal independence attached to ownership of the land.

True, the advanced co-ops could do things beyond the reach of the individual farmer. But few co-ops were rich enough to buy modern tools or build good canals, power dams, roads, mines, cattle breeding stations, local railways, or establish farm equipment, fertilizer and consumer-goods industries. Only the larger multivillage co-ops could do those things. Villages with improved land forged ahead faster than those that had drawn poor land and the former did not readily enter into multivillage planning with the latter. Private plots seldom exceeded a twentieth of an acre but in prosperous villages the smart peasants got hold of the best gardens, lent money to other peasants, established a claim on their output or land and acquired livestock. They soon began to resemble small *kulaks*.

By 1957 about 120,000,000 households, or ninety-six percent of the peasantry, had pooled their cooperative shares (for which they

had exchanged their former land deeds) and their means of production in common 'ownership at the village level'. They formed
740,000 advanced agricultural cooperatives. While the villages were
thus in effect led into rural collectivization, China's machine and
handicraft industry and trade and commerce had been put through
its phased transformation from private to public ownership. By
1958 the state's control over both industrial and agricultural production and distribution was ninety-nine percent complete. Control,
but not absolute ownership – for farms were still collectively owned
by the villages. Otherwise, one quarter of the people on earth had
been added to the 'socialized sector' of the world market.

There was considerable slaughtering of animals and recrudescent
banditry led by rich peasants opposed to cooperatives in 1953, and
again in 1956 and 1957 following the accelerated drive for collectivization. All that was relatively small-scale trouble. Some foreigners said that Chinese peasants were 'too passive' to resort to
violence. But China's history is stained with the bloodiest peasant
rebellions of all time – by virtue of one of which, indeed, the present
régime was founded. I believed there were no peasant strikes or rebellions on anything like a mass scale because the peasants themselves knew that miniature private farms wouldn't work and were
mostly resigned to the inevitability of social ownership.*

The speeded-up collectivization in 1956 did cause considerable
desertion from the land, however. Loss of incentive among the
stronger peasants may have partly accounted for the disappointing
harvest. Despite better weather than in the previous year the food
crop increased only 1·3 percent, or less than the population growth.
This brings us back again to the mystery of the communes and the
way they were launched.

*(1970) Formation of communes in China radically differed from Stalin's
collectivization, which ruined a *majority* of the Russian peasants by
liquidating the *kulaks* as a class. They were not even given beds and work
on the collectives formed from their land but were forced to become urban
laborers, or starve, or end in Siberian slave camps.

At Whose Demand?

SOPHISTICATED observers abroad have ridiculed reports from China that the communes were 'started by the peasants'. To believe that widespread spontaneous demands by cultivators compelled the party to establish communes would of course be absurd. Yet late in 1957 the party actually moved to decentralize cooperatives and to halt more big mergers. On 14 September the Central Committee passed a resolution which stated:

Experiences in different localities during the last few years have proved that *large collectives and large teams are generally not adaptable to the present production conditions* ... all those that are too big and not well managed should be divided into smaller units *in accordance with the wishes of the members*. Henceforth a collective should generally be the size of a village, with over 100 households. ... After the size of the collectives and production teams has been decided upon it should be publicly announced that this organization will remain unchanged in the *next ten years* ...[1]

Collectives 'the size of a village', with an average of a hundred households, and to 'remain unchanged for the next ten years', was certainly no description of the huge commune, embracing scores of villages, which was so soon to follow. A hypothesis advanced by Western analysts is that the origin of the commune lay in a kind of intraparty seizure of power by a left wing in China during the months June to November 1957. Donald Zagoria expounded the theory in great detail in *The Sino-Soviet Conflict, 1956–61*.[2] The left (with Liu Shao-ch'i indicated as its mentor) was supposed from this date to have pushed the challenge to Soviet leadership in the Communist camp, and in foreign policy forced abandonment of the Bandung principles in favor of more militant struggle against colonial and bourgeois régimes, as well as against imperialism.

Internally, according to this surmise, it adopted a more radical agrarian policy as an aspect of rivalry with the Soviet Union for world leadership of the party and as a demonstration of the power of people to build socialism without major Soviet aid.

External and ideological factors undoubtedly played a role in the decision to form communes. As may be seen from the above resolution, however (which Mr Zagoria seemed to have overlooked), the party was actually moving away from agrarian radicalism just at the time his hypothetical left 'coup' should have been in power. The evidence to date suggested that the communes were – like many past Chinese Communist innovations – a synthetic solution, worked out collectively, to meet a set of circumstances which had not been foreseen in the particular combination that occurred, and that they were not adopted until prolonged argument had reconciled differences in a majority opinion.

A starting point in this set of circumstances was that the poor harvest of 1956 had forced an emergency hunt for means of stimulating rural production without reducing capital investment in industry. Among several possible solutions the first would have been new loans from Russia. In November Mao Tse-tung had gone to Moscow to attend the world conference of Communist parties. There he made proposals for a militant international strategy which would have made China more important to Russia and a candidate for additional economic as well as military aid, including atomic support. Mao's trip produced no cash. China was to have new trade credits but no capital. On the contrary, amortization installments due Russia necessitated continued output increases in the agricultural raw materials of industry, particularly cotton.

China could not borrow foreign capital and all domestic wealth had been utilized. Or had it? What about idle man power, the 'poor and blank' millions whom Mao and other leaders had emphasized as China's greatest asset? In January 1956, when Chou En-lai presented the draft Twelve-Year Agricultural Plan – to bring 'food plenty' by 1967 – he had pointed out that farm labor was underutilized. China's 120,000,000 rural households were capable of supplying 45,000,000,000 eight-hour labor days but only about 30,000,000,000 days were needed for farm tasks. Chou said that the plan would eventually use about 15,000,000,000 additional labor days which would be available when all able-bodied rural males worked 250 days a year and able-bodied females worked 120 days a year. (As early as 1925 a respected Western-trained economist had estimated China's combined unemployed and underemployed labor force as 168,000,000.[3])

There was also much urban underemployment. For years the party had opposed the 'blind peasant drift to the cities', a phenomenon characteristic of newly industrializing nations. No measures had been able to halt a growth in the urban population of 23,000,000 in five years; in 1957 it had reached 94,400,000. But this rate of urban increase was two and one half times faster than growth of nonagricultural employment.[4]

It was against that background that the Central Committee on 24 September issued another directive (by no means incompatible with the 14 September directive mentioned above) calling for mass mobilization of labor to construct public works. A month later the revised draft of the Twelve-Year Agricultural Plan was accompanied by slogans exhorting everybody to cut short the period by a couple of years. After the autumn harvest, from November onward, tens of millions of people were put to work repairing dikes, planting trees, digging reservoirs, making roads, collecting all kinds of organic and inorganic fertilizers, and starting small industries.

The wave of socialist construction swept on into 1958, as millions leaped forward along the 'general line' of 'aiming high and going all out to achieve greater, faster, better and more economical results'. Foreign visitors saw a countryside in convulsion, as armies of blue-clad peasants, drums beating and flags waving, attacked their joint tasks of cultivating, digging, building, as if committed to battle. Newspapers carried reports of people 'eating and sleeping in the fields day and night' and of women cadres who 'worked forty-eight and seventy-two hours without a rest'. At this time twelve- and fourteen-hour work days in the fields were common and press reports told of people collapsing from fatigue. In less than *six months* China claimed to have more than *doubled* her irrigated lands. At least seventy million people worked at collecting fertilizer alone. Every machine was in use. To move earth to and from new dike works and canal reservoirs workers began to build miniature wooden railways. A few small native hearths were built to supply them with iron rail strips. The 'back-yard' furnace movement began.

Mass feeding at canteens became common. Strong young women were brought into the work and someone had to take care of their children and household chores; community services were organized. Swarms of office workers, students and intellectuals were sent from towns to help out; some of them set up spare-time schools for the illiterates. To maneuver masses of people on labor projects required organization and discipline, and local militia groups took charge. Common dining rooms, kindergartens, nurseries, sewing groups, cooperative industries, had all been introduced by the army and cadres during the civil war. Many urban factories, government and party organizations already had such arrangements. Now they spread to the countryside in the wake of 'agricultural armies'. Resemblance to the program of the *Communist Manifesto* and to Marx's description of the Paris Commune became striking. For example:

Equal liability of all to labor. Establishment of industrial armies, especially for agriculture. [From the *Manifesto*.]

Combination of agriculture with manufacturing industries; gradual abolition of the distinction between town and country, by a more equable distribution of the population over the country ... Combination of education with industrial production. [From *The Civil War in France*.]

It remained to define this new way of solving mass underemployment in the countryside with a reorganized village life and stamp upon it the name 'commune'.

The Great Leap Forward in production and new employment was not, of course, confined to the rural areas or the agricultural economy. According to a carefully documented and highly significant study of 'Manpower Absorption' during this period made by John Philip Emerson, the nonagricultural labor force by 1958 reached 58,000,000, an increase of forty-three percent in that year alone. Industrial employment increased by 15,500,000 while 'construction and modern transport' absorbed another 5,000,000 persons.[5] A one-year forty-three-percent growth in nonagricultural employment made sensational gains reported in industrial output for the Leap years – as well as subsequent farm labor shortage – somewhat more credible. (Much of this was, of course, unskilled or semiskilled labor on temporary location.)[6]

On his return from Moscow late in November of 1957, Mao had found preliminaries to the Great Leap Forward already in motion. The rectification campaign had subsided in the cities. In the villages it was directed against 'rightist' peasants who resisted advanced cooperatives. In mid-winter Mao made a tour through the South, visiting factories, schools, and housing developments. During a 'surrender your hearts' campaign, youth offered its 'all-out' support to Mao and the big leap. Apparently reassured, Mao settled down for a long investigation of farm cooperatives. In the early spring he spent a month in Honan.

We may now recall that one result of the Hundred Flowers was the revelation of a deep division in the Honan provincial party. A series of reports denouncing 'rightist' leadership in Honan had been accompanied by a purge led by the central party supervisory committee under Liu Shao-ch'i himself. The new Honan secretary, Wu Chih-pu, further clarified the issue as a struggle which followed the dissolution of a number of large-scale cooperatives on orders of the former leadership.

Yielding to the demand of a small number of well-to-do middle peasants, a few rightist opportunists within the Honan provincial Communist party committee indiscriminately tried to compel all the large co-ops to split up.[7]

Throughout 1957 the rectification campaign had been 'conducted in the cities and the countryside as to the two roads – socialism or capitalism', according to Wu. Advocates of collectivization had overcome 'the onslaught of bourgeois rightists, [ex-] landlords, rich peasants and counterrevolutionaries' and 'the spontaneous tendency toward capitalism among the well-to-do middle peasants'. Thereafter the people had resumed their 'march forward along the socialist path'.

With resumption of the merger of small co-ops, public works projects were undertaken along lines already described – 'socialist cooperation on a vast scale'. Various welfare facilities were organ-

ized and 'in the cities, too, an increasing number of factories were
built and more and more community services' initiated. This was
the urban commune (soon abandoned) in embryo. All through
North China experimentation continued in the winter and early
spring of 1957–8. When Mao reached Honan in April,

... people were not yet aware of the real nature of the development.
Only after Comrade Mao Tse-tung gave his directive regarding the
people's communes did they begin to see things clearly, realize the
meaning of this new form of organization that had appeared in the vast
rural and urban areas, and feel more confident and determined to take
this path.[8]

Whether the communes had been discussed and already set up in
Honan and elsewhere in advance of Mao's travels I do not know.
One could recall that when in 1953 the party first published its
resolutions calling for the creation of 'primary cooperatives', thousands already had been formed on the basis of secret directives
issued two years earlier.[9] Now, in any event, Mao Tse-tung was not
openly credited with sponsoring the communes until 16 July 1958,
in an article in *Red Flag*. Here it was asserted that in accordance
with Lenin's advice to 'Communists of Eastern countries' to apply
Marxism 'in the light of special conditions unknown to the European countries ... realizing that the peasants are the principal
masses', Mao Tse-tung had launched the Great Leap and the communes to speed up socialization and help to realize communism 'in
the not distant future'.

Obviously annoyed by Chinese attempts to push ahead of
Russia's own 'stage of socialist development', Khrushchev told
Senator Hubert H. Humphrey on 1 December 1958 :

'You know, Senator, what those communes are based on? They
are based on that principle, "From each according to his abilities, to
each according to his needs." You know that won't work. You
can't get production without incentive.'

Feeling that he was 'about to fall out of his chair', the Senator
said : 'That is rather capitalistic.'

'Call it what you will,' Khrushchev replied. 'It works.'[10]

The Soviet party, then ostensibly still China's close ally and
mentor, evidently had had no advance warning of the Chinese

commune program. This fact in itself lent some weight to the belief that it was a more or less spontaneous development and a name and form applied to conditions which grew out of the 'leap forward'. Moscow's reaction was at first cautious and then increasingly negative. Had not Russia in the earliest days tried a kind of agricultural commune and proved that it would not work? Anti-Stalin though Nikita Khrushchev might be, in this instance he soon made it clear that Stalin's views on premature egalitarian movements were his own.* In a 1934 party report Stalin had declared:

The future agricultural commune will arise ... on the basis of an abundance of products. When will that be? Not soon, of course. But be it will. It would be criminal to accelerate artificially the process of transition from the artel [cooperative, in which the incentive system prevails] to the future commune. ... The transition from the artel to the future commune must proceed gradually, to the extent that all the collective farmers become convinced that such a transition is necessary.[11]

How could China, more backward than Russia, attempt any such transition toward communism? The answer must be found in the party's belief that their people had already 'changed fundamentally' even though the technology had not. In this they were to be proved mistaken, judging by the speedy retreat from claims that they were a means of *early* attainment of communism. Their appearance and continuation even in modified form, however, were to add greatly to the developing tension between Moscow and Peking. For the whole theoretical implication of the Chinese communes was that an *Asiatic form of Marxism* could develop more rapidly toward true communism than Marx, Lenin or Stalin had foreseen.

Not without reason had the Chinese named their prototype commune Sputnik – a pace-breaker of their own launched under 'conditions unknown to European countries'. One may thus imagine Mao's state of mind in the midst of the new 'upsurge in the

---

*(1970) What Khrushchev neglected to point out was that Stalin had attempted the forcible imposition of 'communes' in Russia in 1929–30, with catastrophic results, which he later blamed on his own Central Committee men, including Khrushchev. It was only then that he discovered the virtue of gradualism in collectivizing.

countryside', as he described it. Masses of men and women mobilized, performing prodigious feats, banners flying, seizing nature, changing it, turning rivers and mountains – the wealth of 15,000,000,000 'surplus' labor days put to work at last. What should be done? Send them back to the villages as before the Great Leap? Decapitalize labor? Or make the tempo of the leap a permanent thing, provide a new social and organizational form for it – with a promise of early abundance as reward? Was not this the psychologically correct moment to build in everybody 'the spirit of communism'? Only one more push would bring China into large-scale socialized farming and leave behind, forever, the 'spontaneous tendency toward capitalism among the well-to-do peasants'.

But where would the vast new array of administrators, accountants, technicians of all kinds needed at the township level, be found to organize communes? In 1955, to those who had objected that the cadres were 'not prepared' to lead collectivization Mao had replied: 'If we do not guide the peasants in organizing one or several producers' cooperatives in every *hsiang* or village where will the "cadres' experience" come from, how will the level of that experience be gained?' Leadership 'should never lag behind the mass movement. As things stand today the mass movement is in advance of the leadership.' Those were probably his answers in 1957, also.

And yet, when I asked a Very High Official the direct question, who did give the final 'push' that launched the communes, his answer was, 'The peasant masses started them. The party followed.'

The transfer of much of the responsibility for rural modernization directly to an all-embracing authority offered advantages of decentralization. At the same time it focused political and economy control at a level much easier for the central government to manipulate. Third, the commune administrations would theoretically provide Peking planners with the means to universalize standards of farm production, to limit consumption, and to extract savings for investment on an increased scale. The communes would 'make it easier for leadership', Mao had said. So it would seem – but did it?

53

Communes to Brigadunes

'IF the Commune should be destroyed, the struggle would only be postponed. The principles of the Commune are perpetual and indestructible; they will present themselves again and again until the working class is liberated.' *Karl Marx*

Whatever doubts existed in the party must have been overcome mainly by widespread unpublicized organization of communes, with apparent success, throughout the spring and summer of 1958. When the open directive was issued in August, probably half the countryside was already in transformation. By November all the nation's 740,000 advanced agricultural cooperatives, embracing ninety-nine percent of the peasantry, had been engulfed by 26,000 (later consolidated into 24,000) communes.

Management councils were set up by the former township governments and party committees. In effect they became 'organs of state power', or 24,000 'states within the state'. Commune administrations took over direct management of trade and commerce, small industries, bookkeeping, banking, marketing and supply, education, communal dining halls and kitchens, housing, medical care, and the training and command of the militia as well as public works.

The mutation happened far too suddenly for all the technical problems and social implications to be understood even among the eight or nine million cadres of peasant origin, not to say the peasant masses. Many rushed ahead to establish 'real communism' right away. Wu Chih-pu had reported a 'free supply' system in Honan whereby the costs of 'seven of the ten basic requirements of life are borne by the commune', namely : eating, clothing, housing, childbirth, education, medical treatment, marriage and funeral expenses. Accordingly, at least a few communes began unrationed 'free supply' of food, clothing and other staples. They soon exhausted their reserves. Some commune leaders took command of the new militia to march and countermarch peasants to do jobs for the township, with long hours of work and inefficient food arrangements; in their zeal they often interfered with harvesting and other work.

More experienced party leaders merely supervised local production and management and waited for the village production brigades to agree on plans for joint projects. Such communes showed great progress. Others at once began forming villages into barracks-like military reservations. Some communes turned all personal possessions into public property, right down to pots and pans; others did not. Many canteens and nurseries began mass operations before they had been through a trial period, and dissatisfaction followed. Prosperous peasants and villages leveled by the amalgamation were often the best and strongest farmers. For many of them the welfare advantages offered by the commune must have seemed poor compensation. Malingerers and weak peasants now got the same food and benefits as hard workers. Where was the incentive? The amount of fiscal chaos created by the wholesale pooling of village accounts under the township finance department may be imagined.

Very greatly increased agricultural production quotas were worked out between the state and the commune planners, in which the small village cooperatives had little voice. Whereas in 1957 something like eighty-nine percent of the net farm output was set aside for consumption and only eleven percent was used for accumulation and investment, close students of the economy believed that in 1958 plans might have called for an accumulation as high as fifty percent.[1] To maintain consumption at the 1957 level would have required an overall increase in output of about eighty percent! Did Peking really believe it possible? One reason for transfer of the statistical responsibility to the cadres was said to be impressions on high that well-to-do peasants had been cheating; the output of their farms and the tiny private lots was thought to be much larger than the statisticians had been reporting. With the pooling of all farms, plus gains from new waterworks, improved cultivating methods, more fertilizer, and anticipated mass enthusiasm for the communes, it may be that something like a planned miracle was actually expected. Held answerable for both quota fulfillment and statistics, the cadres provided them, many of them self-deceived.

Despite the gross exaggerations of the 1958 harvest figures, however, other aspects of disorder were already so abundant by the end of the year that the top party leadership abruptly ended the excesses and began what was to become a general retreat. Meeting in Wuhan,* the Central Committee adopted resolutions in which it definitely reversed itself on several points and on others cleared up the ambiguity of the August directive.

Even at a very rapid pace it would 'take a fairly long time to realize, on a large scale, the industrialization of the country'. Ownership 'by the whole people' was no longer something to be attained in 'three to five years' but had to await completion of industrialization. That would take 'fifteen, twenty or more years'. Until then China as a whole would remain in a stage of 'socialist construction' – although as the communes built and financed public projects those would, of course, be owned by all. Meanwhile people would work indefinitely for wages; those who had begun a 'free supply' system were wrong. Food was to be considered part of wages, payments for work would be divided into six or eight grades, and peasants would be supplied in accordance with skill and output. A system of rewards was to be enforced.

Other incentives were restored. The communes which had declared personal possessions – such as bedding, furniture, cooking utensils, bicycles – 'public property' were ordered to rescind the proclamation; where such property had actually been seized it was to be returned immediately to its original owners. The working day was acknowledged to be too heavy. A guarantee of 'eight hours of sleep and four hours for meals and recreation, altogether twelve hours' was declared a minimum, even in busy planting and harvesting seasons. The use of community dining rooms and nurseries and kindergartens became optional. Existing houses were to be restored to private ownership, and members could live in them 'always'. Decisions to build new housing could be taken only by the villages themselves. Such housing should be constructed so that 'the young

* Between 28 November and 10 December, the Sixth Plenary Session of the C.C.C.P.C. reached these decisions, which were made public on 16 December 1958.

and aged of each family can all live together'. The integrity of the three-generation family was thus reaffirmed.

Above all, misuse of the militia as a means of organizing production had to end at once. Many cadres had 'misunderstood'. What was described as 'getting organized along military lines', said the directive, meant 'getting organized on the pattern of a factory' or a factory farm – *not* an army where the member had no voice or vote. Commune chiefs could *not* be militia commanders. 'It is absolutely impermissible to use "getting organized along military lines" as a pretext to make use of the militia system – which is directed against the enemy – to impair, in the least, democratic life in the communes.'

The most astonishing part of the December communiqué was the news that Mao Tse-tung had decided not to be a candidate for a second term as Chairman of the Republic in the elections due in 1959.* Henceforth he would 'concentrate his energies on dealing with questions of the direction, policy and line of the party and the state; he may also be enabled to set aside more time for Marxist-Leninist theoretical work.' At the same time a reform and reorganization movement was launched to 'tidy up the communes'.

More fundamental decisions of the Central Committee were announced (in part) in March 1959. New directives then greatly decentralized the commune. Now 'three levels of ownership' were recognized: commune or township ownership; production brigade or village ownership; and ownership by the production team, or group of ten to twenty families. The commune itself owned only those factories, tractor stations, power plants, new schools, public buildings, reservoirs, railways, and such enterprises as were financed or built by the villages as a whole. These remained great achievements of regimented mass effort but many people were later to question the price paid for them.

'The basic level of ownership' was restored to the village or

*(1970) During the Great Proletarian Cultural Revolution, Red Guard publications alleged that Mao's resignation from chairmanship of the government had not been voluntary but had resulted from what appears to have been a concession made in exchange for the Central Committee's agreement, in 1959, to remove P'eng Teh-huai as defense minister and replace him with Mao's choice, Lin Piao.

brigade – ownership over its land, farming tools, animals, forests, fisheries and local industries and schools built with village funds and labor. Ownership at the family level included houses, personal possessions, private plots, poultry, etc. In 1961 this system of ownership was 'guaranteed'.

Later on it was made clear that 'ownership' carried with it rights of management. The brigade controlled its own labor, tools and animals. Commune authorities could no longer impose quotas or crop plans or commandeer village labor except in agreement with production plans of the brigade and the production teams of ten to twenty families. The latter were recognized as the 'basic accounting units', with wide autonomy conceded to them in the use of their cash income and spare-time labor once collective quotas were fulfilled. With emphasis on collective 'overfulfillment' reduced, the production teams were greatly stimulated (by local loans to buy breeding fowl, pigs, goats, and fertilizer) to increase 'side-line farming' on family plots. It was noted that often the farmers who responded most enterprisingly to these incentives were also those who overfulfilled their brigade tasks.[2] In 1961, for example, the official *People's Daily* reported on one commune in which private plots were as large as ·55 *mou* and where private income accounted for twenty-two percent of the total earnings of the average family, while the collective economy – which remained 'on a priority basis' – increased its grain harvest by 133,000 catties.[3] Here each family 'ate on the average about ten chickens and ducks that they themselves had raised'; during the same year each sold 'an average of fifteen domestic fowl' on the market. Families were reported maintaining from sixty-six to seventy-seven fowl, and from one to two pigs each, largely fed on sweet potatoes grown on their private land.

With the Central Committee's directive of January 1961, which envisaged 'two or three years' of 'consolidation' and of priority development of food production as the fundamental basis of the economy, all new building loans were decided in accordance with the principle of 'letting the communes and the production brigades depend primarily on their own resources'. Beginning late in 1960 and in the austerity years 1961 and 1962, the state granted farm loans only to purchase 'means of production commensurable with the material to be supplied' in exchange. Loans requested had to be kept within 'fifty percent of the commune's public reserves' in cash and materials in any given year.[4]

All this meant in effect a recovery of rights by the advanced agricultural cooperative. By the time I left China many village powers of self-management had been restored. The commune had become a loose federation of brigades. In 1961 the commune bureaucracy was reduced by eighty percent. Cadres 'in overwhelming majority' were sent back to field work in the farms and villages.

Most of these changes were indicated in rectification directives following widespread self-criticism of errors and excesses in open press articles, especially in the latter part of 1960. A sense of reality began to return to the countryside. Grain quotas were greatly lowered. Commune institutions like nurseries, kindergartens, canteens and schools were turned back to village management. The brigade was guaranteed sixty percent of its product for consumption. State controls of the market were modified for all but five basic items and staples. Village fairs were revived, and families were encouraged to sell side-line produce and raise pigs, chickens and goats for private consumption or sale.

Thus the communes survived in name but it was the 'brigadunes' that were running them – with plenty of help from private initiative.

Rural France, Italy, Switzerland and other parts of Europe are still administered under townships called 'communes'. These trace to days of the French Revolution when men also dreamed of the ideal equalitarian society. Many such communes still own certain property in common but they have become bourgeoisized; they have never been able to abolish inequality nor to establish the law of 'to each according to his needs'. Whether the commune in China would in 'fifteen, twenty or more years' have attained that ideal state no one could know. But it was still a very different society from anything ever seen in Europe.

54

Chairman Yen

BEHIND all the communes stood human personalities and countless small beginnings.

Yen Wei-chuan, chairman of the Yellow Ridge Commune, had started from one of those small beginnings. In July, I visited Yen and the farmers on Yellow Ridge's 9,300 acres of grain, vegetable and pasture lands, situated some twenty-five miles east of the city walls of Peking. Yen had been to Peking only once.

He was attired in the peasant's blue cotton jeans, blouse and cloth-soled shoes, but he wore a badge of distinction, a cheap wrist watch – often given as an award to prize workers. His three-room, brick-floored, thatch-roofed cottage boasted a wall clock and several pieces of good Chinese furniture. He looked younger than his thirty-six years and younger than his wife, two years his junior, who was his assistant. His hands were heavily calloused and his head was shaved almost bald. He was all farmer, and fully at ease only when he talked his trade.

After I had listened for hours to the usual outpouring of figures, dates, tributes to Mao Tse-tung, the 'general line', the 'eight-point charter for agriculture', and praise for the communes, he reluctantly answered some questions of personal history :

'My parents were poor tenant peasants of Yellow Ridge. I can remember we were hungry every winter. If there was a flood or famine we had to go into debt to survive. My mother died of sickness and starvation during the Japanese occupation. My father is still alive and a working member of the commune. When I was seven years old I began to do farm chores. I slept under my father's quilt till I was fourteen. At that age I became a full-time farm worker hired out to a local landlord [an indentured laborer]. We belonged to the six families in ten who owned no land and were sharecroppers or laborers.

'Education? I had had two years of character study but had forgotten most of it by the time of liberation. I could not write even "moon" or "sun". Since then I have become fully literate through spare-time study. In ten years we have wiped out illiteracy among about 5,500 adult members of our more than 6,000 commune families.

'Was I a soldier, you asked? No. I have always been a farmer here. I did not take part in the revolution; I knew nothing about it.

'After liberation our landlord fled. I received my portion of land and began to eat better. Party cadres asked me to join a mutual-aid team with three other poor families. As master of my own land for the first time I was grateful and wanted to help. I had few tools and needed help, too. They chose me as team leader.

'The new village council gave us some seeds. I also received a rubber-tired cart and I took charge of transportation. At that time we had no other wheels. In 1951, our first year, our families together made 160 yuan besides food – more cash than we had ever seen before. We bought some tools and better seeds. We recruited four more families and formed a small cooperative. I was again elected chairman.

'Our first year as a co-op was very tough. Floods destroyed both our spring and summer crops except on one farm – and by August we had nothing to eat. In this situation even brothers quarrel. It was a bad year everywhere [the Korean War?] and we could get little help from the government. Some wanted to leave the land for the city. We called a meeting and persuaded the one family with a surplus to lend the co-op seed and food instead of selling at a good profit. We had enough food to eat for one month. Very late in the season, then, we eight families, adults and children all working, planted our land in vegetables for one more try. Other peasants laughed at us; they thought we would never be able to bring in our crop. By intensive cultivation, luck and shock-brigade methods, we brought in a rich harvest in record time. That year our income increased by more than half. We were able to buy not only tools and seeds but eight bales of cloth to make winter clothes for every family and new shoes and new sashes, pay off our debts and still have a surplus. Seven of those families had never before owned a new suit of clothes.

'After our success, neighbors recognized the superiority of co-operative farming. More than fifty families asked to join. We took in twenty-five families and helped the others organize separately. In 1954 we took in the whole village, 106 families, and total income increased by about sixty percent. Already ten other co-ops existed in the whole district. In 1955 we took in another village and had altogether 296 families. We formed an advance cooperative and I was still chairman. By 1957 we had doubled our original assets.

'Since then – well, our co-op joined the commune, and you see the results all around. Great improvements we couldn't have dreamed about in the past – income up twenty percent in 1959 alone, and for us that was a year of floods.'

'Results all around' included the Yellow Ridge first-brigade head-quarters, a long, neat, one-story brick building in which we sat, a combined meeting hall and theater, in a tree-trimmed courtyard and flower garden. In one wing I had already visited a young girl, peasant by birth and a middle school graduate, who operated the brigade broadcasting station. Three other brigades owned stations and also broadcast to the commune's fifty-six villages, each with its receiving sets and amplifiers spreading music, news, lessons, orders of the day, exhortations and messages from local leaders. Another girl operated a switchboard; all villages were now connected by phone.

'– and 5,300 meters of high- and low-voltage electric wire, 370 electric water pumps, eleven tractors, four trucks, 500 rubber-tired carts, 1,500 horses and mules,' said Yen, talking faster than I could write.

'That's what co-ops and communes have done for us. A clinic for every brigade, altogether five doctors, forty-four medical assistants and nurses, ninety-six community dining rooms, our own factories making our own tools, fertilizers and building materials. Who could talk about machines and electric pumps in former times? What poor farmer ever heard of regular meals, good clothes, cash in the bank, schools and medical care for everybody? Even in good years we were hungry and in rags; in bad times our people died of starvation, sold their sons and daughters, or worse –'

'What about your children now? Working or in school?'

'They are in school, of course, and of course they work. Everybody goes to school now and everybody works. My oldest boy is in his second year in junior high school; he wants to be an engineer. My two daughters are in primary school. They do farm work in their spare time – just like Peking students who come to help us sometimes. My children already have a far better education than I had. Schools? We have twenty-three primary schools with 8,000 students; three middle schools, 1,800 students; 120 kindergartens and nurseries, I forget how many little ones – but all our children go to school now. We also have four spare-time and technical schools for adults.'

'And you're the elected head of it all – top man? In America they'd call you a self-made success.'

Yen gave a puzzled glance at Shen Yao, the district party secretary, who had sat quietly listening through all this. They both looked at me curiously.

'You are making a joke,' Yen decided. 'I do not know how it is under capitalism but here nobody is "self-made". I am like everybody else, doing what work I can for socialism. How could I, an ignorant impoverished peasant, "make myself" anything without the party, the leadership of Mao Tse-tung, the methods of Marxism and socialism? We owe everything to them.'

As for Shen Yao, he was in his mid-forties, with short gray hair grizzled like a German Mecki doll's, a lined and deeply sunburned face; in dress a peasant, physically hard as nails, bright, quick, serious and confident in manner, not unpleasant, he was obviously a disciplined, well-trained party veteran. He studied me shrewdly and made occasional asides to a woman secretary who took notes on my questions. I told Shen I'd guess he was an old Eighth Route Army man.

'Right,' he said. 'I fought in the Wu T'ai Shan area.'

Over a luncheon of local vegetables, fresh salad and chicken, I reminisced a moment about Wu T'ai Shan's wartime leaders – Generals Nieh Jung-chen, Tsai Chuan, Ch'en Keng – whom I knew years ago. Shen Yao warmed up. I learned that he was a primary school graduate and had been to party institutes besides having had military training. Child of a rich peasant family of Shansi, he had joined the Red partisans and worked as a peasant organizer for twenty years, the last eight of them in this district, where he had broken in Yen and other brigade leaders. Beside him, Yen was a boy. Shen Yao was the top brain and command of that whole commune.

55

A Commune That Worked

A SUBTLE and vital relationship between the party man and the party-groomed local peasant natural leader, directly elected by the village, existed throughout China's 24,000 communes. (The village, brigade, and township or commune council chairman was usually, but not always, a party member; as a rule he was not the district party *leader*.) On the strength, intimacy and mutual confidence of this relationship largely depended the growth or failure of Chinese agriculture. When the local party leader was a 'foreigner' his task was harder. He had to know both peasant psychology and sound farming practice, make the party's directives understood and accepted by the people, organize enough support to prevent former landlords and able but antiparty peasants from taking dominance, and give the majority a feeling of pride of ownership and active management.

To expect to find 24,000 men at the township level and another 750,000 at the village brigade level, all of equal excellence in experience, intelligence and necessary flexibility in the implementation of generalized and often contradictory or ambiguous party slogans and directives, would be highly illusory. Among the more than eight million party members of peasant origin were many commune, brigade and village team production leaders. The party deeply permeated the entire peasantry but of course the peasants were far from homogeneous. It would be a mistake however to visualize a few party men sitting on top of the peasants; millions sat beside them at all levels and were related to them by village and family ties. In many instances the district party secretary (or boss) was also the elected commune chairman. If such a chairman happened also to be a peasant of local origin who had grown quickly in both practical farming and political knowledge and competence, the chances for a high degree of success were enhanced – as I observed in several instances.

In Yellow Ridge two percent of the adult commune members – about five hundred men and a hundred women – were party members. Here the party secretary and the commune chairman (also a party member) obviously worked in harmony; they had been together for years and the secretary was one of the community. That this relationship was probably equally satisfactory throughout the brigades and teams was, I assumed, an important factor in this commune's prosperity.

More than eighty percent of the party members at Yellow Ridge were local people and seven in ten were actively engaged in production work, according to Shen Yao. They also served as functionaries under the commune management committee's various departments and subdepartments, which included the following: agriculture, industry, animal husbandry, public health and sanitation, culture and welfare, accounting and planning, public security and militia, justice, savings and banking, machinery management, and commerce or supply and marketing.

I was told that about seventy percent of the population had formerly been landless peasants; the rest were middle or rich peasants who had kept their property in the land distribution. Much of the area had been an imperial hunting park in the days of the Empire; half of it was low sandy marshland. During distribution many former tenant peasants got the worst land; the area flooded easily and needed extensive drainage work. When the advanced agricultural cooperatives were organized the 'well-to-do' peasants, finding themselves in a minority, had had to contribute heavily to the common investment in rehabilitating the poorer land.

'Our investment in irrigation had been too small', Shen Yao explained. 'Despite all our work our dikes failed to hold the local floods of 1959, the worst in a century. Four fifths of the land was under water. It wasn't just one flood. We had had very good early crops but our autumn planting was ruined. Our seeds were washed away four times! In the old days that would have meant total ruin for the poorer peasants. They would never have been able to fight such floods as individual families. Those who were not affected would have opposed having their lands dug up into ditches and canals to save the poor families.

'Now it was a different matter. All our brigade leaders got together and drew up an emergency plan for the whole *hsiang*. We selected one half of the land that was easier to drain and mobilized "the whole people" to work on that alone – with the harvest to belong to all. It was very late in the season. By using all our machines, tools and labor, and a maximum of fertilizer, we managed to plant five thousand acres just in time. From then on we had excellent weather. By hard labor we brought in a bumper harvest – better than 1958. Even the prosperous peasants did better than ever. After the harvest we returned to the flooded lands. Again using all our resources we finally completed a whole new system of dikes, dams and drainage ditches. We rebuilt the villages with joint funds. We greatly improved the soil. What was once the poorer half of Yellow Ridge is now almost as good as the wealthy half.'

Distribution of income at Yellow Ridge indicated a very high rate of growth in profits and an extraordinarily rapid rate of capital investment and increase in assets which were fairly typical of *well-run* collective farms. After deductions for taxes, materials, depreciation, loan payments, all the costs of production and marketing – except wages – the net income in 1959 at Yellow Ridge, 8,180,000 yuan ($3,350,000), worked out at 314 yuan per head or 1,362 yuan ($559) per family. The individual peasant-workers did not actually receive any such sums. Of the total collective profit the commune invested about forty-five percent in new construction and equipment, including six more tractors, fifty carts, sixty horses, and seven power lathes. All these were held in common; each brigade or village had ownership rights to their use, and shared in the profits of enterprises. Eighteen percent was budgeted for loan funds, recreation, health, pensions and reserves. Wages amounted to the balance of about thirty-seven percent or 3,026,000 yuan. Their reserves, excluding fodder, amounted to five to eight percent of the product. These sums or credits, as well as wages, were distributed by the production brigades, 'the basic accounting unit'.

Some ten percent of the wages was paid to outside seasonal and part-time labor (mostly in food). That left a theoretical balance of

454 yuan average income per village family. Some families with as
many as four full-time adult workers easily earned as much as 1,000
yuan ($410) annually, according to Chairman Yen Wei-chuan.
The theoretical 'income' of a family with only one actual wage-
earner was about 250 yuan. Wages were figured (as elsewhere) on
a piecework rate. In a mixed farming economy such as that of
Yellow Ridge, rates were highly differentiated, with 'work points'
ranked according to standards commonly agreed upon among the
workers.

How much did the peasant see in cash? One third of all wages
was in the form of food for consumption supplied to members by
the production brigades. This mainly took the form of grain. In
Yellow Ridge, with a heavy truck garden output, all vegetables
consumed were (then) free. Farmers also had private plots of less
than one fifth of an acre. Those I saw were planted in corn to
feed the family chickens and a pig or two for local consumption or
sale.

Deductions for nursery and kindergarten costs and various contributions reduced the average family income by ten to twenty
percent. Normally no more than half the wage was paid over
monthly, the rest being credited to the member's savings account,
theoretically accessible at the end of the year. Shen conceded that
there was strong pressure on the peasant to accumulate, that with-
drawals were made sparingly, and often only after discussion with
the team leaders. (By way of comparison, a 'poor commune where
the soil is infertile and the economic foundation weak' was reported
in February 1962 as having provided for every family 'seventy
yuan in cash on the average [apart from food and basic services]'
in the previous year. There were 888 families; the whole commune
had a 'favorable balance' of 62,000 yuan in cash. Some members
'wanted to buy good clothes' with their cash while others 'wanted
to buy expensive [!] goods'.[1])

All over the country I saw peasant homes with one or more of
the following: wall clocks, radios, vacuum bottles, furniture,
lamps, abundant bedding, spare clothing, and even books and
paintings – which owners told me they had bought with their
savings. It would be a rare home that did not possess one such new
'luxury'. Obviously, however, the semiblocked savings accounts

were a means for capital accumulation and investment in capital construction.

Even with a *cash* income of no more than ten to twenty yuan per month, the families of Yellow Ridge were above average. Add to this their food, free rent (in most instances), welfare benefits, etc., and their standard was close to an urban worker's. Here young couples were permitted to build their own homes, small two- or three-room brick structures, which they financed (cost, about 400 yuan) from savings and money borrowed from the welfare fund. Here also, as in other communes, were some new one- and two-story multiple-family brick flats of one to three rooms. Most families still lived in old-style farmhouses and many preferred them, I was told.

'Our general plan', it was explained to me as we walked through the fields and villages, 'is to organize the whole commune around four modern community centers. Each center will have administrative offices, schools, hospital, theater, playgrounds, parks, a factory zone, repair shops, hostels, clubs, lots of trees – the nucleus of a modern town. We are keeping the old villages and houses where they are worth improving, but the worst are being torn down as soon as new housing is built. When small-plot farming changes into large-scale farms and mechanization increases, we'll need fewer villages. Our farm economy is changing to factory-farm economy. Already here in Yellow Ridge we are no longer a mere farm but a factory farm.'

Yellow Ridge leaders took me to see one of their community centers. Later, south of Shanghai, I saw a commune* in which similar community plants were very well advanced and highly successful, but those at Yellow Ridge were still under construction. A large square had been partly built up with new offices, stores and houses, dominated by a new building, seating capacity eight hundred, which would serve as a dining hall and theater. Bricks, windows and some fittings were locally made. The building would eventually have flush toilets, a distinct innovation in village life. General use of flush toilets in rural China would for some time be too wasteful even if it were more possible today; human manure was still much needed for fertilizer. The use of covered latrines was

*See Chapter 65, 'Building, Building –'.

being widely enforced, however; sanitary squads collected the ordure in the manner already described. I saw such latrines in use here and on other farms, and I was told in Yellow Ridge by a clinic doctor that among some four thousand persons in his brigade only three cases of dysentery had occurred since 1958.

Near the civic center I inspected several new brick homes. Most residents were in the fields, but before a two-room cottage I met a lady of sixty-five working in her tiny garden of sunflowers and cabbages. She invited me in for tea and I sat beside a fine old Chinese table, several chairs and a teak chest. On the large brick family k'ang were piled clean, brightly colored quilts. She was a widow and her husband had been a poor peasant. The furniture had been acquired during the division of land – and landlord's furniture.

Rice simmered in a pot over a new brick cook stove in the tiny vestibule; water was available nearby from a new well. Here the old lady lived with her son and daughter-in-law, both then at work. Mme Wang was full of praise for the 'new life better for all'. For example, she and her husband were illiterates; just look at her grandchildren, both soon to finish primary school. What was more, her son and daughter-in-law were able to study at night school. Who could have saved in the past? Now her son could buy clothes for the children and make payments on a bicycle. Even she herself owned two coats, vests and trousers. Who would have fed a person unable to work in former times? Now she, an old lady, was fed by the brigade.

'You do the family cooking?'

'A little breakfast for everyone, yes. The children eat where they work. We have supper together in our team dining room. It's a great blessing, being able to take meals outside.'

'In what way?'

'Ai-ya! In every way. No scrambling for fuel, preparing food, dish washing, pot washing, smoking up the house! Of course the cooking is not always the best. When we get tired of it we eat at home.'

'Was there ever any attempt here to make your son and daughter-in-law live apart, in separate barracks – to divide men from women?'

My question had to be repeated and explained by the interpreter.

The old lady looked at me in astonishment. Of course not. Could that be 'human'? She wanted to know if it was practiced in my country.

We went on to the older part of the village, with here and there a new brick house, until we reached a nursery-kindergarten and its seventy-two infants. It was (as often) located in a former landlord's home and was simply furnished with roughly made child-size chairs, stools, tables and benches. The little citizens were dressed in cotton playsuits and cloth shoes; there were a few runny noses and no overt signs of malnutrition.

They stood up, as usual, and cried in tiny-voiced chorus, 'Welcome, Foreign Uncle!' Then they rendered a version of 'Socialism Is Good', clapped hands and cheered. A smiling bobbed-hair doll handed me a large bouquet of yellow chrysanthemums picked from the school garden; thereafter she hung onto my hand. This performance, minus the flowers, was enacted in every nursery I visited. Usually I was able to bring some unexpected diversion into their lives by winding up and playing my miniature Swiss keychain music box and holding it to the ears of children daring enough to listen in wide-eyed delight.

This nursery was better than average for a village, but its conditions were poorer than the standards of the well-run urban nurseries to which all aspire. Each child had the usual equipment: his own hooks for toothbrush, comb, washcloth, coat; he had a bowl of his own, chopsticks, and a place at the table and on one of the k'angs where all retired for morning and afternoon naps. Lunch was gruel and vegetables, and the infants had a ration of soya bean milk. Sanitary arrangements included Japanese-style johns, cut to size, and a lavatory through which ran a stream of fresh water in a long low stone basin used for ablutions. The sunny courtyard was equipped with homemade swings, slides and hobbyhorses.

Care and lunches here cost mothers three yuan a month for each child – deductible, however, from book earnings, not cash. There were no boarding children as in some nurseries; neighborhood mothers called for their charges each day after work. Attendants were four local women (one with bound feet) who were themselves all mothers, and who had had some rudimentary training in child care. Their leader was a primary school graduate, bright and energetic. Of her efficiency I know no more than that she kept her charges remarkably clean, considering the circumstances, and reported complete toilet-training success with most of them at three, all by the age of four. A trained nurse visited once a week and was on special call. Vaccinations were complete and the health record for the year showed only minor ailments, principally colds.

Here again I could easily have invested the whole day with pleasure and profit, but I had just spent such a day at a nursery in Peking. As I had asked to see the brigade clinic, one of the new schools and a shop or two, I was hurried along through vegetable fields and acres of gladioli, chrysanthemums, and dahlias – Yellow Ridge grows flowers commercially for the nearby Peking market – until we came to the outskirts of Wei Hsien, the next big village,

'Teng Chia brigade includes fourteen villages of work teams – 4,000 people out of our total commune population of 26,000.' The speaker was the brigade deputy leader and party secretary, Chang Hsuan-hai. We got out of our car and scrambled through a large vegetable field.

'Our income is above average, you say? A little, yes. We have advantages of help from the city, we are more mechanized, with pumps and tractors, and we have good cash crops. We get three crops a year: spring vegetables; summer vegetables and wheat; autumn vegetables and corn. The whole commune averages two thirds in vegetables, one third in grain. We are also doing well with our tree nurseries and flowers; winter hothouses bring a good income. Two thirds of our earnings come from the July crop, which looks very good this year.'

Fields of tomatoes, peppers, fat cabbages and leeks were being weeded and sprayed by turbaned young and old women who plunged their embarrassed pink grinning faces into the vegetables when one turned and caught them staring. I stopped to question some women gardeners but was interrupted by a sudden heavy shower. We took refuge in a farm hut set all by itself in the middle of the field. Inside, a young peasant woman and her teen-age brother welcomed us and a baby stared wide-eyed from the k'ang. The floor was of packed earth, the kitchen hung with drying onions and peppers. It was the house in which she had been born, said the woman; she liked it and had no intention of moving into any communal housing project. Her husband worked in a nearby factory. Her brother, who had been studying a textbook when we entered, said he had just completed higher primary school. How many village children got to middle school these days? About half. And what was he studying to be?

'Serve the needs of socialism. Obey the will of the masses.'

'Yes, but *you* – what do you want to be if you have a choice?'

'I'd like to be a doctor.' He had the bright eager face of hope and he grinned to hide his embarrassment.

'Why?'

'I want to be a soldier for my country,' he replied. 'In white uniform.'

The rain ceased. We walked into the town and entered the brigade clinic, an old converted dwelling with rooms built round a courtyard now half flooded by the shower. A doctor in his early thirties was on duty, and a nurse was in charge of the dispensary. The equipment was crude, the brick floors and whitewashed walls clean.

Wu Chu-ying was a short-course (three-year) doctor – really an interne, under a township graduate physician. He hoped to continue his studies later. Dr Wu was on call for all the villages of the brigade, each of which had a public health team and was now in touch with the clinic by telephone. Major diseases under control; no cholera, smallpox or other epidemics for some years; vaccinations, 100 percent; intestinal diseases down eighty percent since 1952. Colds, bronchitis, the usual complaints. Operable cases were referred to the county hospital or sent to Peking.

'Do you have many requests for instruction in birth control?'

'We provide it when required.'

'Do you encourage it?'

Dr Wu hesitated. 'We don't oppose it. We advise it if the woman's health is affected or she already has enough children – three or four, for example.'

'Are contraceptives available to unmarried people?'

The question produced a puzzled silence. Secretary Shen Yao had rejoined us. It was he who spoke up.

'Our people are always married when they have sex relations.'

'Always? You never have any cases of premarital intercourse?'

This colloquy produced (as on a few other occasions) a distinctly uncomfortable if not painful atmosphere.

'This may be a problem in capitalist societies. It is not so here.'

'Capitalism? I lived for several years in the Soviet Union. Pre-marital sex is about as common there as in any industrialized society. I know that in former times it was a rare thing among peasant women in China, when marriages were arranged early. Now, with women's rights, freedom of choice, sex equality – hasn't it changed at all?'

'It has changed for the better. In feudal days young maidens frequently would be raped or seduced by landlords; sometimes the landlord claimed "first rights". That is gone. Now everybody can get married; the legal age is twenty for men and eighteen for girls; there is no need for sex before then. But I won't say it never happens. We have had only two or three cases that I remember, in the whole commune. Social opinion is strongly against it.'

'What punishment is provided?'

'There is no law against it. We persuade people to get married.'

'What if they simply don't want to get married?'

Shen Yao looked seriously at the others, who seemed depressed by this conversation.

'Usually they respond to education – their duties. I will say there was one such case. It was solved when the young man went to the city to work in a factory. Later, the girl moved to the city also.'

'If a child were involved, what then?'

'The man would be held fully responsible as the legal father, of course. They would certainly be married.'

'What if they were under legal age?'

'Special permission would be granted by the court.'

'And adultery? Is that a crime?'

'It is not a crime unless the injured husband or wife wants to bring it to court. We had some cases at the time the marriage law went into effect but not in recent years. It is very rare now.'

Before I left, Shen Yao asked me for criticism and suggestions. 'If I lived and worked here a year,' I said, 'I might have an informed comment. What can a tourist know of your internal tensions and problems of management? For example, how well satisfied are the peasants with their private plots? Would they like more? I don't know. How do they feel about the disposal made of their surpluses?'

'We have never taken private plots from the people – I know some communes have done so, but not here,' answered Shen Yao. 'Conditions vary. We have marginal land for those who want to work it. They can earn more by working the common lands; that is also their first duty. About management? It is in the hands of the production brigade. Commune management plans in consultation with the brigades and teams who know their own land best. We listen to the masses.'

'Who actually owns the land, the commune or the village?'

'Here ownership is on three levels. The villages own the land, tools, housing sites, and some primary schools and nurseries and they manage all these things. But the brigades also have collective ownership. They exercise supervision and coordinate planning and management. The brigades collectively own the mechanized tools, horses, cattle, small reservoirs, pumps, brigade centers, and secondary schools, where investments were made in common. The commune owns large reservoirs, power plants, telephones, large factories, new technical schools and will own an agriculture college we are building. Basic ownership is at the brigade level and so is basic management.'

'That's a very different picture from 1958, isn't it?'

He smiled. 'We have to learn to walk before we can jump. All the means of production will eventually be owned by the commune. But that's a long way off. We have to wait. Poorer areas must be brought up to the level of the richer ones. We need far more mechanization, our political level must rise, everyone must understand. First, we have to learn a lot from experience. We make mistakes but we learn.'

All these pages! Yet I have condensed only part of my notes and recollections of a visit to just one rural commune! I saw eleven. Yellow Ridge was far ahead of the average commune and benefited greatly from its nearness to Peking, yet it was not so prosperous as one I saw in the Yangtze Valley nor yet so advanced as another in Szechuan. I must content myself with the detailed story of only one more – where I spent three days far off the beaten track in the extremely poor country of north Shensi – before leaving this subject which still holds the key to Communist China's future.

56

Sian: 'Western Peace'

I WANTED to see Shensi province again for several reasons.

By mid-September of 1960 the American press was beginning to publish seasonal famine reports about China from Hongkong. I have already described conditions in one serious drought area – Paotou. Another was said (in Hongkong) to be Shensi, where people were reported to be living on two meals a day of 'watered rice'.[1] Second, impressive though Manchurian industrialization might be, the impact of the new régime could be judged better, as I have said, in regions formerly little touched by modern life. Few had been more backward than hinterland Shensi and the middle reaches of the Yellow River Valley. I had made long treks across that province in wartime days of real austerity, and those fearsome old hills of loess still held a sentimental attraction for me. Finally, no foreign visitor to pre-1949 Yenan had been back there* since the days when it was the mountain base and capital of Mao Tse-tung's guerrilla armies.

Having just completed a book, Rewi Alley was free to make the trip with me, bringing his deep knowledge of and pride in a part of the land to which he had made great personal contributions. We flew in a DC-3 from Peking to Taiyuan, in Shansi, and to Sian, the capital of Shensi; then on to the Yenan country in a smaller Chinese-made plane. We were to return from Sian to Peking by train, making leisurely stops at San Men Gorge, site of the great new Yellow River lower control dam; at Loyang, to see a tractor factory; and at Chengchow – altogether a two weeks' journey.

It was clear, dry, crisp weather, beautiful for flying but not for autumn crops. All the way to Sian we were seldom out of sight of blue-water reservoirs and mountain catch basins. Most of them

*Rewi Alley had been back, but Alley was a resident of China, not a visitor.

were very low and the irrigation life lines which reached out from them stopped far short of much of the thirsting grain, where peasants waited for a last-minute rain that did not come. The Yellow River itself, usually in flood by now, was a thin ribbon twenty feet below its normal level.

On the plane not one but two smartly dressed young army officers each carried a baby a few months old wrapped in soft padded quilts and sucking a pacifier, a public spectacle one would never have encountered in the past. Presently one baby dropped his plug and loudly announced his dissatisfaction with the state of affairs. I went to the man's aid by holding my miniature Swiss music box to his baby's ear; that stopped the bawling until the stewardess (having finished checking freight in the rear of the plane) could render more fundamental repairs.

'Where is your wife?' I asked.

He explained that he had been transferred to a new post; his wife had gone ahead of him by train, taking their two other children. She already had a job and had to report for work. By the time he arrived she would have arranged for nursery care. In South China later I noticed several other baby-toting officers on planes and trains. Warriors seen in this homely role, so different from the Western caricature of the mad-dog, war-hungry Chinese – even as our military differ from the Chinese caricature of them – gave a sudden poignant sense of the profound pathos of man in uniform everywhere today, obsessed by the illusory pursuit of security for his loved ones through the perfection of the means of finally destroying himself and all he most cherishes.

Once we crossed over into Shensi the look of the land improved. Especially around the Wei River Valley, crops were lush and abundant. Here the economy was no longer purely agricultural. Where I remembered only straggling towns and villages along the river there were now forests of factory chimneys below, mazes of railway sidings, and substantial industrial towns.

'The Wei Valley has become a big base for heavy industry,' said Rewi. 'New iron deposits opened up, and coal all over the place. That's just a token of what is going on in Kansu and farther west. Oil? Scads of it; China has plenty for her needs. Takes time to get the stuff out of the ground and then to get it out of the northwest.

So little to start with; had to build the railways, the roads. Takes man power and time, but they're moving fast.'

China's geographical northwest* is larger than India and formerly had less than a tenth of India's population, but the new régime had given high priority to its development. About two thirds of the major enterprises begun during the First Five-Year Plan (1953–7) were centered in this vast region, and millions of technicians and workers had been coming in to complete them. Sian itself, a town of about 200,000 when I had last visited it in 1939, was now seven times that size and spilled far beyond its ancient walls. Meanwhile it had been connected by rail with Turkestan via Lanchow to Urumchi;† with Siberia via Lanchow, Paotou and Ulan Bator; and with the upper Yangtze Valley via Chengtu and Chungking. A three-lane paved highway was being rapidly pushed westward from Sian to Lanchow.

'There it is!' cried Rewi as we lowered over the city. Long straight pennants of asphalt dotted with creeping trucks led into the western horizon and disappeared.

The region we had flown over is hallowed ground for the Chinese: the valleys of the Wei and Lo rivers, the cradle of their civilization. Great battles for supremacy were fought here thirty centuries ago, west of the bend of the Yellow River, between armies equipped with bronze spears and shields, riding in two-wheeled bronze chariots. After the period of 'Warring States', the great imperialist Ch'in Shih Huang Ti (259–210 B.C.) prevailed and built his fabulous palace near Sian. When his vast realm fell apart in the hands of his son, successors founded the illustrious Han Dynasty (202 B.C.–220 A.D.) on the site of the present-day Sian – then known as Ch'ang-an (Long Peace)‡ – and ruled China throughout the life span of the Roman Empire. These four centuries of enlightenment so impressed the people that they remained content, ever afterward, to call themselves *Han-jen*, Men of Han.

---

*Shensi, Kansu, Chinghai, Ninghsia, Sinkiang and part of western Inner Mongolia.

† The railway was projected to extend to Alma Ata, the capital of Kazakhstan. (1970) After the breakdown in Sino-Soviet cooperation (1960–) no effort was made to join Russian and Chinese Turkestan by rail.

‡ An is usually translated 'peace'; the more exact meaning is 'tranquillity'.

During the Han period notable advances were made in astronomy and medicine; tea cultivation and wine making began; and inventions included the Han compass, water clocks, paper, glazed porcelain, and the humble wheelbarrow – which Europe did not import for another thousand years. Sian was next the seat of the Sui Empire, which sent colonists as far as the Penghu Islands (Pescadores) in the Taiwan Strait and to Taiwan itself. On the foundations of the Sui city arose the great capital of T'ang (618–906), and Sian entered its golden age of art and literature. It became the center of the most brilliant empire of its period. T'ang culture was imported bodily by Japan and a Tibetan monarch united his throne with the dynasty by marriage. Foreign ideas, artists and teachers were hospitably received.

As a modern city, Sian dates largely from the Ming Dynasty (1368–1644). I was glad to see the glazed-tile roofs and magnificent gold and red pillars and lattices of the old Ming drum and bell towers handsomely and faithfully restored. Streets had been widened, but the ancient plan of thoroughfares radiating from these central towers to the four great gates (one facing each direction) was kept intact.

Red China's interest in digging up the past increased along with the digging of minerals, canals, reservoirs and foundations. After 1952 more than 2,800 tombs of the T'ang and earlier periods were opened or excavated in Shensi alone. Tons of porcelains, pottery, jades, bronzes, weapons, tools and other artifacts were unearthed by engineers and construction crews briefed on how to identify and preserve objects of historical value. China overflowed with recently recovered historical and cultural treasures. More than three hundred new state museums were opened, and many communes began to collect on their own.

In an old and neglected section of Sian, on a large mound of earth where vegetables were growing, archeologists had recently made a startling discovery. Careful excavation revealed a complete neolithic village in almost perfect condition, which they named Po I-chih. Now roofed over in its entirety, it stood at the summit of a long flight of stone steps flanked by buildings of a new museum. Po I-chih was the best specimen of late-neolithic life yet found in China. Its communal granary and a brick and pottery kiln were still in fair condition. The village was protected by a deep moat which evidently connected with irrigation canals of surrounding fields. Igloo-shaped houses, half sunk into the ground and with a central hearth, resembled Igorot dwellings of the Philippines, except that walls and rounded roofs were made of baked mud bricks and straw. Numerous pottery utensils were found, and ornaments and toys. Buried in the walls were large well-turned earthen jars which served as coffins for children. Archeologists fixed the age of the village as between five and six thousand years.

There was nothing neolithic about our commodious modern hotel: architecture in modified Chinese style, two hundred fifty rooms, modern baths, and good by any standards. Here was more housing for Russian advisers and their families, most of whom had departed leaving behind them industry of fundamental value.

Of the countless new and old structures in and around Sian I shall here mention three of interest to history: the Confucian temple, the Lintung pool, and No. 4 Textile Mill.

Sian's Confucian temple was considered one of the finest and its inner courtyards displayed the best surviving examples of T'ang architecture. These included an exquisitely roofed tea house about twelve hundred years old, with bell-hung eaves and perfectly balanced overall proportions. Now a state museum under the care of Academia Sinica, the temple area contained 30,000 cultural objects. Among historical documents carved in enduring stone, a Nestorian tablet recorded the presence in China of Byzantine Catholics. Introduced in 635, the cult flourished until it was involved in a rebellion a century later and suppressed.

Here also were four of the six world-famous Wei horses from the fifth century. One missing horse had been stolen many years ago and now resided in the Philadelphia Museum of Art; Chinese referred to this crime, as bitterly as if it had happened yesterday, as 'another example of cultural imperialism'.

And the 'Lintung pool'? A pleasure resort ten miles outside Sian, Lintung had as its chief feature large rock-lined hot springs. It was famous in song and story as the retreat of beautiful Yang Kuei-fei, the most celebrated courtesan of the T'ang period. In our time it acquired renewed fame when here, in 1936, Chiang Kai-shek was taken prisoner by his own deputy commander in chief, Marshal Chang Hsueh-liang.

Rewi and I found it now a public park, where another museum portrayed the Sian Incident, giving Yang Kuei-fei second billing as a current attraction. Chiang Kai-shek's bedroom (very simple) was intact; the route of his flight barefoot up a steep stony slope, and the place of his capture by a soldier, were well marked. A glorious role was here ascribed to Chou En-lai and others who opposed demands for Chiang's execution at that time – with some details added which doubtless would be disputed by the Generalissimo as well as by the Manchurian army leaders who actually carried out the coup.

A large enclosed swimming pool was being built at Lintung. After its completion the park area was to be further expanded to include the tomb of Ch'in Shih Huang Ti–if tomb there was. Chinese archeologists awaited this attempted excavation, after 2,200 years, with intense interest. Legend had it that construction of the tomb occupied 700,000 men for eleven years and that a number of false entrances were made. Nobody could be sure whether the authentic vault would be found in the huge mound near Lintung that was said to be the resting place of the great emperor.[2]

No. 4 Textile Mill was a large new plant spread over fifteen acres and self-contained, like many new satellite towns; it had a shopping center, schools, a theater and clubs, paved streets, and landscaped blocks of flats for its 6,000 workers – 3,710 of them women. This was an ultramodern plant: 3,240 automatic weaving looms and 100,000 spindles. The rooms were wide-aisled, glass-roofed, air-conditioned and so hushed and sanitized that one looked beyond white-gowned, gauze-masked operatives expecting to see 'Hospital – Quiet' signs. Battery-driven rubber-tired trolleys provided the transport. Moving parts of the automatic machines were covered and one operator could manage more than a hundred of them.

'Every machine here was made in China,' Manager Chao Ping said proudly. 'The plant was erected in twelve months. Production? We make 44,000,000 meters of cloth a year. We make gabardine, sheeting, dress fabrics – 600 different kinds of textiles. Sian has four other plants of about the same capacity.' (Other foreigners had visited these plants and found them operating a year earlier.

How many were still producing in 1962 I cannot say. China's cotton and textile output fell drastically following crop failures in 1960 and 1961, but no figures were available.)

I had been in Japan the year before and visited cotton mills in Osaka where Japanese women worked the same number of hours as women in Sian's No. 4 plant, received about the same wages and ate almost as meagerly. They had some welfare benefits and could buy more clothes and other cheap consumer goods. One notable difference was that in a Chinese textile plant (and other state factories) husbands and wives worked side by side, their children were cared for in community nurseries and schools, they ate together and their family life was tied in with their common work interests. In Japan, teen-age factory girls slept on the premises and tried to save a few dollars toward marriage and children, but they seldom married 'in the plant'. As a rule there was no housing provision for married couples nor any community life built around the center of their work.

I never tired of looking into the way people were living. It was only after I had seen many instances that I accepted the fact that improvement was widespread though far from universal. To people who live in American ranch-style bungalows, all the new multiple dwellings in China would seem primitive. To workers in Shensi who were born in caves* or unlighted huts with no water and inadequate heat, the new life meant marked gains in basic comfort, aside from the new services and educational and entertainment facilities.

In No. 4 I visited dormitories which provided separate facilities for young unmarried women and men as well as two- and three-room flats for married couples. Bachelor quarters varied from small two-bed to larger four-bed and six-bed rooms. They were clean, austerely furnished, lighted by one or several electric bulbs, and had lavatories and bathing and laundry facilities.

I visited a family flat during the noon hour and met a skilled worker who told me he earned seventy yuan a month and his wife earned forty-two. Their joint income was above average in a mill where apprentices started at eighteen yuan and the median wage was forty yuan. Rent cost them eight yuan, utilities two yuan,

*Millions were, of course, still living in caves.

food (for themselves and three children) fifty to sixty yuan, nursery care six yuan. (In official exchange values their joint monthly income was about $47, but comparison in such terms becomes misleading when one learns that their monthly outlay for rent and food, for five, cost the equivalent of no more than $29.) After budgeting for clothing and miscellaneous items they saved ten to twelve yuan a month. They owned a bicycle and planned to buy a radio.

Framed photographs hung over a table covered with an embroidered cloth. I noticed they were of groups by the seaside, and on inquiry learned that this worker and his wife were natives of Tsingtao. He had been working in a mill there when he was drafted to help open No. 4. Sixty percent of the employees here came from other provinces. Did they fare better or worse here? 'About the same.' Could they go back to visit their relatives? He said he had been back once. Would they have liked to stay in Tsingtao?

'No, we go where we are needed to help build socialism.'

'But Shantung is a socialist province, too. Couldn't you have done just as good a job without leaving home?'

'Home? Shensi is home for all Chinese. Isn't that where China began?'

Nevertheless, I thought, few Americans would like being shifted about with little to say in the matter. Then I read a *New York Times* dispatch wherein Homer Bigart revealed, from Saigon, that the United States was helping in the 'compulsory relocation' of thousands of Vietnamese supposedly infected by the Red virus.[3]

While I was writing these lines I also happened to hear a broadcast of a talk about the American family by Margaret Mead. In the course of it she remarked that 30,000,000 Americans had changed their domiciles (or 'left home') since the end of the Second World War. That would be the equivalent of 110,000,000 migratory Chinese. The uprooting of populations everywhere and the breakup of large families are often not so much arbitrary political actions as consequences of increasing industrialization. But Americans move 'voluntarily', it may be said; they go where 'opportunity' lies. They also move where 'the company needs them'. Their children move elsewhere.

Museum of the Revolution

WE rose in our slow boxcar, a Chinese one-engine plane, and flew over the reforested loess hills and marvelous works of terracing that were reclaiming these old badlands and helping to subdue the Yellow River.

'Probably there is reason to believe in man and his future after all,' said Snow in a banal philosophical observation. 'When one looks down and remembers those people in that primitive neolithic village and the six thousand years of terrors and calamities that their children survived, until humanity finally discovered the riches of nature that were lying about here since the beginning, waiting to be opened – well, one almost believes in the indestructibility of man by man. A thousand years from now people may look down again and wonder how we could have had the courage to go on under our primitive conditions and despite all the ignorance which surrounds us today.'

A young man whom I shall call Mr Chao, assigned (not on request) by China Intourist to accompany us to Yenan, was genuinely shocked.

'How can you compare ignorant neolithic savages with enlightened socialism?' he demanded. 'Men will always regard this time as the true dawning of civilization.'

A paved highway now ran toward Yenan and I congratulated Mr Chao on that improvement. 'There was nothing but a mule track there before liberation,' he replied. Was that so? Rewi and I had both driven over the old dirt road many years earlier.

'By the way,' said Mr Chao, 'don't take any photographs without asking me first. Don't hesitate to ask questions.'

So that's how it was to be. I gave Rewi a pained look. 'Never mind,' he muttered. 'Enjoy the scenery.' Chao was twenty-nine, a native of Kansu, with thick black wavy hair, long nose suggesting

Turkic traces, tight-fitting blue serge suit buttoned to the chin and the brain, and a perpetual false smile like Mona Lisa opened to full diaphragm – full of bowdlerized history, misinformation, the general line, misquotations from Mao, and with three fountain pens in his right breast pocket. I had known a dozen prenatally determined headmaster-bureaucrats like Chao in Russia, but he was the first I encountered in New China. Even Alley, a man of sainted patience, blistered under his condescension. He had no idea that Alley had helped build Yenan when Chao was still in split pants. We were to be stuck with him until our return to Sian – and he with us, poor fellow; we paid scant attention to his injunction against photographs once we had landed in Yenan.

Years ago I spent months riding and walking across north Shensi, Kansu and Ninghsia, through a weird surrealist beauty of hills and mountains pitted, slashed and scored by torrential rains that left behind bald peaks, deep ravines and slanting arroyos – an earth that might have been clawed and torn by herds of angry whale-size centipedes. The transformation that could now be seen from the air was beautiful to behold.

This is a region of the world's deepest and largest deposits of rich loess topsoil. Denuded of trees and overgrazed, the loess had been slipping toward the sea after every heavy rainfall, losing its fertility and filling the Yellow River with silt which piled up in its lower reaches and caused extensive floods. Shensi alone contributed forty percent (half a billion tons) of the river's annual silt burden. The huge new Yellow River power and water conservation program required that the erosion be effectively ended.

Peasants began the tremendous task in the Yenan area soon after farm cooperatives were formed. With the beginning of the whole Yellow River project in 1956, a multiple-province plan was adopted which embraced all villages and townships in a systematic assault on nature gone awry. Now the results in north Shensi were already sufficiently dramatic to offer a scenic attraction for tourists. Thousands of square miles had been contour-terraced and interspersed with pines and other shade trees and extensive orchards and vineyards. Very steep gradients were brought under control and gullies and ravines sealed off by check dams, catch basins and soil banks, between hundreds of leveled-off shelves which stoutly retained and enriched useful land. New land had been won, flood dangers greatly reduced, and clean water reservoirs provided for human needs and for irrigation and power in the valleys.

On the face of a high bluff overlooking Yenan now, large white characters proclaimed from afar: 'Make Green the Fatherland!' From all I saw of that grotesquely eroded and impoverished corner of the country I can say that it was well on its way to fulfilling that slogan, and recovering the lost ground of centuries.

New additions seen on the outskirts of Yenan, as our plane circled in over the old T'ang pagoda: two reservoirs nestling in the ravines; a medium-sized power plant and a number of factories; the stone-walled Yen-hui Canal running from the hills through the city and beyond (where it irrigated four thousand acres); a war memorial with a wide esplanade leading from the river into a mountainside. Our plane lowered over the rebuilt city (intramural Yenan was almost totally demolished by Japanese bombing) and I saw a new stone bridge. I wondered aloud if it was true, as I had heard, that the bridge had been ordered to be built after Chou En-lai, while fording the river, fell off his horse and broke his arm.

'That's an imperialist slander,' said Chao. 'Premier Chou never fell off his horse and there's nothing wrong with his arm.'

I forebore quoting the Premier to contradict him.

At an elevation of about 2,500 feet, Yenan lies athwart the historic invasion route from Mongolia to the Wei Valley; over millennia its environs have seen hundreds of stormy battles. In this century, no territory in China was fought over more continuously nor was more impoverished as a result. Contests between bandits and warlords were followed by class wars organized by Communist intellectuals and army officers who sought refuge in a country ideal for guerrilla warfare; among them, Liu Chih-tan became most famous. Liu led partisan fighting in Shensi for three years before the main Chinese Red forces under Mao Tse-tung reached Shensi at the end of the Long March from South China in 1935, whence they had been driven following the defeat of their first attempt to set up a Soviet state (1927–34) in the Yangtze Valley.

Yenan had now become a special municipality and the administrative center of seven surrounding *hsiang* in the hills south of the Great Wall. As an area under almost continuous Communist control longer than any other it was a place of pilgrimage for young Chinese. Nearly all China's Communist top élite lived and worked here at some time under Mao's leadership. Men trained in the war-time academies in the Yenan hills now enjoyed the prestige of veterans of Valley Forge. Here Mao had mapped out, tried and perfected the tactics and strategy which he followed to victory in the second civil war, 1946-9. Yenan was occupied by the Nation-alists in 1947, but its reconquest by Mao the following year marked the beginning of the end for Chiang Kai-shek.

When I first reached Yenan, in June 1936, the Red forces had occupied most of north Shensi, but Yenan City was still garrisoned by Nationalist forces under Marshal Chang Hsueh-liang. I have re-called* how the Communists had by then won over Chang to a secret truce which ended in the Sian Incident. During that uprising, the Red forces – then numbering about 40,000 – occupied Yenan and another surrounding territory, by agreement with Marshal Chang. After that, north Shensi became the main training base from which the Reds infiltrated the North China plains and carried on guerrilla operations throughout the next eight years of the Sino-Japanese War.

By terms of the September 1937 agreement between Chiang and Mao the old Red Army abandoned its name and flag and took the title Eighth Route Army under the Generalissimo's nominal com-mand. It also abandoned overt class-war slogans in favor of policies of rent reduction and other 'democratic reforms'. In practice Mao was able to continue (in relative security) an intensified program of Marxist indoctrination which attracted thousands of young patriots and intellectuals, and prepared the peasant masses for future revolution while they were organized to resist Japan. It was during this period that the Reds in effect seized political control of the national anti-Japanese war in North China.

Unable to secure Mao's submission or to fight him during the war against Japan, the Generalissimo used 100,000 of his best troops to blockade the Reds from access to any outside aid. Immediately after V-J Day, forces of both sides rushed into and seized as much territory as possible as fast as the Japanese withdrew. By July 1946 heavy fighting had spread to most of the country. Meanwhile,

*In Red Star Over China, op. cit.

formal attempts to achieve a truce and create a coalition government preoccupied American policy makers in China until 1947. By then the two Chinese armies were locked irrevocably in a final struggle for power which engulfed the whole country.

On the Communist side, the brains and source of directives of the high command remained, until national victory was within grasp, concentrated in the inhospitable hills of north Shensi – which still seemed an unlikely place to have sheltered the future leader of 700,000,000 people.

While in Yenan, it was appropriate to recall at least a few basic points in Mao's concepts of war operations which were highly relevant to any interpretation of his thinking about strategic and tactical policy on the 'international front' today.[1] Years ago the 'four principles' of guerrilla warfare which the Red Army evolved from its early struggles were elaborated by Mao Tse-tung in the following set of paradoxes:

Defense, in order to attack; retreat, in order to advance; flanking, in order to take a frontal position; curving, in order to go straight. These are inevitable phenomena in the process of development of any event or material matter.

Such was the general strategy which Mao used to defeat Chiang Kai-shek's forces when they launched a major attack against Yenan in March 1947. Under Hu Tsung-nan and other top commanders, picked Nationalist troops numbering 230,000 invaded the Red bases in north Shensi, Kansu and Ninghsia. Most of the Red troops were east of the Yellow River, scattered across the North China plain to Manchuria, where Chiang had already suffered heavy reverses. Yenan had only 30,000 regular troops at its disposal and did not call for reinforcements from the east.[2]

Of Mao's 'ten principles of operations in the northwest' five may be noted as timeless guerrilla tactics: *

1. Attack small dispersed weak forces first, large strong ones later.
2. Seek to destroy enemy *forces,* not to capture or hold *places.*
3. Fight no battle unless certain of victory; never engage superior forces; use three to six times as many men as the enemy to win decision before the enemy can reinforce.

* In 1960 Mao said, 'We still follow guerrilla tactics.'

4. Replenish with captured arms and soldiers (up to eighty percent of men can be won over after capture) and not with local recruits (to avoid interference with production).

5. Thoroughly indoctrinate troops in the 'new ideological education' (to which Mao attributed 'unity with the people' and 'invincibility').[3]

The enemy arrived well armed but found a dearth of food, animals and able-bodied men in the towns. If he went foraging in the countryside and spread out he was ambushed and quickly wiped out. If he pursued in force the Reds broke contact, countermarched and bit off his tail. Four times the Nationalists circled the province chasing the Reds; each time they dropped a few more brigades isolated and outnumbered in sudden, surprise attacks. By the end of the year the Nationalists were completely defeated and withdrawing in great confusion. Yenan then began sending directives for general offensives on a nation-wide scale.

Even after the war, and despite its historical importance, north Shensi was extremely poor and backward. Yenan itself had no power, modern industries or motor vehicles until after the revolution. By the 1960s Yenan City (population 60,000) had all such conveniences plus a few traffic cops (mostly women using megaphones to warn bumpkin pedestrians against underestimating the speed of trucks), some paved streets, a good provincial hospital, a comfortable hotel, clubhouse, theaters and – above all – museums. After visiting a dozen hallowed caves and other meeting places of Politburo members it seemed to me the place was already in danger of becoming another Benares.

'Merchants may make fortunes here some day selling old Politburo ink brushes, sacred hairs, or Chairman Mao's teeth, if this goes on,' I said to Mr Chao on impulse.

He was so upset that I immediately regretted my irreverence. It would have been all right to address that remark to Chou En-lai or even to Mao – but not to Chao. From then on nothing was done for me that had not already been arranged. The 'Yenan style of party work' was a model constantly publicized throughout China and the Yenan party school would have been worth seeing. We passed it on the road twice and I had seen its exhibit in the town fair. But Chao insisted that it had been closed down; I could not get near it. A foreigner is always wrong in this kind of situation, I knew. Thereafter my behavior was entirely correct. But I never saw Mr Chao smile again until we parted from him at the Sian station.

The Yenan fair was more interesting than any of the 'museums of the living'. It exhibited a variety of abundance of products unknown or rare here in the past, including fruits, grapes, walnuts, honey, and wild silk. I duly inspected an eighty-pound squash, corn fifteen feet tall, and fat fish from new hatcheries. Charts informed me that the Yenan region had afforested 830,000 acres of land and 'basically completed' soil erosion work.

Items of some significance: (1) in 1952, when the area population was 677,000, there were only 266 steel plows in use; in 1960 (area population 919,000) there were 73,100 steel plows, a vast change for a region in which most families still lived in caves; (2) 7,252 people were receiving pensions and 161 old people's homes were in operation; (3) illiteracy among local cadres admitted to the Yenan party school had declined from twenty-six percent in 1952 to zero in 1958.

Finally, *un morceau sentimental*: in a museum that was the former social hall where wartime foreign observers and occasional correspondents used to hobnob with Politburo members and their wives at Saturday night dances and entertainments, there now hung, in testimony to bygone days of comradeship, photographs of a smiling Chairman Mao, arms linked with his American and British guests in agreeable community. Among the faces I recognized Colonel David Barrett, chief of the American mission. Colonel Barrett was denounced by Peking in 1951 for allegedly having aided and abetted an espionage center in the capital. In Yenan, at least, he still held his place of honor with the rest.

Yenan Teachers College

YENAN had no institutes of higher study before it became the Red capital in 1937, when a wartime 'university' was set up with dormitories and classrooms in hillside caves. The descendant of that improvisation was called People's Revolutionary University; it had more than 1,000 students and specialized in agronomy. There was also a Shenpei (North Shensi) College, as well as two middle schools and the party training institute. All these 'plants' consisted of whole buildings as well as half-structures with rear ends that reached into the clay cliffs and front ends conventional in appearance, with round-arched doorways and windows surmounted by several stories of terraced penthouses. They cost little to build, were inexpensive to maintain, and were not unpleasing to the eye.

In a morning at Shenpei College I learned something about the teacher-training program designed to spread middle school education across this whole desolate loess plateau. The nearest college formerly was in Sian, where Kuo Yi, chairman of Shenpei College, graduated from Northwestern University. He was now forty-six and had been working in Yenan since 1948. His assistant or co-administrator was Li Shen-kuei, at thirty-four already a party veteran. A former Eighth Route Army officer, he had been through middle school only. Both men were participating with student workers in helping to build the college, which was still uncompleted when I was there. All students spent ten weeks a year in productive labor.

Shenpei was organized in 1958 with a student body of 210. In 1959 the curriculum was enlarged and a two-year medical course was introduced. It was intended that by 1962 it would become a five-year medical college with a fully qualified faculty. Meanwhile, it had thirty-six teachers and 412 students. Of the latter, eighty-five were girls. About eighty in 100 students were said to be of peasant or working-class origin; the rest came from 'bourgeois' families of mixed background. Tuition, books and rooms were free but food cost twelve yuan ($5) a month. Eighty percent of the students received a monthly stipend of fifteen yuan.

Kuo Yi said there was an immediate demand for all graduates to help staff the 'several score' agricultural and technical junior middle schools already opened in north Shensi. Schools of this type began under the advanced cooperatives in the pre-commune period and by now had branched into a nation-wide half-study, half-farming system similar to the urban schools run for workers.

While the legal age for full-time workers in China was eighteen, I often saw youths who looked no more than fourteen and I found many at that age already doing full-time work on the farms (this is not unknown in the agricultural regions of other countries, of course, including the United States). Schools and teachers for all China's teenagers simply did not exist, even if the economy could have spared their labor from production. Census data of 1953 indicated that China had 13,000,000 youths aged thirteen in 1960, a year when the draft economic plan projected a total of 4,000,000 students in ordinary full-time middle schools. There was a total of 37,000,000 in the thirteen–sixteen age bracket in 1959, according to a party spokesman, Lu Ting-yi.[1]

For the central government to provide facilities obviously would take many years. In line with general aims of decentralizing responsibility and utilizing latent skills and talents at all levels, the party called upon the commune or township councils to organize their own half-work, half-study schools for teenagers. What the Chinese Communists called 'walking on two legs', in industry – what Western economists called 'technological dualism', meaning high-ratio investments of capital in modern industry contrasted with high-ratio investments of labor in rural public works – was applied with great energy in rural education.

Such schools, called *nung-yeh chung-hsueh*, were meeting some of the problems presented by millions of graduates of the primary educational system who did not qualify for the still largely town-focused regular middle schools. Their emphasis was on training youths in the techniques of a more modern and mechanized agriculture. In addition to generally more competent farming, special skills were needed. According to Lu Ting-yi, China would require 1,840,000 agricultural machine operators and 440,000 'technical farming cadres' by the mid-sixties.[2]

Half-study, half-work middle school had flexible schedules, with 'less study during the busy farming season, more during the slack farming season, occasional study during the busiest season and all-day study on rainy days'.[3] Their curricula varied considerably, but generally resembled that of Shenpei College, with the addition of technical courses suited to needs of the local community, where eighty percent of the graduates would remain. As a rule, students spent five months a year in classroom work and five to seven in farm work.

Few agricultural middle schools yet earned all their expenses; most of them seemed to be about two thirds dependent on state and commune support and one third self-sufficient. Their cost of operation was much lower than in full-time schools, and a small fraction of the expense of comparable education in the West. While it cost the state an average of 500 yuan ($200) to put one student through the full three years' training in a standard junior middle school, it was reported that the annual cost per student was as little as thirteen yuan for the state, plus no more than thirty-eight yuan for the commune, in the agricultural middle school[4] supposed to provide the equivalent education in four to five years.

The aim everywhere was to make half-work, half-study schools wholly self-supporting. Besides agricultural commodities, they commonly derived cash income from sericulture, fish hatcheries, pigs, rabbits, woven straw mats and ropes, the manufacture of insecticides, fertilizer and leather products, and the repair of machinery. In Tailing, Manchuria, I saw one such school which appeared to be paying its way entirely by part-time lumbering and forestry.

As with every 'great leap' initiated by the communes in 1958, this one was launched with inadequate preparation and too much was attempted too soon. Dependent largely on amateur, volunteer, poorly paid or unpaid teachers and administrators, such schools ran into grave problems which not all were able to overcome. The party philosophy was that leadership had to 'learn from the masses' by actual practice. Some schools failed to operate in harmony with agricultural production, sometimes slowing it down and depriving it of needed labor, and were dissolved. The best of the survivors still provided only 'second-best' secondary education of a largely improvisatory type.

Sampling some published self-criticism of middle schools one learned that 'the quality of education is not good enough', that 'examinations are learned by heart and without being understood cannot be properly applied', that 'some students, afraid of hard work, do not want to take part in agricultural production', that 'the idea that agricultural production is glorious and pleasant has not yet been firmly set up', and that 'some experimental farms exist in name only'.[5] Remedies advocated included improved training of young teachers 'to take the Red and expert road. "Redness" means support for the Party and for socialism. Expertness means serving socialist education with one's special knowledge ...' To attain these ends, working and living conditions must guarantee that 'teachers can spend five sixths of their time on official duties'.[6]

The foregoing criticisms were applied to a relatively advanced area, in Kwangtung province, and to full-day standard middle schools. One may surmise how still less satisfactory must have been the quality of redness and expertness in half-time schools in so benighted a region as northern Shensi. Yet it might prove less significant in the long run that such weaknesses and low standards existed than that they were acknowledged; and more important that opportunity for higher education existed on an ever broadening scale for those who strove for it than it was that present levels left much to be desired. Anyone familiar with the stagnations of primitive rural life in Shensi in the past could recognize at once the meaning of a single instance of profound change. A certain Shensi village named Wei Tsun, with about two hundred families, which had never in history sent anyone to college, had recently been honored for having produced ten youths who had passed their college entrance examinations – six of whom had already graduated.[7]

Pride of Poor Men

LI YU-HUA, his face crinkled like the hills around him, was burned deep walnut and his hands were roots of the same tree. He wore the peasant garb of Shensi: white toweling around close-cropped hair, a white cotton girdle over old trousers wrapped with cotton bands at the ankles, and a worn jacket hung loosely on bent, broad shoulders, over a white T-shirt. He was fifty-five, a Red partisan farmer since 1935, a native of Hung Shan county, and a brigade leader of Willow Grove Commune, which covered twenty-five square miles of Yenan county.

'Hung Shan,' I said. 'That's the no man's land I crossed when the Red Army smuggled me back across the lines in 1936 – down near Lochuan. Where were you in 1936?'

'I won't forget that year,' he answered, suddenly animated. 'You must have been there about the time I was arrested by the *mint'uan* [landlord militia]. Why? I joined the Poor Men's League when the Red Army occupied our district. After the Kuomintang came back with the landlords, many of us were arrested.'

He had been imprisoned, half starved, and beaten repeatedly for refusing to talk. 'I acted stupid,' he said. Other peasants raised enough money to buy him out of jail, and he went back to work for the landlord again. He had to sell everything he owned and go into debt to pay back his friends. I broke in to ask what was the 'bitterest' time in his life.

'That was it – that winter,' he said. 'We were barely alive. The worst moment was when my starving son said to me, "Let me die, let me die. You are feeding me just enough to keep alive. Please let me die so that the rest of you can live." That was bitter.'

We were sitting in Li's cave, high on an elevation above a rice field in the valley. It was a large clean brick-floored room with a plastered arched ceiling and a wide arched window with paper panes. A two-burner stove stood under a pantry shelf lined with half a dozen glazed jars. Beside the stove were four earthen crocks filled with pickled vegetables. A heavy clothing chest stood beside the great k'ang where five quilts were neatly stacked. Through a connecting doorway which led to another cave I could see three pairs of children's rubber boots and a pair of sneakers beside another k'ang. Four chairs were squared round a teak table holding a giant wicker-covered vacuum bottle and a teapot and china bowls. It occurred to me that several of those items would in the past have been seen only in a landlord's home; I could remember when Shensi bandits would have robbed you for the vacuum flask alone. (Li's furniture probably came to him with his share of landlord's land.) On one wall hung eight framed photographs of Li and his family and friends, taken in younger days, and beside them were yellowed newspaper clippings which told of various honors won by Li's brigade.

After the Reds occupied Yenan, Li had made his way through the lines and over the hills to investigate. He went on:

'Everything was just as in liberated days in Hung Shan. I went back to report to my neighbors and in two days seven families were ready to leave. We had nothing to lose. I carried all the belongings of our family – we had four small children then – in one light bundle. All eight families got away safely at night and reached Yenan two days later.' A pink-faced young girl in braids, who wore a pink-and-white-checked blouse and matching trousers, brought a plate of sunflower seeds and filled our teacups. 'My youngest,' said Li, casting an appraising look after her.

'So you got land when you came to Yenan?'

'Not then. We missed out on the first distribution but we got shelter and food. We got our land in the second distribution, in 1942 – four *mou* [two thirds of an acre]. Our eight families stayed together and organized as a cooperative in 1943. Yes, I was chairman. We did well, with the party's help – bought tools and fertilizer. In 1946 we produced as much as in the two previous years combined. We were able to buy sheep, pigs and a couple of cows.'

'Then you lost it all during the Kuomintang occupation?'

'We lost the crop but we had a year's warning and had places fixed to hide our tools and seed grain. We lost our cows but drove most of the sheep and pigs to the hills, where our families looked after them. We came back the next year and had another good crop that autumn. Since then – well, we can talk about that when you see the farm.'

Mrs Li was her husband's age but still without a gray hair. She sat shyly hiding her bound feet; she must have been conscious that I had noticed them and she refused to be photographed with Li and their children. She had given him three sons and two daughters, and they had four grandchildren. 'Only four?' I asked.

'What poor man could have seen three sons and four grandsons survive in the past?' he asked. 'It was luck if a man lived to see one.'

'So you weren't counting granddaughters? Women have the vote, women count equally now, don't they, Lao Li?'

He grunted. 'Oh, they're equal all right. A woman earns as much as a man nowadays.' As he walked through the doorway he said, 'If you count girls, I've got five grandchildren from my eldest daughter alone.'

To give meaning to Willow Grove I must repeat that north Shensi in the nineteen-thirties was so ravaged a land it was always astonishing to find people living in its crevices at all. The soil seemed worn down, worn out, the topography all against profitable farming: nine tenths of it sloping and eroding, and the valleys so narrow that the good land there provided even landlords with no more than a poor living by our standards. Most of them were as illiterate as the peasants. This country was blighted worse than an Oklahoma dust bowl or the Texas badlands; there were very few trees, and it was arid except for swift summer floods and winter snows. Its best asset was a fine dry healthful climate. That alone probably explained why poor people could survive in their tumble-down caves infested by flies and rats (bubonic plague used to be endemic) and scratch an existence from scabby patches of grain planted on slopes sometimes as steep as thirty degrees, from which they were lucky to bring in three or four bushels an acre.

'Oh, this country always had possibilities.' Alley cut in on my recollections. 'You saw it at its worst. This loess soil is potentially very rich. It just needed work, water, fertilizer and organization.'

We stood on the wide baked-clay terrace before Li's caves, over-looking a lower ledge where a man drove a herd of white goats down the hill to water. There was a view of a ravine on one side and on the other the green and gold of the valley, far down, where half a dozen of the fifty-nine villages of Willow Grove Commune were in sight – each consisting of old caves and two or three new one-story tile-roofed buildings. Several hundred sheep kicked up the dust of a new dirt and gravel highway. In the ravine a team of surveyors was laying out what would be a spur road to the new reservoir. Here a branch of the Yenan River fed into irrigation ditches watering rice fields. *Rice?* Millet and corn were the hardy annuals here, and wheat and vegetables for the good land. Rice was a delicacy I had seldom tasted on my first visit.

Li itemized the landscape: 'See that young pine grove over there? See those apricot trees; they're bearing for the second year. We have planted 47,000 *mou* in pines, nut trees and orchards. Erosion? It's basically [how they love that word!] solved here. Our commune has dry-terraced 6,000 *mou* and terraced another 4,000 in guaranteed irrigation.'

Their total land area was 65,000 *mou* (about 11,000 acres); they must have covered everything but the ridges and peaks.

'How long does it take to terrace a *mou* of land?'

'About seventeen man-labor days. We could do it in two or three with small bulldozers. We don't even have a tractor yet.' With the hand labor of about 2,600 men and women members, Willow Grove had thus terraced 1,500 acres, a third of it since 1957.

We walked a mile through a ravine to see the No. 1 Dam, a well-built, deep-footed stone enbankment about seventy feet high lying in the bed of a small tributary to a minor branch of the Yellow River. Beyond the causeway placid blue waters joined towering cliffs and made a lake half a mile long. Beneath one cliff, where a road was carved, some sun-clad children scampered under willows overhanging a shallow beach.

'Maybe you don't know what it means to us to have dams and reservoirs,' said one of Li's young team leaders, earnest and enthusiastic, who had joined us. 'We've got another dam bigger than this and seven more almost as large. People in these hills never knew the blessings of a good year-round water supply even for bathing, not to say irrigation or power. They hardly knew what soap looked like. It used to be said that a Shensi man bathed only twice in his life, when he was born and when he was married – and that was an exaggeration. Now our children even learn to swim. Our reservoirs are stocked with 640,000 fish! What peasant around here ever ate fresh fish? There's a good life ahead for our children!'

As a 'commune', Willow Grove was in population hardly larger than a big brigade. What are called villages here are mostly small groups of ten or twenty families living in a cluster of caves. Level land is too scarce to be used for villages; even cattle and poultry are quartered in hillside caves. Willow Grove had only 1,592 families; 640,000 fish meant 400 for each family. Fish every day and two on feast days? No. These were commune assets on which to build for the future, and were being consumed only sparingly. The meat and fish ration per member was given as two catties (2·2 pounds) per month, supplemented by such poultry, pigs and goats as each family could maintain on its small private plot. Like most communes, and especially poor communes, Willow Grove was selling much of its meat and saving the proceeds to buy things needed for future development.

Alley and I were Li's guests for two days, on condition – to Mr Chao's dismay – that no feast was spread. We ate *man-t'ou* made of millet, and potatoes, turnips, corn and squash. Yenanites had now learned to eat corn on the cob, in the past considered fit for pigs only. Everything was boiled or baked. There was a 'shortage' of cooking oil. We had fresh tomato salad, also something new here, served with salt and garlic. We ate in the brigade headquarters canteen, at Willow Grove village, for which the whole commune was named. This canteen fed most of the village team at noon – about ninety families. At night it fed fewer, mostly unmarried party workers and young people; married couples ate at home with their children and parents.

The menu varied little from meal to meal except that breakfast was wet *hsiao-mi*, millet gruel. The food at Willow Grove was far better than the unvarying *mien t'iao* (millet noodles) I had eaten out of chipped enamel basins with the old Red Army – a diet which, like Grant's whiskey, did not interfere with winning battles.

Here, as well as anywhere, a brief digression on food values.

Chinese like meat and have no religious taboos against it, but in former times none but 'rich men' ate meat more than three or four times (feast days) a year. Many Europeans and Americans seem to believe that without meat at least once a day a man cannot be properly nourished. The absence of meat is no hardship to habitual vegetarians; George Bernard Shaw and Gandhi proved that genius can thrive to a ripe old age on a noncarniverous diet. Many walrus tears shed abroad over the dying Chinese were inspired by ignorant misinterpretations of reports that meat and fish were rationed at one to two pounds a month (true) and that the people, 'reduced to starvation', were forced to substitute sweet potatoes for meat and grain (which in some areas was true).

One medium sweet potato contains nineteen times more vitamin A units than a whole orange, twice as much B_1, B_2, phosphorus and iron, and nearly three times more calories. One average Chinese yam (or large sweet potato) gives 200 times more vitamin A than a bowl (large cup) of cooked rice, one-third less B_1, nearly four times more B_2, six milligrams of vitamin C (rice has none), forty percent more calcium, and about ten more calories. (It takes two yams to give equal protein value.) The yam has ten percent fewer calories than its weight in beefsteak but many more vitamins and minerals, except phosphorus and iron. The humble dried pea contains five times more calories than its weight in steak, and three times more protein; it provides four times more protein and nearly three times more calories than its weight in pork chops. One cup of Yenan squash contains five times more calcium, two thirds as many calories, and ten percent more vitamin A than one four-ounce serving of calf liver.[1]

Monthly rations of wheat, millet, rice and potatoes here were said to average thirty-four catties (38.4 pounds) per person. This was supplemented by vegetables, which were unrationed in season but rationed in winter. (Cabbage, turnips, etc., were stored in straw in caves or covered pits.) Members also kept a few fowl and a pig or two which could be consumed or sold on the market. The diet was austere and monotonous but certainly provided well above 2,000 calories, more than 'adequate'. For a 'basically poor' commune they were doing well.

Willow Grove already had one small power plant which lighted 120 buildings and supplied a telephone system that reached all its fifty-nine villages. (All the communes were now connected by telephone.) The brigades operated eleven small industries. I saw a slate and tile works, a transportation service (sixty rubber-tired carts and 138 animals), a fertilizer plant, the largest brick kiln in Yenan county, a carpentry shop and a small, open-hearth 'native' blast furnace.

The furnace stood beside a small dam and pleasant reservoir in a village three or four miles from headquarters. It turned out half a ton of iron a day – all consumed by the foundry where plows and tools were made. This was one of the many small native furnaces* that had been found practical and continued operations after the 1958 steel-making drive.

At Willow Grove men got three or four holidays a month, according to the rule throughout China; women got four to six. In Old China the New Year, the equinoctial spring and autumn festivals, and occasional market days were generally the only holidays granted to working people. Now the traditional festivals were observed (with New Year's reduced to one day), but May First, several days on the October anniversary, weekly holidays, and annual vacations (normally ten days) brought the total to more rest days than the average person enjoyed in the past.

When I first went to Shensi there were schools in county towns but none on the village level. Now there was one for every five villages in Willow Grove, where about ninety percent of children over seven were studying. Li claimed that eighty percent of people eighteen to forty here were now literate. The commune's home for childless aged people was a three-chamber cave on a terrace not far from Li's own hilltop castle. There I found eight gentlemen in their late sixties; one of them, with a white beard luxuriant for China, insisted that he was fifty-six. 'He doesn't know when he was born,' said one of the others, laughing at him.

The old gentlemen were given food and a cook who looked after them and they had a few chickens and a tiny garden. None of them could read. What did they do with their time? When they felt energetic they strolled up to the new dam. (Had I seen it? Did we have such things in my country?) They played chess and they

---

*Some of these had their crude beginnings in the Chinese Industrial Co-operatives Rewi Alley and his adopted Chinese sons had started here, with overseas aid, as far back as the 1940s.

gardened a bit, but mostly they drowsed on the terrace or looked down at the familiar valley activity below. Communism? They knew nothing about that and were too old to learn. But the old folks' home? They repeated what I heard everywhere.

'Like it? Who doesn't like a rest after a hard life? Who would feed and shelter old men with no children in former times? Nothing to worry about! Simply unheard of! We'd all be dead.'

Two individualists, however, 'too old to change', still lived in their caves alone, and wanted nothing to do with any 'home' as long as they got food.

60

Willow Grove

THE next day we sat for hours on benches beside a long table in the big cave that was the brigade headquarters and meeting room. Red banners flecked with stars hung on the walls, and photographs, slogans, charts, tables of production, posters, graphs and trophies. Li and two of his team leaders, the chairman of the women's work department, the doctor, the treasurer, the youth leader, were all there. Peasants drifted in, listened curiously to my questions, whispered among themselves, and sauntered outside to discuss answers.

Facts, facts, facts! In other times you couldn't get an exactitude from any peasant: his children were 'several', the next town was 'not ten *li* distant', the size of his farm was '*shang hsia*' – more or less. Now, whether it was the party secretary, a nurse, a cook or a student, he talked percentages, numbers of pigs and piglets, years and increases, high yields and average, things everyone discussed at meetings again and again: how much old Tsai should be paid for weeding, what counts as heavy work and what as light, how much cabbage for the old people's homes, how much wheat to be sold, eaten and reserved, how to increase fertilizer – and what to plan for in 1967! These people knew their taxes to a decimal; they knew their 'four fixed' and their 'three guarantees', and where their labor and money went. 'Fixed' items were land, man power, animals and tools. 'Guarantees' were quotas of production for taxes; state purchasing contracts; and 'outside contract' sales and local consumption. 'Rewards' were fixed bonuses for overproduction.

Li Yu-hua was only one of twenty-four brigade leaders in Willow Grove, but the commune took its name from the village where he organized the first cooperative, and he was the senior captain of them all. His 'success story' was much like that of Yen Wei-chuan of Yellow Ridge. By 1955 the area had twenty-one advanced cooperatives which showed an increased production of more than thirty percent. Remaining skeptics then pooled their assets and joined.

'How did your commune begin?

'We read Mao Tse-tung's article in June 1958,[1] praising the Honan commune, and we discussed it. It made sense to us. We held meetings with other advanced co-ops and the *hsiang* and county officials and decided to organize as a commune.'

'Led by the party, no doubt?'

'Led by the party.'

Li had often seen Mao in his Yenan days and had talked to him.

'Mao is a good farmer. He knows farming. He was right about co-operatives. He was right about communes. We followed his eight-point charter and it produced results for us.'

This magic charter 'everywhere held aloft' by the rural communes consisted of: deep plowing and soil improvement; close planting; more fertilizer; water conservation; improved seeds; pest control; improved management; better farm tools. Li Yu-hua and his practical men of the field had no experience in presenting complex materials to an outsider; they assumed background you didn't possess; they were in no way prepared to impress the foreigner, and no public relations officer handed you a neatly packaged story.

There were dozens of technical traps. To cite one: you could end up with production and income figures per capita which didn't tally at all with aggregates. Unless you could check your translator you might not realize that the speaker was talking about *chia* (family) income, not individual income. Despite man-woman equality, rural Chinese still lumped husband-wife (and grandfather-grandmother) income as a unit and tended to use it interchangeably with 'per capita' in conversation.

Some vital statistics interested me. The total 1959 population of the commune was 6,254 ,of whom 3,655 were dependents, young and old. There were 1,582 families; the average couple had only two dependents. Of the 2,599 able-bodied workers, 1,592 were males, of whom only ten seemed to be still unmarried. The relative insignificance of this commune's industrial output was indicated by its full-time industrial labor force: only 181 workers (male and female) with 128 dependents. 'Able-bodied' here meant from eighteen to retirement age. Veterans were encouraged to settle and there were many 'immigrants' from other provinces. After 1948 the population of Yenan had sharply declined; thousands of youths trained by the party and the army left for the east, and very few of them returned.

In 1950 average output in this area was less than five bushels of grain an acre. By 1956 Li's advanced co-op had raised theirs to nearly twelve bushels. In 1959, a year after the commune was formed, cultivated land had been increased from 3,500 acres to almost 5,000 acres by the twenty-four brigade organization of labor, conservation works, etc. In the same year grain output averaged nineteen bushels an acre. In 1960 weather in north Shensi was good (in contrast with drought in the south) and preliminary returns on the harvest, already in, showed an output for the whole commune well above their target, which was fixed at about twenty-eight bushels of mixed grain (including livestock feed) an acre.

Even for mixed grain, those figures compared favorably with an American average wheat yield of 21·3 bushels per acre, but the investment in labor power in China was still vastly greater. Peking economists had recently pointed out that annual output per farm worker in the U.S. was about 1,000 bushels of grain. In China it required 300 days of labor to take care of 2·1 acres of crops. If China's labor productivity equaled that of the U.S. she would need only about 21,000,000 farm workers to feed the nation at its present level – instead of nearly ten times that number.[2]

Willow Grove's harvest included an average of 55 bushels on each of 1,650 acres of their best land, where a top yield of 118 bushels an acre was claimed. Such figures were phenomenal for north Shensi but they were not much more than average in Szechuan and China's rich delta areas. Near Shanghai a commune chairman told me he had established a record yield of 540 bushels (of mixed grain) an acre.

Irrigation, terracing, steel plows, improved methods and heavy increases in fertilizer were paying off, said Li. Other investments of labor and capital were reflected in increases of Willow Grove's livestock population since 1957 as follows: pigs, 2,370, up fifty-one percent; cattle, 3,220, including 1,540 cows, up ten percent; sheep, 14,690, up forty-two percent; chickens, 8,000, up twenty-five percent.

One reason I took Li seriously was that he gave me such a very low figure on Willow Grove's 1959 net income. I was unable to get a clear answer from him about gross income, or percentage of actual output delivered on compulsory sales contracts to the state. He merely gave me to understand that taxes never exceeded 'ten to twelve percent' and that the brigade was guaranteed a minimum of sixty percent of its output for consumption or 'cash sale' at market prices.

A brief digression about taxes. Up to 1958 direct grain levies had not been as exorbitant as many supposed. According to Mao Tse-tung's report to the National Congress in 1957, output of food crops in 1949 was 'only something over 210,000,000,000 catties'. That would be 105,000,000 tons, perhaps the crop on which taxes were collected but likely not the full crop. By 1956 the harvest was claimed to be 360,000,000,000 catties or 180,000,000 tons – not far from correct, in the view of foreign economists. (The U.S. cereals crop in 1957 was 157,000,000 tons.) Said Mao in 1957 :

The state agricultural tax is not heavy ... only thirty billion catties [fifteen million tons] a year. Grain bought from the peasants at normal prices [he refers to compulsory sales of fixed percentages of the crop to state grain agencies] amounts to something over fifty billion catties a year. These two items together total over eighty billion catties. ... We are prepared to stabilize over a number of years the total amount of grain purchased by the State at approximately something over eighty billion catties [forty million tons] a year.[3]

A tax of 15,000,000 tons on a crop of 180,000,000 tons (a bit more than eight percent) and state grain purchases of 40,000,000 tons would bring the combined levy to roughly thirty percent of the crop. Mao left himself an escape clause in the 'something over' but it is quite possible that in 1957 state taxes and purchases did not much exceed thirty percent. In 1958 and 1959, however, the combined tax and purchases may have been far higher than that figure, if the levies were based on the inflated harvest reports of those years.

Taxes on Willow Grove Commune in 1959 were stated to have been only 5·4 percent of output, whereas in Yellow Ridge they were eleven percent. In other areas I found variations from six to fourteen percent, depending on prosperity. In 1960 many hard-hit cooperatives were forgiven taxes while fortunate ones paid much more heavily. The *People's Daily* for 5 June 1958 stated that average grain taxes for that year were to be 15·5 percent, based on the harvest of 1956 or 1957; this would have meant a low tax if the expected giant 1958 crop had materialized. But I was told by one Chinese official that some communes had so far overestimated their harvest that they paid up to fifty percent of their crop in taxes and obligatory sales. Afterward they had to appeal to the government for relief.

Wages were determined on a basis involving eight to twelve grades of farm tasks, each paid differently. Every team kept daily and monthly records of the amount and kind of piecework accomplished by each member. This system could drive a chartered accountant mad but it seemed satisfactory to Chinese farmers, who agreed on fair rates among themselves. In Willow Grove Commune the income was figured in both cash and grain.

Mr Li's 'net income' figure for 1959 was what remained after operating expenses and payment of taxes and sales to the state – which may have amounted to more than thirty percent of output. Other deductions included 'fifteen to twenty percent' for livestock feed and seed grain, 'fifteen to twenty percent' for depreciation, reserves and welfare fund, and 'about ten percent' for new investments. Of the capital invested in new projects and equipment, sixty percent went to improvements in the land, industries, cattle, etc., owned by the brigades or villages, the rest went to commune projects under joint ownership.

After all these deductions the cash left for distribution amounted to only 187,800 yuan, which worked out at an average of about seventy-two yuan per worker. In addition each averaged an income of 830 catties in grain, including meat equivalents. Out of this grain income the commune set aside 390 catties (429 pounds) per inhabitant (including dependents) for consumption. The member worker was thus left with less than half of his 830 catties as book income. The 'surplus grain' was 'voluntarily' sold collectively at market prices, each member being credited with his proportion in 'share ownership'. The profit was added to capital funds for investment in brigade and commune projects and services.

Stated as take-home cash, the seventy-two yuan pittance sounds intolerable; but here the family paid no rent, nothing for utilities, nothing for nursery, kindergarten and schools (supported jointly by the commune welfare fund and the state), very little for medical care, no personal taxes, and its staple food was supplied. Members kept pigs or poultry and gardened an average family plot of ·10 *mou* for consumption or supplementary income. (A pig sold for forty yuan.) A strong worker could make much more than the average. I was introduced to one who earned 190 yuan ($72) in 1959.

Peasants here never used to see more than a yuan or two in cash at a time; their purchases were limited to salt, light oil, needles and thread, and occasionally a piece of cloth. Poor peasants were always in debt to usurers; now, if a peasant borrowed money to buy a pig or a bicycle it was from his mutual welfare fund and at no more than three percent interest. Not all peasant homes I saw in Willow Grove were as 'richly furnished' as Li's, but even the poorest had chests of clothing and piled-up quilts. Even on such minimal cash they somehow managed to dress their children attractively and I was constantly surprised at the bright, clean 'town-best' clothes of the peasant girls one saw riding donkeys to and from Yenan.

All the land, orchards, local dams, irrigation works, buildings, factories, and livestock were jointly owned by the brigades and village teams at Willow Grove. Mounting assets were thus considerably greater than the current cash income reflected. They might reasonably be expected to pay an increasingly higher return once the basic national construction program in agriculture and industry was completed and consumer goods output could absorb more cash. Since peasant members could not sell their nominal share in the brigade's capital assets, their investment in it tended to keep them stabilized on the land; if they left for another commune it might take them years as hired laborers to win acceptance as members with full rights.

The whole success of collective ownership depended upon maintaining peasant understanding of the reasons for self-denial and saving and on maintaining faith and enthusiasm about the system. Here in Willow Grove at least, the already realized tangible benefits, combined with visible evidence of the new wealth created by their collective labor, had produced a high degree of ambition for the fulfillment of plans. And every worker knew about these plans.

Before I left Willow Grove, I visited the kindergarten-nursery in a cave high on a bluff where one of Li's daughters, a Mrs Chen, kept thirty-three infants busy learning the rudiments of socialist cooperation. A nursery in a cave? The Shensi *yao-fang* is not a hole in the ground but a 'house in a hill'. Except in external appearance a cave can be superior to the average farm hut, drier and cooler in summer, warmer in winter. Terraces dug from the fudge-colored loess provide a suitable façade; chimneys are put in at a slant; the rooms have vaulted ceilings and large arched windows give ample light. Frequently two or more rooms are linked into apartments.

Mrs Chen's rooms were clean, so were the children, and so were the grownups – down to fingernails. (Shensi peasants with clean fingernails? There had been a revolution here.) There used to be dysentery in nearly every family. Mrs Chen said they had had no case for a year. A public health nurse called once a week; all children were vaccinated. I saw no sign of trachoma, formerly very common. The children looked well nourished and healthy and their behavior was energetic. They were dressed in cheap but attractive jumper suits differing in color and design; girls had slashes of red ribbons in their bobbed hair, boys had shaved heads and wide grins.

Taking charge of me, tugging at my hands and jacket, the kindergarteners dragged me to see their piles of squash and pumpkins, their purple corn; these they had tended and hauled up the hill themselves. The usual rows of combs, toothbrushes, wash basins and towels were ranged under health posters, and each child had his bowl and chopsticks. Besides gruel, mashed vegetables and occasional eggs, there was even milk here twice a week – for nursery tots only.

Commune nurseries at Willow Grove were (as in many rural areas) operated only during the busy planting and harvesting seasons, when mothers worked full time in the fields. Most of them were, like the kindergartens, day schools only. Parents left the children in the morning and picked them up after work.

I have described two communes that were more or less typical of nine others I visited except that Yellow Ridge was one of the richest and Willow Grove was the poorest. The best managed I saw was the

Horse Bridge Commune near Shanghai, a very prosperous large ranch farm with yields as good as American ones. It was so much above average that to dwell on it at length would be misleading. For the same reason I have omitted here a detailed report of the highly mechanized state farm I saw at Chia Mu Ssu outside Harbin.

State farms were run like factories and employees on them were wage workers who had no private ownership rights. They were a stage beyond collectivization, in Communist theory; they were 'owned by the whole people' and thus already had 'elements of communism'. Cultivators received high cash wages comparable to those of factory workers, and the general standard of living was much above that of the cooperative farms.

A few model state farms were organized as early as 1950, in Manchuria – where great wheat domains and cattle ranches were first opened by White Russians. Later they were extended to virgin lands in sparsely populated Sinkiang, Mongolia and Yunnan. Since communes were formed such farms had about doubled in area, but by 1961 they still embraced only 12,500,000 acres, or less than five percent of China's cultivated land. Most of them were not affected by the drought that came late in 1960 – a year when they reported a 25,000,000-ton harvest gathered by 2,800,000 workers. If the same rate had prevailed everywhere China could have shown a crop of 550,000,000 tons (3.7 times the estimated 1960 output), needed but 60,000,000 farm hands, and had an abundance of food as well as labor. The state farms' high productivity was explained by heavy use of chemical fertilizer and 28,000 tractors and 3,300 combine-harvesters; they were about five times more mechanized than the communes.

As I have described it, my itinerary in China afforded me a fair sampling of conditions in widely separated parts of the nation. But I could not begin to claim authority as an eyewitness to how people worked and ate 'in every region of the Chinese country-side'. For that, it seemed necessary to see China from the Portuguese colony of Macão, according to Joseph Alsop. So I learned when I returned from Yenan to Sian and found a few letters forwarded from Peking. One enclosed clippings of some articles depicting conditions inside China in November 1959. They were written by Joseph Alsop. Viewing the situation from Macão, Mr Alsop reported that 'gnawing hunger, made worse by chain-gang work conditions, now prevails *in every region of the Chinese country-side*'. He went on to assert that 'fats and proteins ... were mere dreams of the past in the communes' – 'many' of which were requiring '16 hours of work a day for at least half of each month'. He also learned in Macão (which had Kuomintang as well as Communist propaganda centers) of 'numerous cases of grass-eating ... and leaf-eating' in China and of 'peasants driven to work *24 hours a day* for two to four days on end'.[4]

I have had some experience in detecting starvation among wartime refugees. In famine areas of yore I personally saw hundreds of Chinese actually feeding on bark, leaves and even mud. But they were not working sixteen or twenty-four hours a day. They were dying.

After a swift visit to Hongkong and another peep at the bamboo curtain early in 1961, Mr Alsop scored an even more important scoop over resident Hongkong correspondents. He cabled home the news that Chinese were now reduced to dining on human after-births.[5] Mr Alsop attributed this refugee intelligence to 'an obviously well-balanced trained nurse from North China'.

61

The Yellow River Turns Blue

WE took a night express from Sian to the new city of San Men Hsia, Three Gate Gorge, where man had at last put a throttle on the Yellow River. Some people considered this the most spectacular and significant single engineering achievement yet seen in eastern Asia.

If we thought of the known history of China and its civilization as having had a life span of twenty-four hours, then Communist power had been in existence less than five minutes. By comparison, the longest single dynastic reign in China endured for almost five hours. Anyone who had ever found anything admirable in this land or any part of its history must therefore derive pleasure from two remarkable improvements in the landscape brought about mainly during the past 'five minutes'. These were best seen from the air: (1) the numerous blue-water reservoirs I have mentioned; and (2) the advancing forests of young trees flanking the sides of once barren hills, along rivers, canals, highways and railways, and pushing back the northern deserts.

Kuant'ing and Miyun reservoirs, which I had seen, and now the San Men, which we were nearing, were three of a score of major new water-conservation works that had been completed as part of a state program for more than four hundred principal dams which were in various stages of construction or planning. Within the decade since 1950, China had risen from twenty-fifth place as a power producer to seventh place in the world, standing just behind France. Meanwhile a myriad of hands had in twelve years built more than a million small reservoirs and ponds such as those at Willow Grove, and dug nine million wells. They had also developed new canals and storage basins which increased the irrigated area by 120,000,000 acres.

But the whole conservancy scheme waited, for permanence, on

the growth of vast new forested ground cover to contain the anarchy of the rains. Between 1952 and 1960, China had graduated more than 5,000 forestry experts and established a modern forestry service. In north Shensi I saw the southern edge of one great forest belt which stretched for 360 miles above the Yellow River to stop the silt-laden sandstorms from the Gobi. Above it, reaching from Inner Mongolia to the Manchurian provinces, another tree belt had been more than half planted over a length of 720 miles. Elsewhere most of the afforestation labor was provided by agricultural communes, but every able-bodied person had participated and was still planting his annual quota of trees. Most collectives and production brigades now had tree nurseries where billions of seedlings and saplings were nurtured and cultivated.

In the northwest, extensive new resources and industries were being developed around the Tsaidam basin, where it was essential to reclaim marginal land in order to feed the incoming population. Since 1955, it was claimed, some 150,000 acres of land in that region had been successfully desalinized.[1] In Sinkiang alone 'more than 140 mechanized state farms had been set up since 1949 by demobilized army men and other young people'.[2] Much of the 30,000,000 acres of land brought into cultivation since the revolution lay in this area and in Mongolia. Over all China, it was claimed, more than 51,000,000 hectares – 'an area twice as large as Great Britain' – had been tree-planted and reforested between 1949 and 1960.[3]

In Peking's agricultural and industrial exhibition halls I had seen scale models not only of all the major conservation systems but of important projects I had never heard of, many of them already completed, in widely scattered areas. One Wellsian exhibit showed the long-range plan of a canal and river system which would virtually encircle China, reaching from the frontiers of Manchuria to Yunnan, and from Peking to Central Asia, bringing all corners of the realm within reach of motor vessels carrying cargo and passenger traffic. This would involve no less than turning some of the headwaters of the Yangtze River from eastern Tibet into the Taklamakan Desert. It is easy to draw futuristic pictures, of course. What made these schemes notable were the steps already taken toward their realization. Many achievements publicized only locally, which the outside world never heard about, would be considered major events in small countries or even in a large country like India.

'Yes, yes, yes, San Men is a magnificent thing,' Rewi Alley said as we came into the new city, 'but it's the miniature San Mens going up all over the backwoods, like Yenan – and like Yunnan, each one representing untold struggles of little people who had to dream big – that's where you really see the creative force this country is releasing.' Those who were worried about China's launching an aggressive war might have found in Alley's new book, *China's Hinterland*,[4] and its thousands of true stories of unsung heroes at work, some interesting information about how that nation's vast human energies were presently being contained in building activities which should make the world rejoice – unless, of course, all growth in lands of the blue ants must inevitably lead to war, as it had done in the white-ant lands of private capitalism.

In 1956, San Men City was a drowsy village known as Hui Hsin, on the Honan-Shensi border. Now it unexpectedly found itself host to 170,000 workers, with many more to come. Hui Hsin was the point nearest to the gorge accessible by railway and for that reason was chosen as base of operations. The Sian-Chengchow main line had to be relaid to touch here, and double-tracking of the whole Sian-Chengchow line as far as Lanchow was accelerated to accommodate workers on the dam and the reservoir as much as to facilitate access to the new oil fields in the northwest. The reservoir backed up behind the big dam was 194 miles long, and reached to the outskirts of Sian itself. I was told that it was now China's second largest lake.

Nothing was finished in San Men City, but it was laid out with wide, straight paved streets running through block after block of half-completed red-brick apartment buildings and on to many new structures: railway workshops, sidings, spur lines to the steel plant and car repair shops and various other industries I had no time to investigate. I had come to see the dam. We put up at a guest house in a group of modest buildings strung around a courtyard and flower garden with a teahouse in the center.

After breakfast on ham and eggs we drove in a new Ford sedan across a rough dirt road which suddenly gave way to an excellent macadamized highway and immediately entered steep mountain country. The curves were sharp but well banked, the driver fast, the landscape breathtaking: drops to deep ravines on one side, highlands glimpsed on the other – cave dwellers, loess terraces high up, shepherds and cowherds silhouetted on the skyline. Suddenly I saw a group of perhaps a hundred men wearing white hoods and capes like Klansmen and I insisted on stopping. I wanted some pictures.

Who were these men? Monks? Prisoners? Or were they women? We piled out and saw that about half of them were drinking tea. We went up to one sitting in the shade and learned that they had been dynamiting and breaking up stone from a nearby ledge; their felt capes were to protect them from flying debris. When I told them I had thought they were monks, they all threw off their capes and began laughing. They were a work gang from the dam.

As we came out of the pass we entered a plateau of beautiful farmlands and soon afterward reached a bluff where we stopped. Mr Chin motioned me out and led me to the precipice. A thousand feet below us, on either side of the wide new dam which had caught the Yellow River and belted it at its narrowest, lay vast expanses of shimmering water as blue as the Aegean.

'Our yellow dragon has changed color,' said Mr Chin, smiling. 'He is tamed now.'

The Grandest Coolie

PERHAPS *only* a Chinese or someone who had seen something of the past rampages of the Huang Ho would have found the closing of the great gates of San Men particularly exciting. For all Chinese, whether pro- or anti-Mao, San Men was not just another barrage adding 1,200,000 kilowatts to the national power capacity; it was the beginning of a happy ending to an old tragedy.

'If the People's Government did nothing else, and if it perished tomorrow,' someone wrote in the guest book at the dam, 'the Chinese nation would gratefully remember it for a thousand years because of its conquest of the Yellow River !' San Men was No. 37 – but the key control point – of forty-six step-dams in the giant staircase 2,500 feet high and 2,000 miles long, by means of which that conquest was being won.

The Yangtze is China's mightiest river, but the Huang Ho is about equally important to agriculture. Its basin includes sixty percent of her wheat fields, fifty-seven percent of her cotton fields, and sixty-seven percent of her tobacco fields. Starting in the highlands of Chinghai, near Tibet, the river runs eastward through Kansu, flows abruptly north to Inner Mongolia, drops southward through deep gorges which divide Shensi and Shansi provinces, and then marches toward the northeast across the plains of Honan, Hopei and Shantung. Ending its travels of nearly three thousand miles south of Tientsin, the Huang Ho has at times added as much as fourteen square miles of new land a year to the coastline along the Yellow Sea. In places its silt burden has been twenty times that of the Colorado. It has changed its course twenty-six times in recorded history. During the past hundred years overflows occurred more than two hundred times.

By 1950 the habits of the river combined with years of man's neglect and misuse of nature's own controls had created the staggering problems I have described : plateaus and farms of the northwest gradually denuded of trees, overgrazed, and desiccated. Half the annual rainfall in this basin occurs in July and August, when each year sudden torrents would sweep more earth, natural phosphates and nitrates into the river and down upon the central plains. In Shantung the river bed was built up twenty to twenty-five feet above the surrounding countryside and I have watched junks sail overhead at that height. Prodigious amounts of labor were needed to prevent floods even in years of normal flow, and they were labors of Sisyphus repeated for ages past.

Part of the radical solution required to tame the Yellow River was foreseen years ago by American famine-relief engineers, notable among them being O. J. Todd. No Chinese administration ever undertook the gigantic task until 1954, however, when the Peking government established the Yellow River Planning Commission. Extensive surveys were made and a multipurpose Yellow River plan was completed in 1955; with the help of Soviet experts actual work began in 1956. By November 1960 China could justly claim that it had (a year ahead of schedule) 'basically' licked the River Dragon God, propitiated for many centuries past by superstitious peasants.

Victory came a few months too late. As early as the summer of 1960 the San Men dam could have stopped the Yellow River in flood – but that was not the problem. There was no flood; in the lower reaches of the basin, including the whole province of Shantung, with 57,000,000 people, there was for weeks simply *no river*. In 1960, North China suffered its worst drought in a century. By October, when I watched the lake at last filling up from a flow heavy with delayed autumn rains, the harvests had been lost in the parched plains below.

San Men was the Grandest Coolie and the Grand Coulee of China, and there was equal truth in either spelling. Compared to America's largest concrete dam, San Men was fundamentally a drought- and river-control project. It produced only sixty percent as much power as Grand Coulee but its reservoir held 36,000,000,000 cubic meters of water, or more than Grand Coulee and Boulder dams combined. In 1960 it was the world's third-greatest reservoir. San Men was planned to provide irrigation and prevent flood on 6,600,000 acres.

The second largest Yellow River dam, at Lanchow, in Kansu, was scheduled to be operating by 1963, with the same power capacity as San Men. Three other major dams and reservoirs and forty-one smaller ones, some already built, were to complete a system of reservoirs with a total water-reserve capacity exceeding the flow of the Yellow River for an entire year. The whole dam and power system was scheduled to be completed in 1967. Total power capacity should eventually reach 23,000,000 kilowatts, with an annual power output of 110,000,000,000 kilowatts. That is four times China's prewar power capacity and forty percent more than that of India in 1960.

None of this plan would be fully practicable, however, nor could it ultimately double agricultural production on one third of China's grain lands, as promised, if it were not for giant supplementary efforts. All the power dams and reservoirs would have a brief life if the erosion problem affecting a land area inhabited by 150,000,000 people were not simultaneously solved. ·

Antisilting and soil-rationalization measures had begun in some areas ten years ago. Labors of Hercules, mostly done by hand, the program included: reforestation, afforestation, and orchard planting on 15,000 square miles; soil and water retaining, contour terracing, ditching and banking covering 22,000 square miles; soil-banking and dustpan storage (small ponds) on 4,000 square miles of steep slopes; grass-and-crop rotation on 3,300 square miles, and returfing and otherwise improving 50,000 square miles of pasture land.[1]

Battalions, whole divisions, of spade-armed peasants in this general area had been working on a plan which required about 950,000 check dams, gully seals, and silt-precipitation basins, and 37,000 ponds and sumps with a total capacity two thirds as large as San Men Lake. Many of these toy dams were already used for local power, irrigation and soil-restorative purposes such as I saw in Willow Grove. Precipitated silt was helping to reclaim wasteland and desert while the forest belts were beginning to halt the desert in the north. Irrigated land in the whole basin was to be extended sevenfold.

Control systems can work miracles but they cannot make rain. Even in good years the water flow in the Yellow River basin is inadequate. Nearly fifty-one percent of China's cultivated land lies in this basin, which gets only seven percent of the nation's water flow, while the Yangtze Valley, which embraces thirty-three percent of the cultivated land, receives seventy-six percent of the annual water flow. In search of a solution to the water problem, Chinese engineers had completed surveys for a daring project to split the upper Yangtze and divert nearly two billion cubic meters of water into the Yellow River. This would about *quadruple* the volume of the latter.

The Yangtze plan would involve the greatest engineering tasks in Asia. Four dams were planned, each larger than San Men. Three Gorges Dam, between Ichang and Chungking, would serve multiple purposes of power, flood control, irrigation and navigation. It would have a power capacity of 4,000,000 kilowatts, larger than any existing plant in the world. The combined system, including a series of upstream barrages, would add a total of 18,250,000 kilowatts to China's capacity.

Both the river-splitting and the Yangtze barrages would be stupendous undertakings in any country. In China they meant concentrations of capital and engineering resources on a scale which at present probably could be achieved only with considerable technical and material help from abroad. One of the major unpublished Chinese complaints behind the Sino-Soviet dispute was Moscow's decision to build the Aswan dam for Nasser on easy terms denied to China for the Yangtze and Yellow River projects. In the absence of such help, work on both projects was moving very slowly in 1962. Nothing better illustrated the vicious paradox of China's undercapitalized economy than that such basic solutions to agricultural problems had to be deferred while technique and resources were diverted to overcome food crises by means which could provide little more than temporary relief.

Meanwhile, Chinese engineers had by 1958 already completed nineteen other modern hydroelectric systems without Russian help. The largest was the 580,000-kilowatt plant in Chekiang, equipped with the first China-made giant generators, of 75,000- and 100,000-kilowatt capacity. Literally thousands of smaller thermal power stations were now being installed every year by Chinese engineers using Chinese equipment. San Men's power plant of 1,200,000 kilowatts was planned to utilize eight generators, each with a capacity of 150,000 kilowatts. China had produced nothing so large and these generators were ordered from the U.S.S.R. Only one had arrived at the time of my visit. If Russia reneged on deliveries to San Men the power part of the whole Yellow River project would doubtless be delayed – along with other major works dependent on Soviet imports – but by 1963 China expected to be able to make even these very large generators herself.*

So I was assured by the general administrator, Chou Yi-lin, who conducted me through the labyrinth of San Men. 'This has been a field college of priceless value,' said Mr Chou. 'In four years we've trained hundreds of engineers and technicians who will be kept busy for the rest of their lives building dams and power plants and training others.'

There were 21,000 workers directly engaged on the San Men project, including 2,000 women. Kuant'ing, China's first large modern reservoir, which was built in 1954, was less than one tenth the size of San Men Reservoir in area and power capacity. It required 60,000 workers plus assistance at one stage of an army division of diggers. Most of the skilled workers at San Men got their preliminary training at Kuant'ing, but now they had mechanized China-made equipment as well as machines and tools from all over Europe.

Wages for workers ranged from forty to 100 yuan and averaged sixty; the work day was eight hours. Engineers got from 150 to 250 yuan; part-time apprentices (half-study, half-work) began at twenty. Rent, utilities, medical care, movies, opera and clubs were provided free of charge, as were workers' dungarees, helmets,

---

*(1970) The U.S.S.R. did cancel deliveries of the generators and of other essential tools; San Men was not to be completed for several years. Various anti-erosion measures required to make the entire Yellow River control and power complex function as described above were not carried out in time to prevent silting up of the San Men basin (Lake) and of higher basins. The Lanchow dam was, however, able to supply power and water adequate for the operation of a large gaseous diffusion plant built near the Kansu capital. It produced the fissionable materials necessary to make China's first atom bomb (1964) and subsequent nuclear devices. At this writing the San Men dam is operating but not at full efficiency.

goggles, shoes, etc. Their main expense was food, which cost twelve to fifteen yuan a month.

Floodlights were strung everywhere, and work went on day and night. Amplifiers hung at strategic points and opera and symphonic music alternated with the noise of riveting and instructions from on high. Banners hung amidst steel girders, flags flew, squads of drums and cymbals now and then marched to present pennants to bonus-winning 'overfulfillers'.

'When the Yellow River is controlled a genie will appear!' ran a slogan strung out on a long banner against a cliff, and quoting an ancient peasant axiom. 'The genie has appeared: the Chinese people!'

The ancient 'Three Gates' of the Gorge were narrows formed between stone eyots; they had been called Man's Gate, Gods' Gate and Dragon's Gate. Now the eyots had disappeared under the great jaws of the dam. So: 'Where is the Gate of the Gods? Where is the Gate of the Dragon? Only the Gate of Man Remains!' declared another slogan hung from the bamboo stagings.

I stopped to take a color picture of a welder playing his bright torch on a silvery flume and then I asked him to remove his helmet. 'He' was a grinning bobbed-haired girl, agreeably good-looking. Parents? Peasants in a commune. Like the work? Why not? She had tried hard enough to qualify for it. But she was doing spare-time study and hoped to become an engineer, as many had already done before her.

Then I asked to go up the giant crane to meet the slaves up there doing what looked to me like the most responsible job on the set; the lives of hundreds of men below depended upon their accuracy. Cheerfully Chou Yi-lin took me up a hundred feet or more in a fast elevator from which I stepped out to behold a splendid panorama of the whole barrage and the reservoir. Through one open sluice gate the imprisoned river surged and boiled, and now beyond it I could see a canal being dug through solid rock to by-pass the dam; it would permit motor ships to enter the upper lake through a series of locks. I stepped out on the catwalk and watched the great fist of the crane pick up a 200-ton steel and concrete beam and place the load neatly between huge studs where fitters and welders perched far below.

When I went into the control cabin I found two twenty-two-year-old girls second and third in command of the crane. The smaller one was rather shy, a primary school graduate from Tangshan, homely but bright-eyed; short hair; unmarried. She had got her job by passing an examination and had worked at Kuant'ing a year before coming here. Father? A miner. 'From the first time I ever saw a crane – it was in a movie – I knew I wanted to operate one. I studied, I learned the technique. There's nothing I'd rather do.' The other girl, an orphaned daughter of poor peasants, felt exactly the same about it. I don't know how many women operate cranes in other countries, but they seemed to be more trusted than men at the job in China.

I drove on, with Chou Yi-lin, to visit Ta An, the new workers' village. On the cliffs and bluffs rising up on both banks of the river to the plateau 3,000 feet high there clung hundreds of caves where peasants still lived – the same peasants who used to make annual sacrifices to the river dragon. A few years ago people in these rugged mountain fastnesses had never seen a motor. Now their sons were driving trucks and handling pneumatic drills; their daughters and granddaughters were marrying literate workers from other provinces. Some of the workers would settle here, others would go on to the next job. Time had moved ahead ten thousand years.

'Half a million people were displaced by the lake reservoir,' said Chou Yi-lin. 'We had to explain patiently the meaning of the slogan, "One family leaves the valley to guarantee life for 10,000". Now there are fishing and boatbuilding industries and new towns are springing up along the lake. There will be plenty of fish, and canning factories – it will be a big thing. Our servicing industries will go on after we leave. Look at Ta An – nobody could have lived on this river bank before for fear of floods. Now it's already becoming an attractive lake port. It will be a pleasure resort and have commercial importance besides.'

Ta An (Great Peace) was built from scratch to house the personnel for the dam, and it was no shanty town; a planning committee had supervised all building. The straight streets were still unpaved but sewers were being laid and telephones and street lights were working. With a population already numbering 27,000, Ta An was organized as a combination urban-rural commune which took in surrounding farm lands. High above the town, 6,000 people still lived in caves, now lighted also by Mr Edison's magic lanterns.

In one flat I met a man of fifty-four who had been a railway worker all his life; after eight years of spare-time study he had just qualified as a graduate engineer and proudly showed me his diploma. In another place I flushed out two doll-like children to photograph. The prettier, a little girl with large saucy black eyes and beribboned hair her mother must have water-waved, refused to cooperate. 'I just won't do it,' she said with finality, hiding her face but bursting with laughter. Even Chou, who knew her parents, couldn't persuade her.

'She's always that way,' he said good-naturedly, 'but she's clever. Probably going to be an actress.'

We dropped in on a young woman worker preparing a meal. She was at home nursing a leg injury acquired at the dam. As I talked to her Chou Yi-lin looked around and went over to a family-group photograph. 'Is this man related to you?' he suddenly asked her. Yes, he was a cousin. Chou said he knew him very well, he worked in his bureau. Then he was off exchanging small talk with her about mutual acquaintances and when he left they seemed already old friends. A good politician. Somewhat the same thing happened when I stopped a bound-footed woman on the street who told me both her son and daughter-in-law worked on the dam. She greeted Chou warmly and I asked if he knew her.

'Yes,' he said, 'she's a clean-up woman in one of the engineering laboratories.'

And who was Chou Yi-lin?

We had been working together for two days before I found time to ask. He was in his mid-thirties, homely, thin and wiry, with jutting teeth and thick lips: a man ready with precise answers to every question I raised. It occurred to me that I had not once heard him mention American imperialism.

'Let me see if I can guess some of your personal history,' I said as we sat down for tea in the canteen, while Rewi dozed in a corner. He looked amused. 'You're a veteran, of course. Not old enough to be a Long March man, but a veteran. Had to shoot a few people, Japanese and maybe a few others. Known a lot of hunger – and old enough now to know the difference between wanting something and wanting to do something? Where did you come in?'

'Not bad guessing. Yes, I was in the army – wounded once – nearly died. My parents were small landlords but I had only three years in school. We were ruined by the Japanese. I joined the guerrillas under Lo P'ing-hui and fought all through the anti-Japanese war and then the civil war. I ended up at Canton as a regimental commander. After that the party sent me to school. I met my wife; she's a party worker, too. Then I was put in command of military units that helped build the Kuant'ing reservoir. That's how I became an "expert" on dams.' He laughed. 'Of course I did study some engineering along the way. The party sent me here to San Men and I've been working at it ever since.'

'Are you here as an army officer or party leader?'

'Both. My real boss is the Minister of Hydroelectric Works, Fu Tso-yi.'

'So you're working for the general you defeated.'

He smiled. General Fu Tso-yi was the last old North China warlord to surrender. He held onto Peking for a month while he bargained for a peaceful turnover and good conditions for his men and himself. (Peking, like Paris, is always surrounded first, then peacefully surrenders.) Not a mere display-window minister, like some of the ex-Kuomintang officials in the present government, Fu Tso-yi worked hard at his job and was widely respected as an able administrator.

Driving back to the city late in the afternoon we passed many detachments of young men and women carrying spades and farming tools, sometimes arm-in-arm, occasionally clinging to a tractor or a truck loaded with vegetables, sometimes marching battalion style and singing under waving banners. They were students and workers from technical schools and shops in the new city, doing their *hsia fang* or down-on-the-farm harvest labor. They looked strong and healthy.

We picked up our bags in town and drove on to the station. Halfway there we passed about twenty men carrying picks and shovels and marching down the street between two very young armed soldiers. I stared at them intently as we drove by. They did not look at us; they gazed straight ahead and they were not talking or singing.

Their expressionless faces were entirely different from those of all the other groups I had seen that day. There were two or three youths among them but most of them were middle-aged men. They were not in uniform but were dressed about like any other workers, and they were physically sound, as far as I could see at a glance.

It does not matter what crimes a man commits, once he becomes a prisoner he ceases to be an enemy and evokes sympathy like a caged bird or an animal. I remember how it was always that way during the war; we hated the Nazis and Japanese still uncaught or unkilled, but prisoners were lost people in rumpled clothes, needing shaves, lonely, hanging onto torn photographs of girl friends or wives or children; captivity made them pathetic humans again. All this flashed through my mind as I asked Mr Chou whether these were political or ordinary prisoners.

'They're from a reform labor farm,' he replied. 'Some of them may be political; more likely not. They've been building roads.'

'Do you use many prisoners around here?'

'Very few. Most of the time they work on the farm.'

'Any on the dam construction?'

'Did you see any soldiers guarding our workers there?' No, I had not. 'No, and you won't see any. Prisoners have to work, like everybody else, but not until they've been re-educated can they work with good citizens again. It takes time to reform them.'

In fairly wide travels in twelve provinces and over many back-country roads I saw one other detachment of guarded prisoners doing field work – also a small group – as against countless men and women obviously not working under duress.

63

Loyang and Chengchow

LOYANG is more than three thousand years old; it was the capital during several dynastic reigns beginning with the Chou. The old walled city with its narrow streets was still picturesque but now it was swamped by suburbs where most of Loyang's 600,000 inhabitants lived and worked in new enterprises. In 1948 Loyang had a population of 80,000. There had been no modern industry here. Coal and iron resources were plentiful nearby, so it was decided to turn Loyang into a 'major construction city'.

Largest and most significant of the new enterprises was Loyang's Tractor Plant No. 1, which employed 23,000 workers. Around it a model new satellite town had been constructed replete with shopping centers, wide paved streets and sidewalks, and well-landscaped housing for 100,000 people. This was China's largest tractor plant and its assembly line seemed to be working well when I visited it. Output in 1959 was 15,000 tractors and the 1960 target was fixed at 30,000, or capacity. No. 1 was among the initial 156 projects built with the aid of Soviet machines and engineers.

All parts of the tractor from tracks to engines were made in Loyang, where the assembly rate normally was one machine every nineteen minutes. 'Now we are turning out one "East Wind" tractor every few minutes,' the director told me. The East Wind was a sturdy multipurpose machine of fifty-four horsepower with numerous attachments for hauling, water pumping, forging, etc. Some idea of current costs of production in motor-mechanized industry could be gathered from the 'output value' (sales price) of 21,000 yuan ($8,400) which the director placed on an East Wind tractor.

Wages were lower here than in most state industries, but a thirty percent bonus was distributed for fulfillment of quotas. The average wage was given to me as forty yuan, with a top, for engineers ('one to three per workshop'), at 280 yuan. An apprentice started at twenty-one yuan. Rent (in modern housing, with tiny kitchen and shower for married couples) was only sixty cents a month. Food costs averaged ten to twelve yuan per worker. Medical treatment was free to employees and half-rate to their dependents. Medical care, pensions and other benefits came out of the welfare fund to which workers contributed 1·5 percent to three percent of wages.

I saw only about a quarter of this very large plant, from which all Soviet engineers had departed. 'Farewell Soviet Comrades' read signs. 'We shall never forget you!' The director told me that Chinese engineers were able to duplicate No. 1. A copy of it was scheduled to be finished in Paotou in 1962. Smaller tractor plants also existed in Shanghai and Manchuria, and I saw threshing machines made in Kunming on a low production basis.

One afternoon I visited a Loyang primary school where 1,180 students and forty-eight teachers worked in new brick buildings with a vegetable garden at the back. The director, a normal school graduate, took me through some of the twenty-four classrooms and five workshops, pointing out wall slogans along the way which echoed those in the factories: 'Dare to think!' 'Dare to do!' 'Dare to invent!'

'Since we began to combine practical shop work with classroom study in 1957,' he said, 'our superior students have risen from seventy-nine percent to ninety-three percent. It has given them new incentives.'

Students aged nine or above were obliged to spend two hours a week in shop but many volunteered for much more. It seemed to me no different from the manual training and cooking classes we used to have in Norman School in Kansas City, but it was a new idea in China. There was a variety of work and students sold their products. Profits went into the school welfare fund. Each class was led by an elected foreman. Here I saw boys and girls making parts for small table radios and assembling them, mixing and packaging a patent-medicine pain-killer (under a teacher's supervision!), and making furniture and ceramics. About half of them wore Red Pioneer kerchiefs.

Outside Loyang I visited a large rural production brigade called Ku-ch'eng, made up of fifty production teams with about 2,000 members. It was part of Lo-pei township. This brigade was an old advanced agricultural cooperative.

According to information given to me by the cadres, Honan had had rain on only fourteen days of the past 300; the total fall was less than forty millimeters. It was the worst drought for fifty years, yet Honan would have enough of a harvest to feed itself, they said. Ten million *mou* of Honan were now irrigable by canals and well systems. (Millions of Honan peasants were caught in areas without adequate water, however. They did not simply sit there in the desert, waiting to starve, as in the past. Commune organization permitted them to be temporarily shifted to more fortunate farms, where they were put to work on land improvement, construction, workshop and other tasks, in exchange for their rations.)

In the middle of a tomato field I fell behind my hosts to take some pictures of the canal. An old peasant, sunburned black, bare-chested and with a jacket hung over a shoulder, stood watching me. Was he a native? I asked. Yes. He had one brother. They had received land in the distribution? He pointed across the canal where half a dozen men and women were tilling a field of cabbage and spinach. That was it, right there. Good land?

'Very good. Between our families we had six *mou*.'

'Now it belongs to the whole village?'

'It's part of the *tui* [brigade] land.'

'Does it grow more or less than when you tilled it as a family?'

'Oh ho! Four times more! We didn't have the canal then, and who could buy fertilizer, get power and tractors?' At the tractor station I had seen six tractors and a combine – some of the thirty-four tractors and six combines owned jointly by the township.

'Married?'

He had married late in life, he said; they had two children. One was in middle school in the city. One was in primary school. What had happened to his family burial plot? He pointed to a grove of trees. On the whole, were things better or worse?

'I liked it better when we had our own land.' He pulled on his jacket, shrugged and started to leave. Then he turned and added: 'But of course all this –' His hand swept in the canal, the power plant in the distance. He grinned. 'Without the canal we would be starving in a year like this. The young people are probably right. This is the only way.'

Going east, half a day beyond Loyang, we stopped for two days at ancient Chengchow, which was also being transformed. I quote from my diary :

Chengchow, Sept. 27. Awoke at six with the aid of blue cadres singing cadres' blues. My hotel is headquarters for the cadres' autumn training. Their morning opens with party hymns, followed by exercise in the courtyard. There seems to be a choice between *t'ai chi ch'uan* and the conventional physical jerks.

Chengchow's housing development is the most successful I have seen here. The old wall is down completely. Most of the new streets are broad and the new buildings are set well back from them and generously spaced and landscaped. Principal highways are divided by parklike esplanades all of which are now being used as vegetable gardens. Nearly every inch of surface is planted in sunflowers, turnips, cabbage, corn and potatoes. Scattered along the margins are asters, roses, gladioli and hollyhocks. Four fifths of the population is said to be living in new housing, mostly three- or four-story apartment buildings in brick, generally grouped around the new factories. Each zone has its own shopping and recreational centers. There are nine new theaters and six opera houses. On the streets are far more bicycles than in Peking and stores seemed well stocked.

Down a newly opened divided highway flanked by modern buildings come rubber-tired carts filled with bricks, bricks, and more bricks, mortar, sand, lime, bags of cement, carrots, cabbages, apples, potatoes, tomatoes, cardboard boxes, paper, steel reinforcement rods, chemical products, radios, bundles of cloth, household furniture, bathtubs, motors, toilet seats, television sets, coal – and small children ! The pullers are students, teachers, workers, peasants, red-kerchiefed Pioneers, each with a rope around his shoulders, sometimes singing, sometimes following banners; housewives dragging their new commune-made goods to market; professionals with heavy loads, cushioned pads on their shoulders. Made-in-Manchuria trucks drag three or four trailers behind them, each carrying tons of produce from farms or factories – iron bars, agricultural tools, bales of cotton. A giant self-propelled crane, its kangaroo neck reaching twenty to thirty feet ahead of it, is preceded by boys laying down lengths of padded cloth before the tracks to save the pavements. Between bamboo-scaffolded uncompleted buildings graze flocks of sheep and goats and on small isolated ponds are clusters of ducks, indifferent to the oncoming town. Old ladies with bound feet ride donkeys in danger of being crushed by trolleys, trucks and carts. A long street of modern, almost California-Spanish architecture, with low brick walls and moon-gate doorways leading into gardens: casement windows – and flowers on the sills. Who lives there? 'Intellectuals,' said Shih, my Intourist guide.

After watching textile machines being made in a large (2,500 workers) factory, where the whole output was earmarked for export to North Vietnam, I stopped by to see some railway workshops. There I learned about an urban-commune quilt and clothing factory run entirely by women, and on request I was permitted to visit it. Most of the workers were wives of railway workers employed in the nearby locomotive repair shops. The lady in charge, a housewife named Cheng Chih-chi, told me that they had started work in 1958 with twelve sewing machines, eight of them owned by members and four purchased.

Their workshop was a white cement-block building originally designed for a neighborhood meeting hall in the new housing development in which they all lived. Now they owned 108 machines, employed more than two hundred women, and in 1960 output was valued at 28,000 yuan monthly – mostly work clothes, children's jumpers and leather jackets for railway workers. Their wages, on a piecework basis, averaged twenty-two yuan monthly per person. Here the women worked a full eight-hour day, eight to twelve and two to six.

The women workers whose children were in day nurseries paid 1·50 yuan a month each for their care, and three yuan a month each for their lunches. Kindergartens cost the same. Boarding children paid six to seven yuan a month for food. This was about forty percent less expensive than the best nurseries in Peking. The cost of their food was no more than at home. Nursery, kindergarten and community services were paid for from the commune's welfare fund set aside from income. The women had a canteen but it was used by only one in five. This workshop averaged fifteen percent net profit from its output.

I stopped to talk to a young woman worker behind a machine and asked her where her children were. She had two, both in kindergarten. Was she satisfied with their care? Very much so.

They were healthy and learning to dance and sing; she could never have taught them that. She herself now also had time to attend spare-time literacy classes. What was her husband? He was a railway worker but he had won a scholarship for a year's study in Peking. He would be back in a few weeks. How could she live on twenty-two yuan a month while he was gone? They drew his full pay during his absence. She told me that in three years they had saved 500 yuan ($200)! She was doubtless rehearsed to say this? But I had picked her at random from among two hundred.

Before leaving Chengchow I saw one of the oldest rural communes. I shall not go into its finances but the irrigation system and the small hydroelectric power plants had transformed a backward farming area into a highly prospering community. Just a few miles farther north, on our way back to Peking by train, we crossed the Yellow River. Under the long newly double-tracked bridge the river was so low that one could have maneuvered an army division between the water and the towering earthwork dikes to which it normally attained at this season.

Along the way I saw numerous family burial mounds set in groves of old trees entirely surrounded by broad unbroken fields where collectivization had erased other traces of small-scale farming. India had her sacred cows, monkeys and rats which consumed about a sixth of her annual grain crop, but fortunately the Hindus cremated their dead. North China's equivalent (in terms of lost production) had been the family burial plots; in parts of the Yellow River Valley, inhabited for thousands of years, the dead were said to remove as much as ten percent of the land from cultivation by the living. Several years ago the party had begun a drive to consolidate the bones in common cemeteries. Many welcomed the change but some conservative peasants resisted and the pressure relaxed. As with birth control, time and education were needed to win general acceptance. More and more villages and towns in North China were now cremating the newly deceased or burying them in wasteland set aside for collective cemeteries, however, as in the West and as the custom had long been in parts of South China.

Between ten in the morning and dusk we passed five or six wholly new towns, each centered on a small or medium-sized steel mill. They looked like well-planned industrial communities: electrified, with wide tree-lined streets dividing block after block of new two- or three-story apartments interspersed with gardens, schools, hospitals and shopping centers. Our express did not stop at them. But south of one new station, called Yuanshi, a town I didn't remember from when I used to travel the Chengchow–Peking line in the past, our train came to a grinding stop in open country. Slowly we went into reverse. When the train halted Alley and I got out to investigate.

A man riding a bicycle had run into the tail end of our train when his brakes failed. A conductorette happened to see the accident and reported it to the engineer. The train's first-aid team got the injured man onto a stretcher and brought him aboard. They telephoned ahead to Yuanshi, where an ambulance waited when we made an unscheduled stop. (From the past I could recall seeing a truck not even pause when the driver hit a mere 'coolie'.) Our express was delayed half an hour by the incident.

In the afternoon we passed hundreds of peasants who were gathering cotton from already rusting fields. Threshing machines were working in some villages; in others wheat was being winnowed by hand. Here and there tractors were turning freshly harvested soil; on other farms draft animals were used, and occasionally one saw men and women dragging heavy implements across the fields, as of yore. Golden corn and melons were piled mountain high in many fields. Before I went to sleep I looked out the window and beheld a whole village celebrating the harvest. Someone was playing an accordion and young women in costume were dancing on the earthen threshing floor, where flags waved around a circle of corn and pumpkins, lighted by huge bonfires.

Back in the capital I spent three weeks in Peking's glorious October weather and then told Rewi and other friends farewell. I turned southward to the Yangtze Valley for the last leg of my journey and an exit via Kunming.

Part Six

SHANGHAI AND BEYOND

WHILE I was in Loyang, Honan, I drove out over a new paved highway to see the world-famous works of art at Lung-men.

When Loyang was the capital of the T'ang Empire, Wu Tzu-t'ien, loveliest concubine of the enfeebled Emperor Kao Tsung, seized power in the year 660. She became the only female 'emperor' in Chinese history, and ruled until 705. A highly talented woman, she was an enthusiastic Buddhist and was responsible for a great age of religious sculpture in China. She took for her lover a young monk whom she made abbot of the Lung-men monastery on the banks of the Yi River outside the capital. In this period, Wu Tzu-t'ien and her lover lavished funds on the gigantic and beautiful Buddhas which stand on the stone cliffs at Lung-men. Thousands of other Buddhistic sculptures, murals, and works in bas-relief decorate the nearby grottoes.

One of the Lung-men caves held two panels of exquisite bas-relief sculptures of graceful male and female figures from the Chinese Buddhistic pantheon. Both were stolen about thirty years ago by vandals hired by Yueh Pin, a notorious art dealer of Peking. At the gate of the shrine I saw enlarged photographs of these stolen friezes, one of which is on display in the Metropolitan Museum and the other in the Nelson Gallery in Kansas City. Mounted under glass beneath the photos were reproductions of contracts allegedly signed by Alan Priest, the Metropolitan curator, and Yueh Pin. Above them were emblazoned the words 'American Cultural Imperialism!'

Chinese pilgrims who come here read the story and mourn their loss. As my student guide read me the details his voice shook with wrath.

'Egypt and Greece fared much worse,' I said to console him. 'You should see what Lord Elgin left of the Parthenon! After all, isn't it something to know that Americans who see these treasures will appreciate Chinese as artistic and talented people?'

'Who can see them? Only imperialists! How can imperialists like art if they hate people?'

Alas!

64

Shanghai

GONE the glitter and glamour; the pompous wealth beside naked starvation; gone the strange excitement of a polyglot and many-sided city; gone the island of Western capitalism flourishing in the vast slum that was Shanghai.

Good-by to all that : the well-dressed Chinese in their chauffeured cars behind bullet-proof glass; the gangsters, the shakedowns, the kidnapers; the exclusive foreign clubs, the men in white dinner jackets, their women beautifully gowned, the white-coated Chinese 'boys' obsequiously waiting to be tipped; Jimmy's Kitchen with its good American coffee, hamburgers, chili and sirloin steaks. Good-by to all the night life : the gilded singing girl in her enameled hair-do, her stage make-up, her tight-fitting gown with its slit skirt breaking at the silk-clad hip, and her polished ebony and silver-trimmed rickshaw with its crown of lights; the hundred dance halls and the thousands of taxi dolls; the opium dens and gambling halls; the flashing lights of the great restaurants, the clatter of mah-jongg pieces, the yells of Chinese feasting and playing the finger game for bottoms-up drinking; the sailors in their smelly bars and friendly brothels on Szechuan Road; the myriad short-time whores and pimps busily darting in and out of the alleyways; the display signs of foreign business, the innumerable shops spilling with silks, jades, embroideries, porcelains and all the wares of the East; the generations of foreign familes who called Shanghai home and lived quiet conservative lives in their tiny vacuum untouched by China; the beggars on every downtown block and the scabby infants urinating or defecating on the curb while mendicant mothers absently scratched for lice; the 'honey carts' hauling the night soil through the streets; the blocks-long funerals, the white-clad professional mourners weeping false tears, the tiers of paper palaces and paper money burned on the rich man's tomb; the jungle free-for-all struggle for gold or survival and the day's toll of unwanted infants and suicides floating in the canals; the knotted rickshaws with their owners fighting each other for customers and arguing fares; the peddlers and their plaintive cries; the armored white ships on the Whangpoo, 'protecting foreign lives and property'; the Japanese conquerors and their American and Kuomintang successors; gone the wickedest and most colorful city of the old Orient: good-by to all that.

Some of it had been carried by refugees to Hongkong and some of it, with strip-tease added, you might find in Tokyo. Shanghai still held more people than either city, if suburbs were included; in 1961 its population was 10,400,000. Foreigners still said it was the 'one place in China that really looks like a great city'. The tall buildings were there, but the International Settlement and the French Concession,* which used to be the heart of a modern megalopolis, were strangely like a village now, and downtown after dark was as quiet as Wall Street on Sunday.

There was plenty of heavy traffic in the new industrial suburbs, but many downtown office buildings of the Settlement had been turned into schools, dwellings and workers' clubs. Here bicycles, pedicabs (not many) and trams moved leisurely between shops selling necessities and a few luxuries to customers who gave the impression of being village tourists taking in the city where the wicked imperialists used to rule. The once crowded Bund was a recreation center. Into it, each morning and afternoon, the former office buildings debouched swarms of little children to play and exercise in well-kept gardens along the river. Elderly folk also gathered there to read, drowse or play Chinese chess; one of them told me he remembered a time when Chinese (and dogs) were not admitted. So did I.

The Shanghai Club, once very exclusively for British gentlemen, used to boast the world's longest bar. It was now run by the party as an international seamen's club, where sailors could play games

---

*Before the 1840s Shanghai was a fishing village on a mud flat on the Whangpoo; its importance began with the Opium Wars in midcentury, after which Britain and other powers acquired control of Shanghai as a treaty port. For a brief historical account of Shanghai see *Journey to the Beginning.*

or read books or see movies, but find no bedtime companions. Nearby, the ponderous old Hongkong and Shanghai Bank building (the paws of its huge bronze lions still shining from many hands that touched them for good luck) was now a government bureau. The old American Club building had been put to the same use as the National City Bank in Peking; both housed police headquarters.

I stayed at the Cathay Hotel, which was once Asia's finest hostelry. It was now called the Peace Hotel and was exceedingly so: quiet, orderly, the restaurant little used and subdued compared to its former aggressive gaiety, its famous bar and night club extinct, its lobby shops closed at dusk, and few lights on after ten. One got the impression here, as at certain large and empty provincial hotels, that the Chinese had not yet quite decided how to utilize these rooms since the Russians left. But the Cathay was still a fine place to live, furnished much as it was when owned by Sir Victor Sassoon: the simulated Chinese décor a bit tarnished now but the plumbing super, cuisine ditto, and more new American cars for hire outside its doors than anywhere in China.

I was offered my choice of Sir Victor's suite, usually reserved for V.I.P.s, or an ordinary double room about the dimensions of the *Mayflower*. A single would do me nicely, I said, but I asked to see the suite. It was in the tower, high above the river, pseudo-Tudor, handsomely paneled and filled with light from wide leaded windows. The bedroom was sumptuously furnished with king-sized beds adjoining two large tiled bathrooms; there was a dressing room the size of a small flat, a private entrance foyer, servants' quarters, a bar, a kitchen and pantry, a private dining room with a fireplace, and a spacious living room with another fireplace.

'How much?' I asked the China Intourist agent.

'Thirty-five yuan a day.'

'That's less than fifteen dollars. At the Waldorf it would cost me a hundred.' Betraying incurable bourgeois romanticism, I said, 'I'd like to wake up in the morning knowing how Victor Sassoon felt when he owned Shanghai. I'll take it for a night.'

I did not rest comfortably. For a long time, as I looked down at the river life, I was filled with remembrance of things past in this city where I had invested or misspent some years of my youth, fallen in love and into a brief but eventful marriage, seen two wars and many men destroyed in futile combat, until, engulfed by China, I had turned abroad – to more wars. Returning to my present magnificence, I tried the first bed but could not sleep. Then I tried the other, soft and blissful, but had no better luck. I ended on the living room couch and woke up at dawn. If that was the way Sir Victor had felt when he owned Shanghai I did not envy him. Perhaps he had had better company than my thoughts.

At seven o'clock I went down to walk in the Bund gardens, which were already well populated. Eager young and middle-aged people were doing their *t'ai chi ch'uan* steps and some students wearing athletes' red sweat shirts and slacks were practicing sword dancing. Under a tree some small children were being led in song by their teacher. Everyone was much in earnest. I watched a family in a sampan eating a breakfast of rice and greens, waved to them, and they waved back, smiling. Encouraged, I sat down on a bench beside an elderly gentleman who looked my way. I spoke to him in Chinese.

'You are up early,' I said.

'At my age you don't need much sleep.'

'Your age? You don't look over fifty, Elder Born,' I lied.

'Courtesy talk! I'm more than sixty. What does a man my age do in Russia, sir?'

'You take me for a Russian? No, I'm an American.'

'American?' That was a dirty word in China now but they still used the old flattering term for it: *Mei-kuo*, the 'beautiful country'. He repeated it and I nodded. Now he began to speak in stilted but animated English. 'You are certainly the first American I have seen for many years.'

'I don't doubt that. How long is it since you spoke English?'

'Quite some years. I am forgetting it. You have been a long time in China? You speak Chinese.'

I told him that I was a newspaperman and had once worked for the *China Weekly Review* in Shanghai. He remembered it; he had read it, he said. He had learned some English in his youth and had used it in business. Now he was retired.

'I take it you are not a Communist?' I said.

'Oh, no!' He grinned and showed half a dozen large teeth. 'I'm a capitalist! That's what they tell me.' He plucked at the sleeve of his dark blue padded jacket of worn silk. 'I used to own a silk store.'

'How do you live?'

'I get my interest-dividends like other merchants.'

'But how is it compared to the past? Before *chieh-fang* [liberation]?'

'We eat better than most. We live in our old house, my wife and I, sharing now with some others. That's all right. Good people. Hardworking people. We don't need the rooms. My children are married and live away. What is your thinking of China?'

'Officials show me something, then always ask me that. They want criticisms. Now I'll ask you, what are your criticisms?' I repeated the word in Chinese.

'Oh, I know.' He looked at me shrewdly. 'Americans think we have a bad time, maybe? I can say the truth, I have lived much better. But poor people have lived much worse. Everything is for the people. We used to think America was for the people too but it not look so now, eh? Is America only friend of Chiang Kai-shek? How is this?'

'Suppose I oppose that. Can you criticize your government?'

'Oh, I know. It makes bad mistakes. Who is ever right? I could tell you stories of people who have a bad time. Myself too, but not much. China is a socialist country now. Property rights are not the same, you know. One thing: this is an honest government. Hard, but honest. It has made China one great country again. Chinese can hold up their heads in the world. We are not foreign slaves any more.' He drew back proudly. 'What do you think about that, sir? Maybe the government is too strong, sometimes too young to listen to others. But – it does good things for China and does not steal. We forget much against that. Nobody wants Chiang Kai-shek back again, no!'

'Your son? What does he do?'

'Two sons. One is a teacher, all right. The other is in Hongkong. He wants to come back but he should stay there. We are the old generations. We lost something. My grandchildren, they are the new life. They wear it. They like it. Things in China were too bad in old days. Well, they have ended the worst. I won't cry.'

'Many people in jail – prison – arrested?'

'Very few I know. They convince you and convince. I see the

point. All for China. You know old Shanghai? Everybody robbing, cheating. Crimes, gangs, bad men. Tu Yueh-sheng? You know him?* Bad man. Now you see the *hsiao hai-tzu* [children] telling us older ones not even to spit, to use the spit bucket. Not to throw dirty things on the streets, that's good. Everybody working, everybody reading. No more starving people dying. How is that? Better. Building, building, building more – but nobody getting rich. Why? All for China family. I see the point.'

'Maybe you aren't telling me everything. Maybe you're afraid I'll tell the government?' I smiled but he did not.

'Ha! I say the truth. Why should –'

An acquaintance of his stopped and he stood up to exchange greetings. They strolled off together, but before the capitalist left he turned and bowed to me and said, 'So much building. You must see.'

I took scores of pictures at random of all kinds of people in the Bund gardens and along the waterfront and in various Shanghai streets. People at work, people shopping, people unaware they were being photographed. Like the pictures I took everywhere else in China, they showed people poorly dressed, none of them fat. They were all dying but apparently only at about the same rate people are dying everywhere; I did not see any beggars, mangy infants, policemen beating up people, or rice riots. Editors abroad thought my pictures looked too 'posed'. They wanted to see 'the real China'.

---

*Yes, I remembered Tu and had known him. He was for years Shanghai's No. 1 gangster, chief of the *Ch'ing Pang* (Green Circle Secret Society), which ran the narcotics, gambling and prostitution rackets. In 1927 his armed thugs helped Chiang Kai-shek (with aid from the International Settlement's Shanghai Municipal Council) seize power in the native city from the left-wing trade unions' militia. About 5,000 workers were killed. Later on Chiang Kai-shek rewarded Mr Tu with a post on the Opium Suppression Bureau, which continued to run the narcotics traffic, and officially decorated him with the Order of the Brilliant Jade. For details, see *The Battle for Asia*.

65

'Building, Building –'

CHANG YAO-HUI, secretary-general of the Shanghai People's Congress (which elects the municipal government and sends delegates to the National Congress), welcomed me 'as an old resident'. He was a man of about forty, strongly built, erect, son of a rich peasant family, and possessed of some higher education. As a student he had left his native Shantung and joined the guerrillas under Liu Shao-ch'i and Ch'en Yi. Like most veterans he was relaxed and easy to talk to; he ticked off answers sans the usual preliminaries about Mao and the general line.

'Gangsters? They weren't hard to eliminate once they lost their government protection and the people were free to expose them. Gangs are organized to make money for gang leaders; when they succeed they become capitalists no different from the others. The chief of one gang here was chairman of a bank; he fled to Hong-kong. His successor published an ad in the papers, at our suggestion, dissolving the secret organizations. We've had no gangs since 1951. Pimps and prostitutes? Eliminated at the same time, but it took much longer to re-educate the women and find jobs for them. I won't say there are none left but they are rare cases.'

Chang Yao-hui offered to show me anything I wanted to see in Shanghai. I said I'd like to see some housing, the best and the worst.

'That's all right. But what about industry? Shanghai is a lot different from what you knew, and even from the Shanghai of ten years ago. Textile and other light industry used to account for sixty percent of total output here. Now we have a bigger textile industry than ever, but heavy industry amounts to more than half the output. We made more cotton spindles in Shanghai alone in 1959 than total British production. You never thought of Shanghai as a steel city, did you? Shanghai will smelt more than two million tons of steel this year.* Look out on the Whangpoo. Most of those ships were made in China. Shanghai turned out vessels up to 10,000 tons this year. How much time do you have?'

'Five days.'

He was disappointed. 'Anyway, we'll show you more than most people see in ten days.'

I was afraid of that. I was beginning to feel steel running out of my ears. I begged for a day to myself, just to walk the streets in search of forgotten places. Chang reluctantly agreed to this waste of time but he got me down for a tough schedule from then on, under the skilled guidance of an assistant, Li Yi-ming. A bright young Shanghai college graduate, Li spoke fast English and never missed a remark or a cue.

Strolling through the old shopping centers on my own I recognized places but not faces, and no shops I remembered were doing business at the old stands. Consumer goods on sale made a poor contrast with the remembered glory of the silk blocks on Nanking and Bubbling Well roads. Shanghai produced more silk goods than ever and in magnificent designs and fabrics, both modern and traditional, but most of them were exported to buy machinery. (I sometimes thought of Omar, who wondered what the vintner bought one half so precious as the stuff he sold.) I priced rayon at the equivalents of $1·50 a yard, dark silk for $2·25 to $7, wool at $6, cotton at 75 cents to $2. Leather shoes ranged from $3 to $12, shirts were $2·50 to $5, socks 40 cents to $1·50 a pair, leather jackets $25 to $30.

Prices were somewhat higher than those in Hongkong, where China-made consumer goods were sold (for foreign exchange) in an abundance unknown in Shanghai. But I also saw goods in greater variety and quantity and at lower prices in Chungking, Loyang and Kunming. The cloth ration (halved since 1959) allowed each person sixteen feet (one-meter width) a year – the same for infants and adults. That was enough for two Chinese dresses, one and a half adult suits, or two or three children's outfits. Used clothing could be bought in second-hand stores without coupons, but prices were high. For instance : $15 to $25 for a woolen suit.

*(1970) Steel production in Shanghai reportedly rose to about six million tons by 1969.

'Yes, we export a lot of materials,' the Communists said. 'But the average family has two to three times more clothing than it had in the past. If we stopped all our exports we might have perhaps only another suit or two per person. As for silk, let the capitalists wear it for a few more years. When we have all the machines we need we'll have plenty of silk, too.'

The great department stores, Wing On's, Sun Sun's, and Sincere's, were still open; they displayed clothing, shoes, linen goods and cheap merchandise of a wide variety, including some off-ration tinned goods, beer (60 fen), wine (2 yuan), vodka (8 yuan), household equipment and toys and bicycles. A good bicycle cost about $60, two months' wages for a skilled worker.

I walked to the site of a restaurant that used to serve a good light Chinese meal for about thirty cents, which was then too expensive for the average Chinese.* It was now one of those state provision stores which handled odd lots of unrationed goods. 'What's for sale?' I asked the last man on the line. He gave me a hesitant look, then shrugged his shoulders. 'Pu ch'ing-ch'u.' He 'wasn't clear' – nor was the woman in front of him. Who cared? Apparently anyone with the time to spend queued up first and learned what was for sale when he got to it – if anything was left. I stood long enough to see a customer squeeze out the door with a small bundle from which a sickly banana peered. One saw such queues in all the cities. They reminded me of wartime Russia, except that in Russia the queues were longer, more numerous, and for bread, not luxuries like bananas. It is a fair comparison to say that the food situation in China was generally very much better than in Russia when I lived there during the war years, 1942–5.

I looked carefully for signs of undernourishment but saw no certain indications. People were lean, but most Chinese were always lean; 'fat men' and 'moneyed men' were synonyms. I was told by a Chinese doctor in Peking that cases of beriberi and pellagra had appeared in Shanghai hospitals, and in the Bund gardens I saw

*For a detailed description of food shortages and near-famine conditions in 'the different years' 1960–62, see Chapter 75, 'Facts About Food'. By 1970 China's grain production had attained record levels and, as a result of modernization (electrification, irrigation, wide use of chemical fertilizers) seemed at last free from fear of mass famine.

what may have been a case of vitamin deficiency. A woman teacher permitted me to photograph some attractively dressed, laughing children in her care. They at once clammed up and posed. I asked them to look natural and go on playing. While I was with them I noticed that one child had severely blackened teeth. I asked the nurse about it and she insisted that it was from 'eating too much sugar when he was younger'. Pellagra? Perhaps. The nurse turned abruptly and left with her charges. At a kiosk in the park plenty of sweets were for sale, but when I tried to buy some for other children playing nearby I couldn't do so. Candy, like sugar, was rationed and sold to Shanghai residents only, at twelve ounces a month.

There were only about a dozen pedicabs on Nanking Road. They charged a standard fare of forty fen (about sixteen cents) an hour, too much for most Chinese. I hired one for a brief trip and in the course of it asked the pedalist how much rice he was eating. 'Six bowls a day,' he said. Enough? 'Not enough. I need ten.' Six standard bowls are about a pound. He also got greens, he said. 'Yo *fa-tzu, yo pan-fa*,' he added. 'On my free day I work in a garden and get a few eggs.' He was neatly clad and an energetic pedalist.

Shanghai was always an ugly city and no aesthetic values would have been lost if it had been erased and begun anew. The municipality was satisfied to repair, expand and touch up existing buildings which would eventually be replaced. Most new construction lay beyond the old city limits, in satellite towns or suburbs. Wide new highways are being cut through the city and around it, to link town and country. In the suburbs the effects of planned construction contrasted favorably with the aimless and helter-skelter expansion of other Asian cities – the monstrosity that was rebuilt Tokyo, for instance.

We drove for a day through the outskirts, visiting one development after another. Each of these self-contained communities economically centered upon a sprawling new machine-building plant, a textile mill or some other factory among many dozens now built or under construction on a large scale. Some of the surrounding truck gardens, piggeries and poultry farms were owned and managed by the factories. Good highways and sidewalks led to traffic circles with shopping areas, hotels and theaters. Radiating from them were blocks of three- or four-story apartment dwellings for the workers, some built around gardens and playgrounds for children attending the schools also newly set up for the neighborhood. Residents were all within walking distance of their work.

Six satellites of this kind had been completed and five more were under construction. Much of the labor was spare-time effort contributed by the residents. I spent some hours in three of these new developments.

Ming Hong was typical – a community of about 70,000 workers and their families, employed by small neighborhood factories making motors and farm machinery. More than a thousand Ming Hong buildings of simple construction had been completed in less than two years. The town plaza consisted of eleven brick and tile structures, one of which was a hotel, newly opened, where I stopped for tea. It had fifty-five rooms and was built in sixty-seven days. In external appearance it was comparable to any small Middletown hotel, and it was attractively if inexpensively furnished. The manager was a twenty-year-old party member who had been through a special training period. He already had a full house and a backlog of reservations – mostly relatives of residents, workers' delegations, lecturers, teams of visiting technicians and athletes. A two-room suite with bath at the Ming Hong cost three dollars a day; a room for two, without bath, one dollar per person.

Strolling down a tree-planted street of new apartment houses I chose one to enter. From the outside these buildings looked comparable to American lower-middle-class suburban dwellings, but they were crudely finished inside : unpainted plaster walls, stairs of cement, corridors narrow and poorly lighted. They were somewhat better than East Side or West Side New York tenements and better than much housing I remember in Moscow, as well as a great improvement over old Shanghai slums.

It was afternoon in Ming Hong; most people were at work. No one answered our knocks at the first three flats. At the fourth an elderly gentleman opened the door and invited us in. A living room, two bedrooms, tiny kitchen, toilet and shower; sparsely furnished, no carpets, clean floors, white cotton curtains.

'How many? We are eight persons here : my wife, myself, our son and daughter-in-law, and their four children. Comfortable?

Yes, indeed. Before, we were all in one room the size of this kitchen. Now we have space to turn around in. Me? I am a worker but retired, now sixty-five, living on pension. Who would have paid me fifty yuan a month to be idle in the past? I would be starving.'

Next day we drove fifteen miles into the countryside to visit the Horse Bridge rural commune. Large: 48,000 people, 12,000 acres. Well irrigated: twenty-nine power pumping stations. Advanced in mechanization: twenty-three tractors. Prosperous: output up from $900,000 worth in 1952 to $6,100,000 in 1959, when cash income was eighty-five yuan per capita. Literate: ninety-one percent able to read and write, excluding infants and old folks. Food allowance: average adult, thirty-four pounds of grain per month; vegetables, thirty to forty pounds. Members cultivated their private plots and the average person got thirteen eggs and six ounces of meat per month. In 1959 an able-bodied worker could earn about 200 yuan per year, in addition to his food. People here, as on most farms I saw, appeared to be eating better than city-dwellers; they had an ample supply of vegetables in addition to the basic grain rations and bonuses in accordance with work performed.

Horse Bridge Commune's five 'town centers' were rural equivalents of the city's satellite towns. Center No. 1, which I visited, had thirty-two new brick structures, all built by commune workers with bricks made in their own kiln: a large school, a modern kindergarten-nursery, a hospital (four doctors, two operating rooms, X-ray equipment, 150 beds), telegraph and post office, broadcasting station, several shops and stores, dining rooms, a theater, a public bath, and brick flats thus far providing housing for 600 families. The flats were surrounded by trees and flowers. Rent was free, electricity one to two yuan a month per family. Medical examination was free; hospital beds cost twenty fen a day; childbirth, three yuan. (Whenever I inquired I was told that all deliveries by healthy, normal mothers were natural births; anesthesia was rare.) Maternity leave, before and after birth: fifty-four days.

'All right, Mr Li,' I said when we left. 'You've shown me the best, now let's see the worst.'

'What's your idea of the worst?'

'I remember thousands sleeping under mats along the Soochow

Canal,. thousands sleeping in the streets. I remember a jungle of
bamboo huts in the burned-out parts of old Chapei down by the
railroad station. I've seen the canal; that's cleaned up now. Even
the sampans looked sanitized. No more street-sleepers. What about
that jungle?'

'It's still there – Pumpkin Town. We haven't had time to build
new homes for those people yet.'

We got back to the city at dusk and went to see the old crazy
quilt of crooked paths and lanes between 'homes' built of box wood,
pieces of bamboo, matting, old oil cans and newspapers. Refugees of
all kinds, people hanging on the edge of life, traditionally had
camped in Pumpkin Town in squalor worse than the mud cliffs and
filth where derelicts live outside Mexico City – or much like the
mat-shed refugee huts in Kowloon.

Some of the shelters had collapsed or been torn down but thousands survived, with improvements like roofs, glass windows and
dry floors. The lanes and the alleyways were clean now, young
willows were planted everywhere, water had been piped in to public
fountains, and there were few flies. The grinning kids were no
longer in rags and covered with sores. It was still a slum, but there
were health stations in its midst, and tiny nurseries. Various workshops were busy and I saw a reading room and a bookstore. We
had not gone a hundred feet before a businesslike woman appeared,
introduced herself as the lane committee chairman, and asked our
business.

'Most of our families don't want to leave,' she said. 'They're all
squatters but their ownership was confirmed after liberation. The
city needs the land and they'll have to move sooner or later, but
we're making it a decent place to live in the meantime.'

Here I stopped in to talk to another family – again my own
choice. An old lady was getting supper ready in her one-room mat-
floored shanty, which was clean as a pin. A small radio was tuned
to music. Her son and daughter-in-law were away at work. That
was a smart girl, her daughter-in-law, she said. 'She's been through
primary school.' Her three grandchildren who clustered around
were smart, too, learning to read and write. 'Just show the gentlemen how you can write, An-tsai,' she said to one, who blushed
and hid. The daughter-in-law earned sixty-eight yuan a month;

her son earned only sixty. They had no rent to pay. Food cost them seventy yuan; she did the cooking and was economical. Food? She pointed to a charcoal stove where rice was simmering. Look at their supper: a fish tonight! (A one-pound fish for six people, but a fish. Probably their meat-fish ration for a week.) Two kinds of rice, wet and dry: 'Two kinds, just imagine.' There seemed to be a series of bunks behind a curtain but some of them must have slept on the floor.

'Move? Why? We've got our own home here. Quite happy as it is. If we can just get a sewing machine –'

66

The Mayor of Shanghai

INESCAPABLY I overfulfilled my inspection quota of Shanghai industry. Industrial output here in 1960 was valued at 24,000,000,000 yuan, more than ten percent of the national total. I saw only a few of its muscles at work, but I learned that the city was making good steel converters, power generators, rolling machines, giant hammers, drills, forging presses, aluminum-foil-making machines, fertilizer plants, diesel tractors and rubber tires up to sixty tons in weight, not to mention antibiotic drugs, fine surgical equipment, X-ray machines, precision lenses, television and other cameras, and disposable diapers and baby bottles. It would take many pages to describe even one factory adequately, if the people were included. When you have seen a hundred factories they blur together like scenes remembered from a moving car.

I learned more at the Shanghai Industrial Exhibition, which was housed in a very large building of the conventional exposition type. Every big city had at least one. In Peking half a dozen permanent exhibitions were filled with animated displays as entertaining and informative as the Chicago Field Museum. For the Chinese it was all new and exciting. Television sets, hi-fi and radio-TV consoles, pianos, refrigerators, electric shavers, stunning fabrics of all kinds, a wide variety of processed foods, fine porcelains and rugs – things you didn't see in the stores. They were mostly for export or available in China only for collective use. Chinese must have viewed these displays with pride and satisfaction mixed with some envy of countries where individuals could afford to buy them.

Li Yi-ming broke in on my musings. 'I am sorry to tell you that Mme Soong Ching-ling won't be able to see you tonight.'*

*Mme Soong, the revered widow of Dr Sun Yat-sen, lived in her old home in Shanghai most of the time. Her chronic illness had reached a particularly acute stage, she wrote to me from her sickbed. Her letter expressed buoyant

'I'm not surprised; I know she's been very ill.'

'But the mayor has invited you to dinner.'

Shanghai was a special municipality, like Peking, and with its suburban districts it was as important as a province. Mayor K'eh was a Politburo member and outranked most governors. A big man, powerfully built, with a shock of black hair and wide, searching eyes, he looked fortyish but was in his late fifties. He was direct and forceful in his speech.

K'eh Cheng-shih was born in Huangshan, Anhui, north of Nanking, in a middle-class landowning family. After Chiang Kai-shek led the counterrevolution in 1927, K'eh became a 'political miner'. He went underground for ten years, first in Shanghai, later in Peking. With Liu Shao-ch'i he ran the party underground (the North China Bureau), and when Japan invaded China they went into the villages together to organize guerrillas.

The mayor welcomed me in the former home of the Italian Consul General, in the erstwhile French Concession, a rambling old dwelling in well-kept gardens. It was now used as municipal reception chambers and K'eh had an office there. If all the powers ever recognize China, I thought, there will be some frustrated house hunters. The British Consulate General on the Bund was the only former Western property still in 'imperialist' hands.

Others present that evening were the vice-mayor, Tsao Tieh-chien; Chang Yao-hui, the secretary-general; and Li Yi-ming.

The mayor said his evening was entirely free. I could ask any questions I wished; he'd try to answer. To begin, he'd make some prefatory remarks.

'Li Yi-ming has told me that you have two impressions. First, the old surface glamour and prosperity seem gone. Second, the moral tone of the city seems to have improved. Both impressions are correct. Many foreign visitors don't see what the change means. As an old resident you ought to know. A small percentage of rich Chinese and foreigners had more than enough; the glamour and the luxurious shops and hotels on Nanking Road were for them. In the

---

satisfaction with the régime and deep confidence in the future. A brief biographical sketch and an account of Mme Sun's activities in the Communist revolution appear in *Journey to the Beginning*.

dirty back lanes and alleys millions lived in hunger or on refuse or they starved. Now nobody is rich but nobody starves and nobody lives in filth and rags.

'Does everybody have enough? Yes, enough. Do people want more? Of course. Wages and living standards in Shanghai are higher than in the rest of the country. Shanghai produces more; Shanghai should have a higher living standard. The average industrial worker's wage in Shanghai is 74.50 yuan. Rent runs from four to fifteen yuan a family, utilities cost three to four, food about twelve yuan a person. The average family has two wage earners. That leaves a lot of consumer purchasing power, a lot of pressure on us. Production of consumer goods admittedly is still low. We can't get too far ahead. We have 10,000,000 people here. Suppose we raise consumption by only twenty yuan per person. That means 200,000,000 yuan a year taken out of production of farm tools, irrigation machines, steel, all much more urgently needed elsewhere than Shanghai needs more leather shoes. Shanghai makes more than enough textiles to give everybody extra suits and dresses. When you think of increasing living standards you have to think of six hundred seventy million times* whatever the increase is. To double the cloth ration we must double cotton output, textile machines, factories.† You can't do it overnight.

'We ration food now for the same reason. This region grows plenty but we've had two bad-weather years in the north. Crop failures in other parts mean we have to feed them, too. Rations are fixed now at an adequate minimum we can maintain indefinitely. Foreign press reports mistake our careful rationing for famine. We don't have and we won't have famine. When output provides plenty for everyone we'll end rationing.

'You asked about rations here? Our monthly minimum is about the same as elsewhere: for adults, twenty-seven pounds of grain,

*(1970) Mayor K'eh was the only official who, in conversation with me in 1960, used a population figure as high as 670 millions. In 1965, Mao gave me that figure as one result of the 'sampling census' of 1964, but expressed his skepticism.

† In 1959 China's cotton textile output was 7,500,000,000 meters, nearly half of which was exported, chiefly to the U.S.S.R. If the same export ratio were maintained China would have had to produce about eighty percent more than U.S. output of cotton textiles in order to double the cloth ration.

six ounces of meat, twenty-six ounces of fish, thirty-three pounds of vegetables.* Factory workers get thirty to thirty-three pounds of grain and heavy workers get forty-four pounds. Artists and brain workers get the same, plus extra meat allowances. So do capitalists living on dividends; there are special restaurants for them. We try to give people what they consider their honest "need". Altogether, the municipality is feeding more than 800,000 people on those top rations. As for the peasants, they do better than that, of course, with their side-line production.'

Mayor K'eh was full of instances. 'Take rice. There are two edible parts, the husk and the green, rich in vitamins but less calories, and there is the kernel. In the past the peasants ate husks and only a bit of the kernels, which were sold. Now everybody eats the whole rice. On a farm recently I met an old man who was collecting manure from the latrines. Did you ever think you could tell peasants where to *ta-pien*? Well, they do it; the children scold them if they don't. About that old man who was collecting manure. I asked him how things were.

' "See here," he said, "look at this." He showed me the stuff in his buckets. "When we were eating nothing but husks the *ta-pien* was whitish and fluffy, an unhealthy color. Now, you see, it is solid and brown. *Ma-ti!* It's the right color. People are eating better." What are your questions?'

I knew that Vice-Mayor Tsao had himself spent seven years in the Ward Road Jail, where he was imprisoned as a Communist by the authorities of the International Settlement. I asked him if he had been back to visit his old quarters. Yes; he'd seen his former cell but there was nobody there; the door was open. All the doors were open. In his time prisoners were allowed out for exercise half an hour a day and beaten if they spoke to each other. Now prisoners had their recreation time, a library and reading room for use after working hours. There were less than 2,500 prisoners now, Tsao said. (I had no difficulty in arranging a visit, and the routine was much the same as in the Peking prison I have described – except for the absence of gardening.)

'How many prisoners on the Supei reform-through-labor farm?' I asked.

* K'eh used equivalents in Chinese catties.

'About 6,000,' said the mayor. 'I've been there. It's a good farm. You wouldn't know it was a prison – there are very few guards. Prisoners built their own houses. They have a power plant, electric lights, movies. There's a lot of pigs and livestock and their production is above average. When men are trusted they can get leave for a week or so to come back to visit their families – no guards go with them.'

'They always come back?'

'So far, always. Some of them ask to bring their families in and we have let them; they work better. Some prisoners like it so well they stay on and work for wages after their terms expire. They have rights like any other citizens.'

'Mayor K'eh, I wouldn't believe a word you're telling me except that I actually spoke to some women ex-prisoners in the Peking jail who said they were staying on to work there out of choice. I'd like to see this farm for myself.'

'It's quite a trip. You'd have to wait for a boat and it takes two or three days each way. If you've got the time we'll try to arrange it.'

I should have taken him up at once, but a week or ten days then would have meant dropping the rest of my schedule or requesting another visa extension, which I wasn't sure I could get. I was told I'd have other opportunities near Hankow, Chungking and Kunming, but I did not. I cannot, therefore, blame anyone but myself for not being able to confirm or deny Mayor K'eh's account of the only 'labor camps' to which China admitted.

Calculating 8,500 prisoners to the Shanghai population of roughly ten million gave a prison rate of ·0085 per thousand. If that rate prevailed over all China her prison population would then have been 595,000.* Interesting – if true.

'That's not very high, especially if it includes all prisoners, not just political,' I said.

'It includes all, and the majority are not political prisoners,' said

---

* The same rate in the U.S.A. would give a prison population of 161,500. In 1960 it was 207,000. Arrest rates (2,612,000 in 1960) would doubtless be much higher in proportion to prison rates than in China, where the number of convictions closely approximated the number of arraignments. (1970) Political arrests after the G.P.C.R. must have far exceeded any figure since 1952, the end of the land revolution.

K'eh. 'But our actual crime rate today is much lower than that. You must remember that Shanghai had the highest crime rate in the country in the past. Right now we have trouble finding a case in the courts to show foreign visitors who want to hear a trial.'

'I know. I was told in Peking there was not a case in the courts. They told me to try here.'

'We will let you know if there is anything on while you're here. Crime is no real problem now. Ninety percent of the people support what we are trying to do. Only a few would actively oppose us – if they could. We have 6,000 policemen, including the Fire Department. That's not many for a city this size. How many policemen do you have in New York?* Most of ours are for traffic control.'

'They used to say Shanghai had more police, more prisoners, and more prostitutes than there were students in the schools. That was an exaggeration, of course.'

'Not much. You couldn't say that now. We have more than 2,000,000 students in Shanghai. If you count the 1,300,000 people in spare-time schools, almost a third of the population are students. That's another reason the crime rate is low.'

'That doesn't sound like Shanghai is being forcibly depopulated, as was reported a few years ago.'

'That was never true. What we did do was to persuade thousands of college-trained people, professional men and technicians to start new schools and factories in the interior. We had two good medical colleges and far more medical personnel than the rest of the country. We split the colleges and sent personnel to open new colleges and hospitals in Anhui and Wuhan. Today we have two new medical colleges with far more students, hospitals with more personnel – 30,000 hospital beds. That's one example. Altogether, Shanghai has sent 1,600,000 professional people and technical workers into the interior. Shanghai and Manchuria have been the biggest training centers for China's modernization.'

It was past midnight and K'eh † was still going strong. For me it had been a long day. I made a tentative move to adjourn.

---

*New York City police numbered 23,000 in 1960, exclusive of the Fire Department. Shanghai had far less traffic.

† (1970) K'eh Cheng-shih died in 1965. He was succeeded by Tsao Tieh-chun, whose deputy mayor was Chang Yao-hui. Both men were, like K'eh,

'There is one other thing,' he said. 'We haven't talked about your country. We can never restore relations with America as long as you hang on to our territory, of course, and that means we can't trade with you, either. Why aren't American ships carrying on a peaceful trade with us – but only American warships invading our waters and wasting your money? It's not our fault.'

'Premier Chou En-lai has already reminded me that I am not the Secretary of State,' I said, 'but I shall gladly convey your message.'

---

lifelong close associates of Liu Shao-ch'i. In 1966 Tsao was attacked by the Red Guards. Both he and Chang were denounced as 'revisionists' and forced out of office by 'rebel revolutionaries' following Mao's instructions.

67

God and Party

CHRISTIANITY was still proscribed in China when Emperor K'ang Hsi took the throne in 1665, but Jesuit priests were in charge of the Peking observatory. This paradox was chiefly the work of Matteo Ricci (1552–1610), whom John Fairbank has rightly described as 'one of the greatest proponents of boring from within'. No latter-day Comintern agent in China was as subtle in subverting traditional Chinese society as Ricci, who became 'all-Chinese' and ingratiated himself with imperial scholars by preaching a Christianity fully reconciled with Confucian ancestor-worship, ethics and philosophy.

After K'ang Hsi had put down the serious Wu San-kuei rebellion in the South and defeated the Russians at Albazin with the aid of Jesuit cannon, a new tolerance was granted Catholicism. The young Jesuit François Gerbillon taught K'ang Hsi some Euclidian geometry and helped negotiate the Sino-Russian Treaty of Nerchinsk, which was highly favorable to China. In 1693 K'ang Hsi acknowledged these various services in an edict which opened China to Christianity.

Jesuits prospered in China until 1715, when Pope Alexander VII began an egregiously bigoted attack on Confucian 'paganism and idolatry'. K'ang Hsi himself wrote to explain that nobody really believed that Confucius and the Ancients were living in the ancestral stone tablets any more than Christians believed Jesus was living on the crucifix. How could the symbolical 'Rites' of homage to their spirits be called idolatry? The Vatican never got around to answering K'ang Hsi's arguments. Disgusted, the Emperor placated his Confucian reactionaries by issuing a new edict in 1717 which withdrew imperial recognition from the Jesuits.[1]

No massive opportunity to Christianize China arose again until 1850, when the T'ai-p'ing revolution was launched under the leadership of Cantonese converts. Missionaries denounced the T'ai-p'ings as heretics and deviationists, but their armies were blessed with success from Canton to the gates of Peking. When the Manchu throne was saved by the intervention of Western armies, China was finally forced to legalize the importation of opium, Christianity and Western philosophy – including all forms of Protestant heresy and Marxism.

A few representatives of various Protestant groups had visited Red China; as a result, both the Anglicans and the Friends published reports on the state of the faith under the People's Republic.[2] I had attended services of Christian churches in Shanghai and Peking, and I had spoken to an ex-missionary Englishwoman who was visiting some Chinese followers but who did not wish to be quoted about her mission. A young Chinese Anglican bishop whom I met at a state banquet in Peking assured me that the constitutional guarantee of freedom of worship was being upheld. He himself was a delegate to the People's Consultative Conference, as were certain other religious leaders.

Shanghai had always had the largest concentration of native Christians in China and was the base from which both Protestant and Catholic missionaries operated. It was appropriate, therefore, that I should seek out the Chinese Catholic fathers quoted at length below. Their anti-Vatican charges were of course disputed in Rome, where the Church had a very different story to tell.[3] This occasion was, however, a unique opportunity to hear church problems discussed by men responsible for confronting and solving them on the spot.

'For the first time in history we Catholics are in charge of our own church in China. Always before we were under foreign bishops and domination from abroad.'

That is what I was told by Father Chen Fu-ming, forty-eight, a sallow, thin-faced, tense pastor whom I interviewed at Ziccawei Cathedral in Shanghai. Ziccawei was one of the oldest Chinese Christian churches. The seat of a bishopric, with some 40,000 Catholics in the city and 110,000 in the diocese, it had been one of the wealthiest parishes in China. In the former French Concession, and long run by French priests, the fine brick edifice was still encompassed by spacious lawns and gardens.

'Our final break with the Vatican occurred in 1958,' said Pastor Chen. 'In June 1958 the Vatican issued an Encyclical Letter forbidding clergy and laity from participating in any activities backed by the Communist party. Priests were supposed to withhold blessings from such people. By implication the Letter demanded that we become a counterrevolutionary organization dedicated to the overthrow of the régime and the return of Chiang Kai-shek. It expressed the aims of American imperialism. Those bishops and priests who received the Letter were threatened with excommunication if they ignored it.'

'I am not familiar with the Letter you mention. What was the response of the Church as a whole in China?'

'There is no Catholic church under a single head,' said the pastor. 'Each diocese operates autonomously.'*

'And the response?'

'We ignored the order. We consider it a sinful violation of the Commandments, and immoral. Both Pope Pius and Pope John have openly prayed for the downfall of our country. Pope John supported the Tibetan counterrevolution and the Vatican denounced the communes. The Pope said, like Mr Dulles, that their aim was to destroy the family. Of course that is a lie.'

'Under present circumstances, in the eyes of Rome do you have the right to administer the sacraments?'

'We have the right, and we do so. The Vatican uses the threat of depriving us of the right but we ignore it.'

They mentioned only three instances of excommunication. A priest named Li Ying-t'ao who had 'comforted the wounded' during the Korean War (performed Mass and given absolution and communion at the front) was the first to be read out. Li Wei-kiang, now bishop of the Nanking diocese, was the second; he had supported the government's 1951 expulsion from China of Monsignor Ribberi, the Papal Nuncio. Tung Kuan-ch'ing, who permitted himself to be elected bishop of Wuhan at a meeting of clerics and laymen, had been threatened with 'special excommunication', but the threat had not materialized.

According to these priests there was no discrimination against either clergy or lay Catholics 'unless they used religion as a cloak for counterrevolution.' Priests and Catholics had civil rights, including the right to be elected to office and hold seats, up to the National

---

* Father Chen estimated the Chinese Catholic population as three million, about the same as it was before 1949, when Protestant converts were no more than a million.

Congress level. They could not, of course, become members of the Party.

'We believe in God and redemption,' said Father Chen. 'Communists do not. We observe the Sabbath and believe in prayer. On matters of religion we differ profoundly but on secular matters we can cooperate. In practice, the Communists observe the other Commandments and the law respects them.'

What about 'Thou shalt not kill'? The government of course opposed murder; there were fewer crimes in China than ever before. But what about execution of priests and other clerics? There had been cases of misuse of the cloth for espionage and counterrevolution, they said. The Church deplored and could never sanction killing.

'Under foreign domination our church went beyond religious matters in the past and sometimes served as a political instrument of imperialism. We have cut all ties with that past. There is today no use of force against Christians who observe the laws of the land.'

Further questioning explained something of what all this meant in practice. All schools, orphanages, hospitals and other welfare activities formerly run by religious organizations were taken over by the government during early campaigns which sought to arouse public disgust with missionaries, nuns, priests and such acolytes as served them. Foreign superiors once accounted for about half the 13,000 Catholic priests, brothers and nuns in China: Jesuits, Dominicans, Franciscans, Marists and others, Europeans and Americans. 'By August 1954, 126 out of 143 dioceses had lost their superiors,' according to one authority. 'Of the 5,486 foreign religious leaders who were originally resident in China, less than 100 remained.'[4] Highly vilifying reports of their conduct were published, some suffered painful imprisonment and died, and eventually nearly all foreigners departed voluntarily or were deported. Some Chinese loyal to them were also reported persecuted and killed.[5] According to Pastor Chen there were in 1960 two European priests still at the Sacred Heart Church, in Peking.

Judging from my interview, state policy may have had the active support of those Chinese Catholics as well as Protestants who shared the general antiforeign *revanche* sentiments held by many intellectuals against any and all kinds of past 'imperialist' domination and who wanted a 'purely Chinese' church more than Papal blessings. That the Church was still sharply split between 'orthodox' and 'progressive' (anti-Vatican) elements was clearly indicated at a meeting of Church leaders from twenty-six provinces summoned to a Catholic conference in Peking during the 'Hundred Flowers' period. The press then reported that numerous bishops and priests were opposed to the Christian National Front and that one even 'demanded the dissolution of the Communist party leadership and going over to capitalism.'[6] Meanwhile Protestant Christian churches, far less united than the Catholics, proved unable to support effective opposition to the drive for ideological integration of church and state. Now their Chinese leaders were 'supporting socialism' under the National Christian Council.

Members of the Chinese Catholic Patriotic Association obviously held opinions sharply at variance with those of the American Church about the way the situation on this earth looks in the eyes of God. Bishop K. H. Ting, president of the Nanking Union Theological Seminary, reportedly 'denounced the U.S. reactionary authorities for their attack on progressive [American] religious figures.' No matter what 'high-sounding words about peace and democracy' the U.S. President might utter, one should remember the words of St Paul: 'Even Satan fashioneth himself into an angel of light.'[7]

One need not subscribe to this hyperbole in order to recognize linkages of past missionary activity in China with imperialist aggression as indisputable facts of history. When the fanatical Boxer rebels rose in 1900 against Western domination, a number of missionaries in the interior were the only foreign devils available for revenge. Mark Twain's bitterly ironic and classic commentary, 'To a Person Sitting in Darkness', reminds us that some European missionaries secured the retaliatory execution of hundreds of people during the Allied occupation of North China following the rebellion – an event also applauded by a few American evangelists.

While Westerners looked upon missionaries dispatched into the old cultures of the East as messengers of altruism and redemption, they often appeared quite otherwise to peoples whom they sought to deliver. To educated Chinese the arrival of missionaries was always associated with China's military defeats. It must be conceded also that anyone who sets out into an unknown country carrying the only true faith under his arm is not in a frame of mind exactly suited to objective study of conceptions of social living which he is predetermined to supplant. It should not surprise anyone that nationalistic Chinese tended to consider the missionaries' attitude as arrogant if not ignorant.

Chinese Communist hostility toward Christianity had ideological and traditional as well as nationalistic aspects. Most missionaries in China owned property, lived on a far higher standard than Chinese, and were bourgeois in status and outlook. Some Catholic missions owned quite large farms and vineyards and the Communists saw no difference between them and native capitalists and landlords. Much property owned by missionaries had been acquired under extraterritoriality rights that made it nontaxable, and the owners were answerable only to foreign authorities.

Capitalists in Marxist eyes, and also under direct Vatican discipline and control, the Catholics seemed outright imperialists even to many non-Communist Chinese. Periodically, they were attacked by the Kuomintang. Much as the old scholars had seen the Jesuits as a threat to enforcement of uniformity of ritual worship and Confucian thought, so the Communists now looked upon Christian teachers as subversive to the correct system of discipline and conformance. A similarity between Catholic and Chinese indoctrination methods had been noted by more than one Catholic.[8]

Although missionary educational and social institutions and all holdings in farmlands were expropriated by the state, churches and grounds as well as urban commercial real estate nominally remained the property of each Chinese Catholic diocese. The real estate was managed by the government, however, much like joint private-state enterprise. The clergy received their stipends and rents or dividends through the 'ministry of cults'. Other sources of income were minimal: contributions from the laity, payments for Masses and other services, and sale of religious articles. I was told by the Ziccawei priests that they maintained their own shops to make religious articles and that the same was true in other churches.

The Bible had not been touched, but extensive revisions of prayer books were required and neither these nor catechisms were being printed in new editions as yet, according to Pastor Chen. The

Church had practically no press. He cited one example of an 'unsuitable prayer' which had to be revised because of a line stating, 'This land is filled with calamities' (Fatima?). Father Shen agreed that certain statements 'clearly opposed to socialism' must be changed.

Worship was permitted but not proselytization. Missionary activity was not permitted. The interdiction applied not only to private Catholic schools but to Sunday schools and any kind of organized catechismic teaching of youth, as well. Children were expected to learn the elements of faith from their parents.

'That is the way I acquired my faith,' said Pastor Chen. Both he and Father Shen were born in Catholic families. 'Religion is a matter of personal belief. No other private organizations run schools. Why should we?'

No Catholic seminary exists in China today. The pastor said that the Shanghai seminary was dissolved by the members themselves, not on government orders. In 1958, Shen joined others in voting to dissolve it because it was 'riddled with past contaminating influences'. He was now working out with other Chinese priests a suitable curriculum for a new seminary which would 'unquestionably' be permitted to function when they agreed. The property was still theirs, waiting to be utilized.

How much of this was sincere, how much uttered for the ears of Mr Li, the party representative who was present, how much both men still wanted what the Vatican would call the 'free Church' of the past, I do not know. Both emphatically denied that they were doctrinal rebels or in any way wished to 'reform' basic Catholic teachings.

'From what you have told me and from what I have observed for myself,' I said, 'it seems to me that your means of propagation of the faith are extremely limited. All children are taught atheism in the schools, while you cannot proselytize against it. Will it not be difficult to find young men to enlist in your seminary even if you reopen it?'

'We do not think so,' answered the pastor. 'As long as there is freedom of conscience people will seek God. We are masters of our own house; we are independent. Our people like the new Church better than the old one; they are more sincere in their faith. In the past, opportunists joined the foreign-dominated Church seeking advantages in the courts and foreign protection. We attracted lots of rice Christians. We don't want that kind of people, but men of high moral and spiritual convictions. There is no conflict between socialism and the teachings of Jesus.'

'You are more interested in applied Christian ethics than in propagation of the faith?'

Pastor Chen replied: 'They should be one and the same. Under new conditions we can make them so. Our future is the future of the people.'

Clearly this kind of nationalized church, dependent on the state, could offer no serious threat to it. With fewer than six Christians per thousand Chinese, the combined Catholic and Protestant churches never actually constituted such a threat except through their potent foreign connections. By breaking those connections, conflict between church and state had been solved in a manner relatively simple compared to the problem in satellite Communist states of Europe, especially Poland, where Catholicism was part of the national culture. Religion had nothing like so powerful a hold in China. Christianity there never embraced more than a fraction of one percent of the population. Even native Confucianism and Taoism exerted their influence mainly through ethical and philosophical teachings, and Buddhism had long been moribund. The ancient surviving temples of Buddhism's past glory were regarded as state treasures today and had never been so well renovated, so well kept, and so empty. Chinese youths now visited them and stared at the great images as curiously as foreign tourists.

Islam was a different matter. Moslems were called *Hui-min* (Moslem people) and recognized as a minority nationality. Islam had an ancient history in China through its ethnic ties with central Asian peoples who entered the Northwest as invaders and were slowly assimilated culturally but kept their religion. Unlike Christians, Mohammedans could join the party. But they joined as *Hui-min* rather than as members of *Hui-chiao* (Moslem religion). In China as in Russia, 'good' Moslem Communists were atheists, though they did not eat pork and did not publicly renounce the faith. Moslem leaders were cultivated by Communists also because of significant links between them and the anti-imperialistic Islamic world stretching across colonial and ex-colonial Asia and Africa. The combined population of the Hui Autonomous Region of Ninghsia and the Sinkiang Uighur Autonomous Region was about eight million, but Moslems were scattered elsewhere and altogether may have numbered fifteen million, of varying degrees of orthodoxy.

Perhaps news of my interview at Ziccawei preceded me to Wuhan. In that city I met a young Communist member of the city secretariat who, when we were driving back from Tung Lake, suddenly said:

'I hear you are a Catholic.'

'You are misinformed. I was brought up as a Catholic but I lost faith in institutionalized churches many years ago.'

'Do you believe in God?'

'God seems to be a human invention to comfort and control man in his ignorance and fears. I share every man's profound ignorance and his lonely fear of oblivion after death. The organized church exploits both for its own glorification and a power often misused. On the other hand, I agree with Einstein's observation that the universe surrounds us with evidence of a superior reasoning power. That is very far from being a Catholic, and accepting the Pope as God's vice-regent on earth. Do you believe in God?'

'Huh! Not in any sense. Belief in God and scientific Marxism are irreconcilable. I am a Marxist.'

I mentioned the Shanghai padre's comments that Communists also respect and work for the Commandments – or most of them.

'If that is so it is for different reasons. You cannot be a Christian and be a Marxist,' he replied. 'Marxism is modern, scientific truth. Religion belongs to the past. There's no connection between them.'

'Are you sure? Isn't Marxism a product of many historical teachings – among others, the ethical ideals of Judeo-Christianity? Did you ever read Engels' essay comparing early Christian martyrs to early Communist martyrs? When Marx and Engels called religion the opiate of the people they did not mean the Christian ideals of universal brotherhood but the organized church as a capitalist institution participating in the exploitation of man by man.'

'Religion is a class question. If one denies that then one isn't a Marxist. I can see that you are after all still a Catholic.' Red or

Christian, a dogmatist makes a dreary conversationalist. I dropped the discussion. But I was once more reminded by it that Chinese Communists are in general far less concerned with problems of reconciling socialism and religious thought than are Communists of the West.*

In Kunming, some time later, I noticed on the wall of the old Seventh Day Adventist compound a large and recently repainted sign in white Chinese characters: 'Jesus Saves Sinners.' When I expressed curiosity at this 'relic' of proselytization, my Eastern companion, a young professor of Kunming's new Institute of Minority Nationalities, refreshed my memory that *tsui-jen*, as the word 'sinner' is translated, is also the Chinese word for 'criminal'. The language has no exact equivalent for the Western concept of sinner.

'We all believe in saving *tsui-jen*,' he added wryly. 'The rains will eventually wash that sign away, as they will religion itself. In the meantime, it does no harm.'

It is too early to be so sure about that, I thought. Marxism is in solid at the moment, but the rains are indifferent to the slogans of the religions they erase.

* (1970) Christianity as well as Buddhism, and their churches and temples, came under severe attack during the G.P.C.P. In 1966 the only foreign Catholic missionaries still in China were Belgian nuns who operated a French-language school in Peking attended by children of foreign diplomats, including some Russians. They were seized by Red Guards and expelled from China. Their school and convent were wrecked and they were subjected to physical humiliations before Red Guards forced them across the frontier at Hong Kong. One of them died a few hours after her arrival. Christian worship ended for a time; at this writing it is reported that a few 'token' churches may be reopened. 'Freedom to Worship' (guaranteed by Article 88 of the Constitution, and still unrescinded) might again become viable when circumstances change, as had so often happened in China in the past.

68

*Literature and Music**

NOT much need be said about literature in the early years of the People's Republic; its condition was roughly analogous to that in the Soviet Union before the 'thaw' of 1956. Writing was party-functional for most authors. At its best it involved readers in educationally useful facts; at its worst it was vulgar propaganda.

China had produced great literature in the past and would again. Meanwhile, no one but a fool could contend that writers were free to nonconform, and the last person to say so would have been Mao Tse-tung. In his famous *Talks at the Yenan Forum on Art and Literature* in 1942, he made it quite clear that writers must be disciplined to 'serve the masses'; that is, the party's linear view of the masses' needs.[1]

Mao had privately said that absolute individualist freedom of expression would be possible only in a classless world. Literally, he could have been right about that; no such absolute yet exists anywhere outside mental institutions, and they also impose certain limits on exhibitionism. Communists believe that all literature serves one set of class interests or another; objectively speaking, it

*(1970) An opening gun of the G.P.C.R. was fired against a historical play, *Hai Jui Dismissed from Office*. It was written by Wu Han, a deputy Mayor of Peking. Allegedly it was an allegory criticizing Mao (the 'emperor') for dismissing P'eng Teh-huai from office, to make Lin Piao his successor as minister of defense. The attack on Wu Han led to denunciations of his patrons, Lo Ting-yi and P'eng Chen, both Politburo members, and then to their 'protector', Chairman of the Government, Liu Shao-ch'i. All were removed from power during the G.P.C.R. (1966–9). This chapter is retained as a historical description of problems of artists, writers and musicians even before 1966. By 1970 foreign influences were almost totally extinguished. Art, literature, music, drama, opera and cinema were all required to meet idealistic criteria of Mao's *Talks at the Yenan Forum*. Art could not be larger than life – and certainly not larger than Mao or Mao's vision of the Proletarian hero as the maximum man. For better or worse, that was the way it was.

makes no difference whether the writer is a conscious or an unconscious instrument. The world is flooded with as many bourgeois hacks as proletarian hacks, of course. But the view that only the party knows how to serve the masses in a socialist society makes no allowance for the role of the writer as the timeless conscience of humanity as a whole and the voice of dissent or protest against intolerable realities – an aspect of contradictions which exist between any people and its socially organized power. Mao himself noted such contradictions in China.

Under Kuomintang society the writer of any importance was persecuted, driven underground, and sometimes killed. (A few were buried alive.[2]) While he breathed, his work had the meaning of an individual conscience. He helped to expose and reject despotic idiocies of the old order; he served by quickening general awareness of the 'becoming' beyond the 'being'. The present society had corrected some of the ignorance pitilessly exposed by Lu Hsun and his disciples. Yet if Lu Hsun had lived with the same courage in the same frail body today he would not have been able to project life beyond the idiocies and tyrannies in the current set of value-realities – *not before the party itself began to rectify them*. He would not be buried alive; probably he would not even be imprisoned, as had happened periodically to Djilas, in Yugoslavia. But he would certainly be obliged to attempt reform through thought remolding. The artist was thus condemned to silence or to the repetition of party truisms – until self-criticism could work its way to the top and a new set of collective truisms received official sanction.

Still less, however, had any Chinese writers in exile produced any noteworthy literature. Hongkong bourgeois Chinese periodicals and books, for example, were filled with the old prewar puerilities of China or they imitated slick Western prose and poetry just as irrelevant. It could hardly be otherwise, since such writers had left their own ecology. The writer in China meanwhile retained roots in a living society and would one day originate again.

Nonconformist art is an introspective luxury which only relatively affluent and stable societies can afford. Whether led by church or state, reformations are always bigoted. If revolution is a

new birth, postrevolution inevitably involves growing pains and
adolescence; the artist who was creative when he was helping to
make the revolution cannot expect to find the child born with
an understanding of his adult view of the human experience.

In an epoch of this kind literature does have a prosaic but noble
function, however. That is to teach, to educate, to enlighten the
dark corners of imprisoned minds formerly denied both the simplest
liberating truths of universal practical knowledge and an appreciation of classical art and literature. In this respect the literature of
People's China had probably been of greater mass service than in
the past.

Another means of world communication recently opened up in
China was the widespread teaching of Western as well as Eastern
music and technique. It was making contributions of lasting value,
quite apart from the overlay of changing slogans of the time. A
good way to sense the enrichment music had brought to Chinese
culture was to spend a day at the Shanghai Conservatory. Apart
from the cosmopolitanism of the medium itself, it was a pleasure to
me to hear English and French freely spoken by so many conservatory faculty members.

One of the attractions was Chu Ying-hu, a grave little girl
violinist, aged twelve, who had first attended the conservatory's
spare-time school for children three years earlier. Her father was
a middle school teacher, her mother worked in an agricultural research institute. What was her ambition? 'To serve the people –
with good music.' She played a Chopin étude very nicely, bowed
and made way for Hsu Fei-ping.

Hsu Fei-ping was eleven, and he came from Amoy, in South
China. His mother was a musician, they had a piano in their
home – no average home – and he had begun to play when he was
five. Fei-ping's teacher in Amoy had recommended him to the
school, where he had been a boarding student for two years. He
had already given two public concerts. He played a selection from
Mozart with skill and dignity, then bowed to three girl *p'i-p'a*
players who succeeded him. The *p'i-p'a* is a native Chinese instrument something like a zither.

One child followed another, and then a large chorus, singing,
'Socialism is good . . .'

Four sixteen- and seventeen-year-old girls in blue serge skirts, white silk blouses and black pumps played something from Handel on three violins and one cello. Applause won an encore of a Cantonese folk song arranged by a faculty member. The violins were made in the school workshop, tones true and clear. A Tibetan woman of twenty-two, Chaidan Choma, with a fine natural soprano, sang her own highland songs and then a fragment from *Carmen*. She was a large, imposing figure in her bright native costume hung with silver and turquoise ornaments under a smile and a pile of thick glossy hair.

'She was a serf,' explained Tan Hsu-chen, vice-director of the conservatory, a violinist and instrument maker. 'Her voice was famous among the peasants, she used to sing in the fields at work. One of our teachers sent her back to us. She could not read when she arrived two years ago. After another two years she will return to teach music in Tibet.' The school had three other Tibetan students, as well as a dozen youths nominated for their talent by the Mongol, Li, Yao and Chuang minority peoples.

The Shanghai Conservatory was established by foreign sponsors early in this century and provided the nucleus for a prewar symphony orchestra which I used to hear under the leadership of an able Italian maestro named Paci. Tan Hsu-chen had been a violinist in that orchestra and at the outset was its only Chinese member. Old Shanghai had many private music teachers and was the music center of China. But those who could afford to study Western instruments found employment chiefly limited to hotels and dance orchestras. Beyond a few treaty ports, Western and even modern Chinese music had few audiences.

Vastly enlarged and run on socialist principles, the Shanghai Conservatory was still a leading school of the nation but it had a lot of new company. There were literally hundreds of orchestras of Chinese and Western instruments fingering both scales and kinds of music, and at least a score were capable of professional symphonic performances. The armed forces, most large municipalities, universities and great factories (unlikely places such as shipyards and steel mills) had orchestras and choruses of varying quality. With a decade of teaching and practice behind them, some were now quite good. Europeans in Peking in 1960 who heard the Central Orchestra play Beethoven's *Ninth Symphony* acclaimed it as first rate.

The Shanghai Symphony Orchestra, still sponsored by the conservatory, had the oldest tradition, dating from Paci's day, and its partisans called it the nation's best.

'We had fourteen pianos here at the time of liberation,' Director Tan told me. 'Today we have more than five hundred. Most of them are made in China. We make good pianos now, although our grands are not yet quite good enough for concert work. We need more pianos – and more space. That's why' – he pointed to an uncompleted four-story brick and stone building on the campus – 'we're all working to finish the new hall over there. Besides our child students we have 700 students in a middle school and 650 enrolled in the higher institute of the conservatory for four years plus a year of graduate study.'

From its original building on a small plot the conservatory had expanded to include more than ten acres of classrooms in converted residences – one of them Mme Chiang Kai-shek's – and new buildings constructed by student labor with some professional help. Mme Chang Hui-chih, principal of the children's school of music, was the wife of the conservatory director, who was off on a visit to Kiangsi with some students recording folk music. The conservatory was not only the home of the symphony orchestra and a folk music instrumental orchestra; it recorded, broadcasted, collected musical archives, experimented with new instruments, and revived and improved ancient Chinese instruments out of use since the Mongol Dynasty. Mme Chang herself was a violin maker. She showed me an exquisite miniature violin she had made as a model.

'Our children's school is the largest, but there is another such school in Peking and one in Kwangsi,' said Mme Chang. 'To qualify for entrance exams? Children must be recommended by primary school teachers. We take full-time students from the fourth grade on and have a current enrollment of 106. Those from out of town are boarding students; the majority are day students. Tuition? Free. All expenses are paid except food, twelve yuan a month; those whose parents can't pay may receive full scholarships. Difficult to qualify? Last year we had more than a thousand recommendations. We were able to take only sixty.'

Beginning at seven, children could take instruction in spare-time music classes held twice a week. Enrolled in such classes, at all levels, were 1,400 students, including adult workers and factory choruses.

I had intended to spend only a morning at the conservatory. By late afternoon I had seen only a small part of the 'plant' and met only a few of the senior faculty members and advanced students. There were nineteen laureates among the faculty; a number had studied and won honors abroad. Kao Shih-lan, nicknamed 'Ch'i-tan Kao' (a delicious Chinese custard) for reasons abscure to me, sang a duet with Chaidan Choma. Miss Kao was one of China's two most celebrated sopranos. She may be remembered at Juilliard, in New York, under her maiden name, Chia Lan-ko. She studied there until her return to China in 1948. Her husband, a New York University graduate, was now a professor in Shanghai University.

Here an aside seems necessary, in view of Western notions that all Chinese singing is falsetto. Some leading roles in classical operas were taken by female impersonators when women were banned from the stage, but even before the war this practice was becoming obsolete. The trend in today's theater was 'natural', with male and female parts played by men and women and sung accordingly, as anywhere else.

'Don't tell me you're a gardener, too.' I was speaking to Chou Hsiao-yen, the other 'most celebrated' soprano. Daintily clad and lovely to look at, in a black velvet gown, wearing modest make-up with a dash of lipstick emphasis, she seemed right out of a stage dressing room. She smiled agreeably and said, 'You should see me in my working clothes on the farm. We all spend a month a year helping the peasants and learning from them. I was frightened to death of it the first time, but now we look forward to it as the best fun we have. We are better artists and composers and closer to the people.'

I had first heard Hsiao-yen sing a new arrangement of Hsieh Hsing-hai's *Yellow River Cantata*. Then I met Meng Po, a composer and former director of the conservatory, who was now head of the Shanghai Cultural Bureau. It was at a performance of the operetta *Storm Over the Yangtze*, in which Mme Chou starred.

When I expressed a wish to know her story, Meng Po had arranged my visit to the conservatory.

'My story? That's simple,' she said now, 'and brief.'

Chou Hsiao-yen spoke English and French. A native of Hankow, she had studied in Shanghai until she met Nieh Erh,* China's greatest popular composer. She then joined Nieh's wartime traveling Troubadours, who pioneered modern music in China.

'In 1939 my family sent me to France for further voice study,' she continued. 'I was caught there in the war and couldn't escape. I lived with French friends in Biarritz until liberation; then I went to Paris and studied and did concert work. After our Shanghai victory I returned, in 1949. I met my husband here when I was making a picture at the Shanghai film studio. He's chief director there. Chang Chun-hsiang. He's a Yale graduate but in spite of that we lived happily ever after. That's about all – except that I'm terribly glad I came back. We have our problems, but right now this is the most exciting and creative place in the world to be. I wouldn't live anywhere else.'

The Cultural Bureau chief, Meng Po, arrived and organized an impromptu concert. He brought together a forty-piece orchestra and a women's string quartet, a violin soloist, a flutist, two piano soloists, a harpist and a girl *p'i-p'a* trio, with apologies for being able to offer no more on short notice. For two hours I heard brief selections from Bach, Chopin, Brahms and Prokofiev; after that, assorted works of Chinese composers – concertos, folk songs, love songs, political songs.

The mellow and dreamy playing of the Chinese flute enchanted me. I was introduced to Lu Tsung-lin, and learned that his name was famous among millions of radio listeners as the 'pedicab flutist'. He had picked up flute playing by ear in his youth, learned to make his own flutes, composed ballads, and endured constant scolding from an aging mother for wasting time playing when he should have been pulling passengers to buy rice. Ten years ago a music teacher had heard him playing on the street, recognized his talent,

---

*Besides the operetta I heard, Nieh Erh's many stirring compositions included the 'March of the Volunteers', which was now China's national anthem. He died at the age of twenty-four, a hero widely mourned by patriotic youth.

and put him in the conservatory. An illiterate then, he was now a concert artist, instructor, and composer of duets widely played at home and in Eastern Europe.

Tan Hsu-chen took me to see his factory, which was stocked with carefully selected varieties of pine, redwood, lapwood, ivory, ebony and horn. He himself had studied violin making in his youth from an old master, and now he also taught a conservatory course on the subject. I saw about a hundred skilled workers and student amateurs who were making and repairing violins, violas, cellos, oboes, clarinets, brass instruments, reeds and strings. Chinese are among the world's finest artists in wood, ivory, bone and metal; there is no reason to doubt their ability to excel in the making of musical instruments.

Over good Fukien tea with Tan and others I expressed my thanks and pleasure. Modern music had come a long way in China since that first performance of Hsieh Hsing-hai's *Yellow River Cantata* in Yenan, back in 1939. Fresh from Russia then, Hsieh was thirty-four, and it was his first major wartime composition. I happened to be in Yenan for its debut before an audience of roughly clad students and soldiers of the Eighth Route Army, and an overflow crowd of peasants.

'That was a weird orchestra Hsieh put together,' I reminisced. 'The Catholic church organ for a piano, two or three violins, a home-made cello or two, some Chinese flutes, clarinets, *yang-ch'ins* and *hu-ch'ins*, improvised instruments of some kind made of old Standard Oil tins with gut strung over them, a few pieces of battered brass, cymbals, army drums and trumpets. Did he also use a few cannon? Somehow he got his melody and his fugue out of them.

'I wish,' I added, 'that Hsieh could have lived to hear your magnificent full orchestration of his composition today.'

'Hsieh was indeed a talent,' one of them said quietly. 'You Westerners taught a few of our bourgeoisie some music, but it was Hsieh and those who followed him into Yenan – and the students they trained – who were the first to bring modern music to the people. They were the bridge builders between Western and Chinese music.'

Students and professors drifted in as darkness fell; our circle enlarged. They began to question me about American music. They were interested in everything: jazz, ballads, folk music, spirituals, ballet, operettas, musicals, modern and classical styles, trends, subjects, composers. By means of old and new recordings they knew of music and composers scarcely more than names to me. What they missed, they said, was contact with American artists.

'Do you know,' asked Meng Po, 'that we did invite many Americans to come to China? They did not come. Not one artist came. Is it not true that at that time your government forbade them to come?'

I had to admit the truth of that.*

* (1970) For many years the U.S. government continued to deny, through State Department administrative decrees and passport controls, the right of American artists to visit Mainland China. In 1967 the U.S. Supreme Court finally ruled that such State Department passport controls over travel were unconstitutional.

69

Crime and Punishment

THE courtroom was in the former missionary compound in the Hongkew district of Shanghai. About forty people dressed in working clothes were already seated and quiet as church when the young judge, Mo Pen-wan, entered. He was accompanied by two 'people's representatives' in their thirties, with whom the law required a judge to confer before pronouncing sentence. I learned from my companion that Judge Mo was a machinist and labor union leader who had been given special training in a school operated by the judicial department to teach the relatively simple legal codes of the People's Courts.

Yang Kuan-fu was the prisoner, aged thirty-nine. A lean, sallow-faced man with a receding chin, he was escorted into the room and stood at attention before the elevated bench. Yang and his defense lawyer listened as the prosecutor read his summation of the charges:

'You were arrested on 14 September 1960. As a former special policeman under the Kuomintang régime you intrigued with gangsters to blackmail, intimidate and rob citizens, having in instances beaten them. After liberation you stayed on in Shanghai, failed to report your past misdeeds, donned civilian clothes, and took a job with the light and power company. Your duties were to collect bills owed for repairs and maintenance. During the past two years you embezzled 1,527 yuan by falsifying receipts. These facts were first reported by your fellow workers. After your arrest an investigation confirmed the facts, to which you have confessed. Accordingly you are brought to trial under Article Three of the Legal Code. Do you admit your guilt and acknowledge your confession?'

After the prisoner had replied in the affirmative Judge Mo questioned him directly:

Q. 'What did you do before liberation?'

A. 'I was a policeman in Chiang Kai-shek's Loyalty Gendarmerie, engaged in political and intelligence work. Aside from that I arrested and tortured people to extract money from them, part of which I kept for myself. I helped carry out some looting also. With others, I took part in a few highway robberies ...'

Q. 'When did you take your present job?'

A. 'In 1957. I began embezzling on a small scale but soon took as much as thirty yuan at a time. My method was to write one figure on the top receipt but a different and lower one on the carbon copy.'

Several witnesses appeared against the accused. Judge Mo instructed them briefly: 'Tell the truth. Do not exaggerate. Do not try to protect the accused.' The first witness was a worker who asserted that Yang had come to his factory thirty-five times to collect for repairs. A total of 487.82 yuan had been paid to him. The next witness, an accountant in Yang's office, testified that the accused had remitted only 109.34 out of the total mentioned. Becoming suspicious, he had gone to the factory, compared receipts, and discovered the discrepancy. Two more factory representatives provided similar evidence. Most of the audience consisted of men and women workers from the defrauded factories and organizations. They were attending the trial to see that justice was done and to report back to their groups.

When the defendant had admitted all the accusations the Judge asked him whether he realized that he had been robbing the working people and his own family, and whether he realized the seriousness of his crime. He said that he did, and added: 'While the whole country is going forward I have been leaping backward. The government had given me a new way of life despite my corrupt past life. I was not satisfied with ample wages. I was greedy and wanted more.'

The prosecutor then demanded maximum punishment in accordance with the law. The accused had not voluntarily confessed his crimes. Even after his fellow workers had discovered the first instance of embezzlement, the previous May, he had refused to help them by admitting his other crimes. Only after they had gathered all the evidence and had him arrested had he confessed to the police.

Judge Mo next heard from the defense attorney, who spoke in the following sense:

'The accused has confessed and expressed his regret. Article Three is two-sided. It provides for punishment but also for reform through education. With us it is a principle to be lenient to those who repent and to be severe with those who do not. After his arrest the accused did quickly confess and confess thoroughly. After a trip in the countryside he himself has seen how everyone is working to build the country up while he was tearing it down. This is true even in his own family. Now he feels ashamed. We should consider the corrupt life he formerly lived and make allowances. I consider his attitude relatively good. I would recommend leniency.'

Judge Mo turned to the prisoner, who was visibly shaking. 'Have you anything to say?' Yang replied in a quavering voice with one sentence only : 'I shall do my best to carry out whatever punishment is given to me and to reform myself into a morally fit citizen.'

Court was recessed while the judges conferred. It took no longer than a cigarette smoke. In the courtyard I spoke to a young electrician who knew some English. He had worked in the same office with Yang. I asked him what Yang had done with the money he stole.

'He spent it on expensive restaurants where capitalists go. Of course when someone saw him in those places we began to get suspicious. He got hold of some bad women, too, and he wanted money to sleep with them. Prostitutes? No. But there are still some women around who will make love for money.'

Yang could have got ten years for embezzlement. When court reconvened, Judge Mo again reviewed the facts. Then he compared life in the corrupt Shanghai of the past with the present and said that allowances must be made.

'The crime was serious but the prisoner has now fully confessed and seems ready to rehabilitate himself. We consider that after some re-education he can still do something useful in society. Our sentence,' he ended, 'is three years.'

The prisoner was notified that he had a right to file an appeal within ten days. The court then adjourned. Everyone seemed satisfied. In a moment the place was empty. I stared at the gray brick walls of the old compound where missionaries probably had sung hymns and prayed for man's redemption in the past. Then I walked down the gray October streets past the gray Whangpoo River to Mr Sassoon's former hotel.

70

The Triple Cities

AT the Hankow airport I was met by Li Chao, a short, round, energetic party stalwart in his mid-thirties. He was evidently a kind of Man Friday to Li Chih, a member of the city council and local party secretariat, with whom I had an interview over a pot of tea. Li Chih was the mayor's protocol chief; a college graduate, he knew some English and had a modest and agreeable way of speaking, less cluttered with political clichés than most.

Li Chao, 'the Short', was a former 'little Red devil'. He told me he had joined the anti-Japanese guerrillas in Shantung at the age of twelve. Thereafter 'the army was father and mother' to him. In 1949, Liu Shao-ch'i sent him with Li Chih and sixty other young men to begin the reconstruction of Hankow. 'At that time living space was so scarce here all sixty of us lived in four rooms.' Housing had 'more than doubled' since then. Li Chao spoke of new factories, schools, hospitals and bridges with the pride of one who had personally built all of them.

The three mid-Yangtze cities of Hankow, Wuchang and Hanyang – collectively known as Wuhan – had indeed witnessed some startling improvements. None was more pleasing to an old China hand than the railroad and vehicular bridges across the Han and Yangtze rivers, which have their confluence at Hankow. The Yangtze bridge, just short of a mile long, is thoroughly modern and aesthetically satisfying. Completed in 1958 with Soviet aid, it connected North and South China by rail for the first time and provided an unbroken line from Siberia to Canton.

Hankow accounted for two thirds of Wuhan's population of about 2,100,000. Like Shanghai, Peking and other large cities, Wuhan was now a special administrative region which integrated industrial and farm economy. The whole greater municipality covered eight *ch'u** and included some 8,400,000 inhabitants. In the *ch'u* called Ch'ing Shan, Green Mountain, was the mammoth Wuhan Iron and Steel Works.

The Wuhan plant was possibly the largest of all the basic projects built with Soviet aid. Work on it began in 1955 and the first steel was poured from its modern furnaces in 1958. There had been a small iron and steel works in this neighborhood as early as 1908, based on the iron reserves near neighboring Tayeh, but production was negligible. Foreign and Kuomintang geologists had rated Tayeh's reserves as rich (fifty percent iron) but limited; after 1949, thorough surveys revealed new and far more extensive deposits. It was then decided to make Hanyang the center of mid-China's largest integrated iron and steel industry. Indispensable to this were the excellent deposits of coking coal in Pinghsiang, a short haul to Hanyang, now connected by electric railway to the modernized and partly mechanized Tayeh mines.

Huang Ming, general manager of the big works, took me on a tour of as much as one could see in a day of its workshops, furnaces, power and cement plants, laboratories, schools, housing and recreational areas. A Shansi University student who joined the Paluchun in 1937, Huang had received postwar training at the Anshan steel works, where most of Wuhan's leading technicians were recruited. The Wuhan plant still suffered from a lack of skilled workers and technicians as well as engineers, he said. The gap would soon be filled by graduates of Ch'ing Shan's own Iron and Steel Institute, with about 5,000 full-time students (under the Ministry of Metallurgy), supplemented by spare-time technical training schools for workers.

Current output was stated to be 800,000 tons each of pig iron and steel (with one main blast furnace and one giant open hearth operating), but a No. 2 blast furnace was being completed well ahead of schedule which was expected to bring output for 1961 above a million tons each.

To a nonspecialist the Wuhan plant seemed at least as efficient in layout and operations as the modern plant of the Nippon Steel Company, of about the same capacity, which I had visited near Tokyo in 1959. Rather superior to the latter, however, were the

*An urban administration unit, roughly equivalent to a borough.

Wuhan works' arrangements for housing and integrated community facilities. Large blocks of well-spaced three-story apartments, divided by the usual tree-lined streets, provided more than a million square meters of living space. Buildings were of about the same standard as those I saw around many state factories; accommodations varied according to size of family and income. Monthly wages averaged sixty-five yuan per worker, ranging from thirty-two yuan for apprentices to 107 for skilled technicians and as high as 230 for engineers.

In this instance, I asked to see the apartment of an engineer's family. In a building which housed fourteen families I entered, late one afternoon, a flat (two bedrooms, tiny kitchen, toilet and shower) occupied by a family of six persons. One son, aged fifteen, was home from middle school; he wore a gray corduroy jacket, slacks, and serviceable shoes; beside him stood his grinning sister, aged seven, in a bright yellow sweater. Another son, of fourteen, was still at school, as was another daughter, aged nine; both were doing Red Pioneer duties, the mother explained. She described her husband as a graduate engineer of the Peking Iron and Steel Institute, who earned 175 yuan a month. She herself, a primary school graduate, worked part time in a commune factory where she was paid twenty-four yuan. They ate their noon and evening meals at canteens; they had breakfasts and Sunday meals at home. Their monthly budget: canteen food, seventy to eighty yuan (rations, twenty-five to forty pounds each); nonrationed food and miscellaneous, thirty yuan; clothing, books, 'extras', ten to twenty yuan; rent, including utilities, eleven yuan; savings, thirty-six yuan. Why 'thirty-six'? State savings bonds were four yuan each; they were buying nine bonds a month. Could they cash the bonds, I asked. 'When we need the money,' answered the mother. 'Meanwhile, it helps build socialism.'

Undoubtedly the greatest local consumer of Green Mountain steel was the Wuhan Heavy Machine Tool Factory, operating since 1958, when forty-six sets of heavy machine tools were made. In 1959 output rose to 369 sets; the target for 1960 was 670 sets. 'Heavy' meant such things as portal lathes weighing up to 480 tons and a metal cutter on a bed 125 feet long, which I saw in production. Milling machines, grinders, casters and many other cutting tools were being turned out on a scale entirely new for a city that could not make a modern machine tool of any kind when I had last visited it.

Here I was told that eighty percent of all adult workers attended spare-time schools; their average age was twenty-three. The factory also operated a part-time school for 800 youths aged sixteen to eighteen. At seventeen they did two months in the shop, eight months in classroom work, and had two months vacation; at eighteen they worked half-time at the bench, half-time in school. Orchestras, bands, an auditorium where weekly dances were held (20 percent of the workers were women), a football field, a boating pavilion, athletic teams, theatrical troupes and various clubs were part of the organized social life. After a farewell party given to the last three Soviet experts on their departure, a few weeks previously, the big factory was now entirely Chinese run. Eighty percent of its machines were Chinese made, twenty percent imported.

As an industrial city Wuhan's requirements for education and health facilities were recognized in planning that was making it one of China's more advanced cities in those respects. Many new sanatoria and rest homes for workers had sprung up along the shores of Tung Ting, the nation's largest natural lake. The most significant additions to China's third-largest educational center were the T'ung Chi Medical College and hospitals. These were already the focus of a network of smaller hospitals and clinics and a new county health system. I found T'ung Chi's pediatrics hospital and general hospital graceful ultramodern structures; they had a staff of about 250 doctors, of whom ninety-two were women. With 150 full-time professors and lecturers, aided by nearly 300 part-time lecturers from Wuhan University, the T'ung Chi Medical College had a current enrollment of 3,200 students, besides 460 studying in night school and several thousand enrolled in pre-medical correspondence courses.

Wuhan's economic, cultural and political life were of importance far greater than the space devoted to it here might suggest, but many Western scientists and other specialists have published their observations about it. The city was after all on the main 'tourist circuit' – Peking-Shanghai-Hankow-Canton.

Szechuan, 'The Heavenly Land'

CHUNGKING lies about 1,000 miles west of Shanghai as our four-engine Soviet plane flew it, and nearly twice that far if one travels by boat up the Yangtze. I had not seen Chungking since 1943, when it was China's war capital. With more than two million inhabitants, it was the largest city in Szechuan, which is a simply fabulous land. If Szechuan were a separate continent instead of a landlocked province clinging to the eaves of Tibet, it might in itself be a world power. It has an extraordinary abundance of nearly all the resources required by a major nation and a variety of climate – Himalayan to subtropical – that makes it possible to grow any product cultivated anywhere in all China. Since the pre-Christian era Szechuan has been known to the Chinese as 'the heavenly land', but man has often contrived to make it hell on earth.

Including Sikang (recently joined to Szechuan) the province was 220,000 square miles in area,[1] or slightly larger than France. In 1957 its population was officially put at 72,000,000; in 1962 it probably reached 80,000,000, or more than that of Germany. Blessed by numerous streams and rivers (*Sze-ch'uan* means 'four rivers'), it had an enormous hydroelectric power potential. Normally Szechuan produces about one-fourth of all the rice grown in China, and has a large food surplus. If China's transportation system were adequate to effect speedy distribution, this province alone might export enough food to alleviate chronic shortages in the alternately typhoon-swept and drought-stricken areas of the East and South.

At the end of a twenty-mile drive over a macadam road from the Chungking airport – about the size of that of Dayton, Ohio – I was escorted by a China Intourist agent to Szechuan's new provincial House of the People. This assembly hall was surmounted by a massive reproduction of the Temple of Heaven, an architectural curiosity which created in the viewer something of the same state of anxiety as a giant piece of pâtisserie of Mr Wright's Guggen-heim Museum. Beneath the double superstructure there was a two-story hotel, modern and comfortable. Here a room and bath, with a balcony view, cost three dollars; excellent Chinese food was com-parably inexpensive. At the foot of broad steps below the edifice lay a wide plaza and opposite it was the building formerly used by Chiang Kai-shek as his state palace. It now served as a city hall or mayor's office, where I was invited to tea and stayed to dinner the second day after my arrival.

Mayor Jen was fifty-five and bore the *ming-tzu* or given name Pei-kuo. A professional writer until 1938, he left his old master, Lu Hsun, to go to Yenan to join the Eighth Route Army. Another protégé of Liu Shao-ch'i, he was a member of the provincial party standing committee as well as responsible for the administration of West China's largest city. In reply to my request that he discuss his 'most difficult problem', Mayor Jen said that it was the procuring of more food for export to needy areas of China and the means of getting it there. Peasants here were 'eating too much' and 'eating more than ever before'; there had been some drought but still Szechuan would have a surplus for export. I asked whether there was continuing trouble, as reported abroad, with Khamba tribes-men in the Sikang area, where the Tibetan revolt first started, in 1957. He said that the country was thoroughly pacified although isolated assassinations of Han officials still occurred.

Jen emphasized that Szechuan as a whole was still behind the advanced seaboard areas. He added, 'Any fair-minded person who knew the old opium-soaked province of the past could not fail to agree that the people have changed fundamentally.'

In a three-day visit I could not assess his statement nor do much more than observe transformations in Chungking and its environs. Americans who were here during the war may find difficulty in believing that it was now a relatively clean city. Paved streets had replaced dirty alleyways, and 250 miles of sewers, plus the efforts of sanitary squads in every block, had dethroned and almost elimin-ated the rats. Broken stone stairways down which one used to slip precariously, or ride in a human-borne chair to the river front, had been rebuilt and chairs had disappeared along with rickshaws. A steep truck road led to the pier and there was a new funicular railway. The large new gymnasium, a municipal stadium (capacity 50,000), and a park and a 'palace of culture and rest', had given the hilltop something like a city center. Around it were scattered some twelve institutes of higher learning, ranging from the university to a medical college, with a total enrollment of 19,000.

Mayor Jen asserted that housing in the city proper had 'more than doubled' in ten years. Much of the new was shoddy in appearance and bamboo structures still lined the river bluffs. In the growing industrial suburbs one now saw quite large substantial brick apartment buildings, four to six stories high, surrounded by vegetable gardens and trees. From the outside they appeared as good as similar conventional structures in the West but they were cheaply finished within. Vastly better housing than workers hereabouts knew in the past, such apartments were as yet available to only a small percentage of the population.

Beyond doubt the greatest single change in Chungking and the rest of the province was the shattering of Szechuan's traditional isolation by the opening up of modern communications. 'Szechuan has probably been more hampered by inadequate transportation than any other single factor,' wrote George B. Cressey in his prewar and still highly valuable study, *China's Geographic Foundations*. '... Animals are rare, carts unknown, railroads but dreams, canals impossible, and the rivers too swift. ... As Beach has said, man is "the universal animal, the omnibus of commerce and the pack mule of the race. It is cheaper to wear men down than to keep the roads up." '[2]

Under the new régime the Chungking-Chengtu railway (300 miles) was constructed in two years and began operating in 1953. By 1956 the longer (415 miles) and far more difficult Chengtu-Paochi railway was opened for traffic. Involving tens of tunnels through the Min mountains, it connected Szechuan to the northwest and all parts of northern China. Other railways were being pushed southward. One traversed Kweichow province, to reach Yunnan, providing a route to the Vietnam frontier. The Chungking-Hankow railway, said to be about one-third completed, would eventually join Szechuan to the middle Yangtze Valley, formerly accessible only by small river boats which shot the precarious Yangtze rapids on a 780-mile journey to Hankow. Most impressive of the new highways was the 1,400-mile road from Ya-an, near Chengtu, to Lhasa, one of three China-Tibet highways built since 1949. Over it went the made-in-Chungking generators which established Lhasa's first power plant.

Although thousands of trucks, rubber-tired carts and railway cars now crawled across the face of Szechuan, man was still an indispensable pack mule. Ten times more road mileage was needed than the 15,000 miles already built, and ten times more wheels. Szechuan had been rapidly industrializing to provide these and other means of modern transport. Chungking and its environs were the major heavy industry base but machinery was manufactured in many other cities. By 1959 the province claimed an output of 1,060,000 tons of iron and 700,000 tons of steel.[3]

Szechuan was expected to be industrially self-sufficient by 1970. It was now believed to hold China's largest coal reserves; coking coal was plentiful and conveniently located near iron ore. Newly discovered deposits in Yenpien (near the Yunnan border) were reported alone sufficient to satisfy foreseeable iron requirements of local heavy industry.[4] Oil wells were being exploited in Neichiang and Yuehchih, where natural gas was abundant, and uranium deposits were probably second only to those in Turkestan. Szechuan had significant reserves of copper, lead and asbestos, all of which were being mined; it had long been an exporter of salt.

Rewi Alley's description of an exhibit in Chengtu catches some of the atmosphere of popular awe and enthusiasm for dawning industrialization which I felt in many hinterland places – its paradox, its incongruity, its naïveté. 'In the industrial exhibition there were queues waiting to enter,' he wrote, 'middle-aged and even old women with bound feet, country farmers with long blue gowns and white turbans, city folk and innumerable youngsters. They were fascinated with the exhibits, many of which were simplifications of machine tools which could be easily built by the communes.'[5]

Mountain-rimmed by ranges which in the west reach to the lordly height of Minya Konka, at 25,000 feet, and in the north-west to the 10,000-foot Min Shan, Szechuan lowers on the south and east to hill ranges and upland folds which form the gorges of the upper Yangtze. The central part of the province is a basin which was once a vast lake. The 'red basin' ranges from 1,500 feet above sea level in the valleys to 4,000 feet in the mesas or flat hill-tops peculiar to the region, which gets thirty-five to forty inches of rainfall annually. Frost is rare, the farming season is ten months, and double cropping is general. Besides the staple rice and wheat, major crops are cotton, sugar cane, delicious citrus fruit – Szechuan is the home of the mandarin orange – bamboo, rape, tobacco and tung oil.

Even the sober Dr Cressey, not given to superlatives when he eyed China's resources, described the Min plain in the red basin as 'one of the loveliest garden spots on earth' and concluded that 'no-where in the world is there a more fertile, productive, or thickly populated agricultural area of similar size.'[6] Characteristic of Szechuan, long stairways of rice terraces fall from hillsides as steep as forty-five degrees, and the narrow flooded plots are a million mirrors flashing in the sun. Below them varied crops of green and gold in the valleys make a checkerboard pattern; innumerable waterfalls rain down from coniferous forests into fern and bamboo groves bright with exotic flowers and tropical birds. High overhead cloud-dimmed peaks beckon from the Tibetan plateau. Not surprisingly, Szechuan has produced painters and poets since ancient times.

'The region offers a magnificent home for a prosperous and pro-gressive people,' wrote Dr Cressey in the thirties, 'but like so many of the gifts of nature there are limits to its capacity. ...' He con-sidered the population, then well under 50,000,000, already too dense to be sustained by the available land. And so it seemed. One reason : 'Opium poppy is raised very widely,' Dr Cressey noted. In times of nominal 'suppression' farmers were 'fined ... whether the opium was raised or not.'[7] Opium consumption was almost univer-sal; I used to see ignorant parents spread it on sugar cane and feed it to their children as a pacifier.

During the war, poppy cultivation was pushed away from areas where foreigners could see it, but when I traveled overland from Chungking to Sian in 1939 opium was sold in the native inns; doubtless it helped guests overlook the lice and rats. The towns abounded with scrofulous beggars. Swarms of lice-ridden and ragged or completely naked derelict children used to wait in the streets outside restaurants for guests to throw scraps from their tables and amuse themselves by watching the little beggars scramble like boys diving for pennies.

In the past one did not have to look for beggars; in self-defense, one tried to avoid them. There may have been beggars in Szechuan in 1960. I did not see any around Chungking. Waifs had disappeared from the streets. I saw no one in filthy rags although many wore patched clothing. In several other areas of China where I had seen poppies grown in the past (Paotou, Shensi, Hopei, Yunnan) there were none today. I never smelled opium in China in 1960, nor had any foreign traveler whom I asked about it.

Sanitation and public health measures had brought results in Szechuan not far behind the rest of China. Chungking now had 300,000 members of 'health defense' or physical culture associations. In a talk with the municipal director of sports at the central gymnasium I learned that all able-bodied persons were required to take ten minutes of exercises every day. There were 130,000 'qualified' (one of four grades) athletes and one of them had run the 100-meter dash in 10.3 seconds. Athletic instructors now selected 'tall and able' children at primary school age for special instruction. I gathered that China expected to win all the Olympics; thus far, she was represented only by Taiwan. On the gym court I watched two teams of teen-age girls play some fast basketball. (Chungking had 20,000 basketball teams.) China's national teams are now six-footers. These Chungking girls averaged five feet ten – giantesses among old Szechuanese – and short shorts and tight shirts revealed interesting anatomical progress. I asked to photograph them but I had no flash equipment and when they all trooped outside they had modestly covered themselves in pullovers and long cotton slacks. Thus I missed a picture of the best bare legs I saw in China.

Food output in Szechuan had more than doubled since the war, it was claimed;[8] at any rate food was more plentiful than elsewhere although urban rationing was strict. In Shanghai and Hankow I occasionally saw signs of malnutrition among children but I saw none in Chungking. Kindergartens and nurseries I visited at random were poorly housed and equipped (in one, a single hobby horse for twenty-two!) but the children were clean and looked healthy. At one day school I saw steamed rice and wheat rolls and soya bean milk being consumed for breakfast; in another I watched a lunch of noodles and two vegetables being served. Food here cost six yuan a month per child for two meals a day.

Mayor Jen's comment left no doubt that the problem of urban food supply was his major headache. To extract more from the peasants, city-dwellers had to produce more things peasants wanted to buy. Nowhere else, except in Dairen and Kunming, did I see department stores as well stocked as in Chungking; a general drive to increase output for local consumption seemed to show results. Mayor Jen told me the 'big change' was that Chungking was now 'eighty percent self-sufficient' in manufactured consumption goods, whereas before 1949 it had imported eighty percent of its needs.

'Needs' is here a relative term; no one should visualize Saks or Selfridge's. The largest Chungking department store was about the equivalent of the store owned and operated by the People's Republic of Hongkong, which is distinguished mainly for low prices on cheap goods. Peasants who crowded the aisles in Chungking seemed well supplied with money. I saw a bound-footed woman buy a fur-trimmed silk brocade jacket for sixty yuan. Another consulted with her son about children's shoes, priced at four to six yuan, while she cast a sidelong glance at suède shoes of good quality, offered at fourteen yuan.

Many of Chungking's consumer goods were made in urban commune workshops which utilized the labor of housewives in an experiment widely tried throughout China from 1958 onwards. In Chungking, as elsewhere, the urban commune organization had its prototype in former neighborhood street committees. The principal innovation of urban communes was the mobilization of unemployed household dependents, chiefly women, to work in handicraft or small machine factories. Most of them made consumer necessities or parts and supplies for existing state or municipal factories which they served as satellites. Many workers who had never handled a tool or a machine were taught by individual handicraftsmen or small cooperatives of handicraft workers, or by workers from nearby state factories.

I saw a dozen or more urban communes all the way from Peking to Manchuria and down to Yunnan. Working conditions varied from poor to good. In Chungking I saw commune foundries smelting iron and casting metal parts in primitive unheated outdoor sheds and I very much doubted the ultimate usefulness of the product. In Manchuria I saw some efficient, well-lighted factories employing as many as several hundred women producing bicycles, precision meters, ball bearings and electrical parts that looked quite serviceable. Salaries ranged from as low as twenty yuan to thirty-five or forty yuan per month. In most shops workers spent six hours at the bench and two to three hours learning characters and elementary politics, for six days a week.

Use of communal dining facilities in Chungking was optional, as it was said to be elsewhere. The average commune family seemed to be eating the noon meal communally and the evening meal at home. Participation in theory was voluntary but strong pressure was probably brought to bear in some instances. Door-knocking in various places, I did meet stay-at-home mothers who preferred to do their own baby-tending and whose husbands earned good wages. For mothers with two or more children, the take-home pay, after payments for day care of their infants, obviously could offer small inducement in the poorer communes.

Seven Star Ridge Commune, in Chungking, was fairly typical of large urban communes I saw, although it was poorer than some in Shenyang, for example, where communes even operated large suburban vegetable and poultry farms. Seven Star covered the area of an average city precinct, with a total of 76,000 residents. Of these, 22,000 adults were already employed in state or municipal enterprises or services.

Seven Star's largest enterprise made electrical parts, employed about 100 workers, and had a monthly output valued at 40,000 yuan. Other shops made shoes, clothing, leather goods, bricks and bamboo products. Wages averaged only twenty-three yuan per person for a six-hour day, or less than half the average pay in a state factory. The commune operated a total of thirty-six small shops which employed 4,160 persons, some of them part-time, and some 1,400 of whom worked in nurseries, homes for the aged, kindergartens, health stations, dining rooms and services. Service centers did the workers' laundry, tailoring, mending and shoe repairs and sold small daily necessities and theater tickets. They also provided baby-sitters.

In 1959 urban commune industries in all China were reported

to have accounted for production valued at 2,000,000,000 yuan. In 1960 they were scheduled to have an output five times that large. In that year they may have employed as many as 4,000,000 women. With the sharp curtailment of state capital investment in 1961, the de-emphasis on urbanization of the economy at the expense of agriculture, and the adoption of the slogan 'consolidation and improvement in quality' for industry, many commune shops were merged with municipal factories, or closed down. Between 10,000,000 and 20,000,000 people were reported shifted back from the cities and hundreds of county seats to the farms in 1961, in accordance with 'priority given to agricultural production'.[9] These no doubt included dependents of millions of semiskilled peasant laborers moved from urban building and other suspended construction programs.

Everywhere I inspected urban communes I was told that they were still in an 'experimental stage' – in contrast to rural communes – and no one would predict a future for them. By 1962 hordes of cadres had been sent from urban centers to do farm labor and most of the commune social services and productive functions apparently had been skeletalized and placed under direct municipal administration. Many of the women recruited to work in urban communes disappeared from the cities after 1960. Their men folk took them back to the villages after they themselves lost urban jobs following sharp curtailment of building projects abandoned after the Great Leap Forward.

I had a feeling of being more closely watched – or protected – in Chungking than in other places. Every time I attempted to take a walk by myself I was soon discovered by my China Intourist guide. The best I could manage was a few minutes' rummaging in stores and book stalls. I saw not a single other foreigner. Szechuan has long had a reputation for xenophobia, even toward outland Chinese, but I sensed indifference rather more than hostility. When I was introduced people were polite and often animated. But no stranger on the streets proffered me any more attention than an American tourist in provincial France gets from a Frenchman who has nothing to sell him.

A Few Words on Tibet

TIBET was a land I had often wished to see, but when I lived in China time and opportunity had never coincided. Now I could not make a strong case for a visit since I had already expressed a preference to retrace old paths and the Chinese knew I had never been to Tibet. Then Stuart Gelder came to Peking, to write for British papers. He was very anxious to see Tibet and we put in a joint petition for air accommodation.

It was October, heavy snow was already falling in Tibet and there was no regular plane service. China had few army planes equipped to carry passengers above the 20,000-foot level to clear the mountains safely. Chou En-lai told Gelder that if we insisted he would furnish a military plane but we might be held up weeks in Sikang by bad weather. He added that if Britain's Armstrong Vickers had been willing to sell China the high-altitude planes she had been trying to buy, the whole problem would have been simple. Gelder and I had to abandon our trip.[1] I mention it now only because at the time I wondered why China didn't buy the planes from Russia. A few months afterward I read that Khrushchev had sold India high-altitude helicopters to patrol her Tibetan frontier. It was not until December 1961 that Armstrong Vickers announced that five of its giant turbojets had been sold to China. The incident was one of several which suggested a curious Soviet indifference to China's side of the dispute with India over the Tibetan frontier – and Britain's quiet indifference to the American embargo against trade with China.

One man in Peking could have told me a great deal about Tibetans: the Panchen Lama, or Erdeni. I saw him once at a state dinner, resplendent in his priestly yellow robes, but nothing came of my request to interview him before he returned to Tibet. The two living buddhas were the Dalai Lama and the Panchen Lama. After the Dalai Lama fled to India, the Panchen Lama, his ecclesiastical alter ego (as in times of the dual papacy), became the chief figurehead of the Chinese-organized preparatory committee for an autonomous government of Tibet.

Ever since the Manchus suppressed the great Tibetan rebellion of 1751 the ties of the Panchen had been closer to China than those of the Dalai. In that year the Emperor Ch'ien Lung sent an expedition to Lhasa after the lamas, led by the Dalai Lama, had murdered the two Chinese high commissioners – *ambans* – and massacred the entire resident Chinese population. Ch'ien Lung's retaliation was sanguinary. His troops also crossed the Himalayas and descended upon Nepal, where they defeated the Gurkas who had been raiding into Tibet. (Nepal remained a tributary state of Peking until the British established a protectorate there in the nineteenth century.) The Panchen Lama (Panchen Rimpoche) was first in the religious hierarchy of Tibet and was traditionally viewed as the direct incarnation of Buddha, whereas the Dalai Lama was the incarnation of a mere bodhisattva. Ch'ien Lung recognized the Panchen Lama as the principal figure in the political as well as the religious hierachy, reducing the Dalai Lama to a secondary role in both departments. At that time Tibet's frontier on India (then known as Hindustan, and under the loose control of the Mogul kings and their feudatory states), was roughly fixed by Ch'ien Lung near – in some places, far beyond – boundary lines claimed by China today.

No foreign power seriously questioned China's sovereignty over Tibet, although at the time of the collapse of the Ch'ing Dynasty Tibetan authorities had British encouragement when they attempted a coup and proclaimed Tibet's fealty to China at an end. Chinese troops suppressed the rebellion and the British never recognized Tibet as an independent state. They did, however, negotiate a tripartite convention with Chinese and Tibetan representatives at Simla, India, in 1913–14. This conceded China's suzerainty over all Tibet but sought to establish the 'autonomy' of Outer (western) Tibet. Peking repudiated the Chinese envoys at Simla and refused to ratify the convention, regarding it as an infringement on claims to Tibet as 'part of China'. The agreement would also have settled the Indo-Tibetan border on the basis of the so-called McMahon line but its rejection left areas of the lofty frontier still undetermined.

Generations of Chinese attrition by settlement ate away at the grasslands and highlands of eastern Tibet. These areas were loosely administered by petty Tibetan potentates who divided their fealty between Lhasa and Peking. Much of Inner Tibet had thus been effectively Sinicized. During the Kuomintang period these regions were formally incorporated into 'China proper' by the creation of two new provinces, Chinghai and Sikang, but the republican government's hold over Lhasa remained almost entirely nominal – the existence of a true national government of China itself being often in dispute.

During the Second World War China's suzerainty over Tibet was a subject of discussion between Britain, China and the United States. In an aide-memoire in 1943 the British Embassy in Washington conceded 'formal Chinese suzerainty' but also wished to secure for the Lhasa government 'the full enjoyment of local autonomy', and the right to 'exchange diplomatic representatives with other powers'.[2] In reply the State Department unequivocally declined support for the latter aim when it declared : 'The Government of the United States has borne in mind the fact that the Chinese Government has long claimed suzerainty over Tibet and that the Chinese constitution lists Tibet among areas constituting the territory of the Republic of China. This Government has at no time raised a question regarding either of those claims.'[3]

What had all that to do with the wretched existence of a million and a half [4] Tibetan peasants? Very little. The Tibetan wished to be free among his flocks and enjoy the fruits of his toil on the high windy plateaus of the roof of the world. Except for a brief romantic flurry, when Ronald Coleman disappeared behind the *Lost Horizon*, not many people in the West took much interest in the Tibetan's liberation or his lamas in the past. It cannot be said that the United States ever offered to send the Dalai Lama any foreign aid, technicians or even moral support when he was a subject of Kuomintang China. In any case, it is doubtful that the Dalai Lama would have let us carry out such work in competition with the system of taboos, nostrums, charms, belief in his divinity and other magic by which the lamaist hierarchy exorcised evil spirits, sold absolution, indulgences and prayer wheels, and kept their power.

The Tibetan theocracy was an anomaly which inaccessibility alone preserved into the 1950s. Absolute feudalism prevailed and most people were held in serfdom. The lamas and nobility owned nearly all the land, livestock and other wealth. Fear of devils and hellfire for the impious combined with barbaric torture and death for fugitives from the system kept the population in subjugation, as in other feudalisms.

None of that meant that many Tibetans were not anti-Chinese and would not desire independence. They were no more likely to get it than Kashmir was likely to get a plebiscite on the same subject from India. Certainly a reform and an age of enlightenment under Tibet's own leaders was long overdue and might have salvaged something of Tibetan Buddhism, freed of its lamaistic corruptions. They waited too long for a palace revolt. Chinese Communists arrived first. They began at once to organize poor Tibetans against the lamaist system, unquestionably aiming at the subversion of the whole ruling class. Foreseeing their inevitable doom, the lamas and landed nobles refused to play the role assigned to them in the 'period of transition'. They rebelled and fled into exile, thereby hastening their own downfall but that does not mean the end of Tibet or its people. The land, the mountains, the rivers and the people were still there – a proud people, rugged as their peaks, and likely to prove as obdurate.

Tibet was now held by a large army and probably would be for some years to come. Former Tibetan serfs were trained and armed and labor was conscripted to construct public works. Schools and hospitals and barracks were opened in the lama temples and homes, a modern Tibetan army was being trained, highways now linked China and Lhasa, and the capital saw its first power plant and steel mill. Tibetans who received land and property were being prepared for eventual socialization. Even without Marxism, however, mass literacy and access to science and knowledge of the modern world alone would have doomed the anachronistic Tibetan theocracy together with its prayer wheels and sorcerers.

Tibetan party members receiving technical school and higher education in China now numbered many thousands. Most of them had begun as illiterates. The great majority were being trained to teach in a mass education program in Tibet. It was only in 1962 that 'the first group of Tibetan students of the preparatory specialty class of the Central Minorities Institute [Peking] graduated' and took up 'their posts in the building of a new Tibet'.[5] (Most of them were geologists.) It was stated that 'almost all the group' were children of serfs. Meanwhile, *Chinese* geologists, wasting no time, were busily digging in the no longer inaccessible Tibetan mountains and reported finding many valuable resources.

In 1954, India, having recognized the People's Republic, acknowledged its sovereignty in Tibet, as had the British government before it. Peking gave general assurances that it would respect the 'autonomy' of Tibet; the manner in which it would do so was regarded as an internal affair of China. India's boundaries on Tibet remained undefined except as the British raj had asserted claims there during and before the abortive 1914 tripartite convention. Some disagreement over frontiers looked inevitable as the two governments confronted each other for the first time in Himalayan areas formerly hard to reach. Yet China managed to define a border to the satisfaction of the little kingdom of Nepal, and also reached a boundary settlement with Burma in a give-and-take manner. Why did the Sino-Indian impasse rather suddenly assume a character seemingly as insoluble as India's prolonged impasse with Pakistan over Kashmir?

The Sino-Indian dispute had arisen when India challenged China's right to build a highway to link southern Tibet to Chinese Turkestan. The remoteness and unimportance of the frontier area are suggested by the circumstance that the Tibetan highway had apparently been completed for two years before India discovered it. It was not until 1959 that India made its protest, following a clash between Indian and Chinese patrols which resulted in some casualties. That incident had followed hard upon the flight of the Dalai Lama and a revolt which had some foreign backing and large Indian sympathy. It also followed new American loans to India. The United States, of course, continued to recognize Chiang Kai-shek's régime on Taiwan as the national government of all China. Since Tibet was part of China, the United States might, if it found effective means, actively encourage Chiang Kai-shek's ambitions to 'liberate' Tibet. Reports of C.I.A. activity along the Tibetan border (including air drops of arms and money) may or may not have been true, but they were taken quite seriously in Peking. The Chinese leaders were probably also considerably provoked by Moscow's offers of new aid to Nehru's government just at this time. On the Indian side Mr Nehru was under attack for following an appeasement policy toward China; a 'strong stand' over Tibet was demanded by the exigencies of internal politics to restore the Congress party's then dwindling prestige. Putting all these things together, Peking asserted that India was following policies incompatible with the five principles of peaceful coexistence, that she was maneuvering to get both American and Russian aid in order to oppose the unification of the People's Republic.

In December 1959 I had discussed the border dispute with Prime Minister Nehru in New Delhi at considerable length. Mr Nehru seemed more perplexed by some harsh attacks made against him in the Peking press than by the disagreement that had arisen over the frontier – an event he regarded more philosophically. Then, in October 1960, during an official interview with Chou En-lai, I said:

'Last year Prime Minister Nehru told me that perhaps the basic reason for the Sino-Indian dispute was that both were "new nations", ... newly independent and under dynamic nationalistic leaderships. In a sense they were meeting at their frontiers for the first time in history. ... In the past India was a colony and China a semicolony. The boundary was not so clear and for the administrative needs of that time the boundary did not particularly have to be clearly delineated.'

Premier Chou replied that such was not quite the case. 'China and Burma are also newly independent countries,' he reminded me. Why had it 'been possible for Burma to settle the boundary question with China whereas India had not?' He answered his own question: 'Burma took a *positive* attitude ... India doesn't want to settle the boundary questions. The real idea they have in mind is to turn China's Tibet region into a buffer zone. ... They don't want Tibet to become a Socialist Tibet. That's why after the rebellion was quelled in Tibet they became more dissatisfied and shortly afterwards the Sino-Indian boundary question came to the fore.

'Our stand has been very clear. It is to maintain the status quo and seek a friendly settlement. Even in the case of the so-called Mc-Mahon Line [established by the British and claimed by the Indians] we haven't crossed to the south of it in spite of the fact that we don't recognize it. Neither have we put forward any territorial claims as preconditions to negotiations. But the Indian side is using the Sino-Indian boundary question as a card ... against progressive forces at home [the Indian Communist Party] and as capital for obtaining "foreign aid". There is no conflict of basic interests between the Chinese and Indian peoples. We will be friendly to each other. The present situation is but a temporary phenomenon.'

China could not seriously plan war over the uninhabited and frozen highlands of the Tibetan-Indian frontier. Khrushchev had made it clear that he would not sacrifice India's good will to back China's side in the quarrel. This knowledge may have encouraged India to turn her attention southward for the armed conquest of Goa in December 1961 – perhaps also intended to impress China with India's military efficiency and readiness to use force when it was 'unavoidable', as Mr Nehru put it.

An aggravating factor in Sino-Indian relations (which did not appear in the official exchanges over boundary disputes) was the growing cooperation between Nepal and China. A month after he signed a treaty of peace and friendship with Burma, in March 1960, Chou En-lai visited Kathmandu, the Nepalese capital, and concluded a similar treaty there. This was accompanied by statements that Nepal intended to remain neutral – by implication not only in the cold war, but in any Sino-Indian disputes as well. In the time of the British raj Nepal was a *de facto* British protectorate controlled through a Hindu Rajput family who had kept the native kings (ethnically related to the Tibetan–Mongol race) virtual prisoners for a century. In 1951 the heir to the throne recovered power, however, and a constitutional monarchy was established. In 1960 the reigning monarch dissolved the parliament, arrested the premier, and reoriented Nepalese policy toward complete independence based on strict neutrality. To the irritation of New Delhi, part of China's credit grants to Nepal were used to construct a new highway linking Kathmandu and Lhasa, and built by Chinese engineers. King Mahendra further strengthened his ties with

Peking during a state visit in 1961. Many Indian nationalists believed that India had somehow been cheated out of Nepalese allegiance by Chinese intrigue, and feared that a Chinese policy of ethnic attrition was aimed at aligning all the Mongoloid peoples in the Tibetan-border states with China.

Meanwhile, China improved relations with Afghanistan by diplomatic treaties and the extension of trade credits. Between Nepal and Afghanistan lay the disputed Kashmir border. Adjoining Nepal was the principality of Bhutan, separated from Nepal by the former Tibetan principality of Sikkim, over which the British established a protectorate in 1930. Both areas also had populations of Tibetan ethnic affinity. Far to the east, north of Burma, were other undefined borders along tribal highlands which the British designated simply 'The North-east Frontier Agency'. There the Indian army had been busy, ever since the British left, trying to suppress an independence movement among the Naga tribesmen.

On balance, it was clear that China had firmly returned to central Asia as a major Himalayan power for the first time in two hundred years. New Delhi obviously would prefer a softer frontier than she was now likely to get. It was certain, however, that neither India nor China could seriously plan to use major military means to win a 'map victory' in largely uninhabitable wastelands of no real value to either power.*

---

* After this chapter was written, the Chinese launched, early in October 1962, what Peking described as a 'counterattack' against Indian forces attempting to establish Indian outposts, on the flanks of Chinese positions, in order to restore what New Delhi described as the correct international boundary in Ladakh. In a month the Chinese army cleared India's forces from some 35,000 square miles of frontier territory. Just as suddenly, in November, Peking announced a unilateral cease-fire and a withdrawal of Chinese troops behind what were defined as positions held by China's frontier guards as of 1959. Peking asserted that it was India's violation of those lines, after 1959, which had caused the border conflict. Just as vehemently India insisted that the Chinese had precipitated the clash by illegal southward advances between 1957 and 1959 – which India had first formally protested in 1959. At the time of the cease-fire China also offered to withdraw twenty kilometers behind her 1959 line, provided India would refrain from reoccupying a zone of equal size on her side. Following the Chinese with-

drawal, Peking proposed that the two powers confer in order to set up a joint commission to survey new and mutually satisfactory boundaries. In 1963, China carried out her unilateral pronouncements and returned captured Indian soldiers and equipment. New Delhi was considering China's terms, as they applied to eastern Ladakh, to create a forty-kilometer no man's land between the two forces on either side of the 1959 line.

Both parties conceded that maps inherited by India from the British raj left large areas in the disputed frontiers marked 'boundary undefined'. Both India and China had attempted to impose unilateral definitions of those boundaries by force. The resulting limited conflict hardly constituted a Chinese 'war of foreign conquest', however, as some Washington officials, and much of the Western press, alleged.

A compromise whereby India would concede China's claims to the northern Ladakh corridor (and the legality of the existing Chinese strategic Sinkiang–Tibet highway there), in exchange for China's recognition of a boundary north of Assam (which would approximate the McMahon Line but would be resurveyed and renamed), seemed an eventual likelihood.

(1970) It still does. The positions taken up by Chinese troops have been accepted, *de facto*, by India, in a no-war and no-settlement situation which has prevailed till now.

In 1969 Indira Gandhi, India's prime minister, reached for a thaw in Sino-Indian relations; she publicly declared her readiness to reopen discussions, without the conditions previously insisted upon by India. When that offer drew no immediate response from China Mrs Gandhi was rebuked by Indian critics. But in 1970, as Mao emerged triumphant from the Great Proletarian Cultural Revolution, and moved into the arena of foreign diplomacy on a wide front following the opening provided by the American thrust into Cambodia, indications were that Peking might again seek negotiations with India on the basis of the status quo. For a careful study with 'insight' by *The Times'* former South Asia correspondent in a book which brought the Sino-Indian frontier conflict up to date, consult *India's China War*, by Neville Maxwell, Jonathan Cape, London, 1970.

73

National Minorities

'MINORITIES' in China cover a lot more territory than Tibet. The province of Yunnan alone holds about four times as many non-Chinese as there are Tibetans in Tibet. In preparation for a trip to Yunnan I spent a day at the Institute of National Minorities in Peking. There I found 2,600 students of forty-seven different nationalities (including 900 Tibetans), who were using twenty different languages in the acquisition of more or less higher education and training as teachers and party cadres.

That large institution symbolized the fact that more than sixty percent of China's area was 'autonomous' homeland for non-Han peoples. If all the autonomous areas were put together they would about equal the size of Europe without Russia. Most of them were on China's frontiers, but minority communities were scattered all through China. Altogether they numbered about 43,000,000. (See the map of minority nationalities on page 20.)

Autonomous Inner Mongolia had more Mongols than its brother state of Outer Mongolia, and more Tibetans lived in Sikang, Chinghai, Kansu, Szechuan and Yunnan than in Tibet. Autonomous Sinkiang had five million Uighurs and half a million Kazakhs on the borders of Soviet Kazakhstan. In Yunnan lived a million Shans closely related to the northern Burmans and Thais. Above Indochina were other Thai and Chuang cousins of the Lao people of Laos and northern Thailand. Isolated civilizations among more than a hundred tribal and minority peoples of China varied from naked forest folk who had never built houses of any kind, to highly cultured and advanced societies like that of the Shans, who ruled an empire a thousand years ago which covered much of Yunnan and South Asia. Generally speaking, the minorities preceded the Han in eastern Asia and had been very slowly pushed southward by them. Ranging from tribal or semitribal to feudal and semifeudal societies, they had agrarian or mixed pastoral-agrarian economies. Some of the Yi people in Yunnan used to plant grain as the American Indians did. They took a sharp stick, poked it in the ground, dropped a grain of corn into the hole, and uttered a prayer for good weather.

Minority peoples did not readily intermarry with the Han and were hostile to them. The Han looked down on them as barbarians and aborigines. Ruling powers in China recognized chieftains among them and collected taxes and tribute when they could catch them. The Nationalists had barely begun attempts to gather them into the form of a larger Chinese state. Communists were the first to reach them with a fully integrated theory providing a place for them in a 'China Union'. With it began a real effort to proselytize and sinicize on a mass scale.

At the Institute of National Minorities I was met by Professor Lin Yao-hua, director of the History Department. He was a former professor of history and ethnology at Peking University. A graduate of Yenching and Harvard (1941), he had returned to China in 1946 and begun to specialize in nationalities questions. He would not converse with me directly in English. With him was Chang K'ai-yu, a secretary in the dean's office. Chang was obviously the Party representative and Professor Lin the responsible academician.

The Institute covered nearly two acres and had twenty-one buildings, including classrooms and dormitories. Four large halls with Chinese roofs faced a newly tree-planted campus. Flanking the next garden were new homes for a faculty of 370, who managed four departments at the university level, a middle school and a primary school. All food, clothing and living quarters were supplied by the state and students received a stipend.

The populations of Sinkiang, Inner Mongolia, Tibet, the Moslem regions and the Chuang area of Kwangsi accounted for about three fourths of all non-Han peoples. In addition to those territories there were fifty-four autonomous counties and 269 autonomous districts of township size or larger. All these areas had local governments organized like the rest of China, but their school systems were generally more backward. The central nationalities institute trained new teaching personnel qualified both academically and politically to speed up progress and bring literacy and ideological development abreast of the country as a whole. Eight provinces had special training institutes but the central institute was the only university exclusively for the training of national minority party cadres. Non-Hans could and did enter ordinary Chinese schools on an equal footing. Peking had also built a striking multistory edifice called the Museum of National Minorities which offered any visitor a fascinating visual education on the whole subject.

The Chinese Communists carried out a policy of preservation and protection of distinctive cultural characteristics of the different nationalities, their languages, costumes, folklore, music, and traditions, just as in the U.S.S.R. It was a patriarchal relationship. The aim was to give the minorities self-governing socialist systems. Party membership among them in 1961 exceeded a quarter of a million.

I have mentioned that China was now constitutionally defined as a 'unified multinational state' while Russia was merely a 'multinational state'. According to Professor Lin, since the Han Dynasty all peoples had been equally members of a unified China. For 2,000 years China had not been an 'imperialist' state. In the 1840s China became a semicolonial country and all its peoples were alike oppressed. They all finally became free only in 1949, in Professor Lin's theory. Tsarist Russia, on the other hand, was an imperialist country which held many smaller nations in subjugation, Professor Lin continued. When revolution occurred it liberated both Russia's working class and the colonial nations. As these nations were already 'bourgeois nationalist' states they had to be recognized as 'autonomous republics' with national political autonomy. In China the minorities never reached the stage of 'bourgeois nationalist' states. They were minority *nationalities* but minorities of the one *nationality* they shared with the Han majority – that is, 'Chinese'.

That official rationalization was accepted by neither Soviet nor non-Marxist scholars. Chinese history is replete with occasions of aggressive expansion in no significant way different from more modern imperialisms. All China's frontier territories, including Manchuria, Mongolia, Sinkiang, Tibet and even Yunnan, are inhabited by non-Han peoples or tribes conquered, absorbed or minimized within the records of writen history. It is also true that China was often the victim of aggression and for long centuries was dominated by barbarian conquerors who eventually lost their identity in China – most recently the Manchus. Meanwhile, other neighbors, pushed southward by the Chinese, themselves aggressed against weaker peoples – a notable example being the Vietnamese and Thai obliteration of the Khmers, whose survivors, today's Cambodians, once dominated most of Indo-China.

While armed conquests certainly did not end with the Han Dynasty, it might be said that the boundaries of China as we know it today were fixed in the Han *mind*, without yet having been completely fulfilled. That Chinese Communists did not admit that such a thing as Chinese imperialism had ever existed was no more difficult to comprehend than the conviction held among many intelligent Americans (in which category all congressmen may be included to avoid argument) that the United States had never been imperialistic, or overrun weaker peoples and their territories, despite quite recent events which flatly belied them.

In Kunming, Yunnan, I visited another 'national minorities' school with 1,676 students of twenty-two different cultural-linguistic backgrounds. Six million non-Han people lived in Yunnan alone. The Yi were the most numerous and the Pai (close to the Siamese) exceeded 600,000. This province operated a number of party and normal training schools on the county level. Obviously the main emphasis in Kunming was on political training, but a full middle school curriculum was offered, with much music and dancing.

The Kunming Institute had a fine campus with a swimming pool, modern buildings, and an excellent library and science laboratory. Its faculty of ninety teachers included fifty-five non-Hans. Teachers and students to whom I spoke no longer believed in Buddhism, Lamaism, Islamism or Christianity. (Some of the Chins and Kachins among them had been baptized.) They were there solely to master Marxism and science techniques to carry back to their villages as leaders and preachers of the new gospel.

I happened to visit the Kunming school when students were preparing for an autumn festival. The girls wore silk and velvet costumes of vivid colors and sang and danced to orchestras of native instruments. They were as full of vivacity and excitement as teen-agers engaged in the same exhibitionism anywhere else. Their Communist teachers had not forgotten that man does not live by politics alone.

Part Seven

THE LONG MARCH AHEAD

MAO TSE-TUNG told me that as long as he was alive China would never resort to international war as a means of settling disputes, but that China would always oppose the export of counterrevolution.

'We on our part will shoulder the responsibility of world peace,' Mao said he wished the American people to understand, 'whether or not the United States recognizes China, or whether or not we get into the United Nations. We will not defy all laws, human and divine, like the Monkey King who stormed the Palace of Heaven. We want to maintain world peace. We do not want war. We hold that war should not be used as a means to settle disputes between nations. However, not only China but the United States, as well, has the responsibility to maintain peace.'

He added: 'Taiwan is China's affair. We will insist on this.'

'And those who have nothing to lose are beginning to understand that only militant struggles against oppression can assure for them a life worthy of being called human. And they are the immense majority of the world. To them, the thought of Mao Tse-tung is the way to the future. ... China's position and prestige in the world is growing and there is no part of the world where she is not known; and though every effort is made to make her feared, yet many more do not fear but welcome what she is and what she has done.'

Han Suyin, *Asia Today*, 1969

74

South of the Clouds

KUNMING, capital of Yunnan province, was the only city in China where I was awakened by the sound of gunfire. At the airport, enlarged since General Chennault's Flying Tigers used it during the Second World War, I had noticed more than two hundred MIG fighters lined up – the only field I saw in joint use by civilian and military planes. Coming into the old city on a broad paved highway we skirted a collection of two- and three-storey buildings, brown brick with brown tile roofs, spread over many acres. They housed a military academy for cadets of the army and air force. Around it lay extensive fields of grain and vegetables where soldiers could be seen operating tractors and combines. On a nearby artillery range daily target practice gave the city a reveille and a reminder that Yunnan bordered on Vietnam, in the southern half of which were American air bases. 'Imperialist planes', the Chinese alleged, frequently violated the air space of both North Vietnam and Yunnan.

The weather in Kunming was as perfect as I remembered, and the air as bracing. Kunming is called 'the city of eternal spring', and it is. Just above the tropical zone, it has an elevation of 6,400 feet and is rarely too hot or too cold. Rainfall is adequate but the skies are clear most of the year; the Kunming plain, encircled by blue hills, is usually flooded with sunshine. Yunnan means 'south of the clouds' and most of them do stop abruptly where the plateau leaves Kweichow, to the north, shrouded in mists.

When I was twenty-four I traveled by caravan across Yunnan westward from Kunming to Tali Lake and then to the south over the upper Mekong and Salween rivers, down to the Irrawaddy and Upper Burma (fascinating land of giant 'singing' bamboos, parakeets, rhododendrons, camellias, azaleas, flame trees, wild monkeys and wild elephants). There were no roads and the steep trails over the ancient mountains were slow going; the 500-mile trek took six weeks. Much of the time we were in bandit country; we hired Chinese soldiers as bodyguards at one yuan a day, which generally went for opium. It was not until the Second World War that a motor road was opened to Burma.

New highways now linked all neighboring provinces and one saw trucks and buses far in the interior. The spectacular French-built railway from Haiphong and Hanoi, in Indochina, to Kunming, was being changed from narrow to standard gauge. There was still no direct railway connection to the China coast but goods from Kunming could take the roundabout route down to Hanoi and thence overland to Hanoi–Kwangchow-wan and Canton, on a line completed during the Vietnamese war of independence against the French. Two other railways were approaching Yunnan, one from Fukien province, on the seaboard, and the other from Szechuan via Kweichow.

Before 1949 there was virtually no modern industry in Yunnan. A traveler by air today could observe new towns built around small power and steel plants, with blue-water reservoirs nestling in the hills nearby. Amazingly, as far north as Loyang I had seen large lathes and other machine tools marked 'made in Yunnan'. The Yunnan plateau's rich agricultural land was limited to much less than ten percent of the total area, but the province was well endowed with other natural resources: tin, copper, mercury, zinc, antimony, phosphorus, cinnabar, manganese, placer gold, vast hydroelectric potentials, forest reserves, and recently discovered coal and iron said to be adequate for regional industrialization. Yunnan's tin deposits were among the largest in the world and output already accounted for two thirds of China's exports of the metal.

The province had an area as large as Poland and East Germany but less than half (approximately 21,000,000) their combined populations. Much of the western region, of lordly mountains and great river divides, was uninhabitable. In the south, Yunnan's border territories were largely populated by hill peoples closely related to natives of adjoining northern Burma, Laos and Vietnam. Kunming was full of outlanders now. Since 1949 its population had quadrupled, to reach nearly a million by 1961, and its area had tripled. New factories and apartments sprawled far into the suburbs;

structures of brick and cement were rising everywhere. The old city walls seemed entirely gone. Streets were widened and paved and old buildings replaced and renovated so that I could recognize few landmarks except the stately beauty of the eucalyptus trees which still lined the canal that used to fill a city moat. A broad main thoroughfare busy with trucks and buses led me into the wide plaza dominated by a three-story department store fairly well stocked with consumer goods.

A thing new to me: I saw on the clean streets (something new in itself, for Yunnan) white-clad women wearing gauze nose masks and pushing along carts from which they ladled out milk, half a pint to each child for the equivalent of four cents. When I tried to buy some I received an astonished stare; it was for children only. Popsicles were sold to both adults and children, however, and at the industrial fair there were Eskimo pies. In the evening, bookstores were crowded; I saw many cheap prints, lithographs, posters and even some postcard reproductions of Western art, but nothing abstract. Watching a young officer shyly studying a photograph of Rodin's 'The Kiss',* I wondered what he would think of *Playboy*. Stores were offering food, clothing and household articles in some abundance and at relatively low prices. Among items I noted as unusual were a brace of fat ducks for seven yuan, and a five-pound Yunnan smoked ham for ten. It was suggested to me that transportation and export to other provinces being still difficult and expensive, Yunnan's own products largely remained in the home market.

On my last visit to Kunming, in 1945, it had still lacked a single good hotel. Now there were several, including the modern Western-style hotel in the eastern suburb where I had a large room and bath, with meals, for four dollars a day. Across the street stood a new municipal hall and around us were many new apartment buildings. A few blocks down the main street I visited the industrial exhibition, where I saw Yunnan-made buses, pumps, generators, textile machinery, telephone equipment, radios, motorcycles, cigarette-making machines, musical instruments, lathes, diesel engines,

---

*(1970) Even such mildly 'erotic' Western art as reproductions of Rodin disappeared from shops, to correspond to puritanical standards of the Great Proletarian Cultural Revolution (1966–9).

cranes, drills, small tractors, hardware and electrical appliances, scales, surgical instruments, perfume, toilet water, and a variety of textiles – including one cotton print with a design that mystified me: Christmas trees bearing electric lights (possibly for some of the Christian Min Chia people?). A bantam two-cylinder car was also displayed; I was told that production thus far was only 120 vehicles; they cost 4,000 yuan each.

'Yunnanfu [Kunming] smelled of opium everywhere; pipes and lamps were sold in all the markets; the drug was as easy to buy as rice,' I wrote, in *Journey to the Beginning*, of the old city as it was when I first saw it. 'Demoralization and impoverishment were especially apparent in the abuse of children, who are exploited all over China but nowhere quite so unconscionably as in Yunnan … Poverty in other parts of China also obliged the very poor to sell their surplus daughters … but except in deep famine conditions they rarely sold their sons. In Yunnan large numbers of boys were in servitude.'

Poppy cultivation had greatly declined and opium paraphernalia were not so openly sold during the time of American use of Yunnan as an air base, but man's inhumanity to man had not much changed. Whatever evils the new régime had brought, all children now enjoyed fairly equal opportunity to make the most of what was offered: health care, education, recreation – and the 'iron rice bowl'. Goiter, which used to be widespread, had been eliminated by iodinization of the water; trachoma, smallpox and other epidemic diseases were, as elsewhere, disappearing. Stunted, naked runts, illiterate boy slaves, were in former days notoriously exploited in the primitive tin mines at Kochiu. Now those mines were worked by modern methods and by adults who lived in clean dry houses, married, had families, and sent their children to school – in a valley with electric trolleys and tramlines, where tin production was sixteen times the 1949 output.[1] In the hills there were sanatoria for workers, and hot baths and ultraviolet treatments were available.

When I traveled through Yunnan in the 1930s and 1940s most *Han-jen* still regarded the 'barbarians', as they called the non-Hans, with contempt. Distrust and hostility were mutual. For the most part Chinese ruled the plains while the tribal folk lived in the highlands and forests, where Chinese seldom ventured alone. Did the non-Hans now like Red Chinese any better? I could take no poll. I have mentioned the Kunming Institute of National Minorities, which symbolized a very real and systematic effort to improve relations with the Yunnan aborigines. Chinese-speaking students trained there were to become political and cultural leaders of four large autonomous districts and seven autonomous counties of the province. Tribal peoples did obviously share a new equality of opportunity. There was widespread integration; to see the Lolo mingling freely with Chinese in work and social activities was truly remarkable when one remembered the past. They had proportional representation in provincial and national government organs. Under the Communists, stage, screen, television and art were widely used to popularize tribal songs, dances, folklore and differences in physiognomy and stature, dress, coiffure and culture which distinguish the non-Hans from the Hans.

A mixed community of Han and non-Han farmers operated the last commune I saw before I left China. This was in an autonomous administrative area of the Kuan-tu district, on the outskirts of Kunming. Of its 21,000 adults sixty-two percent were Min Chia (San Mei) and Lolo (Yi) and the rest were Han Chinese. The area was divided into four brigades. In the Ala brigade, which I visited, the chairman was a Han, the two vice-chairmen were Lolo, the party secretary was a Min Chia, and the head of the women's work department was a Lolo girl. Through an interpreter I asked the girl just who had elected her.

'My friends,' she said. She was pockmarked, homely, and had an honest smile.

'Why do they like you?'

'Well, it may be like this. I worked hard. I was a serf in the lord's house here doing dirty work until I was eleven. I'm twenty-three now. After liberation I was given some land. I raised more cabbages than the others and was asked to lead a mutual-aid team. Comrades taught me to read and write characters. Then I began teaching others. I took an interest in politics and life became better. I am a hard worker and like to help others.'

'What women's work do you do?'

'Many things. I see that women get their equal rights. For instance, we have three rules that must be observed for expectant mothers : no field work for fifty days, hot water for their feet, and special food such as spinach. What else? I propagandize among women. To do that I must study and understand government policies and be able to explain them to others. It's not easy to get understanding. Many women are timid and don't want to be involved.'

Near the large village that served as brigade headquarters many men and women, some in tribal costume, some Han, were feeding grain into a small red threshing machine, which separated the grain and threw out straw that had to be stacked. It was a new commune purchase and more people were watching, fascinated, than working. According to the chairman the threshing machine had been paid for entirely by cash profits of the commune on its output of rice, wheat, rape and vegetables.

The village was rather dirty and seemed to be getting little attention – compared to the new poultry pens with electric incubators. A few hundred feet away from the commune clinic, which stood apart from the village in a whitewashed mud and straw building, there was a surprisingly modern-looking structure of two stories, with balconies and a tile roof. I was told that it was new commune housing but no one seemed particularly anxious to show it to me. I went off by myself to photograph it and was followed by the party secretary. The building was divided into about forty apartments of one or two rooms each, with wooden floors. Most of the doors were open; in all the building I found only one flat occupied – by a Lolo woman with two small children.

'Nobody seems to be living here !' I said.

'Not many,' the secretary responded.

'Why not?'

'Oh, there will be more. It takes time to persuade people to leave the village. They have to get used to the new ways slowly.'

Here was a commune where it seemed obvious that somebody had gone ahead inflexibly following higher directives calling for communal housing; public opinion may now have been casting a belated veto. Dirty, dark, mud-floored as the old village huts were, they were peasant-owned 'homes' and probably preferred, with their few chickens and pigs moored in the muddy back yards, to the strange new many-familied building – even if it did have glass window panes and a promise of electric lights.

Here, as occasionally elsewhere – though not universally – I sensed that the guarantee of a fixed abode on a fixed piece of land was more important to many conservative peasant families than all the modern improvements. The advanced cooperative was still able to satisfy that traditional attachment. The scrambling of land and dwellings in the early commune often threatened it before the peasants were psychologically prepared to accept personal de-identification with the land in exchange for identification with a broader structure of security. Commune reforms after 1959 were directed largely toward restoring that sense of security in the peasantry. It would remain an important part of peasant incentive until a more advanced and stable industrialization could offer greater guarantees than at present.*

At my hotel I met a number of Burmese army officers who had just come up by highway from Bhamo, and from their accounts I gathered that western Yunnan was also being rapidly transformed. Hsiao-kuan, at the southern end of Lake Erh Hai, near Tali, was building a power plant with a 250,000-kilowatt capacity. Industries there included a small steel mill, a sugar refinery, an agricultural implements factory, and glass and cement works. Numerous dams had been constructed and small hydroelectric plants now provided power and light, generated by dynamos made in Yunnan, to many towns that a decade ago had still depended on wicks burning rape oil, as when I first passed through them.

The secretary of the Kunming branch of the Peace Committee, a Mr Chang, drove me to the airport late in November on another cool, blue-sky-perfect Kunming day. Above the buildings a light breeze snapped the five-starred flag of China as if in farewell to me. A customs officer unpacked my bags and stacked some fifty rolls of Kodachrome and several thousand feet of 8- and 16-millimeter film on the table. Most of it was unprocessed. In Peking I had been assured that I would be permitted to take out unprocessed film; I

*A Central Committee directive in 1961 restored, 'permanently', peasant family ownership of homes and private plots. Communal housing projects were abandoned. Communal dining, made entirely optional by individual choice, largely disappeared.

knew the same courtesy had been granted to Henri Cartier-Bresson*
and others. I had taken hundreds of exposures without any record
being kept of them – many were made during casual walks alone
– and I had no special photographer's permit. Now that I looked at
the collection it seemed quite a lot – for the needs of a historian. I
expressed some apprehension to Mr Chang.

'Don't worry,' he said. He spoke a few words to the official, who
gave me an appraising look. 'American?' he asked. 'You're the only
one we've seen here in ten years!' I exchanged the few yuan (export of which is strictly prohibited) I possessed, the officer replaced
my belongings neatly in my bags, and I was cleared for departure.
'Yi-p'ing hao lu!' he said. 'Peaceful journey!'

'Please tell the American people,' Mr Chang reminded me
gravely, 'that we have the friendliest feelings toward them – always
have had and always will have. It is only –'

'The American imperialist government that you detest?' I finished for him.

'That's right.'

I thanked him for all he had done to show me around the city;
he had been really helpful.

'To peace, then,' he said as we shook hands.

'To peace,' I echoed. 'That is one commodity of which it may be
said that the more we keep it ourselves the more we give it to
others.'

Mr Chang held up his thumb enthusiastically. 'That's good. You
tell that to Washington!'

In three hours I was in Rangoon and the next day I was united
with my family again, in Europe.

---

*Conditional only on his promise that captions used on his photographs
would present the facts they represented, rather than be distorted to suit
cold-war propaganda needs. I made the same commitment.

75

Facts About Food*

THROUGHOUT 1959–62 many Western press editorials and head-lines referred to 'mass starvation' in China and continued to cite no supporting facts. As far as I know, no report by any non-Communist visitor to China provided an authenticated instance of starvation during this period.[1] Here I am not speaking of food shortages, or lack of surfeit, to which I have made frequent reference, but of mass deaths from hunger, which is what 'famine' connotes to most of us, and what I saw in the past. I assert that I saw no starving people in China, nothing that looked like old-time famine (and only one beggar, among flood refugees in Shenyang); and that the best Western intelligence on China was well aware of this. Isolated instances of starvation due to neglect or failure of the rationing system were possible. Considerable malnutrition undoubtedly existed. Mass starvation? No.

On 31 July, 1962, Richard Starnes reported in the *New York World Telegram*, immediately following a trip to eastern Asia: 'There is not one shred of evidence known to the West that famine threatens Communist China. ... Red China's army is still well-fed. There is no indication available to Western observers that the army is no longer loyal or would not fight, and fight very hard. ... The hard, simple truth is that American policy cannot prevail in Southeast Asia or anywhere else in the world as long as it is based on myth and wishful thinking.'

Chinese officials nowadays took starvation very seriously; to believe that, one need not credit the party leadership with humanitarianism. Many Westerners did not understand that in order to

---

*(1970) At this writing China's food supply (for a population of about 750,000,000) had reached a point of stable growth which may make this detailed examination seem unnecessary. The chapter is retained as an aid to perspective in judging the historical achievements of the régime.

maintain its own image of itself the party *must* see that people are fed. 'People are China's asset', but if they do not eat they cannot study or work; if they do not study and work they cannot produce; if they do not produce there is no growth; if there is no growth the system is a failure.

But the food *shortage* remained real. This was nothing new. 'According to a study made from historical records,' a Chinese scholar in exile has said, 'it was found that between 108 B.C. and A.D. 1911 there were 1,828 famines, or one almost every year. Potential or actual famine is so much a part of cultural expectation that official figures included a factor for famine in the normal death rate.' [2] What was new was that millions of people were not starving, as they did throughout chronic famine in the twenties, thirties and forties. What was new was that an equitable rationing system had been enforced for the first time. What was nearly unbelievable was that a government existed in China which (whatever else history could charge against it) actually kept enough foreign currency out of the pockets of officials to be able to pay hard cash for millions of tons of grain imported after the harvest failures of 1960 – rather than beg from the United States, as normal people did.

Were the 1960 calamities actually as severe as reported by Peking – 'the worst series of disasters since the nineteenth century', as Chou En-lai told me? Weather was not the only cause of the disappointing harvest but it was undoubtedly a major cause. With good weather the crops would have been ample; without it, other adverse factors I have cited – some discontent in the communes, bureaucracy, transportation bottlenecks – made things worse. The impact on Chinese peasant psychology of three years of bad weather in *combination* with commune innovations was recognized by policy changes in 1961–2 which, as we have seen, abandoned ultra-advanced socialist aims and restored many incentives to individual enterprise. Agricultural recovery became China's major preoccupation.

In surplus-burdened America we have no rainfall problem comparable to the vagaries of the Yellow River Valley. Bad weather over a few states brings no national hardships. For China, living very close to the margins of want, and where food cereals make up three fourths to four fifths of the average diet (compared to less than one fifth in the United States), a harvest drop of twenty percent in a single year meant immediate privation.

In the best year of her history, 1958, China probably exceeded American cereal output, running at low speed. In highly mechanized, deep-plowed American croplands, using 25,000,000 tons of chemical fertilizer, one farm laborer feeds thirty-six people; in China, with only five or six percent of her farmland mechanized thus far, and producing less than 3,000,000 tons of chemical fertilizer,* one farm laborer could feed only three people [3] – if the weather cooperated. But comparisons between China and the United States – which alone accounted for nearly half the world's exports of grain – were less significant than comparisons between China and other less-favored nations.

China's food reserves had already been severely reduced to compensate for the very disappointing harvest of 1959. In 1960 many reservoirs and shallow wells dried up, the Yellow River again failed the people of Shantung, and other caprices recurred. In these years harvests were lost or minimized over such wide areas that large-scale famine was avoided only because yields in fortunate provinces were extraordinarily good; because state grain collection and distribution was somehow accomplished despite still very backward transportation facilities; because a policy of maximum local self-sufficiency was promoted by utilizing marginal land either as private plots or collectively for emergency gardens; because a strict rationing system was effected with frugality and reasonable equity by people made fully conscious of a national emergency; and because in all these policies the state was able to utilize the interdependent and mutual-help system of collective or commune society.

Finally, in January 1961 – belatedly but just in time – the government reversed itself on its cherished road of priority for the expansion of heavy industry. Having done so, it focused the nation's major efforts on an all-out attempt to produce adequate harvests – a goal which it had boastfully proclaimed solved, and which it now humbly admitted had not been solved, back in 1958.

What was the actual extent of China's harvest failures or successes, how did output compare with that of other nations in

---

*(1970) China's output of chemical fertilizer by 1969 reportedly exceeded 10 million tons.

trouble, what was the average person now getting to eat, and what prospect of improvement was there, if any? I have already given scattered testimony to these questions; here it seems necessary to offer some general perspective. Any attempt of this kind is bound to involve the reader in rather heavy material, to follow the unraveling of a mystery story; it is worth the effort because China's food problem is a matter of cosmic proportions and affects the entire world.

What is an adequate diet? World health authorities do not agree that it is the 3,000 to 3,500 calories which the average American or Englishman is supposed to get. Unless he is expending extraordinary energy, any person consuming that much is overeating, a disease perhaps more common in the United States than malnutrition in China. The average middle-class American family probably wastes and throws away enough food every day to answer the minimal needs of an average Chinese, Japanese or Vietnamese family. For nongourmands a minimum of 2,000–2,200 calories in balanced diet is adequate [4] except for heavy workers; when average consumption falls below 1,750 calories over a considerable period, deficiency diseases develop. It has been calculated by both Western and Chinese specialists that to get this average the Chinese needs about 1,500 calories in grain, in addition to a minimum of 500 he is able to get from other food items.

To provide 700,000,000 people with 1,500 calories in cereals every day requires a gross annual crop of about 180,000,000 metric tons of grain or its equivalent in potatoes and soya beans. A smaller gross crop may suffice only if there is considerable reduction of normal allowances for fodder, seed grain, reserves, waste and nonfood uses or if other sources of food energy are widely developed.

Had China been able to produce 180,000,000 tons? Here we tread upon ground highly speculative after the Great Leap began. The Bureau of Statistics' estimate of 108,000,000 tons output for 1949 is generally considered an understatement designed to indicate a high rate of growth in subsequent years, but most Western economists accepted the following official figures as approximately correct: 1953, at 156,000,000 tons; 1955, at 174,000,000 tons; 1957, at 185,000,000 tons. [5]

I have commented on the 1958 aberrations (which carried over to mid-1959) when 'politics in command of statistics' brought fantastic results. Revisions of overclaims reduced official figures for 1958 grain output to 261,000,000 tons and, still later, to 250,000,000 tons; 1959 output was first put at 281,000,000 tons. Only a government stronger and more self-confident than any modern China had known before could have accepted the 'loss of face' entailed by admissions of error on so humiliating a scale. Even these greatly reduced figures for 1958 and 1959 were indirectly recognized, in conversations I had with Chinese officials in 1960, as still involving serious overstatements.

Since the 1959 'anti-buoyant exaggeration' reform began in the Bureau of Statistics, no comprehensive agricultural returns had been released at all.* Chou En-lai's statement to me that the 1960 harvest was poorer than 1958 and 1959 but 'higher than 1957' remained a principal clue which Western specialists in Chinese agrarian affairs employed in arriving at latest estimates. On this basis one expert suggested that China's grain output in 1960 might have been 'something on the order of 190,000,000 tons'.[6]

I am able to offer some additional information which gives a much lower and, I believe, more realistic estimate of the extent of the 1960 setback. In my interview with Wu Chen, Vice-Minister of Agriculture, he referred to 1956 and 1959 as 'bad years', indicating that the harvest increase, if any, fell below population growth on both occasions. It seems that 1959 not only did not exceed 1958 production but likely fell as low as 190,000,000 tons, or even less. Mr Wu said that the 1960 grain tax of 24,000,000 tons was 'based on a maximum of twelve percent tax on the 1958 crop'. That would indicate a taxable crop of 200,000,000 tons for 1958.† The grain

* (1970) In interviews with the writer in 1964 and 1965 Chou En-lai indicated that the 1963 harvest was between 185,000,000 and 190,000,000 tons, and that the 1964 output was a bit more or less than 200,000,000. In consensus, foreign China specialists in Hongkong reached estimates of between 210,000,000 and 215,000,000 tons for 1966, described by the mainland press as 'the greatest crop year in Chinese history'.

† In a conversation with Yung Lung-kuei, of the Bureau of Statistics, the 'maximum' tax rate was given as thirteen percent, which would mean a slightly lower output for 1958. The taxable harvest was lower than the gross output, however, as it excluded private plots and considerable above-quota peasant production and consumption.

tax was to be held fixed for three or four years. Mr Wu added:
'Even if the 1960 harvest should reach as high as 250,000,000 tons
the tax will still be only 24,000,000 tons.' The intimation to me
was that 250,000,000 tons was now regarded as a high aspiration
yet to be attained.

Chou En-lai's comment, quoted above, was made 18 October
1960. A visiting foreign economist who was consulted by Chou
En-lai on statistical method in the formulation of crop estimates
later told me that in his presence the Prime Minister had berated
top statisticians for bringing him revised figures which showed that
their earlier estimates had been *twenty percent* above what now
seemed the probable expectation. That was in mid-November. If
190,000,000 tons was something like their earlier estimates, a reduction by twenty percent would bring it down to 152,000,000 tons.
That was my own guess for the probable 1960 harvest.

Such an estimate would correspond also with what Marshal
Montgomery was told in a long interview he had with Mao Tse-
tung late in 1961. 'The normal grain harvest in China is about 180
million tons; in 1960 it was 150 million tons and the forecast for
1961 was ten million tons more,' wrote Lord Montgomery in para-
phrasing his conversation with Mao. 'They had used up all their
reserves of grain during the past *three years* to feed the nation; they
now had to build up fresh reserves.' [7]

Nevertheless, it thus seemed probable that China's grain product
in 1960 was seventeen to twenty percent below 'normal grain harvest' and that the full extent of the inflated estimates for 1958 and
1959 had at last been fully recognized. The imperative necessity
for a massive campaign to grow additional food by all means, and
to halt most new capital construction while industry concentrated
its output on improving the tools of agriculture, became obvious.
Measures were initiated such as I have mentioned seeing used –
private gardens, private poultry and pig raising, wide cultivation
of marginal land for fodder (especially sweet potatoes) and for
human consumption – as well as the return of certain acreages
planted in cotton, hemp, tobacco and other 'cash crops' to the production of food.

Reports abroad had given somewhat distorted impressions of the
amount of food exported by China. That seemed to have been held

to less than two percent, more than half of which was soya beans up to 1955, according to figures supplied by Ch'en Yun in a reply to questions raised in the second session of the National Congress. The rice China exported to Cuba – in exchange for much-needed sugar – and the small tonnages sent to a few other countries to fulfill barter contracts, altogether amounted to a bagatelle in relation to internal consumption. The fact was that China became a heavy grain importer in 1961, buying outright 6,466,000 tons of foreign grain, for 1961–3 deliveries, at a cost of $367,000,000.

Crop failures and the drain on foreign exchange to buy food abroad not only halted domestic industrial expansion but depressed a promising foreign trade. Agricultural products still contributed a little over one-third of the value of China's industrial output as a whole. About half the national revenue came 'directly or indirectly from agriculture', while 'over seventy percent of the total volume of exports [was] agricultural products or processed agricultural goods [textiles, etc]'.[8] In 1950, China's exports and imports amounted to only $2,000,000,000; by 1959 they had reached $6,000,000,000, and showed a growing balance in China's favor. Sixty to eighty percent of this trade had been oriented to the Communist bloc; in 1959 a shift to non-Communist countries resulted in an exchange of products valued at $1,500,000,000. That alone was more than China's total world trade before the war. Until 1961 well over ninety percent of all China's imports had been machinery or other capital goods. The proportion of her own exports of industrial and mining products rose from nine percent in 1950 to twenty-seven percent in 1958, while her exports of agricultural raw materials and products fell from fifty-eight percent to thirty-six percent. In 1961, however, trade with the U.S.S.R. declined twenty percent, and with most other countries fell off fifty percent or more.*

Even if the Chinese in one year consumed all the grain scheduled for delivery from abroad, it would have added less than 100 grams to the average daily diet. As I have emphasized, rations in China were not equally distributed, except among children. They were

---

* (1970) In 1967–8 China's trade with Russia and Eastern Europe had declined to about twenty percent of the total, while Japan, Western Europe, and Hongkong were overwhelmingly favored as trading partners.

based on the amount and kind of work performed and, to some extent, on the estimate of his needs which every individual, after 'examining his conscience', was required to make. Late in 1960 I was told by Yao I-lin that the national average minimum grain ration was twenty-five catties (27.5 pounds; in whole rice about 1,500 calories daily) a month for dependents and sedentary workers, and ranged to forty pounds and up for heavy workers. 'Senior intellectuals', incidentally, were classified with miners and steel fabricators as 'heavy workers'. Dependents or nonproducers in the cities were always the first to feel shortages of supply and cases of undernourishment generally were found in this category. Contrary to impressions abroad, peasants ate well (heavy workers' rations) unless they were in areas of grave underproduction or want.

Szechuan boasts that it alone can 'feed five provinces', but it is a long haul from there to coastal Shantung or Canton. Inadequate transportation is a first handicap in fair distribution. Freight priorities on railways (with a mileage still about one thirtieth as much per person as that in the United States) had heavily favored industrialization programs. Motor vehicles, even more inadequate, were likewise needed for the shipment of raw materials and finished products in accordance with industrial ambitions. The movement of food into the cities even from nearby suburbs was, as I saw, still largely accomplished by hand carts or human backs. Raising transport priorities for food and agricultural tools in order to meet emergency needs was in itself enough to impose a slowdown in industrialization. The dispersal of 'nonessential' persons from the cities in 1960 and 1961 was a form of direct food relief; they went *hsia fang* to produce or earn their own food at the source.

China published the results of nutritional surveys for several years. One foreign specialist in agrarian affairs made a study of these surveys for the *China Quarterly*, a London publication sponsored by the Congress for Cultural Freedom. After careful analysis his conclusion was that the Chinese data represented 'results of their investigations in a manner free from political bias'.[9] For example, one survey revealed the existence of protein deficiency ailments in four percent of the students of a Changsha secondary school who had been working 'from 4 A.M. to 10 P.M., preparing for examinations'. By contrast, surveys conducted in 586 commune canteens in 1958 and 1959 showed peasant intake averaging from 2,245 calories per head daily in August, up to 3,000 and 4,000 calories during the busy harvesting seasons. The author's conclusion was that even in 1961 'the diet, though monotonous and lacking the protective foods considered essential in European consumption patterns, is sufficient to sustain the Chinese population in good health and working condition'.[10]

An interesting fact brought out by China's nutritional surveys is that women engaged in productive work generally raise their food consumption at a higher rate than men. In 1960, in Peking, I was told by Mayor Wu Han* that the '250,000 women added to the municipal working force since 1956' had caused demands for food much greater than anticipated. Chinese women put on 'heavy duty' work increased their food intake by 900 calories a day compared to 670 calories for men.

My own estimate, based on observations in the field and available data, was that the minimum 'average diet' or *urban* Chinese in 1960–62 – varying with the seasons – consisted of about 1,350 to 1,450 calories a day in grain or equivalents. This meant a drop in the basic grain ration to slightly below the level of the year 1952. Persons on minimum rations now had to get from 500 to 800 calories a day from increased production and consumption of vegetables, fruit, poultry, fish, eggs, fats, oils or substitutes which normally supplied about 300-500 calories per person. Peasants ate much more, on the average 2,000 to 3,500 calories, with seasonal variations; many nonworker urban people got less than 2,000 calories.

Government officials knew that China must not only catch up with 1958 output but considerably surpass it. 'Now *here*, you see,' said the Red Queen to Alice, 'it takes all the running *you* can do, to keep in the same place. If you want to get somewhere else, you must run at least twice as fast as that!' By 1963 China was expected to add to her population, since 1958, more people than there were in Great Britain. China should in 1962 have increased her

---

* Wu Han became a name, alas, destined to live in infamy after his play, *Hai Jui Dismissed from Office*, was demolished during the opening barrages of the Great Proletarian Cultural Revolution. See footnote, page 534.

output above 1961 by thirteen percent in order to get back to the level of 1958. To catch up with population growth from 1958 to 1962 another eight percent would have to be added to that. To 'get somewhere else', and well ahead of her population increment, output in 1963 would have exceeded 200,000,000 tons * and thereafter increased by a minimum of two to three percent annually.

The nation had suffered and learned the hard way, by experience acquired in do-it-yourself techniques. In their schematic over-emphasis on heavy industry and certain other doctrinaire measures its leaders repeated some of the Russian errors. They made others all their own. They learned that too much haste makes waste; they now knew a great deal more about what won't work; they were at least farther along than countries which were making no basic efforts to solve their own problems. What solutions emerged would be pragmatic and suitable to Chinese conditions. For various other reasons my conclusion was that, given peace and reasonable luck, somewhere between 1963 and 1967 China would astonish the world by demonstrating that she could comfortably feed her population. In this estimate I assumed that China would continue the re-newed emphasis, which began in 1961, on various means of cur-tailment of the rate of population growth, including mass distribution of the means of birth control and advocacy of late marriages.†

Until then, no one could contend that 'socialist construction' had solved China's fundamental problems. What was more, no Communist country anywhere had yet produced anything like what Marxists call 'food abundance'. Over the whole decade 1949–59 China appeared to have made more progress in that direction than Russia was able to make, despite its greater natural wealth, during the first thirty-three years of socialism.

India, where free enterprise, free-world aid and American philan-thropy actively competed with Soviet help, certainly provided no viable alternative. India consumed so little meat that it was not even listed in her production; the staple food of the millions was almost wholly grain or equivalents. China's food supply had steadily improved compared to that of India. According to com-

---

* That figure was not exceeded until 1968.

† (1969) See notes pages 252 and 400.

parative studies made after field trips to India and China by Gilbert Étienne, professor of economics at the Institut des Hautes Études in Geneva, the per capita output for normal years in both countries revealed that China's was more than thirty percent higher than that of India.[11]

But perhaps the American experience could solve China's agricultural problems? Yes, it might – if we could duplicate, in China, the present endowments of the United States system. One way to start might be to reduce China's population by eighty percent, or 550,000,000 people, thereby providing, for the surviving 150,000,000 Chinese, about the same acreage of cropland per person that America has. A less drastic way would be to expand China's croplands by 40,000,000 acres – to equal the United States' cultivated area – to increase China's fertilizer output by ten times, to increase her motor-mechanized agriculture by twenty times, and then to secure a yield some 400 percent better than the United States harvests from *the same amount of land.*

There is still another way in which the American system might work wonders for China. The United States and Canada have about a billion acres of idle croplands and grasslands. Perhaps the surplus Chinese (over and above the equivalent of United States land-per-acre population) could be imported to cultivate this land for their own consumption and export to hungry and poor lands only? The effect might be to quadruple or better the United States–Canadian food output, to provide an abundance not only for China but for the whole world, enormously to increase the wealth and importance of the entire Western hemisphere, to eliminate all future danger of war between West and East, dispose of the have-nots problem and incalculably enrich both Asian and American culture.

These daydreams suggest that the United States will no more solve China's food problem by means of the American system than it will solve Hongkong's overpopulation problem by providing open house for surplus Orientals.

The Chinese were of course mistaken in suspecting that the United States had the Christian intention of reducing their population by eighty percent. But no leader, whether a capitalist nationalist or a communist socialist, could welcome even the possibility of having so radical a solution imposed on his nation. On the contrary, the Chinese had to strive not only to feed and conserve their multitudes; their leaders also felt obliged to build nuclear bombs, to ensure that any invading force would suffer at least a comparable reduction in numbers. This was what both commonsense American capitalist nationalists and commonsense Chinese communist nationalists agreed to call Security.

76

China, the United States, Russia and the Bomb

ON 26 January 1954 Representative Frederic R. Coudert, at a hearing of the House Committee on Appropriations, asked Walter S. Robertson, Assistant Secretary of State under John Foster Dulles:

Q. 'Did I correctly understand you to say that the heart of the present policy toward China and Formosa is that there is to be kept alive a constant threat of military action vis-à-vis Red China in the hope that at some point there will be an internal breakdown?'

Mr Robertson: 'Yes, sir, that is my conception.'

Q. 'Fundamentally, does that not mean that the United States is undertaking to maintain for an indefinite period of years American dominance in the Far East?'

Mr Robertson: 'Yes. Exactly.'

Testifying before the Appropriations Committee on 10 February 1955 Mr Robertson further declared: 'Our hope of solving the problem of China is ... through action which will promote disintegration from within.'

In the summer of 1962 there began a repeat performance of the 1958 Taiwan crisis and brinkmanship contest. For weeks the Generalissimo clamored for support for an invasive action against the mainland. Chiang's Taipei press described the United States as 'cowardly' and 'short-sighted' for delaying a war of liberation. Again Chiang reinforced his isolated garrisons on Quemoy (Chinmen Tao) and Matsu with new American equipment (including howitzers designed to fire nuclear shells) which could be used for an invasion; again his commandos raided the coast; again his American planes dropped propaganda on the mainland promising liberation.

In 1958 both sides had contributed to the long build-up of tension; it was not easy to say exactly who initiated the crisis and for what purposes. 1962 was not quite the same. For many months Communist guns had shelled Quemoy Island only intermittently and with propaganda, not warheads. It seemed possible that Peking was remaining passive while waiting to see whether President Kennedy would act in accordance with his 1960 campaign speeches, which had called for United States 'disengagement' in China's near waters.

Chiang's renewed agitation was probably based in part on the theory that he would now be welcomed by uprisings of 'millions of starving people', and in part on speculation that Sino-Russian relations had so far deteriorated that Khrushchev would not repeat his 1958 guarantee of all necessary aid to China to repulse any United States-supported attack. China's large-scale mobilization on the coast, followed by Khrushchev's renewed offer of support 'by the whole socialist world', demonstrated that the two 'tests' the Generalissimo may have had in mind could not be undertaken without again inviting consequences perilous to all. It is now useful to recall further how the 1958 events strengthened China's determination to become an independent nuclear power.

In December 1954, a year and a half after President Eisenhower had accepted a truce to end the Korean War, he signed a military alliance with Chiang Kai-shek. In effect this established a unilateral United States protectorate over the Taiwan area. While the Generalissimo had been technically 're-leashed' by the alliance, this recognition of his claim to leadership of China seemed to be meaningless unless he was eventually to be helped to recover the mainland from a sanctuary held inviolate by American forces. Chiang used his American naval and air weapons to harass Red China's shipping. Taiwan boasted of landing spies, saboteurs and armed bands of agitators on the coast. By 1958 the exiled dictator had massed more than one fourth of his troops on the islands of Matsu and Quemoy, the latter less than five miles from the mainland and within easy artillery range of Amoy. Taiwan spokesmen announced 'imminent' liberation.

While Chiang issued communiqués about 'preparations' Peking had not been silent. Virulent protests had been made by the mainland government against American 'aggression' in Taiwan. Demands were renewed that the U.S. fleet withdraw from Chinese waters and Chinese territory. In the summer of 1958 high officials in Peking declared their intention to remove Chiang's blockade of Amoy and Foochow, exercised through control of the offshore islands, and promised final liberation of Taiwan itself. Troops, planes and ships were mobilized.

During an earlier Quemoy crisis following signature of the alliance, President Eisenhower had asked for and been given (January 1955) unprecedented powers by Congress to commit the nation to go to war, if necessary, to preserve the Generalissimo's control over the disputed area. Invoking that power now, he ordered the Seventh Fleet battle-mobilized in the Taiwan Strait and it was announced that the U.S. Air Force based in the territory had been issued atomic missiles. Few knew whether to expect a Nationalist landing in China or a Communist attempt on the islands.

Very detailed syntheses of data covering the 1958 'brink' were made for the United States government by RAND Corporation intelligence analysts. Some results of these studies are available in Alice Langley Hsieh's book *China's Strategy in the Nuclear Era*, and Donald S. Zagoria's *The Sino-Soviet Dispute, 1956–1961*, both published in 1962. These are masterpieces of spoor tracking across mountains of translations of the enemy press. Their conclusions support Secretary of State Dulles' belief that he engineered the 'failure of China's Taiwan venture' by brinkmanship – exercised at the end of the longest limb of United States foreign policy and at heavy and continuing expense. (Fleet mobilization in the Taiwan Strait alone reportedly cost $1,000,000,000.[1])

Mrs Hsieh and Mr Zagoria agree that China probably never intended to attempt a landing on Quemoy but sought to interdict it by artillery fire and force a surrender. They see the 'failure of China's Taiwan venture' as a result of United States nuclear threat and use of naval force in running the blockade, and of China's unwillingness to fire on American ships. In judging that success, however, neither Mrs Hsieh nor Mr Zagoria mentioned Secretary of State John Foster Dulles' promise (10 October 1958) to do 'all that we can' to bring about the 'passing' of the mainland régime.

They did not find it relevant to recall Assistant Secretary of State Walter Robertson's provocative statement that the United States' 'hope of solving the problem of China is ... through action which will promote disintegration from within'. Both overlooked the ominous interpretation which China placed on the United States' rejection of Khrushchev's unexpected agreement (in the main) to a long-standing Allied disarmament plan.* They made no mention of the hardening effects on Chinese policy of the Taiwan alliance and of Dulles' studiedly uncompromising rejection of all Peking's overtures (from 1955 on) to open conversations on a ministerial level in search of a Taiwan solution.

Seen against that background of events, China's side of the 'Taiwan venture' was more comprehensible. The result at least allayed Peking's fear that the Quemoy-Matsu islands could be used as a forward invasion base supported by the United States. Mr Dulles' threat to bring about the passing of the People's Republic had now clearly been restrained or modified by Soviet counter-threats which placed precise limitations on the State Department's ambitions in that respect. The American success was further quali-fied by the cessation of Chiang Kai-shek's attempts to blockade China's ports. In cold-war analyses we necessarily see through a glass darkly, but if an acceptable explanation of an event is to be reached it is mandatory to remember that each of the two an-tagonists makes his contribution to the resolution. Opposite num-bers of Mrs Hsieh and Mr Zagoria in the Institute of International Affairs in Peking, on the other hand, talked to me of the 'failure of American imperialism's 1958 adventure', but ignored the fact that the paper tiger had once again frustrated China's 'freedom of action' within her own territorial waters.

Any realistic analysis of the results of Taiwan must concur, however, in the general RAND conclusion that the Taiwan crisis also reflected internal duels between Peking and Moscow over joint means best suited to confront United States arms in the Far East. A basic assumption of the RAND papers (presumably taken seriously in the Pentagon and the State Department) has been in-terpreted to mean that there exists in China a 'professional officer' class which tends to be in rapport with Khrushchev and in sharp

*See page 686.

conflict with 'nonprofessionals' and party leaders. Opposed to the 'professionals' were the men of 'guerrilla mentality'. These were the 'nonprofessional' marshals committed to party leadership and to Mao Tse-tung's general strategic concepts, which emphasize human or political factors as ultimately more decisive than initial mechanical means in any war. Atomic weapons were held by the 'professionals' to be capable of deciding the outcome by eliminating the human base of political power in a lightning blow.

Was not that too oversimplified a view of the Chinese army? There was nothing in China closely comparable to the West Point or Annapolis élite in conflict with the nonprofessional, or to the contradiction between the Prussian Junker class and the 'non-von' plebeian Nazi generals of the last war. (There was also nothing comparable to American intra-service pressure groups lobbying for General Motors v. General Dynamics or Boeing v. Consolidated Vultee.) Thus far China had no professional soldiers in that sense. She had officers' training academies, of course, but most cadets still rose from the ranks. In a manner very different even from Russia, party and army leadership in China were from the beginning inseparable. In a literal sense all general officers in China were guerrillas, all were professionals, and all were party men.

'You can no more cut me off from Mao Tse-tung,' General Chu Teh told Chang Kuo-t'ao in 1935, when Chang held him prisoner and demanded that he denounce Mao and break all ties with him, 'than you can cut a man in half'.[2] Three years later, and again united with his military alter ego, Mao declared, 'Our principle is that the Party commands the gun, and the gun will never be allowed to command the Party'.[3] This policy made it seemingly impossible for individual warlords to arise and break unity, just as it prevented any future *coup d'état* by politicians backed by army conspirators.

Seven of the eight marshals* of the army were in the Politburo itself, and the senior marshal was traditionally in the Standing Committee. All of them were professional if by that is meant per-

---

*(1970) As noted earlier (page 285), the rank of marshal and other officer titles were abolished under Lin Piao. His reforms in the army set a pattern for the 'rebel' mass organizations of the Great Proletarian Cultural Revolution of 1966 and after. (See Preface.)

sons having had technical training of some kind; all of them were also guerrillas if by that is meant battle experience in irregular warfare. There were no nonparty commanders. An élite existed only in terms of prestige acquired as veterans of the Kiangsi campaigns, the Long March, the Patriotic War, the Liberation War and Korea. In both the Liberation and Korean wars the Chinese command displayed great skill in the deployment of large numbers of troops and the use of combined modern weapons of all kinds, first against Chiang's American-trained officers, then against American armies themselves.

That did not mean there were no disagreements in the high command. It did seem to mean that differences might be seen as reflections of *party* disputes over the correct way to reconcile political objectives with available means. These contradictions have to be resolved inside the party, however, not in the army except as the party was the army. Those who persisted in opposing the dominant central line were apt to be called 'antiparty', but that did not make them professionals or guerrillas. From this it seemed evident that any clear knowledge of China's nuclear policies required a study of party debates over national and international strategy. It was also evident that the heart of such debates must concern key problems of relations with the Soviet party and the Red Army, of which few men possessed details. Something could be inferred from history, however.

The People's Liberation Army had an independent character which set it quite apart from European satellite forces. This history began in 1928, when native Communists confounded prevailing Comintern views by basing the revolution on the peasantry and forming an army which Moscow at first considered 'bandits'. In 1935–6 Mao finally consolidated 'native' control over the Moscow-trained 'returned students' and firmly integrated party command in the army. In ensuing years the Chinese party built up vast irregular forces of far greater potential than Stalin realized. In 1947 Stalin advised Chinese party leaders to take a subordinate role in a coalition under Chiang Kai-shek.[4] They 'agreed', but instead engaged in a major armed struggle for power and quickly won victory. Stalin virtually dismantled China's principal modern industrial assets when, in 1945, he stripped Manchuria – two years later the

Chinese Reds' main base – of nearly two billion dollars' worth of machinery.

The Russians helped to restore (at China's expense) the machine basis of Manchurian industry during the Korean War, when the Sino-Soviet alliance (signed in 1950) was first implemented (in a covert way). No outsider knows exactly who signaled that war. When it began, Soviet advisers were still in North Korea but when reverses occurred they quickly withdrew. It was only after President Truman established United States protection over Taiwan, and after two warnings from Peking that China would intervene if American troops continued their march beyond the Thirty-eighth Parallel toward Manchuria, that the 'Chinese Volunteers' entered the war, as Chou En-lai has reminded us. Even high Chinese officials believed that they had won a victory against the Americans – and in a limited sense they had.

The record of the army suggested : (1) an adroit Chinese leadership capable of wide maneuver to achieve its objectives within the concept of a 'socialist camp led by the Soviet Union'; (2) a series of Chinese victories won in subtle 'compliant-defiance' of Moscow's judgment and yet strategically dependent on the implied Soviet shield for success; and (3) a series of restraints on China's political aspirations in East Asia probably rather flatly imposed in the national interests of the U.S.S.R.

China's military and economic dependence on Russia thus had continued to modify her political independence. By 1955 Moscow's policies had made Peking fully aware of the role of nuclear weapons in their relationship, and Russia must have been under constant pressure to supply the means to her ally. While waiting for a decision it is reasonable to assume that Peking's leaders debated three ways in which China could become Russia's nuclear partner : (1) to place their forces as completely under Moscow's command as the Warsaw Pact states; (2) to seek a Soviet-Chinese all-weapons joint command like NATO with an equal division of powers which would recognize China's manpower-strategic resources as balancing Soviet technological superiority; or (3) to attempt to build an independent nuclear arms industry.

The first choice, for the Chinese, would have meant the surrender of supreme military command and placing China in the role of a complete satellite. In view of the history cited, and especially since the period of decision coincided with post-Stalinist transitions and great instability in Moscow, the first choice was unlikely even if the Russians proposed it, as they perhaps did at one time. The third alternative fitted China's aspirations as a great power but it was a costly long-range solution unless Moscow provided the technical and material assistance on a major scale. The second alternative would seem the most practical solution and one which the Chinese may have pursued with great persistence.

Khrushchev wooed Peking leaders in 1956 and 1957 and committed Russia to new agreements to build key basic industries on a generous scale. While he was consolidating power and needed China's cooperation, Khrushchev may have encouraged hopes of an integrated command to buttress Peking's position in the Far East. Following the Soviet launching of the first ICBM and space satellite, Mao's famous speech in Moscow in November 1957 stated that the 'East wind is prevailing over the West wind' and contended that the strength of the socialist camp already exceeded that of the West. It made sense only on an assumption of close integration of Sino-Soviet military command and maximum *combined* use of Soviet military technology. China received nuclear reactor materials from Russia in 1956–7, many Soviet physicists were sent in as advisers, and there were unconfirmed reports [5] from Poland that Russia had agreed to supply China with atomic missiles.*

The Moscow Conference of November 1957 had exposed serious but apparently still friendly differences between Khrushchev and Mao Tse-tung over questions of correct strategy and tactics for the exploitation of the great advances in Soviet nuclear and rocket technology. To Khrushchev the H-bomb and earth satellite meant primarily the attainment of near-absolute national security, which was bound to diminish his dependence on China. To Mao Tse-tung the gains meant the opening of broader possibilities for revolutionary initiatives in Asia under the shield of Soviet power.

*(1970) Subsequent Sino-Soviet polemics revealed that Khrushchev had, in 1956, promised China a 'sample atomic bomb'; then, following his disputes with Mao, he had reneged on the promise, in 1958 – a prime cause of final breakdown in relations.

Peking's dissatisfaction with Khrushchev's intentions was already deeply aroused by December 1957. The Taiwan crisis of 1958 was to provide the first clear test, however, of how far Mr K. would commit his new power in support of both China's interests and the interests of world revolution – which Peking tended to see as identical.

On 11 May 1958 Foreign Minister Ch'en Yi declared that China would 'soon' have atomic missiles. At the same time he announced support for Khrushchev's proposal for an atom-free zone in the Far East. Quite possibly it was not until the Taiwan crisis in that year, when Khrushchev withheld nuclear protection for any offensive operations in the Taiwan area which might result in conflict with the United States forces, that the Chinese party seriously embarked on a program to make nuclear weapons of their own.

Mao was not a man easily taken by bluff. Anyone who studies Mao's tactical doctrines could assume that he was not at all courting a nuclear war in 1958 but was convinced, and with good reason, that Mr Dulles was using the bomb as blackmail on which he dared not make good if called. He *had* been called in Indochina, when the relative balance of political and nuclear forces was much more favorable to Mr Dulles. In 1958 he was dangerously isolated from both Allied support and public opinion in the United States. Mao therefore must have been astonished and disappointed at what he would have considered Khrushchev's quite gratuitous and maladroit tip-off to the United States that the bomb would be withdrawn from Mao's hand if he followed through with an offensive to close down the Quemoy-Matsu bases.

Peking's decision to build a nuclear weapons industry was obviously related to both the leap-forward program of industrialization late in that year, and the deterioration of Soviet-Chinese party harmony.

Contradictions between the new political, economic and social objectives of the communes and the technical needs of the military establishment found their expression, in 1959, in the replacement of Marshal P'eng Teh-huai as Minister of National Defense. P'eng had long been one of China's ablest party military specialists. A soldier all his life and a combat Communist since 1928, when he led an uprising of Kuomintang troops, he was an intrepid warrior with an impressive career. A native of Mao's Hsiang T'an county, he had loyally supported Mao in every test. In 1936 he emerged in Shensi beside Mao and Chou En-lai as leader of the armed survivors of the Long March, after which he held top command posts throughout war and revolution.

As commander-in-chief of the Chinese Volunteers in Korea, P'eng became keenly aware of China's dependence on Soviet material and technical aid. From 1957 onward he came to personify skepticism among party military specialists about innovations such as overuse of regular army units in commune labor, overextension of the militia system, and too much 'politics in command' of training schedules.

P'eng favored continued long-term close technological reliance on the Soviet Union in order to lighten the burden of an independent all-weapons industry which China was now pursuing. It seemed possible that he was held partly responsible for failing to win Khrushchev's agreement to set up a joint Far Eastern command in 1958. In 1959 he and his staff were replaced by Lin Piao, a more compliant and less colorful figure. Lin's task became the restoration, among party military specialists, of complete solidarity behind Politburo leadership in fulfillment of internal tasks and support of Mao's military doctrine and ideological challenge to Khrushchev.*

By late 1958 Khrushchev's internal prestige was secure enough

---

*(1970) In 1967 Red Guard wall posters and journals revealed that P'eng Teh-huai had been dismissed from office and party positions at Mao's insistence. P'eng was accused of subsequently taking part in a conspiracy to overthrow Mao but no facts were advanced to support such charges, which were dropped by the Maoist press. Red Guard publications did, however, expose profound differences between Mao and P'eng, when the latter was described as a 'revisionist' and 'warlord' for his defiant opposition to Mao at the Party conference held in Lushan in 1959. The Mao–P'eng struggle was not so simple as guerrilla-*versus*-professional-mentality but involved fundamental disputes over strategic, tactical, political and ideological concepts of correct doctrine and policy in matters affecting war and peace. P'eng's views were set forth in a lengthy letter of criticism to Mao presented to Central Committee members. *The Case of P'eng Teh-huai, 1959–1968*, Union Research Service, Hong Kong, 1969, contains documents of varying degrees of authenticity.

for him to begin to offer crushing rejoinders to any 'other party' aspirants to master-mind strategy toward the West. In 1960 the Sino-Soviet ideological dispute broke into the open. The Soviet Party Congress in Moscow in October 1961 revealed even to the outside world that Mr K. intended to retain his nuclear monopoly within the bloc. After the fifty-five-megaton explosion Mr K. offered his most direct affront to Peking when he excommunicated the Albanian party, sole European supporter of Mao Tse-tung's strategic concepts within the international Communist movement.

It is significant to recall an incident which probably further convinced Peking leaders, if any convincing was still necessary, that an independent nuclear capability was essential in order to secure equality of treatment for China as a great power. In 1959, Soviet Air Force pilots shot down a United States RB-47 that was allegedly flying reconnaissance inside the twelve-mile coastal zone claimed by the Soviet Union as its national waters. Mr Khrushchev warned that future intruders would be met in the same way. Following that, no further American flights of that nature were reported in that area. Recalling this event, in contrast to American naval action around Quemoy, a Chinese official (quoting Mao) commented, 'In order to get rid of the gun, we must first grasp it in our hand.'

Meanwhile, China's own nuclear efforts were intensified. In 1955, Russia had signed an agreement to assist China's atomic energy program 'for peaceful purposes'. Work in this field actually began much earlier. Chinese assistants were assigned to Soviet scientists in Sinkiang, where atomic test reactors were reported in 1951. When Sino-Soviet 'joint companies' were dissolved in Sinkiang in 1955 some atomic equipment was rumored to have been given to the Chinese. Soviet exploitation of Sinkiang's uranium (discovered as early as 1944) may have been paid for in this way. Subsequently, rich uranium deposits reportedly were found in Szechuan and the Kansu-Chinghai region. A reactor of unknown capacity was said to be located in that general area.

In the General Electric Corporation's comprehensive private study published late in 1960, its experts could see 'no problems which the Chinese are not capable of solving' in the realization of their atomic ambitions.

According to this study, China possessed all the materials necessary and had more than enough scientists and engineers to carry on a program without further Soviet aid or any major diversion of domestic energies from other fields. The highly detailed General Electric report concluded: 'Assuming no large delays in materials, and that all development, design, and construction work in support of the numerous facilities were done by the Chinese [without Soviet aid], it would take at least five and a half years, but more probably six years, before the first bomb would be tested ...'[6]

From the time a nation explodes its first bomb to the time when it accumulates sufficient uranium, plutonium, thorium and other supplies and facilities to become a 'nuclear power' had been shown to be about three years. France exploded her first bomb in 1959 but was not expected to achieve 'bomb plenty' until 1963. My own guess was that China would not successfully test a bomb of her own before 1964 or 1965, and that the attainment of an abundance of bombs might be achieved in about 1967–8.*

The world presumably had four or five years to think over the possible consequences of that event. Would it decisively change the existing military balance of terror? Probably not. Had the French bomb basically altered the East–West military balance? If the United States could not prevent a revolution in Cuba was it likely that nuclear means would provide China with packaged revolutions for export? Junior membership in the club had not helped frustrated France to restore her lost colonial empire or even to satisfy her 'legitimate needs' in North Africa. Nor was senior membership likely to do so. It was unlikely that Mao would (if still alive) begin any suicidal wars of conquest with a few bombs in his pocket. People obsessed with Yellow Peril and Blue Ant forms of paranoia doubted this, but the record showed that Mao had as lively a sense of self-preservation as any man who ever survived forty years of war. If Peking were intent on provoking an apocalypse it already commanded all the means necessary.

Aggressive as Mao Tse-tung's aims against imperialism might

---

*(1970) China exploded her first 'nuclear device' near Lop Nor, Kansu, in October, 1964. Three years later China announced the explosion of a hydrogen bomb. Chou En-lai told the author in 1964, after the successful test, that 'China will never be the first to use nuclear weapons' and would continue to demand their 'complete and total abolition'.

be, he defended only national or revolutionary wars of liberation; nowhere in his writings had he ever advocated *international wars* of conquest. He believed that liberating *class wars* were not only 'inevitable' but existed at all times inside capitalist societies, whether in the form of armed uprisings or by relatively nonviolent class struggles. It was the duty of the 'liberated' countries, as all Communists saw it, to assist 'anti-imperialist struggles' wherever possible, but that did not mean conquests by international wars. In this perspective the *psychological-political* impact of China-made nuclear devices and means of delivering them would be incalculably great. It would mean an end of the white man's monopoly of the Terror and of its use as a threat against China or her allies.

Enforcement of any conceivable world agreement for control and inspection of nuclear arms manufacture could not be made effective without China's participation. This was unalterable official policy, spelled out by the Standing Committee of the National People's Congress on 21 January 1960, and repeated again in my interviews with Chou En-lai. Russia had repeatedly stated that as a fact. China had reiterated it. Nor could China join any such pact while she was excluded from the United Nations and from diplomatic relations with the U.S.A. Both Chou En-lai and Mao Tse-tung made it quite clear to me that no settlement between the U.S.A. and China was possible unless American bases were liquidated 'on Chinese territory' – meaning Taiwan. It was thus unrealistic and illusory to expect results from disarmament talks while that problem remained unsettled. For Western officials to pretend otherwise was a kind of fraud.

Once China became a nuclear power the chances of any cessation in the build-up of weapons of world destruction would become even more remote. China would doubtless adopt the attitude of France that it would be to her political advantage to defer any nuclear agreements until she achieved 'adequate means' both in weapons and in systems of overseas deliveries. For these various reasons alone the prospect was one of heavier and heavier expenditures for weapons that 'cannot be used'. If the United States was still in Taiwan after China attained nuclear 'plenty' the prospect would seem to be more of the same for years to come.

China and Russia:
Point, Counterpoint

'In the last analysis,' wrote Lenin on his deathbed, in 1923, 'the outcome of the struggle will be determined by the fact that Russia, India, China, etc., account for the overwhelming majority of the population of the globe. And it is precisely that majority that, during the past few years, has been drawn into the struggle for emancipation with extraordinary rapidity. . . . In this sense, the complete victory of Socialism is fully and absolutely assured.'

In 1960 a Chinese Politburo spokesman, Lu Ting-yi, wrote (of the 'anti-Leninists' in the Kremlin): 'The modern revisionists are panic-stricken by the imperialist policy of nuclear-war blackmail. They develop from fear of war to fear of revolution, and proceed from not wanting revolution themselves to opposing other people carrying out revolution.'

Agamemnon and Achilles argued bitterly over their beauteous war prizes, Chryseïs and Briseïs; while Achilles sulked in his tent for ten years Troy was safe. On the banks of the Danube the Tartar princes in the thirteenth century massed their invincible forces to invade Western Europe. A courier brought news of the death of their leader; they violently split over the choice of a successor, called off their offensive, and Christendom was saved from sub-jugation. Some people thought a similar fatal collapse of collabora-tion between the two Marxist titans was now imminent.

Behind Greek disunity on the shores of the Hellespont were many issues besides jealousy over the distribution of female status symbols. From and between the lines of the *Iliad* one may infer differences over tribal interests, over interpretation of the oracles, and over strategy, tactics and objectives against the Trojans. The falling out of the Tartar princes was equally complex – and so is the Sino – Russian dispute of today.

Broadly speaking, differences between the two leaderships could be defined as rooted in the geographical, historical, economic, and psychological or cultural – and perhaps above all the demographical ecology which determined the behavior of two large, multinational states. They found overt expression in quarrels over external strategy and tactics toward the non-Communist world, and over complicated problems of intramural management and cooperation. This discontent in turn invoked conflicting interpretations of Marxist–Leninist doctrine and class interests which the two nominally had in common. All these contradictions were called 'ideological disputes'.

The Tsarist empire spread to its present Asian frontiers in the Amur and Primoye region and in Far Turkestan less than two hundred years ago. China reached those frontiers or beyond them, including Korea, Siberia, Mongolia and Turkestan, from one to two thousand or more years ago and has since advanced or receded from them in periods of rise and decline. The frontiers of Russia are relatively recent and unstable compared to China's. The U.S.S.R. sprawls over a land area nearly two and a half times as large as China; it has twenty-four persons per square mile compared to China's 190 per square mile. If we call 'Asia' everything east of the Urals, the greater part of the Soviet Union lies in Asia, and nearly a third of its population is Asian, or non-Slav. The Russian Union Republic alone is nearly twice as large as China; east of the Urals, Soviet territories might accommodate several times their present population. In Central Asia the Kazakh Republic, whose people have cousins in neighboring Chinese Turkestan, is a fertile steppe about one third the size of China, with one seventieth of China's population.

While advancing across the then largely nomadic lands of Asia to reach the Pacific – during roughly the same period the United States took Texas and California from Mexico and the Indians – the Tsars followed a fixed policy of nonalignment with the seapower invasions of China. Russia reached the Pacific largely by a process of attrition. A cardinal aim of her policy was to avoid head-on collisions with China, while encouraging her conflicts with invaders from the sea. In this respect, with the help of Western mistakes, Russia was highly successful.

Following the expulsion of European colonialism from Eastern Asia, and China's recovery as a formidable continental power, however, her attention began to turn in other directions. Those who believe that China seeks living space in South-east Asia fail to note that the area provides little room for expansion; most of its agricultural lands (particularly Vietnam) are as densely populated as China. Northern Laos, Thailand and Burma are relatively less crowded but mostly mountainous areas inhospitable to farming. The 'empty' spaces are not on the coasts but inland, and Chinese are filling them up.

The main migratory movements inside modern China have been toward the north; now the state was also sponsoring mass settlements in the far west.* China had reached Sinkiang by rail and begun modernizing the area with great vigor. She had linked it up with Tibet by roads that flank Soviet Turkestan, which the Romanovs formally incorporated into the Russian empire scarcely a century ago. The Kremlin has not forgotten that when the Mongols were overlords of Russia – for two centuries – Tashkent and Samarkand, as well as Moscow, paid tribute to Peking. Nor does Peking forget that Moscow detached 'independent' Outer Mongolia from the suzerainty formerly exercised there by China.

In the nineteenth century, Russian pressure on the East seemed irresistible; today it has been checked and conceivably may be reversed. The underlying geopolitical facts are possibly of greater long-range significance than the ideological gulf between Peking and Moscow. More accurately, the former are inseparable from the latter.

To trace the origins of Sino-Soviet political rivalries one may recall first that in Marx's view national differences would disappear after proletarian revolution abolished social classes. Once

---

*(1970) Northward and westward Chinese migration intensified during and after the G.P.C.R. More than two million youths reportedly were settled along the Manchurian-Mongolian-Turkestan frontiers in 1968–9, according to an informant (of the author) returned from Peking late in 1969.

the revolution overthrew capitalism the state everywhere would wither away. Marx foresaw this happening in more or less simultaneous world revolutions led by the proletariat in advanced European countries on about the same level of development. He gave no serious thought to the possibility of a victorious revolution in a single, isolated, and relatively backward semi-Asiatic state such as Russia. Lenin and the early bolsheviks at first believed also that no single socialist state, not even one as large as the Russian empire, could long coexist with a capitalist world. Either one or the other would perish because imperialist war was inevitable as long as imperialism (capitalism in its highest stage) existed. Hence arose the theory of the permanent or uninterrupted revolution – basically an offensive–defensive concept.

Only after repeated failures of revolutionary uprisings abroad did the Soviet government under Stalin embark upon a program of 'building socialism in one country'. While preparing for 'inevitable imperialist war' the bolsheviks defensively built 'the base of the world revolution', in isolation, on foundations of Tsarist empire. They took over the Tsarist colonial territories by extending dictatorship to them under the hegemony of the working class (led by the Russian Communist Party) in order to keep them out of the hands of counterrevolutionaries and imperialists. Although the Soviet system provided administratively for the existence of autonomous national republics, in practice the minority peoples were ruled paternalistically from the Kremlin, under the principle of 'democratic centralism'.

For nearly three decades Russia remained the only Communist-ruled country. As defenders of 'the threatened base of the world revolution' and the 'only homeland of the world proletariat', Soviet party leaders demanded and secured recognition from dependent foreign Communist minorities of the paramountcy of their interests over any and all 'local' interests of other parties. In a short time this led, after Lenin's death and Trotsky's exile, to absolute Russian dictatorship, personified by Stalin, over the Communist movement as a whole. Thus the interests of a single socialist nation came to dominate the concept of international proletarianism. During Stalin's era any foreign party leader who openly questioned his infallibility by pointing out contradictions between Soviet national policies and the interests of world revolution, or who sought to place the national interests of his own party on the same level as Soviet interests, was likely to find himself in an act of heresy and be removed.

When the Stalinist pattern of power victoriously advanced into the political vacuum left in Eastern Europe by the defeat of Hitlerism, Russia had had no experience in operating a federative system in which other national parties could reconcile their differences as equals in a commonwealth of truly self-governing bodies. The absence of such an alternative, plus lack of popular support for a revolution imposed by foreign arms – which necessitated violent suppression of counterrevolutionary forces that had originally supported Hitler's invasion of Russia – placed the Eastern European countries in much the same relationship with Russia as the former Tsarist colonial territories. It was a paradox: revolutionary colonialism.

As remarked at the opening of this book, it was not difficult to foresee that Soviet absolutism was certain to be checked as soon as Communist leadership in another country won sovereign victory by its own national efforts and without direct Soviet armed intervention. Stalinist chauvinism led to nationalist thinking in other parties. This is what happened under Tito in Yugoslavia. When Stalin failed to discredit and overthrow Tito in 1948, a limit was set to the use of the world Communist organization as a means of extending Soviet national power. This event marked the beginning of heterodoxy in the world Communist organization – an era which the Italian Communist leader, Palmiro Togliatti, a decade later called 'polycentric communism'.

Stalin's break with Tito resulted in the collapse of the Greek revolution, but Yugoslavia was too small a country to shake Soviet leadership on a world scale. Shortly afterward such a challenge arose in eastern Asia. The Chinese Communist Party emerged as the leader of a victorious revolution in a major nation with a population three times that of the Soviet Union. It was, moreover, unique in that it was the only fraternal party in the world that had for twenty years fought an independent armed struggle for power, built up its own armed forces, held administrative responsibility over wide areas, acquired an immense amount of political and military experience, and learned to apply Marxist doctrine in many pragmatic ways.

Stalin's intelligence on the Chinese Communist forces during the war against Japan was probably poor; he did not have military advisers or even observers with them for many years. There are indications that he and his Politburo simply did not believe that a party could win power by Mao's methods. The Russian bolsheviks themselves had seized the state apparatus at the center and then imposed social revolution on the Russian peasants after a fairly brief civil war. In their minds that became the classic formula for success. On the other hand, Chinese Communists had been defeated in the cities, fallen back on the hinterland, and organized their bases by gradually winning over the peasant masses. Only after many years, and only after uniting mixed class elements against an invading army, did they capture the leadership of the national patriotic war and mass support with which to encompass and take the cities. In this sense the Chinese victory may have been more democratic (popular) than the Russian.

Russia had been a great empire dominating many colonial peoples; China was a semicolonial country still struggling for independence. In spite of their common adherence to Marxist doctrine, differences in the practical political experiences of the two parties led the Chinese to make claims of uniqueness and greater experience than even the Soviet party. It was in 1943, *five years* before the Tito heresy, that Liu Shao-ch'i asserted:

It may be said that within these twenty-two years our Party has witnessed more important changes and accumulated more experiences of the revolutionary struggle in various complicated forms (whether it be armed struggle or mass struggle, civil war or international war, legal struggle or illegal struggle, economic struggle or political struggle, struggles inside the Party or outside the Party) than *any other Communist Party in the world.*[1]

In 1946, and still two years before Tito had begun to speak openly of 'different roads to socialism', Liu Shao-ch'i categorically claimed:

Mao Tse-tung's great accomplishment has been to change Marxism-Leninism from a European to an Asiatic form.... Mao Tse-tung ... uses

Marxist-Leninist principles to explain Chinese history and the practical problems of China. He is the first that has succeeded in doing so. . . . On every kind of problem – the nation, the peasants, strategy, the construction of the party, literature and culture, military affairs, finance and economy, methods of work, philosophy – Mao has not only applied Marxism to new conditions but has given it a new development. *He has created a Chinese or an Asiatic form of Marxism.* China is a semi-feudal, semi-colonial country in which vast numbers of people live at the edge of starvation, tilling small bits of soil. Its economy is agriculture, backward and dispersed. . . . There are similar conditions in other lands of southeast Asia. The courses chosen by China will influence them all.[2]

Following Liu's 1946 assertion, and throughout the 1949–51 postrevolutionary period, Chinese party spokesmen reiterated claims for the originality of 'Mao's ideology' and upheld the Chinese revolution as the 'model' for other semicolonial and colonial countries. The Soviet party press took no recognition of any ideological 'new development' or 'Asiatic form of Marxism'. It continued to cite solely the fountain of all Marxist wisdom, Josef Stalin. China's claims ceased only after the outbreak of the Korean War -- not to be openly revived again until 1958.

Besides underestimating Mao's chances of victory, Stalin thus had reason, before the end of the Second World War, to be skeptical of his ability to fit Mao into his pattern of revolutionary power. The alliance he signed with Chiang Kai-shek in 1945, the day after Russia attacked Japan in Manchuria, plainly advanced Russian national interests. It also advanced Soviet revolutionary interests by creating a regional situation favorable to an extension of Stalinist domination, similar to that in Eastern Europe. By terms of the treaty Chiang Kai-shek in effect abandoned China's claims to Outer Mongolia by agreeing to a Soviet-sponsored plebiscite. He agreed to restore Russia's former rights in Manchurian railways and enterprises which Stalin, to avoid a conflict, had earlier sold to Japan. The treaty even restored Russian control over the old Tsarist Port Arthur (Dalny) naval base on the Pacific. (The Yalta Pact had left Chiang Kai-shek small choice in most of these matters.)

In sponsoring this treaty the United States recognized a Soviet sphere of influence in Manchuria and tacitly drew a line at the

Great Wall beyond which American nationalism might not intervene.

It is probable that in 1945 Stalin believed – as did most observers on the spot – both that Chiang Kai-shek's well-equipped 2,500,000-man army would quickly disperse the poorly armed and heavily outnumbered Communist troops, and that if necessary the United States would massively intervene to save Chiang from destruction. Stalin's advice to the Communists to dissolve their armies and collaborate as a minority in Chiang's government was probably based on those beliefs.[3] Even in Manchuria, according to General George Marshall, who headed America's mediation mission in China, 'In the opinion of all my advisers and intelligence, they [the Russians] were not supporting them [the Chinese Communist forces].'[4]

The swift and total disintegration of Chiang's armies following initial disasters in Manchuria, and the emergence of the Chinese Communists as victors over all China in 1949, made any regional Soviet hegemony in the north an impossibility. From the standpoint of amicable *national* relations with a united China, Stalin would have had no alternative but to shift his alliance from the Generalissimo to the 'new power', even if no revolutionary sympathies had been involved.

No Soviet aid program to China got under way until after Mao Tse-tung's first visit to Russia; a modest loan of $300,000,000 was announced in 1950. During China's war against Japan the Kuomintang régime had received more than that in Soviet materials. But Russia herself was still bleeding from the war against Hitler, having lost at least ten per cent of her population. The loan was a start toward compensation for the equipment removed from Manchuria by the Red Army as 'reparations' in 1945–6. Although at this time China signed a tripartite alliance with Russia and North Korea which probably had protocols providing for the modernization of the Chinese army, no developments prior to the outbreak of hostilities in Korea suggested that China was preparing for a large military operation. But belief among Chinese was then strong that the Sino-Soviet alliance was an earnest of large-scale future economic help rendered in proletarian solidarity which would surmount all differences.

By the spring of 1950 the United States seemed ready to write off Chiang Kai-shek and Taiwan also. The transitional policy was to 'let the dust settle' in China, in the words of Secretary of State Dean Acheson; both he and General MacArthur went on record to the effect that neither Korea nor Taiwan was necessary for the defense of United States positions from the Aleutians through Japan, Okinawa and the Philippines. On 5 January President Truman himself had declared that the United States 'has no desire to establish bases on Chinese territory' and that 'it will not provide military aid and advice to the Chinese Nationalist forces on Formosa.'[5] American forces in South Korea were reduced to training groups. During that same spring Yugoslav and Indian delegates to the United Nations secured a verbal commitment from the United States delegate that he would accept the decision on a resolution in the Assembly to settle the dispute over China's seat as a 'procedural' rather than a 'substantive' question.[6] Procedural matters do not go before the Security Council. The seating of the Peking government therefore could be decided by an Assembly majority without occasion arising for the United States to enter a veto.

It thus appeared that America would accept a general disengagement from China, and the Russians were certainly informed of the Yugoslav-Indian formula. Yet in May, suddenly, the Soviet delegation was withdrawn from the United Nations. Why? Moscow announced that it would not return as long as Nationalist China was seated in the U.N. It was a singularly ill-timed withdrawal, just at a moment when a Soviet veto would have been most useful in opposing a U.N. action shortly to be provoked in Korea. In June a general offensive was launched from North Korea against the South. Soviet Russian political and military advisers (not Chinese) had helped set up the North Korean régime and had remained in key positions. It is impossible to believe that a well-planned, well-supplied offensive could have been undertaken without prior consultation with and approval by Stalin. Owing to Soviet absence from the Security Council, President Truman was able swiftly to win sanction for large-scale American counteroffensive operations as a United Nations police action.

Was that wholly unforeseen in the Kremlin? It is difficult to imagine that. Even had Stalin supposed that North Korea could successfully hold its conquest, he must have realized that the

United States fleet would be obliged to move into Taiwan to cover that flank against any surprise attack by Russia's Chinese allies. It is often observed that Korea provided an Asian diversion from Russia's difficulties in countering Western pressure in Europe. Cynics have gone further, to suggest that the whole Korean adventure was Stalin's design to bring the United States into irreconcilable conflict with China.

The fact remains that Russian advisers were withdrawn from Korea once the issue was fully joined, and were later replaced by Chinese troops. The end result was that Communist China was formally branded an 'aggressor' by the United Nations and excluded from any early possibility of admission there. Peking's dependence on Russia greatly increased. Hostility between China and the United States was fixed for years to come. Soviet Russia avoided direct involvement in the Korean War and resumed her seat in the United Nations without incurring a vote of censure.

After the death of Stalin in 1953, a new era was cautiously introduced as Khrushchev emerged triumphant. Russia had recovered from the Second World War and developed nuclear weapons. Fear of capitalist encirclement diminished, and it was tacitly recognized that a holocaust threatened capitalism and communism alike. Instead of Stalin's offensive-defensive strategy of preserving 'socialism in one country', the new leadership experimented with a more flexible policy aimed at establishing communism on a world scale while avoiding war.

Among the effects of de-Stalinization in China was an enhancement of Mao's prestige as the leading Marxist theoretician, and demands for a greater role at both the Communist and world summits. Khrushchev in his speeches did accord China a special place beside the Soviet Union conceded to no other country. He extended Soviet aid in new ways. Like Russia, China needed time for internal consolidation and growth. China also supported peaceful coexistence. Following the Geneva Conference of 1954, Chou En-lai took a leading part in the 1955 Bandung Conference of twenty-nine nations (largely colonial and ex-colonial) of Asia and Africa. Its principles were noninterference in each other's internal affairs, mutual aid and trade, and mutual resistance to imperialism. China opened talks on an ambassadorial level with the United States –

provided for at the Geneva Conference – in attempts at some settlement of the Taiwan issue. It soon became clear that the American
ambassador at the Warsaw level had no authority to discuss basic
issues or do more than repeat demands for what would amount to
Peking's *de jure* recognition of the legality of the American armed
protectorate in Taiwan.*

The 'Bandung spirit' led to closer Sino-Indian relations for a
time. A loose 'Asian-African' bloc put up a common propaganda
front, but it produced few concrete results for China. American
military power had already created a Southeast Asia Treaty Organization, to include the Philippines and two Asian nations bordering
on China : Pakistan and Thailand.

China withdrew her troops from Korea and invited the United
States to do likewise, with no result. China released what she
asserted to be all the American prisoners of war in her custody.
Peking invited some Americans to visit China and indicated a
desire to reopen people-to-people communications. The United
States adamantly defended its Taiwan protectorate and forbade
Americans to travel in or trade with China. In 1955–7, China
offered visas to some American newspaper correspondents and
editors; Mr Dulles forbade any of them to accept, under threat of
prosecution. Washington sought the support of other nations to
isolate and quarantine the mainland and thus achieve the 'speedy
passing' of the Peking régime. Mr Dulles frigidly repulsed all Chou
En-lai's efforts to open serious high-level talks following the release
of American prisoners of war – which had been understood to be a
precondition of negotiations. The Chinese leaders concluded that
they had been tricked into concessions without receiving a *quid
pro quo*. They saw that their conciliatory moves had been misin-
terpreted. They were being punished for their weakness.

By 1957 China's dissatisfaction with a relatively passive policy
was deepened by developments which suggested to Peking leaders

---

*The United States position demanded a formal declaration by Peking not
to use force in the Taiwan area, acceptance of which would concede the
legality of United States intervention in China's internal affairs. Peking's
position remained that the United States must recognize China's sovereignty
in Taiwan *simultaneously* with a joint declaration rejecting the use of force
in the settlement of Sino-American differences. See pages 25–8 and 118–19.

that the United States was overextending itself in an age when Western imperialism was actually weakening, rather than strengthening, its hold on the world. Colonial empires were in rapid disintegration from Asia to Africa. National liberation movements, winning all across the board, were facing a critical choice between bourgeois nationalist dictatorship and proletarian dictatorship. Failure to support effective leadership on the Maoist model in the newly emerging states seemed to be forfeiting dominance in them to imperialism – that is, to bourgeois nationalist satellites of American power. Did Khrushchev's fear of nuclear war leave Communists no alternative but a peaceful coexistence which led to peaceful surrender or inevitable war?

Climaxing all these doubts, two very important events late in 1957 decisively influenced Chinese Communist thinking. On 26 August Moscow announced that it had successfully launched the first intercontinental ballistic missile. Many had regarded it as an ultimate weapon. On 4 October the Soviet Union put into space the first earth satellite in history. In China this was news of even more stunning importance (as it turned out) than in Moscow. A 'new stage' had been established in the world power balance. Party conferences were called and prolonged sessions worked out a new international strategy. Opinion in the Central Committee led by the Politburo oscillated from right to left, as always. It came to rest on a new center, with Mao Tse-tung still its spokesman – far to the left of the pre-1957 position.

Mao Tse-tung's basic estimate as presented at Moscow in November 1957 was that Russia's lead in ballistic missiles and satellite systems marked a 'new turning point', an idiom indicating the need for rethinking revolutionary strategy. Placing his usual emphasis on man as the decisive factor in all political struggle, Mao asserted during the conference:

The whole world now has a population of 2.7 billion, of which the various socialist countries have nearly one billion; the independent, former colonial countries more than 700 million; the countries now struggling for independence or for complete independence, 600 million; and the imperialist camp only about 400 million . . .[7] I am of the opinion that the international situation has now reached a new turning point. There are two winds in the world: the East wind and the West wind. . . .

I think the characteristic of the situation today is the East wind prevailing over the West wind. ... *The socialist forces are overwhelmingly superior to the imperialist forces* ...[8]

Mao called for a new orientation of policy to recognize that the 700,000,000 people in the newly independent states, combined with the 600,000,000 people in areas 'struggling for independence or complete independence' (including those now dominated by 'Yankee imperialism' in Latin America), would decide the balance of world power. In this sector of humanity, where the average income was scarcely $100 per person per year, the aim of the Communists should be to outflank and encircle Western imperialism by leading 'struggles' which should not shirk from use of force when confronted by force. Mao did not advocate any general assault but rather his old guerrilla strategy of concentrating where the enemy was weakest, and smashing him one by one:

In order to struggle against the enemy, we have formed the concept over a long period, namely, that *strategically we should slight all enemies, and tactically we should take full account of them.* That is also to say, we might slight the enemy as a whole but take full account of him so far as each and every concrete question is concerned. If we do not slight the enemy as a whole, we shall be committing the mistake of opportunism. ... But on concrete questions and on questions concerning each and every particular enemy, if we do not take full account of the enemy, we shall be committing the mistake of adventurism. In war, battles can only be fought one by one and the enemy can only be annihilated bit by bit. ... This is called one-by-one solution. And in military literature, it is called smashing the enemy one by one.[9]

If at first the Russians did not take Mao very seriously, they were soon to learn that he meant every word he said. In his view now, the balance of world power had changed in favor of the socialist forces. Counteroffensive should begin before the enemy could entrench himself in the uncommitted nations and continue preparations for a new war.

To attempt to trace all the subsequent controversies would be impossible in this space. Readers interested in the enormously complex and enormously important details may find them documented elsewhere.[10] Here it must suffice to complete the barest outline of events.

In November 1957 the Russians and their European comrades did not accept Mao's estimate of the situation. Neither did they believe that by his strategy he could safely walk between 'opportunism' and 'adventurism'. They did not consider that a 'turning point' had been reached nor that the socialist forces were now superior. At most they had achieved a deterrent against attack. It was impossible to determine 'who is encircled and who is the encircler', in Khrushchev's words. Second, the main issue before the world was peace or war but peace was indivisible and it must not be combined with methods that could lead to world war. Third, the attainment of communism was still relatively far distant. Since nuclear war was unthinkable, the decision would be won principally by demonstrating the superiority of the socialist system in a relatively peaceful economic contest with capitalism, in which risks of provoking counterrevolutionary wars were minimized. Many local wars of liberation would inevitably occur; they could not be incited by one side without inviting intervention by the other side. One must support them, but mainly by diplomacy. Extremely militant policies might also throw mature bourgeois democracies into deep reaction; that could close the path to socialists seeking power by parliamentary means.

There can be no doubt that Khrushchev's line was a revision of Leninism. It also opened a door to the despised social democrats. But was not imperialism now obliged to work with socialism? The Chinese denied that. Imperialism had not basically changed in the nuclear era; it was only weaker and more desperate. No revision was admissible in rounding the 'new turning point'.

The issues were not resolved by the Manifesto of November 1957, which was a compromise to maintain outer unity. It recognized that the danger of war existed as long as imperialism existed. Yes, there was also now a possibility of peaceful transition to socialism. It could be realized only by the combined struggle of 'popular forces', in terms used by Chou En-lai in his interview with me as late as October 1960.* The Chinese emphasized the manifesto's support for 'just wars' of liberation.

By the time I saw Chou, the Sino-Soviet dispute had broken into semipublic view, after months of heated polemical exchanges in-

* See page 128.

terrupted by meetings which had only intensified differences. If the 1958 Taiwan crisis is seen in this context it may be said to have strengthened Khrushchev's determination not to be drawn into conflicts the outcome of which he could not control. In Peking in July 1958, Mao and the Soviet leader had certainly argued over the obvious contradictions between efforts at a genuine *détente* with the West and Mao's belief that the bloc should 'slight the enemy strategically' while taking him seriously in specific tactical situations, where local force should be met by local force and nuclear weapons could be avoided. Almost certainly, in Mao's opinion, the Taiwan crisis which followed was a test of whether Khrushchev understood the application of this principle, and Khrushchev had played a weak hand, for reasons already Noted.*

Late in 1958 Khrushchev also became fully aware of the inherent challenge to Soviet ideological prestige in China's adoption of communes as a short cut to communism. This aspect of the dispute demands a special study in itself. If Peking had succeeded in imposing the very 'advanced' goals first set up for the communes it would have left Soviet society a stage or two behind China in programmatic development toward communism. Did Mr K.'s objections influence the Chinese party decision in December 1958 to retreat from its extreme positions? If so, the extension of Soviet credits in February 1959, which over a period of several years were expected to supply China with seventy-eight additional complete industries worth five million rubles ($1,125,000,000), on a barter basis, may be regarded as a large Soviet reward to bridge the gap between them. (These were still merely trading credits, however; no gifts were involved.)

The apparent reconciliation did not last long. Continuing his

*(1970) In 1958 Russia did not have completely convincing 'deterrent credibility'; it was therefore conceivable to Khrushchev that Dulles and Eisenhower were not just bluffing when they brandished the bomb against China over Matsu and Quemoy. With President Johnson's failure to subdue North Vietnam by all-out conventional bombing (1965–68), and China's achievement of the bomb (1964), however, Johnson's decision not to risk using nuclear weapons (out of fear of possible Soviet-Chinese retaliation), made Mao's contention that the bomb was a 'paper tiger' seem much less unrealistic than it had seemed, to many, in 1958.

pursuit of peaceful coexistence, Khrushchev visited President Eisenhower at Camp David to discuss a summit conference. This could not have failed to revive Chinese suspicions of betrayal of principle, if not of their own interests. On his return in October, by way of Peking, Khrushchev's reception there was colder than the weather. His published speeches and subsequent Chinese press comment showed wide differences concerning the objectives of peace negotiations with the West.

Mao and Khrushchev never met again. Peking increased its offensive with attacks on Mr K., thinly veiled by the euphemism 'Yugoslav revisionists', with whom China had quarreled over some of the same issues. Moscow organs retaliated with criticisms of unnamed 'dogmatists' and 'left-infantilists', with occasional asides concerning Trotsky's mistakes.

Very many points of fundamental division had already resulted in conflicting foreign policies. Peking was bidding for support in neighboring countries by offering trade credits on easier terms than Moscow. In some instances the Chinese made outright gifts (to Outer Mongolia, Korea, Vietnam, etc.), something Russia had never done. Yet China was herself still dependent on Soviet credits. China recognized the Algerian national government much in advance, and to the embarrassment, of Moscow. Peking disagreed with Khrushchev's policy of aiding bourgeois nationalist governments in Egypt, India and Indonesia while slighting China and other left-wing forces. Quarrels arose over correct policies in Iraq and over disarmament negotiations. In Chinese eyes, Soviet acceptance of U.N. armed intervention in the Congo amounted to counterrevolutionary betrayal.

Behind all such contradictions lay basic disagreements in evaluating the strength of the world 'socialist forces'. The truth probably was also that Mao had not trusted Khrushchev as a political strategist since he had unnecessarily betrayed his hand during Mr Dulles' 'bluff' in the Quemoy-Matsu crisis of 1958.

At the Moscow Conference of November 1960, the dispute became a duel of personalities as well as strategies. As the junior and weaker socialist power, China (represented by Liu Shao-ch'i) seemed to make most of the compromises. The final conference declaration seemed to adopt the main points of the Soviet party, now designated 'the universally recognized vanguard'; in 1957 it had been 'the head' of the world movement. The conference agreed that competitive and peaceful coexistence was the only alternative to war and massive destruction; the road to socialism was gradual erosion of the capitalist system rather than promotion of armed revolutionary struggle. But in underdeveloped areas the parties were to support 'national liberation movements' in which Communists could play a legal role in governments of 'national democracies' to be led, stage by stage, toward socialism. Wording of the resolution was still sufficiently ambiguous on many points to provide scope for an independent Chinese interpretation, however, particularly on ways and means of 'struggle' for proletarian (Communist) hegemony over the liberation movements.

While Mao's leftist strategy was voted down, in the main, China had forced a number of concessions from Khrushchev. For the first time a Soviet leader had been obliged to confront an opposition before the entire world organization. Revolutionary interests beyond those of Soviet power were now clearly recognized as the responsibility of the 'vanguard party' of world revolution. A precedent was set: major Soviet strategy decisions henceforth would require interparty consultation. China's thesis had found wider support than Khrushchev anticipated. Albania was the only European party which openly espoused the Chinese position in 1960, but factions in other parties, including the Soviet, apparently, were in sympathy with it. As a whole, Asian parties attempted to steer a middle course.

Something else happened, the significance of which was probably not at once absorbed by the contestants. The struggle of wills proved Mao's theory of the persistence of contradictions even between socialist states and between socialist governments and their peoples. In attempting to reconcile them a process developed very akin to freedom of speech, assembly, conscience and even publication. How long could such methods be adopted at the summit without having contagious effects within the ranks of the nations themselves?

In Peking, I spoke of conflicting national interests and differences in the geopolitical environments of the two countries to a Soviet historian who was about to join other Russians in the general

departure. At the end he said, 'Yes, we are two large, socialist countries, both opposed to imperialism; on this matter we are united.
But we have had independent national experiences and are at different levels of revolutionary development. The Chinese are very
proud. They want equality in the world. We have won it; they are
still struggling for it. They are going to get it their own way and
by their own efforts – and their way may be best for them. We have
a Russian proverb that sums up the situation. "You can't fit one
man's head on another man's shoulders." '

Among differences in Russian and Chinese national experiences
none was more pertinent than the contrast in United States behavior toward the two revolutions. Following the bolshevik revolution the United States did not establish armed bases on Soviet
territory in support of the defeated régime.[11] In 1920, when there
was a mass famine in Russia, Americans responded by sending in
wheat. In the twenties and thirties the Soviet government hired
American engineers and bought American machines which helped
lay the foundations of Soviet industry. Cultural contacts were
never cut off, and after 1933 normal diplomatic and trade relations
were restored.

In 1941 the United States began to aid Soviet Russia against
Hitler even before Pearl Harbor. This fact confounded all Marxist
dogma, for by orthodox reasoning the imperialist powers should
have united to carve Russia into colonial prizes. Quite the contrary.
The Soviet command was authorized, in armistices signed by the
United States, to remove from power all elements 'hostile to the
Red Army' throughout Eastern Europe. Russia not only recovered
her lost territories but was rewarded by a vast extension of the
pattern of Soviet power.

In the ensuing cold war the United States never broke off diplomatic and trade relations with the Kremlin. Instead, the Soviet
Communist government won full and respectful consideration for
itself at the tables of the capitalists. President Eisenhower invited
the devil into his camp and made efforts to show him how the welfare state really works. Not surprisingly, Mr Khrushchev believed
that peaceful coexistence was possible.

The Chinese saw those facts, however, as a reflection of only one
thing: Soviet power. In their eyes American imperialism respected

nothing but force. It rewarded revolutionary strength and received it as an equal. It despised and punished weakness.

This harsh judgment was based on Chinese Communist experience with an American imperialism which behaved according to their classical expectations. Their struggle began in a part of the world where Japan was the only power free from Western domination. Throughout the joint war against Japan the impoverished Communist forces received no aid from America. The United States armed Chiang Kai-shek alone and continued to support him against the Communists during the civil war. In 1949 the Peking government invited recognition; the United States withdrew.

To the Chinese, their aid to North Korea was an act of self-defense. As firmly as Mr Truman believed he prevented a world war by intervening there, Chinese Communist leaders were convinced that they not only saved North Korea and Manchuria from conquest but prevented an imperialist war against China. As long as imperialism existed – on Chinese soil, at least – Chinese Communists would not feel that 'socialism is secure'.

Frustrated from winning redress for these injuries to national pride, denied recognition as an equal and great power, Communist China naturally looked upon the removal of the American menace as a much more urgent matter than the Russians did. Unable to launch a direct assault on the 'invader', Mao sought to outflank him by stimulating revolutionary victories in the underdeveloped countries.

In the *Communist International Program* adopted in the early days of the bolshevik revolution – a purely Leninist document – it was clearly recognized that successful proletarian-led revolutions in colonial and semicolonial countries 'will be possible only if direct support is obtained from countries in which the proletarian dictatorship is established'. The Chinese Communists received very little help during their lonely revolution – while their enemy always received support from the imperialists. Now they said that to deny it to the weaker and struggling young liberation movements would be pure 'opportunism' and shirking of the great socialist powers' responsibilities.

But overt support of revolution would bring counterrevolution and dangerous showdowns, Russia argued. The present Russian generation consisted not of Lenins but of youth anxious to enjoy the fruits of their parents' sacrifices. Still 'have-nots' by Western standards, the Russians were a 'have-got' nation in the Communist region, and Khrushchev held power by promising greater abundances than under capitalism. Obviously those could not be won by dissipating Russia's resources in conflicts in remote lands, but only by peaceful economic expansion. Eastern European parties still more reflected the same sentiments. Their people dreaded any prospect of new sacrifices imposed to carry out faraway liberating missions — especially under a Chinese leadership which must increase, rather than break down, their isolation from the West.

All that was implicit in the debates of the 1960 conference, where the Chinese accepted the revisions of the manifesto for the sake of unity rather than from conviction. Mutual press recriminations temporarily ceased but the Chinese continued propaganda for their own anti-imperialist line, in preparation for a review of the whole program at another meeting promised for 1962. In action, China did nothing to violate peaceful coexistence and joined efforts to negotiate a Laos settlement with the United States. Inside the bloc she exercised freedom of interparty relationships as well as continued agitation for a more militant strategy. What most infuriated Khrushchev was Mao's defiance of his attempt to isolate Albania. Albania had its own reasons for sympathizing with Mao. Like China, Albania was excluded from the United Nations. With Albania, as with China, the United States had cut off all communications. The party chief, Hoxha, reflected the fears and hates of his tiny nationalism; if Khrushchev won Yugoslavia back into the camp it might be at the price of Tito's domination of Albania. Peking opposed Tito as a strong 'revisionist' influence pulling Khrushchev in the direction of a *détente* with the United States at the expense of China's interests. In October 1961, when foreign delegates appeared at the Twenty-second Party Congress to hear the Premier announce the Soviet draft program and blueprint for the transition from socialism to communism, Khrushchev dramatically rebuked both China and Albania.

During his opening speech he attacked Albania for refusing to abide by the decisions of the Twentieth Congress (de-Stalinization) program. Unexpectedly, he demanded expulsion of its leadership and read it out of the bloc. This action was at once recognized as aimed at China, for setting up a bipolar leadership. The Chinese delegation, led by Chou En-lai, was the only one which did not applaud Khrushchev's long address. After replying the following day, when he criticized the Soviet leader for dictatorial condemnation of Albania without prior consultation with any other party, Chou left the Congress and promptly flew back to Peking. He was warmly welcomed at the airport by both Mao Tse-tung and Liu Shao-ch'i.

Khrushchev's action was clearly a warning that if China continued intransigent he would also read Mao out of the party. The gravity of the threat was already manifest in the economic sanctions Khrushchev had applied against China ever since the trade-unions conference in Peking in June 1960. Shortly afterward Khrushchev had withdrawn nearly all Soviet technical experts from China, leaving many joint Soviet-Chinese projects in an unfinished state. Chinese engineers might eventually complete them but their task was viciously complicated by the withdrawal also of blueprints and specifications as well as by the withholding of vital parts. Given familiarity with the key weaknesses and shortages of Chinese industrial and scientific equipment, it was not difficult to know where denials would hurt most. When the Russians openly announced what amounted to economic sanctions against China, the punishment coincided with the worst harvests China had known in this century.

If Khrushchev, personifying the current Soviet party majority, sought to bluff Mao Tse-tung by such means, he had misjudged the man, the nation, and the Chinese revolution – if not that part of the world revolution personified by Mao. Would this spokesman for 'the poor, the vast majority', in whom still burned the heart of the youth who had defied Chiang Kai-shek's thousand-to-one superiority in firepower, who had ignored Stalin's advice, and who later refused to be intimidated by the American paper tiger, now be taken on the right by a rich peasant riding an H-bomb? Not likely. China was now too big to be driven to surrender. If Khrushchev forbade all bloc trade with China it would still be possible for the nation to go into a severely autarchical economy; it was after all in a somewhat better condition now to do so than Soviet Russia had been in the dark early days of isolation and 'socialism in one country'.

Soon after Chou's return from Moscow, Peking gave its answer by extending increased economic aid to Albania. The Chinese press reprinted Albanian statements attacking Khrushchev as an 'opportunist', and for 'revisionism', 'treachery', 'lies, pressure and threats'. Inside the party now, at even the lower echelons, the whole dispute was threshed out and finally became general public knowledge.

On an earth about to send visitors to other planets all these polemics to many seemed ludicrous. But Mao's view was far from parochial; he had his eye on the multitudes who would not be space men but still lived in rat-infested villages, fearful of disease and starvation. His view took into consideration the coexistence in man's knowledge and condition of Telstars and human beasts of burden, of the infinity of space and matter and the brevity of human life, of a John Foster Dulles carrying a prayer book in one hand and an earth-cracking bomb in the other, of an African tribesman convinced that an electric lamp is god and of the Tibetan aspiring to become a living buddha by way of prayer wheels blessed by the lamas.

Encompassing these changing levels of life there could be discerned a unity of purpose which in political terms might be described as a four-pronged thrust for a new equality in the condition of man. Four cosmic events were occurring simultaneously: national revolution (former slave nations struggling for racial, color and creed recognition as equals); class revolution (poor men everywhere struggling for equality against the rich); technological revolution (backward societies struggling for equality with advanced ones); and international revolution (blocs of have-not nations struggling for equality with have-got powers). The key to political mastery over all these equations was seen by Mao to lie in the overwhelming majority of mankind, the poor people, as against a very small minority of the rich.

Heretofore the idea of 'poor-man's government' had been considered Utopian. Now two large nations and one third of humanity were ruled by régimes where there was indeed no more individual liberty than before, but where the rich had been eliminated by the abolition of private ownership of the means of production, and where relatively egalitarian societies were established which aimed ultimately to secure 'from each according to his ability', and to satisfy 'each according to his needs'. That these societies work had been universally recognized when one of them, the possessor of nuclear weapons, had to be received as an equal by the rich men's nations. Moreover, direct rule by Western have-got nations over the inferior states had dissolved nearly everywhere before the four-pronged revolution. In 'desperation', the monopoly capitalists were driven to alliances on a basis of equality with the minority who were the ruling class in the former slave or semislave states, where the poor were the vast majority.

In his youth Mao wrote an essay entitled 'A Single Spark May Start a Prairie Fire'. He had seen a few dozen determined men convince the poor that they could get along without the rich. In scarcely more than twenty years he led a quarter of the earth's poor to turn the gun around and take power. He was convinced that other poor men could also master the means of completing the four-pronged revolution. Was there anything between them and their liberation, after all, but force controlled by the rich and very small minority?

Mao's belief was that the disintegration of the colonial world marked a 'turning point' which required *immediate* action. If action were delayed too long, the rich minorities in the backward countries might become so entrenched, with the help of the have-got governments, that conditions of struggle 'by the poor' would become extremely difficult. Then the have-got powers (the imperialists) might be able to build such firm bases throughout the lands of the 1,300,000,000 people in the former slave states that they could be turned toward counterrevolution and produce an imperialist war. To win victory and to prevent an imperialist war, the important thing now was to keep the imperialists on the defensive.*

Since the poor were 'the great majority' Mao never doubted that

* (1970) As emphasized on p. 635, China's efforts to outflank the United States served her national interests as well as world revolutionary interests, as long as neither a direct confrontation with the United States in East Asia, nor a negotiated settlement, was possible or practicable.

they would triumph. One could therefore 'slight the enemy strategically'; history had already demonstrated that he could not win. Even if the enemy had a monopoly on the bomb he could not win. But the poor man already had the bomb. The enemy could not use the bomb strategically (against the socialist base defended by the bomb) because he himself would be destroyed.

But one must 'take serious account of the enemy tactically'. Current liberation struggles were not fought in the have-got countries but in underdeveloped ones. The more the imperialist assisted the native rich to defeat the aspirations of the revolution the more he alienated large sectors of the intellectuals as well as the poor population and united them in antiforeign nationalist sentiment. Could the enemy use the nuclear weapons *tactically*? Yes, he could. But in a social revolution the poor arm themselves mainly by capturing weapons commanded by the rich. If the enemy deployed nuclear tactical weapons against the revolution then sooner or later they and their operators would be captured and used against them. That was what happened to Chiang Kai-shek's conventional American weapons. That was what happened to French weapons in the Algerian and Indochina revolutions, and that was what happened in Cuba. 'Man is more important than the weapon.'

Yet international war, Mao had held, was not the way to change matters. 'People who believe that revolution can break out in a foreign country to order, by agreement,' said Peking, quoting Lenin, 'are either mad or provocateurs. ... We know that revolutions cannot be made to order, or by agreement; they break out when tens of millions of people come to the conclusion that it is impossible to live in the old way any longer.'[12]

And how should they be helped to reach that conclusion? The 'imperialists always have two tactics; the tactics of war and the tactics of "peace"; therefore, the proletariat and the people of all countries must also use two tactics to counter the imperialists; the tactics of thoroughly exposing the imperialists' peace fraud, and striving energetically for a genuine world peace, and the tactics of preparing for a just war to end the imperialist unjust war when and if the imperialists should unleash it.'[13]

Lu Ting-yi, of the Politburo, was more explicit about the strategy all parties should follow. 'All the means of revolution and forms of struggle, including the illegal and the "legal", extraparliamentary and parliamentary, sanguinary and bloodless, economic and political, military and ideological – all these are for the purpose of unmasking the imperialists to a fuller extent, showing them up as aggressors, constantly raising the revolutionary consciousness of the people, achieving broader mobilization of the masses to oppose the imperialists and the reactionaries, developing the struggle for world peace, and preparing for and winning victory in the people's revolution and the national revolution.'[14]

It may thus be seen what Mao meant by a one-by-one strategy. The United States could not send occupation forces to every country in the world which was about to have a social revolution. The more it intervened on behalf of the rich minority the more it would be hated by the poor and revolutionary majority.

Now, if we recall Premier Chou's replies to my questions about Sino-Soviet differences we may see that he answered truthfully, if succinctly. The two countries differed 'on theoretical questions and on ways of looking at things'. There were, first: differences on 'how to evaluate the situation with regard to war'; second, the fact that Russia's membership in the United Nations seated her in the Security Council and other bodies where the 'Taiwan clique' was represented. 'Proceeding from this point,' Chou said, 'the policies of the two governments cannot be the same in *many* respects.' (Emphasis mine.)

Differences over bloc policies in the United Nations arose not only because the Soviet delegate and delegates of ten other socialist countries were obliged to engage in limited collaboration with the 'Taiwan clique' and thus give credence to the existence of 'two Chinas'; inevitably they were also obliged to collaborate with an organization dominated by American policies whose aim was to foster counterrevolution, restore Western power on the Asian continent, and destroy Communist China.

With the failure of China's efforts to win recognition in the United Nations through the Bandung policy, or to dislodge the United States from Taiwan by negotiation, Peking undoubtedly re-evaluated the whole bloc relationship to that organization at the 'turning point' supposedly reached in 1957. While membership in the U.N. was a good propaganda issue with which to win sympathy among the uncommitted nations and divide the Western allies, it was not a viable means of pursuing revolutionary aims now demanded by a new situation. Mao's experience led him to believe that the West would never peacefully accept a socialist majority in the United Nations.

Yet there could be no doubt that Peking was dissatisfied with the Soviet failure to unseat the Nationalists and win recognition for China's sovereignty over Taiwan. It would have been unnatural if Mao had not questioned whether the Soviet delegates had really done everything possible. China's distrust of U.N. disarmament talks which excluded her was manifest. One means by which some of the powers fence-sitting on the question of China's admission might be stampeded into an affirmative vote, whereby critical pressure could be imposed on the United States, would be to threaten permanent withdrawal of the bloc in order to form a rival organization including as many neutral and uncommitted powers as possible. This alternative was undoubtedly debated in Peking and Moscow, but Moscow never used that threat.

Why weren't the Chinese satisfied merely to build toward communism in one backward land, instead of pushing the whole world toward revolution? First, they had not yet united all China. Second, they did have neighboring states divided by the presence of American military power. Third, Mao was part Leninist, part Stalinist – and all Chinese. He believed in a strong independent China; he also genuinely believed in its compatibility with an inevitable world revolution as the only way to order and peace. If he had lacked faith in the doctrine as a universal solution he could not have won victory for it as a national solution. *Under present circumstances an 'activist' world program served Chinese national interests.* But power politics were operating on both sides of the curtain. It might be in Russia's interest to keep China embroiled with the American foreign devil, but not vice versa, with China calling the shots. The more the Soviet Union invested in China and revolutions under China's influence, the more Soviet authority was modified by a rival leadership. Where did one draw the limit in using Soviet resources to serve Chinese national aims?

Yet if China were driven to take her own road the whole Soviet Pacific flank might be in jeopardy. Cut adrift, China would surely intensify her struggle by direct appeals to non-Western as well as Western parties to join her in dissidence. Two socialist worlds might arise. China could reorient her trade and economic policies toward other nations ready to exchange with her. France, Western Germany and Japan might be brought into closer relations with China by only slight shifts in emphasis of Peking's policies.

We now begin to see the true complexity of the uterine growth of a 'new society' struggling between viable birth and catastrophic miscarriage, and the difficult choices which faced the Soviet party as midwife of the future. One can sympathize with the Russian leaders. Powerful forces at home pulled them to the right and away from deep commitments in far places which might condemn Russia to continued low standards of living for years to come. Divisive drives in Eastern Europe pulled still farther to the right, in the hope that a *détente* with the West might open the road to close collaboration with the rising new Common Market and to an independent power center in Western Europe, freed from *both* Soviet and American domination. On the East the wind blew hard to the left, demanding greater equality and greater common sacrifices to advance the cause of liberation from pressures of a kind unknown in Europe.

Chou En-lai had said to me that no amount of ideological difference between China and Russia could be allowed to affect their basic military alliance against imperialism; come what might, an attack on one would be considered an attack on the other. But as the contradictions between the interests and prestige of the two Goliaths grew more profound and less rational, it began to seem that any true reconciliation would be possible only if Mao and Maoism were discarded in China, or a coup in Russia brought a radical change in the leadership there.*

---

*By 1963 it was clear that military cooperation between China and the U.S.S.R. had already been seriously affected. An illustration open to the view of the world was Soviet Russia's continued export to India of war planes and the means of producing them, while India had not yet accepted China's offer to negotiate a border settlement. Confronted with Moscow's intensified efforts to isolate China and organize an anti-Peking front in satellite Eastern Europe and among all the non-Chinese Communist parties of the world, the Chinese fell into a still more intransigent and go-it-alone mood. Under these new tensions it seemed inevitable that the pace of

China's economic growth would be further slowed down. With a Soviet parity in nuclear weapons which guaranteed near-absolute security, Moscow's interest in discrediting Mao as peer and political rival in the Communist world tended to increase in direct proportion to the apparently decreased value of China as a strategic buffer.

(1970) It was of course Khrushchev who fell from power (1964), while Mao survived. But Mao recovered his waning control only after an unprecedented battle against 'revisionists' personified – in the idioms of the Great Proletarian Cultural Revolution – by his former heir apparent, Liu Shao-ch'i, whom Mao ridiculed as 'China's Khrushchev'. A principle reason for Mao's break with Liu, and for the G.P.C.R. itself, was their differences over the correct handling of China's relations with post-Stalinist Russia.

By the spring of 1969, however, Mao had eliminated from positions of influence all those who might have disputed his authority in major questions of both domestic and foreign policy. Unity returned to the leadership, with rapid improvements in morale and the social fabric of the nation.

When, in April 1970, President Nixon blundered into a 'second Vietnam' tragedy in Cambodia, he enabled China to re-emerge into regional and international diplomacy with a clear-cut program of a united front against American aggression and its threat to world peace. Prince Sihanouk, exiled from Cambodia by the Lon Nol militant coup – which Nixon found that he could neither repudiate nor decisively aid – formed a liberation government under China's wing. It then became possible for all Indo-China to set up a common program of resistance against American imperialism, backed by China. Russia's anti-Chinese political offensive wavered under the new circumstances. In Eastern and Western Europe sympathies for China's position vis-à-vis both Soviet and American superpower reflected the self-interest of others eager to free themselves from subservience to the two nuclear giants.

78

China and Japan

IN 1960 there were approximately 900,000,000 Asians living in lands other than China, and excluding Asians and Asian mixtures in the Soviet Union, Mesopotamia, North and South America and Europe. Together with China, these people totaled well over half of humanity. The People's Republic had trade and diplomatic relations with the great majority of them, including the non-Communist countries of Pakistan, India, Afghanistan, Nepal, Burma, Ceylon, Cambodia, Laos and Indonesia, and the Communist-controlled halves of Vietnam and Korea.

After the Second World War the United States established military bases on Taiwan, in South Korea and South Vietnam, in Japan and in Thailand. The immediate national-security objective of Chinese foreign policy became not only to prevent any expansion of what it regarded as American military encirclement, but to outflank it, mainly by political means. Its second objective was to push Western military power out of the Far East altogether – and the United States was the only significant Western military power left there. China's third objective was to establish an Asian community run by Asians – a Monroe Doctrine for the Western Pacific. Its long-range objective was to lead the Asian community toward social revolution as part of a future 'one world' united in a Communist society.

Traditional Chinese strategy teaches that a curve is often the shortest line between two points, and Japan is China's shortest line to American vulnerability. Asia's greatest industrial nation, linked to China by a common written language, by race and by ancient cultural ties, by geography and by complementary economic needs, Japan's hundred million technologically advanced people held the ultimate balance of power in China's struggle to end American military dominance in the Western Pacific.

Japan hammered at China for sixty years, seized her territories, plundered and ravaged her people, and did her best to bring the giant under control. The Japanese ended by creating conditions which made Chinese Communist triumph inevitable, as Mr Kennan has told us. Japan also destroyed the crumbling edifice of Western colonialism, in a vain effort to replace it with her own Monroe Doctrine, and at the cost of her eclipse as an empire. Objectively, Chinese Communists recognize that Japan unconsciously thus played a 'progressive' role in history.

China suffered more damage from Japan, and fought her far longer, than any other power. The Nationalist Chinese government confiscated Japan's very large investment in China, which the People's Republic inherited. Peking was not consulted when the United States signed a peace treaty with the vanquished empire. Peking does not recognize that treaty, granted as a condition of a defense pact which obliged Japan to provide the United States with military bases and left Taiwan under American dominance. American occupation policies in Japan under General Douglas MacArthur nevertheless made it possible for Communist and other left-wing movements legally to become powerful voices in Japan. At the same time those policies were wise from the viewpoint of American power interests and Japanese political stability.

Japan was swiftly and totally disarmed, war industries were dismantled, principal war criminals were tried and punished, labor unions were legalized, and totalitarian propaganda was suppressed. Women attained equality of legal status and the Emperor was reduced to a symbolic figurehead. Proconsul MacArthur handed the Japanese a brand-new constitution which *forever renounced armed force as an instrument of Japanese national policy*. Japan, unlike Germany, was saved from an early revival of the militarism that had brought us to Hiroshima.

Two fundamental economic reforms laid a broad basis for a new economic democracy in Japan. Great private and government estates were broken up and millions of tenant farmers were helped to purchase small plots (averaging 2.5 acres) of land on easy terms. (In prewar Japan, seventy percent of peasant families were tenants.) Second, the few great monopoly capitalist families of Japan known as the zaibatsu – who owned the greater part of the nation's industrial assets – were required to dispose of their vast properties to new and supposedly diffuse ownership. The first reform created a new owner-peasant class that became the backbone of the conservative Japanese Liberal Party. The reform of the zaibatsu was less enduring. The American authorities opposed state ownership or socialism. They also would not advance adequate capital or credits to small entrepreneurs to enable them to buy out the 'pulverized' industries and restore production. The economy remained stagnant, reconstruction was difficult and unemployment mounted. The Socialist party steadily extended its following, with the Communists also growing, under the impact of revolution in China.

Ironically, the Korean War solved the zaibatsu problem. Suddenly, America spent billions in army procurement orders in Japan. Under the exigencies of war, laws were 're-reformed' to the benefit of the old owning families, new credit and capital became available, and restrictions against monopoly control were so relaxed as to permit production to be restored under the zaibatsu – much as happened to the Krupps in Germany. Japan's industrial economy resumed much of its prewar ownership pattern, but democratic rights remained. Labor unions became powerful, and so did peasant cooperative unions, but mostly they remained both 'nonmilitant' (conservative) and antimilitarist in leadership. After the Korean War, American policy in Japan favored a revival of Japanese military power, as in Germany. Almost universal pacifist opposition made it impossible to rewrite the Japanese constitution, however, to legalize the restoration of the army, navy and air force.

When the Japanese-American treaty came up for reconfirmation in the Diet in 1960, protests against even the old terms of the alliance threatened the downfall of the Liberal government. Huge nation-wide demonstrations were organized. The Kishi Administration was compelled to cancel arrangements to receive President Eisenhower on a state visit; it could not guarantee his personal safety. The Kishi régime fell, but not before it renewed the treaty – with no provision for Japanese rearmament. In the new elections the Socialist party failed to win a majority, but while the Liberal-Democrats remained in power they could not seriously raise the question of rearming.

By the mid 1950s China had again become a major issue in internal Japanese politics. This was by no means confined to those influenced by the Japanese Communist Party, which tallied as many as three million votes in the national elections but was still a small minority. Most Japanese wished to have normal trade and cultural relations with China. Their inability to do so increased resentment against U.S. domination, the presence of American armed force in Japan, and American occupation of Okinawa.

The United States walked a tightrope in Japan. American civilians were well received but the uniform was not liked; it was, of course, a reminder of Japan's defeat. Soldiers were confined strictly to army reservations, and men on leave in the cities wore mufti. Great care was taken to avoid incidents between American soldiers and the civilian population. 'A single spark can start a prairie fire.' The Japanese in general seemed grateful for an American occupation far more generous than they had expected, and for vital aid in reconstruction. But sentiment heavily favored neutrality.

China is to Japan what Greece is to children of Western culture. Japanese go there not just as tourists but as pilgrims. Few Japanese suffered any real sense of remorse about having made war on the European nations; they felt a secret pride at having dislodged them in Asia and they were after all beaten by America, not by Europe. Among Japanese who knew China, however, I found a curious sense of unexpiated war guilt. This was skillfully exploited by the Peking government, which received its hundreds of Japanese guests in a spirit of let-bygones-be-bygones and with expressions of desire to restore peace and unity in an Asian community of the future. As Mao Tse-tung took delight in his youth in Japan's victory over Tsarist Russia, so many Japanese saw in both China's resurgent demands for Western withdrawal, and her back-talk to Russia, a continuation of Japan's own lost dream of an Asian co-prosperity sphere. A sense of unity in resentment against the white masters' dominance in their Asian world was always latent between them.

It would have been as foolish to believe that Japan must fall into China's arms as to imagine that she could be kept cut off from China indefinitely by American pressure. Japan was not afraid of being conquered by China. In Japan's hundreds of years of borrowing from China there was no attempt by China to invade Japan except by the Mongols, whose fleet was destroyed in a storm.

Japan was now run by hard-headed and hard-pressed business-men. They knew that they must export or perish. Dependent on imports for twenty percent of its food and ninety percent of its raw materials, faced with the necessity to provide a million new jobs every year in a land one twentieth the size of Australia but with nearly ten times its population, Japan could not afford to look at markets with an ideological monocle. After the Korean War the United States provided substantial subsidies and a highly profitable market, but lopsided dependence on America did not make for a stable economy. Japan's extraordinary post-Korean War prosperity was possible partly because of zero expenditures for national defense – in a land which formerly spent eighty percent of its budget on armaments. As long as America continued to buy enough of Japan's goods or otherwise subsidize her economy sufficiently to keep the mass standard of living stable or rising, the businessmen's régime would probably remain in power. If unemployment and economic depression should reach critical proportions, however, radical solu-tions – including fully restored ties with China – might again find widespread appeal in Japan. Building toward leadership for that day, Japan's Socialist party adopted a foreign policy platform which was popular enough nearly to defeat renewal of the Japanese-American alliance.

Postponement of such a day was, curiously, probably helped in part by United States armed intervention in Vietnam. At least that was the opinion of many Japanese economists, who had anticipated a recession. Instead, the Japanese economy, benefiting by billions in profits acquired through renewed United States use of Japan as a war procurement base, enjoyed a continuation of the boom which had begun during the Korean War.*

Before leaving China and her East Asian neighbors let us take a brief look at the strange metaphysics which brought us to the brink of another world holocaust in Vietnam.

* By 1970 Japan passed West Germany, to become the second greatest industrial power in the non-Communist world. In 1969 her national income reached $1,100 per person and her 1970 gross national product was expected to exceed U.S. $200,000,000.

War and Peace in Vietnam

' "ALL men are created equal ... They are endowed by their Creator with certain inalienable rights. Among these are life, liberty, and the pursuit of happiness."

'These immortal words are from the Declaration of Independence of the United States of America in 1776. Taken in a broader sense, these phrases mean: "All peoples on earth are born equal; all peoples have the right to live, to be free, to be happy." ...

'These are undeniable truths ...

'Nevertheless, for more than eighty years, the French imperialists, abusing their "liberty, equality, and fraternity", have violated the land of our ancestors and oppressed our countrymen. Their acts are contrary to the ideals of humanity and justice.' *Preamble to the Declaration of Independence of the Republic of Vietnam, Hanoi, 2 September 1945*[1]

'All people who are prepared for self-government should be permitted to choose their own form of government ... without any interference from any foreign sources.' *Harry S. Truman, enumerating the 'Four Commandments' of United States Foreign Policy, 1945*

I was in Vietnam shortly after that declaration of independence.* For a few weeks then the country was united, for the first time in sixty years. Then it was again divided successively by the British, the Chinese and the French – all assisted by the Americans. The heat of Chinese-American conflict shifted to South-east Asia, and Americans began to be killed there in increasing numbers. We spent billions of dollars trying to shore up the Diem government, and we could end either by putting as many troops there as in Korea, or

---

*(1970) Background material provided here, which brings us to the eve of major American armed intervention, seems of continuing interest as one demonstration, among many, that the facts available in 1961, already abundantly belied later U.S. pretensions to a moral-legal basis for President Johnson's course, as well as the attempt to impose a unilateral political decision by military means in the internal conflict in Vietnam.

by finding a formula for neutralization of the whole country and getting out. It was probably a last test of the viability of ten years of the Dulles policy in the Far East; any solution found there was bound to be directly relevant in Taiwan, in Korea, and in our relations with China and the United Nations. What *was* Vietnam all about?

It is a very long story. I shall try to make it short by stating at the outset what Vietnam is not. The Republic was originally set up not by Communists of China or Russia but by native nationalists of various parties, in which native Communists were in 1945 still a small minority. They did not take possession of the country from the French; the French régime had surrendered to the Japanese in 1940. The Vietnamese never attacked the United States, and Vietnam was never American territory. The United States had no international mandate in Vietnam. How did we happen to be there, 12,000 miles from home, flushing peasants out of the jungles and waiting to see what North Vietnam, China and Russia were going to do about it?

Indochina is not exactly a 'little country' and not a new nation. With Laos and Cambodia it is about 300,000 square miles in area, and more than eighty percent of its inhabitants are Annamites. Even without Cambodia (88,000 square miles) Indochina is as large as France. In the western mountains lies the heavily forested jungle kingdom of Laos – with 91,000 square miles but fewer than 3,000,000 inhabitants. Vietnam proper is a long, rippling dragon with a coastline of about 2,000 miles, 127,000 square miles of territory, and about 30,000,000 inhabitants. Many centuries ago these people migrated from southern China and absorbed or destroyed earlier inhabitants. Cambodians, like the people of Thailand and Upper Burma, are mixed descendants of the same stock as the Thai and other minority peoples of China. Laotians are indistinguishable from the Pai people across the frontier in Yunnan.

From pre-Christian times this whole area was under Chinese political and cultural influence. It was no perfect idyll; China has had frequent periods of aggressive imperialism. Annam won its independence in the tenth century but it was invaded once every hundred years or so to restore China's position as suzerain. (In turn, it dominated Cambodia and Laos.) During most of the post-

Mongol period the kingdom of Annam was probably as independent as the Dominion of Canada. The loose suzerainty of China usually relied mainly upon cultural dominance – with the threat of military occupation as coercion. The written language, Confucianism, court ritual, houses, customs, were imported from China by Vietnam. The name Vietnam ('Distant South') * was probably Chinese in derivation – as was Japan, which means 'Source of the Sun (rise)', or east of China.

French merchants, soldiers and priests began to take over Indochina after the Chinese empire was crippled by the T'ai-p'ing Rebellion and the Opium Wars. At first the Bible was foremost; after that followed the weightier artillery of *la mission civilisatrice*. In midcentury the French seized the Saigon area and the emperor of Annam called upon Peking for military aid. Rocking from Anglo-French invasions at home, the suzerain power could do nothing. The Book and the sword moved steadily northward. In 1882 the emperor of Annam again appealed to China and large forces were sent to his assistance. In 1885 China – again under French attack at home – withdrew in defeat. France had won the potentially richest colonial prize in her realm. After fifty-five years a pro-Nazi governor general, Admiral Decoux, surrendered effective control of Indochina to the Japanese without firing a shot.

During that brief half-century isolated Annam had been introduced to Christian civilization. The Annamites were stubborn, weak and childish; they had to be punished and taught. The French built modern docking facilities at Saigon and Haiphong, laid down a few military highways, built small modern garrison towns, ran the difficult modern railway up to the capital of Yunnan with an official eye to its annexation, established a monopoly of foreign trade, built themselves luxurious homes and clubs, provided employment for native servants, and kept law and order by executing peasants who sometimes became bandits rather than pay taxes. It all brought little return to the motherland, but it was profitable for a French *colon* community of some 40,000 at peak.

When I first saw Hanoi and Haiphong, as a youth, they were

---

*Vietnamese characters for the Chinese term *Yueh-nan*, which literally means 'South of Yueh' (ancient name for Kwangtung), or China's southernmost (distant) province.

miniature French provincial towns at the center, surrounded by slums of cowed and undernourished slaves. The halls of the best hotels smelled of opium. The cafés and restaurants were excellent. There had been recent revolts that year (1930), and whole villages were bombed and wiped out in reprisal. The local press announced the guillotining of 'rebel leaders', whose heads were displayed for salutary effect.[2] That was the hard line. On the softer side of the market, one could literally buy a comely Annamite concubine for less than a hundred dollars, as lonely French *colons* often did.

In balance, French supremacy was doubtless a more enlightened rule than the native despotism which it replaced. It did bring a backward, secluded kingdom into contact with advanced knowledge of the West. A few upperclass Annamites got to France and studied there; they learned to think politically, as well as to appreciate French culture. French history, as well as their own, taught some to become revolutionaries. By the time the Japanese arrived, the French were operating eighty-one prisons, not counting labor-reform camps. After fifty-five years two percent of the children were officially reported to be getting an elementary education, one half of one percent were in secondary schools, and there was a university in Hanoi. In the puppet kingdom of Laos one native doctor had been trained. Harold Isaacs reported in 1943 that 'the colonial government spent 30,000 piastres for libraries, 71,000 piastres for hospitals, 748,000 piastres for schools . . . and 4,473,000 piastres for the purchase of opium distributed through the official opium monopoly'.[3]

Before Pearl Harbor, China was still resisting Japan, alone. The Japanese navy blocked all the China coast and the only way left open was through Haiphong to Yunnan. The French collected heavy duties on China's imports. Then the Japanese spoiled things by demanding control. Governor General Decoux was an Axis sympathizer; in 1940, he obeyed the puppet Vichy government's order to place the colony at Japan's disposal. Symbolically, this act marked the end of Western empire in Asia.

Bringing in their armed forces, the Japanese allowed the French to remain as stewards. The colonial bureaucracy supplied the Japanese with rice and conscripted native labor for them. Using Indochina as a staging base, the Japanese then mobilized the forces with which, in December 1941, they invaded all southern Asia and attacked the Philippines. Japanese demands became excessive; their unhappy stewards had to rob the peasants for them. During the war years, according to American estimates, more than 2,000,000 Annamites starved to death – eight percent of the population, or about four times all the Americans killed in both world wars.[4]

The Annamites always seemed to me the meekest people in the world, but even the meek revolt; in desperation, thousands joined the guerrillas. Some began to attack isolated police posts. Individual soldiers in the puppet militia faded away with rifles. Patriotic intellectuals in the underground national revolutionary movement organized a united front. In 1943 they sent emissaries to the French timidly to suggest a joint *Résistance* to the Japanese. French officials coldly rebuked them; they were accused of seeking arms against France, not Japan. Throughout the war the Foreign Legion and Senegalese forces were busy hunting down Annamese patriots.

By 1945 the Annamite forces had occupied many villages and built small bases. In Yunnan, they had liaison with the Nationalist Chinese. Near the Chinese border a few American O.S.S. men contacted their guerrilla bands and, helped also by a few antifascist Frenchmen, brought them arms and other supplies. The slaves were rising, and the French *colons* were no longer useful. Just before V-E Day the Japanese arrested, disarmed and interned all French forces in Indochina. Except for a small detachment near the border, which crossed over into Yunnan, there was no resistance. After 6 March 1945 no substance or *gloire* remained of French colonial rule.

Now the Japanese belatedly turned to appease nationalist sentiment. The French governor general had been all-powerful, but there was always a window dressing of native rule, headed by a puppet emperor who functioned much like the native princes of British India. Emperor Bao Dai had been France's figurehead ruler since boyhood. Educated in France, he had spent much of his life on the Riviera. At home, his make-believe court of mandarins formed a ruling hierarchy who danced when Frenchmen pulled the strings. Bao Dai's ancestors had once ruled most of independent Indochina, but the French had broken it up for administrative and economic reasons, restricting the emperor to a shrunken state called Annam. In the south they created 'Cochin-China', under direct French rule; in the north they created the 'protectorate' of 'Tonkin'; in the west they had the puppet kingdoms of Laos and Cambodia.

The Japanese now declared that they were restoring 'unity and independence' under Emperor Bao Dai. They revived the pre-French name of the land, 'Vietnam'. Bao Dai was permitted to send envoys to claim Cochin-China and Tonkin, and even to contact the puppet monarchs of Laos and Cambodia. For the first time since French conquest, the country was nominally 'unified'. Behind this façade, the Japanese first sought to destroy, and then sought to reconcile, the free Vietnamese armed forces. These latter were guerrilla groups led largely by the Vietnamese Independence League – Viet Minh, for short. Their partisans spread over extensive areas from north to south. The week of Hiroshima, a Viet Minh congress representing both north and south elected a provisional government for the whole country. They also used the historic name Vietnam. Conceding independence to Cambodia and Laos, the congress invited them to join a Federation of Indochina.

Then an unusual thing occurred: a peaceful transfer of power. Envoys of the Vietnam republic negotiated with the Japanese commanders. On instructions from Tokyo the Japanese agreed to let members of the Viet Minh enter the cities, including the capital, organize freedom parades, and convene assemblies.* Elections were held by different parties. In Hanoi a national assembly met and drafted a declaration of independence. On 25 August the puppet emperor (anxious to be on the Riviera) made a remarkable declaration 'to abdicate and transfer power to the Democratic Republican Government'. He accepted a post as 'Chief Counselor of State'. The mandarins (appointed by the French and Japanese) and other puppets wilted from the scene.

---

*Japan sought to win postwar good will by recognizing, before the Europeans returned, the independence of all the colonies she had overrun – no doubt hoping also to turn hostility from Japan back toward the old masters.

Within a few days Viet Minh forces peacefully occupied government buildings from Hanoi to Saigon, took over administration of the bureaucracy (already nine tenths native), and held power nearly everywhere from north to south. Confined to their barracks, Japanese troops did not interfere and there were few incidents. Vietnamese political prisoners were released; so were Jews and antifascist Europeans. Only the Legionnaires and other French troops remained interned. Amazed French civilians sat unmolested in their cafés. One Frenchman was killed in a street fight; otherwise the Viet Minh police and new troops maintained admirable order. They treated the French politely but no longer obsequiously. Having proclaimed independence, the Republic of Vietnam sent telegrams to France, to the United States – to all the world capitals, impartially – seeking recognition, admission to the United Nations, and authorization to disarm the Japanese.

Here I must greatly condense the history of the amputation and subsequent tragedy that now befell Vietnam, and – while urging the reader to consult the abundant documentation available elsewhere [5] – rely largely upon eyewitness knowledge of the main events which threw the Republic into the Communist camp, brought Mr Dulles to the 'brink' at Dien Bien Phu, and sent our troops into the muddy rice fields for Ngo Dinh Diem.

At Potsdam the 'freedom-loving nations' (Britain, Russia, the U.S.) agreed that France still owned Vietnam. The Allied chiefs also decided that something had to be done for Generalissimo Chiang Kai-shek, who was fretting because he was not getting much attention as the Big Fourth. The Chinese Nationalists were therefore given the satisfaction of disarming Japanese troops in Indochina north of the Sixteenth Parallel. In the southern half of the country the British were to do that job – in a shoehorn operation for the French, who would later on also 'relieve' the Chinese occupational troops in the north. The Allies made no announcements to the Vietnamese that the French were returning.

Officials of the Republic in Saigon welcomed the first British contingent as their antifascist 'allies'. General Douglas Gracey set up his headquarters and at once conferred with the Japanese commander, General Terauchi. Gracey refused to see Vietnamese leaders who wished to negotiate terms of cooperation for disarming the Japanese. On British orders the Japanese released from internment some 5,000 Foreign Legionnaires. They were immediately rearmed. Gracey then declared martial law and ordered Vietnamese troops and police to evacuate Saigon. Before dawn on 23 September the rearmed Legionnaires staged a *coup d'état* and seized the city hall, seat of the new government. State buildings were taken by force, hundreds of people were arrested, and blood spattered the streets. The Vietnamese began to organize resistance in the suburbs. More British troops arrived. (I also arrived then, as a war correspondent, in an American air force plane ferrying O.S.S. and other observers from Thailand.)

Early in October, French troops disembarked from the cruiser *Gloire*, their arms and all their supplies furnished by the United States. Systematically the Saigon perimeter was extended. Instead of disarming the Japanese, General Gracey ordered them to assist in suppressing the Vietnamese. Terauchi's troops were put back on a war footing, with roles now reversed between the French and themselves.

More American-equipped French forces poured into Saigon. These soon included thousands of Nazi prisoners of war who had enlisted in the Foreign Legion. Meanwhile, many former Vichyite officials were busily re-forming the colonial Sûreté and bureaucracy. I saw them herd hundreds of Vietnamese peasants – men, women and children – into open squares where the broiling tropical sun beat down and they waited days for interrogation and summary sentences to long imprisonment or execution. The road was slowly opened to Cambodia, and French protectorate power was restored in its capital, Phnom Penh. Soon France had 50,000 troops in the south, enough to relieve the British. Having finally disarmed and repatriated the Japanese, General Gracey washed his hands of what soldiers were already calling *la sale guerre* – the dirty war. He departed with the last of his men to the strains of 'Auld Lang Syne'.

France was never to recover full control even in the south. In the north, with no British Trojan Horse to lead them, the French first had to dislodge hostile Chinese Nationalist troops. Why 'hostile'? All Chinese, Nationalist and Communist alike, preferred an independent Vietnam to a French Vietnam. Chiang Kai-shek had sent down one of the Yunnan 'opium generals', Lu Han,* to collect back debts from the French as well as from the Japanese. Ho Chi Minh, leader of the new Republic, had first been imprisoned by the Chinese Nationalists and then been released and 'aided'. From the day General Lu Han arrived, he permitted Ho, as head of the free Vietnam régime, to develop an administrative and political apparatus around Hanoi as their capital.

General Lu was interested in cash, and for cash the Vietnamese could even buy the Japanese arms General Lu collected. They were expensive. Lu imposed Chinese currency as official tender at an exchange rate ten times its purchasing power in China. Officers-in-business (rice, opium, anything at all) piled up black-market profits in the millions which by chain of command reached official pockets as far back as Chungking.[6] France was assessed $23,000,000 to cover China's cost of disarming the Japanese. (The United States would pay.) Large blocks of real estate fell to Kuomintang carpet-baggers. Following their generals' example, Nationalist troops helped themselves, impartially, to the contents of French and Vietnamese homes.[7] Desperate to be rid of the locusts, the French paid off Chiang Kai-shek with a humiliating and costly 'evacuation' agreement.

The Vietnamese no more wished to be bossed by Chinese than by Frenchmen, but China's withdrawal left them not even an 'honest broker' among all the powers. The United Nations did not answer appeals for recognition. President Truman replied by sending millions in American lend-lease and military supplies to the French. As the Chinese prepared to be 'relieved' by the French, the Vietnam government at Hanoi, to avoid prolonged war in an already starving

---

*Throughout the war, as before it, Yunnan had been the fiefdom of the regional satraps Lung Yun and Lu Han, who controlled the opium and tin monopolies. Lu Han had the greater army. In a double maneuver the Generalissimo dispatched Lu Han to Indochina, then quickly descended on Lung Yun and seized control of the rich province. Lung Yun later revenged himself on the Generalissimo by accepting Communist assistance to recover control of Yunnan, but his nominal rule there proved short-lived. Until his death in the spring of 1962, he was a supernumerary among the ex-Kuomintang generals in Peking.

land, sought the best possible bargain offering any hope of self-determination under France.

The French would not grant 'independence'. In the agreement France signed with Ho Chi Minh in March 1946, the Republic of Vietnam was recognized as 'A Free State, having its government, its parliament, its army, and its finances, and forming part of the Indochinese Federation and the French Union'. France had already detached Cambodia and Laos as separate states, but the agreement provided for a popular referendum on 'unification' of north and (again French-occupied) south Vietnam. The French were to send no more than 15,000 troops into the north, to share in garrison duties with 10,000 Vietnamese troops, until the referendum was held. Meanwhile, Indochina's international status (as a member of the French Union) was to be decided by negotiation.[8]

Statesmen in Paris believed they had solved the Vietnam problem. Indeed, Ho Chi Minh and the great majority of Vietnamese nationalists were content to remain within the French Union, if only as a guarantee against possible future Chinese aggression. But Paris was not the colonial mind and hand of French Indochina. As events in North Africa were later to make clear to the world, the colonial army and the colonial bureaucracy operated quite independently whenever they could. And in Vietnam they could and did.

Before the ink was long dry on the Franco-Vietnamese accord, the highest French army leaders in the colony issued orders (then secret, later exposed in France)[9] unmistakably aimed at the crushing of all Vietnamese resistance, full restoration of French military and political power, and the complete sabotage of the 'Free State' agreement. By these orders the French military units which moved in to 'relieve' the Chinese were required 'in each garrison' to prepare and set in operation 'plans ... to transform the situation from a purely military operation to a *coup d'état*'. Meanwhile, the Sûreté was to create teams of specialists to locate 'all leaders' of the various parties in the government and to prepare for 'the task of discreetly neutralizing these leaders as soon as the command considers it necessary ...'[10]

French troops were admitted peacefully by agreement in the north, and permitted to garrison key points, but hostilities in the south never stopped. There the French refused to recognize or deal with the resistance forces. In May 1946, Ho Chi Minh and the Vietnamese delegation left for Paris to negotiate terms of all-national elections and relationships within the Union. The day after his departure the French in Saigon announced the formation of their own carefully selected separate government for the south. In August the French called a 'Conference of the Federation' consisting of delegates having no connection with the 'Free State', and launched a *national* puppet régime. In Haiphong the French army seized control of the ports and customs without any agreement. Incidents followed in many areas as the French 'established order' by arrests, by local coups and by disarming native police.

Despite subsequent agreements Ho Chi Minh signed in Paris which called for a French cease-fire and guaranteed Vietnamese 'civil liberties', incidents were provoked which everywhere gave pretext for arrests and wider French military action. The 15,000 limit on French troops was rapidly violated; air, naval and army units soon doubled and trebled that. In December the French seized Haiphong, which was systematically bombarded and pacified, with the cutting of many a throat. In the same month the generals took police control in Hanoi and demanded the evacuation of all Vietnamese troops. Shortly afterward Hanoi became the scene of the first open battle of the two forces, which French troops easily won.

Léon Blum's Colonial Minister (a Socialist) now arrived in Indochina. Back in Hanoi again, Ho Chi Minh was still anxious to confer with Blum to end hostilities. The Minister refused to meet with Ho, and announced that 'only a military solution of the situation was possible'.[11] (The French Communist Party continued to remain in Blum's cabinet.) Leaders of the Republic of Vietnam were driven back to fight in the fields and the hills. War again raged from north to south.

We must now consider that frail wisp of humanity named Ho Chi Minh, whom Americans became committed to destroy in Vietnam. How was it that he, acknowledged leader of the minority Communist Party of Vietnam (in 1946, 20,000 members; in 1960, called the Lao Dong, with a total of more than 500,000 members), came to be the unanimous choice of all the independence parties and groups which supported the Republic – as the man thought best qualified to lead the struggle against the Japanese, the French, and finally the friendly Americans?

'When one recalls,' wrote two American anti-Communist specialists on South-east Asia, Virginia Thompson and Richard Adloff, 'that during its first nine months of existence the Vietnam Republic was occupied by rapacious Chinese troops, whose commander favored the Dong Minh Hoi [Nationalists] above the Viet Minh [Communist-led coalition], and that millions of people within its confines were threatened by famine, the skill with which Ho maneuvered at this time can be better appreciated. . . . Ho was able not only to win the National Assembly's agreement to the concessions he had made to French imperialism [the abortive 1946 agreement] but also to get the Dong Minh Hoi to share his responsibility. . . . Ho's integrity, which has been recognized even by his enemies, suggests that he would not betray the cause [true national independence] to which he has devoted almost all his adult life . . . . Ho's personal prestige, ability, and training are so outstanding that the course which his leadership charts seems to be the determining factor [of the]future.' [12]

Ho Chi Minh, whose real name was Nguyen Ai Quoc, had a background somewhat comparable to Chou En-lai's. He was born in northern Annam in 1890, to a family whose ancestors were officials before the French conquest. Thin as a blade of grass, and small-boned like most Annamite aristocrats, he was a well-educated intellectual. As a student he went to France to interpret for coolie labor hired to dig trenches and latrines in the First World War. He stayed in France four years. Both his French and his English were good. He also knew Chinese, Russian and German. In 1920, he had attended the meeting at Tours where the French Communist Party was founded.

Is it difficult to understand why Ho and hundreds like him saw the Communist party as the only means of national liberation? Review the reasons which drew men toward the same cause in China. Double them; Indochina was all colonial, China only semi-colonial. If you detested being a slave and found one friend who promised freedom, would you reject or embrace him? Like Sun Yat-sen, Ho Chi Minh had eavesdropped at Versailles; he had found that Vietnam was not on President Wilson's self-determination program. Not the Republican party or the Democratic party, but only the Communists, and only Russia after its revolution, offered help to subjugated nations determined to fight for equality against great odds.

As in China, the revolutionary task was to bring leadership and political action to an amorphous mass of peasants – ninety percent of the people, and ninety percent illiterate – who lived under similar or worse conditions of overpopulation, disease (eighty percent had intestinal parasites), despair, underproduction and servitude. Independence and national unity were the powerful elementary aspirations in Indochina, as in all colonies. In 1950, Russia and China recognized the Democratic Republic of Vietnam, as it was now called. Following the Korean truce, Russo-Chinese aid in guns, training and technical assistance reached proportions which began to counterbalance American help to the French. Vietnam's armies multiplied and improved in efficiency. In the south the French still held the upper hand, but in the north they had to go over more and more to the defensive. By 1954 France had an Indochina army of 250,000 men fully engaged in the attempted reconquest – and had spent more there than all the Marshall Plan aid extended to Paris since its liberation from Nazi occupation.

Then, in a great miscalculation, the heart of the French army cracked at Dien Bien Phu. It was not a French error alone. American joint staff officers were deeply involved, for they had approved the great Navarre plan which led to the disaster. Divining the French intentions (which foundered largely on false assumptions of security of supply lines), the Vietnamese commanding general, Giap, followed a 'one by one' strategy, broke the back of the offensive, and succeeded in isolating and entrapping the cream of the French forces in the north. On 20 March 1954 the French chief of staff, General Paul Ely, arrived in Washington fresh from Indochina. He asked for immediate direct American intervention to relieve the besieged armies. Without it, France would have to accept Vietnam's offer of a cease-fire in exchange for an international conference to negotiate terms of French surrender.

French revelations since then have indicated that the first American response was made two months before the Geneva Peace Conference opened. According to Georges Bidault (French Foreign

Minister at that time), Secretary of State Dulles twice offered him the use of American atomic bombs against both China and Vietnam – to back up his verbal threats of 'massive retaliation'.[13] Realizing the somber implications of such a move, M. Bidault instead repeated General Ely's request for American nonatomic air strikes at Dien Bien Phu. Immediate army and naval air force intervention was then advocated by Mr Dulles as well as by Admiral Radford, chief of the Joint Staffs. Before a final commitment was made General Matthew B. Ridgway, army chief of staff, made a detailed logistical study of what was involved. His report to the President showed that direct intervention could not be 'successful' short of a great war of enormous cost. In his memoirs General Ridgway wrote:

> In Korea we had learned that air and naval power alone cannot win a war and that inadequate ground forces cannot win one either. *It was incredible to me that we had forgotten that bitter lesson so soon – that we were on the verge of making the same tragic error.*
>
> That error, thank God, was not repeated ... The idea of intervention was abandoned, and it is my belief that the analysis which the Army made and presented to higher authority [Eisenhower] played a considerable, perhaps a decisive, part in persuading our government not to embark on that tragic adventure.[14]

If we are to understand why, after all, we did embark upon that 'tragic adventure', it is here unavoidable to focus some irreverent inquiry upon a Christian gentleman who appeared to be anything but a swashbuckler: Secretary of State John Foster Dulles. The questions which concern us, however, are in the broadest sense not one man's responsibility but rather concern the collective conscience of a whole nation. It would be a mistake to believe that Mr Dulles acted alone or arbitrarily. The power delegated to him came from the President; behind both of them all Americans who did not say them nay lent their support.

John Foster Dulles was a product of what President Eisenhower later deplored as the 'military-industrial complex' and of the postKorea hysteria which strengthened it. America was in a punitive mood and Mr Dulles was the man best attuned to it emotionally. He was an obstinate and a righteous man. Like many reformers who had gone forth to redeem the heathen in the past, he had no occasion to reflect that Jehovah, as well as his adversary, can take many forms in many places. Mr Dulles' speeches never convinced me that he had troubled to study the history or realities behind the issues in the Far East or that he understood anything about revolutionary China or Indochina. No one in Washington saw much evidence that he had ever given serious attention to anyone who might have enlightened him. The rise of John Foster Dulles unfortunately coincided with the long agony of McCarthyism, which offered the world the spectacle of a great nation reverting to political infantilism – not just for a few days but for four critical years. Mr Dulles' capacity for trusting infidels on the other side of the river was no more generous than Senator Joseph McCarthy's opinion of his fellow countrymen at home. By fortuitous circumstance, McCarthyism so upset the normal administrative, legislative and even judicial equilibrium of a bewildered United States that the Secretary of State was quite free to do some rather egregiously absurd things.

McCarthy never managed to expose a single one of the 'hundreds of card-carrying Communists in the State Department' who he once alleged were there, but he was a highly useful man in isolating the United States from most of the world, in pursuit of Dulles' aims in eastern Asia. One effect of McCarthyism was the rapid separation from the State Department of many of our ablest foreign service specialists on communism. By 1954, Mr Dulles had found so many of McCarthy's 'names' agreeably expendable that he was left without one experienced senior China or Indochina expert on the policy-making level of his staff. The only crime proved against any of those experts was their prophetically correct wartime reporting on China.[15]

Of all Mr Dulles' (and 'our') errors of commission not one was more costly than his success in tying the United States to Chiang Kai-shek on Taiwan, in a unilateral intervention and a wholly unequal alliance without precedent in American history. That is not a mere hindsight view of my own, it exactly corresponds to the estimate made by the State Department's own Asian experts in the year 1949, as recorded in a remarkably prescient official 'policy information paper' issued to explain why the United States would not establish a protectorate in Taiwan.[16] In the most literal sense,

it was that alliance which brought America into undeclared war
in Indochina.

Now we may well ask what would have happened if M. Bidault
had accepted Dulles' offer of the Bomb or if General Ridgway had
not successfully opposed major intervention at that time. To what
significant degree would the individual American citizen have
shared in the responsibility? There now exist international laws,
fixed at the Nuremberg criminal trials, which quite likely would
have been applied to those who dropped the bomb near Dien Bien
Phu or on China – assuming that they had lost yet survived. Had
we overheard conversations among totalitarian leaders solemnly
considering the fateful decisions I have mentioned, might we not
have doubted their sanity – as many doubted the sanity of Mao
Tse-tung? But was it so insane of Mao to seek an atomic bomb of
his own to discourage Mr Dulles? Of course that worst did not
happen, for which we may thank General Ridgway. But it might
still happen elsewhere. Did not the Communists also recommend
the same means? We do not know. Perhaps they did. If so, we may
also thank *their* General Ridgway. But what happened instead?

With Dien Bien Phu, the French people had had enough of the
'dirty war'. In a new election Mendès-France received a mandate to
'end the war in twenty days'. At the Geneva Conference, concluded in July 1954, France unequivocally recognized the complete
independence of *all* Vietnam. Separate treaties provided for independent kingdoms in Cambodia and Laos. All three states were to
be neutral; they were to be free to have diplomatic relations with
both East and West. All foreign troops were to be withdrawn.

Yet as it turned out, the Geneva agreements destroyed the unifi-
cation which they so explicitly confirmed. As early as 1950 the
French had combined Cochin-China, Annam and Tonkin into a
single 'State' over which they persuaded the exiled ex-emperor,
Bao Dai, to preside as Chief Executive. The State was still part of
the French Union, however. Lacking true independence (as usual),
Bao Dai held no more than nominal sway within the perimeter of
French arms – which covered only parts of the whole country.

The Geneva agreement further provided for a national election
as soon as the French forces withdrew. In the first stage the French

were to concentrate south of the Seventeenth Parallel, turning everything north of it over to the Viet Minh forces. Before 1956 they would totally withdraw also from the south. Heterogeneous native military groups (organized by the French in the name of the puppet Bao Dai government) south of the parallel were to police the area until the national election. The electoral procedure was to be negotiated in 1955 between Bao Dai and the Democratic Republic of Vietnam. The vote itself was to be cast not later than July 1956. This election would choose an all-Vietnam government to complete unification.

For Vietnamese seeking unity, the Geneva accord developed two major flaws. First, it left no outside power committed to enforce the terms. France, having finally surrendered all sovereignty to an independent Vietnam, had no more authority there. Like Russia, China, Britain and other signatory foreign powers, she was merely bound not to interfere in Vietnam's internal affairs. Second, the 1956 date set for a national election provided time for reactionary elements around the Bao Dai régime to regroup before the withdrawal of French arms, to bid for American armed support, and to refuse to carry out an election to achieve unification.

Ho Chi Minh was universally known and his following was overwhelming. As a good politician, Ho had minimized his leading Communist party role. He retained the title, President of the Republic, while others rotated as secretary of his party. His prestige as a national patriot first, and party man next, was well established.[*] He was George Washington on the left. So sure of this were the Viet Minh that they were ready to exchange electoral inspectors between north and south, as well as international observers. Mendès-France realized that even in a fair and well-supervised election the D.R.V. (Democratic Republic of Vietnam) would win dominant power. Vietnam was not East Germany.

Mendès-France had no alternative to the treaty, however; his

---

[*](1970) In his own memoirs, *Mandate for Change, 1953–56*, President Dwight D. Eisenhower wrote: 'I have never talked or corresponded with a person knowledgeable in Indochinese affairs who did not agree that, had elections been held as of the time of the fighting [with the French] possibly 80 percent of the population would have voted for the Communist Ho Chi Minh.' N.Y.C., 1963, p. 372–3.

premiership depended upon concluding a peace. Having failed to prevent what looked to him like a sellout, Mr Dulles had first boy-cotted the conference – where he turned his back on Chou En-lai's outstretched hand. But Vietnam, Russia and China would not accept a settlement which left the United States free to intervene in the south. Under great pressure from the NATO allies, Dulles fin-ally gave backhanded recognition to the agreement. On the last day of the conference he stated that the United States would 'not oppose' implementation of the instrument, 'either by force or threat of force', and would view renewed 'aggression' with 'grave concern'.

It shortly became apparent that the electoral arrangements had been sabotaged in advance, by the promise, through Mr Dulles, of a *de facto* United States military alliance with Ngo Dinh Diem, an ex-royalist violently opposed to unification with the D.R.V. In September 1954, Mr Dulles utilized the façade of SEATO behind which to offer military protection to the nascent 'neutral states' of Indochina. In October, Mr Dulles persuaded President Eisenhower to make a declaration of unqualified United States support for Ngo Dinh Diem personally – even though Bao Dai was still 'Chief of State'.

The strategic concept behind SEATO was to extend the arm-ored arc around China stretching from Korea through Japan and Taiwan to Thailand and Eastern Pakistan. Vietnam formed a miss-ing link. It was presumably now to be filled in. China would then 'pass away'.

The Geneva terms had forbidden new arms build-ups in any of the Indochinese states. Only replacements of worn-out equipment were permitted, subject to check by an international commission. The international commission reported that China and Russia were abiding by the agreement. But were their technicians not 'aiding' North Vietnam? Why should not the United States ex-tend 'technical assistance' to South Vietnam? Especially when there were assurances that there was not to be any election or uni-fication? Washington's pledge had sealed the bargain. Ngo Dinh Diem eagerly welcomed the Americans who quietly replaced French military technicians and brought in money and better arms.

Would it not have been pertinent to inquire whether 'the West' could expect to defeat 'the East' in Vietnam by using (or being used by) a Catholic Easterner in a country more than ninety percent non-Catholic? (The Vatican itself had never taken sides in Vietnam.) Pertinent also was whether an anti-Communist military dictatorship could be forced upon half a people more successfully behind American bayonets than by French bayonets tried seven years against a whole people. Even more to the point was whether an aristocrat from the top shelf of the five percent have-gots (and somewhat tainted by past collaboration with French imperialism) could now impose, in a Vietnam already in revolution for a generation, a 'family system' dictatorship of the kind that had already failed under Syngman Rhee and Chiang Kai-shek – whose delusions of adequacy never seemed to trouble Mr Dulles? If the Secretary asked himself these questions about Ngo Dinh Diem he must have speedily found the answers reassuring. This time he acted in a manner which opened him to no possible veto from any Milquetoast chief of staff.

As a French-educated administrator, and a member of the prewar mandarinate, Ngo Dinh Diem had once led the agonizing life of Bao Dai's prime minister, obliged to carry out the decisions of the French governor general. After the Japanese occupation he became a right-wing factional leader in the Vietnamese Catholic League. (Nominal Catholics numbered some 2,000,000; many of them were also Taoists and Buddhists. Perhaps two thirds of them were in the south.) Ngo Dinh Diem might have had a big role to play in the independent monarchy as restored by Japan, but Bao Dai's speedy abdication in favor of the Republic left Diem out of politics. His background of service with Bao Dai opened for him no place of importance in the Viet Minh coalition. Ngo Dinh Diem astutely refused further collaboration with the losing French, however. Not until Bao Dai was made Chief of State for all Vietnam did he again join a French-sponsored government. He was premier of Bao Dai's régime at the time of the Geneva Conference.

From 1954 on, protected by the demilitarized Seventeenth Parallel, and with solid Dulles backing, Diem* quickly became the

---

*The practice of referring to Ngo Dinh Diem as 'Diem' had now been so well established by journalese that I followed it in order to avoid confusion. Ngo is the surname. There were so many Ngos in his régime that use of the given name was adopted to distinguish 'Diem' from the others.

strong man and Bao Dai the petulant figurehead. Diem built around himself a staff of anti-Communists, anti-federalists, and anti-Baodai-ists and anti-Hochiminh-ists. Their handicap was that few had done anything to recommend themselves as national or revolutionary patriots. Diem distrusted anti-Communist nationalists and democrats who had been guerrillas against the French; perhaps they made him feel inferior. He tended to favor the Catholic minority, and especially northern Catholics. Many Catholics had also fought the French, but most had not. Fearing persecution or having already suffered under the now Communist-dominated Republic, thousands of Catholics came down from the north, during an official exchange of sympathizers. (There were about 16,000,000 people in the north, 14,000,000 in the south.) From these new arrivals Diem chose his closest collaborators outside his own family. In Saigon itself he had some support among the few wealthy Vietnamese – many of them French educated – and among anti-Communist middle- and upper-class refugees from the north. There were also the large landowning families of the south, threatened by the Republic's land equalization program; from them many of Diem's army officers were recruited.

Bao Dai, never a man to 'struggle', soon lost control of his cabinet and hand-picked assembly to Diem and his 'National Revolutionary Movement'. Diem ignored all requests from Hanoi to restore postal, telegraph, rail and other communications. He refused to discuss national elections. He denounced the Geneva agreement – to which Bao Dai, as the 'legal person' and heir of French rule, was morally bound. Moreover, as last survivor of a dynasty which once ruled all Vietnam, Bao Dai wished to see it whole again, as one real service he might perform. Ho Chi Minh (politician enough to realize Bao Dai's sentimental value) was prepared to support him in some symbolical role in the elections. Diem doubtless sincerely wanted to save his country (even as Chiang Kai-shek had); for that he needed power. In October 1956 he staged a 'national' referendum on the question of separation and of Diem against Bao Dai. (Less than fifteen percent even of those allowed to vote participated.) He then became the new Chief of State. Three days later he proclaimed formation of a 'Republic of Vietnam' and assumed office as its first president.

One might suppose that in a country with only a handful of highly trained and educated persons, Diem would then have made great efforts to reconcile any and all intellectuals who could be used. In Saigon, at least, many were anti-Communists. Just the opposite occurred, according to Philippe Devillers, an outstanding French (Catholic and anti-Communist) authority on Diem and the Viet Minh. Why should Diem try to use anyone opposed to him when he had fulsome American backing? He had no mass party to restrain him. Diem destroyed all the opposition which might have saved him – imprisoning many, driving others into exile or the jungles. An eyewitness to these events, M. Devillers observed: 'This repression was aimed in theory at the Communists. In fact it affected all those, and there were many – democrats, socialists, liberals, adherents of the religious sects – who were bold enough to express their disagreement ...'[17] The Cao Dai and Hoa Hao were backward but important sects peculiar to South Vietnam who had fought the French on religious grounds. Diem took savage reprisals against them (driving some toward the Communists) in ways embarrassing even to the Vatican.

But after all, perhaps the nation needed a *strong* government? Weren't the really important people the peasants? One could assume that a man of Diem's intelligence would have read and learned something from China, and from North Vietnam and the French experience before him. Where did the Communists get their support? From the 'great majority' – the poor peasants, ready to die for them. Why? Peasants were not interested in revolution, Marxism, or theories. They wanted peace, rice, parcels of land, relief from their agonies, freedom from crushing debts, usury and taxes, and a chance for their children to learn to read and write.

The two billion dollars America had earlier invested in French attempts at reconquest could have financed peaceful national land reform. Now, here was a second opportunity, with billions more of American money to invest. Surely with only half of a small country to handle, a new start would be made?

To confound the Communists it was necessary immediately to provide land for the landless tillers, to show that the régime stood for *some* betterment of the have-nots. With a satisfied peasantry as its foundation the whole countryside might have been stabilized. The compensated landowners might have become a new urban enterpreneur class. From the new peasant landowning class, youths could have been trained to carry out an adequate program of farm cooperatives, irrigation, roads, cleaned-up villages, health centers, schools, hospitals, local self-government, and so on. Plenty of volunteers (cured of TB and parasites) might then have been eager to accept training and provide leadership for the protection of their stake against Communists or any other threat. Indeed, Communists might have been confined to intellectuals in the cafés and opponents of nuclear testing except by the Russians.

Diem did not even have to fight his way back, like the French; the countryside was quiet when he took over. Viet Minh regular armed forces had been withdrawn to the north, and in many places in the south, where Viet Minh leaders had raised volunteers to oppose the French and Bao Dai, rents and taxes had already been reduced. On some large plantations of absentee native and French landlords, the tenants had been given land before the local Viet Minh guerrillas disbanded in 1955. Some refugee landowners and peasants from the north were settled on government land, but Diem carried out no general equalization of ownership. A new law guaranteed a landlord up to 250 acres – many times more than could be tilled without tenant labor. Peasants who had divided the land under the Viet Minh naturally came under suspicion from a régime determined to destroy all influence of the veterans of the *Résistance* throughout the countryside. In many villages such peasants were herded out of the 'infected areas' and transported, after the processing away of contaminated persons, to state reservations.

'In 1958 the situation grew worse,' according to Devillers. 'A certain sequence of events became almost classical: denunciation, encirclement of villages, searches and raids, arrest of suspects, plundering, interrogations enlivened sometimes by torture (even of innocent people), deportations, and "regroupings" of populations suspected of intelligence with the rebels, etc.'[18] Many villages were burned to the ground; charred corpses littered the ruins. Thousands of families were separated and suspects forced into concentration camps. It was not North Vietnam or even local Communists but Ngo Dinh Diem who finally drove the whole countryside into rebellion. Anyone seeking further confirmation could read the facts in a detailed and lengthy report by Homer Bigart, in the *New York Times*, as early as July 1962, written after he had returned from six months of life under Diem's dictatorship and was free of Saigon censors.[19]

In 1957, before Diem began his repressions, and the reprisal policy in the hinterland, his government policed and was able to collect taxes in nearly three fourths of the villages. By 1962 he had lost effective control of nearly everything but Saigon, the principal provincial towns and cities, and main communications. Yet within those years his armed forces had quadrupled. Besides an investment rapidly approaching three billion dollars, the United States had now placed 10,000 army ground and air force personnel in South Vietnam to assist in training and combat operations of Diem's troops. By 1963, according to Bigart, Diem would be using 350,000 men against no more than 25,000 armed partisans – 'who have no anti-aircraft guns, no air power, no trucks, no jeeps, no prime movers, and only basic infantry weapons.' Most of the latter had, as usual in guerrilla wars, been captured from government forces.

M. Devillers describes very dramatically how partisan warfare was provoked and grew to its present proportions.[20] Since 1960 it had organized national leadership for a 'People's Liberation Army', operating under a 'People's National Front', with many well-defended bases and local partisan régimes. Most members of the 'Front' were nationalists and not (yet) Communists. There was a wide underground network. Various anti-Diem parties and groups supported it in the cities. It had sympathizers high in Diem's army. Its program was not Communistic, but bourgeois-democratic and nationalist. It called for land for the peasants, autonomy for ethnic groups and religious minorities, and civil liberties. It was pledged to 'progressive reunification of the country by peaceful means on the basis of negotiation between the two zones', and immediate restoration of national economic, cultural and postal communications.

What embarrassed United States forces was that they were nowhere engaged against 'Chinese Communist aggressors', as they had expected to be. Instead, they found themselves hunting down (sometimes with wolfhounds imported from Germany) and helping to kill native South Vietnamese. How could that be? All that money and power and heavy equipment, and all those tough, well-trained and well-intentioned Rangers, now brought to bear upon barefoot, puny, skeletal, worm-infested peasants and their under-nourished children, fighting not in uniforms but in rags, and not in tanks but from behind trees in their native rice paddies, their hills, their jungles and their malarious swamps? How was it that to them the American liberators looked no different, in the service of Diem, than the French imperialists before them? Or that Diem's American-uniformed troops – well paid, well fed, and glad to have the job and a rifle to sell when things got rough – seemed no different from puppets of the past?

Where was Ho Chi Minh's army? North Vietnam's troops had not invaded the demilitarized and heavily policed parallel to aid the southern partisans. By 1962, however, small-arms aid was being increasingly carried by circuitous routes from the north to support the anti-Diem forces in the south. Obviously, if North Vietnam's now formidable army were to move southward, more than the U.S. Marine 'advisers' and their air support would be needed to prevent a speedy Dien Bien Phu. What was Ho waiting for? Paradoxically, international law would be on his side; it was Diem and the United States that had scrapped the only agreements internationally recognized. What signator could condemn the north for removing the outlaws?

Why had North Vietnam declined to move? The answer was not that they were better Christians but perhaps that they were greater realists. We must refer again to the Sino-Russian dispute, and to North Vietnam's relation to it. Insofar as I was able to study this question in China and afterward, I shall summarize the main points of an explanation.

After United States intervention and support of Diem's repudiation of the agreement to hold a national election in 1956, China and Russia both began open but limited military support to North Vietnam. Contrary to widespread belief in the West, neither North Vietnam nor northern Laos was occupied by Chinese Communists or Soviet troops. Russia and China extended large-scale economic and technical aid to North Vietnam, however, and their technicians in Vietnam included military experts from both countries.[21] China and Russia about equally influenced the Vietnam Communist Party, and elements within it reflected both orientations. But Ho Chi Minh above all sought to retain his independence.

At the start Ho had clearly stated his desire to maintain economic, cultural and diplomatic ties with the United States, as well as with the United Nations. This would have given him a two-world position, valuable in bargaining inside the Communist camp, and useful also in any struggle to assert Vietnam's sovereignty against intervention by any power. Events made that course impossible.

North Vietnam was of course now led by Communists. The régime also embraced other parties and more bourgeois-democratic and intellectual influences than in China. There was land redistribution, establishment of cooperatives, and collectivization. By 1958 the nation had embarked on a Three-Year Plan aimed at rapid industrialization and modernization of agriculture. In 1960 it began its first Five-Year Plan. Where conditions were comparable to those in China – and many were – North Vietnam followed a Chinese pattern. Similar mistakes were made and the régime had much the same sources of strength. It was not purely imitative; like Mao, Ho Chi Minh sought to adapt Marxism to local realities.

North Vietnam had made such progress in industry that it was now capable of carrying out industrialization of the south.[22] In basic industrialization it was already far ahead of Thailand and Burma. But the north very much needed the surplus rice of the south; in the past it had always been dependent upon Saigon for one fifth to one fourth or more of its food imports – in exchange for the north's abundant coal and other raw materials. The whole economic and political viability of Vietnam rested upon a united nation – much as did that of truncated Korea. Unification could greatly strengthen Vietnam as an independent state able to resist outside pressures against its national interests.

For these and more obvious reasons Ho Chi Minh genuinely

hoped for honest implementation of the Geneva agreements. When Diem ruled out peaceful unification, the D.R.V. faced a dilemma. It had no desire for an armed conflict which would further weaken Vietnam, but a permanent amputation of the south was impossible to accept. Ho Chi Minh was torn between Chinese and Russian views on peaceful coexistence. Vietnam was an immediate case in point in their dispute over armed support to 'people's wars of liberation'. If Ho began open movements against the south it might lead to war with the United States, and then to Chinese counterintervention in Vietnam. Ho wanted neither. At the same time he desperately needed rice; increased output in North Vietnam was still twenty to thirty percent under requirements. In 1960 the harvest failure in North Vietnam exactly paralleled that of China – and in that year of Chinese crop failure China could not help.

After Diem's régime rendered even trade exchanges impossible, North Vietnam still did not activate the underground Viet Minh forces in the south. It was Diem's terror against the villages that forced Hanoi to lead an intensified partisan campaign. Communists in the south were in danger both of being exterminated one by one, and of losing leadership over the anti-Diem resistance to the nationalists. In December 1958, after twenty Vietcong leaders were executed in Phui Loi, one of Diem's largest concentration camps, Hanoi finally openly demanded Diem's overthrow in a war which the southern (non-Communist) Veterans of the Resistance had already begun on their own.[23]

Meanwhile, the North Vietnam Communist Party leadership had been reorganized under a new secretary, Le Duan, said to lean toward those favoring support for the Soviet position in the Sino-Soviet dispute. If war came, Ho Chi Minh did not want to be isolated from Russia by accepting China as his only ally. The D.R.V.'s new policy still did not call for violation of the Seventeenth Parallel. The strategy was not a north-south war, but a ubiquitous partisan war confined to the south. What, if not organized armies, could the north supply to the south? Infiltration of technically trained leaders and the development of a well-coordinated program, backed by propaganda and money with which to buy arms and defectors among Diem's soldiers.

Now in the south division of the land was carried out in earnest, every village became a battlefield between have-nots and have-gots, and for those in the middle, who wanted only peace and rice, life became a nightmare. Diem's answer was more 'agrovilles', set up like Chiang Kai-shek's erstwhile models of 'New Life' in Kiangsi. These impressed some American visitors, but the countryside was a sea and a few costly display villages could not halt the erosion of the vast waters around them. Therefore Diem demanded that the Americans finance the construction of 8,000 fortified villages surrounded by moats and barbed wire – in effect the placing of all peasants under village arrest. But the peasants were divided between pro-partisan, pro-landlord, and pro-Diem factions, and fearful of reprisals by all. Many youths deserted for the hills, the swamps and the jungles. More soldiers were needed by Diem to 'protect' peasants in the fields, where cultivation tasks had to go on. But how many soldiers per fortified village – each soldier a sitting duck for well-led guerrillas?

'The American hypothesis regarding the probable effectiveness of these new tactics [in Vietnam] is based upon a failure to appreciate the very essence of guerrilla warfare,' wrote O. Edmund Clubb, the last American consul general to represent the United States after the Communists occupied Peking, and a Chinese- and Russian-language senior officer distinguished as a pioneer student of Asian communism. 'Successful guerrilla warfare depends upon the general support of the population *in resistance to bad government*. It relies upon an understanding of the desperate plight of the people and the identification of the guerrilla with their needs and aspirations. As Chinese guerrilla leader (and later Peking Defense Minister) P'eng Teh-huai put it: "The people are the water and the guerrillas the fish, and without water the fish will die." It would be hard to imagine anything more like a fish out of water than an American guerrilla fighting in the Vietnamese countryside for Diem's dictatorial and reactionary government.'[24]

If it took 350,000 Diem troops to hold down the main arteries against only 25,000 partisans in 1963, would 700,000 be required against 50,000 partisans in 1964? If we must depend upon force alone, why not put the army directly in charge? Why – as American 'technical personnel' saw it – be hamstrung by a civilian Vietnamese President who insisted upon directing and bungling all operations?

'Should the situation disintegrate further,' wrote Homer Bigart in the *New York Times* (1962) 'Washington may face the alternative of ditching Ngo Dinh Diem for a military junta or sending American combat troops to bolster the régime. No one who has seen conditions of combat in South Vietnam would expect conventionally trained United States forces to fight any better against Communist guerrillas than the French did in their seven years of costly and futile warfare. For, despite all the talk here of training men for jungle fighting, of creating counter-guerrillas who can exist in forests and swamps and hunt down the Vietcong, Americans may simply lack the endurance – and the motivation – to meet the unbelievably tough demands of jungle fighting.'

Adoption of the junta solution might or might not make for increased military efficiency, but it *would* mean political defeat. It would end the pretense* that South Vietnam represented, as an anti-Communist alternative, anything like free, democratic or self-determinative government. Large-scale use of American combat troops would even more expose the blatant travesty. Either course would intensify the cold war and neither could long be tolerated by North Vietnam.

For five years Ho Chi Minh had balanced himself between Khrushchev's 'peaceful coexistence' strategy and Mao's more militant approach, which better fitted Ho's aspirations but not his means. In 1958, Ho adopted Mao's line by lending all his political prestige and leadership to the overthrow of Diem's régime by means mobilized within South Vietnam. At the same time he observed discreet limits, in obeisance to Khrushchev's line, by avoiding direct military action involving the North Vietnam government.

If, however, the United States were to deploy great forces over a long period, or directly attack North Vietnam itself, or if the

---

* (1970) I was mistaken. The pretensions about 'self-determination' and 'free Vietnam' increased, under President Johnson, in proportion to the degree of armed American intervention there for the purpose of determining Vietnam's internal political destiny.

Communist-bloc diplomatic offensive should fail to bring about any modifications in the American approach, internal pressures in Ho's own camp would compel him to extend direct military aid to the partisans. He would then have to depend upon the Chinese and other allies to help defend his base territory. This would be the response which General Ridgway earlier anticipated when he foresaw major American intervention in Indochina as a 'tragic adventure'. Could it be that, with all those bombs and the immensely greater material means of which John Foster Dulles was so confident in 1954, the United States might have to ponder again the question whether man and moral force were more important than weapons?

By now the United States could also reflect on the lessons of Laos. In that toy kingdom the C.I.A. (under the direction of Allen Dulles) had dropped half a billion dollars in vain attempts to subvert palace retainers with Cadillacs and buy the Assembly's votes, and on military supplies which ended by arming left-wing anti-American elements [25] – all in violation of guarantees of complete neutrality and independence for Laos, as contained in the Geneva covenants of 1954. Using the crisis provoked by the C.I.A.'s fiasco as a pretext, the United States first shoehorned Marines into neighboring Thailand and began constructing armed bases there, and on the other hand hastily summoned signator powers of the 1954 Geneva covenants to a second conference on Laos. The result was the July 1962 Geneva agreement on Laos. Terms of that treaty unequivocally recognized a unified, sovereign, neutral, and independent Laos, now jointly guaranteed by the United States, Russia and China against any further armed intervention. In signing that agreement, together with Peking, Washington for the first time took *de jure* (though not diplomatic) recognition of the People's Republic. By that token Peking as well as Hanoi had then begun to place greater credence in possibilities of a similar solution for Vietnam itself. It was toward that end that Khrushchev's policy had long been aimed.

The 'National Revolutionary Front' was one means of attempting to convince Washington of the wisdom of accepting a Laos type of peace for all Vietnam. Such a solution might indeed imply a great 'turning point' in the East-West struggle – but not one in exactly the terms Mao Tse-tung had foreseen when he noticed a changed balance of world forces, in 1957.*

* (1970) The 'lessons of Laos' were of course totally ignored by Americans who took the fateful decisions to bomb North Vietnam and bring 600,000 troops into full-scale military occupation of Vietnamese territory in misguided efforts to impose an alien political will in that distant, stubborn land. During the years of macabre fulfillment of that 'tragic adventure' Laotian sovereignty was savagely torn apart. In 1969 its hills and plains and people were still being attacked as targets held legitimate by American bombers because North Vietnamese troops were using the area to run supplies to their anti-American allies in the south.

Nevertheless, it was a cruel jest of history that the above comment on the Laos 'solution', at first glance seemingly rendered irrelevant by all that had happened since, once again took on a new significance after the opening of Vietnamese-American peace talks in 1968. Any accord reached at Paris would almost certainly require the endorsement by a third Geneva Conference, or its equivalent, of signators of both previous Geneva attempts at workable agreements. China's re-entry into the arena of international diplomacy in 1969, and the reopening of Sino-American conversations at Warsaw concerning 'peaceful coexistence', were among portents of a renewed pertinence for binding international agreements to establish neutrality and freedom from all foreign interference across a wide zone in South-east Asia. Independence, national sovereignty, territorial integrity and non-intervention in each other's internal affairs, were indeed the common program adopted by the four Indo-Chinese allied governments – North Vietnam, South Vietnam, Laos and Cambodia – during their summit meetings in the spring of 1970. Their declarations had the full endorsement of China.

80

Childhood's End? [1]

1835:

OF all armies, those most ardently desirous of war are democratic armies, and of all nations, those most fond of peace are democratic nations...

Among democratic nations it often happens that an officer has no property but his pay and no distinction but that of military honors; consequently, as often as his duties change, his fortune changes and he becomes, as it were, a new man ... war makes vacancies and warrants the violation of the law of seniority which is the sole privilege natural to democracy.... Moreover, as among democratic nations the wealthiest, best-educated, and ablest men seldom adopt the military profession, the army, taken collectively, eventually forms a small nation itself.... Now, this small uncivilized nation has arms in its possession and alone knows how to use them; for, indeed, the pacific temper of the community increases the danger to which a democratic people is exposed from the military and turbulent spirit of the army ...

No protracted war can fail to endanger the freedom of a democratic country.... War does not always give over democratic communities to military government, but ... it must almost compulsorily concentrate the management of all things in the hands of the administration.... All those who seek to destroy the liberties of a democratic nation ought to know that war is the surest and the shortest means to accomplish it.... The most effectual means of diminishing that danger would be to reduce the army, but this is a remedy that not all nations are able to apply. *Alexis de Tocqueville, Democracy in America*

1961:

We have been compelled to create a permanent armaments industry of vast proportions. Added to this, three and a half million men and women are directly engaged in the defense establishment. We annually spend on military establishment security alone more than the net income of all United States corporations ...

Now this conjuncture of an immense military establishment and a large arms industry is new in the American experience. The total influence – economic, political, even spiritual – is felt in every city, every state house, every office of the Federal Government. ... Our toil, resources and livelihood are all involved; so is the very structure of our society ...

In the councils of Government, we must guard against the acquisition of unwarranted influence, whether sought, or unsought, by the *military-industrial complex*. The potential for the disastrous rise of misplaced power exists and will persist. We must never let the weight of this combination endanger our liberties or democratic processes. We should take nothing for granted. *Only an alert and knowledgeable citizenry* can compel the proper meshing of the huge industrial and military machinery of defense with our peaceful methods and goals, so that security and liberty may prosper together. [Emphasis added.] *President Dwight D. Eisenhower, in his Farewell Address to the Nation*

'What is it all,' asked Tennyson, 'but a trouble of ants in a million million of suns?' In the timelessness of infinity what remains of the earth will cool, and as that tiny spark dies a myriad of new stars will burst into beginning. Meanwhile, said Emerson, 'we must treat men and women as if they were real; perhaps they are'. Assuming that people are real, we and the Communists have not much time left in which to learn to live the Confucian truth that 'within the four seas all men are brothers' – not much time before the fuse either burns to the detonator or is plucked out to save man for a few more years.

Can we coexist with China? With Russia? With communism? Until tourist tickets are available for mass migrations to fairer planets, where else are we to live? Where else are we coexisting now?

It is no part of my intention to suggest that coexistence is easy, nor will anything in this book support the view that it is going to become easier in the future. The whole world is caught inescapably in the four-pronged revolution. Not just the 'underdeveloped' but all of us are living through a historic end of childhood. Individuals can afford for a few more hours to deny it, but for the nations there is nowhere to withdraw, no way to turn man back from his inexorable course, and no way to prevent the have-nots from struggling for equality and attainment of things now possessed by the have-gots alone. There is no way to refute the most prophetic remark in President Kennedy's inaugural address: '*If a free society cannot help the many who are poor it can never save the few who are rich.*'

The problems of coexistence with China cannot be solved apart from the world-wide four-pronged revolution. Yet China is a continent in itself, and neither can any world solutions work which exclude her. Perhaps it is thought that we are successfully ignoring her now? People frequently ask, 'Should we recognize China?' The answer is that in practice the United States was always compelled to recognize China, and in far more costly and significant ways than ever before in history.

The State Department, the armed services, the C.I.A. and other paramilitary organizations profoundly recognized China not only in the Far East, the Middle East and Africa, but also in Latin America and at home. In Asia alone, the United States recognized China by subsidizing and arming at least 1,700,000 native troops under military dictatorships in Korea, Taiwan, Vietnam, Thailand and Pakistan, in addition to powerful American air, naval and ground forces arrayed on her perimeter. Never before had China received so much recognition and so much respect from the United States.

The cold war from the beginning was a two-way affair, starting with the mistakes of ignorance which Stalin and Truman (and all of us behind them) made in such ways as to provoke the hostile responses necessary to revive the arms race. China was no exception. China is a big country, too. When it blunders it is on a scale almost as big as the United States or Russia.

We have seen how the Chinese revolution grew from internal and external conditions which finally left the nation no other way out. After twenty years of fighting in the hills and remote villages the Communists came down to the great plains and cities and took power among the world's most numerous and most homogeneous people. In the hinterland they had evolved a domestic program based on Marxism – a harsh and relentless program but workable because it broke the worst chains which bound the imprisoned energies of most of the people.

In international affairs, however, the Communists had only the notebooks of Leninist theory and Stalin's advice to guide them. True, Japan and the Western powers in China had heretofore behaved quite in accordance with Lenin's prophecies. America, backing the have-gots to the very last, seemed no exception. Suspicious of any bourgeois Chinese who understood the United States, the Communists would take no advice from them. They knew that 'imperialism will never change'. The United States was given no help by them to make an easy adjustment, but its forces did withdraw to legitimate lines of self-defense.

It was not simply that Peking immediately formed an alliance with Russia; after all, Chiang Kai-shek had also been Stalin's ally. The unsophisticated Chinese from the hills failed to understand internal conditions in the United States which in 1949 still sharply limited the reach of American nationalism. True, the United States was doing nothing to liberate Europe's Asian colonies, but neither had it made colonies of the countries it liberated. Important changes since Lenin's time were never fully analyzed. The Chinese Communists seemed to forget that the United States had been pulled into China involuntarily. They did not see that it was not as important that the United States had (rather reluctantly) supported the losing side in China as it was that American forces did not attempt an all-out intervention. Fear of Russia, they said. No. Russia was then very weak. Yet from 1946 onward they insisted and really seemed to believe that Russia's last-minute occupation of Manchuria had defeated Japan.

The men from the hills did not consider that the great American army of fifteen million men had been demobilized, that democratic American civilian forces were in charge, and that war industry was being dismantled. That was a very good thing, because 'of all armies, those most desirous of war are democratic armies', as De Tocqueville reasoned, and to see the world's most powerful armed forces being dissolved should have comforted the weak. The Chinese failed to realize that only actions which could be construed as overt attacks on the United States could bring armaments and the generals into commanding positions over the American economy and foreign policy. In common with Stalin, the Chinese Politburo forgot the lesson of Pearl Harbor, if they had ever learned it. The American tiger had already left Asia – but it could be yanked back in again by the tail. The Chinese Communists overestimated Soviet strength and underestimated antiwar and anti-interventionist forces in the world and in the United States. In 'leaning to one side' they unnecessarily isolated themselves from powerful neutral and middle interests and they leaned too far – as they were suddenly to realize only when Khrushchev pulled the props away, in 1960, in consequence of which China suffered a severe attack of national vertigo.

Stirred by their exciting new might, the Chinese Communists also overestimated the ripeness of the rest of Asia for China-type social revolution. They did not quite understand the weight of the response which could be provoked by prolonged hostile demonstrations against American prestige. Above all, they did not understand the difficulty of arresting the momentum of American rearmament, once it was invoked in earnest. How could they? Some mistook President Truman for Chiang Kai-shek. Yet China sent no troops beyond her frontiers. Calls went forth for all Asia to follow the Chinese example – and some parties struggled to do so – but there were no supporting Chinese invasions. Propaganda is one thing, action another. Not until the Korean War broke out was it possible to convince the American nation that Russia and China meant to spread communism by national wars of conquest.

Korea provoked and provided excuses for all subsequent American policies of armed intervention and encirclement of China – which paralleled the rearming of Western Europe. The latter development itself gathered momentum only after Stalin's blundering attempt to blockade Berlin in 1949. Yet that move must also be seen as part of a long chain reaction going back as far as President Truman's cut-off of all lend-lease aid to stricken Russia immediately after V-E Day – an action cruel in its abruptness to a wounded comrade-in-arms, but much worse because it was totally senseless. That error appears traceable to thoughtless advice from minor figures in the State Department, but the same charity cannot be extended to Mr Truman's rejection of earlier recommendations from Henry L. Stimson.

Mr Stimson, inherited from Roosevelt, had just proved himself the ablest Secretary of War in the nation's history. His prophetic insight concerning Russia and the atomic bomb has been remarkably fulfilled by history. Anticipating that unless Russia were at once brought in to share the knowledge and responsibility of atomic power there would inevitably begin 'a secret armament race of a rather desperate character', the Secretary of War urged, in a memorandum to the inexperienced new President, that he go directly to Moscow, with British support, and obtain an agreement both to 'limit the use of the atomic bomb as an instrument of war', and 'to encourage the development of atomic power for peaceful and humanitarian purposes'. With the insight of clairvoyance Stimson recognized that the bomb had begun a new age that upset all previous traditions of diplomatic bargaining, and that there was in truth 'no secret' which could long be kept.[2] He therefore recommended that it be handled 'with the naked lack of hypocrisy that it demanded', as Walter Millis later observed in *Arms and the State*.[3] Mr Stimson wrote:

... If we fail to approach them now and merely continue to negotiate with them, having this weapon rather ostentatiously on our hip, their suspicions ... will increase. It will inspire them to an all-out effort to solve the problem. If the solution is achieved in that spirit it is much less likely that we will ever get a covenant we may desperately need. ... The chief lesson I have learned in a long life is that the only way you can make a man trustworthy is to trust him; and the surest way to make him untrustworthy is to distrust him and show your distrust.[4]

Stimson's view was rejected and it was his farewell appearance in the Cabinet. (Even though Stimson's advice was ignored, the Chinese could have learned something by trying to reconcile the mere fact that it could be offered by any Secretary of War, and monopoly-capital representative, with their own rigid conception of American imperialism.) It was not until after the Soviet 'all-out effort' was well along that the seemingly 'realistic' Baruch plan was advanced by Truman, *not to Russia*, but through the then completely American-controlled United Nations. This would have placed an intelligence inspectorate over Russia which even a novice such as myself knew to be totally unacceptable in the milieu of the Soviet government's total distrust of the Western allies. The chance – merely a chance, but the *only* chance – of avoiding the ensuing epoch of world terror was thrown away. We also got the Korean War.

In June 1950 Soviet troops had already evacuated North Korea; only Soviet advisers remained. American troops had also all but evacuated South Korea. Although divided, all Korea was nominally an independent country. Pronouncement by the American Joint Chiefs of Staff and Dean Acheson had excluded both Korea and Taiwan from the strategic defense perimeter of the United States in the western Pacific. China had had special interests in Korea for centuries; it was linked to her by race, language and culture. In 1894–5 China fought a war with Japan over Korea, to defend her position as suzerain. It was again from Korea that Japan launched her invasion of all Manchuria, in 1931. Both Nationalists and Communists of China had long secretly supported Korean revolutionary parties, in years when the United States did nothing to free Korea. The United States had supported Japan in Korea in her war against Russia. That neither Russia nor the United States now even considered giving China a role in the Allied occupation of Korea was considered by all Chinese a national insult. Some of the Korean Communists who took power in North Korea were close comrades of the Chinese, and were aided in their underground resistance against Japan in Manchuria and Korea all through the Second World War. The United States had put the long-exiled Syngman Rhee in power in Seoul and backed him in arresting and killing leftists in South Korea.

Many Americans still believe that China started the Korean War. That is historically untrue, as Chou En-lai has reminded us (in Chapter 12). 'The evidence indicates that China made no early plans to commit the PLA [People's Liberation Army] to combat in Korea', asserts a study made for the United States Air Force by Allen S. Whiting, a RAND Corporation intelligence analyst.[5] It would be naïve to suppose that the North Korean government began the war without China's knowledge. If China approved, that was obviously a disastrous decision based on faulty understanding of the United States. Yet there is no available evidence that China originally planned to intervene. 'The initial decision [to intervene]', in the opinion of Mr Whiting, was not made until 'late in August'. It was not implemented in combat until four months after the outbreak of hostilities – not until Mr Truman had received two warnings* from Peking against sending troops north of the Thirty-eighth Parallel, and not until American (and U.N.) forces were hard upon China's frontier on the Yalu River, which American planes were bombing.

Combining emotional ties with historic fears and strategic national interest, the Peking high command probably had no real alternative but to 'resist in self-defense'. Transfer the scene to Mexico. Would the United States do nothing if a foreign army approached the Rio Grande? Peking had first officially looked upon the struggle as Korea's internal affair. When war reached Manchuria, the historic invasion route to China, the government regarded its own action as counterintervention against an 'American invasion'.

To this day the Peking government maintains – and most of the people of China seem to believe – that South Korea began the attack at American instigation. I have seen no convincing proof of that, I do not believe it, and most of the world does not believe it. (If it should ever be proved, postwar history would have to be completely rewritten.) But it should not be overlooked that the foolish Syngman Rhee and his generals did repeatedly threaten, and appeal for American support of, an armed conquest of the north. There had been numerous reports of border violations of the Thirty-eighth Parallel by Rhee's forces as well as by the Communists. It is in this sense – as a decisive counterattack – that the Chinese Communists undoubtedly rationalized their participation in the war as defensive. It must also be remembered that China was excluded from the United Nations and was not bound by its ukases. None of that was really assimilated by Mr Truman and other

---

*The MacArthur-Truman exchanges at this time have not been fully revealed. Briefly, General MacArthur's intelligence informed the President that the Chinese were bluffing. MacArthur had earlier sought to bomb China's supply lines, but even after the intervention, Truman (hamstrung by the U.N.) denied him that authority. A clear victory being unattainable under such restrictions, MacArthur early favored armistice negotiations. Truman refused, the war dragged on, and an armistice was eventually negotiated on terms worse than MacArthur believed he could have won earlier. For details, consult the Truman and MacArthur papers. (See Bibliography.)

Americans in 1950. To them, Korea was another Pearl Harbor, and the United States had no alternative (nor did the United Nations) but to oppose armed aggression with force.

This lengthy discussion of seemingly dead history is necessary in order to understand why the government of China was quite genuinely unable to see in events in Korea – from which Chinese troops years ago withdrew – any justification for America's continued hold on Taiwan, the embargo, and exclusion of China from the United Nations. The Chinese are proud, still relatively weak, newly independent, and confronted by merciless problems, but they are strongly patriotic. China has an avowedly Communist government, but the United States does not have an avowedly imperialist government. Was there no way that the United States can demolish the myth that it is imperialist and make the Chinese people adopt more 'rational' opinions?

Yes, there were ways. For many years now United States policy had exactly corresponded to Mao's prophecies of imperialist behavior. One way quickly to confound him in the eyes of his countrymen, and to shake the foundations of nationalist faith in the doctrine that there was no way to talk reason to an imperialist except from behind the barrel of a gun, was for the United States to follow a policy *exactly the opposite* of what China expected.

President John Kennedy had a great opportunity to make such an innovation when he first took office. 'So let us begin anew,' he said in his inaugural address, 'remembering on both sides that civility is not a sign of weakness, and sincerity is always subject to proof.' The United States was not under pressure by China; it was a good time to move 'anew', from positions of strength. That turned out to be, alas, sheer rhetoric. One of Kennedy's closest advisers told me that soon after the inauguration he suggested to the President that he make a 'new' move by announcing the withdrawal of the Seventh Fleet from patrol duties in the Taiwan Strait, and await the Chinese reaction. Kennedy told him he hoped he would never make a remark like that in public. What Kennedy did by way of something 'anew' was to back Allen Dulles' abortive attempt to invade Cuba; and though he learned from that experience he did not make any new beginnings with China.

Yet without vitally affecting a single aspect of American *security*, and without any special authorization from Congress, the President could have (1) announced to Chiang Kai-shek that within sixty days the protection of the Seventh Fleet would be withdrawn from China's off-shore islands of Quemoy and Matsu, and suggested that he remove his troops from this provocative forward base; (2) modified the 'enemy trading act' and embargo against China; (3) canceled the United States ban on travel and communications with China; (4) opened the United States to visits by mainland citizens, including Mao Tse-tung; (5) declared it the United States' desire to see a peaceful conclusion to the Chinese civil war through direct negotiations between Taiwan and Peking;* (6) announced the readiness of the United States to extend long-term credits to China for the purchase of American surplus wheat and other commodities.†

Had such measures been taken without any conditions or political strings attached to them, a totally new climate would have been created in the Far East. The effect would have been electrifying. Mao would have been obliged to rethink an entire strategy based upon the assumption that 'imperialism will never change'. Prospects for international peace would have been immeasurably improved everywhere.

No doubt President Kennedy was sincerely a man of peace, yet of course he did not and could not make any such magnanimous gestures. America was not yet that tall. The truth was that America's entire Far Eastern policy then still rested upon the protectorate in Taiwan, the assumptions of United States 'dominance in the Far East' – as Assistant Secretary of State Walter S. Robertson put it – and the dusty illusions of Mr Dulles that armed pressure on the periphery of China and Russia could bring about counterrevolution. Any move which suggested the elimination of the keystone of this scheme, in Taiwan, endangered the entire

---

*Direct, unofficial negotiations between representatives of the Peking government and Chiang Kai-shek for an intra-national settlement of their differences had been going on intermittently for many years. After the Geneva agreement on Laos these talks took on renewed life.

†Of the six remedial measures suggested above, the Nixon administration partly adopted (2) and (3) in 1969, prior to the resumption of Sino-American talks at Warsaw.

mythology and the edifice erected around it, and necessarily must lead to the disengagement of the have-got and have-not nationalisms now locked in limited but perilous undeclared war.

For of course 'beginning anew' would mean continuing an alternative course toward other ends. Encouraging the Generalissimo to negotiate for peaceful unification would result in eventual cancellation of the United States alliance, withdrawal of American forces from Taiwan, admission of China to the United Nations, neutralizing Korea and Vietnam as a basis for their unification and admission to the United Nations, and United States recognition of China as an equal with responsibilities as well as rights among her peers. By such means China's conception of American imperialism could be modified and by such means new and more fundamental solutions to the needs of the have-nots could be found.

The real reason why Mr Kennedy could not make any such 'beginning anew' was not hard to discern. It lay not only in one man's inability to alter the 'military-industrial complex' which dominated American foreign policy and indeed all American society – as President Eisenhower warned in the words which preface this chapter. It lay in the fact that Mr Kennedy would never have got his budget past committee in the first session of his Congress if he had taken even one of the initiatives suggested. And in those facts lay the explanation of why United States policy had failed to evolve any adequate alternative to bombs, bombs and more bombs.

No American President has yet cared to tell that simple truth to the American people. Such a sudden blow to the stability of the American economy might be so disastrous as to bring impeachment. The tragedy of John Foster Dulles was that his original objectives were already unattainable by his means even before he assumed office and futilely defined them in 1952. 'Roll-back', 'liberation', and similar long-since-abandoned slogans of the first Eisenhower campaign were always illusory, but totally so once Russia became a nuclear power, in 1949. Mr Dulles discovered only in 1954 that massive retaliation was not practicable even in Indochina, much less in Europe. Since then the tangible effect of United States cold war offensives had been the arming of numerous dictatorships and an enormous expansion of both the domestic and external consumption of American armaments production. Except for Japan – where Americans continue to work toward the complete correction of General MacArthur's postwar mistake of total disarmament – United States intervention has nowhere yet created a single viable new democracy, while it has resuscitated countless ailing dictatorships.

This was certainly never the intention or conscious will of the American nation. Neither did it evolve from original master blueprints laid down in the Pentagon itself. We were all caught in a trap which the people only partly helped to lay. It had different origins but was nevertheless very similar to the trap in which Japan found herself in the 1930s when her own military-industrial complex became the dominant influence in foreign and domestic policy and emasculated a vigorous postwar democracy. After the Japanese army seized Manchuria it soon became deeply involved in politics, subsidized and intimidated publications and editors, outlawed Communists first, then Socialists, then pacifists, and ultimately all antimilitarist opposition, by equating all with treason. It systematically frightened or cajoled religious leaders, scientists, union leaders and teachers into total conformance. Every town in the country became dependent on military patronage and on war industry. No one could speak the truth without endangering his livelihood if not his life. Yet Japan was not then under attack by China, any more than the United States is today. Support of the 'defense effort' nevertheless became mandatory for each man's comfort, dividends, security and patriotic self-esteem. Gradually, Japan and its colonial markets became saturated with military tools. To consume the weapons output and maintain the economy more and more conquests became necessary – until major war was inevitable.

America had not reached that extreme, but what worried President Eisenhower was that the 'military-industrial complex' even in his time had become far and away the biggest and most dangerous corporation in the United States. It was, moreover, a socialist corporation; that is, it was always in the 'red' in its accounts with the people; everything was free for members and paid for by taxpayers who had nothing to say about its deployment abroad. It was what De Tocqueville called a 'nation by itself'.

'The Pentagon today owns more than 32 million acres of land in the United States', wrote Fred J. Cook in his well-documented work, *Juggernaut: The Warfare State,*'and another 2·6 million acres in foreign countries. Its total ownings are larger than the combined area of Rhode Island, Delaware, Connecticut, New Jersey, Massachusetts, Maryland, Vermont and New Hampshire. ... Out of the 80·9 billion 1962 budget as originally drafted (this is a mere historic curiosity now, of course), fifty-nine cents in every dollar was allotted for military purposes. ... Military assets are three times as great as the combined assets of United States Steel, American Telephone and Telegraph, Metropolitan Life Insurance, General Motors, and Standard Oil of New Jersey. The paid personnel of Defense is triple the number of employees of these great corporations, whose influence on affairs of state have so often worried observers.'[6]

We also get the feedbacks from monies expended for similiar aims abroad. Foreign lobbies, working on funds of American origin to raise more of the same, hold discreet meetings with such congressmen as they can find unoccupied with domestic military lobbies. Most notorious among these feedbacks is the Nationalist Chinese money which found its way from such unlikely places as an early $10,000 contribution to the campaign chest of Richard Nixon's 1960 presidential candidacy,[7] down to the offices of the nation's greatest hoax : The Committee of One Million Against the Admission of Communist China to the United Nations. The only figures published by the Committee up to 1962 showed 368 dues-paying members.[8] But count, among the sponsors listed in its full-page advertisements, the retired officers, congressmen and businessmen. Then pair the names with those serving in directorates of defense corporations, or as advisers to American-subsidized dictatorships in Taiwan and elsewhere abroad – or bidding for new war industries to be located in their constituencies.

Not that the 'military-industrial complex' and its lobbies were undemocratically run; every member of it had a voice in the spending. True, no one outside the Establishment was ever consulted about whether troops went to Taiwan or Vietnam or a billion more went to Diem or General Dynamics or whether we talked or didn't talk with the Chinese, but that was beside the point. Let not the citizen deceive himself, however. Billions in military largesse (plus veterans' payments, foreign military aid and war-debt interest) now dispensed annually, had so geared the entire nation that many a small shop owner, many a grocery store clerk, and even many a plate-passer in the churches felt a personal threat if anyone suggested that every golden river must end in the sea and that this could not go on forever. From the billionaire to the parson, beneficiaries of arms spending were as convinced as the Chinese Communists that they were saving humanity from extinction.

It was the Communists, they said, who had started it all. What could we do if they wouldn't disarm? Certainly it takes two to make a fight, and the Communists have never been slow to burn. No one expects the United States to disarm alone. Not even the Russians. In fact, in 1955 Moscow launched a wholly unexpected change in Soviet policy when its delegate to the London disarmament conference suddenly accepted a long-standing Anglo-French-American proposal for conventional disarmament, for cessation of the manufacture of nuclear weapons, and for their conversion to peaceful purposes – all that to be supervised by United Nations inspectors from control posts in every country. The Soviet acceptances left unsettled only one key item: a final definition of 'adequate guarantees' of inspection.

So stunned was the American delegation by this *volte face* that it made no attempt to reply; instead, the United States called for a three months' adjournment. After that, silence. The American answer did not come until the following September, when the unhappy Harold Stassen, again at the U.N., was obliged to announce what amounted to a new and negative policy which withdrew all previous American disarmament proposals – until a *perfect* system of 'inspection' of nuclear weapons tests and manufacture could be agreed upon. After that all disarmament talk was about different ways to legalize espionage – known as 'adequate inspection'. This was made into an extremely complicated subject and no judgment can here be offered concerning the merits of the American and the Soviet arguments. The significant truth was that the whole question of inspection rapidly became irrelevant. Before any written accord was reached, the development of space satellite espionage and electronic detection devices had so far advanced that all essential information needed to guarantee against surprise attacks was soon in possession of both sides.

Even if inspection became complete, however, the bombs would still be with us. The danger would remain for years to come if it took as long to dismantle weapons and disarm as it had to get past the preliminary talking stage. In 1961 Dr Linus Pauling, the distinguished scientist and Nobel Prize winner, estimated that the United States possessed about 100,000 megatons of atomic and thermonuclear bombs, and the Russians had something like 50,000 megatons.* Due to the vastness of the Soviet Union about twice as many bombs would be required to eliminate it as the United States; hence the two powers had about an equal destructive capacity.

Dr Pauling's study showed that 10,000 megatons would be adequate to burn, fatally maim, poison by radiation, or otherwise kill every living person in the United States.[9] If the very best, deepest and most extensive shelter systems now conceivable were built (estimated cost $100,000,000,000) the Russians would have to use 40,000 megatons to kill every man, woman and child in the United States. The Americans would need 20,000 megatons to burn up a nonshelterized Russia, and about 80,000 megatons if it were profoundly shelterized. Apart from bombs available for American strategic aircraft, the nuclear equivalent of some 20,000,000,000 tons of T.N.T. was also distributed in the form of thousands of smaller American rockets and missiles spread around the earth. The Russians had comparable equipment. A single major blunder of human miscalculation could lead, Dr Pauling feared, to 'some series of catastrophic events' such that even the wisest national leaders would be unable to halt 'the destruction of civilization'.

Many citizens shared Dr Pauling's concern about 'extreme militarism', but as long as the phenomenon was multilateral the answer obviously could not be any one-sided dissolution of American armed forces. Nor could they be expected to abandon their legitimate responsibilities abroad until they could be transferred to a supranational police force. But how could that be, as long as Communists existed in the world?

*(1970) Since then the stockpiles have spawned their second generation.

Walt Whitman Rostow, an excellent and learned professor*
who had the confidence of the President and was policy planning
director of the State Department (something akin to coordinator
of anti-imperialist strategy in the Peking Foreign Office) is often
quoted as having told an Army War College audience that 'communism is a disease of transition'. By that he meant transition
from a backward society to a mature, advanced society, such
as, for example, the United States. Possibly Mr Rostow's remark was oversimplified in journalistic interpretation? It must
engage our attention in its literal form, however, because it
reflected an innocence of thought still widely characteristic of a
nation which had not taken a close and honest look at its war
economy and its own fundamental problems of transition for many
years.

The United States, still the richest and most powerful nation and
potentially several times greater and taller than it has yet discovered, should never be confused by the notion that it is already a
'mature' or a 'finished' society immune from sudden and dramatic
changes yet unforeseeable to any of us. Communism undoubtedly
is a disease in the sense that it proves highly contagious to technologically backward nations. But private plunder of public resources,
unemployment, personal profit from socialized military waste,
racism, corrupt rulers and bribable senators, Birchites, momentary possession of superiority in deadly weapons, and – above all –
chauvinism are equally diseases of transition.

Could it be said that we had a 'mature' society when, in a starving world, we spent five to six billion dollars annually in bribing
farmers not to grow crops – and about two million dollars a day for
storage of surplus commodities? What was grown-up about an
administration whose solution aimed at removing from production
more than two thirds of our farmlands? Or price supports by means
of the destruction of billions of pounds of fruit and other foods
while millions even in the United States remained undernourished? How 'advanced' was a society capable of making
enough fertilizer, water pumps, pest killers, tractors and plows to
double or treble the food output of the nonindustrialized nations
in a few years, which was yet incapable of offering any means of

* (1970) Currently at the University of Texas.

realizing such an operation – seemingly simple compared to hitting the moon?

Did it make adult sense to sit by while tens of millions of illiterate have-nots learned from Soviet and Chinese propaganda that they could get along without their have-gots, that there was a way, not to become rich, but to build a life which at least promised the minimal satisfactions of food, clothes to cover their nakedness, better health, some education and equality of opportunity for their children, employment and freedom from beggary – the socialization of poverty for a generation or two, no doubt, but freedom from hated enslavement to the financially privileged and the constant reminders of denial to their loved ones of any hope of attaining the adequacies of the rich? Or was it still supposed that bombs and Green Berets taught the tricks of guerrilla warfare, and some paltry charities or reforms urged upon the bought army élites in the impoverished lands, would long be enough to contain the force gathering behind the turning barrel of the gun – among 'the poor, the great majority'?

What was 'mature' about waiting for more thousands of wretched usurers, landlords and sheiks to be killed in a struggle over scrubby parcels of land in Asia, in the Middle East, in Africa, in Latin America? For a small percentage of the $400,000,000,000 the United States spent in ten years to prevent the spread of Communist revolutions, enough land could have been purchased to satisfy all the tenant farmers, a stable new class of owner-tillers established, capital created among ex-landlords obliged to invest in modern production, youths trained to destroy rats and lice in the villages, to organize cooperative farming, and to lay a new basis of public health, schooling and stable citizenship, and to complete technical surveys and the foundations of industrialization.

Problems of land shortage and exploited tenants were by no means universally characteristic of underdeveloped countries. What was obvious was that wherever farm ownership was a revolutionary issue, it would make good sense to encourage a nation to seek a peaceful transition by spending a few *millions* to equalize land ownership *before* spending *billions* to arm landlord armies – to provoke peasants to relieve them of their land *and* their weapons. Although land redistribution might provide a temporary political solution it could offer no economic panacea for such countries, which could find stability only by far-reaching modernization.

The United States could not order bad régimes to behave wisely but it could refrain from supporting and compounding their stupidities. It could make known to the world a desire for basic solutions, and offer help to achieve them. It could flatly decline to supply weapons for régimes bent upon their self-destruction. It could at least stop expanding the payrolls of the millions now in sub-armies which rendered us ever more dependent on subsidized overseas arms markets, dangerously dislocated the American economy, and threatened the stability and life of the American democracy.

Had the United States taken the lead in such a world war against poverty, disease and ignorance it would itself have found some means of transition from the 'military-industrial complex' escapism into which it has fallen. Directly and indirectly, by far the greater part of 'foreign aid' funds has gone into military hardware of no value to the poor and often used as a means of repressing and reducing any chance of peaceful change. In machine-poor lands much of the rest went into the pockets of military sycophants, profiteering merchants, landlords, politicians and their bank accounts in Switzerland. It went into cars and gasoline and freezers for the few. The whole process tends to intensify class hatreds, the chasm between rich and poor, and dislike of the Yankees who bring candy bars for the children but not the means of work for their parents.

All civilizations of the past have been built on slavery, but the time of the human slave is nearing an end. That is certain not only because the human-slave societies cannot compete with the mechanical-slave societies but because the human slaves everywhere are becoming aware of the means of their liberation. (Communists are taking care of that, too.) Apart from famine relief, 'help' to backward societies is useless unless it directly contributes to their liberation from human slavery – chiefly by providing them with the means of producing mechanical slaves of their own. And foremost among all the underdeveloped societies of the West has been the oppressed Negro minority, ten percent of the United States population, who have scarcely begun their social emancipation from their past enslavement.

Paul G. Hoffman, manager of the United Nations Special Fund, classified eighty-two non-Communist member nations and 'some forty territories' as 'underdeveloped' – which embraced 'more than a billion people ... undernourished and without the barest of health or educational facilities'. Their national incomes were increasing at the rate of one percent a year, adding 'not a third of a penny a day' to their per capita incomes of less than thirty-five cents daily per person. (The poor were not even getting the extra third of a penny, as Mr Hoffman was talking about *per capita* income, or a statistical assumption that everybody earns equally.) 'This rate of increase,' said Mr Hoffman, '*is too low – dangerously too low.*'[10]

Many billions a year for investment in productive purposes of direct benefit to the poor is one alternative to armaments races. The United Nations is one place to sponsor it. The United States should not provide more than its share, but its share would be large indeed in proportion to the world's wealth. Such a war against poverty cannot be adequately financed by the private capitalist sector. It must be seen as an investment in world construction financed by United Nations bonds underwritten by the various governments, like state savings certificates. In any case only this kind of foreign investment would long be secure, especially in underdeveloped countries.

In 1962 American investments abroad were approaching $75,000,000,000, exceeding by about $25,000,000,000 the private foreign investment in the United States.* The tendency for capital-poor countries to nationalize foreign investments would increase rather than decrease. But no country could afford to isolate itself from a world government by repudiating debts incurred for low-interest, long-term, productive loans.

Much the same thing could be said for the Administration's 'Alliance for Progress' program in Latin America. Historians a generation hence could ask themselves how sensible men could naïvely intervene halfway round the world, in Vietnam and China,

* (1970) In 1966 the two figures were given as $111,000,000,000 and $86,235,000,000 (*U.S. Statistical Abstract*, 1968). Actual U.S. investments abroad far exceeded $111,000,000,000, however; that figure excluded the immense profits made in foreign countries by U.S. corporations and individuals and reinvested there, outside calculations of balances of payments.

in a crisis far past conventional colonial solutions, when they had made no effort to read the revolutionary message left on the Latin-American threshold of the United States itself. Not Vietnam but the Western Hemisphere – Brazil, Venezuela, Argentina, Chile and Mexico – ought to be the focus of the American war: the war against poverty, not against peasants. The eyes of Washington were on the wrong places and on struggles already lost.

How did the United States finance the Second World War, which resulted in an enormous growth in America's assets? That was the only moment in thirty years when unemployment disappeared, our productive and creative energies were in full use, and national morale reached a summit. We fed virtually the whole world and remained a healthy nation. How have we been financing the cold war? Mainly by inflation, because the product is almost total waste and adds nothing to basic output for consumption. But a war against want could take up today's thirty percent slack in American industrial capacity, create new assets, put the land back into use, and increase the nation's gross national product by $150,000,000,000 to $200,000,000,000.*

And how would the poor pay? By their labor – and by their production. By labor all existing wealth was created and all indebtedness discharged. These poor nations are nearly all potentially self-sustaining. They are like unemployed and underemployed Americans; they are not in use. But the poor wish to work. They do not want charity. They want to learn. They want peace. They do not want war. No one doing useful work wants to die. Imagine the desperate resolve it took for a timid, illiterate, fearful Vietnamese peasant to separate himself from his family and the fragile but only margin of security he ever knew, in order to become an outlaw of the revolution, to kill and be killed? It is only a last-hope decision for any man, whether he be a Buddhist or a Hindu

---

*(1970) Ironically, between original publication of the above comment (1962) and 1969, the G.N.P. in fact did rise to about the sum mentioned – reducing unemployment to a postwar low, taking up much of the production slack, and bringing a boom (and inflation) – not because of any 'war against want' or fulfillment of President Lyndon Johnson's 'Great Society' aims, but largely because of a doubled arms budget necessitated by the enormously wasteful prosecution of the 'wider war' in Vietnam which Johnson had pledged himself not to 'seek'.

ryot. But if nothing else is offered he will take that step rather than condemn his children to starvation and inequality – once he becomes convinced that there is no other way.

Suppose, then, that instead of fighting this 'disease of transition' with bombs alone, we try immunizing means such as increased credits and trade with the pariahs, to hasten them onto the high road to maturity? What about starting by easing the heavy arms load of both Russians and Americans by ending insistence upon an unattainable 'perfect' espionage system, and accept the best possible? Whatever it is, won't it work both ways?

What about going further, and fully reopening trade with all 'communist' countries, offering them the means of more rapidly modernizing their agricultural and urban life?

And what about the bomb? By 1962 scientists had told us there never was any real secret to it after 1945. Mr Stimson was not a stupid man; he won the war for which he was our First Secretary, and that may be more than can be said for the cold war fought by his successors. We had lost the one chance to avoid an arms race with Russia when we tried to 'negotiate with them, having this weapon rather ostentatiously on our hip'. China would get the bomb anyway – and after that, what? Until then, we would have a second chance 'to share the knowledge and responsibility of atomic power' in exchange for an agreement to ban the bomb which could not be used and 'to encourage the development of atomic power for peaceful and humanitarian purposes'. Indeed, Chou En-lai had several times made such a proposal – dismissed by the State Department as 'propaganda'.

Obviously, such a decision could have been made – I hasten to add before some literal-minded reader (not you) misapprehends me – only as part of a comprehensive accord reached with China for a 'new beginning'. None of that could happen while we were punishing China and playing war games. But if at any time we make such an agreement with one poor nation, should we not then have to make it with all the others who desperately need atomic power and other peaceful nuclear utilities? Indeed we should – and there is no way of avoiding it if we are to halt the spread of the arms regatta. If ever we are seriously to seek agreement with the Russians, there could be no surer way of accelerating it than by holding a few preliminary talks on the general subject with Peking.

But what about the blue ants, the yellow peril? It is silly to speak of birth control while holding an atomic rifle on China or any other nation. Obviously, sane opinion about limited parenthood cannot prevail while nationalism continues to dominate all political thought and no alternative exists in real world government or world planning. Only if and when the rich powers emerge with solutions and offers to help the poor on the emergency basis outlined here – and in the works of thoughtful scientists far better informed than I am – can the means and practice of effective population control be universalized. It can never be imposed on the assumption that the poor nations must remain poor and have fewer children while the rich white races that settled the fairest parts of the New World a few years ago continue to proliferate.

For what seem to me good reasons I have stressed American more than Chinese responsibility for the present isolation from each other of two nations whose peoples total nearly a third of humanity. Being an American, I have an incurable tendency to expect the United States to grow slightly up. The United States is far richer and more powerful. In 1949, American government and society existed in stability and maximum security. The United States had not just emerged from a century of invasion climaxed by a revolution and an acute sense of persecution. The United States initiated the formal cut-off in communications.

But I do not wish to minimize the heavy contributions made to the conflict by the stubborn pride, self-righteousness, ignorance of the United States, and an understandable but childish desire for retribution in the Chinese leadership. I cannot predict that the Chinese will turn the other cheek, but I do know that they were long in a mood to respond to another approach by the United States. I need not recapitulate their mistakes in domestic policy, which have been candidly reported here. There will be more. Suffice it to say that they have learned that while it is a difficult thing to win a revolution with the help of men ready to fight for farmland, it is even more difficult, once that land is put into the community chest of socialism, to find other incentives to maintain mass enthusiasm and endorsement. To inspire that, without private ownership, they must constantly create other means – satisfactory to the whole people, not just the party – to guarantee equality of rights in all aspects of life. That is something new. It involves no less than the physical and psychological reconstruction of what used to be regarded as the most conservative society on earth.

China's internal tasks would fully occupy her for at least another generation. It would be equally long before China could ever seriously undertake to attack the internal security of the United States. The aggressiveness of her propaganda and policy lines were at least as defensive as offensive, as I have shown. Yet they gratuitously supplied ammunition to the American 'military-industrial complex' with which to frighten many people about China's intentions and vastly exaggerate her capacity to do evil. Mao Tse-tung's greatest blind spot had been his inability to conceive of United States society as it really is. The United States government's great error had been not to have invited him, long ago with the whole Politburo, to visit America for an extended tour to see what it looks like – how people live, talk and act, and to engage in a few balcony arguments, *a là* Khrushchev. The longer the isolation the greater the distrust, the fear, the double-think, the suspicion and the conspiracy and counterconspiracy.

The Chinese had done little to make it easier. Wounded in their prideful isolation, they had somewhat puffed themselves up with too much faith in 'politics in command'. Temporarily fooling others, they had often fooled themselves most of all. Obsessed with the size and power of their reunited nation they had tended to forget that though large in numbers they were a minority in the world as a whole, and smaller still in comparative wealth.

They knew the United States was not made up of ninety percent peasants and ten percent landlords. Yet much of their propaganda about American life reflected an assumption that most Americans are illiterates with no influence, no brains, and no freedom. It was true that the American press was ninety-nine percent against them and probably would be for some time to come. They were right in assuming that most of the press spoke for the interests of its millionaire owners and the advertisers. They were right in their skepticism about 'people's capitalism' in a nation where less than ten percent of the people owned any corporate stocks at all, and about ten percent controlled most of the productive assets. But they were wrong in assuming that the other ninety percent were have-nots, in ignoring class mobility in the United States, and in failing to see that the nation was evolving toward an exclusively middle-class society with guarantees of satisfaction for the 'ten basic needs' for which Chinese communes were just reaching.

The Chinese Communists were mistaken in assuming that the people of the United States always thought and behaved the way they were told to think and behave by the press or even by the 'military-industrial complex'. They misunderstood the time lag between public opinion in favor of a restoration of communications with China (as expressed in the Gallup Poll) and the press and government policy opposed to it. They forgot that eighty to ninety percent of the same press was always violently against Franklin Delano Roosevelt – and that he was the only President ever elected for three terms and the only one ever elected for four terms. Full of awareness of contradictions in their own camp, the Chinese Communists failed to exploit the contradictions in an American society far more complex than they conceived. Nor did they listen either to their own people who knew something about the United States or to strangers speaking in a different idiom who might have translated some facts for them.

China could herself have done some positive things to reach 'the American people' as apart from the imperialist government. In the sense that the President might shake Mao's certainty that imperialism would never change (and thereby go far toward shaking Mao's hand), Chairman Mao could also have altered the American nation's conviction that it was impossible to coexist with China. The People's Republic could have taken the following steps, 'toward friendship with the American people', and without any political strings or trading with the State Department: (1) publicly renew invitations to visit China to friendly American scholars, teachers, scientists, engineers, doctors and nurses – some of them Christian missionaries – who were formerly acknowledged by Communists themselves to have served the people of China selflessly and without participating in 'imperialist exploitation'; (2) publicly renew offers of visas to reputable writers for leading American news media; (3) have an 'American People Week' in China (sponsored by the International Peace Committee) which would show, in its truthful paradox and complexity, a nation capable of electing a man to lead it for four terms against the veto of the foremost publishers – and its achievements in science and education despite some slightly prehistoric congressmen – along with its failures to solve the economic contradictions I have indicated.

I could not predict that the Chinese would remold their thinking in that way. Mao Tse-tung himself could no more change a nation's pace and direction all alone than the President could. I did know that some Chinese leaders had long been prepared to respond to a 'let us begin anew' approach by the United States. Too proud to say so directly, they were obviously hopeful that my visit might help to build a bridge or two. That was what they told me in various ways – always with the knowing added note that my imperialist government was not interested in bridge-building.

I thought they exaggerated the resistance of Washington to the introduction of useful information. When I returned to the United States, however, I had to revise my opinion; the official wall was a great deal more solid than I had supposed. After a brief colloquy with Dean Rusk, the newly appointed Secretary of State, I was left with the impression that the Chinese had been right.

Yet on reflection I felt sympathy for Mr Rusk, himself (like all of us) a prisoner of the 'complex' President Eisenhower mentioned. He was as helpless as Mr Herter before him to change anything with fresh information from Mao Tse-tung, at that moment. It would take a long time and very much hard work by the 'alert and knowledgeable citizenry' to break out of the trap. That it would change, that it was gradually changing, was becoming evident. There would be strong counterattacks against agonizing attempts to reach an objective understanding, which would be denounced as appeasement. The way ahead was hard but the bridges could, and ultimately must, be built.

Alternatives to mounting military expenditures are no certain cure, even if they were adopted *in toto* and put into immediate effect. I have no illusions that they will be. They also involve risks, perhaps great risks, but nothing comparable to the risks of relying solely on present means. The truth is simply that the atomic era manifestly makes a continuation of the anarchy of nationalism impossible for any prolonged period. Today we are suffering through its last stages.

Of course no one imagines that the national form of cultural and social life will not persist just as the infinite variety of nature itself persists. It would be a dull world if different ethnic groups ceased to compete and grow and add to the common fund of civilization. But nationalisms as warfare states, whether right or left, must surely soon yield their sovereign killer capacities to a higher concept of federated world authority based upon the common realization that the security of all nations against attack is henceforth the only reliable condition for the security of any nation to develop in freedom.

Communist prophets at least recognized the necessity to unite the world – of workers. The result brought the conflict of nationalisms to its greatest crisis – and turning point. The 'West' spoke of Communist imperialism and the 'East' spoke of capitalist imperialism. What we really had were nationalisms of the relative have-nots struggling against nationalisms of the relative have-gots, and even differences of principle between them seemed to grow ever less distinct.

The United States, somewhat hysterically anti-Communist and anti-socialist at home, abroad supported a Communist government in Yugoslavia and hopefully looked elsewhere for more revisionists. It rebuilt a France and an Italy in which Communist parties had far larger mass following than any rivals. It pampered a Germany where a 'Socialist' party might soon come to power. It supported what it considered socialist régimes in Britain and India and would even have shipped free wheat to China if Peking had come begging. All the anti-Communist dictatorships armed and financed by the United States were in varying degrees totalitarianisms maintained for the benefit of socialized consumption by the small military élite. Russia meanwhile aided deviationist Yugoslavia, and bourgeois-nationalist régimes in India, Burma, Indonesia, Iraq and elsewhere. Russia also heavily invested in Nasser's government, which put Communists in concentration camps. At the same time Moscow was not above applying severe economic sanctions against Communist China. China itself advanced loans to semifeudal monarchies in Nepal, Afghanistan and Yemen, aided other monarchies in

Cambodia and Laos, and backed nationalistic Algeria and other bourgeois régimes in Africa.

Behind all these maneuvers were the vestigial characteristics of power politics and nationalism, cloaked in the deadly clichés of the cold war, but also the beginnings of inevitable international unification. While mankind groaned under burdens of more than $150,000,000,000 in labor effort wasted every year on bombs as useless as pyramid-building, but far more deadly, we heard also the parting knell of nationalism and the beginning of world planning, which must end in a certain pooling of world resources. For now it was either childhood's end or the end of all children.

Was I dreaming? I had company among the realists. In 1961 I had heard Dr Edward Teller deliver a commencement address. Dr Teller was Dr H-Bomb himself, and a believer in more and better shelters. If he had had something to say to encourage the shelter-seekers he might have made the covers of *Time-Life* that week, but as it was the press ignored his remarks. In the most solemn tones he made two declarations, one of which would have called mockery upon him a few years earlier, and the other of which shocked a young clergyman, who afterward expressed his fear to me that Dr Teller might not be a religious man. Dr Teller's first comment was that within the lifetime of the students there assembled we would be probing far distant planets to discover the secrets of infinity and God. His other prophecy was that East and West would, within an even shorter period, be united under a single world government and world law, with a world police force, and a world economic planning board. 'There is,' he said quite simply, 'no other way.'

But was it not preposterous to suppose that the President, even if he agreed with any of these modest suggestions, could possibly win acceptance for them in the United States Congress? Of course it was. The Congress is traditionally far behind the sentiment of the American nation, however, and opinion was not dead, it was momentarily asleep. If war is 'too serious an affair to be left in the hands of generals' world peace is too imperative a need to be entrusted entirely to politicians. Soon the congressmen would be forced to listen to somebody besides the oil billionaire lobbies, the A.M.A., the corporations, the army lobbies and the veterans' bureaucracy. Many millions of American housewives and mothers (and househusbands and fathers) were beginning to demand some guarantee of peace and assurance that their children would not be exterminated or be born deformed. Pressures would mount. In time it would be realized by more and more American voters that they were not getting a fair shake. People would begin to know that it was not enough to demand disarmament and peace; they must create the means to compel their representatives to find ways of promoting *production for peace*.

No administration to date had proved capable of stunting the growth of the 'military-industrial complex'. It was not expected that any one President could turn it off like a faucet; another tap had to be turned on before the old one could be shut off. The people themselves had to make a start toward recovering control over foreign policy and the machines and setting both to work on new projects. 'Only an alert and knowledgeable citizenry can compel the proper meshing of the huge industrial and military machinery,' President Eisenhower warned, 'with our peaceful methods and goals.' And only that same citizenry could compel Congress to begin at home the necessary support for modernization and re-education of our own nation in preparation for commencement exercises in the years immediately ahead.

But I am not trying to leave anyone with the impression that it is possible for Americans alone to do much more than reduce poverty, inequality and injustice at home, and thus to make it easier for other people to behave in accordance with their best interests; that is, to keep up with the world rather than fall dangerously behind it. Only one man in thirteen is an American and very few others live as Americans do. Nothing is more preposterous than the assumption that the 'American system' can be exported to solve the problems of nations in very different circumstances. We can do no more, essentially, than cooperate with the attempts of others to find decent pathways of their own. The United States is in no serious danger of eclipse by any one power but it cannot forever hold its overwhelming lead in economic development.

No single 'system' or pattern can prevail everywhere or on the same level, nor can any one power control it. Here one must subscribe completely to the views of George Kennan, already quoted.

Communism or socialism is not about to happen in the United States tomorrow or even the day after that, but to maintain some sense of proportion in public thought it seems useful to remind ourselves that even if it did happen the country would not be run by China or Russia or anybody but Americans. Nor would that change eliminate rivalries and competition or clashes of national interest nor even necessarily make them easier to keep under peaceful control. Russia has been unable to dictate to China. China does not rule Vietnam or Korea. Any United States system of the future inevitably would be 'deviationist' – and patriots inevitably would find any American system best.

The prospects of a readjustment to new realities abroad need not arouse undue anxiety in good Americans. Perhaps we shall be able to see this clearly only when we are relieved of excessive armaments (together with others) and relinquish police control to a larger world organization. Perhaps only then may we mature in planning for our own nation, so badly in need of fundamental transformation in many areas (racial discrimination, slums, urban reconstruction, anarchy of traffic, education, housing, prison reform, archaic laws, etc.) ever since the bomb dropped on Hiroshima. In the end it will be what we do here, and not what we do or say to other peoples, that will create a civilization others wish to emulate.

Perhaps the greatest illusion was that America was ever in full charge at any time.

All plans are important only as indications of a general direction and only if they generally cooperate with the likely. Great events of the transition are quite beyond the compass of any single power, right or left, and often they seem to move independently of all. When we glance back at the postwar years we see that few of the really majestic changes followed the plans of the Pentagon or the State Department. It was not their planning that freed the subcontinent of India and released Europe's other colonies in Asia. Nothing that the United States did ordained the turning loose of Africa. China went Communist despite all that the United States government did to save the Nationalists. Even Cuba slipped away despite much that Washington did for Batista. Foreign intervention in Vietnam strengthened communism there, rather than suppressing it. Communism did not disintegrate from within, as Mr Dulles planned that it must; both China and Russia became far more formidable competitors, not weaker, than at the end of the Second World War. The secret of the bomb on which so much strategy was based was after all no secret.

With equal impartiality history also upset Communist plans and prophecies. Stalin least expected a successful revolution to occur in China; in postwar Western Europe high hopes of Communist victories were completely frustrated. All Moscow's efforts to defeat the Marshall Plan seemed only to increase its success in reviving European capitalism and stabilizing the NATO alliance. Russia's sealing off of the satellite states hastened the formation of the Common Market, with the consequence least desired by Moscow: the exclusion of the U.S.S.R. from Western Europe. Stalin's monolithic Communist superstructure was designed to avoid what it now appears to have done most to create: polycentric communism. And despite the grand strategy of the left, most of the newly emerging states followed a bourgeois path of development.

Seen in perspective, end events are always more complex than any plan can foresee, and the synthesis is certain to be a compromise quite different from, and sometimes the very opposite of, anything consciously desired by even the most powerful nations which set in motion forces to contain or direct history.

Of course the United States made numerous and noble contributions to world recovery. Among these were many constructive actions of first importance, but of them all perhaps the greatest, in the eyes of history, was that the United States did pass by numerous opportunities to misuse its vast postwar power to launch a final world holocaust. Over the half-century which has seen two world wars and their aftermath, the policies of the United States in Asia, as in Europe, have been the product both of responses to the aggressions of others and of challenges which helped provoke them. More than a century ago De Tocqueville observed of Russia and the United States that 'each of them seems marked out by the will of Heaven to sway the destinies of half the globe', and his prophecy has been fulfilled by the rapid westward expansion of one and the eastward expansion of the other. Viewing the world over that period one discerns an inexorability in the transoceanic movement of the vast energies generated by Europeans in the New

World into the Orient, there to confront the great Eurasian land power in a rendezvous destined to break forever the isolation of East and West and to create the foundations of a modern international society.

We can still learn from our mistakes and continue to adjust peacefully to an insurgent world in which we shall always have a voice – and a big voice – but not the only voice, and increasingly a more contested voice. I assert again : we do stand at the threshold of childhood's end. We shall be obliged to follow the general direction of accommodation for the irresistible demands I have mentioned. One cannot say when each step will be taken but taken it will be, if not in one year then in another. It may never be that we shall say that on such and such a day war ceased in the world. It may be rather more like the way Rome stopped the practice of watching gladiators murder each other and of feeding Christians to the lions. No law was ever passed but, after Nero, men all at once became revolted with the spectacle and moved on to a higher stage of barbarism.

Toward the end of the fifteenth century the last of the Crusades simply disintegrated under King Peter, from lack of enthusiasm and plain boredom. There was no edict or encyclical which banned Crusades but no more were begun, and one reason men could no longer be rallied to the old holy-war cries was because, a few years after King Peter's fiasco, Columbus discovered America. Merchants thought they had found a new trade route to the East and the Holy Land was no longer so strategically important. During the next four hundred years the aggressive energies of Europe were largely absorbed in the exploitation of new continents and conquests of nature and savage infidels. Today we are being forced into a race for the planets which may prove analogous.

Or again it may be that humanity's triumph will be comparable to the events depicted by Tolstoy in *War and Peace*. Napoleon seemed to win all the battles, the French army was invincible, the nation was conquered, and yet the Russian people were victorious. The fine plans drawn up for the Russian armies by the Polish and Austrian and Prussian staff professionals repeatedly came to naught; nothing ever happened the way they anticipated because they did not understand the general direction of events. To their mounting fury, General Kutuzov ignored them and saw logic and moral triumph even in the seeming defeat at Borodino. The old man somehow understood that far vaster and more complex forces than the outcome of any battle would decide everything. Kutuzov rode the storm with his people, in the moments of their greatest defeats he understood that they were winning, the French army perished, and the storm subsided.

We must have faith that the American nation also has a better sense of the general direction of history and in the end will have more to say about the future than some of the strategists of the moment, so large with great plans for small ends. Whether we shall eventually carry the republic and the union onto the higher ground of a victory shared with all men depends, of course, upon the ability of our 'alert and knowledgeable citizenry' to see beyond immediate selfish interests, and act far more objectively than they have ever been required to do before.

Wars will face us for many years, and for the first time in history there is no prospect but defeat for the victor in any attempted armed conquest of one nation by another. Dr Hugo Boyko has reminded us that the whole world has now shrunk to a state smaller in time dimensions than Israel was three thousand years ago, when it took fourteen days to travel from the northern border to Elath. Tomorrow our entire planetary system will be reduced to less space than the world of Ulysses' Aegean Islands. Between men who inhabit this earth there are no more seas; there are only rivers.

Notes

Abbreviations used are as follows:

C.Q.: *China Quarterly*, London.

C.R.: *China Reconstructs*, F.L.P.

F.L.P.: Foreign Languages Press, Peking.

J.T.T.B.: *Journey to the Beginning*, Random House, N.Y., 1958; Gollancz, London, 1959.

N.C.N.A.: New China News Agency (*Hsin Hua Hsin-wen Shih*).

P.D.: *People's Daily* (*Jen-min Jih-pao*), official newspaper, Peking.

P.R.: *Peking Review*, F.L.P.

R.S.O.C.: *Red Star Over China*, Gollancz, London, 1937; Random House, N.Y., 1938; reprint, Grove Press, N.Y., 1961. Revised edition, Grove Press, N.Y., 1968; Gollancz, London, 1969.

S.W.: *Selected Works of Mao Tse-tung*, Vols. I, II, III and IV, F.L.P., 1961.

T.B.F.A.: *The Battle for Asia*, Random House, N.Y., 1941.

T.Gl.Y.: *Ten Glorious Years*, nineteen articles and speeches by leaders of the party and government, F.L.P., 1960.

T.G.Y.: *Ten Great Years*, Statistics of the Economic and Cultural Achievements of the People's Republic of China, Compiled by the State Statistical Bureau, F.L.P., 1960.

Many but not all of my excerpts from translations of the Chinese press and magazines derive from services published by the United States Consulate General of Hongkong, namely: *Survey of the China Mainland Press* (*S.C.M.P.*), *Current Background* and *Extracts from China Mainland Magazines*.

INTRODUCTION

1. See listing above.
2. See listing above.
3. George F. Kennan, *Russia and the West Under Lenin and Stalin*, Boston, 1961, p. 276.

PART ONE · Rediscovering China

Chapter 1. Arrival in Peking

1. See T.B.F.A.

Chapter 4. Confucius to Mao

1. T.G.Y., p. 8: area 9,597,000 sq. kilometers.
2. U.S. Statistical Abstract, 1961, p. 618.
3. For a brief, excellent review and evaluation of Chinese civilization consult Derk Bodde, *China's Cultural Tradition*, N.Y., 1957.
4. *Chinese Thought from Confucius to Mao Tse-tung*, Chicago, 1953; reprint, N.Y., 1960, p. 32.
5. R.S.O.C., p. 134.
6. S.W., Vol. IV.
7. Kennan, *op. cit.*, p. 275.

Chapter 5. Paotou Retrospect

1. See Alley's *Sandan*, Caxton Press, Christchurch, N.Z., 1959, for his story of an inspiring adventure in creative education.
2. See J.T.T.B.

Chapter 6. Steel in Mongolia

1. See R.S.O.C.

Chapter 7. White Cloud

1. Alley's *China's Hinterland*, F.L.P., 1961, covers his travels through eighteen provinces and is an enormously informative guide.

Chapter 8. Mongol Commune

1. See 'Cultural Changes in Inner Mongolia', by Li Fang, in the P.R., 10 February 1961.

Chapter 9. Why China Went Red

1. See R.S.O.C. and Edgar Snow, *Random Notes on Red China*, Cambridge, Mass., 1957, 1969.
2. For interesting comparisons between present-day Chinese Communist philosophy and bureaucratic sanctions, and Confucian and neo-Confucian techniques of power, consult A *History of Chinese Philosophy*, by Fung Yu-lan, translated by Derk Bodde, Princeton University Press, 1952; and *The United States and China*, by John K. Fairbank, Harvard University Press, Cambridge, 1948, 1958.
3. T.B.F.A., p. 290, and J.T.T.B., 'That "Agrarian Reformer" Myth'.

Chapter 10. Aboard the Premier's Special Train

1. T.B.F.A.
2. Ibid.

Chapter 11. New Shores on Ancient Mountains

1. George Babcock Cressey, *China's Geographic Foundations*, N.Y., 1934.
2. T.G.Y., p. 128.

Chapter 12. Chou En-lai and America

1. *United States Relations With China*, With Special Reference to the Period 1944–9, Washington, August 1949.
2. See Allen S. Whiting, *China Crosses the Yalu: The Decision to Enter the Korean War*, N.Y., 1960.

Chapter 13. Table Talk

1. S.W., Vol. IV, p. 99.

Chapter 14. Sino-Russian 'Differences'

1. H. Arthur Steiner has made some interesting contributions on this point, e.g. 'Ideology *v.* National Interest in Chinese Foreign Policy', a paper presented at the University of Hongkong Golden Jubilee Congress, 11–16 September 1961.

PART TWO · *Where the Waves Beat*

Chapter 15. The Big Change

1. In a speech made in Peking, 1 July 1951, as reported in *Current Background*, No. 89, 5 July 1951. Italics added.

Chapter 17. Flashback to Pao An

1. *An Analysis of Classes in Chinese Society* (1926), F.L.P., 1956.
2. *Report on An Investigation into the Peasant Movement in Hunan* (1927), F.L.P., 1953.
3. Ibid.
4. See, for example, exchanges between Prof. Benjamin Schwartz and Dr Karl August Wittfogel in C.Q., Nos. 1, 2, 3.

Chapter 18. The Long March

1. *On the Tactics of Fighting Japanese Imperialism* was a series of political lectures delivered in Pao An in 1935 (F.L.P., 1953); a year later Mao evolved the military strategy in another series of lectures published in Yenan, May 1938: *Strategic Problems in China's Revolutionary War*, followed shortly by *On the Protracted War* (1938), both published by F.L.P., 1953. *On Coalition Government*, 1945 (F.L.P., 1955), completed Mao's major writings during the Patriotic War.
2. Mao rewrote this poem in the more classical form in which it appears entitled, 'The Long March', in his *Poems*, Peking, 1959.

Chapter 19. Power Personality

1. S.W., Vol. IV; and Anne Freemantle, *Mao Tse-tung: An Anthology of His Writings*, 'Strategic Problems . . .', N.Y., 1962, p. 77.
2. S.W., Vol. IV, p. 380.

3. S.W., Vol. IV, pp. 185, 202, 215.
4. *Report on an Investigation* . . . , p. 10. The virtues listed were attributed to Confucius by a disciple.
5. S.W., Vol. III.

Chapter 20. Mao at Home

1. Considerable confusion has been created concerning the account of Mao Tse-tung's early life story as told to me, which was Part Four ('Genesis of a Communist') of *Red Star Over China*. To clarify: I wrote up part of my trip to the northwest late in 1936, and early in 1937 gave copies of my newspaper articles to Chinese professors in Peking who brought out a volume in Chinese called *Chung Kuo Hsi-pei Yin-Hsiang Chi*, or *Impressions of Northwest China*. In July 1937 I gave a copy of the completed manuscript of R.S.O.C. to a team of Chinese professors and writers who were members of the National Salvation Association, to which I granted translation rights gratis on condition that book earnings were to be contributed to the Chinese Red Cross. The translated volume, called *Hsi-Hsing Man-Chi*, *Travels in the West*, appeared in 1937 and is the only authorized Chinese version of R.S.O.C. The book was immediately pirated in China – in English, as were most foreign books in those days. Later on (1938), Part Four of R.S.O.C. was pirated in a Chinese version, which appeared in Canton under the title *The Autobiography of Mao Tse-tung*. Some Western scholars have translated the Canton piracy back into English, and thus established for themselves 'a new source'. For example, *Mao Tse-tung and I Were Beggars*, by Siao-yu (published in the United States in 1959), contains a long commentary by Robert North which, alternately quoting (unauthorized) excerpts from R.S.O.C. and from the so-called *Autobiography of Mao Tse-tung*, states that the latter is a quite independent 'source . . . in the Chinese language'. Mao Tse-tung has never written an 'autobiography' nor authorized any 'life' account except my own. Both authorized and unauthorized versions of R.S.O.C. are out of print in China, although copies are occasionally found in bookstores.
2. Mao Tse-tung, *Poems*.
3. *On the Correct Handling of Contradictions Among the People*, F.L.P., 1957.

PART THREE · *Socialist Construction*

Chapter 21. Steel Decade

1. T. J. Hughes and D. E. T. Luard, *The Economic Development of Communist China, 1949–1958* (London, 1959), p. 6.
2. Quoted in Ygael Gluckstein, *Mao's China*, Boston, 1957, p. 23, from *Chinese Farm Economy*, Chicago, 1930. See also George Babcock Cressey, *op. cit.*, p. 100, for U.S. comparisons.
3. Hughes and Luard, *op. cit.*, p. 24, put the prewar average at two thirds of an acre.

4. 'On Co-operatives', N.C.N.A., Peking, 31 July 1955.
5. U.S. Statistical Abstract, 1961, pp. 318, 619, 207.
6. Betty Feinberg, 'Report on the AAAS [American Association for the Advancement of Science] Symposium [on the Sciences in Communist China],' *C.Q.*, No. 6, April–June 1961, pp. 93–94. Italics added.
7. Special Supplement No. 59, March 1960, U.S. Dept. of the Interior, Bureau of Mines, Washington, D.C. Italics added.

Chapter 23. Of Leaps Forward

1. Li Fu-ch'un, 'The First Five-Year Plan', *Ta Kung Pao*, Tientsin, 16 September 1953.
2. W. W. Hollister, *China's Gross National Product and Social Accounts, 1950–1957* (Center for International Studies, M.I.T., Boston), Glencoe, Ill., 1958, p. xix.
3. *Ibid.*, pp. 4, 5.
4. *Ibid.*, p. 141.
5. *Ibid.*, p. 132.
6. Chairman Liu Shao-ch'i in T.G.Y., p. 2.
7. Quoted in Li Choh-ming (Univ. of California, Berkeley), 'The First Decade: Economic Development', *C.Q.*, No. 1, January–March, 1960.
8. The N.Y. *Times*, 4 July 1961, in a report by Harry Schwartz, quoted *Ekonimicheskaya Gazeta*, Moscow, on the Chinese industrial output figures for 1960 which are used here.
9. N.Y. *Times*, *op. cit.* Earlier, Peking officials gave the figure 18,450,000 tons (P.R., 27 January 1961), which was the exact target for 1960. The British Iron and Steel Institute estimate of 17,000,000 tons was reported in a U.P.I. dispatch from London in the N.Y. *Herald Tribune*, 24 March 1961.
10. See T.Gl.Y.
11. The 1959 figures are from Li Fu-ch'un, *op. cit.*; the 1960 figures are from the N.Y. *Times*, *op. cit.*

Chapter 24. And Leaps Backward

1. A. Doak Barnett, *Communist China and Asia: Challenge to American Policy*, N.Y., 1960, p. 402.
2. Li Choh-ming, *op. cit.* Italics added. Li Choh-ming's *The Statistical System of China* (Berkeley, 1962) helps to explain Chinese overestimates of capacity to invest in capital construction in 1959–61 as well as reasons for the 1958 aberrations.
3. *Ibid.* Italics added.
4. Li Hsien-nien, P.R., 5 April 1960. Budget figures here are from Li Fu-ch'un, *op. cit.*, and Li Hsien-nien.
5. P.R., 27 January 1961. Italics added.

Chapter 25. Yao Wei and Private Enterprise

1. By 1969 Han Suyin had produced several important works, including

three volumes of autobiography, *The Crippled Tree, The Mortal Flower,* and *Birdless Summer,* all highly readable, as well as a book of mixed reporting, history and prophecy, *China: 2001.*

2. Hughes and Luard, *op. cit.;* and Robert Loh, *Atlantic Monthly,* December 1959, p. 84.

3. S.W., Vol. IV, p. 203.

4. See Hughes and Luard, *op. cit.,* pp. 83–95, for a more extended discussion of 'The Treatment of Private Enterprise'.

Chapter 26. Manchuria: Industrial Heartland

1. 'The United States and China', an address given before the China Institute, New York City, 18 May 1951. Reprinted by the Committee of One Million, 1961.

2. René Grousset, *Histoire de la Chine,* Paris, 1941, pp. 178ff.

Chapter 29. Science and Education

1. General Electric Co., TEMPO: *Science and Technology in Communist China* (RM60 TMP-72), by John Berberet, Santa Barbara, 1960, p. 110.

2. John M. H. Lindbeck, 'The Organization and Development of Science', a report presented to the Symposium on the Sciences in Communist China, sponsored by the American Association for the Advancement of Science, December 1960. C.Q., No. 6, April–June, 1961.

3. General Electric Co., *op. cit.,* p. 57.

4. Olga Lang, *Chinese Family and Society,* New Haven, 1946, p. 73.

5. On 26 August 1960.

6. *Professional Manpower and Education in China,* U.S. Government Printing Office, 1961, p. 13. Mr Orleans' work is mandatory reading for any deeper study of a cultural revolution which must soon engage the close attention of pedagogues throughout the world.

7. During the Great Leap Forward, in 1958, it is said to have fallen as low as forty percent.

8. N.C.N.A., 12 May 1960. Italics added.

9. Joseph C. Kun, C.Q., No. 8, October–December 1961, contains a more detailed study of 'Higher Education: Some Problems of Selection and Enrollment'.

Chapter 30. 'Ministry' of Spare-Time Education

1. P.D., 9 April 1960.

2. *On the Correct Handling . . . ,* pp. 60–61. Italics added.

Chapter 33. Doctor Horse

1. R.S.O.C. and J.T.T.B.

2. Agnes Smedley, a remarkable American rebel, is the only American woman buried in the National Revolutionary Martyrs Memorial Park, in Peking. *Daughter of Earth,* an autobiography of her youth, is an American

classic; her major work on China is *The Great Road: The Life and Times of Chu Teh*, N.Y., 1956, 1967.

3. For a dramatic account of Dr Bethune's life and work, see Ted Allan and Sydney Gordon, *The Scalpel and the Sword*, Boston, 1952. Dr Bethune is memorialized in *Quotations from Chairman Mao Tse-tung*, the 'Little Red Book'.

Chapter 36. The Family: Fact and Fancy

1. Quoted in Lang, *op. cit.*, p. 113.
2. Now in English. See Bibliography, Chinese Publications.
3. Lang, *op. cit.*, p. 108.
4. *Ibid.*, p. 16.
5. Hu Chang-tu, ed., *China, Its People, Its Society, Its Culture*, New Haven, 1960, p. 173.
6. *Ibid.*
7. Denis Lazure, M.D., 'The Family and Youth in New China: Psychiatric Observations', *Canadian Medical Association Journal*, Montreal, 27 January 1962, Vol. 86.

Chapter 37. Medical History, Personal and Otherwise

1. *Lancet*, London, 9, 16, 23 November 1957.
2. For Dr W. Y. Chen's condensed report, from which all these quotations are taken, see 'Medicine and Public Health', C.Q., No. 6, April–June, 1961. Italics added.
3. Dr R. K. S. Lim and Dr C. C. Chen, 'State Medicine', *Chinese Medical Journal*, 1937. Cited in Dr W. Y. Chen's report.
4. The figure '467,000 beds' probably included those of many primitive commune clinics and health stations. In 1959 Premier Chou En-lai reported only '775 hospitals and sanatoria with over 34,000 beds; in addition there were over 14,000 clinics and health centers' (T.Gl.Y., p. 44).
5. *New Scientist*, London, 31 December 1957.

Chapter 38. From John D. to Acupuncture

1. W. Y. Chen, *op. cit.*
2. *Ibid.* Italics added.
3. *Ibid.*
4. *Observer*, London, 22 October 1961.

PART FOUR · The Democratic Dictatorship

Chapter 39. State and Superstructure

1. S.W., Vol. II, 2nd ed., Peking, 1952.
2. S.W., Vol. III, Peking, 1953.
3. See *Electoral Law of the People's Republic of China*, F.L.P., 1953.
4. *On the Correct Handling* . . .

5. This is a rough estimate used by Communist officials. For detailed discussion of scientifically and technically trained personnel available in China at the time of the take-over in 1949 see John M. H. Lindbeck, *op. cit.*

Chapter 40. *The 800*

1. Speech delivered before the Eighth National Congress of the C.C.P., 16 September 1956, F.L.P., 1956. Italics added.
2. *Ibid.* Italics added.
3. *The Historical Experience of the Dictatorship of the Proletariat*, F.L.P., 1959. The first article was published in the *People's Daily*, 5 April 1956, some weeks after the Politburo meeting on which it was 'based'. The second originally appeared 29 December 1956.
4. 'From that time on to the defeat of the first great revolution [1927] Liu Shao-ch'i led the revolutionary trade union movement in China', according to an official sketch in Liu's *Internationalism and Nationalism*, F.L.P., 1951, N.Y., 1952.
5. Both published, along with other writings of Liu Shao-ch'i, by F.L.P., 1951; also *On Inner Party Struggle*, N.Y., 1952.
6. F.L.P.
7. N.C.N.A., 23 November 1949.

Chapter 41. *The Party and the People*

1. In an address commemorating the fortieth anniversary of the C.C.P., P.R., Nos. 26–7, 1961.
2. 'Almost all [expert analyses] yield a 1958 population estimate within the range of 650,000,000 plus or minus 25,000,000', according to John S. Aird of the U.S. Bureau of Census. Cited in *C.Q.*, No. 7, July–September 1961.
3. Report before the Eighth National Congress of the C.C.P., 16 September 1956, F.L.P., 1956, p. 91.
4. Li Hsien-nien, P.R., 6 April 1960. Italics added.
5. Li Fu-ch'un, *op. cit.*
6. See example in 'Report of the Northeastern Bureau, C.C., C.C.P.', P.D., 24 January 1952.

Chapter 42. *Security*

1. My correspondence on this subject with *Time Magazine* and the State Department is open to inspection.

Chapter 43. *'Slave Labor'*

1. Forced Labour, Supplement: Report of the I.L.O. on Forced Labour, Geneva, 1957.
2. P.D., 4 August 1957, contains the full text of the law.
3. P.D., 26 August 1954.
4. P.D., 7 September 1954.

5. *White Book on Forced Labor in the People's Republic of China*, Commission Internationale Contre le Régime Concentrationaire, Paris, 1956.

6. J.T.T.B., pp. 52-3.

7. Lang, *op. cit.*

8. *Foreign Relations of the United States, 1943, China*, Washington, 1957, pp. 391-3.

Chapter 44. Hsueh-Hsi and Reform-Through-Labor

1. R. J. Lifton, *Thought Reform and the Psychology of Totalism: A Study of 'Brainwashing'*, N.Y., 1961.

2. 'Thought Reform: Ideological Remolding in China', *Atlantic Monthly*, December 1959. See also Allyn and Adele Rickett, *Prisoners of Liberation*, N.Y., 1957; and Harold W. Rigney, *Four Years in a Red Hell: The Story of Father Rigney*, Chicago, 1956.

Chapter 46. Prelude to the Hundred Flowers

1. See especially Roderick MacFarquhar, *The Hundred Flowers*, London, 1960 (published N.Y., 1960, under the title *The Hundred Flowers Campaign and the Chinese Intellectuals*). An invaluable reference work of the period.

2. Lu Ting-yi, *Let a Hundred Flowers Blossom, a Hundred Schools of Thought Contend*, Peking, F.L.P., 1958. Lu's original speech was delivered 26 May 1956.

3. See, for example, *Ta Kung Pao*, 26 March 1956.

4. N.C.N.A., 17 July 1956. Italics added.

5. 17 May 1956.

Chapter 47. Unity-Criticism-Unity

1. Tung Chih-ming, *An Outline History of China*, F.L.P., 1958, p. 403.

2. *On the Correct Handling . . .*, pp. 9-10.

3. *The Way of Chinese Painting*, by Mai-Mai Sze (N.Y., 1956; reprint, N.Y., 1960), contains a brilliantly lucid discussion of these analogies.

4. *On Contradiction* (1942), F.L.P., 1958.

5. In *Rectify the Party's Style in Work*, which launched the party rectification movement of February 1942, Mao wrote: 'Our party members must realize the truth that they are always a minority compared with non-party people. . . . [It is] utterly impossible to . . . attain the goals of the revolution unless the Communists are united with the non-party cadres and the people.' F.L.P., 1953; see also S.W., Vol. III.

6. Extracts are all from *On the Correct Handling. . . .* Italics added.

7. *On the Correct Handling . . .*, pp. 66-7.

Chapter 48. Wild Flowers

1. I am especially indebted to Clare McDermott, then the Reuters correspondent in Peking, who made available his file on the period.

2. P.D., 23 March 1957.

Chapter 49. Counterattack and Paradox

1. *Ch'ang Chiang Daily*, Hankow.
2. P.D., 16 June 1957. Italics added.
3. MacFarquhar, *op. cit.*
4. *People's Daily*, Kaifeng, 4 July 1957.

PART FIVE · Northwest: Old Cradle of New China

Chapter 50. Of Blue Ants and White

1. Cambridge, Mass., 1959.
2. *Op. cit.*, p. 353; but census figures then were educated guesses.
3. Lang, *op. cit.*, p. 153.
4. Hu Chang-tu, *op. cit.*, p. 54.
5. *Look*, 31 January 1961.
6. Japan Statistical Year Book, Bureau of Statistics, Tokyo, 1959.
7. *Ibid.*

Chapter 51. Co-ops to Communes

1. *People's Communes in China*, F.L.P., 1958.
2. *Ibid.* Italics added.
3. *Ibid.*
4. *The Question of Agricultural Co-operation*, 31 July 1955, F.L.P., 1956, p. 34. Italics added.
5. *Ibid.* Italics added.
6. T.G.Y., p. 27. Cf. figures in Hu Chang-tu, *op. cit.*, pp. 337–40.
7. S.W., Vol. IV, 1960, p. 229.
8. See T.B.F.A., p. 322.

Chapter 52. At Whose Demand?

1. *People's Handbook* (for 1958), Peking, 1958. Italics added. This excerpt is taken from the article 'The First Decade: Economic Development', by Li Choh-ming, C.Q., No. 1, January–March 1960, to which I am indebted in discussing this period.
2. Princeton, N.J., 1962, pp. 66ff.
3. Quoted in Ygael Gluckstein, *op. cit.*, p. 23.
4. N.C.N.A., 25 July 1957.
5. John Philip Emerson, 'Manpower Absorption', C.Q., No. 7, July–September 1961.
6. From 1958 to 1961 'the population in the cities and in the industrial and mining districts . . . increased by twenty millions'. *Ta Kung Pao*, Peking, 2 February 1961.
7. *People's Communes . . .*, *op. cit.*
8. *Ibid.*
9. *The Question of Agricultural Co-operation.*
10. *Life*, 12 January 1959.

11. J. V. Stalin, 'Report on the Work of the Central Committee to the 17th Congress of the CPSU', *Selected Writings*, N.Y., 1942, p. 343.

Chapter 53. Communes to Brigadunes

1. Li Choh-ming, *op. cit.*
2. P.D., 5 November 1961.
3. *Ibid.*
4. Ta Kung Pao, Peking, 22 February 1962.

Chapter 55. A Commune That Worked

1. Ta Kung Pao, Peking, 22 February 1962.

Chapter 56. Sian: 'Western Peace'

1. *Wall Street Journal*, 20 August 1960.
2. A dispatch in the N.Y. *Herald Tribune* datelined Tokyo, 22 March 1962, quoted a N.C.N.A. report that the capital of the Ch'in Dynasty had been unearthed six miles northeast of the modern city of Sienyang, fifty miles from Sian.
3. 3 April, 1962.

Chapter 57. Museum of the Revolution

1. S.W., Vol. IV, will be of interest to those who want a full discussion from Mao himself.
2. S.W., Vol. IV, p. 130, contains abundant data on Mao's directives in this period.
3. These were basic tactics used by Cuban revolutionary leaders; internal evidence in Che Guevara's book, *Guerrilla Warfare* (N.Y., 1960), suggests that he and Castro were both students of Mao's works.

Chapter 58. Yenan Teachers College

1. Quoted in Robert D. Barendson, 'The Agricultural Middle Schools', C.Q., No. 8, October–December 1961.
2. *Ibid.*
3. *Ibid.* See also 'New Developments in Agricultural Middle Schools in China', N.C.N.A., 24 November 1961.
4. *Ibid.*
5. Nan-fang Jih-pao, 15 February 1962.
6. *Ibid.*
7. N.C.N.A., 7 February 1962.

Chapter 59. Pride of Poor Men

1. From charts used by Adelle Davis, 'Table of Food Analysis', *Vitality Through Planned Nutrition*, N.Y., 1949; and 'Nutritive Value of Selected Foods', U.S. Dept. of Agriculture, World Almanac, N.Y., 1961.

Chapter 60. Willow Grove

1. In 'Introducing a Co-operative', _Red Flag_, 1 June 1958, Mao Tse-tung discussed views which must have been formed during his Honan tour in April. He did not use the word 'commune', but here employed the now famous 'poor and blank' metaphor. China's people, said Mao, are 'first of all poor and secondly blank. This seems a bad thing but in fact it is a good thing. Poor people want change, want to do things, want revolution. A clean sheet of paper has nothing on it, so that the newest and most beautiful words can be written and the newest and most beautiful pictures painted on it.'

2. See 'Balance in Agriculture and Industry', by Yang Chien-pai and Hsu Ping-wen, _Ta Kung Pao_, Tientsin, 22 May 1961.

3. _On the Correct Handling_ . . . , p. 37.

4. _N.Y. Herald Tribune_, 19 November 1959. Italics added.

5. _Ibid._, 12 May 1961.

Chapter 61. The Yellow River Turns Blue

1. N.C.N.A., 4 March 1962.

2. N.C.N.A., 6 February 1962.

3. See Chang Chao, 'China's Fast-Growing Tree Cover', in _China Reconstructs_, Peking, 20 September 1960.

4. F.L.P., 1961.

Chapter 62. The Grandest Coolie

1. For further details see Teng Tse-hui, _Report on the Multiple-Purpose Plan for Controlling the Yellow River and Exploiting Its Resources_, Peking, 1955.

PART SIX · Shanghai and Beyond

Chapter 67. God and Party

1. Grousset, _op. cit._

2. The Quaker report on China is available from the Society of Friends, Philadelphia or London.

3. In 1961 the International Fides Service of the Vatican reported: 'A very feeble number of priests surround the thirty-five illegitimate ['Patriotic Chinese Catholic'] bishops. Certain ones seem to be completely blinded and drawn by false patriotism but others are suffering and would turn back if they had the occasion or the courage.' U.P.I., Rome, 13 September 1961.

4. Hu Chang-tu, _op. cit._

5. _Ibid._

6. MacFarquhar, _op. cit._, p. 253.

7. N.C.N.A., 23 January 1962.

8. See Eleutherius Winance, *The Communist Persuasion: A Personal Experience in Brain Washing*, N.Y., 1958. See also further comment by Mary C. Wright, *Pacific Affairs*, N.Y., April 1960.

Chapter 68. *Literature and Music*

1. F.L.P., 1956.
2. See J.T.T.B.

Chapter 71. *Szechuan, 'The Heavenly Land'*

1. Wu Chun-hung, *A Simple Geography of China*, F.L.P., 1958, puts the area at 570,000 square kilometers.
2. Cressey, *op. cit.*, p. 320.
3. Rewi Alley, *China's Hinterland*, F.L.P., Peking, 1961, p. 422.
4. Wu Chun-hung, *op. cit.*, p. 183.
5. Alley, *op. cit.*, p. 423.
6. Cressey, *op. cit.*, p. 317.
7. Ibid., p. 316.
8. Alley, *op. cit.*
9. Private letter from Clare McDermott, Peking.

Chapter 72. *A Few Words on Tibet*

1. Stuart Gelder did get to Tibet later. See Stuart and Roma Gelder, *The Timely Rain*, London, 1963; N.Y., 1965.
2. *Foreign Relations of the United States, 1943, China*, Washington, 1957, p. 728.
3. Ibid., p. 630.
4. The 1953 census gave the population of Tibet as 1,273,000, but there were 2,755,000 Tibetan-speaking persons, including 800,000 in Sikang (now part of Szechuan), 450,000 in Chinghai, and 200,000 in Kansu. The Tibetans have had a written language since the seventh century and have 'one of the best developed cultures among the national minorities of China', Theodore Shabad, *China's Changing Map*, N.Y., 1956, pp. 40–44. See also Anna Louise Strong, *When Serfs Stood Up in Tibet*, New World Press, Peking, 1960.
5. *Kuang-ming Jihpao*, 3 March 1962.

Chapter 74. *South of the Clouds*

1. Alley, *op. cit.*, pp. 391–400.

PART SEVEN · *The Long March Ahead*

Chapter 75. *Facts About Food*

1. There was certainly some starvation in the first years of the P.R.C.; after 1954, no further incidents were reported, until 1957. In June of that year it was revealed by press reports that 14,700 Kwangsi peasants caught in a

severe drought in 1956 had been transported but not until 550 of their number had died of starvation. It was a major public scandal; senior officials of the province and responsible party members were reported dismissed and punished for concealing the facts.

2. Hu Chang-tu, *op. cit.*, p. 397.
3. 'Proportional Relationship Between Industry and Agriculture', *Ta Kung Pao*, Peking, 2 February 1961.
4. William Kaye, 'The State of Nutrition in Communist China', C.Q., No. 7, July–September 1961.
5. T.G.Y., p. 119.
6. William Kaye, 'Communist China's Agricultural Calamities', C.Q., No. 6, April–June 1961. Mr Kaye's tables are especially valuable.
7. *Sunday Times*, London, 15 October 1961.
8. 'Proportional Relationship . . .'
9. Kaye, 'The State of Nutrition . . .'
10. *Ibid.*
11. Gilbert Étienne, *De Caboul à Pékin*, Geneva, 1959, Chapter IV.

Chapter 76. China, the United States, Russia and the Bomb

1. Demaree Bess, *Saturday Evening Post*, 21 March 1959.
2. Agnes Smedley, *The Great Road*, N.Y., 1936, p. 331; N.Y., 1967.
3. S.W., London, Vol. II, p. 272, as quoted in T.Gl.Y., p. 86.
4. See Vladimir Dedijer, *Tito*, N.Y., 1958.
5. N.Y. *Times*, 18 August 1958.
6. General Electric Co., *op. cit.*, pp. 110, 123.

Chapter 77. China and Russia: Point, Counterpoint

1. Quoted in S. B. Thomas, *Government and Administration in Communist China*, N.Y., 1953, p. 79, from Liu Shao-ch'i, *Liquidate the Menshevist Ideology Within the Party*, F.L.P., 1951, p. 1. Italics added. Chinese original, Yenan, 1943.
2. Anna Louise Strong, 'The Thought of Mao Tse-tung', *Amerasia*, June 1947. Italics added.
3. Dedijer, *op. cit.*
4. *Institute of Pacific Relations Hearings*, etc., Washington, pp. 1653–4. But the Red Army did not *interfere with*, and probably facilitated, disarming of Japanese troops by the Communists in some areas.
5. N.Y. *Times*, 6 January 1950.
6. Ales Bebler, later foreign minister, at this time headed the Yugoslav delegation at the U.N. In a conversation in April, and subsequently in May, he told me the substance of what is related here.
7. N.C.N.A., 18 November 1957.
8. Mao Tse-tung, *Imperialism and All Reactionaries Are Paper Tigers*, F.L.P., 1958. Italics added.
9. *Ibid.* Italics added.

10. See A *Documentary Analysis of the Sino-Soviet Dispute*, published as a supplement to the *C.Q.*, London, 1961; Zbigniew, Brzesinski, *The Soviet Bloc: Unity and Conflict*, Cambridge, Mass., 1960; and Donald A. Zagoria, *The Sino-Soviet Conflict 1956–61*, N.Y., 1962.

11. The United States sent 7,000 troops to Siberia. The expedition was withdrawn in 1920. It was largely U.S. pressure which secured the subsequent withdrawal of more than 70,000 Japanese troops from northeastern Asia. In 1933 Maxim Litvinov officially withdrew all claims 'of whatsoever character . . . arising out of the activities of the military forces of the United States in Siberia'. George F. Kennan, *Russia and the West Under Lenin and Stalin*, Boston, 1961, p. 113.

12. P.R., 26 April 1960, from Lenin, *Selected Works*, Vol. VII, p. 414, N.Y., 1936.

13. P.R., 26 April 1960.

14. *Ibid.*

Chapter 79. War and Peace in Vietnam

1. Quoted in Harold R. Isaacs, *New Cycle in Asia, Selected Documents on Major International Developments in the Far East, 1943–47*, N.Y., 1947, p. 163.

2. See J.T.T.B., pp. 42–6.

3. Harold R. Isaacs, *No Peace in Asia*, N.Y., 1947, p. 144.

4. *Ibid.*, p. 169.

5. For example, Philippe Devillers, *Histoire du Vietnam, 1945–51*, Paris, 1952; Virginia Thompson and Richard Adloff, *The Left Wing in Southeast Asia*, N.Y., 1950; Harold Isaacs, *New Cycle in Asia*, N.Y., 1947, and *No Peace in Asia*, N.Y., 1947; Anna Louise Strong, *Cash and Violence in Laos*, published officially in Peking, 1961.

6. Isaacs, *No Peace in Asia*, pp. 168–9.

7. *Ibid.*

8. Isaacs, 'Agreement Between France and Vietnam', *New Cycle in Asia*, p. 169.

9. *Ibid.*

10. *Ibid.*, pp. 172–3.

11. *Ibid.*, p. 174.

12. Thompson and Adloff, *op. cit.*, pp. 32, 49.

13. Roscoe Drummond and Gaston Coblentz, *Duel at the Brink*, N.Y., 1960, pp. 116–23.

14. Quoted in Drummond and Coblentz, *op. cit.*, p. 119, from Matthew B. Ridgway and H. H. Martin, *Soldier: Memoirs of Matthew B. Ridgway*, N.Y., 1956. Italics added.

15. See *Foreign Relations of the United States, 1943, China*, especially 'Political Conditions in China', pp. 191–457, and reports by John Carter Vincent, John Paton Davies, John Stewart Service, George Atcheson, Jr., and Ambassador C. E. Gauss, all of whom were senior China specialists,

and all of whom were separated from the foreign service under McCarthy's pressure except George Atcheson, Jr., and Ambassador Gauss, who died prior to Dulles' tenure and the breakup of the China service.

16. In the 'State Department Policy Paper' on China released in September 1949, Formosa was described as having 'no special military significance'. The principal reasons given therein for rejecting the suggestion that the United States establish a protectorate position in Formosa are here summarized for the sake of brevity. It was stated that such a policy would: (a) accomplish no material good for China or its Nationalist régime; (b) involve the United States in a long-term venture producing at best a 'bristling stalemate' and, at worst, possible involvement in open warfare; (c) subject the United States to a violent propaganda barrage and to reaction against American 'militarism, imperialism and interference' even from friendly peoples, and particularly from Chinese, who would be turned against the United States anew; and (d) eminently suit the purposes of the U.S.S.R., which would like to see the United States 'substantiate' its propaganda, and dissipate the energies and weaken the effectiveness of American policies generally by such action.

17. Philippe Devillers, 'The Struggle for Unification', C.Q., No. 9, January–March, 1962.

18. *Ibid.*

19. N.Y. *Times*, 25 July 1962.

20. Devillers, *op. cit.*

21. 'Total Soviet economic assistance to North Vietnam now stands at U.S. $365 million compared with offers worth more than U.S. $450 million made by China (of which roughly half is in the form of free grants and half credits). Total Soviet bloc aid offered to North Vietnam since 1955, including contributions by East European members of the bloc, amounts to more than U.S. $900 million.' William Kaye, 'A Bowl of Rice Divided: The Economy of North Vietnam', C.Q., No. 9, January–March 1962.

22. *Ibid.*

23. Devillers, *op. cit.*

24. O. Edmund Clubb, 'Trap in Vietnam', *The Progressive*, Madison, Wisc., April 1962.

25. Fred J. Cook, 'The CIA', *The Nation*, Special Issue, 24 June 1961, pp. 557–61. Mr Cook presents many other details concerning this episode, including C.I.A. use of refugee Nationalist troops in northern Burma, Thailand and Laos. See also O. Edmund Clubb, 'The Lesson of Laos', *The Progressive*, Madison, Wisc., May 1961.

Chapter 80. *Childhood's End?*

1. With apologies to Arthur Clarke, astronomer, and author of one of the best space-fiction books ever written.

2. Major General Leslie A. Groves's famous 'error' in officially publishing the Smyth Report on the Manhattan project had in 1945 already released

vital information necessary to construct the bomb which was of incalculably greater value than the trivial data obtained by the Rosenbergs, for which they were executed. General Groves himself later won renown before the Un-American Activities Committee as an expert on 'atomic espionage'.

3. Quoted in Fred J. Cook, 'Juggernaut: the Warfare State, *The Nation*, Special Issue, 28 October 1961, p. 293.

4. *Ibid.*

5. *China Crosses the Yalu: The Decision to Enter the Korean War*, N.Y., 1960, p. 126.

6. Cook, *op. cit*, pp. 281–2.

7. Charles Christian Wertenbaker and the *Reporter* staff, 'The China Lobby', *The Reporter*, 5, 19 April 1952.

8. 'United States China Policy', *War/Peace Report* (monthly), July 1961, p. 4.

9. Linus Pauling, 'Why I Am Opposed to Fall-out Shelters', *Liberation*, November 1961.

10. Paul G. Hoffman, 'Economic Development: The United Nations and Business Partnership', United Nations Office of Public Information, PR SPF/6, 20 April 1959.

Acknowledgments

I AM indebted to many authors for permission to use excerpts from their works and to their publishers for granting me the same privilege, especially:

Harvard University Press, Cambridge, Mass., for permission to quote from John King Fairbank, *The United States and China*. Copyright, 1948, 1958, by the President and Fellows of Harvard College.

The *China Quarterly*, London, for permission to quote from several articles that have appeared therein.

Cambridge University Press, New York, for permission to quote from C. P. Snow, *Two Cultures and the Scientific Revolution*, The Rede Lecture. Copyright, Cambridge University Press, 1959.

Yale University Press, New Haven, for permission to quote from Olga Lang, *Chinese Family and Society*. Copyright, 1947.

General Electric Company, for permission to quote from TEMPO: *Science and Technology in Communist China*, by John Berberet, Santa Barbara, 1960 (RM60TMP-72).

James K. Hotchkiss, for permission to quote from *Russia and the West Under Lenin and Stalin*, by George F. Kennan, Boston, 1961.

I also wish to thank Mr Aldous Huxley, Miss Harriet Mills, Mr Fred Cook and Dr Denis Lazure for personal permission to quote from their articles.

O. Edmund Clubb read the manuscript of this book with his customary meticulous and scholarly care, and his many valuable suggestions have contributed to whatever merit the result may possess.

My wife, Lois Wheeler, somehow contrived to combine management of our household with typing most of the manuscript; that did not lead to divorce, but solely because she is a special kind of angel.

I am indebted to Chang Hsin-hai, Chang Siang-mei, Harriet Mills and Philip Kuhn for careful readings and helpful suggestions.

To Mary Heathcote I am most grateful for editorial advice and never-failing help, but

> Not for these I raise
> The song of thanks and praise;
> But for those obstinate questionings
> Of sense and outward things . . .

Bibliography

I⊤ is impossible for me to trace all the sources of works by Chinese as well as non-Chinese writers in a bibliography which would adequately express my indebtedness to others during the many years of reading and study that have contributed to the making of this book. Periodical and newspaper sources are in the Notes and Index. In the brief selected reading list below I have included in the first section works by foreign students of China, or by Chinese abroad, as well as a second section of publications of the Foreign Languages Press of Peking, which have all been of immediate and varying degrees of help which I wish to acknowledge. It would also be presumptuous of me to offer an extensive bibliography on China when so many comprehensive ones have been compiled on the various subjects which I have briefly touched upon. Most of the books listed were published before 1963; in the present edition (1970) there is space to add only a few books published since 1963 which were useful in this revision.

An excellent summary of basic books about ancient, modern and Communist China may be found in 'Suggested Reading' at the back of *The United States and China*, John K. Fairbank, Harvard University Press, Cambridge, 1958. Harvard's Center for Chinese Social and Political Studies has also prepared extensive bibliographies of works on nearly every subject and period of contemporary and historic China. 'A Selected Bibliography', in *China: Its People, Its Society, Its Culture*, compiled by Hu Chang-tu, H.R.A.F. Press, New Haven, 1960, together with a 'Bibliographic Note' in Doak Barnett's *Communist China and Asia*, Harper, 1960, give comprehensive references to available literature in English and some other languages. Li Choh-ming, in *Economic Development of Communist China*, University of California Press, 1959, provides a bibliography of current mainland publications in the Chinese language which is impressive for its scope and its demonstration of vast fields of information now open to scholars. In September each year the *Journal of Asian Studies*, New York, devotes an entire issue to current publications on Asia which includes not only important new literature in English and Chinese but in other languages of the Orient as well as in principal European languages.

SELECTED DOCUMENTS

Adler, Solomon, *The Chinese Economy*, New York, 1957.
Barnett, A. Doak, *Communist China and Asia: Challenge to American Policy*, N.Y., 1960.

Communist Economic Strategy, New York, 1959.

Belden, Jack, *China Shakes the World*, New York, 1949.

Beloff, Max, *Soviet Policy in the Far East, 1944–51*, London, 1953.

Bodde, Derk, *China's Cultural Tradition*, New York, 1957.

Boorman, Howard L., Eckstein, Alexander, Mosley, Philip E., and Schwartz, Benjamin, *Moscow-Peking Axis: Strengths and Strains*, New York, 1957.

Brandt, Conrad, Schwartz, Benjamin, and Fairbank, John K., A *Documentary History of Chinese Communism*, Cambridge, 1952.

Brandt, Conrad, *Stalin's Failure in China*, Cambridge, Mass., 1958.

Brine, Lindsay, *The Taiping Rebellion*, London, 1862.

Buck, J. Lossing, *Land Utilization in China*, 3 vols., Chicago, 1937.

Buck, Pearl, *All Men are Brothers*, translation of the *Shui-Hu Chuan*, 2 vols., New York, 1933.

Callis, Helmut G., *China, Confucian and Communist*, New York, 1959.

Center for Chinese Studies, Berkeley, Calif., Reprint series, C–1 to C–16, 1967–70.

Ch'en, Jerome, *Mao and the Chinese Revolution*, London, 1965.

Chiang Kai-shek, *China's Destiny*, notes by Philip Jaffe, New York, 1947.

Chou Ching-wen, *Ten Years of Storm*, New York, 1960.

Clubb, Edmund, *Twentieth Century China*, N.Y., 1964.

Compton, Boyd, *Mao's China: Party Reform Documents, 1942–4*, Seattle, 1952.

Creel, H. G., *Chinese Thought from Confucius to Mao Tse-tung*, Chicago, 1953.

Cressey, George Babcock, *China's Geographic Foundations*, New York, 1934.

Delza, Sophia, *Body and Mind in Harmony*, *T'ai Chi Ch'uan*, New York, 1961.

Drummond, Roscoe, and Coblentz, Gaston, *Duel at the Brink, John Foster Dulles' Command of American Power*, New York, 1960.

Dumont, René, *Revolution dans les Campagnes Chinoises*, Paris, 1957.

Eckstein, Alexander, *Communist China's Economic Growth and Foreign Trade*, N.Y., 1966.

Elegant, Robert, *Dragon Seed*, New York, 1959.

Epstein, Israel, *The Unfinished Revolution in China*, Boston, 1947.

Étienne, Gilbert, *De Caboul à Pékin*, Geneva, 1959.

La Voie Chinoise, Paris, 1962.

Fairbank, John King, *The United States and China*, new and revised edition, Cambridge, 1958.

Fan, K. H., ed., *The Chinese Cultural Revolution*, N.Y., 1968.

Fei Hsiao-t'ung, *Peasant Life in China*, New York, 1939.

Fitzgerald, C. P., *China: A Short Cultural History*, revised edition, New York, 1954.

Foreign Relations of the United States, 1943, China, Washington: U.S. State Department, 1957.

Foreign Relations of the United States. Vol. VI, 'China, 1944', U.S. Government Printing Office, Washington, 1967.

Freemantle, Anne, *Mao Tse-tung, An Anthology of His Writings*, New York, 1962.

Fung Yu-lan, *A History of Chinese Philosophy*, Vols. I and II, translation by Derk Bodde, Princeton, 1952, 1953.

Gelder, Stuart, *The Chinese Communists*, London, 1946.

Gittings, John, *Survey of the Sino-Soviet Dispute*, London, 1968.

Gluckstein, Ygael, *Mao's China*, Boston, 1957.

Greene, Felix, *Awakened China*, New York, 1961.

Griswold, A. Whitney, *The Far Eastern Policy of the United States*, New York, 1938.

Grousset, René, *Histoire de la Chine*, Paris, 1942.

Guillermaz, *Histoire du Parti Communiste Chinois, 1921–49*, Paris, 1968.

Guillermaz, Jacques, *La Chine Populaire*, Paris, 1959.

Han Suyin, *Asia Today*, Montreal, 1969.
  China in the Year 2001, London, 1967.

Ho Ping-ti, *Studies on the Population of China, 1368–1953*, Cambridge, 1959.

Hsieh, Alice Langley, *Communist China's Strategy in the Nuclear Era*, Englewood Cliffs, New Jersey, 1962.

Hsu, C. Y., *The Rise of Modern China*, N.Y., 1970.

Hu Chang-tu, ed., *China, Its People, Its Society, Its Culture*, New Haven, 1960.

Hudson, G. F., Lowenthal, Richard, and MacFarquhar, Roderick, *The Sino-Soviet Dispute*, London, 1961.

Hughes, T. J. and Luard, D. E. T., *The Economic Development of Communist China, 1949–1958*, London, 1959.

Isaacs, Harold R., *New Cycle in Asia*, New York, 1947.
  No Peace in Asia, New York, 1947.

Kennan, George F., *Russia and the West Under Lenin and Stalin*, Boston, 1961.

Kuo Ping-chia, *China, New Age and New Outlook*, revised edition, New York, 1959.

Lang, Olga, *Chinese Family and Society*, New Haven, 1946.

Lattimore, Owen, *The Desert Road to Turkestan*, New York, 1929.

Lifton, R. J., *Thought Reform and the Psychology of Totalism: A Study of 'Brainwashing'*, New York, 1961.

(MacArthur, Douglas, see Willoughby.)

MacFarquhar, Roderick, *The Hundred Flowers*, London, 1960 (published N.Y., 1960, under the title *The Hundred Flowers Campaign and the Chinese Intellectuals*).

McLane, Charles B. *Soviet Policy and the Chinese Communists, 1931–46*, New York, 1958.

Marx, Karl, and Engels, Friedrich, *Basic Writings*, Lewis S. Feuer, ed., New York, 1959.

Maxwell, Neville, *India's China War*, London, 1970.

Meadows, T. T., *The Chinese and Their Rebellions*, London, 1859.

Meisner, Maurice, *Li Ta-chao and the Origins of Chinese Marxism*, Cambridge, Mass., 1967.

Mende, Tibor, *China and Her Shadow*, New York, 1962.

Needham, Joseph, *Science and Civilization in China*, Vol. II, *History of Scientific Thought*, London, 1956.

Orleans, Leo A., *Professional Manpower and Education in Communist China*, Washington: U.S. Government Printing Office, 1961.

Peffer, Nathaniel, *The Collapse of a Civilization*, New York, 1930.

Rickett, Allyn and Adele, *Prisoners of Liberation*, New York, 1957.

Rigney, Harold W., *Four Years in a Red Hell: The Story of Father Rigney*, Chicago, 1956.

Romanus, C. F., and Sunderland, R., *Stilwell's Mission to China*, Office of the Chief of Military History, Department of the Army, Washington, 1953.
Stilwell's Command Problems, Office of the Chief of Military History, Department of the Army, Washington, 1956.

Rue, John E., *Mao Tse-tung in Opposition*, 1927–35, Stanford, 1966.

Saeki, P. Y., *The Nestorian Documents and Relics in China*, Tokyo, 1951.

Salisbury, Harrison, *A New Russia?* New York, 1962.

Schram, Stuart, *The Political Thought of Mao Tse-tung*, N.Y., 1963.

Schurmann, Franz, *Ideology and Organization in Communist China*, Berkeley, 1963.

Schwartz, Benjamin I., *Chinese Communism and the Rise of Mao*, Cambridge, 1952.

Shabad, Theodore, *China's Changing Map*, New York, 1956.

Simmons, Ernest J., *U.S.S.R.: A Concise Handbook*, Ithaca, 1947.

Smedley, Agnes, *The Great Road: The Life and Times of Chu Teh*, New York, 1956.

Sze, Mai-mai, *The Way of Chinese Painting*, N.Y., 1956.

Tawney, R. H., *Land and Labour in China*, London, 1932.

Thomas, S. B., *Government and Administration in Communist China*, New York, 1953; revised edition, 1955.

Thompson, Virginia, and Adloff, Richard, *The Left Wing in Southeast Asia*, New York, 1950.

Tocqueville, Alexis de, *Democracy in America*, Vols. I & II, New York, 1961. The text used is the Phillips Bradley edition published by Vintage Books, with notes, etc., added to the Henry Reeve translation of the French original, Paris, 1835.

Truman, Harry S., *Memoirs*, 2 vols., New York, 1958.

United States Relations with China, With Special Reference to the Period 1944–49, Washington: U.S. State Department, 1949.

Wales, Nym, *Inside Red China*, New York, 1939.
Red Dust, Palo Alto, 1952.

Walker, Richard L., *China Under Communism: The First Five Years*, New Haven, 1955.

White, Theodore H. and Jacoby, Annalee, *Thunder Out of China*, New York, 1946.

Whiting, Allen S., *China Crosses the Yalu: The Decision to Enter the Korean War*, New York, 1960.

Whiting, Allen S., *Soviet Policies in China, 1917–24*, N.Y., 1954.

Willoughby, Charles A., and Chamberlain, John, *MacArthur: 1941–1951*, New York, 1954.

Williams, S. Wells, *The Middle Kingdom*, 2 vols., New York, 1891, 1904.

Winance, Eleutherius, O. S. B., *The Communist Persuasion: A Personal Experience of Brainwashing*, New York, 1959.

Wong K. Chimin and Wu Lien-teh, *History of Chinese Medicine*, 2nd edition, Shanghai, 1936.

Zagoria, Donald S., *The Sino-Soviet Conflict 1956–1961*, Princeton, 1962.

SELECTED CHINESE PUBLICATIONS IN ENGLISH

Many works in this bibliography are basic documents of which Western scholars and intelligence research analysis have long made intensive use. References to a few others will be found in my Notes. A complete catalog of publications issued with the approval of the Chinese government by the Foreign Languages Press of Peking may be obtained from the authorized distributing agencies mentioned below.*

Geography of China: Peoples and Regions

A *Simple Geography of China*, Wang Chun-heng. Charts, maps and illustrations covering all regions of China. 256 p. 1958.

Peking. China's capital city in photos of today and yesterday, reproductions of ancient paintings in color. Captions in Chinese with English translation in accompanying booklet.

Water Control and Climate

Report on the Multiple-Purpose Plan for Permanently Controlling the Yellow River and Exploiting Its Water Resources, Teng Tse-hui. Map. 49 p. 1955.

*Foreign Languages Press publications are distributed by the Guozi Shudian, P.O. Box 399, Peking, China. United States distribution is handled by China Books and Periodicals, 334 Schiller Street, Chicago, Ill., and by China Publications, 95 Fifth Avenue, New York, N.Y., 10003. In London the official distributors are Collets Holdings, 70 New Oxford Street, London W.1.

China in Transition

The People Have Strength, Rewi Alley. Description of a New Zealander's travels through many parts of China in the early days of the People's Republic. 281 p. 1954.

Miscellaneous

Chinese Therapeutical Methods of Acupuncture and Moxibustion, Academy of Traditional Chinese Medicine. Illustrated. 18 p. 1960.

Embroidery Designs of the Miao People of China, People's Fine Arts Publishing House. 40 illustrations. 50 p. 1956.

China's Hinterland in the Leap Forward, Rewi Alley, Peking, 1961.

Chinese Agriculture

The Question of Agricultural Co-operation, Mao Tse-tung. Report delivered 31 July 1955. 39 p. 1956.

The Draft Programme for Agricultural Development in the People's Republic of China 1956–1967. 44 p. 1956.

People's Communes in China. Articles and documents. 90 p. 1958.

History of China

An Outline History of China, Tung Chi-ming. From Peking Man to 1949 A.D. Table of Dynasties. Illustrated. 469 p. 1959.

A Record of the Buddhist Countries, Fa-hsien, being an account of his travels through Central Asia and India in the 5th century, Chinese Buddhist Assoc., Peking. 94 p. 1957.

Thirty Years of the Communist Party of China, Hu Chiao-mu. 99 p. 1954.

A History of the Modern Chinese Revolution, Ho Kan-chih. From the May Fourth Movement (1919) to the first half of 1956. A detailed analysis of recent Chinese history. 627 p. 1959.

International Relations

Important Documents Concerning the Question of Taiwan. Cairo Declaration, reports by Chou En-lai, etc. 184 p. 1955.

Oppose U.S. Occupation of Taiwan and 'Two Chinas' Plot. A selection of important documents. 162 p. 1958.

1960: Documents of the Sino-Indian Boundary Question. Exchange of letters between Chou En-lai and Nehru. 144 p. 1960.

The Democratic Republic of Vietnam. An Official Report of the Government of the D.R.V., F.L.P., Hanoi. 157 p, 1960.

Two Tactics, One Aim. 'An Exposure of the Peace Tricks of U.S. Imperialism.' Institute of Foreign Affairs. 146 p. May 1960.

Long Live Leninism. Contains the much publicized articles from *Hung Chi (Red Flag)* and *Renmin Ribao (People's Daily)* on the danger of war and the struggle for peace and coexistence. Also an article by Lu Ting-yi. 106 p. Revised edition August 1960.

Tibetan Interviews, Anna Louise Strong. 210 p. 1959.

Imperialism and Chinese Politics, Hu Sheng. 1955.

China's Economy: The Five-Year Plans

Report on National Economic Development and Fulfillment of the State Plan of the People's Republic of China in 1954. With Statistical Summary. 48 p. 1956.

First Five-Year Plan, 1953–1957. Documents on capital construction, heavy industry, agriculture, transport and communications, commerce, etc. 231 p. 1956.

China Will Overtake Britain, Niu Chung-huang. Plan to surpass British industrial level within 15 years. 66 p. 1958.

The Second Five-Year Plan Fulfilled in Two Years. Charts and photographs of the development of the national economy in 1959. Brief text. 40 p. 1960.

The Socialist Transformation of the National Economy in China, Hsueh Mu-chiao, Su Hsing, Lin Tse-li. 287 p. 1960.

Labor

Labor Laws and Regulations. Trade union law, constitution of the trade unions, labor insurance, award for inventions & technical improvement, spare-time education, etc. 86 p. 1956.

Political Reports and Documents

Proposals of the 8th National Congress, C. P. of China, for 2nd 5-Yr. Plan 1958–62). *Report* by Chou En-lai. 105 p. 1956.

Constitution of the Communist Party of China. Report on the Revision of the Constitution of the Communist Party of China by Teng Hsiao-ping, 16 September 1956. 110 p. 1956.

Historical Experience of the Dictatorship of the Proletariat, Editorial in *Renmin Ribao* of 5 April 1956, on the 20th Congress, C. P. of the U.S.S.R., F.L.P., 64 p. 1959.

The Victory of Marxism-Leninism in China, Liu Shao-ch'i. 36 p. 1959.

A History of the Modern Chinese Revolution, Ho Kan-chih, Peking, 1960.

Thirty Years of the Communist Party of China, Hu Chiao-mu, Peking, 1959.

'Let a Hundred Flowers Blossom, a Hundred Schools of Thought Contend' (1956), Lu Ting-yi. 37 p. 1958.

Lin Piao, *Report to the Ninth National Congress of the C.P.C.,* Peking, 1949. *Long Live the Victory of People's War!,* Peking, 1965.

The Constitution of the Communist Party of China (New), Peking, 1969.
Communiqué of the Enlarged Twelfth Session of the Eighth Central Committee of the C.P.C., Peking, 1968.
Communiqué of the Ninth Congress of the C.P.C., 1969.

Selected Books, Articles and Speeches by Mao Tse-tung
(English editions, F.L.P.)

(Date of original issue is given in parentheses if earlier than date of publication.)

Analysis of the Classes in Chinese Society (1926). 17 p. 1956.
The Chinese Revolution and the Chinese Communist Party (1939). 43 p. 1959.
Combat Liberalism (1937). 6 p. 1956.
Communiqué of the Enlarged Twelfth Session of the Eighth Central Committee of the C.P.C., Peking, 1968.
Communiqué of the Ninth Congress of the C.C.P., 1969.
Comrade Mao Tse-tung on 'Imperialism and All Reactionaries Are Paper Tigers'. 32 p. 1958.
On Contradiction (1937). 55 p. 1958.
On the Correct Handling of Contradictions Among the People (1957). 70 p. 1959.
On Methods of Leadership (1943). 10 p. 1955.
On the New Democracy (1940). 84 p. 1955.
On Practice (1937). 26 p. 1953.
On the Protracted War (1938). 140 p. 1954.
On the Question of Agricultural Co-operation (1955). 39 p. 1956.
On the Rectification of Incorrect Ideas in the Party (1929). 19 p. 1953.
Our Study and the Current Situation (1944). 116 p. 1955.
Questions of Tactics in the Present Anti-Japanese Front (1939). 38 p. 1954.
Rectify the Party's Style in Work (1942). 29 p. 1955.
Reform Our Study (1941). 19 p. 1955.
Report of an Investigation into the Peasant Movement in Hunan (1927). 64 p. 1953.
Report to the Second Plenary Session of the Seventh Central Committee of the Communist Party of China, Peking, 1968.
A Single Spark Can Start a Prairie Fire (1930). 22 p. 1953.
Strategic Problems in the Anti-Japanese War (1937). 55 p. 1954.
Why Can China's Red Power Exist? (1928). 17 p. 1953.
Selected Works of Mao Tse-tung, Vol. I, 1952; Vol. II, 1952; Vol. III, 1953; and Vol. IV, 1961, contain most of the foregoing material published as separate pamphlets or books.

Commentary on Mao Tse-tung

Notes on Mao Tse-tung's 'Report of an Investigation into the Peasant Movement in Hunan', Chen Po-t'a. 88 p. 1954.

Classical Literature

Ancient Chinese Fables. From the 4th century B.C. to the 5th century A.D. Illustrated. 60 p. 1957.

The Dragon King's Daughter. Stories of love and the supernatural from the Tang Dynasty (618–907). 178 p. 1954.

Verse

The People Speak Out. Ancient and modern popular songs and poems translated by Rewi Alley. Illustrated. 107 p. 1954.

Poems, Mao Tse-tung. 1959.

Literature and Philosophy

A Brief History of Chinese Fiction, Lu Hsun. From the beginnings to the 20th century. 462 p. 1959.

A Short History of Classical Chinese Literature, Feng Yuan-chun. From the beginnings to 1919. 132 p. 1958.

Talks at the Yenan Forum on Art and Literature (1942), Mao Tse-tung. 51 p. 1956.

Modern Fiction

The Family (1931), Pa Chin. In a feudal household a younger generation breaks with tradition. Illustrations. 323 p. 1958.

Spring Silkworms (1932–1943), Mao Tun, 13 stories dealing with the collapse of China's rural economy, the Japanese invasion, Chinese industrialists, etc. 278 p. 1956.

Uncle Kao, Ouyang Shan. The struggle to develop a village consumer's co-op in the northern Shensi area. 297 p. 1957.

Modern Drama

Chu Yuan, Kuo Mo-jo. Five-act tragedy of the ancient poet of the third century B.C. with a modern meaning. 126 p. 1953.

The Long March, Chen Chi-tung. Six-act epic. 99 p. 1956.

Chinese Opera

Peking Opera, A Traditional Chinese Art. Brief history, training of actors, performances and costumes. 82 photos & illustrations. 102 p. 1957.

Chinese Language

English-Chinese Conversation. For beginners. 176 p. 1959.
Reform of the Chinese Written Language. 70 p. 1958.

Periodicals in English

China Pictorial. Semimonthly. The day-to-day story in pictures of life in modern China. Many photos in color.

China Reconstructs. Illustrated monthly. Popular articles on China's economic, social and cultural development. Language corner, reader's comments, modern art, stamps.

Peking Review. Weekly journal. Authoritative analysis and commentary on international relations and Chinese news and views. Cultural calendar of events in Peking.

Chinese Medical Journal. Monthly official organ of the Chinese Medical Association. Research, surgery, etc.

Index

VINTAGE POLITICAL SCIENCE
AND SOCIAL CRITICISM

VINTAGE HISTORY—AMERICAN

VINTAGE BIOGRAPHY AND AUTOBIOGRAPHY